A PRACTICAL GUIDE
TO THE UNIX® SYSTEM

A PRACTICAL GUIDE TO THE UNIX® SYSTEM

THIRD EDITION

Mark G. Sobell

Addison-Wesley Publishing Company
Menlo Park, California • Reading, Massachusetts
Harlow, U.K., • Amsterdam • Bonn • Sydney • Singapore
Tokyo • Madrid • San Juan, Puerto Rico • Paris
Milan • Taipei • Seoul • Mexico City

Acquisitions Editor: J. Carter Shanklin
Executive Editor: Dan Joraanstad
Production Editor: Teri Holden
Editorial Assistant: Melissa Standen
Marketing Manager: Mary Tudor
Manufacturing Coordinator: Janet Weaver

Composition: Sobell Associates Inc.
Illustrator: Alex Clemens
Cover Designer: Michael Rogandino
Text Designer: David Healy, The First Image
Copyeditor: Nick Murray
Proofreader: Eleanor Renner Brown

Cover photo © Digital Art/Westlight

This book was typeset by Sobell Associates Inc. using FrameMaker on an Intel 80486-based computer running SCO UNIX and Open Desktop. Photos were scanned on a UMAX scanner attached to a Macintosh which was networked to the 486 UNIX machine. Line art was rendered with FrameMaker. Proof copies of the book were printed on an HP 4 laser printer running PostScript, and final film was output directly by a Sprint Imagesetter with a resolution of 2540 dpi. The paper used in this book meets the EPA Standards for recycled fiber.

Many of the designations used by manufacturers and sellers to distinguish their products are claimed as trademarks. Where those designations appear in this book, and Addison-Welsey was aware of a trademark claim, the designations have been printed in initial caps or all caps.

UNIX is a registered trademark in the United States and other countries, licensed exclusively through X/Open Company Ltd.; SunOS is a trademark of Sun Microsystems, Inc.; XENIX, Windows, Windows-NT, and MS-DOS are trademarks of Microsoft, Inc.; PostScript is a trademark of Adobe Software, Inc.; Macintosh is a trademark of Apple Computer; SCO is a registered trademark of the Santa Cruz Operation; FrameMaker is a trademark of Frame Technology Corporation.

Library of Congress Cataloging in Publication Data
Sobell, Mark G.
        A practical guide to the UNIX system / Mark G. Sobell - 3rd ed.
              p.   cm.
        Includes index.
        ISBN 0-8053-7565-1
        1. UNIX (Computer file) I. Title.
QA76.76.063S595 1994   94-8434
005.4'3-dc20   CIP

ISBN 0-8053-7565-1

    4 5 6 7 8 9 10 DOC 98 97 96

Addison-Wesley Publishing Company
2725 Sand Hill Road
Menlo Park, CA 94025

for Laura
Max
Zachary
and the B

See, the human mind is kind of like . . .
a piñata. When it breaks open,
there's a lot of surprises inside.
Once you get the piñata perspective,
you see that losing your mind
can be a peak experience.

Jane Wagner
The Search for Signs of Intelligent Life in the Universe

Preface

This book is *practical* because it uses tutorial examples that show you what you will see on your terminal screen each step of the way. It is a *guide* because it takes you from logging in on your system (Chapter 2) through writing complex shell programs (Chapters 10, 11, 12), using sophisticated software development tools (Chapter 13), and administrating a system (Chapter 14). Part II is a *reference guide* to 76 UNIX utilities. *A Practical Guide to the UNIX System* is intended for people with some computer experience but little or no experience with the UNIX system. However, more experienced UNIX system users will find the later chapters and Part II to be useful sources of information on such subjects as basic and advanced shell programming, C programming, networks, graphical user interfaces, and system administration.

This book covers Berkeley Software Distribution (BSD) Release 4.3 and SunOS version 4.1.x, It is intended for users of versions of UNIX based on Berkeley UNIX. In addition, Appendix B covers DEC's ULTRIX, explaining the differences between what you will find in this book and what you will find on a machine running ULTRIX. The following list highlights some of the features of this book.

Networking

This new chapter is devoted to explaining what a network is, how it works, and how you can use it. It tells you about types of networks, various network implementations, distributed computing, how to use the network for communicating with other users via **talk** and **Mail**, and using various networking utilities (such as **telnet**, **ftp**).

Internet and the World Wide Web

Chapter 7 also discusses the use of the Internet and shows, with examples, how to use **archie** and **gopher**, two user-friendly interfaces to the Internet. It details the World Wide Web and its use of hypertext, and explains how to use the powerful browser named **Mosaic**.

Graphical User Interfaces (GUIs)

Chapter 6, another new chapter, discusses various graphical user interfaces, including Motif and OPEN LOOK. It explains the X Window system, how to open and control windows, how to customize your X work environment, and how to customize the Motif window manager.

The Korn Shell and Advanced Shell Programming

The newest of the three major shells, the Korn Shell, is becoming more popular. Chapter 12 covers the latest version of this shell (ksh93) as well as older versions. This chapter extends the concepts of shell programming introduced in Chapter 10 into more advanced areas, including more information on the locality of variables, recursion, and the coprocess.

The vi Editor

This screen-oriented editor, which was originally a part of Berkeley UNIX, is still one of the most widely used text editors. Chapter 8 continues from the introduction in Chapter 2 and goes on to explain how to use many of the advanced features of **vi** including special characters in search strings, the general-purpose and named buffers, parameters, markers, and executing commands from **vi**. The chapter concludes with a summary of **vi** commands.

The emacs Editor

Produced and distributed (for minimal cost) by the Free Software Foundation, this editor has grown in popularity and is now available on many UNIX machines. Chapter 9 explains how to use many of the features of this versatile editor from a basic orientation to the use of the (META), (ALT), and (ESCAPE) keys; key bindings, buffers, the concept of Point, the cursor, Mark, and Region, incremental and complete searching for both character strings and regular expressions; using the on-line help facilities, cutting and pasting, using multiple windows; and C Mode, which is designed to aid a programmer in writing and debugging C code. The chapter concludes with a summary of **emacs** commands.

Job Control

The job control commands, which originated on Berkeley UNIX, allow a user to work on many jobs at once from a single window, and switch back and forth between the jobs as desired.

Shell Functions

A new feature of the Bourne and Korn Shells, shell functions, enables users to write their own commands that are similar to the aliases provided by the C Shell, only more powerful.

Source Code Management: SCCS and RCS

The Source Code Control System (SCCS) and Revision Control System (RCS) are convenient sets of tools that enable programmers to track multiple versions of files on a number of different types of projects.

POSIX

The IEEE POSIX committees have developed standards for programming and user interfaces based on historical UNIX practice, and new standards are under development. Appendix C describes these standards and their direction and effect on the UNIX industry.

Part I and Part II

A Practical Guide to the UNIX System shows you how to use the UNIX system from your terminal. The first fourteen chapters comprise Part I, which contain step-by-step tutorials covering the most important aspects of the UNIX operating system. (If you have used a UNIX system before, you may want to skim over Chapters 2 and 3.) The more advanced material in each chapter is presented in sections marked "Optional," which you are encouraged to return to after mastering the more basic material presented in the chapter. Review exercises are included at the end of each chapter for readers who want to hone their skills. Some of the exercises test the reader's understanding of material covered in the chapter, while others challenge the reader to go beyond the material presented to develop a more thorough understanding.

Part II offers a comprehensive, detailed reference to the major UNIX utilities, with numerous examples. If you are already familiar with the UNIX system, this part of the book will be a valuable, easy-to-use reference. If you are not an experienced user, you will find Part II a useful supplement while you are mastering the tutorials in Part I.

Organizing Information

In Chapters 2, 3, and 4, you will learn how to create, delete, copy, move, and search for information using your system. You will also learn how to use the UNIX system file structure to organize the information you store on your computer.

Electronic Mail and Telecommunications

Chapters 2 and 3 and Part II include information on how to use the UNIX system utilities (**Mail**, **talk**, and **write**) to communicate with users on your system and other systems. Chapter 7 details how to address electronic mail to users on remote, networked systems.

Using the Shell

In Chapter 5 you will learn how to redirect output from a program to the printer, to your terminal, or to a file—just by changing a command. You will also see how you can use pipes to combine UNIX utilities to solve problems right from the command line.

Shell Programming

Once you have mastered the basics of the UNIX system, you can use your knowledge to build more complex and specialized programs (shell scripts) using a shell programming language. Chapter 10 shows you how to use the Bourne Shell to write your own scripts composed of UNIX system commands. Chapter 11 covers the C Shell. Chapter 12 covers the Korn Shell, which combines many of the popular features of the C Shell (such as history and aliases) with a programming language similar to that of the Bourne Shell. This chapter also covers many concepts of advanced shell programming. The examples in Part II also demonstrate many features of the UNIX utilities that you can use in shell scripts.

Using Programming Tools

Chapter 13 introduces you to the C compiler and the UNIX system's exceptional programming environment. This chapter describes how to use some of the most useful software development tools: **make**, the Source Code Control System (SCCS), and the Revision Control System (RCS). The **make** utility automates much of the drudgery involved in ensuring that a program you compile contains the latest versions of all program modules. SCCS and RCS help you to track the versions of files involved in a project.

System Administration

Chapter 14 explains the inner workings of the UNIX system. It details the responsibilities of the superuser and explains how to bring up and shut down a UNIX system, add users to the system, back up files, set up new devices, check the integrity of a filesystem, and more. This chapter goes into detail about the structure of a filesystem and explains what administrative information is kept in the various files.

Using UNIX Utilities

The UNIX system includes hundreds of utilities. Part II contains extensive examples of how to use many of these utilities to solve problems without resorting to programming in C (or another language). The example sections of **awk** (over 20 pages starting on page 447), and **sort** (page 603), give real-life examples that demonstrate how to use these utilities alone and with other utilities to generate reports, summarize data, and extract information.

Regular Expressions

Many UNIX utilities allow you to use regular expressions to make your job easier. Appendix A explains how to use regular expressions so that you can take advantage of some of the hidden power of your UNIX system.

Perspective

This book is now in its third edition. Over ten years ago when I went peddling my UNIX manuscript, most publishers were polite, but I had the feeling that they had a good chuckle when I left after trying to explain what UNIX was, and how it was going to catch on. UNIX? Never heard of it.

Silicon Valley was hot, the Santa Cruz Operation was starting to sell Xenix, which was Microsoft's version of UNIX, and I worked for Cromemco, a small microprocessor manufacturer. Those were the days of the Z-80 and 8086 chips; 16KB was a lot of memory, and a 10MB hard disk was really special. CP/M was the operating system, and Osborne made a splash with its "portable" computer. UNIX really didn't fit in.

At that time I chose some names to use throughout the book—notably those of my 15-year-old nephew Alex and his younger sister, Jenny. Cute. Now Jenny has a son, and Alex helped me work on this edition of the book (he did the illustrations using FrameMaker).

In producing the first edition of the book, I used Cromemco's text editor. I had limited, 1200-baud dial-up access to a UNIX system—an Onyx machine (the first commercial attempt at a UNIX box) at RDS (later to become Informix). I was bold enough to send the files from my computer to the typesetter via a modem—we had no common medium for exchanging information. Translation from my text files into galleys was marginal at best.

I wrote the second edition on a 386-based computer running UNIX. I used **vi** and **troff** for editing and formatting, a 300 dpi PostScript printer for proofing, generating final output on a Linotronic phototypesetter. Illustrations were hand-drawn, and photos were stripped in at the printer's.

For this edition I decided it was time to join the real world: desktop publishing, scanning, and so on. Although many people said it would be easier to use a Macintosh, I wanted to see if UNIX had matured to the point where I could produce a what-you-see-is-what-you-get book on a UNIX machine. It almost has. I chose to use a Mac for scanning, but that is all. And I access the Mac over a TCP/IP network as a window in a graphical user interface on my X terminal. Now I use an 80486-based computer running Santa Cruz Operation's Open Desktop. A 1,000-megabyte hard disk is no big deal—almost as small as a deck of cards. Screen shots are mostly dumps (using **xwd**) of X windows. Illustrations and all text were produced using FrameMaker. On my screen, I saw what I was going to get before I ever put a piece of paper in the printer. Proofing was still done on a PostScript laser printer (now at 600 dpi), and I used an 88MB Syquest removable hard disk to ship the PostScript file to the printer. The printer took the file and produced negatives, eliminating the paste-up and camera-ready-copy stages of book production.

I miss writing and debugging **troff** macros. Somehow that seemed real—you didn't just click on a button that said "superscript" to get a superscript—you had to tell **troff** how high up to raise the type with a series of arcane commands. Osanna's **troff** manual is a work of art—so dense that even years after reading it for the first time, I could still find new information in it. Quite a challenge and obviously not suitable for most commercial offices. I still use **vi** for writing code. It, too, is dense—even after more than ten years I still learn a new command every once in a while.

Thanks

But as times have changed, so the book and the way it is produced have changed. Many people have helped write, edit, proof, and produce this, the third edition of *A Practical Guide to the UNIX System.*

First, a big *THANKS* to my Production Editor at B/C, Teri Holden, for her gentle yet firm hand in dealing with major procrastination, for her continued support and understanding, and for her being there during the hard part. My Editor, Carter Shanklin, also gets a big *Thank You* for standing behind the project even when things looked pretty dim. Unfortunately, he is the one who takes the flak from both sides, so here's a little de-flakking. Carter, I wouldn't have finished the project without your help and support. Thanks to the many others at B/C who remain mostly invisible to me, but who are an integral part of this project.

Pat Parseghian researched, wrote, analyzed reviews, and coordinated all of the efforts that went into this edition. From her large-scale system-administration experience at Princeton and her interest in data networks, she brings a breadth to this book that ties together the technobabble of computers and their use in the real world. Pat is responsible for much of the work on the Networking and GUI chapters.

Thanks to the Texan, JFP (Dr. John Frank Peters), for his many hours on the **emacs** chapter. His understanding of this editor gives this chapter a depth and breadth that makes you want to dive right in. Fred Zlotnick, author of *The POSIX.1 Standard,* did a lot of work on the Korn Shell chapter and the POSIX Appendix.

Also, many thanks to those whose time and energy went into improving the quality of the Third Edition through the process of review: Arnold Robbins, Georgia Tech. University (Ksh & POSIX), Behrouz Forouzan, DeAnza

College (Ksh & GUI), Mike Keenan, Virginia Polytechnic Institute and State University (GUI), Mike Johnson, Oregon State University (GUI), Jandelyn Plane, University of Maryland (Networking & **emacs**), Sathis Menon, Georgia Tech. University (Networking), Cliff Shaffer, Virginia Polytechnic Institute and State University (**emacs**), and Steven Stepanek, California State University, Northridge (ULTRIX).

I continue to be grateful to the many people who helped with the first and second editions. This book would not have been possible without the help and support of everyone at Informix Software, Inc. Special thanks to Roger Sippl, Laura King, and Roy Harrington for introducing me to the UNIX system. My mother, Dr. Helen Sobell, provided invaluable comments on the manuscript at several junctures.

Isaac Rabinovitch provided a very thorough review of the system administration chapter. Prof. Raphael Finkel and Prof. Randolph Bentson each reviewed the manuscript several times, making many significant improvements. Bob Greenberg, Prof. Udo Pooch, Judy Ross, and Dr. Robert Veroff also reviewed the manuscript and made useful suggestions. In addition, the following people provided critical reviews and were generally helpful during the long haul: Dr. Mike Denny, Joe DiMartino, Dr. John Mashey, Diane Schulz, Robert Jung, and Charles Whitaker.

I am also deeply indebted to many people whose help with different parts of the revision process greatly improved the second edition. Darlene Hawkins and Diane Blass handled countless administrative details. Numerous people helped by providing technical information about of the UNIX system: Don Cragun, Brian Dougherty, Dr. Robert Fish, Guy Harris, Ping Liao, Gary Lindgren, Dr. Jarrett Rosenberg, Dr. Peter Smith, Bill Weber, Mike Bianchi, and Scooter Morris. Brian Reid provided the USENET map of site locations and news exchange paths shown on page 9. Clarke Echols, Oliver Grillmeyer, and Dr. Stephen Wampler reviewed a draft of the manuscript.

Dr. David Korn and Dr. Scott Weikart's reviews of the Bourne Shell chapter and the original Korn Shell appendix caused me to step back and rethink my approach to shell programming, and finally to make significant revisions, particularly to Chapter 10.

Dr. Brian Kernighan and Rob Pike graciously allowed me to reprint the **bundle** script from their book, "The UNIX Programming Environment," and Dr. Richard Curtis provided several other shell scripts used in Chapter 10.

Dr. Kathleen Hemenway researched, wrote, analyzed reviews and generally coordinated all the efforts that went into the Second Edition. From her work on the UNIX system at Bell Labs and her teaching experience, she brought a breadth to this book that greatly increases its value as a learning tool. Of course I must take responsibility for any errors or omissions. If you find one, or just have a comment, let me know (at sobell!mark@igc.org or c/o the publisher), and I'll fix it in the next printing.

Finally, I must also thank the black cat without a tail who harassed me during the preparation of the initial manuscript and who is now sitting upstairs somewhere laughing at us mortals who work all day in front of CRTs instead of stretching out in the sun. This book is for you too, Odie.

Mark G. Sobell
Menlo Park, California

Table of Contents

PART II   THE UNIX UTILITY PROGRAMS

PART I

The UNIX System

CHAPTER 1

The UNIX Operating System

UNIX is the name of a computer operating system and its family of related utility programs. Over the past decade, the UNIX operating system has matured and gained unprecedented popularity. This chapter starts with a definition of an operating system and a brief history and overview of the UNIX system that explains why it is so popular. It continues with a discussion of some of the features that have emerged in the Berkeley and SunOS versions of the UNIX System.

What Is an Operating System?

An operating system is a control program for a computer. It allocates computer resources and schedules tasks. Computer resources include all the hardware: the central processing unit, system memory, disk and tape storage, printers, terminals, modems, and anything else that is connected to or inside the computer. An operating system also provides an interface to the user—it gives the user a way to access the computer resources.

An operating system performs many varied functions almost simultaneously. It keeps track of filenames and where each file is located on the disk, and it monitors every keystroke on each of the terminals. Memory typically must be allocated so that only one task uses a given area of memory at a time. Other operating system functions include fulfilling requests made by users, running accounting programs that keep track of resource use, and executing backup and other maintenance utilities. An operating system schedules tasks so that the central processor is working on only one task at a given moment, although the computer may appear to be running many programs at the same time.

The History of the UNIX Operating System

The UNIX operating system was developed at AT&T Bell Laboratories in Murray Hill, New Jersey—one of the largest research facilities in the world. Since the original design and implementation of the UNIX system by Ken Thompson in 1969, it has gone through a maturing process. When the UNIX operating system was developed, many computers still ran single jobs in a *batch* mode. Programmers fed these computers input in the form of punch cards (these were also called IBM cards) and did not see the program again until the printer produced the output. Because these systems served only one user at a time, they did not take full advantage of the power and speed of the computers. Further, this work environment isolated programmers from each other. It made it difficult to share data and programs, and it did not promote cooperation among people working on the same project.

The UNIX time-sharing system provided three major improvements over single-user, batch systems. It allowed more than one person to use the computer at a time (the UNIX operating system is a *multiuser* operating system), it allowed a person to communicate directly with the computer via a terminal (it is *interactive*), and it made it easy for people to share data and programs.

The UNIX system was not the first interactive, multiuser operating system. An operating system named Multics was in use briefly at Bell Labs before the UNIX operating system was created. The Cambridge Multiple Access System had been developed in Europe, and the Compatible Time Sharing System (CTSS) had also been used for several years. The designers of the UNIX operating system took advantage of the work that had gone into these and other operating systems by incorporating the most desirable aspects of each of them.

The UNIX system was developed by researchers who needed a set of modern computing tools to help them with their projects. The system allowed a group of people working together on a project to share selected data and programs while keeping other information private.

Figure 1-1   DECstation 5000 Model 200 Workstation Running ULTRIX, a BSD-based UNIX operating system. (Courtesy Digital Equipment Corporation.)

Universities and colleges have played a major role in furthering the popularity of the UNIX operating system through the "four-year effect." When the UNIX operating system became widely available in 1975, Bell Labs offered it to educational institutions at minimal cost. The schools, in turn, used it in their computer science programs, ensuring that computer science students became familiar with it. Because the UNIX system is such an advanced development system, the students became acclimated to a sophisticated programming environment. As these students graduated and went into industry, they expected to work in a similarly advanced environment. As more of these students worked their way up in the commercial world, the UNIX operating system found its way into industry.

In addition to introducing its students to the UNIX operating system, the Computer Systems Research Group at the University of California at Berkeley made significant additions and changes to it. They made so many popular changes that one of the two most prominent versions of the system in use today is called the Berkeley Software Distribution (BSD) of the UNIX system. The other major version is UNIX System V, which descended from versions developed and maintained by AT&T and UNIX System Laboratories. This book covers the features commonly found on BSD systems and systems derived from Berkeley UNIX, in particular SunOS.

It is this heritage—development in a research environment and enhancement in a university setting—that has made the UNIX operating system such a powerful software development tool.

Why Is the UNIX System Popular with Manufacturers?

Two trends in the computer industry have set the stage for the recent popularity of the UNIX system. First, advances in hardware technology have created the need for an operating system that can take advantage of available hardware power. In the mid-1970s, minicomputers began challenging the large mainframe computers, because in many applications minicomputers could perform the same functions less expensively. Today, microcomputers are challenging the minis in much the same way, far surpassing even newer minicomputers in cost and performance. Powerful 32-bit processor chips, plentiful, inexpensive memory, and lower-priced hard-disk storage have allowed manufacturers to install multiuser operating systems on microcomputers.

Second, with the cost of hardware continually dropping, hardware manufacturers can no longer afford to develop and support proprietary operating systems. They need a generic system that they can easily adapt to their machines. In turn, software manufacturers need to keep the prices of their products down—they cannot afford to convert their products to run under many different proprietary operating systems. Like hardware manufacturers, software manufacturers need a generic operating system.

The UNIX system satisfies both needs: It is a generic operating system and it takes advantage of available hardware power. Because the UNIX system was written almost entirely in a machine-independent language, it can easily be adapted to different machines, and it can easily be adapted to meet special requirements. Because the UNIX system was initially designed for minicomputers, the file structure takes full advantage of large, fast hard disks. Equally important, it was originally designed as a multiuser operating system—it was not modified to serve several users as an afterthought. Sharing the computer's power among many users and giving users the ability to share data and programs are central features of the system. Because the UNIX system is easily adapted and because it can take advantage of the available hardware, it now runs on a wide range of machines—from microcomputers to supercomputers.

The UNIX system offers an additional advantage to software companies. Having been originally designed by highly skilled programmers to support their own projects, it provides an ideal software development environment.

The advent of a standard operating system aided the development of the software industry. Now software manufacturers can afford to make one version of one product available on many different machines. No longer does one speak of "the company that makes the MRP package for the IBM machine" but rather "the company that makes the MRP package for the UNIX operating system." The hardware manufacturer who offers a UNIX-based system can count on third-party software being available to run on the new machine.

Figure 1-2   New 3.5-inch hard disk drives store 2 Gigabytes of information in a 1" high design, and 4GB in a 1.6" design. The SCSI (Small Computer Systems Interface) drives are targeted at high-end PCs, workstations, servers, and disk arrays. (Courtesy of Conner Peripherals, Inc.)

The UNIX System Is Widely Accepted

The UNIX operating system has gained widespread commercial acceptance. UNIX system user groups have been started in many cities throughout the world; national and international organizations have been established; several conferences and trade shows are held each year; UNIX system books and magazines can be found in bookstores; and articles on the UNIX operating system are abundant. The UNIX operating system is available on many machines, including microcomputers, minicomputers, mainframes, and supercomputers. Even non-UNIX operating systems, such as MS-DOS and Windows NT, have adopted some of the traits of the UNIX system.

The UNIX system has become so important in the computer industry that in recent years there has been widespread concern that the UNIX system itself be standardized. While hardware manufacturers were adapting the UNIX system to their hardware, many of them made changes to it. Ironically, these changes make it difficult for software developers to develop applications that will run on all versions of the system. In the process of making the generic operating system a standard for a variety of machine architectures, changes were made to it that made it less standard.

To standardize the UNIX system, and in turn improve the market for applications, AT&T melded their version of the system, System V, with features of other prominent versions: XENIX, Berkeley Software Distribution (BSD), and SunOS. The result was System V Release 4. AT&T also established a written standard, the System V Interface Definition (SVID). Meanwhile, individuals from companies throughout the industry have joined together to develop a standard called POSIX (Portable Operating System Interface for Computer Environments), which is largely based on the System V Interface Definition and other earlier standardization efforts. These efforts have been spurred by the federal government, which needs a standard computing environment in order to minimize training and procurement costs. As these standards gain widespread acceptance, software developers will be able to develop applications that run on all conforming versions of the UNIX system.

The Future of the UNIX System

As the UNIX system grew larger and more complicated, it became less attractive as a platform for operating system research. Individual manufacturers added value to the system, extending it with unique features. They also made it difficult for others to learn enough about their computers to be able to replace their version of the UNIX system with a different one. In 1993, the Berkeley Computer Systems Research Group exhausted their last source of funding for their continuing UNIX work and the group was dissolved. The last version of BSD UNIX is 4.4; many of its features will undoubtedly be adopted in other versions of the UNIX system, but the BSD 4.4 release (as a whole) will run on very few systems. Thanks to the portability of the UNIX system, it runs on so many different types of computers that one group (such as the CSRG) cannot hope to serve them all.

Some of the Berkeley researchers joined a new company called BSDi, where they have created an inexpensive operating system that runs on PCs, based on the Berkeley Software Distribution. BSDi is an unusual company in that its employees are distributed over a wide geographic area; they interact electronically, over the network. The goal of another organization, the Free Software Foundation, is to create a UNIX-like system that they distribute free of charge. Their project is known as GNU (which stands for "GNU's Not UNIX"), and although they have not written a complete operating system yet, they have contributed many useful, highly portable versions of popular utilities (compiler, debugger, etc.) Both BSDi and the Free Software Foundation are committed to releasing the source code for their software (at low or no cost) whenever possible. This tradition dates back to the earliest days of the UNIX system and contributed to its success and portability.

The largest computer market today is for personal computers, most of which run MS-DOS or Windows. PCs were meant to be used by a single user at a time, so the multiuser, multitasking benefits of the UNIX system were of little interest in the PC community. The UNIX system, however, is typically the operating system of choice for workstations and many larger systems. In response, Microsoft has created a new operating system, Windows NT, that it hopes will come to displace the UNIX system in the workstation market. At this time, it is still too early to tell whether Windows NT is powerful enough to succeed; many UNIX system manufacturers have responded by porting NT to their hardware platforms and by pooling their efforts in a consortium (COSE, which stands for Common Open Software Environment) to define a new standard.

How Can UNIX Run On So Many Machines?

An operating system that can run on many different machines is said to be *portable*. About 95 percent of the UNIX operating system is written in the C programming language, and C is portable because it is written in a higher-level, machine-independent language. (Even the C compiler is written in C.)

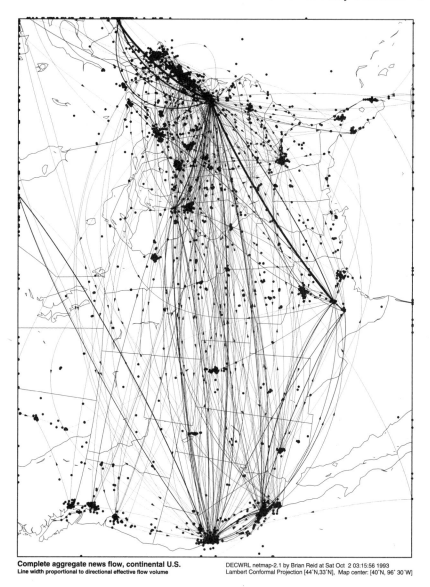

Complete aggregate news flow, continental U.S.
Line width proportional to directional effective flow volume

DECWRL netmap-2.1 by Brian Reid at Sat Oct 2 03:15:56 1993
Lambert Conformal Projection [44˚N,33˚N], Map center: [40˚N, 96˚ 30´W]

Figure 1-3   Site locations and news exchange paths for major USENET sites in the continental U.S. The USENET is a decentralized electronic mail and news network that links more than one million users worldwide. (Map courtesy of Brian Reid.)

The C Programming Language

Ken Thompson originally wrote the UNIX operating system in PDP-7 assembly language. Assembly language is a machine-dependent language—programs written in assembly language work on only one machine or, at best, one family of machines. Therefore, the original UNIX operating system could not easily be transported to run on other machines.

In order to make the UNIX system portable, Thompson developed the B programming language, a machine-independent language. Dennis Ritchie developed the C programming language by modifying B and, with Thompson, rewrote the UNIX system in C. After this rewrite, the operating system could be transported more easily to run on other machines.

That was the start of C. You can see in its roots some of the reasons why it is such a powerful tool. C can be used to write machine-independent programs. A programmer who designs a program to be portable can easily move it to any computer that has a C compiler. As both C and the UNIX operating system become more popular, more machines have C compilers—including many non-UNIX machines.

C is a modern systems language. You can write a compiler or an operating system in C. It is highly structured, but it is not necessarily a high-level language. C allows a programmer to manipulate bits and bytes, as is necessary when writing an operating system. But it also has high-level constructs that allow efficient, modular programming.

C is becoming popular for the same reasons the UNIX operating system is successful. It is portable, standard, and powerful. It has high-level features for flexibility and can still be used for systems programming. These features make it both useful and usable. A standards organization, the American National Standards Institute, defined a standard version of the C language in the late 1980s that is commonly referred to as *ANSI C*. The original version of the language is often referred to as *Kernighan & Ritchie* (or just *K&R*) C, named for the authors of the book that first described it. Another researcher at Bell Labs, Bjarne Stroustrop, created an object-oriented programming language called C^{++} that is built upon the foundation of C.

Overview of the UNIX System

The UNIX operating system has many unique features. Like other operating systems, the UNIX system is a control program for computers. But it is also a well-thought-out family of utility programs (Figure 1-4) and a set of tools that allows users to connect and use these utilities to build systems and applications. This section discusses both the common and unique features of the UNIX operating system.

Utilities

The UNIX system includes a family of several hundred utility programs, often referred to as *commands*. These utilities perform functions that are universally required by users. An example is **sort**. The **sort** utility puts lists (or groups of lists) in order. It can put lists in alphabetical or numerical order and thus can be used to sort by part number, author, last name, city, ZIP code, telephone number, age, size, cost, and so forth. The **sort** utility is an important programming tool and is part of the standard UNIX system. Other utilities allow users to create, display, print, copy, search, and delete files. There are also text editing, formatting, and typesetting utilities. The **man** (for manual) utility provides on-line documentation of the UNIX system itself.

Figure 1-4   The UNIX Operating System

The UNIX System Can Support Many Users

Depending on the machine being used, a UNIX system can support from one to over one hundred users, each concurrently running a different set of programs. The cost of a computer that can be used by many people at the same time is less per user than that of a computer that can be used by only a single person at a time. The cost is less because one person cannot generally use all of the resources a computer has to offer. No one can keep the printer going constantly, keep all the system memory in use, keep the disk busy reading and writing, keep the tape drives spinning, keep the modem in use, and keep the terminals busy. A multiuser operating system allows many people to use all of the system resources almost simultaneously. Thus, utilization of costly resources can be maximized, and the cost per user can be minimized. These are the primary objectives of a multiuser operating system.

The UNIX System Can Support Many Tasks

The UNIX operating system allows each user to run more than one job at a time. You can run several jobs in the background while giving all your attention to the job being displayed on your terminal, and you can even switch back and forth between jobs. This *multitasking* capability enables users to be more productive.

The UNIX System Kernel

The kernel is the heart of the UNIX operating system, responsible for controlling the computer's resources and scheduling user jobs so that each one gets its fair share of the resources (including the CPU as well as access to peripheral devices such as disk storage, printers, and tape drives). Programs interact with the kernel through special functions with well-known names, called *system calls*. A programmer can use a single system call to interact with many different kinds of devices. For example, there is one **write** system call, not many device-specific ones. When a program issues a **write** request, the kernel interprets the context and passes the request along to the appropriate device. This flexibility allows old utilities to work with devices that did not exist when the utilities were originally written, and it makes it possible to move programs to new versions of the system without rewriting them (provided that the new system recognizes the same system calls).

File Structure

A *file* is a collection of information, such as text for a memo or report, an accumulation of sales figures, or object code created by a compiler. Each file is stored under a unique name, usually on a disk storage device. The UNIX filesystem provides a structure where files are arranged under directories, and directories in turn are arranged under other directories, and so forth, in a treelike organization. This structure assists users in keeping track of large numbers of files by enabling them to group related files into directories. Each user has one primary directory and as many subdirectories as required.

Another mechanism, *links*, allows a given file to be accessed by means of two or more different names. The alternative names can be located in the same directory as the original file or in another directory. Links can be used to make the same file appear in several users' directories, enabling them to share the file easily.

Security—Private and Shared Files

Like most multiuser operating systems, the UNIX system allows users to protect their data from access by other users. The UNIX system also allows users to share selected data and programs with certain other users by means of a simple but effective protection scheme.

The Shell

The shell is a command interpreter that acts as an interface between users and the operating system. When you enter a command at a terminal, the shell interprets the command and calls the program you want. There are three popular shells in use today: the Bourne Shell, the C Shell, and the Korn

Shell. Because different users can use different shells at the same time on one system, a system can appear different to different users. The choice of shells demonstrates one of the powers of the UNIX operating system: the ability to provide a customized user interface.

Besides its regular function of interpreting commands from a terminal keyboard and sending them to the operating system, the shell can be used as a high-level programming language. Shell commands can be arranged in a file for later execution as a high-level program. This flexibility allows users to perform complex operations with relative ease, often with rather short commands, or to build elaborate programs that perform highly complex operations, with surprisingly little effort.

Filename Generation

When you are typing commands to be processed by the shell, you can construct patterns using special characters that have special meanings to the shell. These patterns are a kind of shorthand: Rather than typing in complete filenames, users can type in patterns and the shell will fill them in, generating matching filenames. A pattern can save you the effort of typing in a long filename or a long series of similar filenames. Patterns can also be useful when you know only part of a filename and when you cannot remember the exact spelling.

Device-Independent Input and Output

Devices (such as a printer or terminal) and disk files all appear as files to UNIX programs. When you give the UNIX operating system a command, you can instruct it to send the output to any one of several devices or files. This diversion is called output *redirection*.

In a similar manner, a program's input that normally comes from a terminal can be redirected so that it comes from a disk file instead. Under the UNIX operating system, input and output are *device-independent;* they can be redirected to or from any appropriate device.

As an example, the **cat** utility normally displays the contents of a file on the terminal screen. When you enter a **cat** command, you can cause its output to go to a disk file instead of to the terminal.

Interprocess Communication

The UNIX system allows users to establish both pipes and filters on the command line. A *pipe* sends the output of one program to another program as input. A *filter* is a program designed to process a stream of input data and yield a stream of output data. Filters are often used between two pipes. A filter processes another program's output, altering it in some manner. The filter's output then becomes input to another program.

Pipes and filters frequently join utilities to perform a specific task. For example, you can use a pipe to send the output of the **cat** utility to **sort**, a filter, and then use another pipe to send the output of **sort** to a third utility, **lpr**, that will send the file to a printer. Thus, in one command line you can use three utilities together to sort a file and print it.

Additional Features of the UNIX System

Over the years, many people have contributed to the maturation of the UNIX system. The two most prominent versions of the system in use today, Berkeley UNIX and UNIX System V, share a common ancestor—a version of the UNIX system developed by researchers at AT&T Bell Laboratories in the late 1970s called Version 7. Berkeley UNIX originated as a result of additions and modifications made to Version 7 by the Computer Systems Research Group at the University of California at Berkeley. Early versions of Berkeley UNIX added a full-screen text editor (**vi**), a new user interface (the C Shell), and virtual memory management, which enabled the UNIX system to support large applications. Later additions included a new filesystem for higher performance, and a networking subsystem for the support of a wide range of networking protocols. With the networking subsystem, users can log in on one machine and easily copy files to remote machines, run commands on remote machines, and log in on remote machines.

While the Computer Systems Research Group at Berkeley was making its changes to UNIX, AT&T was enhancing it in ways that ultimately resulted in System V. AT&T incorporated work done on the Programmer's Workbench UNIX system (originally developed for use within the Bell System) as well as features produced for other versions in use within AT&T. The result was System III, the predecessor of System V. Notable additions to System V were virtual memory management and new interprocess communication mechanisms. Recent releases of System V include a new filesystem that can span machines and a new networking subsystem.

Many manufacturers have based their operating systems on the BSD version of UNIX; most manufacturers include at least some BSD features and utilities in their versions of the UNIX system. One of the first companies to do so was Sun Microsystems, whose SunOS is descended directly from BSD 4.2. Sun's researchers and developers are responsible for some key innovations that have been widely adopted throughout the UNIX community, such as the Network File System (NFS) and Network Information Service (NIS). The popularity of Sun's workstations and their software has been recognized in the System V community; the latest version, System V Release 4, merged popular features from SunOS, Berkeley UNIX, and XENIX with System V. The following sections describe some of these additional features.

Job Control

Job control allows users to work on several jobs at once, switching back and forth between them as desired. Frequently, when you start a job, it is in the foreground, so it is connected to your terminal. Using job control, you can move the job you are working with into the background so that you can work on or observe another job while the first is running. If a background job needs your attention, you can move it into the foreground so that it is once again attached to your terminal. The concept of job control originated with Berkeley UNIX, where it appeared in the C Shell.

Advanced Electronic Mail

The Berkeley UNIX **Mail** utility

- allows users to reply to a message, automatically addressing the reply to the person who sent the message
- allows users to use an editor (such as **vi** or **emacs**) to edit a piece of electronic mail while they are composing it
- presents users with a summary of all messages waiting for them when they call it up to read their mail
- can automatically keep a copy of all electronic mail users send
- allows users to create aliases that make it easier to send mail to groups of people
- allows users to customize features to suit their needs

See page 46 for a tutorial, and see **mail** in Part II for a detailed summary of this utility.

Screen-Oriented Editor

The **vi** editor, created at Berkeley, is an advance over its predecessor, **ed**, because it displays a context for editing: where **ed** displayed a line at a time, **vi** displays a screenful of text.

This book explains how to use **vi** in stages, from the introduction in Chapter 2 (page 30) through "Advanced Editing Techniques" (page 205). Most of the **vi** coverage is in Chapter 8, which is dedicated to the use of this editor.

Scrolling Through a File

The Berkeley UNIX utility called **more** allows users to display files on their terminals one screenful at a time. When you finish reading what is on the screen, you ask for another screenful by pressing a single key. This utility also has the ability to scroll backward through a file. See **more** in Part II for more information.

Networking Utilities

Berkeley UNIX integrated support for networking, including many valuable utilities that enable users to access remote systems over a variety of networks.

Shell Functions

One of the most important features of the shell (the UNIX command interpreter) is that users can use it as a programming language. Because the shell is an interpreter, it does not compile programs written for it but interprets them each time they are loaded in from the disk. Interpreting and loading programs can be time-consuming.

Two of the most popular shells, the Bourne Shell and the Korn Shell, allow you to write shell functions that the shell will hold in memory, so it does not have to read them from the disk each time you want to execute them. The shell also keeps functions in an internal format, so it does not have to spend as much time interpreting them. Shell functions first appeared in System V, but have been adopted by other versions of the UNIX system such as SunOS. Refer to pages 333 and 387 for more information on shell functions.

Although the third major shell, the C Shell, does not have shell functions, it has a similar feature: aliases. Aliases allow you to define new commands and to make standard utilities perform in nonstandard ways. The C Shell provides aliases but not shell functions; the Korn Shell provides both.

Figure 1-5 A Sun SPARCstation 20 which can house multiple processors. This workstation is based on a SuperSPARC RISC chip running at 60MHz and can hold up to 512MB of main memory. (Courtesy Sun Microsystems, Inc.)

SunOS

SunOS was one of the first UNIX systems to support computer graphics, on a bit-mapped display, including a window system and graphical user interface. Sun's Network File System allows users to work with files that are actually stored on remote computers without any special tools, just as if the files were really stored on a user's local computer system. Sun's Network Information Service simplifies the task of administering common system configuration files, allowing them to be shared by many systems. Changes made by Sun to the organization of the UNIX filesystem hierarchy have made it easier to separate system-independent information that can be shared (such as utilities and on-line documentation) from system-specific data (such as system log files). Just as Berkeley's work has been incorporated in other versions of the UNIX system, SunOS has had a similar influence on the evolution of the UNIX system.

Graphical User Interfaces

The X Window System, developed in part by researchers at the Massachusetts Institute of Technology, provides the foundation for the graphical user interface available with most versions of UNIX today, including SunOS. Given a terminal or workstation screen that supports X Windows, a user can interact with the computer through multiple windows on the screen, display graphical information, or use special-purpose applications to draw pictures or preview typesetter output. The most widely supported graphical user interface on UNIX systems today, built to run under the X Window System, is called OSF/Motif. Another interface, OPEN LOOK, runs on Sun workstations, but is being phased out in favor of Motif.

What Are the Limitations of the UNIX System?

The most commonly heard complaints about the UNIX operating system are that it has an unfriendly, terse, treacherous, unforgiving, inconsistent, and nonmnemonic user interface. These complaints are well founded, but the shortcomings of the user interface were largely a by-product of the original design goals of the system. The designers of the UNIX system intended it to be used by highly skilled programmers for whom ease of use is much less important than power and flexibility.

As the UNIX system became popular with a wider variety of users, many of the worst problems were rectified by newer versions of the operating system and by some application programs. Also, new features of the shells have made them easier to use. In particular, aliases and shell functions enable you to rename and redefine commands so that they are more user-friendly and forgiving, and so you can avoid some of the peculiarities of command line syntax. Although these features make the shells easier to use, they have not changed the basic nature of the user interface. The shells have stayed basically the same for a good reason—many of the features that make them difficult to learn are the same ones that make them so useful for experienced users.

The UNIX system is called unfriendly and terse because it follows the philosophy that "no news is good news." The **ed** editor does not prompt you for input or commands, the **cp** (copy) utility does not confirm that it has copied a file successfully, and the **who** utility does not display column headings before its list of users. It just presents information with no titles or explanation.

This terseness is useful because it facilitates the use of the *pipe* facility, which allows the output from one program to be fed into another program as input. Thus, you can find out how many people are using the system by sending the output of **who** into **wc**, a utility that counts the number of lines in a file. If **who** displayed a heading before it displayed the list of users, you would have to remember to subtract one from the number of lines counted.

In a similar manner, although it would be nice if **ed** prompted you when you were using it as an interactive editor, it would not be as useful when you wanted to feed it input from another program and have it automatically edit a group of files.

The UNIX system was originally designed for slow hard-copy terminals. The less copy a program printed out, the sooner it was done. With high-speed terminals and CRT displays, this is no longer a problem. Editors that display more information (e.g., **vi**) were soon created to take advantage of those technological advances.

The shell user interface can still be treacherous, however. A typing mistake on a command line can easily destroy important files, and it is possible to log off the system inadvertently. You must use caution when working with a powerful operating system. If you want a foolproof system, you can use the tools the UNIX system provides to customize the shell. Some manufacturers are producing menu-driven user interfaces that make it very difficult to make mistakes that have such far-reaching consequences. The C Shell and Korn Shell both have optional built-in safeguards against many of these problems.

Due to its simplicity, the UNIX operating system has had, and still has, some limitations. In older versions, mechanisms to synchronize separate jobs were poorly implemented, as were mechanisms for locking files—important features in a multiuser operating system. The objection that is perhaps the most serious and difficult to overcome is that the UNIX operating system does not have a guaranteed hardware-interrupt response time. This prevents a standard UNIX system from being used in some real-time applications. Other new features that are available from certain manufacturers include concurrency, fault tolerance, and parallel processing. As the system continues to evolve, future versions will undoubtedly provide these and other new features, meeting a wider variety of users' needs.

SUMMARY

Although the UNIX operating system has some shortcomings, most of them can be rectified using the tools that the UNIX system itself provides. The unique approach that the UNIX operating system takes to the problems of standardization and portability, its strong foothold in the professional community, its power as a development tool, and its chameleonlike user interface are helping it to emerge as the standard first choice of users, hardware manufacturers, and software manufacturers.

REVIEW EXERCISES

1. What is a time-sharing system? Why are they successful?

2. Why is the UNIX system popular with manufacturers? Why is it popular in academia?

3. What language is the UNIX system written in? What does the language have to do with the success of the UNIX system?

4. What is a utility program?

5. What is the shell? Why was it designed to be terse?

6. How can you use utility programs and the shell to create your own applications?

7. Why is the UNIX filesystem referred to as a *hierarchical* (or *treelike*) filesystem?

8. Although the UNIX system is a generic operating system, there are different versions of it. Explain this apparent contradiction.

9. Why is it important to software developers that the different versions of the UNIX system converge? What is being done in the industry to promote convergence?

CHAPTER 2

Getting Started

*This chapter explains how to log in on and use the UNIX system. It discusses several important names and keyboard keys that are specific to you, your terminal, and your installation. Following a description of the conventions used in this book, this chapter leads you through a brief session with your UNIX system. After showing you how to log in and out, it explains how to correct typing mistakes and abort program execution. Finally, it guides you through a short session with the **vi** editor and introduces other important utilities that manipulate files. With these utilities you can obtain lists of filenames, display the contents of files, and delete files.*

Before You Start

The best way to learn is by doing. You can read and use Chapters 2 through 14 while you are sitting in front of a terminal. Learn about the UNIX system by running the examples in this book and by making up your own. Feel free to experiment with different utilities. The worst thing that you can do is erase one of the files that you have created. Because these are only practice files, you can easily create another.

Before you log in on a UNIX system for the first time, take a few minutes to find out the answers to the following questions. Ask the system administrator or someone else who is familiar with your installation.

What Is My Login Name?

This is the name that you use to identify yourself to the UNIX system. It is also the name that other users use to send you electronic mail.

What Is My Password?

On systems with several users, passwords can prevent others from accessing your files. To start with, the system administrator assigns you a password. You can change your password at any time.

Which Key Ends a Line?

Different terminals use different keys to move the cursor to the beginning of the next line. This book always refers to the key that ends a line as the (RETURN) key. Your terminal may have a (RET), (NEWLINE), (ENTER), or other key. Some terminals use a key with a bent arrow on it. (The key with the bent arrow is not an arrow key. Arrow keys have arrows on straight shafts—you will use them when you use the **vi** editor.) Figure 2-1 shows a standard terminal keyboard. The key that ends a line on this keyboard is the (RETURN) key. Each time this book asks you to "press the (RETURN) key" or "press (RETURN)," press the equivalent key on your terminal.

Which Is the Erase Key?

The default erase key under Berkeley UNIX is (BACKSPACE) while on Sun machines it is (DELETE) (labeled (DELETE), (DEL), or **RUBOUT**—you may have to hold the (SHIFT) key down while you press this key to make it work). This key will back up over and erase the characters you just entered, one at a time. If these keys do not work, try (CONTROL)-**H** (press H while holding the (CONTROL) or (CTRL) key down). If none of these keys erases characters, you may be able to use the # key. Ask your system administrator or refer to page 708 for examples of how to determine which key is your *erase* key and how to change it to one that is more convenient.

Which Is the Line Kill Key?

Usually, the key that deletes the entire line you are entering is (CONTROL)-**U**; however, @ is used occasionally. This key is called the line kill or simply kill

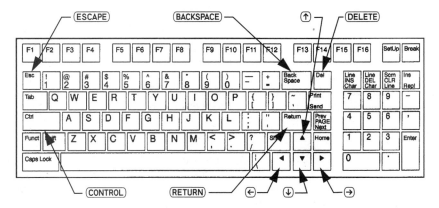

Figure 2-1   A Standard Terminal Keyboard (Courtesy of Wyse Technology.)

key. Refer to page 708 for examples of how to determine which key is your line kill key and how to change it.

Which Key Interrupts Execution?

On Berkeley UNIX the default key that interrupts almost any program you are running is the (DELETE) (or (DEL)) key. On Sun systems (CONTROL)-C is the standard interrupt key. Refer to page 706 for a description of the interrupt key.

What Is the Termcap or Terminfo Name for My Terminal?

A Termcap or Terminfo name describes the functional characteristics of your terminal to any program that requires this information. Berkeley and SunOS systems use Termcap names. Terminfo is available on a SunOS system that has been installed with the System V software option. You will need to know this name if you use **vi** (the visual editor). Some application programs also require this information.

Although the two methods for specifying a terminal are different, the way you use the names is the same. If your system uses Termcap names, use the Termcap name for your terminal when this book calls for a Terminfo name.

Which Shell Will I Be Using?

The shell interprets the commands you enter from the keyboard. You will probably be using the Bourne Shell, the C Shell, or the Korn Shell. They are similar in many respects. The examples in this book show the Bourne Shell but are generally applicable to all three shells. Chapters 5, 10, 11, and 12 describe the shells and the differences between them.

Which Version of UNIX Will I Be Using?

This book tells you what to expect when you are using a Berkeley UNIX based or SunOS system. If you are using another version of UNIX, you may notice subtle differences between what is described here and the behavior of your system.

How Can I Send Files to a Printer?

Most UNIX systems have at least one printer for producing hard copy. Typically, you will be able to use a utility called **lpr** to send output to a printer. However, if your system has more than one printer, you will use different commands, or different variations of one command, to send output to the various printers. Ask the system administrator how the printers are set up on your system. Refer to Chapter 3 for more information about printing.

Where Can I Find the UNIX Manuals?

Most versions of the UNIX system come with reference manuals. You may want to refer to them to get more information about specific topics while reading this book or to determine what features are available on your version of UNIX. The reference pages are also stored online, and you can view them with the **man** utility (page 51).

Conventions

This book uses conventions to make its explanations shorter and clearer. The following paragraphs describe these conventions.

Keys and Characters

This book uses key caps to show three different kinds of items:

- Important terminal keys, such as the (SPACE) bar and the (RETURN), (ESCAPE), and (TAB) keys.

- The characters that keys generate, such as the (SPACE)s generated by the (SPACE) bar.

- Terminal keys that you press with the (CONTROL) key, such as (CONTROL)-D. (Even though **D** is shown as an uppercase letter, you do not have to press the (SHIFT) key; enter (CONTROL)-**D** by holding the (CONTROL) key down and pressing **d**.)

Utility Names

Within the text, names of utilities are printed in **this typeface**. Thus, you will see references to the **sort** utility and the **vi** editor.

Filenames

Within the text, all filenames appear in lowercase letters in a **bold** typeface. Examples of files that appear in the text are: **memo5**, **letter.1283**, and **reports**. Filenames can include uppercase letters, but this book uses only lowercase filenames.

Items You Enter

Within the text, all commands that you can enter at the terminal are printed in a **bold** typeface. This book refers to the **ls** utility, or just **ls**, but instructs you to enter **ls –a** on the terminal. Thus, a distinction is made in the text between utilities, which are programs, and the instructions you give the computer to invoke the utilities.

In the screens and examples shown throughout this book, the items that you would enter are printed in **boldface** type, as they are in the text. However, unlike in the text, where items you enter are in **this boldface** type, in screens and examples the items you enter are in **this boldface** type. In the first line of Figure 2-2, for example, the word login: is printed in a regular typeface because the UNIX system displayed it. The word **jenny** is in boldface to show that the user entered it. The word **jenny** appears in the text.

Prompts and (RETURN)s

All examples include the shell prompt—the signal that the UNIX system is waiting for a command—as a dollar sign ($). Your prompt may differ—another common prompt is a percent sign (%). The prompt is printed in a regular typeface because you do not enter it. Do not enter the prompt on the terminal when you are experimenting with examples from this book. If you do, the examples will not work.

Examples *omit* the (RETURN) keystroke that you must use to execute them. An example of a command line follows:

```
$ vi memo.1204
```

To use this example as a model for calling the **vi** editor, enter **vi memo.1204** and then press the (RETURN) key. This method of giving examples makes the example in the book and what appears on your terminal screen the same. See the next section for a complete example.

Optional Information

A single line at the left margin and the word **OPTIONAL** mark the information that you can skip the first time you read a chapter. Passages that are marked as optional are not central to the concepts presented in the chapter, and they are often difficult. A good strategy is to read a chapter, skipping the optional sections, and return to them later after you are comfortable with the main ideas presented in the chapter. An example follows:

OPTIONAL

You can skip this information the first time you read the chapter.

Using the UNIX System

Now that you are acquainted with some of the special characters on the keyboard and the conventions this book uses, it will be easier to start using the UNIX system. This section leads you through a brief session, explaining how to log in, change your password, and log out.

```
login: jenny
Password:

Welcome to UNIX!

$
```

Figure 2-2　Logging In

Logging In

Since many people can use the UNIX operating system at the same time, it must be able to differentiate between you and other users. You must identify yourself before the UNIX system will process your requests.

Figure 2-2 shows how a typical login procedure appears on a terminal screen. Your login procedure may look different. If your terminal does not have the word login: on it, check to see that the terminal is turned on, then press the (RETURN) key a few times. If login: still does not appear, try pressing (CONTROL)-Q. You can also try pressing the (BREAK) key and the (RETURN) key alternately. If these procedures do not work, check with the system administrator. (If LOGIN: appears in uppercase letters, proceed. This situation is covered shortly.)

You must end every message or command to the UNIX system by pressing the (RETURN) key. Pressing (RETURN) signals that you have completed giving an instruction and that you are ready for the operating system to execute the command or respond to the message.

The first line of Figure 2-2 shows the UNIX system login: prompt followed by the user's response. The user entered **jenny**, her login name, followed by a (RETURN). Try logging in, making sure that you enter your login name exactly as it was given to you. The routine that verifies the login name and password is *case-sensitive*—it differentiates between uppercase and lowercase letters.

The second line of Figure 2-2 shows the Password: prompt. If your account does not require a password, you will not see this prompt. In the example, the user *did* respond to the prompt with a password followed by a (RETURN). For security, the UNIX operating system never displays a password. Enter your password in response to the Password: prompt, then press (RETURN). The characters you enter will not appear on the terminal screen.

You will see a message and a prompt when you successfully log in. The message, called the *message of the day*, generally identifies the version of the operating system that is running along with any special local messages added by your system administrator. If you are using the Bourne Shell or the Korn Shell, the prompt is usually a dollar sign ($). The C Shell generally prompts you with a percent sign (%) or a number followed by a percent sign. Either of these prompts indicates that the system is waiting for you to give it a command.

The Uppercase LOGIN Prompt

If the login prompt appears in all uppercase letters (LOGIN:), everything you enter will also appear in uppercase letters. The UNIX system thinks you have a terminal that can display only uppercase characters. It sends uppercase characters to the terminal and translates everything you enter to lowercase for its internal use. If you are having this problem and your terminal is capable of displaying both uppercase and lowercase characters, make sure the key on your keyboard that causes it to send uppercase characters has *not* been set. (This key is typically labeled **SHIFTLOCK** or (CAPS LOCK).) If it is set, unset it. Once you have logged in, give the following command. Press (RETURN) after you enter the command.

   $ STTY –LCASE

Incorrect Login

If you enter your name or password incorrectly, the **login** utility displays the following message, after you finish entering both your login name *and* password:

   Login incorrect

   This message tells you that you have entered either the login name *or* password incorrectly or that they are not valid. The message does not differentiate between an unacceptable login name and an unacceptable password. This discourages unauthorized people from guessing names and passwords to gain access to the system.

After You Log In

Once you log in, you are communicating with the command interpreter known as the shell. The shell plays an important part in all your communication with the UNIX operating system. When you enter a command at the terminal (in response to the shell prompt), the shell interprets the command and initiates the appropriate action. This action may be executing your program, calling a standard program such as a compiler or a UNIX utility program, or giving you an error message telling you that you have entered a command incorrectly.

Changing Your Password

When you first log in on a UNIX system, either you will not have a password or you will have a password that the system administrator assigned. In either case, it is a good idea to give yourself a new password. A good password is seven or eight characters long and contains a combination of numbers, uppercase letters, lowercase letters, and punctuation characters. Avoid using control characters (e.g., (CONTROL)-H) because they may collide with system operation, making it impossible for you to log in. Do not use names or other familiar words that someone can guess easily.

   Figure 2-3 shows the process of changing a password using the **passwd** utility. Depending on the version of UNIX you are using, the messages the **passwd** utility presents and the sequence of the interaction may differ

```
$ passwd
Changing password for jenny
Old password:
New password:
Re-enter new password:
```

*Figure 2-3   The **passwd** Utility*

slightly from the examples shown on the following pages, but the gist of the interaction is the same. For security reasons, none of the passwords that you enter is ever displayed by this or any other utility.

Give the command **passwd** (followed by a (RETURN)) in response to the shell prompt. This command causes the shell to execute the **passwd** utility. The first item **passwd** asks you for is your *old* password (it skips this question if you do not have a password yet). The **passwd** utility verifies this password to ensure that an unauthorized user is not trying to alter your password. Next, **passwd** requests the new password.

Your password must meet the following criteria:

- It must be at least six characters long.
- It must contain at least two letters and one number.
- It cannot be your login name, the reverse of your login name, or your login name shifted by one or more characters.
- If you are changing your password, the new password must differ from the old one by at least three characters. Changing the case of a character does not make it count as a different character.

After you enter your new password, **passwd** asks you to retype it to make sure you did not make a mistake when you entered it. If the new password is the same both times you enter it, your password is changed. If the passwords differ, it means that you made an error in one of them; **passwd** displays the following message:

```
Mismatch - password unchanged.
```

After you enter the new password, **passwd** will—as it did before—ask you to reenter it.

If your password does not meet the criteria listed above, **passwd** displays the following message:

```
Please use a longer password.
New password:
```

Enter a different password that meets the criteria in response to the New password: prompt.

When you successfully change your password, you change the way you will log in. You must always enter your password *exactly* the way you created it. If you forget your password, the system administrator can help straighten things out. Although no one can determine what your password is, the administrator can change it and tell you your new password.

Logging Out

Once you have changed your password, log out and try logging back in using your new password. Press (CONTROL)-**D** in response to the shell prompt to log out. If (CONTROL)-**D** does not work, try giving the command **exit** or **logout**. The **logout** command is typically used with the C Shell, whereas the Bourne Shell and Korn Shell use (CONTROL)-**D** or **exit**.

Correcting Mistakes

This section explains how to correct typing and other errors you may make while you are logged in. Log in on your system and try making and correcting mistakes as you read this section.

Because the shell and most other utilities do not interpret the command line (or other text) until after you press the (RETURN) key, you can correct typing mistakes before you press (RETURN). There are two ways to correct typing mistakes. You can erase one character at a time, or you can back up to the beginning of the command line in one step. After you press the (RETURN) key, it is too late to correct a mistake; you can either wait for the command to run to completion or abort execution of the program. Refer to the section "Aborting Program Execution" on page 28.

Erasing Characters

While entering characters from the keyboard, you can backspace over a mistake by pressing the erase key ((CONTROL)-**H**) one time for each character you want to delete. (In place of (CONTROL)-**H**, use the erase key you identified at the start of this chapter.) As the cursor moves to the left, the characters it moves over are discounted, even if they still appear on the screen. The erase key backs up over as many characters as you wish. It does not, however, back up past the beginning of the line.

Deleting an Entire Line

You can delete the entire line you are entering, any time before you press (RETURN), by pressing the line kill key ((CONTROL)-**U** or the line kill key you identified on page 20.) The cursor moves to the left, back to the beginning of the line, erasing the characters you had entered.

On some systems, when you press (CONTROL)-**U**, instead of erasing the line the cursor moves down to the next line and all the way to the left. The shell does not give you another prompt, but it is as though the cursor is sitting just following a shell prompt. The operating system does not remove the line with the mistake on it but ignores it. Enter the command (or other text) again, from the start.

Deleting a Word

You can delete the word you are entering by pressing (CONTROL)-**W**. When you press (CONTROL)-**W**, the cursor moves to the left to the beginning of the current word, removing the word. A *word* is any sequence of nonblank characters (that is, a sequence of characters that does not contain a (SPACE) or (TAB)). If you type (CONTROL)-**W** while in the process of typing in a word, the cursor moves to the beginning of the current word. If you type (CONTROL)-**W** after ending a word with a (SPACE) or (TAB) character, the cursor moves to the beginning of the previous word.

Redrawing a Line

If you use the erase key to change characters on the command line, and the erase key on your system does not remove the characters, it may become difficult to read the command line. You can press (CONTROL)-**R**, and the cursor will move down to the next line, and the system will redraw the command line. You can then continue entering characters to complete the command.

Aborting Program Execution

Sometimes you may want to terminate a running program. A UNIX program may be performing a task that takes a long time, such as displaying the contents of a file that is several hundred pages or copying a file that is not the file you meant to copy.

To terminate program execution, press the interrupt key ((DELETE)). (In place of (DELETE), use the interrupt key you identified at the start of this chapter.) When you press this key, the UNIX operating system sends a terminal interrupt signal to all your programs, including the shell. Exactly what effect this signal will have depends on the program. Some programs stop execution immediately, whereas others ignore the signal. Some programs take other, appropriate actions. When the shell receives a terminal interrupt signal, it displays a prompt and waits for another command.

Creating and Editing a File Using vi

A *file* is a collection of information that you can refer to by a *filename*. It is stored on a disk. *Text* files typically contain memos, reports, messages, program source code, lists, or manuscripts. An *editor* is a utility program that allows you to create a new text file or change a text file that already exists. Many editors are in use on UNIX systems. This section shows you how to create a file using **vi** (visual), a powerful (although sometimes cryptic), interactive, visually oriented text editor. This section also covers elementary **vi** editing commands. Chapter 8 explains how to use more advanced **vi** commands.

The **vi** editor is not a text formatting program. It does not justify margins, center titles, or provide the output formatting features of a word processing system. The **emacs** editor (Chapter 9) provides some of these features, but if you want different sizes and types of fonts, you must use a word processing application.

Specifying a Terminal

Because **vi** takes advantage of features that are specific to various kinds of terminals, you must tell it what type of terminal you are using. The Terminfo or Termcap name for your terminal that you identified at the beginning of this chapter communicates this information to **vi**.

On many systems your terminal type may already be set for you automatically. When you log in you may be prompted to identify the type of terminal you are using:

```
TERM = (vt100)
```

If you press (RETURN) your terminal type will be set to the name in parentheses. If that name does not describe the terminal you are using, enter the correct name before you press (RETURN).

```
TERM = (vt100) wyse50
```

If the system does not recognize the name you enter, you may need to ask your system administrator for help. In place of a specific model name, you may be able to use the name **ansi**, which describes a standard set of terminal capabilities defined by the American National Standards Institute. Many types of terminals conform to this standard, which provides sufficient capability to run **vi**.

To check whether your terminal type has been set, give the following command:

```
$ echo $TERM
```

If the system responds with the wrong name, a blank line, or an error message, you can set or change the terminal name as follows.

If you are using the Bourne Shell or Korn Shell, you type in commands similar to those below to identify the type of terminal you are using. If you always use the same type of terminal, you can place these commands in your **.profile** file so the UNIX system will automatically execute them each time you log in (page 71). Replace **name** with the Terminfo or Termcap name for your terminal.

```
TERM=name
export TERM
```

Following are the actual commands you would enter if you were using a Digital Equipment Corporation (DEC) VT-100 terminal:

```
$ TERM=vt100
$ export TERM
```

The C Shell requires the following command format:

```
setenv TERM name
```

You can place a command such as this one in your **.login** file for automatic execution (page 71). Again, replace **name** with the appropriate name for your terminal.

```
~
~
~
~
~
~
~
~
"practice" [New file]
```

Figure 2-4 Starting **vi**

An Editing Session

This section describes how to start **vi**, enter text, move the cursor, correct text, and exit from **vi**. Most **vi** commands take effect immediately. Except as noted, you do not need to press (RETURN) to end a **vi** command.

When giving **vi** a command, it is important that you distinguish between uppercase and lowercase letters. The **vi** editor interprets the same letter as two different commands, depending on whether you enter an uppercase or lowercase character. Beware of the key that causes your keyboard to send uppercase characters. It is typically labeled **SHIFTLOCK** or (CAPS LOCK). If you set this key to enter uppercase text while you are in Input Mode and then you exit to Command Mode, **vi** will interpret your commands as uppercase letters. It can be very confusing when this happens, because **vi** does not appear to be doing what you want.

Starting vi

Start **vi** with the following command line to create a file named **practice**. Terminate the command line with (RETURN).

    $ vi practice

The command line will disappear, and the terminal screen will look similar to the one shown in Figure 2-4.

The tildes (~) indicate that the file is empty. They will go away as you add lines to the file. If your screen looks like a distorted version of the one shown, your terminal type is probably not set correctly. If your screen looks similar to the one shown in Figure 2-5, your terminal type is probably not set at all.

To set your terminal type correctly, press (ESCAPE) and then give the following command to exit from **vi** and get the shell prompt back:

    :q!

When you enter the colon, **vi** will move the cursor to the bottom line of the screen. The characters **q!** tell **vi** to quit without saving your work. (You will not ordinarily exit from **vi** in this way because you will typically want to save your work.) You must press (RETURN) after you give this command. Once

```
$ vi practice
[Using open mode]
"practice" [New file]
```

Figure 2-5   Starting **vi** *Without Your Terminal Type Set*

you get the shell prompt back, refer to the preceding section, "Specifying a Terminal," and then start **vi** again.

The **practice** file is new; there is no text in it yet. The **vi** editor displays the following message on the status (bottom) line of the terminal to show that you are creating and editing a new file. Your system may display a different message.

```
"practice" [New file]
```

When you edit an existing file, **vi** displays the first few lines of the file and gives status information about the file on the status line.

Command and Input Modes

The **vi** editor has two modes of operation: *Command Mode* and *Input Mode*. While **vi** is in Command Mode, you can give **vi** commands. For example, in Command Mode you can delete text or exit from **vi**. You can also command **vi** to enter the Input Mode. While in the Input Mode, **vi** accepts anything you enter as text and displays it on the terminal screen. You can press (ESCAPE) to return **vi** to Command Mode.

The **vi** editor does not normally keep you informed about which mode it is in. If you give the **:set showmode** command, **vi** will display the mode at the lower right of the screen while it is in Input Mode.

```
:set showmode
```

When you enter the colon, **vi** moves the cursor to the status line. Enter the command and press (RETURN). There are three types of Input Mode: OPEN, INSERT, and APPEND. Refer to page 203 for more information about **showmode**.

Entering Text

After you start a new session with **vi**, you must put it in Input Mode before you can enter text. To put **vi** in Input Mode, press the **i** key. If you have not set **showmode**, **vi** will not respond to let you know that it is in Input Mode.

If you are not sure whether **vi** is in Input Mode, press the (ESCAPE) key; **vi** will return to Command Mode if it was in Input Mode or beep (some terminals flash) if it is already in Command Mode. You can put **vi** back in Input Mode by pressing the **i** key again.

While **vi** is in Input Mode, you can enter text by typing on the terminal. If the text does not appear on the screen as you type, you are not in Input Mode.

Enter the sample paragraph shown in Figure 2-6, pressing the (RETURN) key to end each line. As you enter text, you should prevent lines of text from

```
vi (visual) is a powerful,
interactive, visually oriented
text editor.
This section shows you how to create a
file using vi.
It also covers beginning editing commands.
Chapter 8 goes into detail about using
more advanced vi commands.
~
~
~
~
~
~
~
~
~
~
~
~
~
~
"practice" New file                    INSERT MODE
```

Figure 2-6   Entering Text with **vi**

wrapping around from the right side of the screen to the left by pressing the
(RETURN) key before the cursor reaches the far right side of the screen. Also,
make sure that you do not end a line with a (SPACE). Some **vi** commands (such
as the **w** command) will not behave properly when they encounter a line
that ends with a (SPACE).

While you are using **vi**, you can always correct any typing mistakes you
make. If you notice a mistake on the line you are entering, you can correct
it before you continue. Refer to the next paragraph. You can correct other
mistakes later. When you finish entering the paragraph, press the (ESCAPE) key
to return **vi** to Command Mode.

Correcting Text as You Insert It

The keys that allow you to back up and correct a shell command line serve
the same functions when **vi** is in Input Mode. These keys include the erase
and line kill keys you inquired about earlier (usually (CONTROL)-**H** and
(CONTROL)-**U**) as well as the word kill key ((CONTROL)-**W**). Although **vi** may not
remove deleted text from the screen as you back up over it, **vi** will remove
it when you type over it or press (ESCAPE).

There are two restrictions on the use of these correction keys. They allow you only to back up over text on the line you are entering (you cannot back up to a previous line), and they back up only over text that you just entered. As an example, assume that **vi** is in Input Mode—you are entering text and press the (ESCAPE) key to return **vi** to Command Mode. Then you give the i command to put **vi** back in Input Mode. Now you cannot back up over text you entered the first time you were in the Input Mode, even if the text is part of the line you are working on.

Moving the Cursor

When you are using **vi**, you will need to move the cursor on the screen so that you can delete text, insert new text, and correct text. While **vi** is in Command Mode, you can use the (RETURN) key, the (SPACE) bar, and the **ARROW** keys to move the cursor. If your terminal does not have **ARROW** keys, you can use the **h, j, k,** and **l** keys to move the cursor left, down, up, and right, respectively.

Deleting Text

You can delete a single character by moving the cursor until it is over the character you want to delete and then giving the command **x**. You can delete a word by positioning the cursor on the first letter of the word and giving the command **dw** (delete word). You can delete a line of text by moving the cursor until it is anywhere on the line you want to delete and then giving the command **dd**.

The Undo Command

If you delete a character, line, or word by mistake, give the command **u** (undo) immediately after you give the Delete command, and **vi** will restore the deleted text. If you give the command **u** again immediately, **vi** will undo the undo command, and the deleted text will be gone.

Inserting Additional Text

When you want to insert new text within text that you have already entered, move the cursor so that it is on the character that will follow the new text you plan to enter. Then give the **i** (insert) command to put **vi** in Input Mode, enter the new text, and press (ESCAPE) to return **vi** to Command Mode.

To enter one or more lines, position the cursor on the line above where you want the new text to go. Give the command **o** (open). The **vi** editor will open a blank line, put the cursor on it, and go into Input Mode. Enter the new text, ending each line with a (RETURN). When you are finished entering text, press (ESCAPE) to return **vi** to Command Mode.

Correcting Text

To correct text, use **dd, dw,** or **x** to remove the incorrect text. Then use **i** or **o** to insert the correct text.

For example, one way to change the word *beginning* to *elementary* in Figure 2-6 is to use the **ARROW** keys to move the cursor until it is on top of the *b* in *beginning*. Then give the command **dw** to delete the word *beginning*. Put **vi** in Input Mode by giving an **i** command, enter the word *elementary* followed by a (SPACE), and press (ESCAPE). The word is changed and **vi** is in Command Mode, waiting for another command.

```
vi (visual) is a powerful,
interactive, visually oriented
text editor.
This section shows you how to create a
file using vi.
It also covers elementary editing commands.
Chapter 8 goes into detail about using
more advanced vi commands.
~
~
~
~
~
~
~
~
~
~
~
"practice" [New file] 8 lines, 235 characters
$
```

Figure 2-7   Exiting from **vi**

Ending the Editing Session

While you are editing, **vi** keeps the edited text in an area called the *Work Buffer*. When you finish editing, you must write out the contents of the Work Buffer to a disk file so that the edited text will be saved and available when you next want it.

Make sure **vi** is in Command Mode and use the **ZZ** command (you must use uppercase **Z**'s) to write your newly entered text to the disk and end the editing session. After you give the **ZZ** command, **vi** displays the name of the file you are editing and the number of characters in the file; then it returns control to the shell (Figure 2-7).

Listing the Contents of a Directory

If you followed the preceding example, you used **vi** to create a file named **practice** in your directory. After exiting from **vi**, you can use the **ls** (list) utility to display a list of the names of the files in your directory. The first command in Figure 2-8 shows **ls** listing the name of the **practice** file. Subsequent commands in Figure 2-8 display the contents of the file and remove the file. These commands are described next.

```
$ ls
practice
$ cat practice
vi (visual) is a powerful,
interactive, visually oriented
text editor.
This section shows you how to create a
file using vi.
It also covers elementary editing commands.
Chapter 8 goes into detail about using
more advanced vi commands.
$ rm practice
$ ls
$ cat practice
cat: cannot open practice
$
```

Figure 2-8   Using **ls**, **cat**, *and* **rm**

Displaying the Contents of a Text File

The **cat** utility displays the contents of a text file. The name of the command is derived from *catenate*, which means to join together one after another. As Chapter 5 explains, one of **cat**'s functions is to join files together in this manner. To use **cat**, enter cat followed by a (SPACE) and the name of the file that you want to display.

Figure 2-8 shows **cat** displaying the contents of **practice**. This figure shows the difference between the **ls** and **cat** utilities. The **ls** utility displays the *names* of the files in a directory, whereas **cat** displays the *contents* of a file.

If you want to view a file that is longer than one screenful, you can use the **more** utility in place of **cat**. The **more** utility pauses after displaying a screenful, waiting for you to press the (SPACE) bar. At the end of the file **more** returns you directly to the shell. Give the command **more practice** in place of the **cat** command in Figure 2-8 to see how it works. Part II describes **more** in greater detail.

Deleting a File

The **rm** (remove) utility deletes a file. Figure 2-8 shows **rm** deleting the **practice** file. After **rm** deletes the file, **ls** and **cat** show that **practice** is no longer in the directory. The **ls** utility does not list its filename, and **cat** says it cannot open the file. Consequently, you should be very careful when using **rm** to delete files.

Special Characters

Special characters—those that have a special meaning to the shell—are discussed in Chapter 5. These characters are mentioned here so that you can avoid accidentally using them as regular characters until you understand how the shell interprets them. For example, you should not use any of these characters in a filename. A list of the standard special characters includes:

     & ; | * ? ' " ` [ ] ( ) $ < > { } ^ # / \

In addition, %, !, and ~ are special characters to the C Shell and the Korn Shell.

Although not considered special characters, (RETURN), (SPACE), and (TAB) also have special meanings to the shell. (RETURN) usually ends a command line and initiates execution of a command. The (SPACE) and (TAB) characters separate elements on the command line and are collectively known as *white space* or *blanks*.

Quoting Characters

If you need to use as a regular character one of the characters that has a special meaning to the shell, you can *quote* it. When you quote a special character, you keep the shell from giving it special meaning. The shell treats a quoted special character as a regular character.

To quote a character, precede it with a backslash (\). One backslash must precede each character that you are quoting. If you are using two or more special characters, you must precede each with a backslash (e.g., ** must be entered as **). You can quote a backslash just as you would quote any other special character—by preceding it with a backslash (\\).

Another way of quoting special characters is to enclose them between single quotation marks (e.g., '**'). You can quote many special and regular characters between a pair of single quotation marks (e.g., 'This is a special character: >'). The regular characters remain regular, and the shell also interprets the special characters as regular characters.

You can quote the erase character ((CONTROL)-H) and the line kill character ((CONTROL)-U) (and the exclamation point in the C Shell) by preceding any one with a backslash. Single quotation marks will not work.

SUMMARY

After reading this chapter and experimenting on your system, you should be able to log in and use the utilities and special keys listed below. Chapter 8 explains more about **vi**, and Part II has more information on **ls**, **rm**, and **cat**.

- the **passwd** command changes your password.

- (CONTROL)-**D**, **logout**, or **exit** logs you off the system.

- The (CONTROL)-**H**, (BACKSPACE), or another key is the erase key. It erases a character on the command line.

- The (CONTROL)-**R** (or another) key is the redraw line key. It redraws the current command line.
- The (CONTROL)-**U** (or another) key is the line kill key. It deletes the entire command line.
- The (CONTROL)-**W** (or another) key is the word erase key. It erases a word on the command line.
- The (DELETE) (or another) key interrupts execution of the program you are running.
- **vi** creates and edits a text file.
- **ls** lists the names of files.
- **cat** catenates the contents of files and displays them.
- **more** displays a file a screenful at a time.
- **rm** removes a file.

REVIEW EXERCISES

1. Is **fido** an acceptable password? Why or why not?
2. If you start **vi** and your screen looks strange, what might be wrong? How can you fix it?
3. When you first start **vi**, what mode are you in?
4. When you are in **vi**, what are the three ways you can tell whether you are in Input Mode?
5. How can you change from Command Mode to Input Mode in **vi**? How can you change back again?
6. What **vi** command(s) would you use to:
   a. delete a line
   b. undo your last command
   c. leave the **vi** editor

ADVANCED REVIEW EXERCISES

7. What are the differences between the **cat** and **ls** utilities? What are the differences between **more** and **cat**?
8. What is special about the *special characters*? How can you cause the shell to treat them as regular characters?

CHAPTER 3

An Introduction to the Utilities

UNIX utility programs allow you to work with the UNIX system and manipulate the files you create. Chapter 2 introduced the shell, the most important UNIX utility program, and **passwd,** *the utility that allows you to change your password. It also introduced some of the utilities that you can use to create and manipulate files:* **vi, ls, cat, more,** *and* **rm.** *This chapter describes several other file manipulation utilities, as well as utilities that allow you to find out who is logged in, communicate with other users, display system documentation, print files, and perform other useful functions.*

About the Utilities in This Chapter

Some of the utilities included in this chapter were chosen because you can learn to use them easily and they allow you to communicate with other people using the system. Others were chosen because they were designed to help users learn UNIX. Still others were chosen because they form the bases for examples in later chapters. Part II of this book covers many of these utilities as well as other utilities more concisely and completely.

Who Is Using the System?

There are several utilities that you can use to find out who is using the computer system, each varying in the details they provide and the options they support. The oldest utility, **who**, produces a short list of user names along with the terminal connection each person is using and the time the person logged into the system.

Two newer utilities, **w** and **finger**, show more detail (such as each user's full name and the command line each user is running). The **finger** utility can also be used to retrieve information about users on remote systems if your computer is attached to a local area network (see Chapter 7).

Using finger

You can use **finger** to display a list of the people who are currently using the system. In addition to login names, finger supplies each user's full name, along with information about which terminal line the person is using, how recently the user typed something on the keyboard, when the user logged in, and information about where the user is located (if the terminal line appears in a system database). If the user has logged in over the network, the name of the remote system is shown as the user's location (**bravo**, in Figure 3-1, for the user hls).

In Figure 3-1, the star (*) in front of the name of Helen's terminal (TTY) line indicates that she has blocked others from sending messages directly to her terminal (using the **mesg** utility, described on page 45).

You can also use **finger** to learn more about a particular individual by specifying more information on the command line. Figure 3-2 displays detailed information about the user Alex.

```
$ finger
Login         Name          TTY   Idle      When      Where
hls      Helen Simpson      *p0      1    Wed  8:34    bravo
scott    Scott Adams        02   23:48    Tue 15:21    Room 307
jenny    Jenny Chen         03            Wed  9:07    Room 201
alex     Alex Watson        06            Wed  9:15    Room 219
```

*Figure 3-1   The **finger** Utility I*

```
$ finger alex
Login name: alex              In real life: Alex Watson
Directory: /home/alex         Shell: /bin/csh
On since Aug 11  9:15:37 on tty06
New mail received Wed Aug 11 9:13:14 1994;
   unread since Wed Aug 11  9:01:40 1994
Plan:
For appointments contact Jenny Chen, x1693.
   .
   .
   .
```

Figure 3-2   The **finger** *Utility II*

Figure 3-2 shows that Alex is currently logged in and actively using his terminal (if he were not, **finger** would report how long he had been idle), some new mail has arrived for Alex that he has not yet read, and if you want to set up a meeting with him you should contact Jenny at extension 1693. Most of the information above was collected by **finger** from system files. The information shown after the heading Plan:, however, was supplied by Alex. The **finger** utility searched for a file named **.plan** in Alex's home directory and displayed its contents. You may find it helpful to create a **.plan** file for yourself; it can contain any information you choose, such as your typical schedule, interests, phone number, address, etc.

If Alex had not been logged in, the **finger** utility would have reported the last time he had used the system. If you do not know a person's login name, you can user the **finger** utility to learn it. For example, you might know that Helen's last name is Simpson, but you might not guess that her login name is hls. The **finger** utility can also search for information on Helen using her first or last name. The following commands will find the information you seek, along with information on other users on the system whose names are Helen or Simpson.

```
$ finger helen
   .
   .
   .
$ finger simpson
   .
   .
   .
```

Using w

The **w** utility displays a list of the users currently logged in. In Figure 3-3, the first column **w** displays shows that hls, Scott, Jenny, and Alex are logged in. The second column shows the designation of the terminal that each person is using. The third column shows the date and time that the person logged in. The fourth column indicates how long the person has been idle (how many minutes have elapsed since the last key was pressed on the key-

```
$ w
   9:19am  up 15 days, 12:24,  4 users,  load average: 0.15, 0.03, 0.01
User      tty       login@ idle   JCPU   PCPU  what
hls       ttyp0      8:34am   1     11      1  vi .profile
scott     tty02   Tue 3pm 23:48    16      1  -sh
jenny     tty03      9:07am                    w
alex      tty06      9:15am                    telnet bravo
```

Figure 3-3   The w Command

board). The next two columns give measures of how much computer processor time the person has used during the current login session and on the task that is currently running. The last column shows what the person is currently running.

The first line that the **w** utility displays is the same as that provided by the **uptime** command. This report includes the current time of day, how long the computer has been running (in days, hours, and minutes), how many users are logged in, and how busy the system is (load average). The three load average numbers represent the number of jobs waiting to run, averaged over the past minute, five minutes, and 15 minutes.

The **who** utility displays a report that is similar to that produced by **w**, but it includes less information. If you need to find out which terminal you are using or what time you logged in, you can use the command **who am i**.

```
$ who am i
alex       tty06        May 11  9:15
```

The information that **w** displays is useful if you want to communicate with someone at your installation. If the person is logged in and recently active, you can use **talk** or **write** (below) to establish communication immediately. If **w** does not show that the person is logged in or if you do not need to communicate immediately, you can send that person UNIX system mail (page 46).

Using talk to Communicate with Another User

You can use the **talk** utility to carry on a two-way conversation with another person who is logged in on your system. If your system is connected to a network, you can also use **talk** to communicate with someone on a different computer (see Chapter 7). When you use **talk**, your display screen will be split into two sections; once you establish contact with the other person, the messages you type will appear in the top half of your screen and the messages from the other person will be displayed in the bottom half. In this example, Alex needs some information from Jenny.

```
$ talk jenny
```

```
Alex's screen:                          Jenny's screen:

[Connection established]                [Connection established]
Did you finish the slides               Hi, Alex, what's up?
for the 9:30 meeting today?             Yes, they're all set.  Should
Sounds good, see you in a few           I just meet you in the conference
minutes!                                room?
                                        Bye.
-------------------------------         -------------------------------
Hi, Alex, what's up?                    Did you finish the slides
Yes, they're all set.  Should           for the 9:30 meeting today?
I just meet you in the conference       Sounds good, see you in a few
room?                                   minutes!
Bye.
```

Figure 3-4   *The* **talk** *Utility*

Alex's display is immediately split into two sections, and the following message appears at the top of his screen:

[Waiting for your party to respond]

Meanwhile, this message appears on Jenny's screen and she responds:

```
Message from Talk_Daemon@bravo at 9:22 ...
talk: connection requested by alex@bravo.
talk: respond with: talk alex@bravo
$ talk alex@bravo
```

Alex and Jenny are both using a computer named **bravo**; **alex@bravo** is Alex's network address, which will be described in more detail in Chapter 7. Figure 3-4 shows what Jenny's and Alex's screens look like as they type their messages.

To end the **talk** session, one person interrupts by pressing (DELETE), and the following message appears before a new shell prompt is displayed:

[Connection closing. Exiting]

If you see the following message when you try to use **talk** to reach someone, he or she has used the **mesg** command to block out interruptions. See the section on **mesg** on page 45.

[Your party is refusing messages]

Before the **talk** utility was available, people used the write command to interact with each other on the same computer. The **talk** utility has a few advantages over write: With **talk**, the other person's messages appear on your screen, letter by letter, as they are typed; write, on the other hand, sends only a whole line at a time. If you use **write**, sometimes you are not sure whether the other person is still connected at the other end (or just a slow typist). Also, unlike **write**, **talk** has been extended to support communication over the network. Still, if you need to exchange a quick message with another person logged in on your system, without disrupting your current screen display, you may want to use **write** instead.

```
$ write alex
Hi Alex, are you there? o
```

Figure 3-5   The **write** *Utility I*

Using write **to Send a Message**

You can use the **write** utility to send a message to another user who is logged in. When the other user also uses **write** to send you a message, you establish two-way communication.

When you give a **write** command (Figure 3-5), it displays a banner on the other user's terminal saying that you are about to send a message. The format of a **write** command line is as follows:

write destination-user [terminal]

The **destination-user** is the login name of the user you want to communicate with. You can find out the login names of the users who are logged in by using the **who** utility (above).

If the person you want to write to is logged in on more than one terminal, you can direct **write** to send your message to a specific terminal by including the **terminal** designation. Replace **terminal** on your command line with the terminal designation that **who** displays. Do not enter the square brackets ([])—they just indicate that the **terminal** part of the command is optional.

To establish two-way communication with another user, you and the other user must each execute **write**, specifying the other's login name as the **destination-user**. The **write** utility then copies text, line by line, from one terminal to the other. When you want to stop communicating with the other user, press (CONTROL)-**D** at the beginning of a line. Pressing (CONTROL)-**D** tells **write** to quit, displays EOT (End Of Transmission) on the other user's terminal, and returns you to the shell. The other user must do the same.

It is helpful to establish a protocol for carrying on communication using **write**. Try ending each message with **o** (for *over*) and ending the transmission with **oo** (for *over and out*). This protocol gives each user time to think and to enter a complete message, without the other user wondering if the first user is finished. Because **write** copies one line at a time, if you write several short lines of text rather than one long line, the other user will be reassured that you are still there.

The following example shows how one side of a two-way communication using **write** appears to Jenny. Figure 3-5 shows Jenny initiating communication by calling the **write** utility and specifying **alex** as the **destination-user**. She enters a message terminated by **o** and then waits for a reply.

As soon as Alex has a chance to respond and execute **write**, the utility sends a banner to Jenny's terminal. Then, Alex sends a message indicating that he is ready to receive Jenny's message (Figure 3-6).

```
$ write alex
Hi Alex, are you there? o
   Message from alex on bravo (tty11) [Mon May 23 15:08]...
Yes Jenny, I'm here. o
```

Figure 3-6   The **write** *Utility II*

Following the protocol that he and Jenny have established, Alex terminates his message with **o**.

At this point, Jenny and Alex can communicate back and forth. Each time one of them types a line and presses (RETURN), the line appears on the other's terminal. When they are done, Jenny enters a final message terminated by **oo** and presses (CONTROL)-**D** (as the first and only thing on a line) to sign off (Figure 3-7). The shell prompt appears. Then Alex signs off, and Jenny sees the EOT that results from Alex pressing (CONTROL)-**D**.

Alex's final message appears after Jenny's shell prompt. Because Jenny did not give any commands, she can display another shell prompt by simply pressing the (RETURN) key.

Throughout this communication, Alex and Jenny followed the convention of using **o** after each message. This is just a convention and is not recognized by **write**. You can use any convention you please or none at all.

Using mesg to Deny or Accept Messages

If you do not want to receive messages, you can give the following command:

```
$ mesg n
```

After giving this command, another user cannot send you messages using **write** or **talk**.

```
$ write alex
Hi Alex, are you there? o
   Message from alex on bravo (tty11) [Mon May 23 15:08]...
Yes Jenny, I'm here. o
.
.
.
Thank you, Alex - bye oo
(CONTROL)-D
$ Bye, Jenny oo
<EOT>
(RETURN)
$
```

Figure 3-7   The **write** *utility III*

If Alex had given the preceding command before Jenny tried to send him a message, she would have seen the following:

```
$ write alex
Permission denied.
```

You can allow messages again by entering **mesg y**.

If you want to know if someone can write to you, give the command **mesg** by itself. The **mesg** utility will respond with a **y** (for yes, messages are allowed) or **n** (for no, messages are *not* allowed).

Using Mail **to Send and Receive Electronic Mail**

You can use the mail utility programs to send and receive electronic mail. Electronic mail (or *e-mail* as it is sometimes called) is similar to post office mail except it is quicker and does not involve any paper or stamps. You can use it to send and receive letters, memos, reminders, invitations, and even junk mail.

You can use electronic mail to communicate with users on your system and, if your installation is part of a network, with other users on the network. Many UNIX systems are attached to networks that allow worldwide communication.

The mail utilities differ from the **write** utility, described on page 44. Although the mail utilities allow you to send a message to a user whether or not that user is logged in on the system, **write** allows you to send messages only if the user is logged in and willing to receive messages.

There are usually several mail utilities available on a UNIX system, and their names can lead to confusion. The original mail utility, called **mail**, has limited functionality and a primitive user interface. The most popular mail program supplied with UNIX systems today was created at Berkeley and is known as **Mail**. This section describes **Mail** (with a capital M, though it may be available as **mail** also).

The UNIX operating system mail utilities have two distinct functions: sending electronic mail and receiving it. The following example demonstrates these two functions. Try it on your system, replacing `alex` with your login name. First, Alex uses **Mail** to send himself a message:

```
$ Mail alex
Subject: Test Message
This is a test message that I am sending myself.
(CONTROL)-D
$
```

After he starts **Mail** by typing **Mail alex**, Alex is prompted to enter the subject of the message. On your system, **Mail** may or may not prompt you for a subject, depending on how it is set up (refer to **Mail** in Part II for more information). After he types in the subject (**Test Message**) and presses (RETURN), Alex types his message. He ends each line with a (RETURN), and, when he is finished, he enters a (CONTROL)-**D** on a line by itself. The **Mail** utility sends the mail and returns Alex to the shell.

Sometimes **Mail** is set up to prompt you for a copy-to list after you press (CONTROL)-**D**. At that time you can enter the login names of users who should receive copies of the message. After you finish the list and press (RETURN), the **Mail** utility will send the mail and return you to the shell.

To read his mail, Alex can run **Mail** without a user name (just **Mail**, not **Mail alex**). The **Mail** utility displays two lines of information about **Mail** that include the version number of the **Mail** program he is using, instructions for getting help, the mailbox that is being read, and the number of messages. The string **/usr/spool/mail/alex** identifies the location of Alex's mailbox in the hierarchical filesystem. (See Chapter 4 for an explanation of this terminology.) Following the header information is a list of any messages that are waiting for him. The list includes a header for each message, composed of the status of the message (**N** means new), the name of the person who sent it, the date it was sent, its length (number of lines/number of characters), and the subject of the message.

```
$ Mail
Mail version SMI 4.1-OWV3 Mon Sep 23 07:17:24 PDT 1991 Type ? for help.
"/usr/spool/mail/alex": 2 messages 2 new
>N  1 alex           Wed Aug 10 10:49    6/120    Test message
 N  2 jenny          Wed Aug 10 10:50    6/115    lunch?
&
```

Alex has two messages, the one he just sent and one from Jenny. The *greater than* sign (>) to the left of the first header indicates that the message from Alex is the current message. After the list of headers, **Mail** displays a prompt (usually a question mark or ampersand) indicating that it is waiting for Alex to give it a command. Alex can simply press (RETURN) to look at the current message. Alex could have used the **t** (for *type*) command with a message number argument, such as **t 1**, to print a specific message. The **t** command used without an argument always prints the current message, as does (RETURN) by itself.

```
& (RETURN)
Message 1:
From alex Wed Aug 10 10:49 PDT 1994
To: alex
Subject: Test Message
Status: R

This is a test message that I am sending myself.

& d  (RETURN)
```

The first four lines of the message are header lines. They list who the message is from, who it is to, the subject, and the status. Depending on how your system is set up, and depending on whether the message was sent to you from your machine or from another machine, the header may be as simple as the one above or much more complicated. In any case, the **To**, **From**, and **Subject** lines are the ones you will typically be interested in.

After reading his message, Alex uses a **d** command (followed by a (RETURN)) to delete the message. If Alex did not delete the message, **Mail** would have saved the message in a file named **mbox** in Alex's home directory.

As the first line of the **Mail** display indicates (Type ? for help.), **Mail** has a built-in help feature. Alex can enter ? in response to the **Mail** prompt (&) to get a list of other commands he can use. Also see Part II of this book for more information on **Mail** commands.

After Alex presses **d** and (RETURN), **Mail** displays the mail prompt. Alex types **2** (RETURN) to see message 2:

```
& 2 (RETURN)
Message 2:
From jenny Wed Aug 10 10:50 PDT 1994
To: alex
Subject: Lunch?
Status: R

Alex, can you meet me for lunch today at noon?

& (RETURN)
At EOF
& q (RETURN)
Saved 1 message in /home/alex/mbox
$
```

In response to this message, Alex presses (RETURN). Because he has no more messages, the **Mail** utility displays At EOF, indicating that Alex is at the *End Of* his mailbox *File*. Alex then types **q** to quit reading his mail, and **Mail** tells him that one message (the second message) was saved in his **mbox** file. (Pathnames such as **/home/alex/mbox** are described in Chapter 4). If there were any messages left in his mailbox that Alex had not looked at, they would be there for him to read the next time he read his mail.

You can send mail to more than one person at a time. Below, Jenny sends a reminder to Alex, Barbara, and hls (Helen's login name). The characters :–) in the message represent a "smiley face" (look at it sideways). Because it can be difficult to tell when the writer of an electronic message is saying something in jest or in a humorously sarcastic way, electronic mail users often use :–) to indicate humor.

```
$ Mail alex barbara hls
Subject: Meeting Reminder
Please remember to bring your notes from our
last meeting to the meeting on Friday at 9:00 am
in my office.

And don't forget the doughnuts :-) ...

Jenny
(CONTROL)-D
$
```

When Alex, Barbara, and hls each log in, the system will tell them they have mail.

If your system is part of a network, you can send mail to and receive mail from users on other systems. If you are on a **uucp** network, you can send mail to a user on a system that is linked to yours by preceding the user's name with the name of a remote system and an exclamation point (which is commonly referred to as a *bang*). If your system is connected to a local area or other network—such as the Internet or BITNET,—you may need to use a different format for addressing mail to users on other systems. For more information about networks, see Chapter 7 or check with your system administrator.

The following examples show you how to send mail to remote systems on a uucp network. The following command line sends mail to Bill on the system named **bravo**:

```
$ Mail bravo!bill
```

If you are using the C Shell, you must quote the exclamation point by preceding it with a backslash:

```
% Mail bravo\!bill
```

You can also send mail to a user on a system that is not directly networked to your computer as long as your system has a link to a system that, in turn, has a direct or indirect link to the destination system. Your system may have a database that specifies how to reach remote systems, or it may use a name service if it is attached to a local area network (see Chapter 7). If not, you will need to specify the path your message should take by listing all the systems in order on the command line. For example, if you have a login on a system that is connected to the Internet, you can send the author mail with the following command. The @ symbol is part of the address that the Internet uses.

```
$ Mail sobell!mark@igc.org
```

To deliver a message to the author using this address, your system will first contact the system named **igc.org** over the Internet. That system, in turn, recognizes that the message needs to be passed along to the system named **sobell**, using **uucp**. When the message arrives on **sobell**, it will be delivered to Mark's mailbox.

You can also mix the names of users on your system and on other systems on one command line:

```
$ Mail alex bravo!bill hls
```

You may be able to obtain a list of machine names and users that are part of your network from the system administrator.

Incoming Mail Notification

If Alex checks his mail after having already looked at all his messages, he will see the following:

```
$ Mail
No mail for alex
```

However, you do not have to type **Mail** in order to find out whether you have mail. At specified intervals (usually every ten minutes) while you are logged in, the shell checks to see whether mail has arrived since the last time you read your mail. If mail has arrived, the shell presents the following message before the next prompt:

```
You have new mail.
$
```

Another service, **biff**, is available to let you know when new mail arrives. You subscribe to this service by typing:

```
$ biff y
```

When new mail for you arrives, your terminal will beep and the first few lines of the new message will appear on your screen. Seeing the Subject line and first line or two of text can help you decide whether you should read the whole message right away; however, some people find this service intrusive (because it tends to disrupt what you are working on). To turn off the service, type

```
$ biff n
```

If you are wondering about the unusual name for this service, Biff was the name of a student's dog at Berkeley who always barked when the postal carrier delivered the mail.

Using learn **to Learn About UNIX**

UNIX provides **learn** to introduce novice users to the system (not available on all systems). The **learn** utility is a computer-aided instruction program that guides you through a series of lessons in several different courses. If **learn** is available on your system, the following topics are probably included, although the courses vary somewhat from one manufacturer's system to another:

- manipulating files

- using text editors

- formatting documents

- formatting equations

- programming in C

To use **learn**, type **learn** on the command line. It will present the information shown in Figure 3-8.

If you press (RETURN) without typing in a course name, **learn** will present descriptions of the courses and ask you to choose one. Then if you select the first course in the series, **learn** will present instructions about how to answer the questions it asks you, how to exit from the **learn** program, and so on.

```
$ learn


These are the available courses -
  files
  editor
  vi
  morefiles
  macros
  eqn
  C


If you want more information about the courses,
or if you have never used 'learn' before,
press RETURN; otherwise type the name of
the course you want, followed by RETURN.
```

*Figure 3-8   The **learn** Facility*

Using man **to Display the System Manual**

The **man** (manual) utility displays pages from the system documentation on the terminal. This documentation is useful if you know what utility you want to use but have forgotten exactly how to use it. Because the descriptions in the system documentation are often quite terse, they are most helpful if you already understand basically what a utility does. If a utility is new to you, the descriptions provided by this book are typically easier to understand.

To find out more about a utility, give the command **man** followed by the name of the utility. The following command displays information about the **w** utility. If the information **man** displays runs off the top of the screen, give the second form of the command, which uses a pipe (the | symbol—pipes are explained in Chapter 5) and **more** to cause the output to pause after each screenful.

$ `man w`

or

$ `man w | more`

You can use the command **man man** (or **man man | more**) to find out more about the **man** utility.

When you use the preceding format for **man**, the utility displays a prompt at the bottom of the screen after each screenful of text and waits for you to request another screenful. When you press (SPACE), **more** displays a new screenful of information from the **man** utility. Pressing (DELETE) stops **man** and gives you a shell prompt.

Organization of the System Manual

Traditionally, the UNIX system manual has been divided into eight sections that describe related tools:

- 1 user commands
- 2 system calls
- 3 C library functions
- 4 devices and network interfaces
- 5 file formats
- 6 games and demos
- 7 environments, tables, and **troff** macros
- 8 system maintenance

Most users find the information they need in sections 1, 6, and 7; programmers and system administrators frequently need to consult the other sections. In some cases you will find that there are manual entries for different tools with the same name. For example, if you type the following command you will see more than one manual page:

```
$ man write
```

If you wanted to see just the manual page for the **write** utility described earlier in this chapter, you would enter:

```
$ man 1 write
```

The manual page for the user command **write** is contained in section 1. To see the manual page for the write system call from section 2, you would run:

```
$ man 2 write
```

Searching with Keywords

If you do not know the name of the command you need to carry out a particular task, you can use the **man** utility to search for it using a keyword. For

```
$ man -k sort
bsearch (3) - binary search a sorted table
comm (1)      - display lines in common, and lines not in common, between two sorted lists
look (1)      - find words in the system dictionary or lines in a sorted list
qsort (3)     - quicker sort
scandir, alphasort (3) - scan a directory
sort (1V)     - sort and collate lines
sortbib (1) - sort a bibliographic database
tsort (1)     - topological sort
```

*Figure 3-9   The **man** Utility with the –k Option*

example, to find a utility that you can use to sort a list of words, use the –**k** (keyword) option.

The list in Figure 3-9 includes the name of the command, the section of the manual that contains it, and a brief description. This list includes the utility that you need (**sort**) and also identifies other related tools that you might find useful for specialized problems in the future.

As you read this book and learn new utilities, you may want to use the **man** command or refer to the system documentation to find out more about the utilities. Since the information displayed by the **man** command is an electronic version of the system documentation, the same information should be available in hard copy in the manuals that came with your system. If you would rather use paper documents than read about utilities on the screen, refer to your system manuals. You may find, however, that the online (electronic) copy of the manual is more up-to-date than any paper copy.

Using echo **to Display Text on the Terminal**

The **echo** utility copies to the terminal anything you put on the command line after **echo**. Some examples are shown in Figure 3-10.

The **echo** utility is a good tool for learning about the shell and other UNIX programs. In Chapter 5, **echo** is used to learn about special characters. In Chapter 10, it is used to learn about shell variables and about how to send messages from a shell program to the terminal.

```
$ echo Hi
Hi
$ echo This is a sentence.
This is a sentence.
$ echo Good morning.
Good morning.
$
```

Figure 3-10   The **echo** *Utility*

Using date **to Display the Time and Date**

The **date** utility displays the current date and time. An example of **date** follows:

```
$ date
Wed Aug  10 11:23:30 PDT 1994
```

Using cp to Copy a File

The **cp** (copy) utility makes a copy of a file. It can copy any file, including text and executable program files. Among other uses, you can use **cp** to make a backup copy of a file or a copy to experiment with.

A **cp** command line specifies source and destination files. The format is as follows:

cp **source-file destination-file**

The **source-file** is the name of the file that **cp** is going to copy. The **destination-file** is the name that **cp** assigns to the resulting copy of the file.

> **CAUTION**
>
> If the **destination-file** exists *before* you give a **cp** command, **cp** overwrites it. Because **cp** overwrites (and destroys the contents of) an existing **destination-file** without warning you, you must take care not to cause **cp** to overwrite a file that you need.

The following command line makes a *copy of the file* named **output**. The copy is named **outputb**. The initial **ls** command below shows that **output** is the only file in the directory. After the **cp** command, the second **ls** shows both files, **output** and **outputb**, in the directory.

```
$ ls
output
$ cp output outputb
$ ls
output outputb
```

Sometimes it is useful to incorporate the date in the name of a copy of a file. In the following example, the period is part of the filename—just another character:

```
$ cp memo memo.0130
```

Although the date has no significance to the UNIX operating system, it can help you to find a version of a file that you saved on a certain date. It can also help you avoid overwriting existing files by providing a unique filename each day. Chapter 4 discusses rules for naming files.

Using mv to Change the Name of a File

If you want to rename a file without making a duplicate copy of it, you can use the **mv** (move) utility.

An **mv** command line specifies an existing file and a new filename. The format is as follows:

mv **existing-file new-file**

The following command line *changes the name* of the file **memo** to **memo.0130**. The initial **ls** command below shows that **memo** is the only file in the current directory. Following the **mv** command, **memo.0130** is the only file in the current directory. Compare this with the **cp** example above.

```
$ ls
memo
$ mv memo memo.0130
$ ls
memo.0130
```

The **mv** utility can be used for much more than changing the name of a file. Refer to Chapter 4 and **mv** in Part II.

Using lpr to Print a File

So that several people or jobs can use a single printer, the UNIX system provides a means for *queuing* printer output so that only one job gets printed at a time. The **lpr** (line printer) utility places a file in the printer queue for printing.

The following command line prints the file named **report**:

```
$ lpr report
```

You can send more than one file to the printer with a single command line. The following command line prints three files:

```
$ lpr memo letter text
```

Refer to **lpr** on page 628 for more information.

Using grep to Find a String

The **grep** (*g*lobal *r*egular *e*xpression *p*rint) utility searches through a file to see if it contains a specified string of characters. This utility does not change the file it searches through but displays each line that contains the string.

```
$ cat memo

Helen:

In our meeting on June 6th we
discussed the issue of credit.
Have you had any further thoughts
about it?

                    Alex
$ grep 'credit' memo
discussed the issue of credit.
```

Figure 3-11   The **grep** *Utility*

The **grep** command in Figure 3-11 searches through the file **memo** for lines that contain the string **credit**, and displays a single line.

If **memo** contained words like *discredit, creditor,* and *accreditation,* **grep** would have displayed those lines as well because they contain the string it was searching for.

You do not need to enclose in single quotation marks the string you are searching for, but doing so allows you to put (SPACE)s and special characters in the Search String.

The **grep** utility can do much more than search for a simple string. Refer to **grep** in Part II and to Appendix A, "Regular Expressions," for more information.

Using head **to Look at the Top of a File**

The **head** utility displays the first ten lines of a file. It is useful for reminding yourself about what a particular file contains. If you have a file named **months** that contains the twelve months of the year in order, **head** will display January through October (Figure 3-12).

The **head** utility can display any number of lines, so you can use it to look at only the first line of a file or at a screenful or more. To specify the number of lines **head** will display, include a hyphen followed by the number of lines in the **head** command. For example, the command on the next page prints only the first line of **months**.

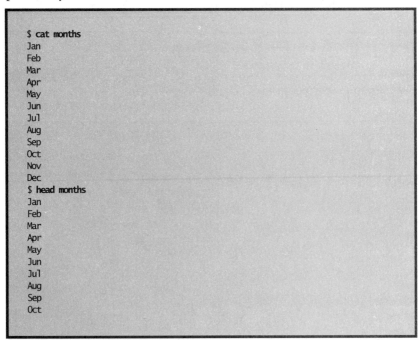

```
$ cat months
Jan
Feb
Mar
Apr
May
Jun
Jul
Aug
Sep
Oct
Nov
Dec
$ head months
Jan
Feb
Mar
Apr
May
Jun
Jul
Aug
Sep
Oct
```

*Figure 3-12   The **head** Utility*

```
$ head -1 months
Jan
```

If the **head** utility is not available on your system, you can use the **sed** command to look at the top of a file. The following command displays the first ten lines of the file **months**.

```
$ sed 10q months
```

The first argument to **sed** tells **sed** to display ten lines and quit. You can specify any number of lines for **sed** to display. The next command displays only the first line of **months**.

```
$ sed 1q months
```

Refer to Part II for more information about **sed** and **head**.

Using tail to Look at the End of a File

The **tail** utility displays the last ten lines of a file. It displays Mar through Dec from the **months** file (Figure 3-13).

Depending on how you invoke it, the **tail** utility can display fewer or more than ten lines, and it can also display parts of a file based on a count of blocks or characters rather than lines. Refer to **tail** in Part II for more information.

```
$ cat months
Jan
Feb
Mar
Apr
May
Jun
Jul
Aug
Sep
Oct
Nov
Dec
$ tail months
Mar
Apr
May
Jun
Jul
Aug
Sep
Oct
Nov
Dec
```

*Figure 3-13   The **tail** Utility*

```
$ cat days
Monday
Tuesday
Wednesday
Thursday
Friday
Saturday
Sunday
$ sort days
Friday
Monday
Saturday
Sunday
Thursday
Tuesday
Wednesday
```

Figure 3-14   The **sort** *Utility*

Using sort **to Display a File In Order**

The **sort** utility displays the contents of a file in order by lines. If you have a file named **days** that contains the names of each of the days of the week on separate lines, **sort** displays the file in alphabetical order, as shown in Figure 3-14.

The **sort** utility is useful for putting lists in order. Within certain limits, **sort** can be used to order a list of numbers. Part II describes the features and limitations of **sort**.

Using uniq **to Remove Duplicate Lines in a File**

The **uniq** (unique) utility displays a file, skipping adjacent duplicate lines. If the file named **phone_list** has two successive entries for the same person, **uniq** skips the extra lines (Figure 3-15).

If the file has been sorted before **uniq** is used, **uniq** ensures that no two lines in the file are the same. Chapter 5 describes how to use a combination of commands, such as **sort** and **uniq**, to make changes to a file. See Part II for a description of other features of **uniq**.

Using whereis **and** which **to Find Utilities**

When you type the name of a utility on the command line, the shell searches a list of directories for the program and runs it. This list of directories is called a *search path* and you will learn how to change it in the chapters that describe each shell; if you do not change the list, the Shell will search a standard set of directories. There may be other directories on your system that contain useful utilities—check with your system administrator or other users for hints.

```
$ cat phone_list
Alex     856-3462
Jenny    451-7339
Jenny    451-7339
Barbara  328-3078
Helen    249-0348
Jenny    451-7339
$ uniq phone_list
Alex     856-3462
Jenny    451-7339
Barbara  328-3078
Helen    249-0348
Jenny    451-7339
```

Figure 3-15   The **uniq** *Utility*

There are two utilities that you can use to find the full pathname associated with a command, **whereis** and **which**. Chapter 4 contains more information on pathnames and the structure of the UNIX filesystem.

To find a particular tool, you can use the **whereis** utility. This utility is helpful if you have heard of a command and think it may be available on your system but you do not know where it is stored. In the next example the user wants to run **ping** but the shell does not find it in any of the standard places. (The **ping** utility uses a network connection to communicate with a remote system—see page 159).

```
$ ping bravo
ping: not found
$ whereis ping
ping: /usr/etc/ping /usr/man/man8/ping.8c
```

In addition to locating the command, **/usr/etc/ping**, **whereis** reports the location of the corresponding manual page (**/usr/man/man8/ping.8c**). If the C source code for the command is available on your system, **whereis** will report where that is stored as well. Now that you know the location of the **ping** program, you can run it directly by running its full pathname:

```
$ /usr/etc/ping bravo
bravo is alive
```

Another useful utility is the **which** command. There may be multiple commands on your system that have the same name (such as **mail**). When you type the name of a command, the shell examines your search path in the order you have specified and runs the first one it finds. You can find out which copy of the program the shell will run by using the **which** utility. In the following example, **which** reports the location of the **cat** command.

```
$ which cat
/bin/cat
```

The **which** utility can be very helpful when a command seems to be working in unexpected ways. By running **which**, you may discover that you are running a non-standard version of a tool or a different one than you expected. For example, if you find that you are running **/usr/local/bin/cat** instead of **/bin/cat**, you might suspect that the local version is broken.

Using diff to Compare Two Files

The **diff** (difference) utility compares two files and displays a list of the differences between them. This utility does not change either file; it just displays a list of the actions you would need to take to convert one file into the other. This is useful if you want to compare two versions of a letter or report, or two versions of the source code for a program.

The **diff** utility produces a series of lines containing instructions to add (**a**), delete (**d**), or change (**c**) followed by the lines that you need to add, delete, or change. If you have two files called **colors.1** and **colors.2** that contain names of colors, **diff** compares the two files and displays a list of their differences (Figure 3-16).

The **diff** utility assumes that you want to convert the first file (**colors.1**) into the second file (**colors.2**). The first line that **diff** displays (**4d3**) indicates that you need to delete the fourth line. (You can ignore the number following the **d** since it is only important if you want to convert the second file into the first.) The next line of the display shows the line to be deleted; the *less than* symbol indicates that the line is from the first file (a *greater than* symbol is used to identify lines that are from the second file). See **diff** in Part II for a more complete description of its features.

```
$ cat colors.1
red
blue
green
yellow
$ cat colors.2
red
blue
green
$ diff colors.1 colors.2
4d3
< yellow
```

Figure 3-16   The **diff** *Utility*

Using compress to Shrink Files

Large files can use up a lot of disk space quickly, and they are slow to transfer from one system to another over a network. If you will not need to look at the contents of a large file very often, you may want to save it on a magnetic tape and remove it from the disk. If you have a continuing need for the file, however, retrieving a copy from a tape is inconvenient. There is another way to reduce the amount of disk space you use without removing the file entirely; you can compress (shrink) the file without losing any of the information.

The **compress** utility examines the contents of a file, searching for repeated patterns. Once it has analyzed a file, **compress** applies a formula that recodes the file more efficiently. The new version of the file looks completely different (and is usually smaller); in fact, the new file will contain many nonprintable characters, so you do not want to try to read it directly. The **compress** utility works well on large files that contain many repeated patterns, especially text files. On many systems, the electronic copy of the system manual is stored in compressed form.

The following example uses a boring file: Each of the 8,000 lines of this file, **letter_e**, contains 72 letter e's. The file occupies more than half a megabyte of disk storage.

```
$ ls -l
-rw-r--r--  1 alex          576000 Oct 15 10:57 letter_e
```

The **–v** (verbose) option below causes **compress** to report how much it was able to reduce the size of the file; in this case, by more than 99%!

```
$ compress -v letter_e
letter_e: Compression: 99.27% -- replaced with letter_e.Z
$ ls -l
-rw-r--r--  1 alex          10113 Oct 15 10:57 letter_e.Z
```

The **compress** utility also renamed the file—it appended .Z to the file's name. This naming convention helps to remind you that the file is compressed; you would not want to display or print it, for example, without first uncompressing it. The **compress** utility did not change the modification date associated with the file, even though it completely changed the file's contents.

You can use the **file** utility to learn about the contents of any file on a UNIX system without having to examine the file yourself. (Refer to Part II for more information on **file**.) In this example, **file** reports that **letter_e.Z** contains data that has been compressed in a particular way:

```
$ file letter_e.Z
letter_e.Z:          compressed data block compressed 16 bits
```

You can also use the **zcat** utility to display the file. The **zcat** utility is the equivalent of **cat** for .Z files; unlike **cat**, **zcat** interprets the compressed data and displays the contents of the file as though it were not compressed.

```
$ zcat letter_e.Z | head -2
eeeeeeeeeeeeeeeeeeeeeeeeeeeeeeeeeeeeeeeeeeeeeeeeeeeeeeeeeeeeeeeeeeeeeeeeee
eeeeeeeeeeeeeeeeeeeeeeeeeeeeeeeeeeeeeeeeeeeeeeeeeeeeeeeeeeeeeeeeeeeeeeeeee
```

After running **zcat**, the contents of **letter_e.Z** are unchanged—the file is still stored on the disk in compressed form. If you need to restore the file to its original size and form, use the **uncompress** utility, as shown below.

```
$ uncompress letter_e.Z
$ ls -l
-rw-r--r--  1 alex          576000 Oct 15 10:57 letter_e
```

SUMMARY

Below is a list of the utilities that have been introduced up to this point. Because you will be using these utilities frequently, and because they are integral to the following chapters, it is important that you become comfortable using them. The particular editor that you use is not important. If your installation has an editor other than **vi** that you prefer, learn to use that editor.

- **biff** displays the first lines of incoming mail messages.
- **cat** displays the contents of a file on the terminal.
- **compress** shrinks files in size.
- **cp** makes a copy of a file.
- **date** displays the time, day of the week, and date.
- **diff** displays a list of the differences between two files.
- **echo** displays a line of text on the terminal.
- **file** displays information about the contents of a file.
- **finger** displays detailed information about users.
- **grep** searches for a specific string in a file.
- **head** displays the beginning of a file.
- **learn** provides lessons on how to use the system.
- **lpr** prints text files.
- **ls** displays a list of files.
- **Mail** sends and receives mail.
- **man** displays information on utilities.
- **mesg** permits or denies messages sent by **write** or **talk**.
- **more** displays the contents of a text file one screenful at a time.
- **mv** changes the name of a file.
- **passwd** changes your password.
- **rm** deletes a file.
- **sed** can display the beginning of a file.
- **sort** puts a file in order by lines.
- **tail** displays the end of a file.
- **talk** supports an online conversation with another user who is logged in.
- **uncompress** restores a compressed file to its original size.
- **uniq** displays the contents of a file, skipping successive duplicate lines.
- **vi** creates or edits a text file.
- **w** displays a list of who is logged in.
- **whereis** displays the pathname of a utility program on the system.
- **which** displays the full pathname of a command you can run.
- **write** sends a message to another user who is logged in.
- **zcat** displays the contents of a compressed file.

1. What command can you use to determine who is logged in on a specific terminal?

2. List some differences between **talk** and **write**. Why are three different communications utilities (**talk, write, Mail**) useful on a UNIX system? Describe a situation where it makes sense to use:

   a. **Mail** instead of **talk** or **write**.

   b. **talk** instead of **write**.

   c. **write** instead of **talk**.

3. How can you send a single mail message to **agnes** on the system named **cougar** and to **jim** on the system named **ucsf**? Assume your computer has network links to **cougar** and **ucsf**.

4. Describe a method for synchronizing communication with another user when you are using **write**.

5. How can you keep other users from using **write** to communicate with you? Why would you want to?

6. What happens if you give the following commands when the file called **done** already exists?

   ```
   $ cp to_do done
   $ mv to_do done
   ```

7. What command will send the files **chapter1**, **chapter2**, and **chapter3** to the printer?

8. How can you find the phone number for Ace Electronics in a file called **phone** that contains a list of names and phone numbers? What command can you use to display the entire file in alphabetical order? How can you remove adjacent duplicate lines from the file?

9. Try giving these two commands:

   ```
   $ echo cat
   $ cat echo
   ```

   Explain the differences between them.

10. How can you tell whether the file **memo** is the same as the file **memo.bak**? (The .bak extension is often used to identify a backup copy of a file.)

11. How can you use the **tail** utility to display the last line of a file? (*Hint:* Refer to **tail** in Part II, page 709.)

12. What command can you use to look at the first few lines of a file called **status.report**? What command can you use to look at the end of the file?

13. Alex is expecting a mail message from Scott. How can he find out if he has received one?

ADVANCED REVIEW EXERCISES

14. Suppose you have typed the following commands:

    ```
    $ biff y
    $ mesg n
    ```

    What appears on your screen if someone sends you a **mail** message? if someone tries to run **talk** to communicate with you?

15. How might you look at the last mail message someone sent you, without running the **Mail** utility?

16. How can you find out which utilities are available on your system for editing files?

17. Repeat exercise 8 above using the file **phone.Z**, a compressed version of the list of names and phone numbers. Try to consider more than one approach to each question, and explain how you chose your answer.

CHAPTER 4

The File Structure

This chapter discusses the organization and terminology of the file structure of the UNIX system. It defines ordinary and directory files and explains the rules for naming them. It shows how to create and delete directories, move through the file structure, and use pathnames to access files in different directories. This chapter also covers file access permissions that allow you to share selected files with other users. The final section describes links, which can make a single file appear in more than one directory.

The Hierarchical File Structure

A *hierarchical* structure frequently takes the shape of a pyramid. One example of this type of structure is found by tracing a family's lineage: A couple has a child; that child may have several children; and each of those children may have more children. This hierarchical structure, shown in Figure 4-1, is called a *family tree*.

Like the family tree it resembles, the UNIX system file structure is also called a *tree*. It is composed of a set of connected files. This structure allows users to organize files so they can easily find any particular one. In a standard UNIX system, each user starts with one directory. From this single directory, users can make as many subdirectories as they like, dividing subdirectories into additional subdirectories. In this manner, they can continue expanding the structure to any level according to their needs.

Using the Hierarchical File Structure

Typically, each subdirectory is dedicated to a single subject. The subject dictates whether a subdirectory should be subdivided further. For instance, Figure 4-2 shows a secretary's subdirectory named **correspondence**. This directory contains three subdirectories: **business**, **memos**, and **personal**. The **business** directory contains files that store each letter the secretary types. If there are many letters going to one client (as is the case with **milk_co**), a subdirectory can be dedicated to that client.

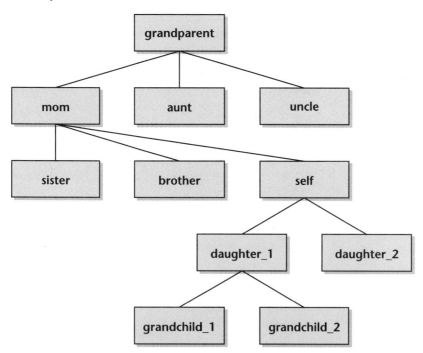

Figure 4-1   A Family Tree

One of the strengths of the UNIX system file structure is its ability to adapt to different users' needs. You can take advantage of this strength by strategically organizing your files so they are most convenient and useful for you.

Directory and Ordinary Files

Like a family tree, the tree representing the file structure is usually pictured upside down, with its *root* at the top. Figures 4-2 and 4-3 show that the tree "grows" downward from the root, with paths connecting the root to each of the other files. At the end of each path is an ordinary file or a directory file. *Ordinary files*, frequently just called *files*, are at the ends of paths that cannot support other paths. *Directory files*, usually referred to as *directories*, are the points that other paths *can* branch off from. (Figures 4-2 and 4-3 show some empty directories.) When you refer to the tree, *up* is toward the root, and *down* is away from the root. Directories directly connected by a path are called *parents* (closer to the root) and *children* (farther from the root).

Filenames

Every file has a *filename*. On SunOS and Berkeley UNIX systems you can use as many as 255 characters in a filename; older versions of UNIX had a maximum length of 14 characters. Although you can use almost any character in a filename, you will avoid confusion if you choose characters from the list on the next page:

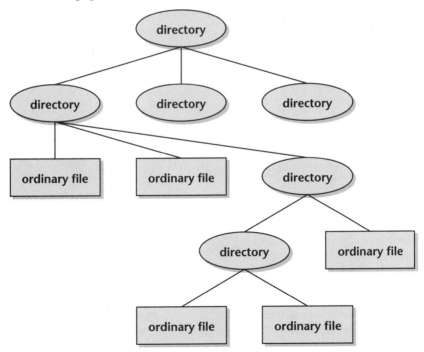

Figure 4-2   Directories and Ordinary Files

- uppercase letters (A-Z)
- lowercase letters (a-z)
- numbers (0-9)
- underscore (_)
- period (.)
- comma (,)

The only exception is the root directory, which is always named / and referred to by this single character. No other file can use this name.

Like children of one parent, no two files in the same directory can have the same name. (Whereas parents give their children different names because it makes good sense, UNIX requires it.) Files in different directories, like children of different parents, can have the same name.

The filenames you choose should mean something. Too often, a directory is filled with important files with names such as **foobar, wombat,** and **junk.** Names like these are poor choices because they will not help you recall what you stored in a file.

The following filenames conform to the required syntax *and* convey information about the contents of the file:

- **correspondence**
- **january**
- **davis**
- **reports**
- **1994**
- **acct_payable**

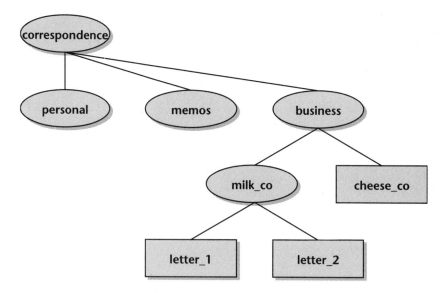

Figure 4-3   The Directories of a Secretary

UNIX systems that support longer filenames are becoming more common. If you share your files with users on other UNIX systems, you should probably make sure that long filenames differ within the first 14 characters. If you keep the filenames short, they will be easy to type, and later you can add extensions to them without exceeding the 14-character limit imposed by some versions of UNIX (see the following section). Of course, the disadvantage of short filenames is that they are typically less descriptive than long filenames.

The length limit on filenames was increased to enable users to select descriptive names. A feature was added to the C Shell, *filename completion*, that helps users select among files in the working directory without typing in entire filenames. Refer to "Filename Completion" on page 353.

Although they are not used in examples in this book, you can use uppercase letters within filenames. The UNIX operating system is case-sensitive, however, and files named **JANUARY**, **January**, and **january** would represent three distinct files.

Filename Extensions

In the following filenames, filename extensions help describe the contents of the file. A *filename extension* is the part of the filename following an embedded period. Some programs, such as the C programming language compiler, depend on specific filename extensions. In most cases, however, filename extensions are optional. Use extensions freely to make filenames easy to understand. If you like, you can use several periods within the same filename (for example, **notes.4.10.88**).

Filename	Meaning of Filename Extension
compute.c	A C programming language source file
compute.o	The object code for the program
compute	The same program as an executable file
memo.0410	A text file

Invisible Filenames

A filename beginning with a period is called an invisible filename because **ls** does not normally display it. The command **ls –a** displays *all* filenames, even invisible ones. Startup files are usually invisible so that they do not clutter a directory (page 71). Two special invisible entries, a single and double period (. and ..), appear in every directory. These entries are discussed on page 73.

Absolute Pathnames

As shown in Figure 4-4, every file has a *pathname*. Figure 4-4 shows the pathnames of directories and ordinary files in part of a filesystem hierarchy.

You can build the pathname of a file by tracing a path from the root directory, through all the intermediate directories, to the file. String all the filenames in the path together, separating them with slashes (/) and preceding them with the name of the root directory (/).

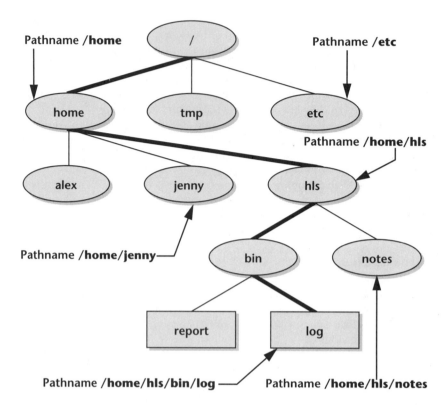

Figure 4-4   Pathnames

This path of filenames is called an *absolute pathname* because it locates a file absolutely, tracing a path from the root directory to the file. The part of a pathname following the final slash is called a *simple filename*, or just a *filename*.

Directories

This section covers creating, deleting, and using directories. It explains the concepts of the *working* and *home directories* and their importance in *relative pathnames*.

The Working Directory

While you are logged in on a UNIX system, you will always be associated with one directory or another. The directory you are associated with, or are working in, is called the *working directory*, or the *current directory*. Sometimes this association is referred to in a physical sense: "You are *in* (or *working in*) the **jenny** directory." The **pwd** (print working directory) utility displays the pathname of the working directory (Figure 4-5).

```
login: alex
Password:

Welcome to UNIX!

$ pwd
/home/alex
```

Figure 4-5   Logging In

To access any file in the working directory, you do not need a path-name—just a simple filename. To access a file in another directory, however, you *must* use a pathname.

Your Home Directory

When you first log in on a UNIX system, the working directory is your *home* directory. To display the absolute pathname of your home directory, use **pwd** just after you log in. Figure 4-5 shows Alex logging in and displaying the name of his home directory.

The **ls** utility displays a list of the files in the working directory. Because your home directory has been the only working directory you have used so far, **ls** has always displayed a list of files in your home directory. (All the files you have created up to now are in your home directory.)

Startup Files

An important file that appears in your home directory is a *startup file*. It gives the operating system specific information about you as a user. Frequently, it tells the system what kind of terminal you are using and executes the **stty** (set terminal) utility to establish your line kill and erase keys. Refer to Part II for more information about **stty**.

Either you or the system administrator can put a startup file, containing shell commands, in your home directory. The shell executes the commands in this file each time you log in. With the Bourne Shell and the Korn Shell, the filename must be **.profile**. Use **.login** with the C Shell. Because the start-up files have invisible filenames, you must use the **ls –a** command to see if either of these files is in your home directory. For more information on start-up files and other files the shell automatically executes, refer to Chapters 10, 11, and 12.

Creating a Directory

The **mkdir** utility creates a directory. It does *not* change your association with the working directory. The *argument* (the word following the name of the command) you use with **mkdir** becomes the pathname of the new directory.

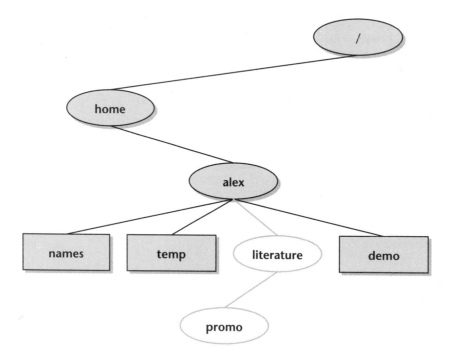

Figure 4-6   The File Structure Developed In the Examples

Figure 4-6 shows the directory structure that is developed in the following examples. The light lines represent directories that are added.

In Figure 4-7, **mkdir** creates a directory named **literature** as a child of the /**home/alex** directory. When you use **mkdir**, enter the absolute pathname of *your* home directory in place of /**home/alex**.

The **ls** utility verifies the presence of the new directory and shows the files Alex has been working with: **names, temp,** and **demo.**

By itself, **ls** does not distinguish between a directory and an ordinary file. With the –F option, **ls** displays a slash after the name of each directory (and an asterisk after each executable file). When you call **ls** with an argument that is the name of a directory, **ls** lists the contents of the directory. If there are no files in the directory, **ls** does not list anything.

```
$ mkdir /home/alex/literature
$ ls
demo          literature    names         temp
$ ls -F
demo          literature/   names         temp
$ ls literature
$
```

*Figure 4-7   The **mkdir** Utility*

```
$ pwd
/home/alex
$ ls ..
alex     barbara  hls       jenny
.
.
```

Figure 4-8   Using .. with ls

The . and .. Directory Entries

The **mkdir** utility automatically puts two entries in every directory you create. They are a single and double period, representing the directory itself and the parent directory, respectively. These entries are invisible because their filenames begin with periods.

Because **mkdir** automatically places these entries in every directory, you can rely on their presence. The . is synonymous with the pathname of the working directory and can be used in its place; .. is synonymous with the pathname of the parent of the working directory. Figure 4-8 lists the contents of the /**home** directory from /**home/alex** by using .. to represent the parent directory.

Changing to Another Working Directory

The **cd** (change directory) utility makes another directory the working directory—it does *not* change the contents of the working directory. In this context, you can think of the working directory as a place marker. The first **cd** command in Figure 4-9 makes the /**home/alex/literature** directory the working directory, as verified by **pwd**.

Without an argument, **cd** makes your home directory the working directory, as it was when you first logged in. The second **cd** in Figure 4-9 does not have an argument and makes Alex's home directory the working directory.

Deleting a Directory

The **rmdir** (remove directory) utility deletes a directory. You cannot delete the working directory or a directory that contains files. If you need to delete

```
$ cd /home/alex/literature
$ pwd
/home/alex/literature
$ cd
$ pwd
/home/alex
```

Figure 4-9   The cd Utility

a directory with files in it, first delete the files (using **rm**) and then delete the directory. You do not have to delete the . and .. entries; **rmdir** removes them automatically. The following command deletes the directory that was created in Figure 4-7.

```
$ rmdir /home/alex/literature
```

Relative Pathnames

A *relative pathname* traces a path from the working directory to a file. The pathname is *relative* to the working directory. Any pathname that does not begin with the root directory (/) is a relative pathname. Like absolute pathnames, relative pathnames can describe a path through many directories.

Alex could have created the **literature** directory (Figure 4-7) more easily using a relative pathname, as shown here:

```
$ pwd
/home/alex
$ mkdir literature
```

The **pwd** command shows that Alex's home directory (**/home/alex**) is still the working directory. The **mkdir** utility will display an error message if a directory or file called **literature** already exists—you cannot have two files or directories with the same name in one directory.

The pathname used in this example is a simple filename. A simple filename is a kind of relative pathname that specifies a file in the working directory.

The following commands show two ways to create the same directory, **promo**, a child of the **literature** directory that was just created. The first assumes that **/home/alex** is the working directory and uses a relative pathname; the second uses an absolute pathname.

Because the location of the file that you are accessing with a relative pathname is dependent on (relative to) the working directory, always make sure you know which is the working directory before using a relative pathname. When you use an absolute pathname, it does not matter which is the working directory.

```
$ pwd
/home/alex
$ mkdir literature/promo
```

or

```
$ mkdir /home/alex/literature/promo
```

Virtually anywhere that a UNIX utility program requires a filename or pathname, you can use an absolute or relative pathname or a simple filename. You can use any of these types of names with **cd**, **ls**, **vi**, **mkdir**, **rm**, **rmdir**, and other UNIX utilities.

Significance of the Working Directory

Typing long pathnames is tedious and increases the chances of making mistakes. You can choose a working directory for any particular task to reduce the need for long pathnames. Your choice of a working directory does not allow you to do anything you could not do otherwise—it just makes some operations easier.

Files that are children of the working directory can be referenced by simple filenames. Grandchildren of the working directory can be referenced by relative pathnames, composed of two filenames separated by a slash. When you manipulate files in a large directory structure, short relative pathnames can save time and aggravation. If you choose a working directory that contains the files used most for a particular task, you will need to use fewer long, cumbersome pathnames.

Using Pathnames

The following example assumes that **/home/alex** is the working directory. It uses a relative pathname to copy the file **letter** to the directory named **/home/alex/literature/promo**. The copy of the file has the simple filename **letter.0610**. Use **vi** to create a file named **letter** if you want to experiment with the examples that follow.

```
$ cp letter literature/promo/letter.0610
```

Assuming that Alex has not changed to another working directory, the following command allows him to edit the copy of the file he just made:

```
$ vi literature/promo/letter.0610
    .
    .
```

If Alex does not want to use a long pathname to specify the file, he can, before using **vi**, use **cd** to make the **promo** directory the working directory.

```
$ cd literature/promo
$ pwd
/home/alex/literature/promo
$ vi letter.0610
    .
    .
```

If Alex wants to make the parent of the working directory (named **/home/alex/literature**) the new working directory, he can give the following command, which takes advantage of the .. directory entry:

```
$ cd ..
$ pwd
/home/alex/literature
```

Moving Files from One Directory to Another

The **mv** (move) utility can be used to move files from one directory to another. Chapter 3 discussed the use of **mv** to rename files. However, the **mv** utility is actually much more general than that—it can be used to change the pathname of a file as well as changing the simple filename.

When it is used to move a file to a new directory, the format of the **mv** utility is:

mv **existing-file-list directory**

If the working directory is **/home/alex**, Alex can use the following command to move the files **names** and **temp** from the working directory to the directory **literature**:

```
$ mv names temp literature
```

This command changes the absolute pathname of **names** and **temp** from **/home/alex/names** and **/home/alex/temp** to **/home/alex/literature/names** and **/home/alex/literature/temp**. Like most other UNIX commands, **mv** accepts either absolute or relative pathnames.

As you work with the UNIX system, you will create more and more files, and you will need to create directories to keep them organized. The **mv** utility is a useful tool for moving files from one directory to another as you develop your directory hierarchy.

Important Standard Directories and Files

The UNIX system file structure is usually set up according to a convention. Aspects of this convention may vary from installation to installation. Figure 4-10 shows the usual locations of some important directories and files.

/ (root)   The root directory is present in all UNIX system file structures. It is the ancestor of all files in the filesystem.

/home   Each user's home directory is typically one of many subdirectories of the **/home** directory. On some systems, the users' directories may not be under the **/home** directory (e.g., they might all be under **/inhouse**, or some might be under **/inhouse** and others under **/clients**). As an example, assuming that users' directories are under **/home**, the absolute pathname of Jenny's home directory is **/home/jenny**.

/usr   This directory traditionally includes subdirectories that contain information used by the system. Files in subdirectories of **/usr** do not change often and may be shared by multiple systems.

/usr/bin, /bin   These directories contain the standard UNIX utility programs. On some systems, both names are used to refer to the same directory..

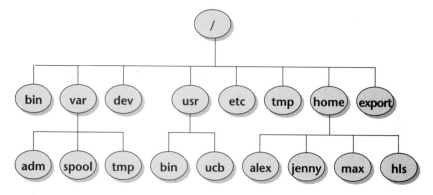

Figure 4-10   A Typical UNIX System File Structure

/usr/ucb   The utilities stored in **/usr/ucb** were developed at the University of California, Berkeley. You can find the networking utilities here.

/etc, /usr/etc   Administrative, configuration, and other system files are kept here. The **/etc** directory typically includes utilities needed during the booting process, and **/usr/etc** holds those utilities that are most useful after the system is up and running. One of the most important is the **/etc/passwd** file, containing a list of all users who have permission to use the system. See Chapter 14 for more information.

/var   Files with contents that vary as the system runs are found in subdirectories under **/var.** The most common examples are temporary files, system log files, spooled files, and user mailbox files. Older versions of UNIX scattered such files through several subdirectories of **/usr** (**/usr/adm, /usr/mail, /usr/spool, /usr/tmp**).

/dev   All files that represent peripheral devices, such as terminals and printers, are kept in this directory.

/tmp   Many programs use this directory to hold temporary files.

/export   A common place to locate files on a fileserver that are to be shared by many systems (e.g., manual pages and other system files that do not change).

Access Permissions

Three types of users can access a file: the owner of the file (*owner*), a member of a group to which the owner belongs (*group*—see Chapter 14 for more information on groups), and everyone else (*other*). A user can attempt to access an ordinary file in three ways—by trying to *read from, write to,* or *execute* it. Three types of users, each able to access a file in three ways, equals a total of nine possible ways to access an ordinary file:

The owner of a file can try to:	read from the file
	write to the file
	execute the file
A member of the owner's group can try to:	read from the file
	write to the file
	execute the file
Anyone else can try to:	read from the file
	write to the file
	execute the file

The ls **Utility with the –l and –g Options**

When you call **ls** with the –l (long) option and the name of a file, **ls** displays a line of information about the file. When called with –**g** (group) it displays information about the group the file belongs to. The following example calls **ls** with both the –l and –**g** options and displays information for two files. The file **letter.0610** contains the text of a letter, and **check_spell** contains a shell script (a program written in the high-level shell programming language).

```
$ ls -lg letter.0610 check_spell
-rw-r--r-- 1 alex   pubs   3355   May   2 10:52 letter.0610
-rwxr-xr-x 2 alex   pubs    852   May   5 14:03 check_spell
```

From left to right, the lines contain the following information:

- the type of file (first character)
- the file's access permissions (the next nine characters)
- the number of links to the file (page 80)
- the name of the owner of the file (usually the person who created the file)
- the name of the group that has group access to the file
- the size of the file in characters (bytes)
- the date and time the file was created or last modified
- the name of the file

If the first character is a **d**, the file is a directory; if the character is a –, it is an ordinary file. Both of the files in the above example are ordinary files. The next three characters represent the access permission for the owner of the file: **r** indicates that the owner *has* read permission, – indicates that the owner *does not have* read permission; **w** indicates that the owner *has* write permission, – indicates that the owner *does not have* write permission; **x** indicates execute permission for the owner, and – indicates no execute permission.

In a similar manner, the next three characters represent permissions for the group, and the final three characters represent permissions for everyone else. In the preceding example, the owner of the file **letter.0610** can read from the file or write to it, whereas others can only read from it and no one is allowed to execute it. Although execute permissions can be allowed for any file, it does not make sense to assign execute permissions to a file that contains an ordinary document such as a letter. However, the file **check_spell** is an executable shell script, and execute permissions are appropriate. (The owner, group, and others have execute access permission.)

Changing Access Permissions

The owner of a file controls which users have permission to access the file and how they can access it. If you own a file, you can use the **chmod** (change mode) utility to change access permissions for that file. Below, **chmod** adds (+) read and write permission (**rw**) for all (**a**) users.

```
$ chmod a+rw letter.0610
$ ls -lg letter.0610
-rw-rw-rw- 1 alex  pubs    3355  May  2 10:52 letter.0610
```

In the next example, **chmod** removes (–) read and execute (**rx**) permissions for users other than Alex and members of the pubs group (**o**).

```
$ chmod o-rx check_spell
$ ls -lg check_spell
-rwxr-x--- 2 alex  pubs     852  May  5 14:03 check_spell
```

In addition to **a** (for *all*) and **o** (for *other*), you can use **g** (for *group*) and **u** (for *user*, although user actually refers to the owner of the file, who may or may not be the user of the file at any given time) in the argument to **chmod**. For more information on changing access permissions, refer to the discussion of **chmod** in Part II.

The UNIX system access-permission scheme lets you give other users access to the files you want to share and keep your private files confidential. You can allow other users to read from *and* write to a file (you may be one of several people working on a joint project); only to read from a file (perhaps a project specification you are proposing); or only to write to a file (similar to an in-basket or mailbox, where you want others to be able to send you mail but you do not want them to read your mail). Similarly, you can protect entire directories from being scanned.

There is an exception to the access permissions described above. The system administrator or another user who knows the special password can log in as the *Superuser* and have full access to *all* files, regardless of owner or access permissions. Refer to Chapter 14 for more information.

Directory Access Permissions

Access permissions have slightly different meanings when used with directories. Although a directory can be accessed by the three types of users and can be read from or written to, it can never be executed. Execute access permission is redefined for a directory. It means you can search through the directory. It has nothing to do with executing a file.

Alex can give the following command to ensure that Jenny, or anyone else, can look through, read files from, write files to, and remove files from his directory named **info**:

```
$ chmod a+rwx /home/alex/info
```

You can view the access permissions associated with a directory by using the –**d** (directory), –**l**, and –**g** options, as shown in the following example. The **d** at the left end of the line indicates that /**home/alex/info** is a directory.

```
$ ls -ldg /home/alex/info
drwxrwxrwx 3 alex  pubs 112  Apr 15 11:05 /home/alex/info
```

Links

A *link* is a pointer to a file. Every time you create a file using **vi**, **cp**, or any other means, you are putting a pointer in a directory. This pointer associates a filename with a place on the disk. When you specify a filename in a command, you are pointing to the place on the disk where the information that you want is (to be) located.

Creating Additional Links

Sharing files can be useful if two or more people are working on a project and need to share some information. You can make it easy for other users to access one of your files by creating additional links to the file.

To share a file with another user, you first give the user permission to read and write to the file. (In addition, you may have to use the **chmod** utility to change the access permissions of the parent directory of the file to give the user read, write, and execute permissions.) Once the permissions are appropriately set, you allow the user to create a link to the file so that each of you can access the file from your separate directory hierarchies.

A link can also be useful to a single user with a large directory hierarchy. You can create links in order to cross-classify files in your directory hierarchy, using different classifications for different tasks. For example, if your directory hierarchy is the one depicted in Figure 4-3, you might have a file called **to_do** in each of the subdirectories of the **correspondence** directory— that is, in **personal**, **memos**, and **business**. Then if you find it hard to keep track of all the things you need to do, you can create a separate directory called **to_do** in the **correspondence** directory and link each to-do list into that directory. For example, you might link the file called **to_do** in the **memos** directory to a file called **memos** in the **to_do** directory. This set of links is shown in Figure 4-11.

Although this may sound complicated, in this way you can keep all of your to-do lists conveniently in one place. The appropriate list is also easily accessible in the task-related directory when you are busy composing letters, writing memos, or handling personal business.

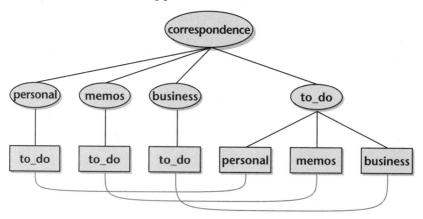

Figure 4-11   Cross-Classification of Files Using Links

Using ln to Create a Link

The **ln** (link) utility creates an additional link to an existing file. The new link appears as another file in the file structure. If the file appears in the same directory as the one the file is linked with, the links must have different filenames. This restriction does not apply if the linked file is in another directory.

The following command makes the link shown in Figure 4-12. It assumes that /**home/jenny** is the working directory and that Jenny is creating a link to the file named **draft**. The new link appears in the /**home/alex** directory with the filename **letter**. In practice, it may be necessary for Alex to use **chmod**, as shown in the previous section, to give Jenny write access permission to the /**home/alex** directory.

```
$ ln draft /home/alex/letter
```

The **ln** utility creates an additional pointer to an existing file. It does *not* make another copy of the file. Because there is only one file, the file status information (such as access permissions, owner, and the time the file was last modified) is the same for all links. Only the filenames differ. You can verify that **ln** does not make an additional copy of a file by creating a file, using **ln** to make an additional link to the file, changing the contents of the file through one link (use **vi**), and verifying the change through the other link.

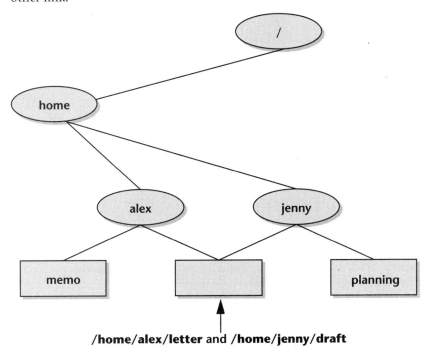

/**home/alex/letter** and /**home/jenny/draft**

Figure 4-12   /**home/alex/letter** *and* /**home/jenny/draft** *Are Two Links to the Same File*

```
$ cat file_a
This is file A.
$ ln file_a file_b
$ cat file_b
This is file A.

$ vi file_b
.
.
.
$ cat file_b
This is file B after the change.
$ cat file_a
This is file B after the change.
```

If you try the same experiment using **cp** instead of **ln** (and make a change to a *copy* of the file), the difference between the two utilities will become clearer. Once you change a *copy* of a file, the two files are different.

```
$ cat file_c
This is file C.
$ cp file_c file_d
$ cat file_d
This is file C.
$ vi file_d
.
.
.
$ cat file_d
This is file D after the change.
$ cat file_c
This is file C.
```

You can also use **ls** with the –l option, followed by the names of the files you want to compare, to see that the status information is the same for two links to a file and is different for files that are not linked. In the following example, the **2** in the links field (just to the left of **alex**) shows there are two links to **file_a** and **file_b**:

```
$ ls -l file_a file_b file_c file_d
-rw-r--r-- 2 alex 33  May 24 10:52 file_a
-rw-r--r-- 2 alex 33  May 24 10:52 file_b
-rw-r--r-- 1 alex 16  May 24 10:55 file_c
-rw-r--r-- 1 alex 33  May 24 10:57 file_d
```

Although it is easy to guess which files are linked to one another in the example above, **ls** does not explicitly tell you. If you use **ls** with the –i option, you can determine without a doubt which files are linked to each other. The –i option lists the *inode number* for each file. An *inode* is the control structure for a file. If the two filenames have the same inode number, then they share the control structure, and they are links to the same file. Conversely, if two filenames have different inode numbers, they are different files. The following example shows that **file_a** and **file_b** have the same inode number and that **file_c** and **file_d** have different inode numbers:

```
$ ls -i file_a file_b file_c file_d
3534 file_a    3534 file_b    5800 file_c    7328 file_d
```

All links to a file are of equal value—the operating system cannot distinguish the order in which two links were made. If a file has two links, you can remove either one and still access the file through the remaining link. You can even remove the link used to create the file and, as long as there is a remaining link, still access the file through that link.

Removing Links

When you first create a file, there is one link to it. You can delete the file or, using UNIX system terminology, remove the link, with the **rm** utility. When you remove the last link to a file, you can no longer access the information stored in the file, and the operating system releases the space the file occupied on the disk for use by other files. If there is more than one link to a file, you can remove a link and still access the file from any remaining link.

Symbolic Links

The links that are described above are *hard links*. In addition to hard links, most modern UNIX systems also support links called *symbolic links*. A hard link is a pointer to a file, and a symbolic link is an *indirect pointer* to a file. It is a directory entry that contains the pathname of the pointed-to file.

Symbolic links were developed because of the limitations of hard links. Only the Superuser can create a hard link to a directory, but anyone can create a symbolic link to a directory. Also, a symbolic link can link to any file, regardless of where it is located in the file structure, but all hard links to a file must be in the same filesystem. Typically, the UNIX file hierarchy is composed of several filesystems. Because each filesystem keeps separate control information (that is, separate inodes) for the files it contains, it is not possible to create hard links between files in different filesystems. If you are creating links only among files in your own directories, you probably will not notice this limitation.

Although symbolic links are more general than hard links, they have some disadvantages. Whereas all hard links to a file have equal status, symbolic links do not have the same status as hard links. When a file has multiple hard links, it is like a person having multiple, full legal names (as most married women do). In contrast, symbolic links are like pseudonyms. Anybody can have one or more pseudonyms, but pseudonyms have a lesser status than legal names. Some of the peculiarities of symbolic links are described in the following sections.

Creating a Symbolic Link

To make a symbolic link, use **ln** with the –s option. The example below creates a symbolic link, **/tmp/s3**, to the file **sum**. When you use the **ls** –l command to look at the symbolic link, **ls** displays the name of the link as well as the name of the file to which it is an indirect pointer. Also, the first character of the listing shows **l** for link. Note that the sizes and times of last modification of the two files are different. Unlike a hard link, a symbolic link to a file does not have the same status information as the file itself.

```
$ ln -s sum /tmp/s3
$ ls -lg sum /tmp/s3
-rw-r--r-- 1 alex pubs 981 May 24 10:55 sum
lrwxrwxrwx 1 alex pubs 4 May 24 10:57 /tmp/s3 -> sum
```

You can also use a command such as the one above to create a symbolic link to a directory. When you use the –s option, **ln** does not care whether the file you are creating a link to is a regular file or a directory.

Using Symbolic Links to Change Directories

When you use a symbolic link as an argument to **cd** to change directories, the results can be confusing, particularly if you did not realize you were using a symbolic link. The **pwd** command lists the name of the linked-to directory rather than the name of the symbolic link.

```
$ ln -s /home/alex/grades /tmp/grades.old
$ cd /tmp/grades.old
$ pwd
/home/alex/grades
```

Because **pwd** does not identify the symbolic link, the C Shell provides a variable, **cwd** (current working directory), that contains the name of the symbolic link (assuming you used a symbolic link to access the working directory). If you did not use a symbolic link to access the working directory, **cwd** contains the name of the hard link to the working directory. Because it is a variable, **cwd** is preceded by a dollar sign in the following example. When you use the **echo** command followed by a dollar sign and a variable name, **echo** displays the value of the variable. Shell variables and the use of the dollar sign are explained in Chapters 10, 11, and 12.

```
% pwd
/home/alex/grades
% echo $cwd
/tmp/grades.old
```

Changing directories to the parent directory of a directory that you accessed through a symbolic link can also be confusing. When you use the **cd ..** command, the parent of the linked-to directory becomes the working directory (rather than the parent directory of the symbolic link itself). In the following example, the **cd ..** command makes the working directory the parent of the linked-to directory, **/home/alex**, rather than the parent of the symbolic link, **/tmp**:

```
% echo $cwd
/tmp/grades.old
% cd ..
% echo $cwd
/home/alex
```

Removing Hard and Symbolic Links

A file exists only as long as a hard link to it exists, regardless of any symbolic links. Consequently, if you remove all the hard links to a file, you will not be able to access it through a symbolic link. In the following example, **cat** reports that the file **total** does not exist because it is a symbolic link to a file that has been removed:

```
$ ls -lg sum
-rw-r--r-- 1 alex pubs 981  May 24 11:05 sum
$ ln -s sum total
$ rm sum
$ cat total
total: No such file or directory
$ ls -lg total
lrwxrwxrwx 1 alex pubs 6  May 24 11:09 total -> sum
```

When you remove a file, be sure to remove all symbolic links to it. You can remove a symbolic link in the same way you remove other files:

```
$ rm total
```

SUMMARY

The UNIX system has a *hierarchical*, or treelike, file structure that makes it possible to organize files so that you can find them quickly and easily. The file structure contains *directory* files and *ordinary* files. Directories contain other files, including other directories, whereas ordinary files generally contain text or programs. The ancestor of all files is the *root* directory, named /.

Older releases of the UNIX system allowed you to use up to 14 characters to name a file; most UNIX systems today support 255-character filenames, including SunOS and Berkeley UNIX. Nonetheless, it is a good idea to keep filenames simple and meaningful. *Filename extensions* help make filenames more meaningful.

An *absolute pathname* starts with the root directory and contains all the filenames that trace a path to a given file. Such a pathname starts with a slash representing the root directory and contains additional slashes between the other filenames in the path.

A *relative pathname* is similar to an absolute pathname, but the path it traces starts from the working directory. A *simple filename* is the last element of a pathname and is a form of a relative pathname.

When you are logged in, you are always associated with a *working directory*. Your *home directory* is your working directory from the time you first log in until you use **cd** to change directories.

A *link* is a pointer to a file. You can have several links to a single file, so that you can share the file with other users or have the file appear in more than one directory. Because there is only one copy of a file with multiple links, changing the file through any one link causes the changes to appear in all the links. Hard links cannot connect directories and cannot span file-systems, but symbolic links can.

This chapter introduced the following utilities:

- **pwd** displays the pathname of the working directory.
- **mkdir** creates a directory.
- **cd** associates you with another working directory.
- **rmdir** deletes a directory.
- **chmod** changes the access permissions on a file.
- **ln** makes a link to an existing file.

REVIEW EXERCISES

1. How are directories different from ordinary files?

2. Determine whether each of the following is an absolute pathname, a relative pathname, or a simple filename:

    a. **milk_co**

    b. **correspondence/business/milk_co**

    c. **/home/alex**

    d. **/home/alex/literature/promo**

    e. **..**

    f. **letter.0610**

3. Should you ordinarily start your filenames with a period (.)? Why or why not?

4. List the commands you can use to:

    a. make your home directory the working directory

    b. identify the working directory

5. If your working directory is **/home/alex/literature**, what two different commands can you use to create a subdirectory called **classics**?

6. What sequence of commands can you use to remove a directory called **/home/jenny/temp** and all its contents?

7. Is the **to_do** file below a directory or an ordinary file? Do members of the pubs group have permission to read the file?

```
$ ls -lg to_do
-rw-r--r-- 1 alex  pubs    1338 May 24 17:01 to_do
```

What command can Alex use to give everyone permission to write to the file? What will the ls –lg command display after he does so?

8. What does it mean to have execute permission for a directory?

9. Suppose you have a file named **andor** in the current directory. What happens if you run the following command line?

   mv andor and\/or

   Explain.

10. Create a file called –x in an empty directory. Explain what happens when you try to rename it. How can you rename it?

11. If **/home/jenny/draft** is linked to **/home/alex/letter** and Alex changes **letter**, will Jenny see the changes when she looks at **draft**? What should Jenny do if she does not want Alex's changes to **letter** to affect **draft**?

12. If **/home/jenny/draft** and /home/alex/letter are links to the same file and the following sequence of events occurs, what will the date be in the opening of the letter?

    a. Alex gives the command **vi letter**.

    b. Jenny gives the command **vi draft**.

    c. Jenny changes the date in the opening of the letter to January 31, 1994, and exits from **vi** with the **ZZ** command.

    d. Alex changes the date to February 1, 1994, and exits from **vi** with the **ZZ** command.

13. What problems do you run into with multiple writable links to a file?

14. Given the directory structure shown in Figure 4-3 and the following directory permissions:

    ```
    d--x--x--x 3 jenny  pubs   512 May 15 10:01 correspondence/business
    drwxr-xr-x 3 jenny  pubs   512 May 15 10:01 correspondence/business/milk_co
    ```

    What happens when you run each of the following commands? (Assume that the files **cheese_co**, **letter_1**, and **letter_2** are readable by everyone.)

    a. **cd correspondence/business/milk_co**

    b. **ls –lg correspondence/business**

    c. **cat correspondence/business/cheese_co**

CHAPTER 5

The Shell

This chapter takes a close look at the shell and explains how to use some of its features. It discusses command line syntax, how the shell processes a command line, and how it initiates execution of a command. The chapter shows how to redirect input to and output from a command, construct pipes and filters on the command line, and run a command as a background task. The final section covers filename generation and explains how you can use this feature in your everyday work. Everything in this chapter applies to the Bourne Shell, the C Shell, and the Korn Shell. Refer to Chapters 10, 11, and 12 for information on using the shell programming language to write shell scripts.

The Command Line

The shell executes a program when you give it a command in response to its prompt. For example, when you give the **ls** command, the shell executes the utility program called **ls**. You can cause the shell to execute other types of programs—such as shell scripts, application programs, and programs you have written—in the same way. The line that contains the command, including any arguments, is called the *command line*. In this book, the term *command* is used to refer to the characters you type on the command line as well as the program that action invokes.

Command Line Syntax

Command line syntax dictates the ordering and separation of the elements on a command line. When you press the (RETURN) key after entering a command, the shell scans the command line for proper syntax. The format for a command line is:

command [arg1] [arg2] ... [argn] (RETURN)

The square brackets in the example enclose optional elements. One or more (SPACE)s or (TAB)s must appear between elements on the command line. The **command** is the command name, **arg1** through **argn** are arguments, and (RETURN) is the keystroke that terminates all command lines. The arguments are enclosed in square brackets above to show that they are optional: not all commands have arguments; some commands do not allow arguments, other commands allow a variable number of arguments, and others require a specific number of arguments.

Command Name

Some useful UNIX commands consist only of the name of the command. For example, **ls** without any arguments lists the contents of the current directory. However, most UNIX commands accept one or more arguments. Commands that require arguments typically give a short error message when you use them without arguments.

Arguments

An *argument* is a filename, string of text, number, or some other object that a command acts on. For example, the argument to a **vi** command is the name of the file you want to edit.

The following command line shows **cp** copying the file named **temp** to **tempcopy**:

```
$ cp temp tempcopy
```

The **cp** utility requires two arguments on the command line. The first is the name of an existing file, and the second is the name of the file that it is creating. Here, the arguments are not optional; both arguments must be present for the command to work. If you do not supply the right num-

```
$ ls -r
test personal names
temp oldstuff hold
$ ls -x
hold      names oldstuff
personal temp  test
```

Figure 5-1   Using Options

ber or kind of arguments, **cp** displays an error message. Try it—just type **cp** and (RETURN).

Options

An option is an argument that modifies the effects of a command. Frequently, you can specify more than one option, modifying the command in several different ways. Options are specific to and interpreted by the program that the command calls.

By convention, options are separate arguments that follow the name of the command. Most UNIX utilities require you to prefix options with a hyphen. However, this requirement is specific to the utility and not the shell.

Figure 5-1 shows that the –r (reverse order) option causes the **ls** utility to display the list of files in reverse alphabetical order. The –x option causes **ls** to display the list of files in horizontally sorted columns. (The **ls** utility normally displays files in vertically sorted columns.) It allows you to view a list of many filenames sorted across the screen. (If your version of **ls** displays a list of filenames in one long column that scrolls off the screen and does not have the –x option, use the –C option or see page 103 for an example of how to use **more** with **ls**.)

If you need to use several options, you can usually (but not always) group them into one argument that starts with a single hyphen; do not put (SPACE)s between the options. Specific rules for combining options depend on the utility. Figure 5-2 shows both the –r and –x options with the **ls** utility. Together, these options generate a list of filenames in horizontally sorted columns, in reverse alphabetical order. Most utilities allow you to list options in any order; **ls –xr** produces the same results as **ls –rx**. The command **ls –x –r** will also generate the same list.

```
$ ls -rx
test      temp  personal
oldstuff names hold
```

Figure 5-2   Using Two Options at Once

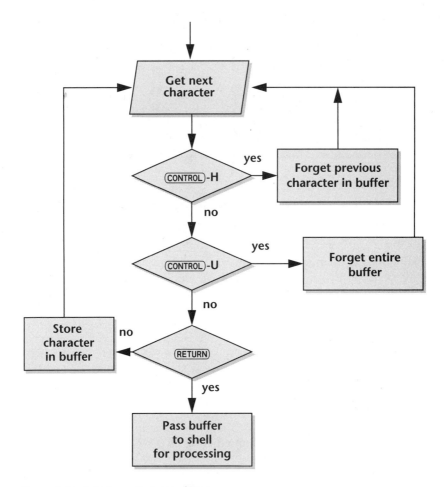

Figure 5-3   Entering a Command Line

Processing the Command Line

As you enter a command line, the UNIX operating system examines each character to see if it must take any action (Figure 5-3). When you enter a (CONTROL)-**H** (to erase a character) or a (CONTROL)-**U** (to kill a line), the operating system immediately adjusts the command line as required—the shell never sees the character you erased or the line you killed. The system also adjusts the line when you enter (CONTROL)-**W** (to erase a word) or (CONTROL)-**R** (to redraw the command line). If the character does not require immediate action, the operating system stores the character in a buffer and waits for additional characters. When you press (RETURN), the operating system passes the command line to the shell for processing.

When the shell processes a command line, it looks at the line as a whole and breaks it down into its component parts (Figure 5-4). Next, the shell looks for the name of the command. It assumes that the name of the command is the first thing on the command line after the prompt (that is, argu-

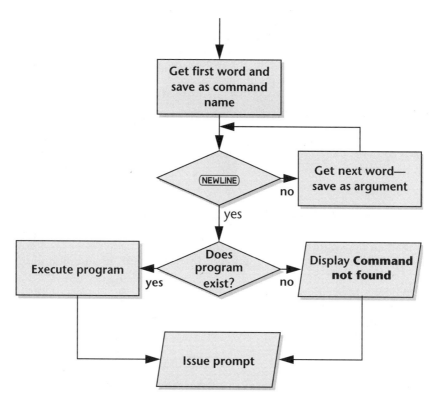

Figure 5-4   Processing the Command Line

ment zero), so it takes the first characters on the command line, up to the first blank (⟨TAB⟩ or ⟨SPACE⟩), and looks for a command with that name. On the command line, each sequence of nonblank characters is referred to as a *word*. The command name (the first word) can be specified on the command line either as a simple filename or as a pathname. For example, you can call the **ls** command in either of the following ways:

```
$ ls
$ /bin/ls
```

If you give an absolute pathname on the command line or a relative pathname that is not just a simple filename (that is, any pathname that includes at least one slash), the shell looks in the specified directory (/**bin** in this case) for a file that has the name **ls** and that you have permission to execute. If you do not give a pathname on the command line, the shell searches through a list of directories for a filename that matches the name you specified and that you have execute permission for. The shell does not look through all directories—it looks only through the directories determined by a *shell variable* called the **PATH** variable. This variable is described in Chapters 10, 11, and 12.

If the Bourne Shell cannot find the command, it displays the message xx: not found, where xx is the name of the command you called. If the Bourne Shell finds the program but cannot execute it (if you do not have execute access to the file that contains the program), you will see the following message: xx: execute permission denied. The messages presented by the C Shell and the Korn Shell are worded differently, but their gist is the same.

The shell has no way of knowing whether a particular option or other argument is valid for a given command. Any error messages about options or arguments come from the command itself. Many UNIX utilities ignore bad options.

Executing the Command Line

If the shell finds an executable file with the same name as the command, it starts a new process. A *process* is the UNIX system execution of a program. The shell makes each command line argument, including options and the name of the command, available to the command. While the command is executing, the shell waits, inactive, for the process to finish. The shell is in a state called *sleep*. When the command finishes executing, the shell returns to an active state (wakes up), issues a prompt, and waits for another command.

Standard Input and Standard Output

A command's *standard output* is a place to which it can send information, frequently text. The command never "knows" where the information it sends to its standard output is going. The information can go to a printer, an ordinary file, or a terminal. This section shows that the shell directs the standard output from a command to the terminal and describes how you can cause the shell to redirect this output to another file. It also explains how to redirect the *standard input* to a command so that it comes from an ordinary file instead of the terminal.

The Terminal As a File

Chapter 4 introduced ordinary files and directories. The UNIX system has an additional type of file, a *device file*. A device file resides in the UNIX file structure, usually in the /dev directory, and represents a peripheral device such as a terminal, printer, or disk drive.

The device name that the **who** utility displays after your login name is the filename of your terminal. If **who** displays the device name **tty06**, the pathname of your terminal is probably **/dev/tty06**. Although you would not normally have occasion to, you could read from and write to this file as though it were a text file. Writing to it would display what you wrote on the terminal screen, and reading from it would read what you entered on the keyboard.

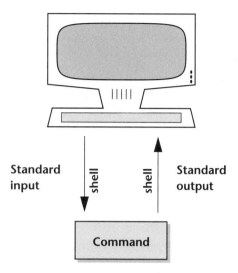

Figure 5-5   Standard Input and Output

The Terminal As the Standard Input and Output

When you first log in, the shell directs your commands' standard output to the device file that represents your terminal (Figure 5-5). Directing output in this manner causes it to appear on your terminal screen. The shell also directs the standard input to come from the same file, so that your commands receive as input anything you type on your terminal keyboard.

The **cat** utility provides a good example of the way the terminal functions as the standard input and output. When you use **cat**, it copies a file to its standard output. Because the shell directs the standard output to the terminal, **cat** displays the file on the terminal.

Up to this point, **cat** has taken its input from the filename (argument) you specified on the command line. If you do not give **cat** an argument (that is, if you give the command **cat** immediately followed by a (RETURN)), **cat** takes input from its standard input.

The **cat** utility can now be defined as a utility that, when called without an argument, copies its standard input file to its standard output file. On most systems, it copies one line at a time.

To see how **cat** works, type cat (RETURN) in response to the shell prompt. Nothing happens. Enter a line of text and a (RETURN). The same line appears just under the one you entered. The **cat** utility is working. (Some versions do not display anything until you signal the end of the file by pressing (CONTROL)-**D**; see below.) What happened is that you typed a line of text on the terminal, which the shell associated with **cat**'s standard input, and **cat** copied your line of text to its standard output file, which the shell also associated with the terminal. This exchange is shown in Figure 5-6.

The **cat** utility keeps copying until you enter (CONTROL)-**D** on a line by itself. Pressing (CONTROL)-**D** sends an *end-of-file* signal to **cat** that indicates it has

```
$ cat
This is a line of text.
This is a line of text.
Cat keeps copying lines of text
Cat keeps copying lines of text
until you press CONTROL-D at the beginning
until you press CONTROL-D at the beginning
of a line.
of a line.
(CONTROL)-D
$
```

Figure 5-6   **cat** *Copies Its Standard Input to Its Standard Output*

reached the end of the standard input file and that there is no more text for
it to copy. When you enter (CONTROL)-**D, cat** finishes execution and returns control to the shell, which gives you a prompt.

Redirection

The term *redirection* encompasses the various ways you can cause the shell to
alter where a command gets its standard input from or where it sends its
standard output to. As the previous section demonstrated, the shell, by default, associates a command's standard input and standard output with the
terminal. Users can cause the shell to redirect the standard input and/or the
standard output of any command by associating the input or output with a
command or file other than the device file representing the terminal. This
section demonstrates how to redirect output from and input to ordinary text
files and UNIX utilities.

Redirecting the Standard Output

The *redirect output* symbol (>) instructs the shell to redirect a command's output to the specified file instead of to the terminal (Figure 5-7). The format of
a command line that redirects output follows:

  command [arguments] > filename

The **command** is any executable program (e.g., an application program
or a UNIX utility), **arguments** are optional arguments, and **filename** is the
name of the ordinary file the shell redirects the output to.

> **CAUTION**
> Use caution when you redirect output. If the file already exists, the
> shell may overwrite it and destroy its contents.

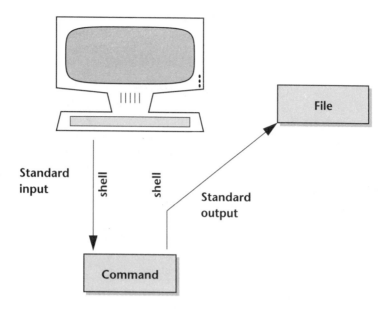

Figure 5-7   Redirecting the Standard Output

In Figure 5-8, **cat** demonstrates output redirection. This figure contrasts with Figure 5-6, where both the standard input *and* standard output were associated with the terminal. In Figure 5-8, only the input comes from the terminal. The redirect output symbol on the command line causes the shell to associate **cat**'s standard output with the file specified on the command line, **sample.txt**.

Now **sample.txt** contains the text you entered. You can use **cat** with an argument of **sample.txt** to display the file. The next section shows another way to use **cat** to display the file.

Figure 5-8 shows that redirecting the output from **cat** is a handy way to make files without using an editor. Its drawback is that, once you enter a line and press (RETURN), you cannot edit the text. While you are entering a line, the erase and kill keys work to delete text. This procedure is useful for making short, simple files.

```
$ cat > sample.txt
This text is being entered at the keyboard.
Cat is copying it to a file.
Press CONTROL-D to indicate the
end of file.
(CONTROL)-D
$
```

*Figure 5-8   **cat** with Its Output Redirected*

```
$ cat stationery
2000 sheets letterhead  ordered: 10/7/94
$ cat tape
1 box masking tape      ordered: 10/14/94
5 boxes filament tape   ordered: 10/28/94
$ cat pens
12 doz. black pens      ordered: 10/4/94
$ cat stationery tape pens > supply_orders
$ cat supply_orders
2000 sheets letterhead  ordered: 10/7/94
1 box masking tape      ordered: 10/14/94
5 boxes filament tape   ordered: 10/28/94
12 doz. black pens      ordered: 10/4/94
$
```

Figure 5-9   Using **cat** *to Catenate Files*

Figure 5-9 shows how to use **cat** and the redirect output symbol to *catenate* (join one after the other) several files into one larger file. The first three commands display the contents of three files: **stationery, tape,** and **pens**. The next command shows **cat** with three filenames as arguments. When you call **cat** with more than one filename, it copies the files, one at a time, to its standard output. Here, the standard output is redirected to the file **supply_orders**. The final **cat** command shows that **supply_orders** contains the contents of all three files.

Redirecting the Standard Input

Just as you can redirect **cat**'s standard output, you can redirect its standard input. The *redirect input* symbol (<) instructs the shell to redirect a command's input from the specified file instead of the terminal (Figure 5-10). The format of a command line that redirects input follows:

command [arguments] < filename

The **command** is any executable program (e.g., an application program or a UNIX utility), **arguments** are optional arguments, and **filename** is the name of the ordinary file the shell redirects the input from.

Figure 5-11 shows **cat** with its input redirected from the **supply_orders** file that was created in Figure 5-9 and its standard output going to the terminal. This setup causes **cat** to display the sample file on the terminal. The system automatically supplies an end-of-file signal at the end of an ordinary file, so no (CONTROL)-D is necessary.

Using **cat** with input redirected from a file yields the same result as giving a **cat** command with the filename as an argument. The **cat** utility is a member of a class of UNIX utilities that function in this manner. Other members of this class of utilities are **lpr, sort,** and **grep**. These utilities first examine the

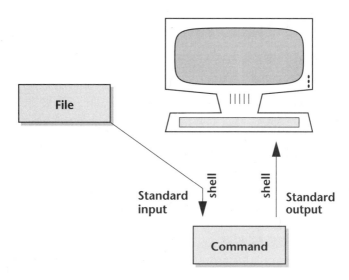

Figure 5-10   Redirecting the Standard Input

command line you use to call them. If you include a filename on the command line, the utility takes its input from the file you specify. If there is no filename, the utility takes its input from its standard input. It is the program, not the shell or the operating system, that functions in this manner.

```
$ cat < supply_orders
2000 sheets letterhead    ordered: 10/7/94
1 box masking tape        ordered: 10/14/94
5 boxes filament tape     ordered: 10/28/94
12 doz. black pens        ordered: 10/4/94
$
```

Figure 5-11   cat with Its Input Redirected

Following is an example of how to use redirected input with **mail**. Frequently, it is convenient to compose your thoughts in a file before you send someone electronic mail. You can use **lpr** to print the file, check that it is correct, and send it at your leisure. The following command sends the contents of the file **memo.alex** to Alex, using **mail**. The redirect input symbol redirects **mail**'s standard input to come from **memo.alex** instead of the terminal.

```
$ mail alex < memo.alex
```

CAUTION

Depending on what shell you are using and how your environment has been set up, the shell may display an error message and

CAUTION Continued

overwrite the contents of the **orange** file when you give the following command:

```
$ cat orange pear > orange
cat: input orange is output
```

Although **cat** displays an error message, it goes ahead and destroys the contents of the existing **orange** file. If you give the command above, the new **orange** file will have the same contents as **pear**, because the first action of the command is to remove the contents of the original **orange** file. If you want to catenate two files into one, use **cat** to put the two files into a third, temporary file, and then use **mv** to rename the third file as you desire.

```
$ cat orange pear > temp
$ mv temp orange
```

What happens with the typo in the next example can be even worse. The person giving the command meant to redirect the output from the **grep** command (page 55) to the file **a.output**. Instead, the person entered the filename as **a output**, omitting the period and leaving a (SPACE) in its place. The shell obediently removed the contents of **a** and then called **grep**. The error message takes a moment to appear, giving you a sense that the command is running correctly. Even after you see the error message, though, you may not know that you destroyed the contents of **a**.

```
$ grep apple a b c > a output
grep: output: No such file or directory
```

The C Shell and Korn Shell provide a feature called **noclobber** that stops you from inadvertently overwriting an existing file using redirection. If this variable is set and you attempt to redirect output to an existing file, the shell presents an error message and the command is not executed. If the examples above result in a message such as a: file exists., then the **noclobber** variable is in effect. This feature is described on page 363.

Appending the Standard Output to a File

The *append output* symbol (>>) causes the shell to add the new information to the end of a file, leaving intact any information that was already there. This symbol provides a convenient way of catenating two files into one. You can use the following command to accomplish the catenation described above:

```
$ cat pear >> orange
```

This is simpler to use than the two-step procedure described in the previous section, but you must be careful to include both *greater than* signs. If you accidentally use only one and the **noclobber** variable is not set (or you are us-

```
$ date > whoson
$ cat whoson
Thu Aug  11 09:24:19 PDT 1994
$ who >> whoson
$ cat whoson
Thu Aug  11 09:24:31 PDT 1994
hls          console       Aug  11 08:47
jenny        tty02         Aug  11 07:21
alex         tty06         Aug  10 11:01
$
```

Figure 5-12   Redirecting and Appending Output

ing the Bourne Shell), the **orange** file will be overwritten. Generally, even if you have the **noclobber** variable set, it is a good idea to keep backup copies of files you are manipulating in these ways in case you make a mistake. Although **noclobber** protects you from making an erroneous redirection, it cannot stop you from overwriting an existing file using the **cp** or **mv** utility. The **cp** and **mv** utilities include an option that protects users from those mistakes by making the commands verify your intentions if you try to overwrite a file. Refer to **cp** and **mv** in Part II.

The example in Figure 5-12 shows how to create a file that contains the date and time (the output from the **date** utility) followed by a list of who is logged in (the output from **who**). The first line in Figure 5-12 redirects the output from **date** to the file named **whoson**. Then **cat** displays the file. Next, the example appends the output from **who** to the **whoson** file. Finally, **cat** displays the file containing the output of both utilities.

Pipes

The shell uses a *pipe* to connect the standard output of one command directly to the standard input of another command. A pipe has the same effect as redirecting the standard output of one command to a file and then using that file as the standard input to another command. It does away with separate commands and the intermediate file. The symbol for a pipe is a vertical bar (|). The format of a command line using a pipe follows:

  command_a [arguments] | command_b [arguments]

This command line uses a pipe to generate the same result as the following command lines:

  command_a [arguments] > temp
  command_b [arguments] < temp
  rm temp

The preceding sequence of commands first redirects the standard output from **command_a** to an intermediate file named **temp**. Then it redirects the standard input for **command_b** to come from **temp**. The final command line deletes **temp**.

You can use a pipe with a member of the class of UNIX utilities that accepts input either from a file specified on the command line or from the standard input. Other commands accept input only from the standard input, and you can also use pipes with these commands. For example, the **tr** (translate) utility takes its input only from the standard input. In its simplest usage, **tr** has the following format:

tr **string1 string2**

The **tr** utility translates each character in **string1** in its standard input to the corresponding character in **string2**. (The first character in **string1** is translated into the first character in **string2**, and so forth.) In the example below, **tr** displays the content of the **abstract** file with the letters a, b, and c translated into A, B, and C, respectively. Like other UNIX filters, **tr** does not change the content of the original file (see page 104 for more information about filters).

```
$ cat abstract | tr abc ABC
```

or

```
$ tr abc ABC < abstract
```

Refer to page 723 for more information about **tr**.

The **lpr** (line printer) utility is among the commands that accept input from either a file or the standard input. When you follow **lpr** with the name of a file, it places that file in the printer queue. If you do not specify a filename on the command line, **lpr** takes input from its standard input. This feature allows you to use a pipe to redirect input to **lpr**. The first set of commands in Figure 5-13 shows how you can use **ls** and **lpr**, with an intermediate file, to send to the printer a list of the files in the working directory. The second set of commands sends the same list to the printer using a pipe.

```
$ ls > temp
$ lpr temp
$ rm temp

or

$ ls | lpr
$
```

Figure 5-13   A Pipe

```
$ who > temp
$ sort temp
barbara      tty03        May 26 12:53
chas         tty06        May 26 10:31
hls          console      May 26 12:48
scott        tty02        May 25 09:07
$
```

Figure 5-14   Simulating a Pipe with **who** *and* **sort**

The commands in Figure 5-14 redirect the output from the **who** utility to **temp** and then display this file in sorted order. The **sort** utility takes its input from the file specified on the command line or, if a file is not specified, from its standard input. It sends its output to its standard output. The **sort** command in Figure 5-14 specifies **temp** as the input file. The output that **sort** sends to the terminal lists the users in sorted (alphabetical) order.

Figure 5-15 achieves the same result with a pipe. Using a pipe, the shell directs the output from **who** to the input of **sort**. The **sort** utility takes input from its standard input because no filename follows it on the command line.

If a lot of people are using the system and you want information about only one of them, you can send the output from **who** to **grep** using a pipe. The **grep** utility will display the line containing the string you specify—chas in the following example.

```
$ who | grep 'chas'
chas         tty06        May 26 10:31
```

Another way of handling output that is too long to fit on the screen, such as a list of files in a crowded directory, is to use a pipe to send it through the **more** utility:

```
$ ls | more
```

The **more** utility allows you to view text on your terminal a screenful at a time. To view another screenful, press (SPACE). To view one more line, press (RETURN).

```
$ who | sort
barbara      tty03        May 26 12:53
chas         tty06        May 26 10:31
hls          console      May 26 12:48
scott        tty02        May 25 09:07
$
```

Figure 5-15   A Pipe

Filters

A *filter* is a command that processes an input stream of data to produce an output stream of data. A command line that includes a filter uses a pipe to connect the filter's input to the standard output of one command. Another pipe connects the filter's output to the standard input of another command. Some utilities that are interactive, such as **vi** and **mail**, cannot be used as filters.

Below, **sort** is a filter, taking its standard input from the standard output of **who** and using a pipe to redirect its standard output to the standard input of **lpr**. The command line sends the sorted output of **who** to the printer.

```
$ who | sort | lpr
```

This example demonstrates the power of the shell combined with the versatility of UNIX utilities. The three utilities, **who**, **sort**, and **lpr**, were not specifically designed to work with each other, but they all use the standard input and standard output in the conventional way. By using the shell to handle input and output, you can piece standard utilities together on the command line to achieve the results you want.

The tee Utility

You can use the **tee** utility in a pipe to send the output of a command to a file while also sending it to its standard output. The utility is aptly named—it takes a single input and sends the output in two directions. In the following example, the output of **who** is sent via a pipe to the standard input of **tee**. The **tee** utility saves a copy of the standard input in a file called **who.out** while it also sends a copy to the standard output. The standard output of **tee** goes, via a pipe, to the standard input of **grep**, which displays lines containing the string **chas**.

```
$ who | tee who.out | grep chas
chas       tty06       May 26 10:31
$ cat who.out
hls        console     May 26 12:48
scott      tty02       May 25 09:07
barbara    tty03       May 26 12:53
chas       tty06       May 26 10:31
```

Running a Program in the Background

In all the examples you have seen so far in this book, commands were run in the *foreground*. When you run a command in the foreground, the shell waits for it to finish before giving you another prompt and allowing you to continue. When you run a command in the *background*, you do not have to wait for the command to finish before you start running another command. Running a command in the background can be useful if the command will be running a long time and does not need supervision. The terminal will be free so you can use it for other work.

To run a command in the background, type an ampersand (&) just before the (RETURN) that ends the command line. The shell will display a Process Identification (PID) number that identifies the command running in the background and give you another prompt.

The following example runs a command line in the background. The command sends its output through a pipe to the **lpr** utility, which sends it to the printer.

```
$ ls -l | lpr &
31725
```

If a background task sends output to the standard output and you do not redirect it, the output appears on your terminal, even if you are running another job. If a background task requests input from the standard input and you have not redirected the standard input, the shell supplies a null string (Bourne Shell) or stops the job and waits for you to give it input (C Shell).

You will probably want to redirect the output of a job you run in the background or send it through a pipe to keep it from interfering with whatever you are doing at the terminal. See page 278 for more detail about background tasks in the section "Command Separation and Grouping."

The interrupt key (usually (DELETE) or (CONTROL)-**C**) cannot abort a process you are running in the background; you must use the **kill** command for this purpose. If you want to kill *all* processes that you are running *in the background*, you can use the following command.

```
$ kill 0
```

Alternatively, when you use **kill** to halt selected processes, you must give it the PID number of the process you want to abort.

If you forget the PID number, you can use the **ps** (process status) utility to display it. The following example runs a **tail** job in the background, uses **ps** to display the PID number of the process, and aborts the job with **kill**. Refer to Part II for more information on **kill** and **ps**.

```
$ tail -f outfile &
1466
$ ps
    PID TT STAT   TIME COMMAND
   1456 03 S     0:05 sh
   1466 03 S     0:07 tail
   1514 03 R     0:03 ps
$ kill 1466
```

Filename Generation

When you give the shell abbreviated filenames that contain *special characters* (or *metacharacters*—characters that have a special meaning to the shell), the shell can generate filenames that match the names of existing files. When one of these special characters appears in an argument on the command line, the shell expands that argument into a list of filenames and passes the list to the program that the command line is calling. Filenames that contain these special characters are called *ambiguous file references* because they do not refer to any one specific file.

The special characters are referred to as *metacharacters* or *wild cards* because they act as the jokers do in a deck of cards. The process of expanding an ambiguous file reference used to be called *globbing*. Ambiguous file references allow you to quickly reference a group of files with similar names, saving you the effort of typing the names individually. They also allow you to reference a file whose name you do not remember in its entirety.

The ? Special Character

The question mark is a special character that causes the shell to generate filenames. It matches any single character in the name of an existing file. The following command uses this special character in an argument to the **lpr** utility:

```
$ lpr memo?
```

The shell expands the memo? argument and generates a list of the files in the working directory that have names composed of **memo** followed by any single character. The shell passes this list to **lpr**. The **lpr** utility never "knows" that the shell generated the filenames it was called with. If no filename matches the ambiguous file reference, the Bourne Shell and Korn Shell pass the string itself (memo?) to the command. Depending on how it is set up, the C Shell may display an error message (No match) or pass the string itself.

The following example uses **ls** to display the filenames that memo? does and does not match:

```
$ ls
mem          memo12      memo9      memoalex  newmemo5
memo         memo5       memoa      memos
$ ls memo?
memo5   memo9   memoa   memos
```

The memo? ambiguous file reference does not match **mem, memo, memo12, memoalex,** or **newmemo5**.

You can also use a question mark in the middle of an ambiguous file reference:

```
$ ls
7may4report     may14report    may4report.79  mayqreport
may.report      may4report     may_report     mayreport
$ ls may?report
may.report   may4report   may_report   mayqreport
```

To practice with filename generation, you can use **echo** as well as **ls**. The **echo** utility displays the arguments that the shell passes to it. Try giving the following command:

```
$ echo may?report
may.report   may4report   may_report   mayqreport
```

The shell expands the ambiguous file reference into a list of all files in the working directory that match the string **may?report** and passes this list to **echo,** as though you had entered the list of filenames as arguments to **echo.** The **echo** utility responds to this command by displaying the list of filenames.

The * Special Character

The asterisk performs a function similar to that of the question mark, except that it matches any number of characters, *including zero characters,* in a filename. The following example shows all the files in the current directory and then all the filenames that begin with the string **memo**:

```
$ ls
amemo        memo          memoa        memosally    user.memo
mem          memo.0612     memorandum   sallymemo
$ echo memo*
memo memo.0612 memoa memorandum memosally
```

The ambiguous file reference memo* does not match **amemo**, **mem**, **sallymemo**, or **user.memo**.

<hr>

OPTIONAL

An asterisk does not match a leading period (one that indicates an invisible filename). Consequently, if you want to match filenames that begin with a period, you must explicitly include the period in the ambiguous file reference.

The **ls** utility also has an option, **–a**, that causes it to display invisible filenames:

```
$ ls -a
.    .aaa     aaa          memo.sally  sally.0612  thurs
..   .profile memo.0612    report      saturday
$ echo *
aaa memo.0612 memo.sally report sally.0612 saturday thurs
$ echo .*
. .. .aaa .profile
```

The command **echo *** does not display . (the working directory), .. (the parent of the working directory), **.aaa** or **.profile**. The command **echo .*** displays only those four names.

```
$ ls -a
.           .private     memo.0612    reminder
..          .profile     private      report

$ echo .p*
.private .profile
```

In the final example, .p* does not match **memo.0612**, **private**, **reminder**, or **report**. The following command causes **ls** to list **.private** and **.profile** in addition to the entire contents of the . directory (the working directory) and the .. directory (the parent of the working directory).

```
$ ls .*
.private .profile

.:
memo.0612  private     reminder    report

..:
.
.
```

If you establish conventions for naming files, you can take advantage of ambiguous file references. For example, if you end all your text file filenames with .txt, you can reference that group of files with *.txt. Following this convention, the command below will send all the text files in the working directory to the printer. The ampersand causes **lpr** to run in the background.

```
$ lpr *.txt &
4312
```

The [] Special Characters

A pair of square brackets surrounding a list of characters causes the shell to match filenames containing the individual characters. Whereas **memo?** matches **memo** followed by any character, **memo[17a]** is more restrictive— it matches only **memo1**, **memo7**, and **memoa**. The brackets define a *character class* that includes all the characters within the brackets. The shell expands an argument that includes a character class definition, substituting each member of the character class, *one at a time*, in place of the brackets and their contents. The shell passes a list of matching filenames to the command it is calling.

Each character class definition can replace only a single character within a filename. The brackets and their contents are like a question mark that will substitute only the members of the character class.

The first of the following commands lists the names of all the files in the working directory that begin with **a**, **e**, **i**, **o**, or **u**. The second command displays the contents of the files named **page2.txt**, **page4.txt**, **page6.txt**, and **page8.txt**.

```
$ echo [aeiou]*
.
.
.
$ cat page[2468].txt
.
.
.
```

A hyphen defines a range of characters within a character class definition. For example, [6-9] represents [6789], and [a-z] represents all lowercase letters.

The following command lines show three ways to print the files named **part0**, **part1**, **part2**, **part3**, and **part5**. Each of the command lines calls **lpr** with five filenames.

```
$ lpr part0 part1 part2 part3 part5
```

```
$ lpr part[01235]
```

```
$ lpr part[0-35]
```

The first command line explicitly specifies the five filenames. The second and third command lines use ambiguous file references, incorporating character class definitions. The shell expands the argument on the second command line to include all files that have names beginning with **part** and ending with any of the characters in the character class. The character class is explicitly defined as 0, 1, 2, 3, and 5. The third command line also uses a character class definition, except it defines the character class to be all characters in the range from 0–3 and 5.

The following command line will print 36 files, **part0** through **part35**:

```
$ lpr part[0-9] part[12][0-9] part3[0-5]
```

The next two examples list the names of some of the files in the working directory. The first lists the files whose names start with **a** through **m**. The second lists files whose names end with **x**, **y**, or **z**.

```
$ echo [a-m]*
.
.

$ echo *[x-z]
.
.
```

SUMMARY

The shell is the UNIX command interpreter. It scans the command line for proper syntax, picking out the command name and any arguments. Many programs use options to modify the effects of a command. Most UNIX utilities identify options by their leading hyphens.

When you give the shell a command, it tries to find an executable program with the same name as the command. If it does, it executes the program. If it does not, it tells you that it cannot find or execute the program.

When the shell executes a command, it assigns a file to the command's *standard input* and *standard output*. By default, the shell causes a command's standard input to come from the terminal keyboard and its standard output to go to the terminal screen. You can instruct the shell to *redirect* a command's standard input or standard output to any reasonable file or device. You can also connect the standard output of one command to the standard input of another by using a pipe.

When a command runs in the *foreground*, the shell waits for it to finish before it gives you another prompt and allows you to continue. If you put an ampersand (&) at the end of a command line, the shell executes the command in the *background* and gives you another prompt immediately.

The shell interprets special characters on a command line for *filename generation*. It uses a question mark to represent any single character and an asterisk to represent zero or more characters. A reference to a file that includes one of these characters is called an *ambiguous file reference*.

REVIEW EXERCISES

1. What does the shell ordinarily do while a command is executing? What should you do if you do not want to wait for a command to finish before running another command?

2. What command line will redirect the standard output from the **sort**

command into a file called **phone_list**? Assume the input file is called **numbers**.

3. Can the **grep** utility be used as a filter? Explain your answer.

4. Describe two ways you can create a file called **book** that contains the contents of two other files, **part1** and **part2**.

5. Rewrite the following sequence of commands using **sort** as a filter:

```
$ sort list > temp
$ lpr temp
$ rm temp
```

6. What is a PID number? Why are they useful when you run processes in the background?

7. Assume the following files are in the working directory:

```
$ ls
intro     notesb    ref2     section1    section3    section4b
notesa    ref1      ref3     section2    section4a
```

What command(s) (including wild cards) can you use to

a. list all files that begin with **section**.

b. list the files **section1**, **section2**, and **section3**.

c. list the **intro** file only.

d. list the files **section1**, **section3**, **ref1**, and **ref3**.

ADVANCED REVIEW EXERCISES

8. Why do command names and filenames usually not have embedded spaces? If you wanted to create a filename containing a space, how would you do it? (This is a thought exercise—it is not a recommended practice.)

9. If you accidentally create a filename with a nonprinting character in it (e.g., a (CONTROL) character), how can you rename the file?

10. Create a file called **answers** and then give the following command:

```
$ > answers.0194 < answers cat
```

Explain what the command does and why.

11. Why can the **noclobber** variable not protect you from overwriting an existing file with **cp** or **mv**?

## CHAPTER 6

Graphical User Interfaces

The ability of UNIX to run several jobs at the same time is one of the reasons it is popular. As you become familiar with UNIX, you may find that working with one terminal screen can be awkward. Suppose you are editing a report and need to read your electronic mail periodically for information you want to add to the report. You can only run one job in the foreground— **mail** *or the editor. These programs are both interactive, so it does not make sense to run one in the background. You need to alternate between the two programs: edit for a while, write the results to a file, quit the editor, start up* **mail**, *read your mail, quit* **mail**, *start the editor, and so on. There are other ways to alternate between two utilities), but they are not much more convenient. As long as you are alternating between jobs on a single terminal, you can see only one thing at a time—the contents of your mailbox or the report.*

Why Use a GUI?

If you could work at two terminals, side by side, you could read your mail on one and edit the report on the other. Soon, however, you might wish you had a third terminal—suppose the mail message referred you to an online database for more information?

A graphical user interface (GUI) solves this problem by allowing you to create multiple windows on one terminal screen. Each window is a box that encloses a separate area on the screen. You can run a different utility in each window: special-purpose tools, such as a clock or calculator program, or a shell so you can run familiar UNIX commands. As before, you can interact with only one program (window) at a time; but now you can create three windows on one terminal screen and see your report, your email, and the database at the same time.

After describing the common attributes of a GUI and providing a short background on the X Window System, this chapter describes how to use one of the most popular user interfaces, Motif. Although you can configure X and Motif in complex ways, this chapter will acquaint you with the basic terminology and operations. For clarity, this chapter focuses on examples that are straightforward; it does not describe every method or shortcut available under X or Motif.

What Is a GUI?

A user interface is the connection between the user and, in this case, the computer system. The user interface controls how the user interacts with the system. The typical UNIX system user interface is the command line interface: In response to a shell prompt, you type a command line (ending with the (RETURN) key). For example, to remove a file named **junkfile** you would type:

```
$ rm junkfile
```

One of the most common complaints about UNIX is that the command names and the command line interface are difficult to learn and use. To use a command, you must know its exact name; most are abbreviated and nonintuitive. For example, if you are not familiar with a UNIX system, you might guess that the command to get rid of an old file would be remove or delete. You probably would not guess that the command is named **rm**.

Contrast that with the graphical user interface on a Macintosh computer, which is designed so that you manipulate pictures of objects on your screen (Figure 6-1). To get rid of an unwanted file on a Macintosh system, you highlight the picture of the file and drag it across the screen until it collides with a picture of a trash can. This approach is so straightforward that many people can begin to use a Macintosh system immediately, without being trained or reading instructions.

Once you are familiar with a system, however, a purely graphical interface can be tedious to use. Suppose you want to remove several files, named **junkfile1**, **junkfile2**, and **junkfile3**. Dragging a picture of each file into a trash can is time-consuming, compared with the powerful shorthand of a command-line interface:

```
$ rm junkfile?
```

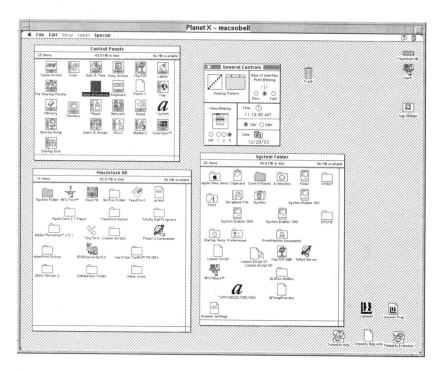

Figure 6-1   A Macintosh Screen as Seen on an X Window System Display

Components of a GUI

A graphical user interface typically runs on a *bit-mapped* display, a device that is designed so that each dot (pixel) on the screen can be drawn independent-ly. A *character-based* display is equipped to draw only a set of specific symbols on the screen (such as alphanumeric characters), using fixed combinations of pixels. With a bit-mapped display it is possible to plot lines and draw pic-tures, as well as to form many styles and sizes of alphanumeric characters.

A typewriter-style keyboard is an effective way to enter numbers and let-ters, but an awkward interface for drawing lines or selecting a particular point on a display screen—it is much easier to use a *mouse*. In addition to the cursor associated with your keyboard, which determines where the next character you type on the keyboard will appear on the screen, the mouse controls a separate cursor that points to some location on the screen. As you slide a mouse around on your tabletop, this cursor, called the *mouse pointer*, moves on the screen relative to the movement of the mouse.

A mouse is equipped with one, two, or three buttons that you use to car-ry out certain operations. To *click* a mouse button, press and release it (you will hear an audible click); to *double-click*, press and release the mouse button twice in quick succession without moving the mouse. You will often select something pictured on your screen by moving the mouse pointer on top of it and clicking a particular mouse button. Sometimes you will need to posi-tion the mouse pointer, press and hold down one of the buttons while you

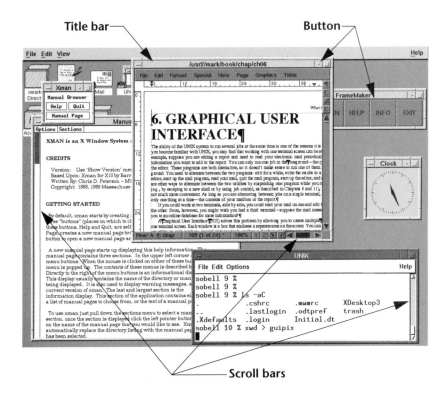

Figure 6-2 A Graphical User Interface

drag (move) the mouse to a new location, and then release the button. This method is commonly used to highlight sections of text.

Windows

When you use a window system, you may work with several windows on your screen, each running a different program. A common window on UNIX systems is a terminal emulator, which typically provides a familiar shell command-line interface to the system. Other windows may run more specialized utilities, such as a text previewer, a drawing program, or multimedia tools such as an audio/video playback program. Figure 6-2 shows several applications running in different windows, including a terminal emulator, clock, publishing system, and **xman**—the graphical version of **man** that allows you to browse through the system's on-line manual pages.

Regardless of the program running in a window, most windows have a few properties in common, as illustrated in Figures 6-2 and 6-4. Each of these properties of the window system is described below.

Title Bar

The *title bar* appears at the top of the window and usually contains the name of the program that controls the window, along with a few buttons.

Buttons

Buttons are usually shown as small squares or rectangles, meant to be pressed to carry out some operation. To press a button on your screen, move the mouse pointer on top of it and click a mouse button. Although you will typically find some buttons on a title bar, they appear in many other contexts as well. Buttons are commonly used to turn simple attributes on or off, or to make other simple yes/no choices.

Sliders

A *slider* is a type of bar that lets you adjust some attribute within a range, like the sliding controls on a stereo system's graphic equalizer that allow you to minimize or boost certain audio frequencies. To use a slider on your screen, position your mouse pointer on the bar, hold down a mouse button, and slide the mouse pointer in one direction or the other along the bar. A button is usually drawn inside the slider to mark the current setting on the bar. Figure 6-4 includes a window that provides three sliders that allow the user to adjust certain attributes of a mouse.

Scroll Bars

A *scroll bar* is a type of slider that appears along the side of a window. When a window is too small to display a full copy of some text or graphic, you can use a scroll bar to browse through more of the image than will fit on the screen. Scroll bars can appear vertically, along one side, to allow you to move up and down through the text or graphic, or horizontally, usually across the bottom, to allow you to scroll a wide page left and right. Three of the windows shown in Figure 6-2 include scroll bars.

Icons

If you are working with several windows, you may find it handy to be able to put one or more of them aside temporarily. This can be helpful to clear up some space on your screen; but it would also be convenient if you could restart the application quickly, at the point where you left it. An *icon* is a small picture that represents a window. When you *iconify* a window, you can no longer see the contents of the window; instead, an icon represents it somewhere on the screen. The method you use to iconify a window varies from one window system to another; usually, you select the operation from a menu or click on a button. To restore an application from the icon, you position the mouse pointer over the icon and double-click a mouse button. Figures 6-4 and 6-5 show many icons.

Menus

When you need to choose among several options, it is often easier to work with a list of options (a *menu*) than an array of individual buttons. To select an item from a menu, position the mouse pointer over that item and click on it. If a menu item does not make sense in a particular context (e.g., to expand a window that is already full-size), the text for that item is usually displayed in a lighter color. By making the text hard to read, the system is giving you a cue that an option is not available or that choosing it will have no effect.

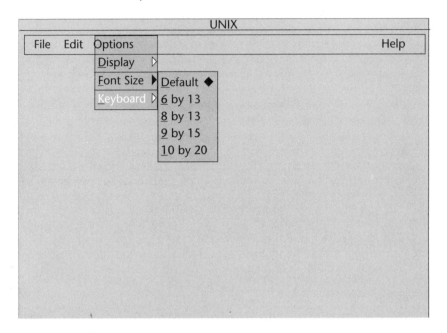

Figure 6-3   A Pull-Down Menu

Instead of cluttering your screen, menus often stay out of sight until you need them. To access a pull-down menu, you typically click on a word or button displayed on your screen; this type of menu usually stays attached to the word or button you clicked (Figure 6-3). In contrast, a pop-up menu appears when you press a particular mouse button somewhere inside a larger region (e.g., inside a window, or on its border). Menu items that contain submenus are known as *cascading* menus; these are usually identified by a right-hand arrow after an item name as shown in Figure 6-3. The next menu level appears when you select one of these items.

Dialog Boxes

A *dialog box* is a small window that appears when an application needs to notify you about something, such as a result or an error message (Figure 6-4). Like a regular window, a dialog box has a title bar and some buttons, but there is little you can do with it. Typically, the application will expect you to acknowledge that you have read the message by clicking your mouse on a button drawn inside the box; after you have done so, the box will disappear from the screen.

Screen Layout

You can arrange the windows on your screen in many ways. Just as you might stack or overlap pieces of paper on your desk, you can position one

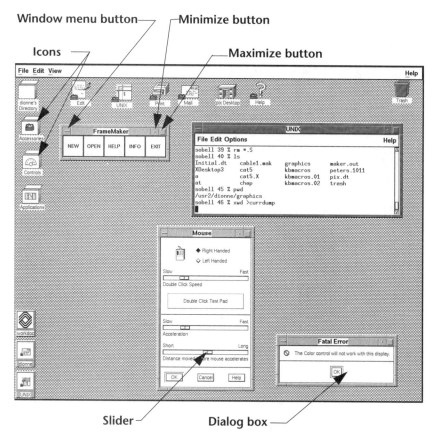

Figure 6-4 Additional Components of a Graphical User Interface

window on top of another (Figure 6-2). The topmost window is fully visible, covering up pieces of the windows below. If you choose to overlap windows, it is a good idea not to cover the lower windows completely. It is easier to bring a window to the top of the stack if you can position the mouse pointer somewhere on its border.

Another approach is to set up your windows so that none of them overlap one another, like floor tiles; in fact, this layout is commonly referred to as *tiling* (Figure 6-4). This arrangement is useful if you need to see the full contents of all your windows at the same time. Unfortunately, the space on your screen is limited; one of the disadvantages of tiling is that if you need more than a few windows, you will need to make each one quite small.

Window Manager

A window manager is the program that controls the look and feel of the graphical user interface. The window manager defines the appearance of the

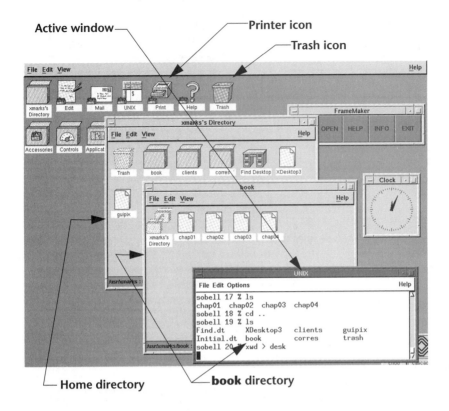

Figure 6-5   A Desktop Manager

windows on your screen, as well as how you operate them: open, close, move, and resize. The window manager may also handle some session-management functions, such as how to pause, resume, restart, or end a session of the window manager.

Desktop Manager

A picture-oriented interface to common commands is often referred to as a *desktop manager*. For example, on a UNIX system, a desktop manager allows you to copy, move, and delete files by manipulating icons instead of typing the corresponding commands to a shell (Figure 6-5).

People who are unaccustomed to working with computers, or with a UNIX system, often feel more comfortable working with a desktop manager. Desktop managers are available today from most UNIX system vendors as well as from a few independent software companies. The screen dumps in this chapter show Santa Cruz Operation Open Desktop (SCO ODT).

Workspace Manager

If you are working in a complex environment, using many windows to run a variety of programs simultaneously, a workspace manager may help you

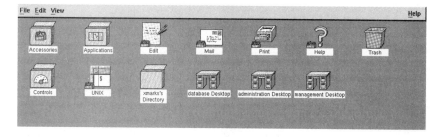

Figure 6-6   A Workspace Manager, Showing Several Desktops

organize and separate your tasks. Using a window system is like working on several terminals at the same time; using a workspace manager is like working with several windowing sessions at the same time. A workspace manager allows you to switch between multiple screen contexts (Figure 6-6).

A system administrator, for example, might be working on several distinct activities, each of which involves more than one window. One workspace might consist of a series of windows set up to edit, compile, and debug software. In another workspace, the task might be to locate and restore some lost user files. A third workspace might be dedicated to reading mail messages and news. The advantage of a workspace manager is the ease of switching between sets of tasks—without having to fuss with icons or reposition overlapping windows. Each desktop icon in Figure 6-6 represents a separate task environment.

The X Window System

The X Window System was created in 1984 at the Massachusetts Institute of Technology (MIT) by researchers working on a distributed computing project at the Laboratory for Computer Science and on a campus-wide distributed environment, Project Athena, with support from Digital Equipment Corporation (DEC) and International Business Machines (IBM). It is not the first windowing software to run on a UNIX system, but it was the first to become widely available. In 1985, MIT released X (version 9) to the public, license-free. Three years later, a group of vendors formed the X Consortium to support the continued development of X, under the leadership of MIT. In 1993 version 11, release 5 (commonly called X11R5) was released.

X was inspired by the ideas and features found in earlier, proprietary window systems, but it was written to be portable and flexible. X was designed to run on a workstation, a small computer with a bit-mapped graphical display, keyboard, and mouse, that is typically attached to a local area network. The designers built X with the network in mind. If you can communicate with a remote computer over a network, it is straightforward to run an X application on that computer and send the results to your local display screen. The X Window System includes the X Toolkit, a library of powerful routines that handle the common graphics operations. As a result, programmers need to know little about the low-level graphical display details and can develop portable applications more quickly.

*Figure 6-7   An X Terminal Provides Simultaneous Access to Multiple Computers and
Applications via a Multiwindow GUI. (Courtesy Network Computing Devices.)*

The popularity of X has extended outside the UNIX community and
beyond the workstation class of computers it was conceived for. X is available for Macintosh computers, as well as for PCs running Microsoft Windows or Windows NT. It is widely available on a special kind of display
terminal, known as an *X terminal,* that has been developed specifically to
run X.

The X Terminal

Workstations are more expensive than terminals, and many users do not
need powerful computers dedicated for personal use. Since each UNIX workstation runs its own copy of the operating system, someone (a system administrator) must look after it: installing and maintaining software,
managing user accounts, and so on. Several entrepreneurs saw a market for
a new device, the X terminal (Figure 6-7), which is customized to run the X
Window System. Like an ordinary character terminal, an X terminal must
communicate with a computer to be useful. Like a workstation, the X terminal includes a graphical display, keyboard, and mouse. Since it does not include a full-blown computer (with a hard disk, back-up device, printer, etc.)
or an entire operating system, it is less expensive and much easier to install
and maintain than a workstation. Unlike character terminals, which are usu-

ally directly connected to computers or modems using serial lines, X terminals are usually attached to a local area network and can easily operate with all the computers on the network.

An X terminal has a Central Processing Unit (CPU) and memory. It runs a control program that is downloaded over the network or is stored in the terminal in Read Only Memory (ROM). The control program is the equivalent of an operating system for an X terminal, but it is much smaller and less complex than an operating system such as UNIX. It does not support peripheral devices and is very limited in functionality. The control program only needs to know how to set a few terminal-specific parameters, how to communicate over the network, and how to run the X protocol (the language that controls X).

X Window Managers

There are many different window managers available for the X Window System, each with different characteristics. Choosing a window manager is largely a matter of individual taste; all window managers allow you to perform the basic operations described in this chapter, but how you perform them will differ. You should be able to run any X application under any window manager.

OSF/Motif

The examples in this chapter are based on the Motif Window Manager, **mwm**, which was developed by a consortium of several leading computer manufacturers known as the Open Software Foundation (OSF). It was designed to be similar to the leading windowing packages for PCs (Microsoft Windows and OS/2 Presentation Manager). Motif has been widely accepted and is provided by most UNIX workstation vendors. As a result, many third-party software developers have written applications to run under Motif.

Although most vendors provide the basic Motif Window Manager, the default user interface on a particular workstation is often an enhanced version. These enhancements typically include additional menus, allowing you to start a window application by clicking on its name rather than typing a command line. In addition to the standard applications supported by the X Consortium, vendors also tend to supply a few specialized or customized applications (e.g., unique tools or standard tools with additional features).

Applications designed to be run in a Motif environment conform to a common style that has been specified by OSF. Motif, like X, is highly configurable; because vendors set different defaults for many characteristics and provide different extensions to the basic window manager, you will notice slight differences if you use more than one Motif-based window manager. For example, although **mwm** should behave in the same way on both DEC and Silicon Graphics computers, the Motif-based window managers DECwindows (DEC) and 4Dwm (Silicon Graphics) differ from each other and from the basic **mwm**. Overall, however, you will find more similarities than differences among Motif window managers.

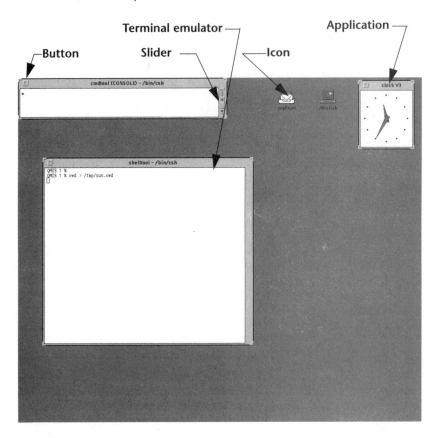

Figure 6-8   An OPEN LOOK Desktop

OPEN LOOK

The OPEN LOOK GUI was developed by AT&T and Sun Microsystems. OPEN LOOK was the basis of Open Windows (**olwm**), the standard window manager on Sun's workstations, but was not adopted on other computer platforms as widely as Motif. Although both window systems support the usual GUI components such as menus, buttons, scroll bars, and icons (Figure 6-8), after several years in the UNIX marketplace, Motif is displacing OPEN LOOK even on Sun workstations.

The differences in style and terminology between two window managers (Figure 6-8) can easily confuse (or mislead) a user. For example, both Motif and Open Windows allow you to copy text by selecting it with the left mouse button; but instead of clicking the middle button to paste the text, under Open Windows you need to press the right mouse button and select "paste" from the menu that pops up.

If you compare the window menus for the two window managers you will uncover another important difference. Not only do they use different terms for the operations they support, in one case they use the same term to refer to different operations! In Motif, "close" *closes* (deletes) the window; in Open Windows, "close" *iconifies* the window.

If you need to work with more than one type of computer, you will find it easier if you choose one window manager that runs on all the systems. If you do not, the subtle differences in their user interfaces are liable to confuse you and cause you to make unfortunate mistakes (such as deleting a window that you meant to iconify!).

Other Window Managers

Using the X Toolkit, individual programmers have created other window managers such as **twm** (Tab Window Manager) and **vtwm** (Virtual Tab Window Manager). Although they may be widely available, these window managers are in the public domain and are typically not well supported. Nonetheless, you may find that you prefer the style or added features provided by one of these window managers. The **vtwm** window manager for example, allows you to manage a workspace that is larger than your physical display. A small box is drawn in one corner of the screen to represent the entire workspace; each window you open appears as a miniature outline within this box. The **vtwm** window manager provides a way for you to move around in the larger workspace, controlling which portion of it is visible in full size on your physical display.

Using a Motif Window Manager

Motif is emerging as the common denominator for UNIX systems running X windows, much as Microsoft Windows dominates the PC arena. Third-party software developers can rely on the Motif library in order to write applications that will run on a variety of UNIX platforms, with the same appearance and functionality. Available applications include high-level application, workspace and desktop managers, as well as many specialized tools (e.g., database interfaces, desktop publishing, and spreadsheets).

While you may find some of the tools listed on menus defined by your vendor or system administrator, you will discover that most are not listed there. X application programs are commonly found on UNIX systems in /usr/bin/X11; look on your system to see which tools are available. Read the manual pages for them or just experiment. Some of the most useful tools are listed at the end of this chapter (Figure 6-16).

The background area that fills in the area of the screen between the application windows is called the *root window*. As you move the mouse pointer around on the screen, the shape of the pointer changes. When it is positioned over the root window, the pointer is shaped like the letter X (or like a pointing hand under SCO Open Desktop). If you move the pointer inside a terminal window, the pointer changes to a large I shape (called an *I-beam*). These changes in the appearance of the cursor serve as cues to the operations you can perform with the mouse. The I mouse pointer, for example, is easy to position between individual characters on your screen. When you move it to a button or the title bar, the mouse pointer changes into an arrow (or other pointer) that is obviously directed at that object.

Selecting the Current Window

When you type on your keyboard, the window manager needs to know which window should receive the characters you are sending. You can distinguish your current window from the others on your screen by comparing their borders; the border of your current (active) window is darker (or a different color) than the others. For example, see the UNIX terminal emulator windows in Figures 6-4 and 6-5. There are two common ways to specify the *keyboard focus*; that is, which window is currently accepting input from your keyboard. One method (called *pointer*) is to position the mouse pointer inside the window and keep it there, even though you will be using the keyboard (not the mouse) as you type characters. With the second method (known as *explicit*), you select a window by clicking on it; that window will continue to accept input from your keyboard regardless of the position of the mouse pointer.

By default, Motif recognizes the explicit, or click-to-type, method. Position the mouse pointer in the window you wish to use, and click the left mouse button. The border of that window should darken (or change color), and the shape of the keyboard cursor should change from an open rectangle to a solid rectangle. Any characters you type now will appear in that window. If you move the mouse pointer outside the window and the border changes back to its normal appearance, you will need to use the *pointer* method to activate that window. To change your keyboard focus, move the mouse pointer inside the window you wish to use (and keep it there).

> **CAUTION**
>
> With Motif, how you control your keyboard focus is a matter of personal preference; you can customize your environment to use one method or the other (see the end of the sample .**Xdefaults** file on page 135). If you do not use the click-to-type method and the pointer strays outside the window, the characters you type will be lost (if the pointer is positioned on the root window) or sent to another window unintentionally (if positioned on a different window).

Starting and Ending a Session

The basic Motif Window Manager is a program named **mwm**, but it is unlikely that you will need to run it as a command. In most cases, a workstation or X terminal is set up so that a window manager starts up automatically whenever you log in. Because local policies and configurations vary from one site to another, consult your system administrator for help if the window manager does not start up automatically.

The basic Motif Window Manager does not include a standard method for ending a session, so you may need to consult your system administrator or local documentation for advice. Individual vendors have addressed this need, however, so you may find a Quit or Log Out option on a menu. For example, Silicon Graphics added a Quit option to the basic Motif window manager's Root Menu, which pops up when you position the mouse pointer on the root window and press the left mouse button. If you run their enhanced window manager (4Dwm) instead, a short menu pops up if you click the left mouse button on the root window. If you then click on Log Out, the system will ask you to confirm your choice (using a dialog box) before it ends your session. SCO includes a Log Out option on the root menu, that pops up when you click the left mouse button while the mouse pointer is outside the root window.

Opening a Window

When the Motif Window Manager starts up, one window may be opened for you automatically. This window is a terminal emulator (or terminal window); that is, you can interact with it just as you would work at a regular character terminal. You will see a shell prompt in the window; you can run any UNIX system command that you choose. Because this window looks like an ordinary character terminal to the UNIX system, you can run utilities such as **vi** that will manipulate the display within that window. A terminal window may seem like a disappointing way to interact with a window system, since it is restricted to operating on characters (not graphical objects). However, a terminal window is a powerful tool because it allows you to run all the existing UNIX command-line programs—even if they have not been converted to run in a graphical environment and without having to learn new versions that were specifically designed to run with a graphical user interface.

You may also be able to open a window by choosing one from a menu. The Motif Root Menu, which pops up when you press the right mouse button when the mouse pointer is positioned anywhere over the root window, includes the item "New Window." Motif-based window managers supplied by individual vendors may include other menus to help you start terminal windows and other X applications. On a system from the Digital Equipment Corporation running DECwindows, for example, you will find an enhanced terminal emulator called DECterm on a menu under the item named Applications. On SCO Open Desktop, you open a new window by clicking on the UNIX icon.

If you can interact with the UNIX shell in a window, you can also open a new window by running an application by name. To open a new terminal window, type **xterm** in response to a shell prompt; to start up a basic clock, type **xclock**. Start an application such as **xterm** or **xclock** in the background [by ending the command line with an ampersand (&)], so you can continue to interact with the UNIX shell in the original window.

The Motif Window Title Bar

The Motif title bar includes three buttons, as shown in Figures 6-4 and 6-9. To bring up a menu of operations you can perform on a window, click the left mouse button while pointing to the Window Menu button (the button with a horizontal bar in it at the left side of the title bar). To enlarge a window so that it fills the entire screen, click on the Maximize button (the button containing a large square, at the right end of the title bar). To restore this window to its previous size and position, click on the Maximize button again. To iconify a window, click on the Minimize button (the button containing a tiny square, adjacent to the Maximize button).

Closing a Window

Just as there are several ways to open a window, you can use different methods to close a window. The method that is common to all windows is to select the Close entry from the associated Window Menu. You access this menu, which includes some other choices that can change the appearance of the window, by pointing and clicking on the leftmost button on the window's title bar (the button with a horizontal line in it). This menu will also appear if you point anywhere on the window's border or title bar and press the right mouse button. You can close a window running a UNIX shell by giving an **exit** command. This command terminates the shell and closes the window automatically. Individual applications may provide other ways to close their windows, such as a specialized Quit button or menu selection.

It is good practice to close all windows before exiting from the session completely, for two reasons: Some applications may not shut down cleanly if you do not close them, while others may try to protect your work for you. For example, if you try to close a text editor application without first saving changes to the file you were editing, the editor will prompt you regarding saving your work before exiting.

Moving a Window

To move a window to a different location on the root window, place your mouse pointer on the title bar, hold down the left mouse button, and slide your mouse around. As you move the mouse, you drag an outline of the window on your screen. When you have placed the outline where you want the window, release the mouse button.

If the title bar is obscured, you can also move the window by positioning the mouse pointer anywhere on the window's border and then clicking and holding the middle mouse button while dragging the window to its new location.

Changing Window Size

As described above, you can toggle between two window sizes by using the Maximize button.

You can also use your mouse to resize a window by an arbitrary amount. To make a window larger or smaller, position the mouse pointer on one of the corners of the window (on the window's border). The mouse pointer will change shape, to an arrow pointing toward the inside of a right angle. To make the window larger, hold down the left mouse button and slide the mouse away from the window; to shrink the window, slide the mouse toward the interior of the window. You can change the shape of the window along one side at a time (by moving the mouse up/down or left/right) or along adjacent sides (by moving the mouse diagonally). As you move the mouse, you will see an outline of the window change dimensions on your screen (Figure 6-9).

Raising and Lowering Windows

As you position windows on the screen, chances are that some of them will overlap. Any window can be your active window, even one that is partially obscured, but it is usually easier to work with a window when you can see all

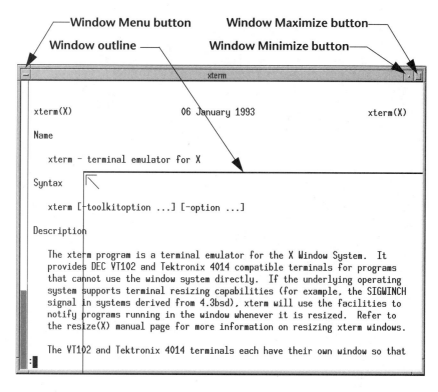

Figure 6-9   Changing Window Size

of it. To raise a window to the top, click on its border with the left mouse button. Similarly, you can lower a window by raising other windows on top of it.

There are two menus available that you can use to change how the windows on your screen are stacked. The Window Menu available for each window includes Raise and Lower options, and the Root Menu includes Shuffle Up and Shuffle Down options. Raise and Lower affect one window at a time, whereas Shuffle Up and Shuffle Down cyclically rearrange several windows in a stack each time you click on one of those options.

Using Icons

To change a window into an icon, click on the Minimize button. When you iconify a window, the window disappears, and a small picture (usually labeled with the name of the application) appears on the screen, as shown in Figure 6-4. If the system chose an inconvenient location for the icon, you can move it by positioning the mouse pointer on the icon, holding down the left mouse button, and dragging the icon to a new place.

To restore the original window from the icon, double-click on it with the left mouse button. The window will reappear exactly as it was before you iconified it: the contents of the window, as well as its size and original position on your screen, will be restored.

You can also use menu options to switch between windows and icons. On the Window Menu, select Minimize to iconify a window, Restore to re-

Pasted copy of error message in mail to
the system administrator (root)

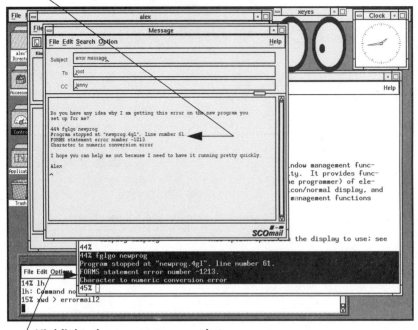

Highlighted error message ready to copy

Figure 6-10   Copying an Error Message from One Window and Pasting It into Another

turn the window to its previous (normal-sized) state, or Maximize to open
the window to the full size of the screen. To access the Window Menu for an
icon, position the mouse pointer on the icon and press the right button.

Copying and Pasting Text

Using the mouse, it is easy to copy text from one part of the screen and insert
(paste) it in another location. This is useful when you want to move a block of
text around, not only within a particular window but also between windows.
For example, suppose you want to send mail to your system administrator to
find out more about an error message that appeared on your screen. Instead
of retyping the message (and possibly introducing mistakes in the process),
you can use the mouse to copy the text and insert it in a mail message.

The first step is to select the text you want to copy. Position the mouse
pointer in front of the first character in the message, hold down the left
mouse button, and drag the mouse over the text you want to copy; if the
message is long, you can continue dragging the mouse over multiple lines.
As you drag the mouse over the text, the characters on your screen are highlighted; release the mouse button when you have positioned the cursor after
the last character you want to include. If you change your mind about the
selection (e.g., you selected too little or too much), you can cancel it by clicking the left mouse button and starting over.

Backward arrow button ⎯⎯

Slider button ⎯⎯

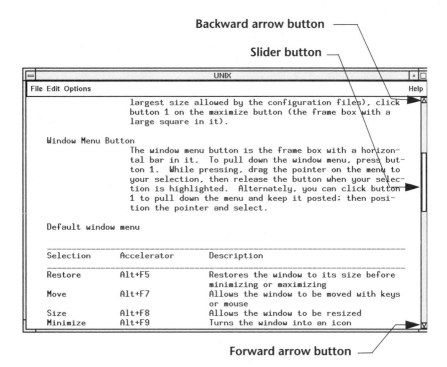

```
┌─┬────────────────────────────────── UNIX ──────────────────────────────┬─┬─┐
│─│                                                                      │□│□│
├─┴──────────────────────────────────────────────────────────────────────┴─┴─┤
│ File Edit Options                                                       Help │
│                    largest size allowed by the configuration files), click ▲│
│                    button 1 on the maximize button (the frame box with a   ││
│                    large square in it).                                     ││
│                                                                             ││
│     Window Menu Button                                                      ││
│                    The window menu button is the frame box with a horizon- ││
│                    tal bar in it. To pull down the window menu, press but-  ││
│                    ton 1. While pressing, drag the pointer on the menu to   ││
│                    your selection, then release the button when your selec- ││
│                    tion is highlighted. Alternately, you can click button▶ ││
│                    1 to pull down the menu and keep it posted; then posi-   ││
│                    tion the pointer and select.                             ││
│                                                                             ││
│     Default window menu                                                     ││
│                                                                             ││
│     ─────────────────────────────────────────────────────────────          ││
│     Selection      Accelerator      Description                             ││
│     ─────────────────────────────────────────────────────────────          ││
│     Restore         Alt+F5           Restores the window to its size before ││
│                                      minimizing or maximizing               ││
│     Move            Alt+F7           Allows the window to be moved with keys ││
│                                      or mouse                               ││
│     Size            Alt+F8           Allows the window to be resized         ││
│     Minimize        Alt+F9           Turns the window into an icon          ▼│
└─────────────────────────────────────────────────────────────────────────────┘
```

Forward arrow button ⎯⎯

Figure 6-11   Motif Scroll Bar in an **scoterm** *Window*

To paste the text, move the mouse pointer to the new location and click the middle mouse button. The text you have just pasted should appear on the screen at the new location.

Another useful application for copying and pasting text is to run one or more commands without retyping them. You can use this method to run commands that are displayed anywhere on your screen—in a set of instructions displayed from a file, a mail message, etc.

CAUTION

When copying and pasting text, work with only a few lines at a time. If you copy too many lines, you may trigger a bug in the system, and your window will become unusable.

Scrolling Text

There are two common types of scroll bars: the Motif scroll bar and the Athena scroll bar. Each of these is described in the next sections.

The Standard Motif Scroll Bar

If a scroll bar appears along one side of a window and there is more text to be displayed than will fit in that window (Figure 6-11), you can use the scroll bar to control which section of the text is visible in the window. To move backward through the text, or scroll up, use the left mouse button to click on the arrow button at the top of the scroll bar. Each time you click on the arrow, one more line is displayed at the top of the window. If you hold down the left mouse button while the pointer is on the arrow button, the text will scroll continuously until you release the button. To move forward through the text, or scroll down, use the arrow button at the bottom of the scroll bar.

You can also scroll through the text one full window at a time. To move back, position the mouse pointer on the scroll bar *above* the slider button and click the left button. To move forward one window, position the mouse pointer *below* the slider button and click the left button.

As you scroll through the text, the position of the slider in the center portion of the scroll bar changes. If the section of text displayed in the window is near the end of what is available, the slider will be near the bottom of the scroll bar. Similarly, if you scroll up to the beginning of the text, the slider will move to the top of the scroll bar. The size of the slider button represents the proportion of the text that is displayed in the window in relation to the entire text available for viewing. If all the text is displayed, you cannot scroll up or down, and the slider button is not present. Instead of using the arrow buttons to scroll through the text, you can move the slider directly. This can be helpful if you know roughly where a particular section is located (e.g., two-thirds of the way through the text).

The Athena Scroll Bar

Some X applications were designed before Motif was available, and provide a scroll bar that differs from the Motif scroll bar in operation and appearance (Figure 6-12). This scroll bar, which is used by **xterm** and some other standard X tools, is known as an Athena scroll bar because it was built with a library of X tools from Project Athena at MIT. The Athena scroll bar lacks Motif's slider and arrow buttons; whether you scroll up or down depends on which mouse button you apply in the scroll region.

Although the Athena scroll bar does not have a slider button, a portion of the scroll bar is highlighted and serves the same function; this part of the scroll bar is called the *thumb*. As with Motif's slider, you can scroll through the text by dragging the thumb up or down; in contrast to Motif, you must use the middle mouse button for this purpose. To scroll back through the text, hold down the middle mouse button and drag the thumb toward the top of the scroll bar; to scroll forward, drag the thumb toward the bottom of the bar.

Another similarity to Motif's slider is that the vertical size of the thumb represents the proportion of the text that you can scroll through and the position of the thumb indicates the relative location of the text that is visible in the window. As in Motif, you can move to a specific place in the text; to do this, position the mouse pointer at a particular point on the scroll bar and click the middle mouse button. For example, if you want to move to the last quarter of the text, position the mouse pointer about three-fourths of the way from the top of the scroll bar and click the middle mouse button.

Unlike the Motif scroll bar, the Athena scroll bar does not allow you to move through the text one line or one window at a time. You can, however, move through the text in blocks by clicking the left or right mouse buttons in the scroll bar. To move forward through the text (toward the bottom of the window), click the left mouse button. If you click the right mouse button, you will move backward through the text.

Scroll region

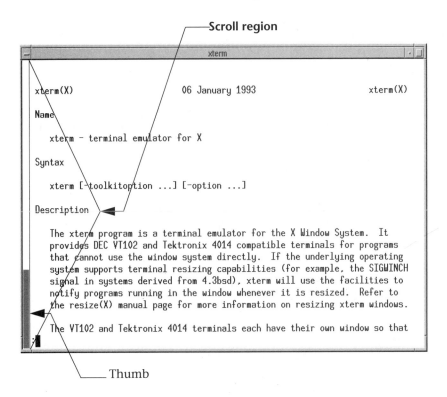

```
 ─                                      xterm                                    ▪ ⌐

    xterm(X)                  06 January 1993                      xterm(X)

    Name

       xterm - terminal emulator for X

    Syntax

       xterm [-toolkitoption ...] [-option ...]

    Description  ◄

       The xterm program is a terminal emulator for the X Window System.  It
       provides DEC VT102 and Tektronix 4014 compatible terminals for programs
       that cannot use the window system directly.  If the underlying operating
       system supports terminal resizing capabilities (for example, the SIGWINCH
       signal in systems derived from 4.3bsd), xterm will use the facilities to
       notify programs running in the window whenever it is resized.  Refer to
       the resize(X) manual page for more information on resizing xterm windows.

       The VT102 and Tektronix 4014 terminals each have their own window so that
```

Thumb

Figure 6-12   Athena Scroll Bar in an **xterm** *Window*

Customizing Your X Work Environment

Chances are that your system administrator or vendor has configured your system so that working with X or Motif is quite straightforward. Both X and Motif, however, are highly configurable. This section introduces some of the techniques you can use to configure applications to match your preferences, to control which applications run automatically whenever you start the window manager, and to change menu listings to meet your needs.

Remapping Mouse Buttons

Throughout this chapter, each description of a mouse click referred to the button by its position (left, middle, or right). The position of a mouse button is more intuitive than an arbitrary name for the button, but you should be aware that in X terminology, the leftmost mouse button is named button 1, the middle one is button 2, and the right one is button 3.

If you are right-handed, you can conveniently press the left mouse button with your index finger and you will find that X programs take advantage of this by relying on button 1 for the most common operations. If you are left-handed, your index finger rests most conveniently on button 3 (the right button).

You can change how X interprets the mouse buttons by using the **xmodmap** utility. If you are left-handed, the following command will cause X to interpret the right mouse button as button 1 and the left mouse button as button 3:

```
$ xmodmap -e 'pointer = 3 2 1'
```

If you remap the mouse buttons, remember to reinterpret the descriptions in this chapter accordingly: When this chapter refers to the left button, you would use the right button instead.

Customizing X Applications

The possibilities for customizing your environment can seem daunting. The manual page for **mwm**, the Motif Window Manager, is more than 50 pages long; the manual page for the **xterm** terminal emulator exceeds 30 pages. Before you try to customize a particular application, you will probably want to get some experience with its default performance. After you are somewhat familiar with an application, you will find it easier to read the manual page and explore the details of its features and how to invoke or change them. This chapter describes some of the basic methods that allow you to set up your X environment. Each X application understands certain attributes (called *resources*), such as typeface, font size, color, and so on. There are several ways you can change the resources to match your personal preferences. One method is to specify options on the command line when you start up an application. The following example invokes the scrolling feature in **xterm**, using the –**sb** (scroll bar) option; if you do not change **xterm**'s default characteristics, it will not start up with a scroll bar.

```
$ xterm -sb &
```

If you are working at a color display, the following example will start a terminal window titled "Hard to read!" that presents characters in yellow (foreground) on a blue background.

```
$ xterm -bg blue -fg yellow -title "Hard to read!" &
```

You can also control where windows appear on your screen. By default, the Motif Window Manager will place the windows in the upper left portion of the screen. You can control the placement (and size) of X applications with the –**geometry** option. The default size of an **xterm** window includes 24 lines of 80 characters each. The following line creates an **xterm** window that has 30 lines of 132 characters:

```
$ xterm -geometry 132x30 &
```

For most X applications, the –**geometry** option recognizes pixels as the unit of size; for some applications, such as a terminal emulator, it is more natural to think in terms of rows and columns and the application was designed to interpret the values accordingly. The following line will start up a clock that is 200 pixels wide by 200 high (larger than the default):

```
$ xclock -geometry 200x200 &
```

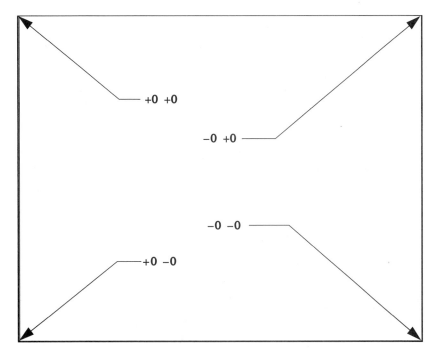

Figure 6-13   Window-Offset Placement

To place a window in a particular location on the screen, you must specify *x*- and *y*-axis offset values, where each unit represents one pixel. The following line places a terminal window 25 pixels in from the left edge of the screen and 15 pixels down from the top edge:

```
$ xterm -geometry +25+15 &
```

Positive offset values refer to the distance from the upper left corner of the screen; negative values refer to the distance from the lower right corner. Figure 6-13 summarizes the effects of the four possible window offset combinations. You can specify both the size and location of a window with one **–geometry** specification. The following command places a large terminal window toward the bottom right of the screen:

```
$ xterm -geometry 132x50-10-10 &
```

Although you probably find it awkward to estimate pixel offsets to place windows on your screen, you will begin to develop a feeling for these values as you work with Motif. When you move a window on your screen, the Motif Window Manager displays a box that reports the approximate offset values (updating them as you slide the window around on your screen). You can also use the **xwininfo** tool to display properties associated with a particular window, including the offset values.

The .xsession **File**

If your system manages X sessions using **xdm**, the X Display Manager, you can set up a **.xsession** file to specify which applications should start automatically when you log in. The **xdm** program is typically configured by your system administrator as a convenient way to prompt each user to enter a login name and password and then start up a window manager.

If you create a file named **.xsession** in your home directory, **xdm** will run the commands listed in the file. For example, if you want a clock and one terminal window to start up whenever you log in, your **.xsession** file would contain the two lines shown below.

```
xclock &
xterm &
```

Because **xdm** treats your **.xsession** file as a shell script, it is important to include an ampersand (&) on each line to run each command in the background. In the example above, if **xdm** started running **xclock** in the foreground, it would not move on to the next line in the **.xsession** file and would not start the terminal emulator.

You can also customize how individual applications start up by specifying appropriate options on each command line in your **.xsession** file. In addition to the clock, the **.xsession** file below creates two instances of **xterm**. The first line starts **xterm** as an icon; when you need it, you can "restore" it to full size. The last line starts another **xterm**, with a scroll bar.

```
xterm -iconic &
xclock &
xterm -sb &
```

When you log in on any X terminal or workstation whose display is controlled by **xdm**, your **.xsession** file should be recognized and run. The files that control how **xdm** is configured on a particular system may start additional applications for you automatically or change other characteristics of your X work environment. Most of the files that control the behavior of **xdm** are shell scripts; if you are curious to learn more about them, they are usually located in the **/usr/lib/X11/xdm** directory.

CAUTION

Be careful when experimenting with your **.xsession** file; if the file contains an error, you may find yourself unable to log in (because the window manager will not start up properly). You may be able to type a sequence of characters that will cause **xdm** ignore your **.xsession** file (check with your system administrator if you do not know what to type) or, you may be able to log into your account in some other way, without trying to start the window manager (e.g., from a character terminal), and move the **.xsession** file aside. If you are unable to resolve the problem yourself, your system administrator will be able to help you.

The .Xdefaults **File**

While it is convenient to specify command-line attributes for a few applications in a .xsession file, it is awkward to type complicated option specifications on a command line each time you start a new application during the course of your session. You may also find that you will always want to run certain applications with particular options (such as **xterm**'s scroll bar). To accomplish this, you can store your preferences in a file in your home directory named .Xdefaults. The format of the .Xdefaults file is

name-of-application*name-of-resource: value

The system-wide application defaults are controlled by files in the directory **/usr/lib/X11/app-defaults**. Any settings in your personal .Xdefaults file will override the system default values.

The following entries in a .Xdefaults file will start all **xterm** windows with yellow characters on a blue background:

```
XTerm*background:    blue
XTerm*foreground:    yellow
```

If you specify different options on the command line when you start a new **xterm** window, however, those values will override the settings in your .Xdefaults file. If you omit the name of the application, the resources and values you list will be used for all applications that recognize them. For example, the following entries will cause all windows to have a blue background, with the exception of **xclock**, which will have a turquoise background.

```
*background:          blue
XClock*background:    turquoise
```

The asterisk acts as a special wildcard that represents only the whole name of an application or resource component. A specification such as XT*background would apply to an application named XT, if one existed, and would have no effect on other applications with names that start with the letters XT (such as **xterm**). The following example includes some useful entries to guide you in setting up your own .Xdefaults file. You can include comments in the file by starting a line with an exclamation point (!).

```
! Resources for xterm:
!
! Turn on the scroll bar.
XTerm*scrollBar:    True
! Use a large font (10 pixels wide, 20 pixels high).
XTerm*Font:         10x20
! Retain more lines to scroll through.
XTerm*saveLines:    150
!
! Comment out default click-to-type.
! Mwm*keyboardFocusPolicy: explicit
!
! Mouse pointer location now determines
! which window is active.
Mwm*keyboardFocusPolicy: pointer
```

Unlike options that you specify on the command line when you start an application, changes you make to a **.Xdefaults** file will not take effect until you load them into the window manager. If your session is managed by **xdm**, your .Xdefaults file will probably be loaded for you automatically when the window manager starts up. If you change your .Xdefaults file during your login session, you can load the specifications immediately by typing the following command at a shell prompt:

```
$ xrdb -load $HOME/.Xdefaults
```

If **xdm** does not load your .Xdefaults file when it starts the window manager for you, add the **xrdb** command line to your **.xsession** file.

Customizing the Motif Window Manager

In addition to using resource attributes to customize how Motif or X applications behave, you can change or add menus that you use to interact with Motif, as well as how you access them. The default configuration for Motif is specified by the file **/usr/lib/X11/system.mwmrc**, including how you access each menu, the names of the items that appear on each menu, and the action associated with each item.

> **CAUTION**
>
> If you run into trouble as you customize Motif, you should be able to restore your session to the defaults specified in the **system.mwmrc** file by holding down the ⟨ALT⟩, ⟨SHIFT⟩, and ⟨CONTROL⟩ keys and pressing the exclamation point key (!). When you do so, a dialog box will appear, asking you to confirm your choice.

The .mwmrc **file**

The **.mwmrc** file tells the window manager what action to take when a mouse button is pressed and/or released. It takes into account where the mouse pointer is located (in a window, on a window border, or on the root window). Each action is specified by calling a Motif function (all of whose names begins with **f.**).

To customize the Motif window manager at this level, you must copy the **system.mwmrc** file to your home directory and give it the name .mwmrc. Changes you make to your .mwmrc file will take effect the next time you start the Motif window manager.

The entry shown below specifies what happens when you press mouse button 1 or 3. If the mouse pointer is on an icon or a window frame (border) and you press button 1, the icon or window moves to the top of the stack of the windows that overlap it by invoking Motif's raise function, **f.raise**. If you press button 3, the function **f.post_wmenu** will display the associated window menu. If the pointer is positioned on the root window and you press button 3, the **f.menu** function will cause the root menu (specified by the DefaultRootMenu entry) to appear. Nothing will happen if you press button 1 on the root window.

```
Buttons DefaultButtonBindings
{
  <Btn1Down>      icon|frame      f.raise
  <Btn3Down>      icon|frame      f.post_wmenu
  <Btn3Down>      root            f.menu  DefaultRootMenu
}
```

The middle mouse button, button 2, is available for you to define a menu of your own. If you add the next line to this menu definition in your **.mwmrc** file, when you press button 2 while pointing to the root window, you will see the menu defined by the entry MyPrivateMenu.

```
  <Btn2Down>      root            f.menu          MyPrivateMenu
```

The simplest menu definition includes two columns, one that lists the names of the items and one that specifies which Motif function is associated with each name. You might find it convenient to create your own menu as a way to start up the tools you use most often. The following entry, available through button 2 as shown above, will carry the title *Favorite Tools*. It includes three entries: one to start up an X interface to the online manual pages, one to start up a calculator application, and one that will open a terminal emulator window and start running **Mail** automatically. The Motif **f.exec** function executes the argument that follows it as though you typed it on the command line.

```
Menu MyPrivateMenu
{
  "Favorite Tools"        f.title
  "Manual Pages"          f.exec "xman &"
  "Calculator"            f.exec "xcalc &"
  "Read Mail"             f.exec "xterm -e Mail &"
}
```

In addition to creating new menus, you can extend any of the standard menus defined in **.mwmrc**. For example, if your root menu does not include an option to quit the window manager, you can add one (or you may find that the Quit entry is already present, but commented out). The following definition adds a menu item that will cause Motif to exit when it is chosen:

```
  "Quit"                  f.quit_mwm
```

To make it less likely that you will choose the Quit item accidentally, you may want to set it apart from the rest of the menu. To draw a line as a separator above the item, add two lines to the menu:

```
  no-label                f.separator
  "Quit"                  f.quit_mwm
```

This section of the chapter has introduced you to the format of the Motif start-up file and provided a few basic examples you can follow if you want to customize the window manager. To learn more about other features of Motif you can change, read the manual page for **mwm**.

Remote Computing and Local Displays

Computer networks are central to the design of X. It is possible to run an application on one computer and display the results on a screen attached to a

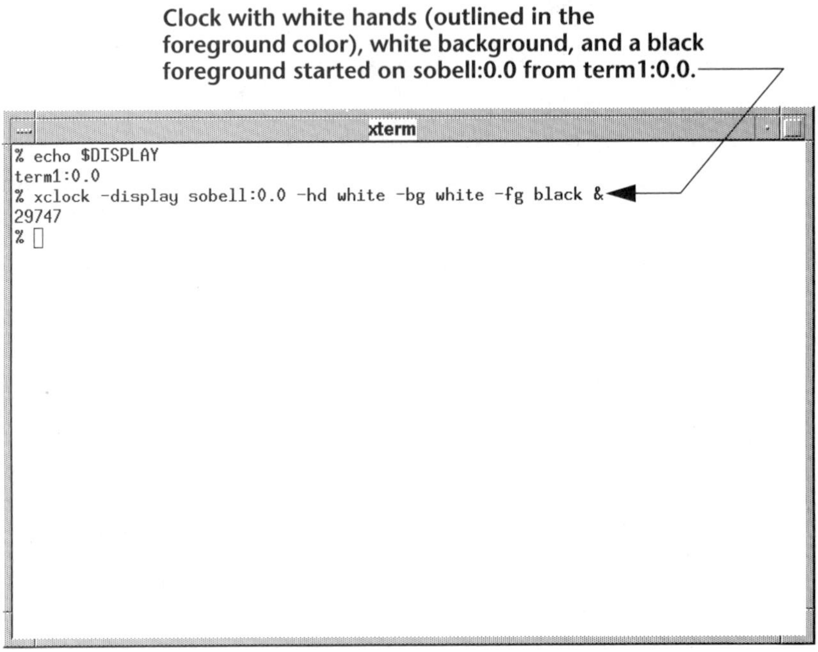

Clock with white hands (outlined in the foreground color), white background, and a black foreground started on sobell:0.0 from term1:0.0.

```
xterm
% echo $DISPLAY
term1:0.0
% xclock -display sobell:0.0 -hd white -bg white -fg black &
29747
%
```

Figure 6-14   Starting a Clock on a Remote Display

different computer; the ease with which this can be done distinguishes X from other window systems available today. Because X has this capability, a scientist can run a program on a powerful supercomputer in another building (or even another state) and view the results directly on his or her personal workstation.

There are two ways to identify the display that an X application should use. The most common method is through the environment variable **$DISPLAY**, which is set automatically when the window manager starts up (Figure 6-14).

You can also specify a display on the command line, using the option **–display**. This option is useful if you want to send the output to a particular display (other than the one you are currently using). Figure 6-15 shows the display screen for a workstation, **sobell:0.0**, including the clock window that was opened remotely from the X terminal display, **term1:0.0**.

If you get an error message when you try to open a window on a remote display, you will need to have the remote user run the **xhost** utility to grant you access to the display. For example, if you are logged in on a system named **kudos** and you want to create a window on Alex's display, which is controlled by the system named **bravo**, Alex needs to run the following command:

```
$ xhost kudos
```

If Alex wants to allow anyone to create windows on his display, the following command line will grant access to all hosts:

```
$ xhost +
```

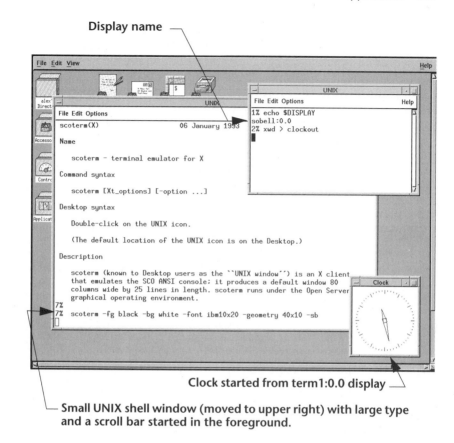

Display name

Clock started from term1:0.0 display

Small UNIX shell window (moved to upper right) with large type and a scroll bar started in the foreground.

Figure 6-15   Remote Display with Clock

If your X session is controlled by **xdm** and you frequently work with others over the network, you may find it convenient to add an **xhost** command line to your .xsession file. Be selective about granting access to your X display; if you allow everyone to send information to your display, you may find that your work is often interrupted by others.

X Applications

Motif is emerging as the common denominator for UNIX systems running X windows, much as Microsoft Windows dominates the PC market. Third-party software developers can rely on the Motif library in order to write applications that will run with the same appearance and functionality on a variety of UNIX platforms. These include high-level applications such as workspace and desktop managers as well as many specialized tools such as database interfaces, desktop publishing applications, and spreadsheets. In addition to buying Motif applications, many organizations have adopted Motif internally, so that the tools they create for their own use have a consistent look and feel.

Part of the power of the X Window System is that applications are independent of window managers; a window manager, such as **mwm**, is really just another application. As a result, you can run any X application while using the Motif window manager, and you should be able to run Motif applications with other window managers. X applications that were not designed to use Motif's features and were not written with the Motif Toolkit library will not share Motif's three-dimensional appearance or controls (such as sliders or particular types of buttons). An application does not inherit properties from the window manager. The Athena scroll bar used by the **xterm** terminal emulator appears and operates the same way under all window managers, for example; it does not turn into a Motif- style scroll bar when you invoke **xterm** while running the Motif window manager.

If you work on a system that supports X, you will be able to use many applications from a variety of sources: tools that are part of the standard distribution from the X Consortium, others supplied by your vendor or purchased from third-party suppliers, free applications that are publicly available, and maybe some that were created locally. Figure 6-16 lists some of the tools you should find in **/usr/bin/X11** on your system. For detailed information about these applications, consult the online manual or the documentation supplied with your system.

Application	Function
appres	List resource values that apply to particular tools.
showrgb	List names of available colors.
xcalc	Emulate a hand-held calculator.
xclipboard	Store and display text cut or copied from other applications.
xclock	Display a running time-of-day clock.
xfontsel	Display available fonts and font names.
xhost	Control access to an X display.
xload	Display a running graph of how busy the system is.
xlsfonts	List names of available fonts.
xmag	Display a magnified image of part of the screen.
xman	Browser interface to the online manual pages.
xmodmap	Remap mouse buttons and keyboard keys.
xpr	Print an image created by **xwd**.
xrdb	Load resource settings into the active database.
xset	Set display, keyboard, or mouse preferences.
xsetroot	Change appearance of the root window.
xterm	Emulate a character terminal.
xwd	Store a screen image (window dump) in a file.
xwininfo	Display information about a particular window.

Figure 6-16   Some Standard X Applications

SUMMARY

A graphical user interface allows you to interact with many different applications and utilities conveniently by dividing your display screen into separate windows, each capable of running a different program. It also provides a way for you to work with pictures of objects and to select options from menus, an approach that many novice users find less intimidating than the traditional UNIX shell's command-line interface.

The X Window System was designed to be portable and flexible, allowing programmers to write applications that work on many different types of systems without having to know the low-level details about each individual system. It was also designed to operate in a networked environment, allowing a user to run a program on a remote system and send the results to a local display.

The look and feel of an X graphical user interface is determined by an application program called a *window manager*. Window managers control the appearance and operation of windows: how to open, resize, move, and close them. Many X window managers have been written, and although they offer different styles of interaction, they have many features in common. The Motif window manager is provided by most UNIX workstation vendors today. Motif is popular because it is easy to use, and it supports the features that most people need, without requiring extensive customization.

The window managers, and virtually all X applications, are designed to permit each user to tailor his or her work environment in simple or complex ways. Users can designate applications that will start up automatically, set attributes such as colors and fonts, and even alter the way keyboard strokes and mouse button presses are interpreted.

REVIEW EXERCISES

1. What is the difference between a workstation and an X terminal? Between an X terminal and a character terminal?

2. What is a window manager? Name two X window managers, and describe how they differ.

3. What happens if you position the mouse pointer in an **xterm** window's scroll bar and click the middle button? The right button? The left button? Do these techniques work for all scroll bars?

4. Describe three ways to

   a. change the size of a window.

   b. delete a window.

   c. uncover a small window that is completely obscured by another, larger window.

5. If the characters you type do not appear on the screen, what might be wrong? How can you fix it?

6. Given two computer systems that can communicate over a network, **bravo** and **kudos**, explain what the following command line does:

   ```
   bravo% xterm –sb –title bravo –display kudos:0.0 &
   ```

7. Consider the following files:

    a. **/usr/lib/X11/system.mwmrc**

    b. **/usr/lib/X11/app-defaults/XTerm**

    c. **$HOME/.mwmrc**

    d. **$HOME/.Xdefaults**

    e. **$HOME/.xsession**

    f. **$HOME/.xterm**

    In which file(s) would you expect to find each of the following entries:

    (1) `xterm -sb &`

    (2) `XTerm*background: pink`

    (3) `Menu DefaultWindowMenu`

    (4) `XClock*chime: True`

    (5) `Menu MyRootMenu`

8. Many X applications interpret the option **–fn** to specify the name of a particular font. Given that the following **.Xdefaults** entries exist on the system named **bravo** (but not on **kudos**),

    ```
    XTerm*saveLines: 100
    *Font: 10x20
    XTe*title: Terminal Emulator
    ```

    describe fully the characteristics of the **xterm** window that is opened by each of the following (on **bravo**):

    a. Using the "New Window" entry on the root menu to open a new **xterm** window

    b. Typing **xterm –sb &** on the command line

    c. Typing **xterm –fn 5x8 &**

    d. Typing **xterm –display kudos:0.0 &**

    On **kudos**, what is the effect of the following command line:

    e. **xterm –display bravo:0.0 &**

9. Add the following customization: When you position the mouse pointer anywhere on the border of a window and press the middle mouse button, that window drops below any of the windows that overlap it.

10. Given the following specification,

    ```
    Menu ToolsMenu
    {
    "Tools"          f.title
    "Calculator"     f.exec "xcalc &"
    "Clock"          f.exec "xclock &"
    "Manual"         f.exec "xman &"
    }
    ```

    what is the effect of adding the following entry to the root menu?

    ```
    "Tools"          f.menu          ToolsMenu
    ```

CHAPTER 7

Networking

This chapter presents an overview of some common networking utilities. First it explains different kinds of networks, and then describes the networking utilities that you will commonly use. Next, it summarizes some system-level services, including three major packages that support distributed computing. Finally, the chapter describes some tools that allow you to locate information on computers around the world and retrieve it remotely.

Of special interest is the coverage of the Internet and various ways of navigating it including **archie** *and* **gopher**. *The chapter closes with a description of the World Wide Web.*

Background

The communications facilities that link computers together are constantly improving, allowing faster and more economical connections. The earliest computers were stand-alone machines—not interconnected at all. To transfer information from one system to another, you had to store it in some form (usually magnetic tape or paper punch cards), carry it to a second, compatible system, and read it back in. It was a notable advance when computers began to exchange data over serial lines, though the transfer rate was slow (hundreds of bits per second). People quickly invented new ways to take advantage of this computing power, such as electronic mail, news retrieval, and bulletin-board services. With the speed of today's networks, it is normal for a piece of electronic mail to cross the country or even travel halfway around the world in a few minutes.

The current administration of the U.S. government has taken a keen interest in building a "national information infrastructure," a data-communications superhighway that will make information resources available to citizens at an unprecedented level. Today, not only is it possible to retrieve electronic copies of speeches and other government materials over the existing network, it is also possible to send electronic mail to the President of the United States (using the address **president@whitehouse.gov**).

It would be hard to find a modern computer facility, with more than one computer, that does not include a local area network (LAN) to link the systems together. UNIX systems are typically attached to an Ethernet network. Large computer facilities usually maintain several networks, often of different types, and almost certainly have connections to larger networks (company- or campus-wide, and beyond). The Internet is a loosely administered network of networks (an "internetwork") that links computers on diverse local area networks around the globe. It is the Internet that makes it possible to send an electronic mail message to a colleague located thousands of miles away and receive a reply within minutes.

Network Services

At the system level, many new services have appeared and are becoming standard. On UNIX systems, special processes called *daemons* run constantly to exchange particular types of messages over the network, such as mail traffic. Several software systems have been created to allow computers to share their filesystems with one another, making it appear to users as though remote files are actually stored on disks attached to their local computer. Sharing remote filesystems allows users to share information without knowing where the files physically reside, without making unnecessary copies, and without learning a new set of utilities to manipulate them. Because the files appear to be stored locally, you can use the standard UNIX utilities (**cat**, **vi**, **lpr**, **mv**, etc.) to work with them.

To take advantage of the higher speeds available on computer networks, some new utilities have been created, and existing commands have been extended. The **ruptime** and **rwho** utilities provide status information about computers and users on a local area network. The **rlogin** and **telnet** utilities allow users to log in on remote computers on their local network or at a distant site through interconnected networks. Users rely on commands such as **rcp** and **ftp** to transfer files from one system to another across the network. Communication utilities, such as **mail** and **talk**, have been adapted to understand remote network addresses and to set up the connections necessary to exchange information with a remote computer.

Common Types of Networks

If a UNIX system is attached to a network today, it is most likely one of three types: *broadcast, token ring,* or *point-to-point.* On a *broadcast* network, such as Ethernet, any system attached to the network cable can send a message at any time; each system examines the address in every message and picks up the messages that are addressed to it. Since there are multiple systems on the cable and any one of them can send a message at any time, messages sometimes collide and become garbled. When that happens, the sending system notices the problem and resends, after waiting a short (but variable) amount of time to try to avoid another collision. The extra network traffic that results from collisions can put quite a load on the network; if the collision rate gets too high, the retransmissions result in more collisions and the network becomes unusable.

On a *token ring* network, such as FDDI, only one system can send a message at any time. A token (a small, special message) is constantly being passed from one host to the next, around the ring. A system can only send a message if it currently has the token. This prevents the collision problems that are troublesome in broadcast networks, but it can have a serious impact on performance if the ring is large (a host may have to wait a long time before it gets the token that allows it to send a message). Another drawback is that if the ring breaks, the token passing is interrupted, and none of the systems can transmit a message.

A *point-to-point link* does not seem like much of a network at all, since only two endpoints are involved. However, most connections to wide area networks are through point-to-point links, using wire cable, radio, or satellite links. The advantage of a point-to-point link is that the traffic on the link is limited and well understood, since only two systems are involved. A disadvantage is that each system can typically be equipped for a small number of such links, and it is impossible to establish point-to-point links that connect every computer to all the rest.

Local Area Networks (LANs)

Local area networks, as the name implies, are confined to a relatively small area—within a single computer facility, building, or campus. Today, most LANs run over copper or fiber optic cable, but researchers are experimenting with other technologies, such as infrared (similar to most television remote control devices) and radio waves.

Figure 7-1 Thinnet Cabling and Connectors. (Courtesy of AMP, Harrisburg, PA.)

Ethernet

If a UNIX system is connected to a LAN today, that network is probably an Ethernet that can support a peak rate of 10 million bits (10 megabits) per second. Due to computer load as well as competing network traffic, file transfer rates on an Ethernet are typically lower than 10 megabits per second.

The Ethernet network is typically composed of one of three types of copper cabling, though it is also possible to use fiber optic (glass) cable with special equipment. In the original design, each computer was attached to a thick coaxial cable (sometimes called *thicknet*) at tap points spaced at fixed intervals along the cable. The thick cable was awkward to deal with, so other solutions were developed: a thinner coaxial cable known as *thinnet* (Figure 7-1), as well as devices to run Ethernet over twisted pair wire (the type of wire used for telephone lines and serial data communications).

Computers communicate over networks using unique addresses that are assigned by system software. A message sent by a computer, called a *packet*, includes the address of the destination computer (as well as the sender's return address). On an Ethernet, each computer checks the destination address in every packet that is transmitted on that network. When a computer finds its own address as the destination, it accepts that packet and processes it appropriately. If a packet's destination address is not on the local network, it must be passed on to another network by a router. A router may be a general purpose computer or a special purpose device that is attached to multiple networks to act as a gateway among them.

FDDI

A less common type of network supported by UNIX systems is the Fiber Distributed Data Interface, or FDDI. The peak data rate on an FDDI network is 100 megabits per second (ten times faster than an Ethernet). Despite the speed, there are many reasons why FDDI has not become the popular network choice. Fiber optic cable is more expensive and difficult to work with than copper cable, and the computer interfaces that attach to the cable are also more expensive (because they are more complex, involving lasers to transmit and receive the optical signals). The technology exists to use the FDDI data format over copper wire, but may never become prevalent, as other networks are emerging that offer new advantages in features and performance.

Wide Area Networks (WANs)

As the name implies, a wide area network covers a large geographic area. The technologies used for local area networks (such as Ethernet or FDDI) were designed to work over limited distances and for a certain number of host connections. A wide area network may span long distances over dedicated data lines (leased from a telephone company) or radio or satellite links. Wide area networks are often used to interconnect local area networks. In the United States today, a wide area network known as NSFnet forms a major part of the Internet that links universities, research centers, and corporations together.

There is another term used to refer to networks that do not fit the designation local or wide area. A metropolitan area network (MAN) is one that is contained in a smaller geographic area, such as a city. Like wide area networks, metropolitan area networks are typically used to interconnect local area networks.

Internetworking Through Gateways and Routers

A local area network connects to a wide area network through a gateway. A gateway might be a computer or another special device with multiple network connections. The purpose of the gateway is to convert the data traffic from the format used on the local area network to that used on the wide area network. Data that crosses the country today from one Ethernet to another over NSFnet, for example, will be repackaged from the Ethernet format to a different format that can be processed by the T3 communications equipment that makes up the NSFnet backbone. (T3 is a standard for communicating at 45 megabits per second.) When it reaches the end of its journey over NSFnet, the data will be converted back to its original format so it can be properly received. For the most part, these details are of concern only to the network administrators; the end user does not need to know anything about how the data transfer was carried out.

Routers play an important role in internetworking. Just as you might study a map to plan your route when you need to drive to an unfamiliar place, a computer needs to know how to deliver a message to a system attached to a distant network by passing through intermediary systems and networks along the way. You could imagine using a giant network road map to choose the route that your data should follow, but a static map of computer routes is usually a poor choice for a large data network. Computers and networks along the route you choose may be overloaded or down, without providing a detour for your message. Routers communicate with one another dynamically, keeping each other informed about which routes are open for use. To extend the analogy, this would be like heading out on your car trip without ever consulting a map; instead, you would stop at one highway information center after another and get directions to find the next one.

Figure 7-2 shows an example of how local area networks might be set up at three sites interconnected by a wide area network (Internet). In network diagrams such as this, rings are typically drawn as such; Ethernet LANs are usually drawn as straight lines, with devices attached at right angles; and a wide area network is represented by a cloud, indicating that the details have been left out. In this figure, a single gateway relays messages between each LAN and the Internet. Three of the routers in the Internet are shown (e.g., the one closest to each site). Site A has some workstations and X terminals sharing a single Ethernet with a super-minicomputer. Site B has two LANs: one Ethernet, which serves several workstations, a printer and a minicomputer, and one FDDI ring that includes a supercomputer as well as some workstations. There are no X terminals at site B; instead, users rely on ordinary character terminals attached directly to the minicomputer over serial lines. A router passes data between the Ethernet and the FDDI ring. There are three LANs at site C, linked by a single device that serves as a router as well as a gateway to the Internet. Site C's FDDI ring includes a minicomputer and some workstations. There are two Ethernet segments at site C, perhaps to reduce the traffic load that would result if they were combined, or to keep workgroups or locations on separate networks. One Ethernet includes a PC as well as a workstation and printer; the other supports a minicomputer as well as workstations, a printer, and a terminal server. A terminal server is a device that attaches serial devices, such as modems and character-based terminals, to a network.

Network Protocols

In order to exchange information over a network, computers must communicate using common protocols. The protocol determines the format of the message packet. The predominant network protocol used by UNIX systems is TCP/IP, which is an abbreviation for Transmission Control Protocol/Internet Protocol. Network services that need highly reliable connections, such as **rlogin** and **rcp**, tend to use TCP/IP. A less reliable protocol used for some UNIX system services is UDP, the User Datagram Protocol. Network services such as **ruptime** and **rwho** tend to operate satisfactorily with the simpler UDP protocol.

Other network protocols developed by particular manufacturers, such as XNS (Xerox Network Software) and DECnet (DEC Network), are less widely supported on UNIX systems. Different protocols do not interfere with one another; they can coexist on a single network cable and be used simultaneously on the same computer.

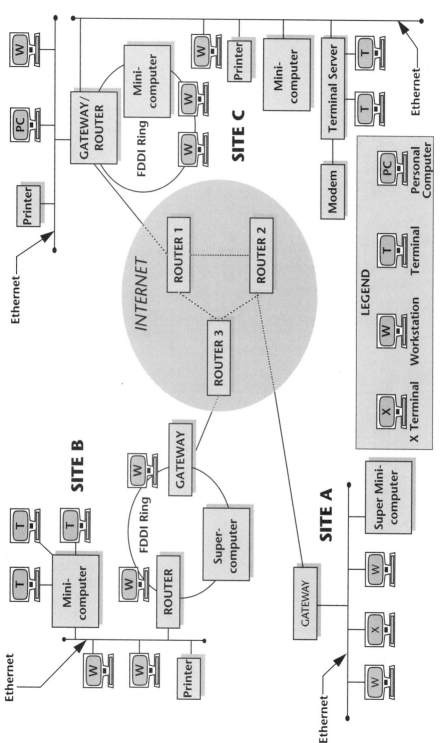

Figure 7-2   A Slice of the Internet

Host Addresses

Each computer is identified by a unique address, or host number, on its network. If a system is attached to more than one network, it will have multiple unique addresses—one for each network. The address you will see on most UNIX systems is an IP (Internet Protocol) address, which is represented as four sets of numbers separated by periods (e.g., **192.192.192.5**). The address assignments are handled by a central authority, an organization called the Network Information Center, or NIC. The NIC does not get involved in handing out addresses for individual host computers; instead, when an organization registers with the NIC, they receive a block (range) of addresses that they can use as needed.

Typically, the leftmost two sets of numbers in an IP address represent a large network (campus- or company-wide); the third set identifies a subnetwork (perhaps a department or single floor in a building), and the rightmost number specifies an individual computer. How the numbers are interpreted is determined by your system or network administrator, who may prefer a different breakdown to support your particular mix of networks and hosts. The operating system uses the address in a different, lower-level form (converting it first to a binary equivalent, a series of 1s and 0s).

People generally find it easier to work with symbolic names rather than numbers, and UNIX systems provide several ways to associate hostnames with IP addresses. The oldest method is to consult a list of names and addresses that are stored in the **/etc/hosts** file.

```
127.0.0.1     localhost
130.128.52.1  sobell.sro.com sobell
130.128.52.2  bravo.sro.com bravo
130.128.52.3  hurrah.sro.com hurrah
130.128.52.4  kudos.sro.com kudos
```

The address **127.0.0.1** is reserved for the special hostname **localhost**, which serves as a hook for the system's networking software to operate on the local machine without actually going out onto a physical network. The names of the other systems are shown in two forms: first in a fully qualified domain format that is meant to be unique, and second as a nickname that is unique locally, but probably is not unique over all the systems attached to the global Internet.

Using a regular text file (**/etc/hosts**) for these name-to-address mappings proved to be inefficient and inconvenient, as more hosts joined networks and the file grew ever larger and impossible to keep up to date. On Sun computers and other systems that run the Network Information Service (NIS—page 163), the host information may be stored in a special database format. This solution makes it easier to search the database using special tools, but does not solve the update problem. The most popular solution today is for systems to subscribe to the Domain Name Service (DNS—page 162). The Domain Name Service effectively addresses the efficiency and update issues.

Communicating Over the Network

Many commands that you can use to communicate with other users on a single computer system have been extended so that they will work over the network. Three examples of such utilities are **finger**, **mail**, and **talk** (introduced in Chapter 3). This is a good example of the UNIX philosophy: Instead of creating a new, special-purpose tool, modify an existing one.

These utilities understand a common convention for the format of network addresses: **user@host** (often read as *user at host*). When you use an @ sign in an argument to one of these commands, it interprets the text that follows as the name of a remote host computer. When your command line argument does not include an @ sign or hostname, the utility assumes that you are requesting information from or corresponding with someone on your local host (as shown in Chapter 3).

The prompt shown in the examples in this chapter differs from the simple prompts carried through the rest of this book. If you frequently use more than one system over a network, you will probably find it hard to keep track of which system you are using at any particular moment. If you set your prompt to include the hostname of the current system, it will always be clear which system you are using. To identify the name of the computer you are using, run the **hostname** command.

```
% hostname
kudos
```

See pages 294, 362, and 385 for information on how you can change your prompt.

On many networked systems, **hostname** reports the name of the system in a longer, DNS format. There is no reason why you could not set your prompt to this fully qualified name, but it is probably intrusively long. You can shorten the name; try using **hostname** with the –s option:

```
% hostname
bravo.sro.com
% hostname -s
bravo
```

If the version of **hostname** on your system does not recognize the –s option, you can filter the output of hostname through another UNIX utility, such as **sed**, to strip off the domain portion of the name.

Using finger to Learn About Remote Users

You can use the **finger** utility to display information about users on remote systems. The **finger** command was originally designed for local use, but when networks became popular, it was obvious that **finger** should be enhanced to reach out and collect information remotely. In this example, **finger** displays information about all the users logged in on the system named **kudos**:

```
bravo% finger @kudos
[kudos]
Login  Name          TTY    Idle    When        Where
alex   Alex Watson   tty01  21      Mon 10:54
roy    Roy Wong      ttyp0  5       Wed 14:2    kudos
```

A user's name (or login name) in front of the @ sign will cause **finger** to retrieve the information from the remote system only for the user you have specified. If there are multiple matches for that name on the remote system, **finger** will display the results for all of them.

```
bravo% finger alex@kudos
[kudos]
Login name: alex               In real life:Alex Watson
Directory: /home/alex           Shell: /bin/csh
On since Sep 19 10:54:49 on tty01
21 minutes Idle Time
 .
 .
 .
bravo%
```

The **finger** utility works by querying a standard network service, the **finger** daemon, that runs on the remote system. Although this service is supplied with most UNIX systems today, some sites choose not to run it in order to minimize load on their systems as well as to reduce security risks, or simply to maintain privacy. If you try to use **finger** to obtain information about someone at such a site, the result may be an error message, or nothing at all. It is the remote **finger** daemon that determines how much information to share with your system, and in what format. As a result, the report displayed for any given system may differ from the examples shown above.

The information for remote **finger** looks much the same as it does when **finger** runs on your local system, with one difference: Before displaying the results, **finger** reports the name of the remote system that answered the query (**kudos**, as shown in brackets in the preceding example). The name of the host that answers may be different from the system name you specified on the command line, depending on how the **finger** daemon service is configured at the remote end. In some cases, several hostnames may be listed, if one **finger** daemon contacts another to retrieve the information.

Some remote sites have set up special services that you can contact using **finger**. For example, you can retrieve information about recent earthquakes from a system run by the U.S. Geological Survey.

```
bravo% finger quake@gldfs.cr.usgs.gov
[gldfs.cr.usgs.gov]
Login name: quake          In real life: see Ray Buland
Directory: /home/gldfs/quake   Shell:/home/gldfs/quake/run_quake
Last login Sun Oct 10 7:23 on ttyi2
Mail last read Sun Oct 10 01:36: 1993
Plan:
Earthquake information following is provided by the National
Earthquake Information Service (NEIS) of the U.S. Geological
Surve

DATE-TIME (UT)  LAT    LON    DEP   MAG     LOCATION AREA
93/10/04  20:54 21:2S 174.5W  33   5.9   TONGA ISLANDS
93/10/05  02:00 42.8N  88.3E  10   5.8   NORTHERN XINJIANG, CHINA
93/10/05  05:09  6.4S  19.7E  33   6.1   BANDA SEA
93/10/07  16:35 13.9S  75.4W  50   5.5   CENTRAL PERU
93/10/08  18:23 46.0N 150.0E 100   5.6   KURIL ISLANDS
```

Sending Mail to a Remote User

If you know a user's login name on a remote system, you can use the standard **mail** program to send a message over the network, using the @ form of address:

kudos% `mail jenny@bravo`

Using talk with a Remote User

Similarly, you can communicate interactively with a remote user over the network by using the **talk** utility:

kudos% `talk jenny@bravo`

See page 42 for an introduction to the **talk** utility.
    Although the @ form of network address is recognized by many UNIX utilities, you may find that you can reach more remote computers with **mail** than with the other networking utilities described in this chapter. The reason for this disparity is that the **mail** system can deliver a message to a host that is not attached to the Internet, even though it appears to have a network address. The message might be routed over the network, for example, until it reaches a remote system that has a point-to-point, dialup connection to the destination system. Other utilities, such as **talk**, rely on special protocols that only operate between networked hosts.

Networking Utilities

In a networked environment, it was clear that it made sense to extend certain tools to utilize it; some of those were described above. Having a network also created a need for new utilities to control and monitor it and led to ideas for new tools that take advantage of network speed and connectivity. The commands described in this section were created to be used on systems attached to a network; without a network connection, they are of little use.

Using rlogin and telnet to Access a Remote Computer

If you have an account on a remote system, you can use the **rlogin** utility to connect to it over the network and start up a login session there. You might choose to use a remote system in order to access a special-purpose application or device that is available only on that system or because you know that the remote system is faster or less busy than your local computer. When you log out, your connection will be broken and you can resume using your local computer. If you are using a window system on your local computer (see Chapter 6), you can use many systems simultaneously by logging into each one through a different window on your screen.

To use **rlogin**, you must specify the name of the remote system you want to connect to:

```
kudos% rlogin bravo
Password:
Last login: Wed Oct 6 21:12:33 from kudos
bravo%
```

Refer to page 673 for more information about the **rlogin** utility.

You can also use **telnet** to interact with a remote computer. The **telnet** utility is similar to **rlogin**, but it can also be used to connect to a non-UNIX system (**rlogin** is available only on UNIX systems).

```
kudos% telnet bravo
Trying 130.128.52.2 ...
Connected to bravo.
Escape character is '^]'.
SunOS UNIX (bravo)
login: watson
Password:
Last login: Wed Oct 6 21:29:07 from sobell
bravo%
    .
    .
    .
kudos% logout
Connection closed by foreign host.
kudos%
```

The remote system presents you with a regular login: prompt when you connect through **telnet**, whereas **rlogin** assumes that your login name on the remote system matches that on your local system. Because **telnet** is designed to work with non-UNIX systems, it does not make such assumptions. You can specify a different name with **rlogin** by using the –l option:

```
kudos% rlogin -l watson bravo
Password:
Last login: Wed Oct 6 21:47:18 from kudos
bravo%
```

Another difference between these two utilities is that **telnet** allows you to configure many special parameters, such as how carriage returns or interrupts are processed. When using **telnet** between two UNIX systems, you will rarely need to access or change any parameters. If you do not specify the name of a remote host on the command line, **telnet** will run in an interactive mode. The following two examples are equivalent:

```
kudos% telnet bravo
Trying 130.128.52.2 ...
Connected to bravo.
Escape character is '^]'.
SunOS UNIX (bravo)
login: watson
Password:
Last login: Wed Oct 6 21:53:20 from kudos
bravo%
kudos% telnet
```

```
telnet> open bravo
Trying 130.128.52.2 ...
Connected to bravo.
  .
  .
  .
  .
```

Before **telnet** connects you to a remote system, it tells you what your *escape character* is—in most cases, it is ^-] (the ^ represents the (CONTROL) key on your keyboard). If you type (CONTROL)-], you will escape to **telnet**'s interactive mode. Continuing the preceding example:

```
bravo% (CONTROL)-]
telnet> ?
```

(displays help information)

```
telnet> close
Connection closed by foreign host.
kudos%
```

The question mark above, typed in response to a telnet> prompt, causes **telnet** to print a help list of the commands it recognizes. The close command ends the current **telnet** session, returning you to your local system.

It is also possible to use **telnet** to access special remote services at sites that have chosen to make such services available. For example, you can use **telnet** to connect to the U.S. Library of Congress Information System:

```
kudos% telnet locis.loc.gov
L O C I S: LIBRARY OF CONGRESS INFORMATION SYSTEM
To make a choice: type a number, then press ENTER

1 Library of Congress Catalog    4 Braille and Audio
2 Federal Legislation            5 Organizations
3 Copyright Information          6 Foreign Law
*    *    *    *    *    *    *    *    *    *
7 Searching Hours and Basics
8 Documentation and Classes
9 Library of Congress General Information
12 Comments and Logoff

Choice: 1
  .
  .
  .
  .
READY: display
     1. 90-29049: Sobell, Mark G. A practical guide to UNIX
     System V / 2nd ed.  Redwood City, Calif. :
     Benjamin/Cummings Pub., c1991. xxvii, 700 p. :
     ill. ; 24 cm.
     LC CALL NUMBER: QA76.76.O63 S6 1991
     2. 88-34230: Sobell, Mark G. A practical guide to the
  .
  .
```

Trusted Hosts and the .rhosts File

Some commands, including **rcp** and **rsh**, will work only if the remote system trusts your local computer (that is, it believes that your computer is not pretending to be a different system and that your login name on both systems is the same). Trusted systems are listed in the file /etc/hosts.equiv.

If your login name is not the same on both systems, or if your system is not listed in the remote /etc/hosts.equiv file, you can arrange for the remote system to trust you by creating a file named **.rhosts** in your home directory there. Suppose that Alex's login name on the local system, **kudos**, is **alex**; but on the remote system, **bravo**, his login is **watson**. A .rhosts file on **bravo** that contains the entry

```
kudos alex
```

will allow alex to use **rcp** to copy files from **kudos** to **bravo** by typing

```
kudos% rcp memo.921 watson@bravo:memos/memo.921
```

Similarly, a **.rhosts** file on **kudos** that contains the entry

```
bravo watson
```

will permit him to transfer files in the opposite direction.

The system name you specify in a **.rhosts** file must match the name you see when you run **hostname**. That is, if **hostname** returns **bravo.sro.com**, then you must put the fully qualified name in your **.rhosts** file on the remote system.

> **CAUTION**
>
> Note that you can use a **.rhosts** file to allow another user to log in as you on a remote system, without knowing your password. This is not recommended! Do not compromise the security of your files, or the entire system, by sharing your login account.

Using rcp and ftp to Transfer Files over a Network

You can use the **rcp** (remote copy) utility to transfer files between two computers attached to a network. The **rcp** utility works like **cp**. In the following example, given that you have an account on a system named **bravo** and that a directory named **memos** exists in your home directory there, the file **memo.921** is copied from the working directory on the local system to your **memos** directory on **bravo**:

```
kudos% rcp memo.921 bravo:memos/memo.921
```

Because **rcp** works like **cp**, if Alex had not specified the filename on the remote system in the preceding example, the system would have used the original filename. That is, the following command line is equivalent to the preceding one.

```
kudos% rcp memo.921 watson@bravo:memos
```

(Refer to page 666 for more information on **rcp**.)

You can also use the **ftp** (*f*ile *t*ransfer *p*rotocol) utility to transfer files between systems on a network. Unlike **rcp**, **ftp** is interactive—it allows you to browse through a directory on the remote system to identify files you may want to transfer. Instead of **rcp**, Alex could have used **ftp** to transfer **memo.921** to **bravo**:

```
kudos% ftp bravo
Connected to bravo.
220 bravo FTP server ready.
Name (bravo:alex): watson
331 Password required for watson.
Password:
230 User watson logged in.
ftp> put memo.921 memos/memo.sept
200 Port command successful.
150 Opening ASCII mode data connection for 'memos/memo.sept'.
226 Transfer complete.
local: memo.921 remote: memos/memo.sept
14876 bytes sent in 0.08 seconds (181.94 Kbytes/s)
ftp> quit
221 Goodbye.
kudos%
```

In the preceding example, the remote system prompts you for a login name and password. By default, it expects that your login name is the same; in this case it is not, so Alex enters **watson**. When using **ftp**, you must tell the remote system the name of the file that it will create to hold your data. Given that the directory **memos** exists on **bravo**, the following command would result in an error and the file would not be transferred:

```
ftp> put memo.921 memos
553 memos: Is a directory.
```

Unlike **rcp**, the **ftp** utility makes no assumptions about filesystem structure because you can use **ftp** to exchange files with non-UNIX systems (whose file naming conventions may be different).

In the following example, Alex connects to the remote system on the Internet named **ftp.uu.net** as the anonymous user and picks up a **README** file, from a subdirectory named **info**, that will tell him more about the archives stored on that system. Although any password is acceptable for anonymous **ftp**, by convention you are requested to give your login name and system name. In this case, Alex would have entered **alex@kudos** in response to the password prompt.

```
kudos% ftp ftp.uu.net
Connected to ftp.uu.net.
220 ftp.UU.NET FTP server (Version 2.0WU(13)
Fri Apr 9 20:44:32 EDT 1993) ready.
Name (ftp.uu.net:alex): anonymous
331 Guest login ok, send your complete e-mail address as password.
Password:
230-
230- Welcome to the UUNET archive.
230- A service of UUNET Technologies Inc, Falls Church, Virginia
   .
   .
   .
```

```
230 Guest login ok, access restrictions apply.
ftp> ls
200 PORT command successful.
150 Opening ASCII mode data connection for file list.
```

(lots of directories listed)

```
226 Transfer complete.
489 bytes received in 0.089 seconds (5.4 Kbytes/s)
ftp> cd info
250 CWD command successful.
ftp> ls
```

(more directories listed)

```
ftp> get README
200 PORT command successful.
150 Opening ASCII mode data connection for README (676 bytes).
226 Transfer complete.
local: README remote: README
690 bytes received in 0.087 seconds (7.8 Kbytes/s)
ftp> quit
221 Goodbye.
kudos%
```

Another important difference between **rcp** and **ftp** is that **ftp** is sensitive to the contents of the files it transfers. If you need to transfer a file containing non-ASCII data, such as a binary program or a compressed file, you need to set up **ftp** accordingly:

```
ftp> binary
```

If you fail to do this, you will not get the results you expect. The transfer may take a long time to complete and the size and contents of the file will be incorrect. This is the most common mistake that is made when using **ftp**. To correct it, turn on the binary option (as above), and transfer the file again.

While using **ftp**, you can type **help** at any `ftp>` prompt to see a list of valid commands. Refer to Part II for more information on **ftp**.

Using rsh to Run a Command Remotely

The **rsh** utility allows you to run a command on a remote system without logging in. If you need to run more than one command on a remote system, it is probably easier for you to log in on the remote system to do so. Sometimes, however, you only want to run a single command.

```
kudos% rsh bravo ls memos
memos/memo.draft memos/memo.0921
```

Suppose there is a file named **memo.new** on your local machine, and you cannot remember whether it contains certain changes to the memo you have been working on, or if you made these changes to the file named **memo.draft** on the system named **bravo**. You could copy **memo.draft** to your local system and run the **diff** utility on the two files, but then you would have three similar copies of the file spread across two systems; if you are not careful about removing the old copies when you are done, you will probably be confused again in a few days. Instead of copying the file, you can use **rsh**:

```
kudos% rsh bravo cat memos/memo.draft | diff memos.new -
```

When you run **rsh**, the standard output of your command line on the remote machine is passed back to your local machine. Also, unless you put quotation marks around characters that have a special meaning to the shell, they will be interpreted by the local machine. In this example, the output of the **cat** command on **bravo** is sent through a pipe on **kudos** to **diff**, which compares the local file **memos.new** to its standard input (–). The following command line has the same effect, but causes the **diff** utility to run on the remote system instead:

```
kudos% cat memos.new | rsh bravo diff - memos/memo.draft
```

The standard output from **diff** on the remote system is sent back to the local system, which displays it on the screen (because it was not redirected).

The **rsh** and **rlogin** utilities are similar; both will prompt you to enter a password if the remote system does not trust your local system. Like **rlogin**, you can specify the login name you use on the remote system if it is different. The following command will list the files in Watson's home directory on **bravo**.

```
kudos% rsh bravo -l watson ls -l
```

If you do not specify a command line to run on the remote system, the **rsh** utility runs **rlogin** for you.

```
kudos% rsh bravo
Last login: Wed Oct 6 21:53:39 from kudos
bravo%
```

Using ping to Test a Network Connection

The **ping** utility sends a particular kind of data packet to a remote computer that causes the remote system to send back a reply. This is a quick way to verify that a remote system is available, as well as to check how well the network is operating, such as how fast it is or whether it is dropping data packets. The name **ping** mimics the sound of a sonar burst used by submarines to identify and communicate with each other.

```
kudos% ping bravo
bravo is alive
```

In this case, the remote system named **bravo** is up and available to you over the network.

Your search path may not include the directory where the **ping** program is kept on your system; if that is the case, use the **whereis** utility (page 58) to find it. If the remote system does not answer, **ping** will keep trying for a short time (usually 20 seconds by default) before reporting back to you.

```
kudos% /usr/etc/ping hurrah
no answer from hurrah
```

There may be several reasons why a system does not answer. The remote computer may be down, the network interface or some part of the network between your systems may be broken, or there may be a software failure.

One of the options available with the **ping** command causes **ping** to provide more detail on the network connection to the remote system. On some systems, **ping** provides the detailed report by default.

```
kudos% ping -s ftp.uu.net
PING ftp.uu.net: 56 data bytes
64 bytes from ftp.UU.NET (192.48.96.9): icmp_seq=0. time=59. ms
64 bytes from ftp.UU.NET (192.48.96.9): icmp_seq=1. time=95. ms
64 bytes from ftp.UU.NET (192.48.96.9): icmp_seq=2. time=46. ms
64 bytes from ftp.UU.NET (192.48.96.9): icmp_seq=3. time=53. ms
(CONTROL)-C
----ftp.UU.NET PING Statistics----
4 packets transmitted, 4 packets received, 0% packet loss
round trip (ms) min/avg/max = 46/64/95
```

The –**s** option causes **ping** to send one packet per second to the remote system. By default, each packet contains 64 bytes (56 data bytes and 8 bytes of protocol header information). In this example, four packets were sent to the system **ftp.uu.net** before the user interrupted ping by typing (CONTROL)-**C**. If the user had not interrupted it, **ping** would have run indefinitely. The four-part number shown on each line in parentheses is the remote system's IP address. A packet sequence number is also given (called **icmp_seq**); if a packet is dropped, you will notice a gap in the sequence numbers. The round-trip time is listed last, in milliseconds; this represents the time that elapsed from when the packet was sent to the remote system until the reply was received by the local system. This time is affected by the distance between the two systems as well as by other network traffic and the load on both computers. Before the program terminates, **ping** summarizes the results—indicating how many packets were sent and received, as well as the minimum, average, and maximum round-trip delays it measured.

Using ruptime to Display Remote Computer Status

If your UNIX system is attached to a local area network, you may be able to use the **ruptime** utility to learn the status of other computers attached to the same network. This information is valuable for a system administrator who must watch over several machines. It can also be useful for individual users—for example, if you have accounts on several computers, you might choose to work on one that is less busy. The **ruptime** utility reports the system names, the status of each system, the amount of time it has been up (or down), the number of users logged in on each system, and the load factor for each machine.

```
kudos% ruptime
bravo     up 29+03:42, 1 users, load 0.37, 0.00, 1.09
hurrah down    12:39
kudos     up  4+14:09, 2 users, load 2.68, 2.09, 1.16
```

If there are many systems attached to your local area network, you may discover that the **ruptime** service has been turned off. To keep the information up to date, each system regularly broadcasts information on its status to all the hosts on the network. On large networks the resulting traffic can impose a serious load on the network, interfering with more important services (such as file transfers, electronic mail, etc.). If you see a message like the one shown below, the **ruptime** service is not running on your system:

```
kudos% ruptime
no hosts!?!
```

Using rwho to List Users on Remote Computers

The **rwho** utility reports the login names of users who are actively using remote systems. The information is presented in four columns: user name, remote system name and the terminal line the user is connected to, when the user logged in, and how long ago the user last typed on the keyboard. If the last column is blank, the user is actively typing at the terminal. This information is especially useful when users work at individual workstations rather than on a central computer system; **rwho** is a **who** command that reports on a network-wide, rather than a computer-specific, basis.

```
kudos% rwho
alex      kudos:tty01    Sep 19 10:54
jenny     bravo:tty03    Sep 21 10:19    :01
roy       kudos:p0       Sep 21 14:24    :33
```

Distributed Computing

When there are many similar systems on a network, it is often desirable to share common files and utilities among them. For example, a system administrator might choose to keep a copy of the system documentation on one computer's disk and to make those files available for all remote systems. In this case, the system administrator would configure the files so that users who needed to access the online documentation would not be aware that the files were actually stored on a remote system. In addition to conserving disk space, it is also easier to keep a central copy up-to-date than it is to track copies scattered throughout the network on many individual systems.

Figure 7-3 illustrates a fileserver that stores the system manual pages and user home directories. With this arrangement, a user will always have access to his or her files—no matter which workstation he or she uses. The workstation's disk might contain a directory to hold temporary files, as well as a copy of the operating system (/**vmunix**).

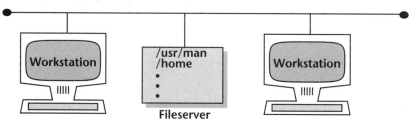

Figure 7-3   A Fileserver

The Client/Server Model

Although there are many ways to distribute computing tasks on hosts attached to a network, the client-server model dominates UNIX system networking. A server system offers services to its clients, and is usually a central resource. In the preceding example, the system that acts as the documentation repository is a server, and all the systems that contact it to display information are clients.

The client/server terminology also applies to processes (which may be running on one or more systems). A server process may control some central database, and client processes send queries to the server and collect replies. In this case, the client and server processes may be running on the same computer.

The client/server model underlies most of the network services described in this chapter.

Domain Name Service (DNS)

The Domain Name Service is a distributed service—name servers on thousands of machines around the world cooperate to keep the database up to date. The database itself, which contains the information that maps hundreds of thousands of alphanumeric hostnames into numeric IP addresses, exists in no one place. That is, no system has a complete copy of the database. Instead, each system that runs DNS knows about the hosts that are local to that site and how to contact other name servers to learn about other, nonlocal hosts.

Like the UNIX filesystem, the DNS is organized hierarchically. There are seven top-level domains; outside the United States, each country uses its ISO country code designation as its domain name (e.g., AU represents Australia, IL is Israel, JP for Japan, etc.). Although it might seem logical to represent the United States in the same way (US) and to use the standard two-letter Postal Service abbreviations to identify the next level of the domain, that is not how the name space was structured. There are six common top-level domains in the United States:

- COM   commercial enterprises
- EDU   educational institutions
- GOV   nonmilitary government agencies
- MIL   military government agencies
- NET   networking organizations
- ORG   other (often nonprofit) organizations

As with Internet addresses, domain names are assigned by the Network Information Center. A system's full name, referred to as its fully qualified domain name, is unambiguous in the way that a simple hostname cannot be. The system **okeeffe.berkeley.edu** at the University of California (Figure 7-4) is not the same as one named **okeeffe.mma.org**, which might represent a host at the Museum of Modern Art. Not only does the domain name tell us something about where a system is located, it adds enough diversity to the name space to avoid confusion when different sites choose similar names for their systems.

Unlike the UNIX filesystem hierarchy, the top-level domain name in the United States appears last (reading from left to right). Also, the DNS is not

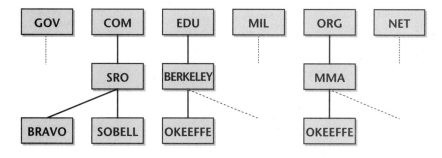

Figure 7-4   United States Top-Level Domains

case-sensitive. The names **okeeffe.berkeley.edu, okeeffe.Berkeley.edu** and **okeeffe.Berkeley.EDU** refer to the same computer. Once a domain has been assigned, the local site is free to extend the hierarchy to meet local needs.

Consider the sample hosts file presented earlier. The domain name, **sro.com**, represents a fictitious entertainment company named Standing Room Only, Inc. Using DNS, mail addressed to **user@sro.com** could be delivered to the computer that handles the corporate mail and knows how to forward messages to user mailboxes on individual machines. As the company grows, the site administrator might decide to create organizational or geographical subdomains. The name **sobell.ca.sro.com** might refer to a system that supports California offices, while **bravo.co.sro.com** is dedicated to Colorado. Functional subdomains might be another choice, with **sobell.sales.sro.com** and **bravo.dev.sro.com** representing the sales and development divisions, respectively.

On UNIX systems, the most common interface to the DNS is the Berkeley Internet Name Domain (BIND) software. BIND follows the client/server model. On any given local network there may be one or more systems running a name server, supporting all the local hosts as clients. When a system wants to send a message to another host, it queries the nearest name server to learn the remote host's IP address. The client, called a *resolver*, may be a process running on the same computer as the name server, or it may pass the request over the network to reach a server. To reduce network traffic and accelerate name lookups, the local name server has some knowledge of distant hosts. If the local server has to contact a remote server to pick up an address, when the answer comes back the local server will add that to its internal table and reuse it for a while. The name server deletes the nonlocal information before it becomes outdated.

How the system translates symbolic hostnames into addresses is transparent to most users; only the system administrator needs to be concerned with the details of name resolution. Systems that use DNS for name resolution are generally capable of communicating with the greatest number of hosts—more than it would be practical to maintain in an **/etc/hosts** file or private Network Information Service database.

Network Information Service (NIS)

The Network Information Service is another example of a client/server paradigm. Sun Microsystems developed NIS to simplify the administration of certain common administrative files by maintaining them in a central database and having clients contact the database server to retrieve information. Just as the DNS addressed the problem of keeping multiple copies of the **hosts** file up-to-date, NIS was created to keep system-independent configuration files current (such as /etc/passwd). Most networks today are heterogeneous (that is, they include systems supplied by many different manufacturers), and even though they run different varieties of the UNIX system, they have certain common attributes (such as the **passwd** file). Thus, many manufacturers have adopted NIS and supply it with the systems they sell.

NIS was formerly called the *Yellow Pages*; many people still refer to it by this name. Sun renamed the service because another corporation holds the trademark to the name *Yellow Pages*. The NIS utilities, however, are still reminiscent of the old name: **ypcat** (display an NIS database), **ypmatch** (search), and so on.

Consider the file /etc/**group**, which maps symbolic names to group ID numbers. If NIS is being used to administer this configuration file on your system, you might see the single following entry, instead of a list of group names and numbers:

```
$ cat /etc/group
+:*:*
$
```

When a utility needs to map a number to the corresponding group name, it encounters the + and knows to query the NIS server at that point for the answer. You can display the group file with the **ypcat** utility:

```
$ ypcat group
pubs::141:alex,jenny,scott,hls,barbara
  .
  .
  .
```

Or, you can search for a particular group name using **ypmatch**:

```
$ ypmatch pubs group
pubs::141:alex,jenny,scott,hls,barbara
```

You can retrieve the same information by filtering the output of **ypcat** through **grep**, but **ypmatch** is more efficient because it searches the database directly, using a single process. The database name is not the full pathname of the file it replaces; the NIS database name is the same as the simple filename **group**, not /etc/group.

As with the Domain Name System, ordinary users need not be aware whether the NIS is used to manage system configuration files. Setting up and maintaining the NIS databases is a task for the system administrator; individual users rarely need to work directly with the system configuration files.

Network File System (NFS)

Using the Network File System, it is possible to work locally with files that are stored on a remote computer system's disks, as if they were present on your own computer. The remote system acts as the file server; the local system is the client, making requests.

NFS is configured by your system administrator; when you work with a file, you are probably not aware of where the file is physically stored. In many computer facilities today, it is common for user files to be stored on a central fileserver that is equipped with many large-capacity disk drives and devices that easily make backup copies of the data. A user's workstation may be entirely *diskless*—in which case it contacts another system that acts as a boot server, loading UNIX and its applications into the workstation's memory—or *dataless*. A dataless workstation client does have a disk, but no user data is stored on it (only the system software, UNIX, and the applications are kept on the disk).

The **df** utility displays a list of the filesystems available on your system, along with how much disk space is available in each one. Filesystem names that are prepended with **hostname:** are available to you through NFS.

```
bravo% df
Filesystem      kbytes    used    avail    capacity    Mounted on
/dev/sd6a       14983     4963    8522     37%         /
/dev/sd6d       139823    102348  23493    81%         /usr
kudos:/home     845086    613857  146991   81%         /kudos/home
sobell:/home    273754    217385  28994    88%         /sobell/home
bravo% pwd
/kudos/home/jenny
```

In this example, Jenny's home directory is actually stored on the remote system **kudos**. The **/home** filesystem on **kudos** is mounted on **bravo** using NFS; as a reminder of its physical location, the system administrator has made it available using a pathname that includes the remote server's name. Refer to Part II for more information on the **df** utility.

The physical location of your files should not matter to you; all the standard UNIX utilities work with NFS-remote files in the same way that they operate on files that are stored locally on your computer. At times, however, you may lose access to your files: your computer may be up and running, but a network problem or a remote system crash may make your files temporarily unavailable. In this case, when you try to access a file, you will probably see an error message like NFS server kudos not responding. When your system can contact the remote server again, you will see a message like NFS server kudos OK.

OPTIONAL

Network Services

On UNIX systems, most network services are provided by daemons that run continuously or are started automatically by the system when a request comes in. The network services that your system supports are listed in a file named **services**, which is typically found in **/etc**. The daemons themselves are usually stored in **/usr/etc**; the name of a daemon ends with the letter **d** by convention, to distinguish it from utilities. (On a system running SunOS, daemon names also have a conventional prefix of **in.** or **rpc..**) When you run **rsh**, for example,

OPTIONAL Continued

your local system contacts the **rsh** daemon (**rshd**) on the remote system to establish the connection. The two systems negotiate the connection according to a fixed protocol. Each system identifies itself to the other, and then they take turns asking each other specific questions and waiting for valid replies. Each network service follows its own protocol.

In addition to the daemons that support the utilities described up to this point, there are many other daemons that support system-level network services that users typically do not interact with. Some of these are described below.

gated

The Gateway daemon manages the routing tables so that your system knows where to send messages that are destined for distant networks. One of the advances offered by **gated** over the simpler routing daemon, **routed**, is enhanced configurability and support for a larger number of routing protocols. If your system has more than one network interface, it is probably running one of these daemons to listen to incoming routing messages as well as to advertise outgoing routes to other systems on your network.

named

The Name daemon supports the Domain Name System, which has replaced the use of the /**etc**/**hosts** table on most networked UNIX systems today for hostname-to-IP address mappings.

nntpd

The Network News Transfer Protocol is designed for the efficient exchange of USENET news articles. It attempts to minimize network traffic by determining whether a remote system already has a copy of a particular message before transferring it.

smtpd

The Simple Mail Transfer Protocol is designed for the exchange of electronic mail messages. One of its responsibilities is to accept an incoming message only if the address is valid. If it is not, the daemon immediately informs the sending system of the problem, and the sending system typically returns the faulty message to the user who originated it.

snmpd

The Simple Network Management Protocol provides access to a wide range of information about devices attached to a network using a standard format, allowing a system manager to monitor remote systems and make adjustments.

xntpd

The Network Time Protocol keeps system clocks synchronized. Clocks on individual computers are not always accurate. When you share files

among computers, it can be a serious problem if one computer in
teprets a file's timestamp as some time in the future while another one
recognizes it as a time in the past. A computer that runs the Network
Time Protocol listens to other systems, including clocks that are certified for accuracy, and continuously monitors and makes small adjustments to its own clock.

USENET

USENET is an informal, loosely connected network of systems that exchange
electronic mail and news items (commonly referred to as *netnews*) (see Figure
1-3, page 9). USENET was formed in the early 1980s when a few sites decided
to share some software and information on topics of common interest. They
agreed to contact one another and to pass the information along over dial-
up telephone lines (at that time, running at 1200 baud at best) using the
UNIX system's **uucp** utility (UNIX-to-UNIX copy program).

The popularity of USENET led to major changes in **uucp** to handle the
ever-escalating volume of messages and sites. Today, much of the news flows
over network links using a sophisticated protocol designed especially for this
purpose (NNTP). The news messages are stored in a standard format, and
there are many public domain programs available to let you read them. An
old, simple interface is named **readnews**. Others, such as **rn** and its X Windows cousin **xrn**, have many features that help you browse through the articles that are available and reply to or create articles of your own. The
USENET software has been ported to non-UNIX systems as well, so the community has grown more diverse.

In the true UNIX tradition, categories of netnews articles are structured
hierarchically. The top level includes designations such as comp (computer-
related), misc (miscellaneous), rec (recreational topics), sci (science), soc (so-
cial issues), and talk (ongoing discussions). There is usually at least one regional category at the top level, such as ba (San Francisco Bay Area), that
includes information about local events. The names of news groups resemble domain names, but read from left to right (like UNIX file names):
comp.lang.c, **misc.jobs.offered**, **rec.skiing**, **sci.med**, **soc.singles**,
talk.politics. Below is an example of an article that appeared in the group
devoted to discussion of issues related to Berkeley UNIX.

```
kudos% rn comp.unix.bsd
Article 14476 (49 more) in comp.unix.bsd:
From: c9020@rrzc1a (Hubert Feyrer)
Subject: Re: root passwd
Date: 30 Sep 1993 18:03:56 GMT
Organization: University of Regensburg, Germany
Lines: 16
Message-ID: <28f72dINNk7m@rrzs3.uni-regensburg.de>
References: <CE6AA1.Mot@cs.uiuc.edu>
Reply-To: feyrer@rrzc1.rz.uni-regensburg.de
NNTP-Posting-Host: rrzc1.rz.uni-regensburg.de
X-Newsreader: TIN [version 1.2 PL0]

John Doe (jdoe@cs.uiuc.edu) wrote:
> Forgot my root passwd on my sun workstation, a stand alone workstation.
> Is there a way to break the startup and reset /etc/passwd?
```

```
I'd suggest booting from CD or tape ...
Regards,
      Hubert

--MORE--(67%)
```

There is a great deal of useful information available on USENET, but it requires patience and perseverance to find what you are looking for. You can ask a question, as did the user above at the University of Illinois, and someone from halfway around the world may answer it (Germany, in this case). Before posing such a simple question and causing it to appear on thousands of systems around the world, ask yourself if there is a straightforward way to get help locally. In this case, John Doe might have asked his system administrator or another Sun user for help; he might have found a paper copy of the system documentation and read it; he might have contacted Sun directly, using electronic mail or the telephone, for help. The last thing he should have done was to pose the question to the world-wide USENET community.

One way to find out about new tools and services is to read the USENET news. People often announce the availability of free software there, along with instructions on how to get a copy for your own use (e.g., through anonymous **ftp**). Other tools exist to help you find resources, both old and new, on the network. Two of these are described in the next section.

Browsing Around the Internet

By now you are probably wondering how you would know that you could use **finger** to display earthquake reports from the U.S. Geological Survey or **telnet** to search the card catalogue at the Library of Congress. Through the Internet you can access a wealth of information stored on computers around the world, but how do you find the resources that are available to you?

When the network was small, it was easy to find what you were looking for. There were a few well-known sites that maintained archives of public domain (free) software and information, and they set up file hierarchies on their systems with logical, descriptive names. As the archives grew larger, they created indexes that you could pick up and study at your leisure. The "one-stop shopping" that a central archive server provides is convenient, but it does not scale up: no one site can store a copy of every piece of useful information. As a network grows in size and popularity, a central server cannot keep up with the demand. The system and the limited network paths that connect to it become clogged with traffic.

In some cases, regional archive servers have addressed the second problem, but the first problem is more difficult. Disk storage space is a finite resource, so regional servers tend to offer collections of information that are interesting to the widest audience. The network is also a valuable tool for specialists, however; it is possible for anyone with a UNIX system attached to a network to set up his or her own server to share information with the rest of the networked world.

At first, it was possible to keep track of these far-flung archives informally through word-of-mouth, advertisements on mailing lists, or bulletin boards. The explosive growth of the network soon made the informal approach impractical. There are several tools now available that are indispensable for browsing through Internet resources; two of these, **archie** and **gopher**, are described below, followed by a brief introduction to the World Wide Web. The best way to become familiar with these tools, and the Internet, is to try them out.

Archie

To use **archie**, you need to contact an **archie** server. There are several **archie** servers available on the Internet; to minimize network traffic, you should contact the server nearest you. In addition to an interactive network interface, you can use electronic mail to retrieve information from **archie**. In late 1993, these **archie** servers were available for public use:

- archie.rutgers.edu   128.6.18.15   (Rutgers University)
- archie.sura.net   128.167.254.179 (SURAnet archie server)
- archie.unl.edu   129.93.1.14   (U of Nebraska in Lincoln)
- archie.ans.net   147.225.1.2   (ANS archie server)
- archie.au   139.130.4.6   (Australian server)
- archie.funet.fi   128.214.6.100   (European server–Finland)
- archie.doc.ic.ac.uk   146.169.11.3   (UK/England server)
- archie.cs.huji.ac.il   132.65.6.15   (Israeli server)
- archie.wide.ad.jp   133.4.3.6   (Japanese server)
- archie.ncu.edu.tw   140.115.19.24   (Taiwanese server)

Over time, this list will change (as new servers come online or old ones are retired). One way to get started with **archie** is to use electronic mail to locate the **archie** server nearest to you. The body of the message you send should contain the **archie** command that will return the information you need; in this case, start with the command **servers** or **help**. Address your mail to the user **archie** at one of the servers listed above.

```
kudos% mail archie@archie.rutgers.edu
help
CONTROL-D
```

The **archie** server will send you a reply that contains a helpful description of the commands it recognizes; if you had specified servers (instead of help) above, the reply would have contained the latest list of **archie** servers. To use **archie**, **telnet** to your nearest server and make a request. The next example shows how to ask for information on Shakespeare (find shakespeare). The **archie** program returned almost 100 matches from organizations around the globe, a sample of which are shown on the next page.

```
kudos% telnet archie@archie.rutgers.edu
SunOS UNIX (dorm.rutgers.edu) (ttyp9)
login: archie
.
.
.
# Bunyip Information Systems, 1993
# Terminal type set to 'vt100 24 80'.
# 'erase' character is '^?'.
# 'search' (type string) has the value 'sub'.
archie> find shakespeare
# Search type: sub.
# Your queue position: 1
# Estimated time for completion: 00:04
working... \       ─
.
.
.
Host ftp.uwp.edu (131.210.1.4)            # University of Wisconsin-Parkside
Last updated 23:25 2 Oct 1993

    Location: /pub/etext
        DIRECTORY drwxrwxr-x 512 bytes 23:07 1 Oct 1993 shakespeare

Host ftp.denet.dk (129.142.6.74)          # Denmark
Last updated 13:00 6 Oct 1993
    Location: /pub/wordlists/literature
        FILE -r--r--r-- 3251 bytes 00:00 12 Jul 1991 shakespeare.Z

Host ring.kotel.co.kr (147.6.1.2)         # Korea
Last updated 10:18 6 Oct 1993

    Location: /pub/mac/hypercard
        FILE -rw-rw-r-- 113869 bytes 00:00 9 Jul 1992
            shakespeare-sonnets-ii.hqx

Host think.com (131.239.2.1)              # Thinking Machines Corporation
Last updated 02:55 3 Oct 1993

    Location: /random/images/sun/backgrounds
        FILE -rw-r--r-- 96562 bytes 00:00 12 Oct 1988
            shakespeare.im1

archie> quit
# Bye.
Connection closed by foreign host.
kudos%
```

The names of files and directories above give you some clues as to their content: electronic text, a MacIntosh Hypercard stack, a bitmap image for a Sun workstation. If any of these matched your interests, the next step you would take would be to use **ftp** to connect to the site that **archie** identified and retrieve the file.

The file named **shakespeare.Z** is a compressed file. Because compressed files typically contain non-ASCII (non-printing) characters, be sure to set binary mode on before retrieving such a file. For more information on **compress**, see page 60.

In the example above, although you requested a connection to the system named **archie.rutgers.edu**, your connection was actually established to a computer named **dorm.rutgers.edu**. The Domain Name Service can map multiple names to a single IP address; this is especially useful in cases like this, where it is intuitive to access a server by using a particular name but you may not want to devote a whole system to that single function. For example, a common convention for identifying anonymous **ftp** servers is to prefix the domain name with **ftp**, as you have seen above—**ftp.uu.net**, **ftp.uwp.edu**, **ftp.denet.dk**.

If you are not connected to the Internet, you can use electronic mail to conduct the same search (the results will be mailed back to you):

```
kudos% mail archie@archie.rutgers.edu
find Shakespeare
(CONTROL)-D
```

Gopher

To experiment with **gopher**, you need to run a **gopher** client program on your system (which will interact over the network with a **gopher** server). To start a **gopher** client, type **gopher** (or if you are running X windows, a window-oriented interface named **xgopher** may be available on your system). If **gopher** is not installed on your system, contact your system administrator for help. You may be able to contact a public **gopher** client at the University of Minnesota (where **gopher** was developed):

```
kudos% telnet consultant.micro.umn.edu
Trying 134.84.132.4...
Connected to hafnhaf.micro.umn.edu
AIX telnet (hafnhaf)
To run gopher on this system login as "gopher"
IBM AIX Version 3 for RISC/System/6000
(C) Copyrights by IBM and by others 1982, 1991.
login: gopher
TERM=(vt100)
.
.
```

In the following examples, the **gopher** client is shown running on a system at an imaginary place named Fredonia University. When it starts up, **gopher** displays a menu of items that you can choose from. The arrow at the left of an item indicates which one will be selected if you press (RETURN). A status line appears at the bottom of your screen, reminding you of some basic commands as well as indicating how many pages of information are available (along with the current page). In this case, the main menu is only one page long. If you choose an item with a / at the end, a new menu will be displayed (one that is specific to that item).

```
           Internet Gopher Information Client v1.11
           Root gopher server: gopher.fredonia.edu
     --> 1. Bringing You a Better Information System.
         2. Help and Information/
         3. News and Weather/
         4. Entertainment and Events/
         5. Especially for Students/
         6. University Departments and Services/
         7. Fredonia University Libraries/
         8. Other Libraries and Reference/
         9. Fredonia News Network/
         10. Search Menu Items at Fredonia <?>
         11. Phone Books and E-mail Addresses/
         12. Explore the Internet/
         Press ? for Help, q to Quit, u to go up a menu        Page: 1/1
```

In this example, you decide to explore the Internet, so you choose item 12. When you enter the number, the arrow moves to the corresponding item

number, and the line at the bottom of the screen changes accordingly. The
next menu appears, and you select item number 10:

```
View item number: 12
Internet Gopher Information Client v1.11
Explore the Internet
1. About the Internet/
2. Some guided exploration/
3. Search document titles (using veronica)/
4. Search for files to transfer (ftp)/
5. InterNIC directory and database services/
6. WAIS based information/
7. University of Minnesota Gopher (top level gopher)/
8. Fredonia Experimental gopher/
9. Navigating the Internet: an interactive course.
--> 10. Other gopher and information servers/
View item number: 10
```

This item retrieves a list of more than 900 **gopher** servers around the
world, the first page of which follows:

```
Internet Gopher Information Client v1.11
All the Gopher Servers in the World
--> 1. Search Gopherspace using Veronica/
2. ACADEME THIS WEEK (Chronicle of Higher Education)/
3. ACM SIGGRAPH/
4. ACTLab (UT Austin, RTF Dept)/
5. AMI -- A Friendly Public Interface/
6. AREA Science Park, Trieste, (IT)/
7. Academic Position Network/
8. Academy of Sciences, Bratislava (Slovakia)/
9. AgResearch Wallaceville, Upper Hutt, New Zealand/
10. Alamo Community College District/
11. Albert Einstein College of Medicine/
12. Alpha Phi Omega/
13. American Mathematical Society/
14. American Philosophical Society/
15. American Physiological Society/
16. Andrews University/
17. Anesthesiology Gopher/
18. Appalachian State University/
Press ? for Help, q to Quit, u to go up a menu          Page: 1/51
```

You can step through the other pages on your display by entering + to move
forward and – to go backward.

Unlike **archie**, which just tells you where to find things over the network, **gopher** allows you to run commands that will retrieve copies for you
as you browse. After you have found an item you would like to save (having
navigated your way through several menus, no doubt), the options on your
status line will include:

```
Press <RETURN> to continue, <m> to mail, <s> to save:
```

If you started the **gopher** client on your own system, you can use the
s command to save the file in your working directory. If you are running
gopher on a different (e.g., public) host, you will probably want to mail
the file to yourself instead.

The World Wide Web

The World Wide Web (WWW or W3) is a project that seeks to provide a unified, interconnected interface to the vast amount of information stored on computers around the world. The Web was designed at CERN, the European Laboratory for Particle Physics, where some researchers created new tools that allowed them to share complex information effectively. By designing the tools to work with existing protocols such as **ftp** and **gopher**, they created a system that is generally useful for many types of information and across different types of hardware and operating systems.

In the simplest case, a WWW server offers another view of existing information. For example, a server at a particular site may supply a list of the files it makes available for anonymous **ftp**. You can use a WWW client application, or browser, to display and retrieve this information.

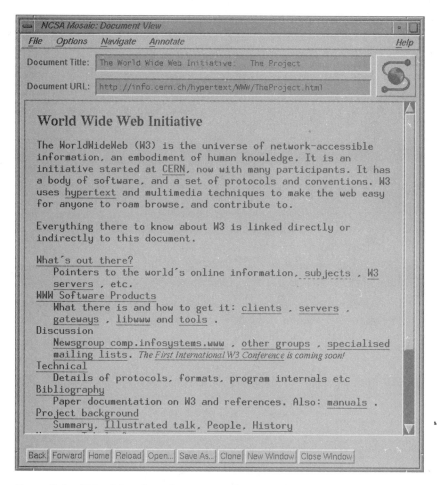

Figure 7-5   Using **Mosaic** *to learn more about WWW*

The power of WWW is, in its use of *hypertext*, a way to navigate through stored information by following cross-references (called links) from one piece of information to another. If this book were available as a hypertext document, you would have an easy way to get more detail about some of the topics described here. Your hypertext client would highlight certain terms that were linked to servers that could provide additional information. For example, if you selected CERN, your client would contact the appropriate server and display the results, which might be a page or two of information about the laboratory. To use the Web effectively, you need to be able to run interactive network applications. The most powerful browser available for the Web today is a tool called **Mosaic**. It was designed at the National Center for Supercomputer Applications at the University of Illinois and is available as an X Window system application for many UNIX systems, as well as for Macintoshes and PCs (running Windows). You can use **ftp** to obtain a copy of **Mosaic** from the system **ftp.ncsa.uiuc.edu**, if it is not already installed on your system.

The Mosaic browser (Figure 7-5) provides a graphical user interface that allows you to display pictures as well as text, giving you access to hypermedia. That is, a picture on your screen may be a link to more detailed, non-verbal information such as a copy of the same picture at a higher resolution or a short animation. If you run Mosaic on a system that is equipped for audio playback, you will be able to listen to audio clips that have been linked into a document. For example, if you selected the picture of the loudspeaker in Figure 7-6, you would hear an audio clip about the Magnetic Resonance Imaging work at the University of Texas. All the underlined words and phrases in Figures 7-5 and 7-6 are hypertext links.

The easiest way to learn about **Mosaic** and the Web is to run **Mosaic** and begin exploring. When you start **Mosaic**, it automatically displays a document that will help you get going. The content of this document, known as a *home page*, varies widely but should include a few hypertext links that will lead you in the right direction. Other client applications, with more limited capabilities, are also available for browsing the Web. If there is no browser on your system, you can get started by running the command:

```
$ telnet info.cern.ch
```

This command connects you to a simple browser (in Switzerland) that you can use to learn about the Web. Following is an example of one of the pages of information available from the server at CERN, as displayed by this simple browser:

```
The World Wide Web Initiative:  The Project
               WORLD WIDE WEB INITIATIVE

The WorldWideWeb (W3) is the universe of network-accessible information, an
embodiment of human knowledge. It is an initiative started at CERN[1], now
with many participants. It has a body of software, and a set of protocols
and conventions. W3 uses hypertext[2] and multimedia techniques to make the
web easy for anyone to roam browse, and contribute to. Everything there is
to know about W3 is linked directly or indirectly to this document.

What's out there?[3]        Pointers to the world's online information,
                            subjects[4], W3 servers[5], etc
```

```
WWW Software Products[6]
            What there is and how to get it: clients[7],
            servers[8], gateways[9], libwww[10] and tools[11].

Discussion     Newsgroup comp.infosystems.www[12], other
            groups[13], specialised mailing lists[14]. The First
            International W3 Conference[15] is coming soon!

1-28, Back, Up, <RETURN> for more, Quit, or Help:
```

In the example above, each hypertext link is identified with a number, shown in brackets. The last line in the example prompts you to enter the number for the link you wish to follow or one of the listed commands. Note that this is the same information displayed in Figure 7-5. There is one copy of this information stored on the computer at CERN; the browser you use to access the information controls how it appears on your screen.

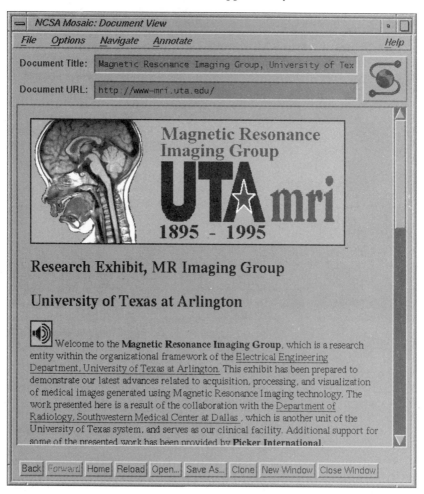

Figure 7-6   Example of some hypermedia on the WWW

If you do not have direct access to the Internet, you can use electronic mail to retrieve information from the Web by sending a message to the address **listserv@info.cern.ch**. The text of your message should be the word HELP on a single line. You should receive a copy of the instructions in return, via electronic mail.

OPTIONAL

Uniform Resource Locator (URL)

In addition to navigating through the Web by links, you can also specify a particular resource by name. The URL for the page of information shown in the previous example is:

```
http://info.cern.ch/hypertext/WWW/TheProject.html
```

Each browser provides a way to jump to a particular resource: **Mosaic** prompts you to type the name after you select a URL menu item; the line-oriented browser shown above recognizes a **Go** command.

The first component in the URL indicates the type of resource; in this case, http (HyperText Transfer Protocol). There are a few other valid resource names, such as **gopher**, to represent information that is available through the Web using other protocols. The next component, following the double slash (//), is the full name of the host that acts as the server for the information (**info.cern.ch**). The rest of the URL is a relative pathname to the file that contains the information (**TheProject.html**). The suffix on this particular file, **html**, suggests that its contents are expressed in the HyperText Markup Language (HTML), which is used to specify the hypertext links.

By convention, many sites identify their WWW servers by prefixing a host or domain name with **www**. For example, you can reach the Web server at the New Jersey Institute of Technology at www.njit.edu. When you use a browser to explore the World Wide Web, you may never need to use a URL directly. However, as people make more information available in hypertext form, you are bound to encounter references to specific URL names (in mail messages, USENET articles, etc.).

Innovations like the World Wide Web and the Mosaic browser give us a glimpse into the future, showing us a potential for practical, global information sharing that is unprecedented in human history.

SUMMARY

Support for network communication was introduced in Berkeley UNIX 4.2 and was soon added to other versions of UNIX by individual manufacturers. UNIX systems today usually communicate on Ethernet or FDDI local area networks, which may be linked in turn to other local and wide area networks.

Basic networking tools allow users to check on the status of remote computers and their users (**ruptime**, **rwho**), to log in on remote systems (**rlogin**, telnet), to run commands on remote systems (**rsh**), and to copy files quickly from one system to another (**rcp**, **ftp**). Standard UNIX tools (such as **mail**, **finger**, and **talk**) have also been extended to recognize network addresses, thus allowing users on different systems to interact with one another. New applications, such as remote filesystems, have extended the basic UNIX model and simplified information sharing.

Two major advantages of computer networks are that they enable systems to communicate at high speeds and that they require few connections (typically one per system, on a common cable). Two UNIX systems that are not attached to a network can still communicate over dial-up or hard-wired serial lines, but it is not feasible to set up direct links from one computer to every system with which it might need to exchange data. Dial-up lines tend to be slow and busy as more and longer connections are needed, and long-distance, hard-wired connections tend to be expensive. Sometimes two computers that need to exchange data can do so without establishing a direct connection, by using intermediary systems to forward their messages, but this approach tends to introduce long delays–often measured in days.

Technological advances continue to improve the performance of both computer systems and the networks that link them together. The backbone of the NSFnet, a major portion of the Internet in the United States, currently runs at 45 megabits per second; some experimental networks today are capable of transferring data at the rate of one billion bits per second (one gigabit). The availability of higher-speed networking encourages the development of new applications and services that can use it to full advantage.

REVIEW EXERCISES

1. Describe the similarities and differences between these utilities:

   a. **rcp** and **ftp**

   b. **rlogin** and **telnet**

   c. **rsh** and **rlogin**

2. Suppose **rwho** is disabled on the systems on your local area network. Describe two ways to find out who is logged in on some of the other machines attached to your network.

3. Explain the client/server model, and give three examples of UNIX services that take advantage of this model.

4. What is the difference between a diskless and a dataless workstation? Name some advantages and disadvantages of each approach.

5. There is an interesting language named Perl that was developed for UNIX systems. It is in the public domain (free). How can you use the network to find a copy and install it on your system?

6. Refer to the network shown in Figure 7-2. Someone at site A sends a message to three users, one at each site. The message is delivered to a workstation on an Ethernet at each site. Which message is likely to arrive first? last? Explain your answer.

7. Suppose the link between routers 1 and 3 is down in the Internet shown in Figure 7-2. What will happen if someone on the PC at site C sends a message to a user on a workstation attached to the Ethernet at site B? What will happen if the router at site B is down? What does this tell you about designing network configurations?

CHAPTER 8

The vi **Editor**

This chapter shows how to use the vi editor to change existing text files. It assumes that you have read the part of Chapter 2 that explains how to specify your terminal and get started using vi. This chapter goes into detail about many of the vi commands and explains the use of parameters for customizing vi to meet your needs. At the end of the chapter is a quick reference summary of vi commands.

About vi

The **vi** editor is very large and powerful, and only some of its features are described here. Nonetheless, if **vi** is completely new to you, you may find even the set of commands described here overwhelming. The **vi** editor provides a variety of different ways to accomplish any specified editing task. A useful strategy when learning **vi** is to learn a subset of commands that enables you to accomplish basic editing tasks and then to learn other commands that will enable you to do things more quickly and efficiently as you become more comfortable with the editor.

Introduction to vi

This section contains historical information on **vi**, some useful facts about how **vi** operates, and suggestions on what you can do when you encounter exceptional conditions, such as system crashes or not being able to exit from **vi**. It also summarizes some of the information on **vi** that was presented in Chapter 2.

History of vi

The **vi** editor was developed at the University of California, Berkeley, as part of Berkeley UNIX (BSD), though it is widely available on other versions of the UNIX system. Before **vi** was developed, the standard UNIX system editor was **ed**. The **ed** editor was line-oriented, which made it difficult to see the context of your editing. Then **ex** came along—**ex** was a superset of **ed**. The most notable advantage that **ex** had over **ed** was a display editing facility that allowed users to work with a full screen of text instead of with only a line at a time. While you were using **ex**, you could use the display editing facility by giving **ex** the command vi (for visual mode). People used the display editing facility of **ex** so extensively that the developers of **ex** made it possible to start the editor so that you were using the display editing facility at once, without having to start **ex** and give the **vi** command. Appropriately, they named the new facility **vi**.

You can still call the visual mode from **ex**, and you can go back to **ex** while you are using **vi**. Give **vi** a **Q** command to use **ex**, or give **ex** a **vi** command to switch to visual mode.

Modes of Operation

The **ex** editor has five modes of operation:

- **ex** Command Mode
- **ex** Input Mode
- **vi** Command Mode
- **vi** Input Mode
- **vi** Last Line Mode

While you are using **vi**, you will mostly use **vi** Command Mode and Input Mode. On occasion you will use Last Line Mode. While in Command Mode, **vi** accepts keystrokes as commands, responding to each command as you enter it. In Command Mode, **vi** does not display the characters you type. In Input Mode, **vi** accepts keystrokes as text, displaying the text as you enter it. All commands that start with a colon (:) put **vi** in Last Line Mode. The colon moves the cursor to the bottom line of the screen, where you enter the rest of the command.

In addition to the position of the cursor, there is another important difference between Last Line Mode and Command Mode. When you give a command in Command Mode, you do not have to terminate the command with (RETURN). However, you must terminate all Last Line Mode commands with a (RETURN) ((ESCAPE) also works).

You will not normally use the **ex** modes. When this chapter refers to Input and Command Modes, it refers to the **vi** modes, not to the **ex** modes.

At the start of an editing session, **vi** is in Command Mode. There are several commands, such as Insert and Append, that put **vi** in Input Mode. When you press the (ESCAPE) key, **vi** always reverts to Command Mode.

The Change and Replace commands combine Command and Input Modes. The Change command deletes the text you want to change and puts **vi** in Input Mode so you can insert new text. The Replace command deletes the character(s) you overwrite and inserts the new one(s) you enter. Figure 8-1 shows the modes as well as the methods for changing between them.

Correcting Text as You Insert It

While **vi** is in Input Mode, you can use the erase and line kill keys to back up over text that you are inserting so you can correct it. You can also use (CONTROL)-**W** to back up to the beginning of the word you are entering. Using

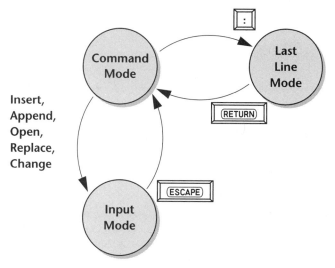

Figure 8-1   Modes in **vi**

these techniques, you cannot back up past the beginning of the line you are working on or past the beginning of the text you entered since you most recently put **vi** into Input Mode.

Command Case

Be certain to observe the case of commands as this chapter describes them. The same letter serves as two different commands, depending on whether you enter it as an uppercase or lowercase character.

If **vi** seems to be behaving strangely, make sure the terminal key **SHIFT LOCK** (or (CAPS LOCK)) is off.

The Work Buffer

The **vi** editor does all its work in the *Work Buffer*. At the start of an editing session, **vi** reads the file you are editing from the disk into the Work Buffer. During the editing session, **vi** makes all changes to this copy of the file. It does not change the disk file until you write the contents of the Work Buffer back to the disk. Normally, when you end an editing session, you command **vi** to write out the contents of the Work Buffer, which makes the changes to the text final. When you edit a new file, **vi** does not create the file until it writes the contents of the Work Buffer to the disk, usually at the end of the editing session.

Storing the text you are editing in the Work Buffer has advantages and disadvantages. If you accidentally end an editing session without writing out the contents of the Work Buffer, all your work is lost. However, if you unintentionally make some major changes (such as deleting the entire contents of the Work Buffer), you can end the editing session without implementing the changes. The **vi** editor will leave the file as it was when you last wrote it out.

If you want to use the **vi** editor to look at a file but not to change it, you can use the **view** command:

```
$ view filename
```

This command calls the **vi** editor with the –R (read-only) option. Once you have invoked the editor in this way, it will not let you write the contents of the Work Buffer back to the file on the disk.

Abnormal Termination of an Editing Session

You can end an editing session in one of two ways: either **vi** saves the changes you made during the editing session, or it does not save them. Chapter 2 explained that the ZZ command saves the contents of the Work Buffer and exits from **vi**.

You can end an editing session without writing out the contents of the Work Buffer by giving the following command. (The : puts **vi** in Last Line Mode—you must press (RETURN) to execute the command.)

```
:q!
```

When you use this command to end an editing session, **vi** does not preserve the contents of the Work Buffer—you lose all the work you did since the last time you wrote the Work Buffer to disk. The next time you edit or use the file, it will appear as it did the last time you wrote the Work Buffer to disk. Use the :q! command cautiously.

You may run into a situation where you have created or edited a file, and **vi** will not let you exit. When you give the **ZZ** command, you will see the message No current filename if you forgot to specify a filename when you first called **vi**. If **vi** will not let you exit normally, you can use the Write command (:w) to name the file and write it to disk before you quit using **vi**. To write the file, give the following command, substituting the name of the file in place of **filename** (remember to follow the command with a (RETURN)):

    :w filename

After you give the Write command, you can use :q to quit. You do not need to use the exclamation point (that is, **q!**) because the exclamation point is necessary only when you have made changes since the last time you wrote the Work Buffer to disk. Refer to page 201 for more information about the Write command.

OPTIONAL

It may also be necessary to write a file using :w **filename** if you do not have write permission for the file you are editing. If you give the **ZZ** command and see the message Permission denied or the message File is read only, you do not have write permission for the file. Use the Write command with a temporary filename to write the file to disk under a different filename. If you do not have write permission to the working directory, **vi** may still not be able to write your file to the disk. Give the command again, using an absolute pathname of a dummy (nonexistent) file in your home directory in place of **filename**. (Alex might give the command :w **/home/alex/temp**.)

Recovering Text After a Crash

If the system crashes while you are editing a file with **vi**, you can often recover text that would otherwise be lost. If the system saved a copy of your Work Buffer, it may send you mail telling you so. However, even if you did not get mail when the system was brought up, give the following command to see if the system saved the contents of your Work Buffer:

    $ vi -r filename

If your work was saved, you will be editing a recent copy of your Work Buffer. Use :w immediately to save the salvaged copy of the Work Buffer to disk, and then continue editing.

The Display

The **vi** editor uses the status line and several special symbols to give information about what is happening during an editing session.

The Status Line

The **vi** editor displays status information on the bottom line—the twenty-fourth line of most terminals. This information includes error messages, information about the deletion or addition of blocks of text, and file status information. In addition, **vi** displays Last Line Mode commands on the status line.

Redrawing the Screen

In some cases, **vi** uses an @ symbol at the left of the screen to replace deleted lines. The **vi** editor does this rather than refreshing the screen so that users, especially those using a UNIX system over slower telephone lines, do not have to wait through unnecessary pauses when text is deleted from the screen. This symbol appears only on the screen and is never written to the Work Buffer or file. If the screen becomes cluttered with these symbols, enter (CONTROL)-**L** (some terminals use (CONTROL)-**R**) while **vi** is in Command Mode to redraw the screen.

You may also want to redraw the screen if another user writes to you while you are in **vi**. When this happens, the other user's message becomes intermixed with the display of the Work Buffer, and this can be confusing. The other user's message *does not* become part of the Work Buffer—it only affects the display. If this happens when you are in Input Mode, press (ESCAPE) to get into Command Mode, and then press (CONTROL)-**L** (or (CONTROL)-**R**) to redraw the screen.

Be sure to read the other user's message before redrawing the screen, since redrawing the screen causes the message to disappear. You can write back to the other user while in **vi** (page 206) or quit **vi** and use the **write** command from the shell.

The Tilde (~) Symbol

If the end of the file is displayed on the screen, **vi** marks lines that would appear past the end of the file with a tilde (~) at the left of the screen. When you start editing a new file, the **vi** editor marks every line on the screen, except for the first line, with these symbols.

Command Mode—Moving the Cursor

While **vi** is in Command Mode, you can position the cursor over any character on the screen. You can also display a different portion of the Work Buffer on the screen. By manipulating the screen and cursor position, you can place the cursor on any character in the Work Buffer.

You can move the cursor forward or backward through the text. As illustrated in Figure 8-2, *forward* always means toward the bottom of the screen

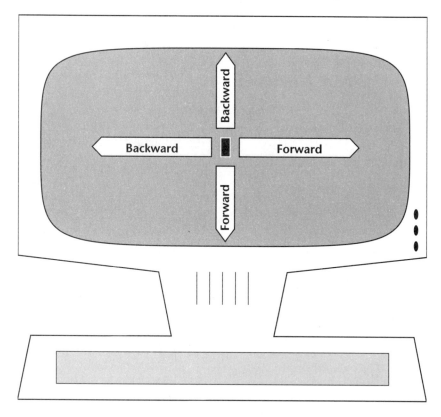

Figure 8-2   Forward and Backward

and the end of the file. *Backward* means toward the top of the screen and the beginning of the file. When you use a command that moves the cursor forward past the end (right) of a line, the cursor generally moves to the beginning (left) of the next line. When you move it backward past the beginning of a line, it moves to the end of the previous line.

You can move the cursor through the text by any *Unit of Measure* (i.e., character, word, line, sentence, paragraph, or screen). If you precede a cursor-movement command with a number, called a *Repeat Factor,* the cursor moves that number of units through the text. Refer to pages 208 and 210 at the end of this chapter for more precise definitions of these terms.

Moving the Cursor by Characters

The (SPACE) bar moves the cursor forward, one character at a time, toward the right side of the screen. The l (ell) key and the ⊖ key (Figure 8-3) do the same thing. The command 7 (SPACE) or 7l moves the cursor seven characters to the right. These keys *cannot* move the cursor past the end of the current line to the beginning of the next.

The h and ⊖ keys are similar to the l key but work in the opposite direction.

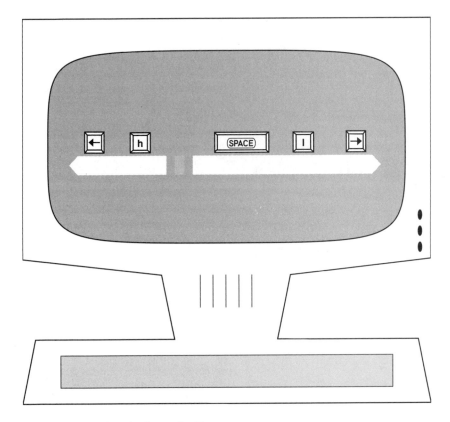

Figure 8-3   Moving the Cursor by Characters

Moving the Cursor by Words

The **w** key moves the cursor forward to the first letter of the next word (Figure 8-4). Groups of punctuation count as words. This command goes to the next line if that is where the next word is, unless the line ends with a (SPACE). The command **15w** moves the cursor to the first character of the fifteenth subsequent word.

The **W** key is similar to the **w** key, except that it moves the cursor by blank delimited words, including punctuation, as it skips forward over words. (See "Blank Delimited Word," page 208.)

The **b** key moves the cursor backward to the first letter of the previous word. The **B** key moves the cursor backward by blank delimited words.

Moving the Cursor by Lines

The (RETURN) key moves the cursor to the beginning of the next line (Figure 8-5), and the **j** and ⊕ keys move it down one line to the character just below the current character. If there is no character immediately below the current character, the cursor moves to the end of the next line. The cursor will not move past the last line of text.

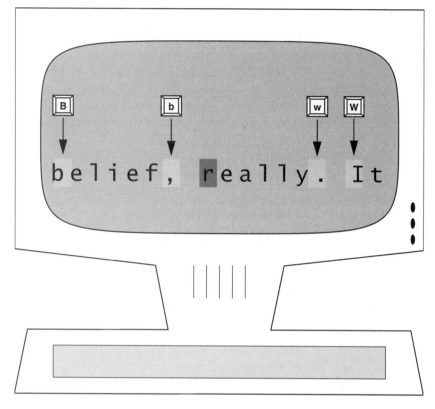

Figure 8-4   Moving the Cursor by Words

The **k** and ⊕ keys are similar to the **j** key, but they work in the opposite direction. Also, the minus (–) key is similar to the (RETURN) key, but it works in the opposite direction.

Moving the Cursor by Sentences and Paragraphs

The) and } keys move the cursor forward to the beginning of the next sentence or paragraph, respectively (Figure 8-6). The (and { keys move the cursor backward to the beginning of the current sentence or paragraph.

Moving the Cursor Within the Screen

The **H** key positions the cursor at the left end of the top, or Home, line of the screen. The **M** key moves the cursor to the Middle line, and **L** moves it to the bottom, or Lower line. See Figure 8-6.

Viewing Different Parts of the Work Buffer

The screen displays a portion of the text that is in the Work Buffer. You can display the text preceding or following the text on the screen by *scrolling* the display. You can also display a portion of the Work Buffer based on a line number.

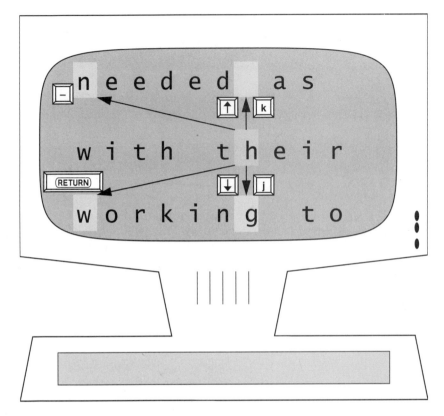

Figure 8-5 *Moving the Cursor by Lines*

Press (CONTROL)-**D** to scroll the screen Down (forward) through the file so that **vi** displays half a screenful of new text. Use (CONTROL)-**U** to scroll the screen Up (backward) the same amount. The (CONTROL)-**F** (Forward) or (CONTROL)-**B** (Backward) keys display almost a *whole* screenful of new text, leaving a couple of lines from the previous screen for continuity. See Figure 8-7.

When you enter a line number followed by **G** (Goto), **vi** displays a specific line in the Work Buffer. If you press **G** without a number, **vi** positions the cursor on the last line in the Work Buffer. Line numbers are implicit; your file does not need to have actual line numbers for you to use this command. Refer to "Line Numbers," page 203, if you want **vi** to display line numbers.

Input Mode

The Insert, Append, Open, Change, and Replace commands put **vi** in Input Mode. While **vi** is in Input Mode, you can put new text into the Work Buffer. Always press the (ESCAPE) key to return **vi** to Command Mode when you finish entering text. Refer to "Show Mode" in the "Parameters" section (page 203) if you want **vi** to remind you when it is in Input Mode.

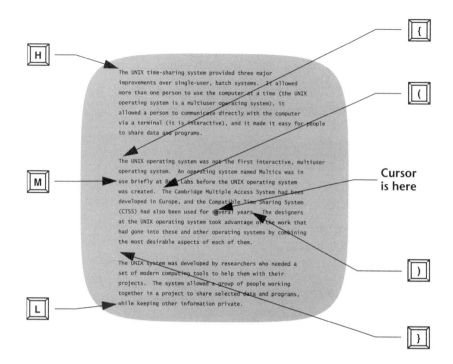

*Figure 8-6   Moving the Cursor by Sentences, Paragraphs, **H**, **M**, and **L***

The Insert Commands

The **i** command puts **vi** in Input Mode and places the text you enter *before* the character the cursor is on (the *current character*). The **I** command places text at the beginning of the current line (Figure 8-8). Although **i** and **I** commands sometimes overwrite text on the screen, the characters in the Work Buffer are not changed (only the display is affected). The overwritten text will be redisplayed when you press (ESCAPE) and **vi** returns to Command Mode. Use **i** or **I** to insert a few characters or words into existing text or to insert text in a new file.

The Append Commands

The **a** command is similar to the **i** command, except that it places the text you enter *after* the current character (Figure 8-8). The **A** command places the text *after* the last character on the current line.

The Open Commands

The **o** and **O** commands open a blank line within existing text, place the cursor at the beginning of the new (blank) line, and put **vi** in Input Mode. The **O** command opens a line *above* the current line; **o** opens one below. Use the Open commands when entering several new lines within existing text.

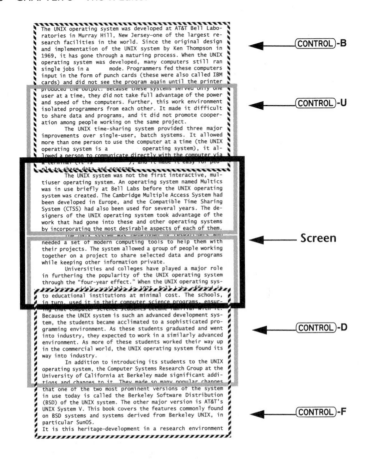

The UNIX operating system was developed at AT&T Bell Laboratories in Murray Hill, New Jersey—one of the largest research facilities in the world. Since the original design
and implementation of the UNIX system by Ken Thompson in
1969, it has gone through a maturing process. When the UNIX
operating system was developed, many computers still ran
single jobs in a   mode. Programmers fed these computers
input in the form of punch cards (these were also called IBM
cards) and did not see the program again until the printer
produced the output. Because these systems served only one
user at a time, they did not take full advantage of the power
and speed of the computers. Further, this work environment
isolated programmers from each other. It made it difficult
to share data and programs, and it did not promote cooperation among people working on the same project.
        The UNIX time-sharing system provided three major
improvements over single-user, batch systems. It allowed
more than one person to use the computer at a time (the UNIX
operating system is a   operating system), it allowed a person to communicate directly with the computer via
        The UNIX system was not the first interactive, mul-
tiuser operating system. An operating system named Multics
was in use briefly at Bell Labs before the UNIX operating
system was created. The Cambridge Multiple Access System had
been developed in Europe, and the Compatible Time Sharing
System (CTSS) had also been used for several years. The designers of the UNIX operating system took advantage of the
work that had gone into these and other operating systems
by incorporating the most desirable aspects of each of them.
needed a set of modern computing tools to help them with
their projects. The system allowed a group of people working
together on a project to share selected data and programs
while keeping other information private.
        Universities and colleges have played a major role
in furthering the popularity of the UNIX operating system
through the "four-year effect." When the UNIX operating sys-
to educational institutions at minimal cost. The schools,
in turn, used it in their computer science programs, ensur-
Because the UNIX system is such an advanced development system, the students became acclimated to a sophisticated programming environment. As these students graduated and went
into industry, they expected to work in a similarly advanced
environment. As more of these students worked their way up
in the commercial world, the UNIX operating system found its
way into industry.
        In addition to introducing its students to the UNIX
operating system, the Computer Systems Research Group at the
University of California at Berkeley made significant additions and changes to it. They made so many popular changes
that one of the two most prominent versions of the system
in use today is called the Berkeley Software Distribution
(BSD) of the UNIX system. The other major version is AT&T's
UNIX System V. This book covers the features commonly found
on BSD systems and systems derived from Berkeley UNIX, in
particular SunOS.
It is this heritage—development in a research environment

Figure 8-7   Moving the Cursor by (CONTROL) *Characters*

The Replace Commands

The **R** and **r** commands cause the new text you enter to overwrite (replace) existing text. The single character you enter following an **r** command over-writes the current character. After you enter that character, **vi** automatically returns to Command Mode. You do not need to press the (ESCAPE) key.

The **R** command causes *all* subsequent characters to overwrite existing text until you press (ESCAPE) to return **vi** to Command Mode.

CAUTION

These commands may appear to behave strangely if you replace (TAB) characters. (TAB) characters can appear as several (SPACE)s—until you try to replace them. They are actually only one character and will be re-placed by a single character. Refer to "Invisible Characters," page 204, for information on how to display (TAB)s as visible characters.

OPTIONAL

The Quote Command

You can use the Quote command, (CONTROL)-**V**, while you are in Input Mode. The Quote command enables you to insert into your text characters that have special meanings to **vi**. Among these characters are (CONTROL)-**L** (or (CONTROL)-**R**), which redraws the screen; (CONTROL)-**W**, which backs the cursor up a word to the left; and (ESCAPE), which ends Input Mode.

To insert one of these characters into your text, type (CONTROL)-**V** and then the character. (CONTROL)-**V** quotes the single character that follows it. For example, to insert the sequence (ESCAPE)[2J into a file you are creating in **vi**, you type the character sequence (CONTROL)-**V** (ESCAPE)[2J. This is the character sequence that clears the screen of a DEC VT-100 terminal. Although you would not ordinarily want to type this sequence into a document, you might want to use it or another (ESCAPE) sequence in a shell script you are creating in **vi**. Refer to Chapters 10, 11, and 12 for information about writing shell scripts.

Command Mode—Deleting and Changing Text

The Undo Commands

The Undo command, **u**, undoes what you just did. It restores text that you deleted or changed by mistake. The Undo command restores only the most recently deleted text. If you delete a line and then change a word, Undo restores only the changed word—not the deleted line. The **U** command restores the current line to the way it was before you started changing it, even after several changes.

The Delete Character Command

The **x** command deletes the current character. You can precede the **x** command by a Repeat Factor to delete several characters on the current line, starting with the current character. A Repeat Factor specifies the number of times a command is performed.

The Delete Command

The **d** command removes text from the Work Buffer. The amount of text that **d** removes depends on the Repeat Factor and the Unit of Measure you enter after the **d**. After the text is deleted, **vi** is still in Command Mode.

A list of some Delete commands follows. Each of the commands, except the last group that starts with **dd**, deletes *from* the current character.

CAUTION

The command **d** (RETURN) deletes two lines: the current line and the following one. Use the **dd** command to delete just the current line, or precede **dd** by a Repeat Factor to delete several lines.

Delete Command	Action
d0	Delete to beginning of line.
dw	Delete to end of word.
d3w	Delete to end of third word.
db	Delete to beginning of word.
dW	Delete to end of blank delimited word.
dB	Delete to beginning of blank delimited word.
d7B	Delete to seventh previous beginning of blank delimited word.
d)	Delete to end of sentence.
d4)	Delete to end of fourth sentence.
d(	Delete to beginning of sentence.
d}	Delete to end of paragraph.
d{	Delete to beginning of paragraph.
d7{	Delete to seventh paragraph preceding beginning of paragraph.
dd	Delete the current line.
d7{	Delete to seventh paragraph preceding beginning of paragraph.
dd	Delete the current line.
5dd	Delete five lines starting with the current line.
dL	Delete through last line on screen.
dH	Delete through first line on screen.
dG	Delete through end of Work Buffer.
d1G	Delete through beginning of Work Buffer.

The Change Command

The **c** command replaces existing text with new text. The new text does not have to occupy the same space as the existing text. You can change a word to several words, a line to several lines, or a paragraph to a single character.

The Change command deletes the amount of text specified by the Unit of Measure that follows it and puts **vi** in Input Mode. When you finish entering the new text and press (ESCAPE), the old word, line, sentence, or paragraph is changed to the new one.

When you change less than a line of text, **vi** does not delete the text immediately. Instead, the **c** command places a dollar sign at the end of the text that it will change and leaves **vi** in Input Mode. You may appear to overwrite text, but only the text that precedes the dollar sign changes in the Work Buffer. Other text remains in the Work Buffer and will be redisplayed when you press (ESCAPE). When you change a line or more, **vi** deletes the lines as soon as you give the Change command.

A list of some Change commands follows. Each of the commands, except the last two, changes text *from* the current character.

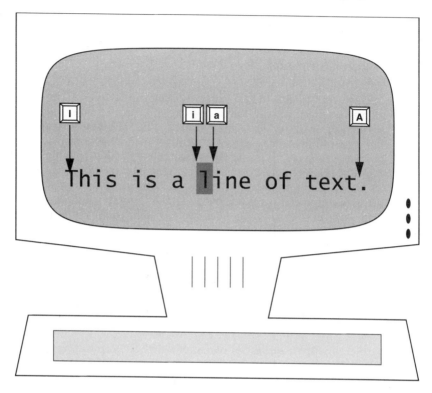

Figure 8-8   The i, I, a, and A Commands

Change Command	Action
cw	Change to end of word.
c3w	Change to end of third word.
cb	Change to beginning of word.
cW	Change to end of blank delimited word.
cB	Change to beginning of blank delimited word.
c7B	Change to beginning of seventh previous blank delimited word.
c)	Change to end of sentence.
c4)	Change to end of fourth sentence.
c(	Change to beginning of sentence.
c}	Change to end of paragraph.
c{	Change to beginning of paragraph.
c7{	Change to beginning of seventh preceding paragraph.
cc	Change the current line.
5cc	Change five lines starting with the current line.

Searching for a String

The Search Commands

The **vi** editor will search backward or forward through the Work Buffer to find a specific string of text. To find the next occurrence of a string (forward), press the forward slash (/) key, enter the text you want to find (called the *Search String*), and press (RETURN). When you press the slash key, **vi** displays a slash on the status line. As you enter the string of text, it too is displayed on the status line. When you press (RETURN), **vi** searches for the string. If **vi** finds the string, it positions the cursor on the first character of the string. If you use a question mark (?) in place of the forward slash, **vi** searches for the previous occurrence of the string. If you need to include a forward slash in a forward search or a question mark in a backward search, you must quote it by preceding it with a backslash (\).

The N and **n** keys repeat the last search without the need for you to enter the Search String again. The **n** key repeats the original search exactly, and the N key repeats the search in the opposite direction of the original search.

Normally, if you are searching forward and **vi** does not find the Search String before it gets to the end of the Work Buffer, it will *wrap around* and continue the search at the beginning of the Work Buffer. During a backward search, **vi** will wrap around from the beginning of the Work Buffer to the end. Also, **vi** normally performs case-sensitive searches. Refer to "Wrap Scan" (page 204) and "Ignore Case in Searches" (page 204) for information about how to change these search parameters.

Special Characters in Search Strings

Because the Search String is a regular expression (refer to Appendix A), some characters take on a special meaning within the Search String. The following paragraphs list some of these characters. The first two (^ and $) always have their special meaning (unless you quote them–page 191), and the rest can have their special meaning turned off by a single command. Refer to "Allow Special Characters in Searches," page 204.

The Beginning-of-Line Indicator (^)   When the first character in a Search String is a caret or circumflex, it matches the beginning of a line. The command /^the finds the next line that begins with the string the.

The End-of-Line Indicator ($)   Similarly, a dollar sign matches the end of a line. The command /!$ finds the next line that ends with an exclamation point.

The Any Character Indicator (.)   A period matches *any* character, anywhere in the Search String. The command /l..e finds line, followed, like, included, all memory, or any other word or character string that contains an l followed by any two characters and an e. To search for an actual period, use a backslash to quote the period (\.).

The End-of-Word Indicator (\>)   This pair of characters matches the end of a word. The command /s\> finds the next word that ends with an s. Notice that, whereas a backslash (\) is typically used to *turn off* the special meaning of a character, the character sequence \> has a special meaning, and > alone does not.

The Beginning-of-Word Indicator (\<)   This pair of characters matches the beginning of a word. The command /\<**The** finds the next word that begins with **The**. The Beginning-of-Word Indicator uses the backslash in the same, atypical way as the End-of-Word Indicator.

The Character Class Definition ([ ])   Square brackets surrounding two or more characters match any *single* character located between the brackets. The command /**dis[ck]** finds the next occurrence of *either* disk or disc.

There are two special characters you can use within a character class definition. A caret (^) as the first character following the left bracket defines the character class to be *any but the following characters*. A hyphen between two characters indicates a range of characters. Refer to the examples below.

Command	Result
/and	Finds the next occurrence of the string and **Examples:** sand, and, standard, slander, andiron
/\<and\>	Finds the next occurrence of the word and **Example:** and
/^The	Finds the next line that starts with The Examples: The... There...
/^[0-9][0-9]	Finds the next line that starts with a two-digit number followed by a right parenthesis. Examples: 77)... 01)... 15)...
/\<[adr]	Finds the next word that starts with an a, d, or r **Examples:** apple, drive, road, argument, right.

Substituting One String for Another

A Substitute command is a combination of a Search command and a Change command. It searches for a string just as the / command does, allowing the same special characters that the previous section discussed. When it finds a string, the Substitute command changes it. The format of the Substitute command is shown below. As with all commands that begin with a colon, **vi** executes a Substitute command from the status line.

:[address]s/search-string/replace-string[/g]

The next sections discuss the **address**, **s** command, **search-string**, **replace-string**, and **g** flag.

The Substitute Address   If you do not specify an address, Substitute searches only the current line. If you use a single line number as the address, Substitute searches that line. If the address is two line numbers separated by a comma, Substitute searches those lines and the lines between. Refer to "Line Numbers," page 203, if you want **vi** to display line numbers.

Within the address, a period represents the current line, and a dollar sign represents the last line in the Work Buffer. In many versions of **vi**, a percent sign represents the entire Work Buffer. You can perform address arithmetic using plus and minus signs. Some examples of addresses are shown in the following list.

Address	Portion of Work Buffer Addressed
5	Line 5
77,100	Lines 77 through 100 inclusive
1,.	The beginning of the Work Buffer through the current line.
.,$	The current line through the end of the Work Buffer.
1,$	The entire Work Buffer.
%	The entire Work Buffer (in some versions of **vi** only).
.,.+10	The current line through the tenth following line (eleven lines in all).

The Search and Replace Strings   An **s**, indicating that a Substitute command follows, comes after the address. A delimiter, marking the beginning of the Search String, follows the **s**. Although the examples in this book use a forward slash, you can use any character that is not a letter or number as a delimiter. You must use the same delimiter at the end of the Search String.

Next comes the Search String. It has the same format as the Search String in the / command and can include the same special characters. (The Search String is a regular expression; refer to Appendix A for more information.) Another delimiter marks the end of the Search String and the beginning of the Replace String. The Replace String is the string that will replace the Search String. The only special characters in the Replace String are the ampersand (&), which represents the text that was matched by the Search String, and the backslash, which quotes the character following it. Refer to the following examples and Appendix A.

To replace only the *first occurrence* of the Search String on each line within the specified address, press the (RETURN) or (ESCAPE) key after you enter the Replace String. If you want a *global* substitution—that is, if you want to replace *all* occurrences of the Search String on all addressed lines—enter a third delimiter (/) and a **g** (for *global*) before you press (RETURN) or (ESCAPE).

Command	Result
s/bigger/biggest	Replaces the string bigger on the current line with biggest Example: bigger → biggest
1,.s/Ch 1/Ch 2/g	Replaces every occurrence of the string Ch 1, before or on the current line, with Ch 2 Examples: Ch 1 → Ch 2 Ch 12 → Ch 22
:1,$s/ten/10/g	Replaces every occurrence of the string ten by the string 10 Examples: ten → 10 often → of10 tenant → 10ant
:1,$s/\<ten\>/10/g	Replaces every occurrence of the word ten by the string 10 Examples: ten → 10
:.,.+10s/every/each/g	Replaces every occurrence of the string every by the string each on the current line through the tenth following line Examples: every → each everything → eachthing

Miscellaneous Commands

The Join Command

The Join command, **J**, joins two lines of text. **J** joins the line below the current line to the end of the current line. It inserts a (SPACE) between what was previously two lines and leaves the cursor on this (SPACE). If the current line ends with a period, exclamation point, or question mark, **vi** inserts two (SPACE)s.

You can always "unjoin" (break) a line into two lines by replacing the (SPACE) or (SPACE)s where you want to break the line with a (RETURN).

The Status Command

The Status command, (CONTROL)-**G**, displays the name of the file you are editing, the line number of the current line, the total number of lines in the Work Buffer, and the percent of the Work Buffer preceding the current line.

The . Command

The . (period) command repeats the most recent command that made a change. If, for example, you had just given a **d2w** command (delete the next two words), the . command would delete the next two words. If you had just inserted text, the . command would repeat the insertion of the same text.

This command is useful if you want to change some, but not all, occurrences of a word or phrase in the Work Buffer. Search for the first occurrence of the word (use /), then make the change you want (use **cw**). Following these two commands, you can use **n** to search for the next occurrence of the word and . to make the same change to it. If you do not want to make the change, use **n** again to find the next occurrence.

The Put, Delete, and Yank Commands

The **vi** editor has a General-Purpose Buffer and 26 Named Buffers that can hold text during an editing session. These buffers are useful if you want to move or copy a portion of text to another location in the Work Buffer. A combination of the Delete and Put commands removes text from one location in the Work Buffer and places it in another. The Yank and Put commands copy text to another location in the Work Buffer without changing the original text.

The General-Purpose Buffer

The **vi** editor stores the text that you most recently changed, deleted, or yanked (see following) in the General-Purpose Buffer. The Undo command uses the General-Purpose Buffer when it restores text.

The Put Commands

The Put commands, **P** and **p**, copy text from the General-Purpose Buffer into the Work Buffer.

If you delete or yank characters or words into the General-Purpose Buffer, **P** inserts them before the current *character,* and **p** inserts them after. If you delete or yank lines, sentences, or paragraphs, **P** inserts the contents of the General-Purpose Buffer before the *line* the cursor is on, and **p** inserts it after.

The Put commands do not destroy the contents of the General-Purpose Buffer, so it is possible to place the same text at several points within the file by using one Delete or Yank command and several Put commands.

Because **vi** has only one General-Purpose Buffer and **vi** changes the contents of this buffer each time you give a Change, Delete, or Yank command, **you can use only cursor positioning commands between a Delete or Yank command and the corresponding Put command.** Any other commands change the contents of the General-Purpose Buffer and therefore change the results of the Put command. If you do not plan to use the Put command immediately after a Delete or Yank, you should use a Named Buffer rather than the General-Purpose Buffer (see "The Named Buffers," on the next page).

The Delete Commands

Any of the Delete commands that were described earlier in this chapter (page 191) automatically places the deleted text in the General-Purpose Buffer. Just as you can use the Undo command to put the deleted text back where it came from, you can use a Put command to put the deleted text at another location in the Work Buffer.

For example, if you delete a word from the middle of a sentence using the **dw** command and then move the cursor to a (SPACE) between two words and give a **p** command, **vi** will place the word you just deleted at the new location. Or, if you delete a line using the **dd** command and then move the cursor to the line *below* the line where you want the deleted line to appear and give a **P** command, **vi** will place the line at the new location.

The Yank Commands

The Yank commands are identical to the Delete commands, except that they do not delete text from the Work Buffer. The **vi** editor places a *copy* of the yanked text in the General-Purpose Buffer, so that you can use Put to place another copy of it elsewhere in the Work Buffer. Use the Yank command, y, just as you use **d**, the Delete command.

> **CAUTION**
>
> Just as **d** (RETURN) deletes two lines, **y** (RETURN) yanks two lines. Use the **yy** command to yank the current line. For example, if you yank three lines by using a **3yy** command and then move the cursor to the line *above* the line where you want a copy of the yanked lines to appear and give a **p** command, **vi** will copy the lines to the new location.

OPTIONAL

The Named Buffers

You can use a Named Buffer with any of the Delete, Yank, or Put commands. There are 26 Named Buffers, each named by a letter of the alphabet. Each Named Buffer can store a different block of text so that you can recall each block as needed. Unlike the General-Purpose Buffer, **vi** does not change the contents of a Named Buffer unless you use a command that specifically overwrites that buffer. The **vi** editor maintains the contents of the Named Buffers throughout an editing session.

The **vi** editor stores text in a Named Buffer if you precede a Delete or Yank command with a double quotation mark (") and a buffer name (e.g., "**kyy** yanks a copy of the current line into buffer **k**). You can use a Named Buffer in two ways. If you give the name of the buffer as a lowercase letter, **vi** overwrites the contents of the buffer when it deletes or yanks text into the buffer. If you use an uppercase letter, **vi** appends the newly deleted or yanked text to the end of the buffer. This feature enables you to collect blocks of text from various sections of a file and then deposit them at one place in the file with a single command. Named Buffers are also useful when you are moving a section of a file and do not want to use Put immediately after the corresponding Delete, and when you want to insert a paragraph, sentence, or phrase repeatedly in a document.

If you have one sentence that you will be using throughout a document, you can yank the sentence into a Named Buffer and put it wherever you need it by using the following procedure. After inserting the first occurrence of the sentence and pressing (ESCAPE) to return to Command Mode, leave the cursor on the line containing the sentence. (The sentence must appear on a line or lines by itself for this procedure to work.) Then yank the sentence into buffer **a** by giving a **"ayy** command (or **"a2yy** if the sentence takes up two lines). Now, as you are entering text, any time you need the sentence, you can return to Command Mode and give the command **"ap** to put a copy of the sentence below the line the cursor is on.

This technique provides a quick and easy way to insert text that you use frequently in a document. For example, if you were editing a legal document, you might use a Named Buffer to store the phrase The Plaintiff alleges that the Defendant to save yourself the trouble of typing it in every time you want to use it. Similarly, if you were creating a letter that frequently used a long company name, such as National Standards Institute, you might put it into a Named Buffer.

Reading and Writing Files

The **vi** editor reads a disk file into the Work Buffer when you call **vi** from the shell. The ZZ command that terminates the editing session writes the contents of the Work Buffer back to the disk file. This section discusses other ways of reading text into the Work Buffer and writing it out.

The Read Command

The Read command reads a file into the Work Buffer. The new file does not overwrite any text in the Work Buffer but is positioned following the single address (or the current line if you do not specify an address). You can use an address of 0 to read the file into the beginning of the Work Buffer. The format of the Read command follows:

:[address]r [filename]

As with other commands that begin with a colon, when you enter the colon, it appears on the status line. The **filename** is the pathname of the file that you want to read and must be terminated by (RETURN). If you omit the **filename**, **vi** reads the file you are editing from the disk.

The Write Command

The Write command writes part or all of the Work Buffer to a file. You can use an address to write out part of the Work Buffer and a filename to specify a file to receive the text. If you do not use an address or filename, **vi** writes the entire contents of the Work Buffer to the file you are editing, updating the file on the disk.

During a long editing session, it is a good idea to use the Write command occasionally. Then, if a problem develops, a recent copy of the Work Buffer is safe on the disk. If you use a **:q!** command to exit from **vi**, the disk file will reflect the version of the Work Buffer at the time you last used the Write command. The formats of the Write command follow:

> :[address]w[!] [filename]
> :[address]w>> filename

You can use the second format of the Write command to append text to an existing file. The next sections discuss the components of the Write command.

The Address   If you use an address, it specifies the portion of the Work Buffer that you want **vi** to write to the disk. The address follows the form of the address that the Substitute command uses. If you do not use an address, **vi** writes out the entire contents of the Work Buffer.

The w and !   Because Write can quickly destroy a large amount of work, **vi** demands that you enter an exclamation point following the **w** as a safeguard against accidentally overwriting a file. The only times you do not need an exclamation point are when you are writing out the entire contents of the Work Buffer to the file being edited (using no address, no filename) and when you are writing part or all of the Work Buffer to a new file. When you are writing part of the file to the file being edited, or when you are overwriting another file, you must use an exclamation point.

The Filename   The optional filename is the pathname of the file you are writing to. If you do not specify a filename, **vi** writes to the file you are editing.

Identifying the Current File

The File command identifies the file you are currently editing in the Work Buffer. The filename the File command identifies is the one the Write command uses if you give a :w command (rather than :w **filename**). The File command follows:

> :f

The File command displays the filename, the current line number, the number of lines in the Work Buffer, and the percentage of the Work Buffer that is above the current line. The File command also displays [Modified] if the Work Buffer has been changed since the last time it was written to disk. An example of the display produced by the File command follows:

```
"practice" [Modified] line 6 of 8 --75%--
```

Setting Parameters

You can adapt **vi** to your needs and habits by setting **vi** parameters. These parameters perform many functions, such as displaying line numbers, automatically inserting (RETURN)s for you, and establishing nonstandard searches.

You can set parameters in several different ways. You can set them while you are using **vi**, to establish the environment for the current editing session. Alternatively, you can set the parameters in your **.profile** (Bourne and Korn Shells) or **.login** (C Shell) file or in a startup file that **vi** uses, **.exrc**. When you set the parameters in any of those three files, each time you use **vi** the environment has been established, and you can begin editing immediately.

Setting Parameters from vi

To set a parameter while you are using **vi**, enter a colon (:), the word **set**, a (SPACE), and the parameter (see the "Parameters" section, following). The command appears on the status line as you type it and takes effect when you press (RETURN).

Setting Parameters in a Startup File

If you are using the Bourne or Korn Shell, you can set **vi** parameters by putting the following lines in the **.profile** file in your home directory:

    EXINIT='set param1 param2 . . .'
    export EXINIT

Replace **param1** and **param2** with parameters selected from the list in the next section. **EXINIT** is a variable that **vi** reads.

If you are using the C Shell, put the following line in the **.login** file in your home directory:

    setenv EXINIT 'set param1 param2 . . .'

Again, replace **param1** and **param2** with parameters from the following section.

Instead of setting **vi** parameters in your **.login** or **.profile** file, you can create a **.exrc** file and set them there. If you set the parameters in a **.exrc** file, use the following format:

    set param1 param2 . . .

When you start **vi**, it looks for a **.exrc** file in your current directory. If it does not find one there, it looks in your home directory. If you set parameters in your **.profile** or **.login** file, as well as in **.exrc**, the parameters in **.exrc** will take precedence since **.exrc** is executed later than **.profile** and **.login**.

Parameters

This section contains a list of some of the most useful **vi** parameters. The **vi** editor displays a complete list of parameters and how they are currently set when you give the command **:set all** followed by a (RETURN) while using **vi**.

Because **vi** looks for a .exrc file in your current directory and then in your home directory, you can use several .exrc files to customize your environment for editing different kinds of files. For example, you could set the parameters you like to use for most editing tasks in a .exrc file in your home directory. For special editing tasks, such as creating program source code or writing a long article, you could put a .exrc file in the directory you use when working on that task. When you start **vi** from a directory with a .exrc file in it, **vi** will execute the .exrc file in that directory. Whenever you start **vi** from a directory that does not have a .exrc file, **vi** will execute the .exrc file in your home directory.

Line Numbers   The **vi** editor does not normally display the line number associated with each line. To display line numbers, set the parameter **number**. To cause line numbers not to be displayed, set the parameter **nonumber**.

Line numbers—whether displayed or not—are not part of the file, are not stored with the file, and are not displayed when the file is printed. They only appear on the screen while you are using **vi**.

Line Wrap Margin   The line wrap margin causes **vi** to break the text that you are inserting at approximately the specified number of characters from the right margin. The **vi** editor breaks the text by inserting a (NEWLINE) character at the closest blank delimited word boundary. Setting the line wrap margin is handy if you want all your text lines to be about the same length. It relieves you of the burden of remembering to press (RETURN) after each line of input.

Set the parameter **wrapmargin=nn**, where **nn** is the number of characters *from the right side of the screen* where you want **vi** to break the text. This number is not the column width of the text but the distance from the end of the text to the right edge of the screen. Setting the wrap margin to 0 (zero) turns this feature off. By default, **vi** sets the wrap margin to 0.

Shell   While you are in **vi**, you can cause **vi** to spawn a new shell. You can either create an interactive shell (if you want to run several commands) or run a single command. The **shell** parameter determines what shell **vi** will invoke. By default, **vi** sets the **shell** parameter to your login shell. To change it, set the parameter **shell=pathname**, where **pathname** is the full pathname of the shell you want to use.

Show Mode   The **vi** editor does not normally give you a visual cue to let you know when it is in Input Mode. On some versions of **vi**, however, you can set the parameter **showmode** to display the mode at the lower right of the screen when **vi** is in Input Mode. There are three types of Input Mode: OPEN, INSERT, and APPEND. Set **noshowmode** to cause **vi** not to display the message. This parameter is not available on all versions of **vi**.

Flash   The **vi** editor normally causes the terminal to beep when you give an invalid command or press (ESCAPE) when you are in Command Mode. Setting the parameter **flash** causes the terminal to flash instead of beep. Set **noflash** to cause it to beep. This parameter is not available on all versions of **vi**.

Ignore Case in Searches   The **vi** editor normally performs case-sensitive searches, differentiating between uppercase and lowercase letters. It performs case-insensitive searches when you set the **ignorecase** parameter. Set **noignorecase** to restore case-sensitive searches.

Allow Special Characters in Searches   Each of the following characters and character pairs normally has a special meaning when you use it within a Search String. Refer to "Special Characters in Search Strings," page 194.

.   \<   \>   [   ]

When you set the **nomagic** parameter, these characters no longer have special meanings. The **magic** parameter gives them back their special meanings.

The ^ and $ characters always have a special meaning within Search Strings, regardless of how you set this parameter.

Invisible Characters   To cause **vi** to display (TAB)s as ^I and to mark the end of each line with a $, set the parameter **list**. To display (TAB)s as white space and not mark ends of lines, set **nolist**.

Wrap Scan   Normally, when a search for the next occurrence of a Search String reaches the end of the Work Buffer, **vi** continues the search at the beginning of the Work Buffer. The reverse is true of a search for the previous occurrence of a Search String. The **nowrapscan** parameter stops the search at either end of the Work Buffer. Set the **wrapscan** parameter if you want searches to once again wrap around the ends of the Work Buffer.

Automatic Indention   The automatic indention feature works with the **shiftwidth** parameter to provide a regular set of indentions for programs or tabular material. This feature is normally off. You can turn it on by setting **autoindent** (or **ai**) and turn it off by setting **noautoindent** (or **noai**).

When automatic indention is on and **vi** is in Input Mode, (CONTROL)-**T** moves the cursor from the left margin (or an indention) to the next indention position, (RETURN) moves the cursor to the left side of the next line under the first character of the previous line, and (CONTROL)-**D** backs up over indention positions. The (CONTROL)-**T** and (CONTROL)-**D** characters function in a manner analogous to (TAB) and (SHIFT)(TAB) keys, but they function only before text is placed on a line.

Shift Width   The **shiftwidth** parameter controls the functioning of (CONTROL)-**T** and (CONTROL)-**D** in Input Mode when automatic indention is on. Set the parameter **shiftwidth=nn**, where **nn** is the spacing of the indention positions. Setting the shift width is similar to setting the (TAB) stops on a typewriter; however, with **shiftwidth** the distance between (TAB) stops is always constant.

Advanced Editing Techniques

This section presents several commands that you may find useful once you have become comfortable using **vi**.

Using Markers

While you are using **vi**, you can set and use as many as 26 markers. Set a marker by giving the command **ma**, where **a** is any letter from **a** to z. Once you have set a marker, you can use it in a manner similar to a line number. The **vi** editor does not preserve markers when you stop editing a file.

You can move the cursor to a marker by preceding the marker name with a single quotation mark. For example, to set marker **t**, position the cursor on the line you want to mark, and give the command **mt**. Unless you reset marker **t** or delete the line it marks, during this editing session you can return to the line you marked with the command **'t**.

You can delete all text from the current line to marker **r** with the following command:

    d'r

You can use markers in addresses of commands in place of line numbers. The following command will replace all occurrences of The with THE on all lines from marker **m** to the current line (marker **m** must precede the current line):

    :'m,.s/The/THE/g

Editing Other Files

The following command causes **vi** to edit the file you specify with **filename**:

    :e[!] [filename]

If you want to save the contents of the Work Buffer, you must write it out (using **:w**) before you give this command. If you do not want to save the contents of the Work Buffer, **vi** insists that you use an exclamation point to show that you know that you will lose the work you did since the last time you wrote out the Work Buffer. If you do not supply a **filename**, **vi** edits the same file you are currently working on.

You can give the command **:e!** to start an editing session over again. This command returns the Work Buffer to the state it was in the last time you wrote it out, or, if you have not written it out, the state it was in when you started editing the file. This is useful when you make mistakes editing a file and decide that it would be easier to start over than to fix the mistakes.

OPTIONAL Continued

Because this command does not destroy the contents of the Named Buffers, you can store text from one file in a Named Buffer, use a :e command to edit a second file, and put text from the Named Buffer in the second file. A :e command does destroy the contents of the General-Purpose Buffer and any markers you have sent.

Executing Shell Commands from vi

You can execute shell commands in several ways while you are using **vi**. You can create a new, interactive shell by giving the following command and pressing (RETURN):

   : sh

The **shell** parameter determines what kind of shell is created (usually a Bourne, C, or Korn Shell). By default, **shell** is the same as your login shell.

After you have done what you want to do in the shell, you can return to **vi** by exiting from the shell (press (CONTROL)-**D** or give the command **exit**).

CAUTION

When you create a new shell in this manner, you must remember that you are still using **vi.** A common mistake is to start editing the same file from the new shell, forgetting that **vi** is already editing the file from a different shell. Because each invocation of **vi** uses a different Work Buffer, you will overwrite any work you did from the more recent invocation of **vi** when you finally get around to exiting from the original invocation of **vi** (assuming that you write the file to disk when you exit).

You can execute a shell command line from **vi** by giving the following command, replacing **command** with the command line you want to execute. Terminate the command with a (RETURN).

   : ! command

The **vi** editor will spawn a new shell that will execute the **command**. When the command runs to completion, the newly spawned shell will return control to the editor.

Users frequently use this feature to carry on a dialog with the **write** command. If Alex gets a message from Jenny while he is using **vi**, he can use the following command to write back to Jenny. After giving the command, Alex can carry on a dialog with Jenny in the same way he would if he had invoked **write** from the shell.

   : !write jenny

If Alex has modified the Work Buffer since he last wrote the file to disk, **vi** will display the following message before starting the **write** command:

[No write since last change]

When Alex finishes his dialog with Jenny, he presses (CONTROL)-**D** to terminate the **write** command. Then **vi** displays the following message:

[Hit return to continue]

When Alex presses (RETURN), he can continue his editing session in **vi**.

You can execute a command from **vi** and have **vi** replace the current line with the output from the command. If you do not want to replace any text, put the cursor on a blank line before giving the command.

! ! command

Nothing will happen when you enter the first exclamation point. When you enter the second one, **vi** will move the cursor to the status line and allow you to enter the command you want to execute. Because this command puts **vi** in Last Line Mode, you must end the command with a (RETURN).

Finally, you can execute a command from **vi** with the standard input to the command coming from all or part of the file you are editing and the standard output from the command replacing the input in the file you are editing. You can use this type of command to sort a list in place in a file you are working on.

To specify the block of text that is to become the standard input for the command, move the cursor to one end of the block of text. Then enter an exclamation point followed by a command that would normally move the cursor to the other end of the block of text. For example, if the cursor is at the beginning of the file and you want to specify the whole file, give the command !G. If you want to specify the part of the file between the cursor and marker **b**, you will give the command !'b. After you give the cursor movement command, **vi** will display an exclamation point on the status line and allow you to give a command.

For example, to sort a list of names in a file, move the cursor to the beginning of the list and set marker **q** with an **mq** command. Then move the cursor to the end of the list and give the following command:

! 'qsort

Press (RETURN) and wait. After a few moments, you will see the sorted list replace the original list on the screen. If the command did not do what you expected, you can undo the change with a **u** command.

Units of Measure

Many **vi** commands operate on a block of text—from a character to many paragraphs. You can specify the size of a block of text with a *Unit of Measure*. You can specify multiple Units of Measure by preceding a Unit of Measure with a number, called a Repeat Factor. This section defines the various Units of Measure.

Character

A character is one character, visible or not, printable or not, including (SPACE)s and (TAB)s. **Some examples of characters follow.**

a   q   A   .   5   R   –   >   (TAB)   (SPACE)

Word

A word is similar to an ordinary word in the English language. It is a string of one or more characters that is bounded on both sides by any combination of one or more of the following elements: a punctuation mark, (SPACE), (TAB), numeral, or (NEWLINE). In addition, **vi** considers each group of punctuation marks to be a word.

Word Count	Text
1	pear
2	pear!
2	pear!)
3	pear!) The
4	pear!) "The
11	This is a short, concise line (no frills).

Blank Delimited Word

A blank delimited word is the same as a word, except that it includes adjacent punctuation. Blank delimited words are separated from each other by one or more of the following elements: a (SPACE), (TAB), or (NEWLINE).

Blank Delimited Word Count	Text
1	pear
1	pear!
1	pear!)
2	pear!) The
2	pear!) "The
8	This is a short, concise line (no frills).

Line

A line is a string of characters bounded by (NEWLINE)s. It is not necessarily a single, physical line on the terminal. You can enter a very long single (logical) line that wraps around (continues on the next physical line) several times. It is a good idea, however, to avoid long logical lines by terminating lines with a (RETURN) before they reach the right side of the terminal screen. Terminating lines in this manner ensures that each physical line contains one logical line and avoids confusion when you edit and format text. Some commands do not *appear* to work properly on physical lines that are longer than the width of the screen. For example, with the cursor on a long logical line that wraps around several physical lines, pressing (RETURN) once will appear to move the cursor down more than one line.

Sentence

A sentence is an English sentence or the equivalent. A sentence starts at the end of the previous sentence and ends with a period, exclamation point, or question mark, followed by two (SPACE)s or a (NEWLINE).

Sentence Count	Text
One: only 1 (SPACE) after the first period - (NEWLINE) after the second period	That's it. This is one sentence.
Two: 2 (SPACE)s after the first period - (NEWLINE) after the second period	That's it. This is two sentences.
Three : 2 (SPACE)s after the first two question marks - (NEWLINE) after the exclamation point	What? Three sentences? One line!
One: (NEWLINE) after the period	This sentence takes up a total of three lines.

Paragraph

A paragraph is preceded and followed by one or more blank lines. A blank line is composed of two (NEWLINE) characters in a row.

Paragraph Count	Text
One: blank line before and after text	One paragraph
One: blank line before and after text	This may appear to be more than one paragraph. Just because there are two indentions does not mean it qualifies as two paragraphs.

(Continued)

Paragraph Count	Text
Three: 3 blocks of text separated by blank lines	Even though in English this is only one sentence, vi considers it to be three paragraphs.

Screen

The terminal screen is a window that opens onto part of the Work Buffer. You can position this window so that it shows different portions of the Work Buffer.

Repeat Factor

A number that precedes a Unit of Measure is a Repeat Factor. Just as the *5* in *5 inches* causes you to consider *5 inches* as a single unit of measure, a Repeat Factor causes **vi** to group more than one Unit of Measure and consider it as a single Unit of Measure. For example, the command **w** moves the cursor forward one word. The command **5w** moves the cursor forward five words, and **250w** moves it 250 words. If you do not specify a Repeat Factor, **vi** assumes that you mean one Unit of Measure.

SUMMARY

This summary of **vi** includes all the commands covered in this chapter, plus some additional ones.

Starting vi

Command	Function
vi filename	Edit **filename** starting at line1.
vi +n filename	Edit **filename** starting at line **n**.
vi + filename	Edit **filename** starting at the last line.
vi +/pattern filename	Edit **filename** starting at the first line containing **pattern**.
vi −r filename	Recover **filename** after a system crash.

Moving the Cursor by Units of Measure

You must be in Command Mode to use commands that move the cursor by Units of Measure. They are the Units of Measure that you can use in Change,

Delete, and Yank commands. Each of these commands can be preceded with a Repeat Factor.

Command	Moves the Cursor
(SPACE), l, or →	Space to the right
h or ←	Space to the left
w	Word to the right
W	Blank delimited word to the right
b	Word to the left
B	Blank delimited word to the left
$	End of line
e	End of word to the right
E	End of blank delimited word to the right
0	Beginning of line (cannot be used with a Repeat Factor)
(RETURN)	Beginning of next line
j or ↓	Down one line
−	Beginning of previous line
k or ↑	Up one line
)	End of sentence
(	Beginning of sentence
}	End of paragraph
{	Beginning of paragraph

Viewing Different Parts of the Work Buffer

Command	Moves the Cursor
(CONTROL)-D	Forward one-half screenful
(CONTROL)-U	Backward one-half screenful
(CONTROL)-F	Forward one screenful
(CONTROL)-B	Backward one screenful
nG	To line n (without n, to the last line)
H	To the top of screen
M	To the middle of screen
L	To the bottom of screen

Adding Text

All the following commands (except **r**) leave **vi** in Input Mode. You must press (ESCAPE) to return it to Command Mode.

Command	Insert Text
i	Before cursor
I	Before first nonblank character on line
a	After cursor
A	At end of line
o	Open a line below the current line.
O	Open a line above the current line.
r	Replace current character (no (ESCAPE) needed).
R	Replace characters, starting with current character (overwrite until (ESCAPE)).

Deleting and Changing Text

In the following list, **M** is a Unit of Measure that you can precede with a Repeat Factor. The **n** is a Repeat Factor.

Command	Effect
nx	Delete the number of characters specified by **n**, starting with the current character.
nX	Delete **n** characters before the current character, starting with the character preceding the current character.
dM	Delete text specified by **M**.
ndd	Delete the number of lines specified by **n**.
D	Delete to end of the line.

The following commands leave **vi** in Input Mode. You must press (ESCAPE) to return it to Command Mode.

Command	Effect
ns	Substitute the number of characters specified by **n**.
cM	Change text specified by **M**.
ncc	Change the number of lines specified by **n**.
C	Change to end of line.

Searching for a String

In the following list, **rexp** is a regular expression that can be a simple string of characters.

Command	Effect
/rexp(RETURN)	Search forward for **rexp**.
?rexp(RETURN)	Search backward for **rexp**.
n	Repeat original search exactly.
N	Repeat original search, opposite direction.
/(RETURN)	Repeat original search forward.
?(RETURN)	Repeat original search backward.

String Substitution

The format of a Substitute command follows:

:[address]s/search-string/replace-string[/g]

Element of Command	Contains
address	One line number or two line numbers separated by a comma. A . represents the current line, $ represents the last line, and % represents the entire file in some versions of **vi**. You can use a marker in place of a line number.
search-string	A regular expression that can be a simple string of characters.
replace-string	The replacement string.
g	Indicates a global replacement (more than one replacement per line).

Miscellaneous Commands

Command	Effect
J	Join the current line and the following line.
.	Repeat the most recent command that made a change.
:w filename	Write contents of Work Buffer to **filename** (to current file if there is no **filename**).
:q	Quit **vi**.
ZZ	Write contents of Work Buffer to the current file and quit **vi**.
:f or (CONTROL)-G	Display the filename, the status, the current line number, the number of lines in the Work Buffer, and the percent of the Work Buffer preceding the current line.
(CONTROL)-V	Insert the next character literally (use in Input Mode).
~	Change uppercase to lowercase and vice versa.

Yanking and Putting Text

In the following list, **M** is a Unit of Measure that you can precede with a Repeat Factor. The **n** is a Repeat Factor. You can precede any of these commands with the name of a buffer in the form of "x where **x** is the name of the buffer (**a–z**).

Command	Effect
yM	Yank text specified by **M**.
nyy	Yank the number of lines specified by **n**.
Y	Yank to end of line.
P	Put text before or above.
p	Put text after or below.

Advanced Commands

Command	Effect
mx	Set marker **x**, where **x** is a letter from **a** to **z**.
' '	Move cursor back to its previous location.
' x	Move cursor to marker **x**, where **x** is a letter from **a** to **z**.
:e! filename	Edit **filename**, discarding changes to current file (use :w first if you want to keep the changes).
:sh	Start a shell.
:!command	Start a shell and execute command.
!!command	Start a shell, execute a command, place output in file replacing the current line.

REVIEW EXERCISES

1. How can you cause **vi** to enter Input Mode? How can you make it revert to Command Mode?

2. What is the Work Buffer? Name two ways of writing the contents of the Work Buffer to the disk.

3. If you have a file that contains the following paragraph and the cursor is on the second tilde (~), how can you

   a. move the cursor to the end of the paragraph?

   b. move the cursor to the beginning of the word Unfortunately?

c. change the word `character` to `letter`?

> The vi editor has a command, tilde (~),
> that changes lowercase letters to
> uppercase and vice versa.
> Unfortunately, the ~ command does
> not work with a Unit of Measure or
> a Repeat Factor, so you have to change
> the case of one character at a time.

4. In **vi**, with the cursor positioned on the first letter of a word, give the command x followed by **p**. Explain what happens.

5. What are the differences between the following commands?

   a. **i** and **I**

   b. **a** and **A**

   c. **o** and **O**

   d. **r** and **R**

   e. **u** and **U**

6. What command would you use to search backward through the Work Buffer for lines that start with the word **it**?

7. What command will substitute all occurrences of the phrase **this week** with the phrase **next week**?

8. Consider the following scenario. You start **vi** to edit an existing file. You make many changes to the file and then realize that you deleted a critical section of the file early in your editing session. You want to get that section back, but you do not want to lose all the other changes you made. What would you do?

9. Consider the following scenario: Alex puts the following line in his **.login** file:

   ```
   setenv EXINIT 'set number wrapmargin=10 showmode'
   ```

   Then Alex creates a **.exrc** file in the directory **/home/alex/literature** with the following line in it:

   ```
   set nonumber
   ```

   What will the parameter settings be when Alex runs **vi** while the working directory is **/home/alex/bin**? What will they be when he runs **vi** from the directory **/home/alex/literature**? What will they be when he edits the file **/home/alex/literature/promo**?

10. What commands can you use to take a paragraph from one file and insert it in a second file?

11. Create a file that contains the following list, and then execute commands from within **vi** to sort the list and display it in two columns. (*Hint:*
See the **pr** command in Part II).

```
Command Mode
Input Mode
Last Line Mode
Work Buffer
General-Purpose Buffer
Named Buffer
Regular Expression
Search String
Replace String
Startup File
Repeat Factor
```

12. How do the Named Buffers differ from the General-Purpose Buffer?

CHAPTER 9

The emacs **Editor**

In 1956, the Lisp (LISt Processing) language was developed at MIT by John McCarthy. In its original conception, Lisp had only a few scalar (called atomic) data types and only one data structure, a list. Lists could contain atomic data or perhaps other lists. Lisp supported recursion and non-numeric data (exciting concepts in those Fortran and COBOL days) and, in the Cambridge culture at least, was once the favored implementation language. Richard Stallman and Guy Steele were part of this MIT Lisp culture, and in 1975 they collaborated on **emacs**.

About emacs

Initially, **emacs** was prototyped as a series of editor commands or macros for the late-1960s text editor TECO (Text Editor and COrrector). The acronymic name, Editor MACroS, reflects these beginnings, although there have been many humorous reinterpretations including (ESCAPE)(META)(ALT)(CONTROL)(SHIFT), Emacs Makes All Computing Simple, and the unkind translation Eight Megabytes And Constantly Swapping.

Since then, **emacs** has grown and evolved through more than twenty major revisions to the mainstream GNU version alone. The **emacs** editor is coded in C, and it contains a complete Lisp interpreter. It fully supports the X Window System and mouse interaction, and until very recently has been maintained by Stallman himself. The original TECO macros are long gone.

The **emacs** editor has always been considerably more than a text editor. Not having been developed originally in a UNIX envirnonment, **emacs** does not adhere to the UNIX philosophy. Where a UNIX utility is typically designed to do one thing and to be used in conjunction with other utilities, **emacs** is designed to "do it all." Because there is a programming language (Lisp) underlying it, emacs users tend to customize and extend the editor rather than to use existing utilities or create new general-purpose tools. Instead, they share their **.emacs** (customization) files.

 Well before the X Window System, Stallman put a great deal of thought and effort into designing a window-oriented work environment, and he used **emacs** as his research vehicle. Over time, he built facilities within **emacs** for reading and composing email messages, for giving shell commands, for compiling programs and analyzing error messages, for running and debugging these programs, and for playing games. Eventually, it became possible to enter the **emacs** environment and not come out all day, switching from window to window and from file to file. If you had only an ordinary, serial, character-based terminal, **emacs** gave you tremendous leverage.

In an X Window System envirnonment, **emacs** does not need to control the whole display, usually operating only one or two windows. However, part or all of the original work environment is still available for those who want to use it.

A *language-sensitive* editor, **emacs** has special features that you can turn on to help edit text, **nroff**, TeX, Lisp, C, Fortran, and so on. While these feature sets are called *modes*, they are not related in any way to the Command Mode and Input Mode found in **vi** and other editors. Because you never need to switch **emacs** between Input and Command Modes, **emacs** is called a *modeless* editor.

emacs **vs.** vi

Like **vi**, **emacs** is a display editor: it displays the text you are editing on the screen, and changes the display as you type each command or insert new text.

Unlike **vi**, **emacs** does not require you to keep track of whether you are in Command Mode or Insert Mode: commands always use a (CONTROL) or other special key. The **emacs** editor always inserts ordinary characters.

This is called *modeless* editing, and for many people, it is convenient and natural.

As in **vi**, you edit a file in a work area, or *buffer,* and have the option of writing this buffer back to the file on the disk when you are finished. With **emacs**, however, you can have many work buffers, changing among them without having to write out and read back in. Furthermore, you can display multiple buffers at one time, each in its own window. This is often helpful in cut and paste operations or to keep C declarations in one window while editing related code in another part of the file in another window.

Like **vi**, **emacs** has a rich, extensive command set for moving about in the buffer and altering text, but in **emacs** this command set is not "cast in concrete." You can change or customize commands at any time. Literally any key can be coupled, or *bound,* to any command, to better match a particular keyboard or just to fulfill a personal whim. Usually key bindings are set in the .emacs startup file, but they can also be changed interactively during a session. All the key bindings described in this chapter are standard on GNU **emacs** version 18.59. Although version 19 added many visual, mouse-oriented capabilities, all of the commands described in this chapter still work with the new version.

> **CAUTION**
>
> If you change too many key bindings, you can easily produce a command set that you will not remember, or that will make it impossible for you to get back to the standard bindings again in the same session.

Finally, and *very* unlike **vi**, **emacs** allows you to use Lisp to write new commands or override old ones. Stallman calls this feature *on-line extensibility,* but it would take a gutsy Lisp guru to write and debug a new command while editing live text. It's much more common to add a few extra debugged commands to the .emacs file where they will be loaded automatically when **emacs** starts up.

Getting Started

The **emacs** editor has many, many features and there are many ways to use it. Its complete manual had 29 chapters *before* the X window upgrade in Version 19. However, you can do a considerable amount of meaningful work with a relatively small subset of the commands. This section describes a simple editing session, explaining how to start and exit from **emacs**, and how to move the cursor and delete text. It postpones or simplifies some issues in the interest of clarity.

Starting emacs

To edit a file named **sample**, type the shell command:

```
$ emacs -q sample
```

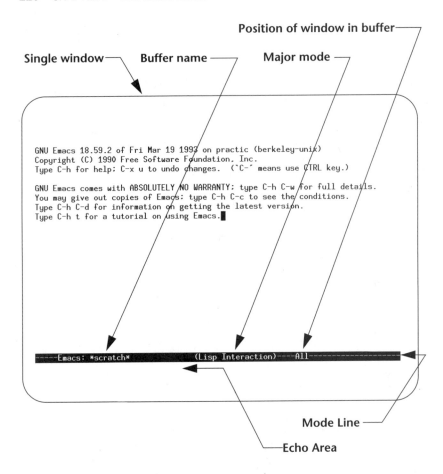

Position of window in buffer

Single window ¬   Buffer name ¬   Major mode ¬

```
GNU Emacs 18.59.2 of Fri Mar 19 1993 on practic (berkeley-unix)
Copyright (C) 1990 Free Software Foundation, Inc.
Type C-h for help; C-x u to undo changes.  (`C-' means use CTRL key.)

GNU Emacs comes with ABSOLUTELY NO WARRANTY; type C-h C-w for full details.
You may give out copies of Emacs; type C-h C-c to see the conditions.
Type C-h C-d for information on getting the latest version.
Type C-h t for a tutorial on using Emacs.█
```

`----Emacs: *scratch*            (Lisp Interaction)----All----------------`

Mode Line ¬

Echo Area

Figure 9-1   An Empty Window for a New File

This command starts **emacs**, reads the file named **sample** into a buffer, and displays its contents on the screen. If there is no file by this name, it displays a blank screen with New File at the bottom (Figure 9-1). The **−q** option tells emacs *not* to read the **.emacs** startup file from your home directory. This will guarantee that you get standard uncustomized behavior, and is sometimes useful for beginners or for other users wanting to bypass a .emacs file.

The screen starts out with a single *window*. At the bottom of this window is a reverse-video title bar called the *Mode Line*. The Mode Line, at a minimum, shows the name of the buffer that the window is viewing, whether the buffer has been changed, what major and minor modes are in effect, and how far down the buffer the window is currently positioned. When you have more than one window, there is one Mode Line in each window. At the bottom of the screen **emacs** leaves a single line open called the *Echo Area* or *Minibuffer*. This line is for short messages and special one-line commands.

There is a cursor in the window or Minibuffer. All the input and nearly all the editing takes place at the cursor. As you type ordinary characters, **emacs** inserts them at the cursor position. If there are characters under the cursor or to its right, they get pushed over as you type, so that no characters are lost.

Stopping emacs

The command to exit from **emacs** is the two-key sequence (CONTROL)-**X** (CONTROL)-**C**. You can give this command at any time. It will stop **emacs** gracefully, asking you if you wish to save the changes you made during the editing session.

If you want to cancel a half-typed command or stop a running command before it is done, you can *quit* by typing (CONTROL)-**G**. The **emacs** editor displays Quit in the Echo Area and waits for your next command.

If you quickly type (CONTROL)-**G** two times or more, **emacs** enters the *Emergency Escape* sequence and asks two questions:

Auto-save? (y or n)
Abort (and dump core)? (y or n)

If you answer **y** to the first question **emacs** will save each modified buffer to a new file (named **#filename#**) in the original file's parent directory. If you answer **y** to the second question, **emacs** will abort and produce a core image (a file named **core**, which you should probably remove). You will be left at the shell prompt, unable to return to your former **emacs** session. If you get into Emergency Escape by accident, answer **n** to both questions and **emacs** will wait for another command.

Inserting Text

Typing an ordinary (printing) character pushes the cursor and any characters to the right of the cursor one position to the right and inserts the new character in the position just opened. Backspacing pulls the cursor and any characters to the right of the cursor one position to the left, erasing the character that was there before.

CAUTION

With standard default key bindings, you backspace with the (CONTROL)-**D** key while the backspace key ((CONTROL)-**H**) is bound to the on-line help function (page 232). For the moment it is easiest to backspace with (DELETE).

The (RETURN) key inserts an invisible end-of-line character in the buffer, and returns the cursor to the left margin, one line down.

Start **emacs** and type a few lines of text. If you make a mistake, back up using (DELETE). It is possible to back up past the start of a line and up to the end of the line just above. Figure 9-2 shows a sample buffer.

In 1975, Richard Stallman and Guy Steele wrote Emacs. They implemented it
as a series of editor commands for an even more historic (late 60's) text
editor, TECO (Text Editor and Corrector). The acronymic name Editor MACroS,
reflects these beginnings, but there have been many humorous reinterpretations including ESCAPE-META-ALT-CONTROL-SHIFT and Emacs Makes All
Computing Simple.

Since then, Emacs has grown and evolved through more than twenty major
revisions to the mainstream GNU version alone. The Emacs editor is now
coded in C, and contains a complete Lisp interpreter.

```
--**-Emacs: sample            (Fundamental)----All----------------------
Save file /u1/jfp/sample? (y or n) █
```

Figure 9-2   Sample Buffer

Moving the Cursor

You can position the cursor over any character in the **emacs** window and
move the window so it displays any portion of the buffer. You can move the
cursor forward or backward through the text (Figure 8-2, page 185) by various textual units (e.g., characters, words, sentences, lines, paragraphs). Any
of the cursor movement commands can be preceded by a repetition count
((CONTROL)-**U** followed by a numeric argument) that causes the cursor to move
that number of textual units through the text. More discussion of numeric
arguments appears on page 228.

Moving the Cursor by Characters

Pressing (CONTROL)-**F** moves the cursor forward one character. If the cursor is at
the end of a line, this command wraps it to the beginning of the next line.
The command (CONTROL)-**U** 7 (CONTROL)-**F** moves the cursor seven characters to
the right.

Pressing (CONTROL)-**B** moves the cursor backward one character. (CONTROL)-**B**
works in a manner similar to (CONTROL)-**F** (Figure 9-3).

Moving the Cursor by Words

Pressing (META)-**f** moves the cursor forward one word. To press (META)-**f** hold the
(META) or (ALT) key down while you press **f**; if you do not have either of these
keys, press (ESCAPE) and after releasing it press **f**. It leaves the cursor on the first

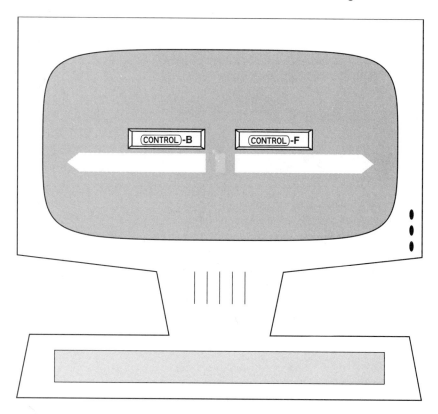

Figure 9-3   Moving the Cursor by Characters

character that is not part of the word the cursor started on. The command
(CONTROL)-**U** **4** (META)-**f** moves the cursor forward one space past the end of the
fourth word. See page 227 for more about keys.

Pressing (META)-**b** moves the cursor backward one word so the cursor is on
the first letter of the word it started on. It works in a manner similar to (META)-**f**
(Figure 9-4).

Moving the Cursor by Lines

Pressing (CONTROL)-**A** moves the cursor to the beginning of the line it is on;
(CONTROL)-**E** moves it to the end. Pressing (CONTROL)-**P** moves the cursor up one
line to the position directly above where the cursor started; (CONTROL)-**N** moves
it down. As with the other cursor movement keys, you can precede (CONTROL)-**P**
and (CONTROL)-**N** with (CONTROL)-**U** and a numeric argument to move up or down
multiple lines at a time.

You can use pairs of these commands to move the cursor up to the beginning of the previous line, down to the end of the following line, and so
on (Figure 9-5).

Figure 9-4 Moving the Cursor by Words

Moving the Cursor by Sentences, Paragraphs, and Window Position

Pressing (META)-**a** moves the cursor to the beginning of the sentence the cursor is on; (META)-**e** moves the cursor to the end. (META)-**[** moves the cursor to the beginning of the paragraph the cursor is on; (META)-**]** moves it to the end. You can precede any of these commands by (CONTROL)-**U** and a repetition count to move the cursor that many sentences or paragraphs.

Pressing (META)-**r** moves the cursor to the beginning of the middle line of the window. You can precede this command with a (CONTROL)-**U** and a line number (here (CONTROL)-**U** does not indicate a repitition count, but a screen line number). The command (CONTROL)-**U 0** (META)-**r** moves the cursor to the beginning of the top line (line zero) in the window. You can replace zero with the line number of the line you want to move the cursor to or a minus sign (–), in which case the cursor will move to the beginning of the last line of the window (Figure 9-6).

Editing at the Cursor Position

You can type in new text and push the existing text to the right. Entering new text requires no special commands once the cursor is positioned. If you type in so much that the text in a line goes past the right edge of the window,

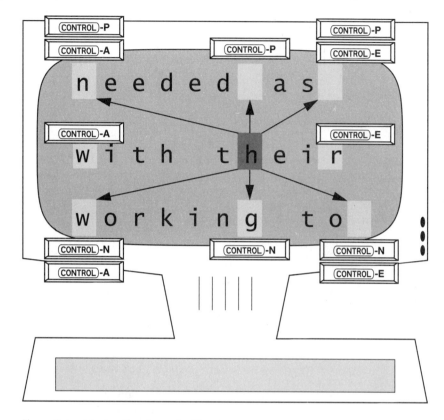

Figure 9-5   Moving the Cursor by Lines

emacs puts a backslash (\) in column 80 and then wraps the remainder of the text to the next line. The backslash only appears on the screen and is never printed out. Although you can create an arbitrarily long line, some UNIX tools will have problems with text files containing these very long lines. You can split a line at any point by positioning the cursor and pressing (RETURN).

Pressing (DELETE) removes characters to the left of the cursor. The cursor and the remainder of the text on this line both move to the left each time you press (DELETE). To join a line with the line above it, position the cursor on the first character of the second line and press (DELETE).

Press (CONTROL)-**D** to delete the character under the cursor. The cursor remains stationary, and the remainder of the text on this line moves left to replace the deleted character.

Saving and Retrieving the Buffer

No matter what happens to a buffer during an **emacs** session, the associated file is not changed until you save the buffer. If you leave **emacs** without saving the buffer (this *is* possible if you are insistent enough), the file is not changed, and the session's work is discarded.

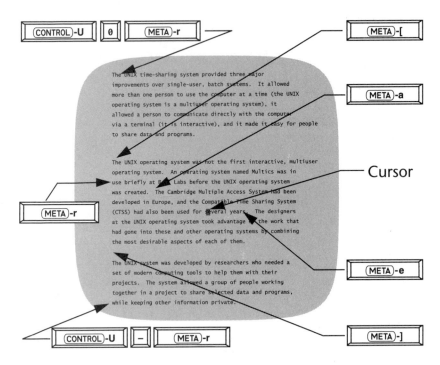

Figure 9-6   *Moving the Cursor by Sentences, Paragraphs, and Window Position*

As mentioned previously, **emacs** will prompt you about unsaved changes to the buffer contents. As **emacs** writes a buffer's edited contents back out to the file, it may optionally first make a backup of the original file contents. You can choose between no backups, one level (default), or an arbitrary number of levels. The one level backup filenames are formed by appending the ~ character to the original filename. The multilevel backups append **.~n~** to the filename where **n** is the sequential backup number starting with 1.

The command (CONTROL)-**X** (CONTROL)-**S** saves the current buffer in its associated file. The **emacs** editor will confirm a successful save with a message in the Echo Area.

If you are already editing a file with **emacs** and wish to begin editing another file (also called *visiting* a file), you can copy the new file into a new **emacs** buffer by giving the command (CONTROL)-**X** (CONTROL)-**F**. The **emacs** editor will prompt you for a filename, read that file into a new buffer, and display that buffer in the current window. Having two files open in one editing session is more convenient than exiting out of **emacs** and back to the shell and starting a new copy of **emacs** when you want to edit a second file.

Basic Editing Commands

This section takes a more detailed look at the fundamental editing commands in **emacs**. It covers straightforward editing of a single file in a single window.

Keys: Notation and Use

Mainstream **emacs** uses 128-character ASCII codes. ASCII keyboards have the typewriter-style (SHIFT) key, and a (CONTROL) key. In addition, some keyboards have a (META) (or (ALT)) key that controls the eighth bit (it takes seven bits to describe an ASCII character—the eighth bit of an eight-bit byte can be used to communicate other information). Since so much of the **emacs** command set is in the nonprinting (CONTROL) or (META) case, Stallman was one of the first to confront the problem of developing a notation for writing about keystrokes.

His solution, although not popular outside the **emacs** community, is clear and unambiguous. It uses the capital letters **C** and **M** to denote holding down the (CONTROL) and (META) keys respectively, and a few simple acronyms for the most common special characters such as **RET** (this book uses (RETURN)), **LFD** ((LINEFEED)), **DEL** ((DELETE)), **ESC** ((ESCAPE)), **SPC** ((SPACE)), and **TAB** (TAB). Most **emacs** documentation, including the on-line help, uses this notation.

Character	Classic emacs Notation
(lowercase) **a**	a
(uppercase) (SHIFT)-**a**	A
(CONTROL)-**a**	C-a
(CONTROL)-**A**	C-a (do *not* use (SHIFT)) Equivalent to preceding character
(META)-**a**	M-a
(META)-**A**	M-A (*do* use (SHIFT))
(CONTROL)-(META)-**a**	C-M-a
(CONTROL)-(META)-**a**	M-C-a (not used frequently)

There were some problems with this use of keys. There were many keyboards without a (META) key, and some operating systems discarded the (META) bit. The **emacs** character set clashes with XON-XOFF flow control, which also uses (CONTROL)-**S** and (CONTROL)-**Q**, and continues to do so to this day.

Although the flow-control problem still exists, the (META) key issue was resolved by making it an optional two-key sequence starting with (ESCAPE). For instance, you can type (ESCAPE) **a** in place of (META)-**a** or (ESCAPE) (CONTROL)-**A** to get (CONTROL)-(META)-**a**. If your keyboard does not have a (META) or (ALT) key, you can use the two-key (ESCAPE) sequence by pressing the (ESCAPE) key down (and releasing it) and then pressing the key following the (META) key in this book. For example, if this book says "Press (META)-**r**" you can either press the (META) or (ALT) key while you press **r**, or you can press and release (ESCAPE) and then press **r**.

An aside on notation: this book uses an uppercase letter following the (CONTROL) key and a lowercase letter following the (META) key. In either case you *do not ever have to hold down the* (SHIFT) *key while entering a* (CONTROL) *or* (META) *character.* Although (META) uppercase character (i.e., (META)-**A**) is a different character, it is usually set up to cause no action or the same effect as its lowercase counterpart.

Even though all PC keyboards have an (ALT) key, it is sometimes not noticed or handled properly by the resident UNIX system or the terminal emulator. However, the (ESCAPE) sequence will always work. If your terminal does not have an (ESCAPE) key, you can use (CONTROL)-[in its place.

Key Sequences and Commands

In **emacs**, the relationship between key sequences (one or more keys that are pressed together or in sequence to issue an **emacs** command) and commands is very flexible, and there is considerable opportunity for exercising your personal preference. You can translate and remap key sequences to other commands, and replace or reprogram commands themselves.

Although most **emacs** documentation glosses over all the details and talks about keystrokes as though they were the actual commands, it is important to know that the underlying machinery is separate from the key sequences, and to understand that the behavior of the key sequences and the commands can be changed (page 258).

Running a Command Without a Key Binding: (META)-x

The **emacs** keymaps (the tables, or vectors, that **emacs** uses to translate key sequences to commands—page 260) are very crowded, and often it is not possible to bind every single command to a key sequence. You can execute any command by name by preceding it with (META)-x. The **emacs** editor will prompt you for a command in the Echo Area and execute it after you enter the command name and press (RETURN).

Sometimes, when there is no common key sequence for a command, it will be described as (META)-x *command-name*. The **emacs** editor has a *smart completion* for most prompted answers, using (SPACE) or (TAB) to complete, if possible, to the end of the current word or the whole command respectively. Forcing a completion past the last unambiguous point, or typing ?, displays a list of alternatives. You can find more details on smart completion in the on-line **emacs** manual.

Numeric Arguments

Some of the **emacs** editing commands will take a numeric argument and interpret it as a repetition count. The argument immediately prefixes the key sequence for the command, and the most common case of no argument is almost always interpreted as a count of 1. Even ordinary alphabetic characters can have a numeric argument, which means "insert this many times." The two ways of giving a command a numeric argument are shown below.

- Press (META) with each digit (0-9) or the minus sign (–) (e.g., to insert 10 z characters, type (META)-1 (META)-0 z).

- Use (CONTROL)-U to begin a string of digits (including the minus sign) (e.g., to move the cursor forward 20 words, type (CONTROL)-U 20 (META)-f.)

For convenience (CONTROL)-U defaults to *multiply by four* when you do not follow it with a string of one or more digits. For example, entering (CONTROL)-U r means insert rrrr (4∗1) while (CONTROL)-U (CONTROL)-U r means insert rrrrrrrrrrrrrrrr (4 ∗ 4 ∗ 1).

Point and the Cursor

Point is the place in a buffer where editing takes place, and this is where the cursor is positioned. Strictly speaking, Point is the left edge of the cursor—it is thought of as always lying *between* characters.

Each window has its own Point, but there is only one cursor. When the cursor is in a window, moving the cursor also moves Point. Switching the cursor out of a window does not change that window's Point; it will be in the same place when the cursor is switched back to that window.

All of the cursor positioning commands previously described also move Point. In addition you can move the cursor to the beginning of the buffer with (META)-< or to the end of the buffer with (META)->.

Scrolling Through a Buffer

A buffer is likely to be much larger than the window through which it is viewed, and there has to be some way of moving the display of the buffer contents up or down to put the interesting part in the window (Figure 9-7). *Scrolling forward* refers to moving the text upward, with new lines entering at the bottom of the window. Use (CONTROL)-V to scroll forward one window (mi-

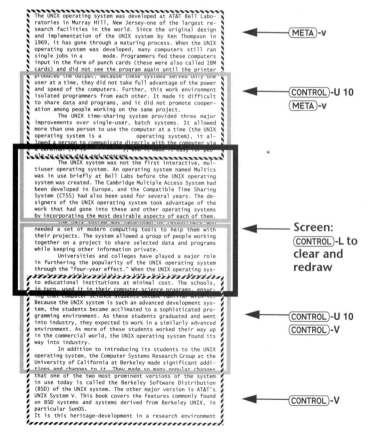

Figure 9-7   Scrolling through a Buffer

nus two lines for context). *Scrolling backward* refers to moving the text downward, with new lines entering at the top of the window. Use (META)-**v** to scroll backward one window (again leaving two lines for context). Pressing (CONTROL)-**L** clears the screen and repaints it, moving the current line to the center of the window. This command is useful if the screen display becomes garbled.

A numeric argument to (CONTROL)-**V** or (META)-**v** means "scroll that many lines"; thus, (CONTROL)-**U 10** (CONTROL)-**V** means scroll forward ten lines. A numeric argument to (CONTROL)-**L** means "scroll the text so the cursor is on that line of the window," where 0 means the top line and –1 means the bottom, just above the Mode Line. Scrolling occurs automatically if you exceed the window limits with (CONTROL)-**P** or (CONTROL)-**N**.

Erasing Text

When text is erased, it can be discarded, or it can be moved into a holding area and optionally brought back later. The term *delete* means *permanent discard,* and the term *kill* means *move to a holding area.* The holding area is called the *Kill Ring*—it can hold several pieces of killed text. You can use the text in the Kill Ring in many ways (see "Cutting and Pasting," page 238).

The (DELETE) key deletes the character to the left of the cursor, while (CONTROL)-**D** deletes the character under the cursor. The (META)-**d** command kills from the cursor forward to the end of the current word, and the (META)-(DELETE) command kills the text from the cursor backward to the beginning of the previous word.

(CONTROL)-**K** kills forward to the end of the current line. It will *not* delete the line ending (LINEFEED) character unless Point (and the cursor) are just to the left of the (LINEFEED). This allows you to get to the left end of a line with (CONTROL)-**A**, kill the whole line with (CONTROL)-**K**, and then immediately type a replacement line without having to reopen a hole for the new line. Another consequence is that (from the beginning of the line) it takes (CONTROL)-**K** (CONTROL)-**K** (or (CONTROL)-**U1**(CONTROL)-**K**) to kill the text and close the hole.

Searching

The **emacs** editor has several types of search commands. You can search in the following ways:

- incrementally for a character string
- incrementally for a regular expression (possible but very uncommon)
- for a complete character string
- for a complete full regular expression (page 741)

You can run each of the following four searches either forward or backward in the buffer.

The *complete* string searches behave in the same manner as a search on other editors. Searching begins only when the search string is complete. In contrast, an *incremental* search begins as you type the first character of the search string and keeps going as you enter additional characters. Initially this sounds confusing, but it is surprisingly useful and is the preferred search technique in **emacs**.

Incremental Searches

A single command is required to select the direction of and start an incremental search: (CONTROL)-**S** starts a forward incremental search, and (CONTROL)-**R** starts a reverse incremental search.

When you start an incremental search, **emacs** starts a special one-line dialog in the Echo Area. You are prompted with I-search: to enter some characters. When you enter a character, **emacs** begins searching for that character in the buffer. If it finds that character, it moves Point and cursor to that position so you can see the search progress.

After you enter each character of the search string, you can take any one of several actions:

1. The search reaches your target in the buffer, and the cursor is positioned just to its right. In this case, exit from the search and leave the cursor in its new position by entering (ESCAPE). (Actually, any **emacs** command not related to searching also takes you out, but remembering exactly which ones can be difficult. For a new user, (ESCAPE) is safer.)

2. The search reaches the current search string, but it's not yet at the target you want. Now you can refine the search string by adding another letter, reiterate your (CONTROL)-**R** or (CONTROL)-**S** to look for the next occurrence of this search string, or enter (ESCAPE) to stop the search and leave the cursor at its current position.

3. The search hits the beginning or end of the buffer and reports Failing I-Search. You can proceed in several ways at this point:

   a. If you mistyped the search string or reiterated (CONTROL)-**S** too often, press (DELETE) to back out some of the wrong characters or search reiterations. The text and cursor in the window will jump backward in step with you.

   b. If you want to wrap past the beginning or end of the buffer and continue searching, you can force a wrap by entering (CONTROL)-**R** or (CONTROL)-**S** again.

   c. If the search has not found what you want but you want to stay at the current position, press (ESCAPE) to stop the search at that point.

   d. If the search has gone wrong and you just want to get back to where you started, press (CONTROL)-**G** (the quit character). From an unsuccessful search, a single (CONTROL)-**G** backs out all the characters in the search string that could not be found. If this takes you back to a place you wish to continue searching from, you can add characters to the search string again. If you do not want to continue the search from here, a second (CONTROL)-**G** ends the search and leaves the cursor where it was to begin with.

Nonincremental Searches

If you prefer that your searches just succeed or fail without showing all the intermediate results, you can give the nonincremental commands (CONTROL)-S (ESCAPE) to search forward or (CONTROL)-R (ESCAPE) to search backward. Searching does not begin until you enter a search string in response to the **emacs** prompt and press (RETURN). Neither of these commands will wrap past the end of the buffer.

Regular Expression Searching

You can perform both incremental and nonincremental regular expression searching in **emacs**. To begin a regular expression search, you can use the following commands:

(META)-(CONTROL)-S

> Incremental search forward for regular expression—prompts for a regular expression one character at a time.

(META)-x *isearch-backward-regexp*

> Incremental search backward for regular expression—prompts for a regular expression one character at a time.

(META)-(CONTROL)-S (ESCAPE)

> Prompt for and then search forward for a complete regular expression.

(META)-x *isearch-backward-regexp* (ESCAPE)

> Prompt for and then search backward for a complete regular expression.

On-line Help

The **emacs** help system is always available. With the default key bindings, you can start it with (CONTROL)-H. The help system then prompts you for a one-letter help command. If you do not know which help command you want, type ? or (CONTROL)-H. This gives you a one-line list of the help command letters, and again requests a one-letter help command.

If you still do not know which help command you want, you type ? or (CONTROL)-H again. This switches the current window to a list of help commands, each of them with a one-line description, and again requests a one-letter help command.

If, while still being prompted about what help you want, you decide you do not really want help after all, you can type (CONTROL)-G to cancel your help request and get back to your former buffer.

If the help output is only a single line, it will appear in the Echo Area. If it is more, then the output will appear in its own window. To scroll this output, you can use (META)-v, or select the window with (CONTROL)-X o and scroll back and forth. When you are done with the help window, you can delete it. More on working with multiple windows appears on page 245.

Some help commands such as **news** ((CONTROL)-**M n** for recent **emacs** changes) and **tutorial** ((CONTROL)-**M** t) have so much output that they give you a whole window right away. When you are done with this help window, you can delete it in the usual way (i.e., (CONTROL)-**X 1** if the cursor is not in the window, (CONTROL)-**X 0** if it is).

On many terminals, the (BACKSPACE) or ← key generates (CONTROL)-**H**. If you forget you are using **emacs** and try to back over a few characters, you may find yourself in the help system unintentionally. There is no danger to the buffer you are editing, but it can be unsettling to lose the window contents and not have a clear picture of how to restore it. In this case, type (CONTROL)-**G** to return to editing the buffer. Some users elect to put help on a different key (page 260).

These are some of the help commands:

(CONTROL)-**H a**

> Prompt for **string**, then show a list of commands whose names contain **string**.

(CONTROL)-**H b**

> Show a table (it will be long) of all the key bindings now in effect.

(CONTROL)-**H c key-sequence**

> Print the name of the command bound to this **key-sequence**. Multiple key sequences are allowed; however, for a long key sequence where only the first part is recognized, the command will describe the first part and quietly insert the unrecognized part into your buffer. This can happen with 3-character function keys ((F1), (F2), etc. on the keyboard) that generate character sequences such as (ESCAPE) [M.

(CONTROL)-**H k key-sequence**

> Print the name and documentation of the command bound to this **key-sequence**. (See the notes on the preceding command.)

(CONTROL)-**H f**

> Prompt for the name of a Lisp function, and print the documentation for it. Because commands are Lisp functions, you can use a command name with this command.

(CONTROL)-**H i**

> Takes you to the top menu of Info, a documentation browser. Generally, a complete Info manual and **emacs** manual are kept on-line, and other GNU packages may have manuals here too. Info has its own help system. Type **?** for a summary or **h** for a tutorial.

(CONTROL)-**H l**

> (lowercase ell) Show the last 100 characters typed. The record is kept *after* the first-stage keyboard translation. If you have

customized the keyboard translation table, you must make a mental reverse translation.

(CONTROL)-**H m**

> Show the documentation and special key bindings for the current major mode (i.e., Text, C, Fundamental, etc.)

(CONTROL)-**H n**

> Show the **emacs** news file (new changes made to **emacs**, ordered with most recent first).

(CONTROL)-**H t**

> Runs an **emacs** tutorial session. When you are finished with the tutorial you can reselect your original buffer with (CONTROL)-**X b** or kill the help buffer with (CONTROL)-**X k.**

(CONTROL)-**H v**

> Prompts for a Lisp variable name, and gives the documentation for that variable.

(CONTROL)-**H w**

> Prompts for a command name, and gives the key sequence, if any, bound to that command. Multiple key sequences are allowed. However, for a long key sequence where only the first part is recognized, the command will describe the first part and quietly insert the unrecognized part into your buffer. This can happen with 3-character function keys (**F1**, **F2**, etc. on the keyboard) that generate character sequences such as (ESCAPE) **[M.**Even in this

CAUTION

After a long Info session, the q command (quit Info) may take your window back to an Info help buffer instead of your original buffer. This is a bug. You can reselect your original buffer with (CONTROL)-**X b**, or kill the help buffer with (CONTROL)-**X k.**

abridged presentation, it is clear that you can use the help system to browse through the **emacs** internal Lisp system. For the curious, here is Stallman's suggested list of strings that will match many names in the Lisp system:

char	line	word	sentence	paragraph	region	page
sexp	list	defun	buffer	screen	window	file
dir	register	mode	beginning	end	forward	backward
next	previous	up	down	search	goto	kill
delete	mark	insert	yank	fill	indent	case
change	set	what	list	find	view	describe

(CONTROL)-**H a**

> This command is part of the help system; it prompts for a string and then shows the commands whose names contain **string**.

(META)-**x** *apropos*

> Prompts for a **string** and shows all the Lisp commands and variables whose names contain **string**.

Advanced Editing Topics

The basic **emacs** commands are sufficient for many editing tasks, but the serious user will quickly find the need for more power. This section presents some of the more advanced **emacs** capabilities.

Undoing Changes

An editing session begins when you read a file into an **emacs** buffer. At that point, the buffer content matches the file exactly. As you insert text and give editing commands, the buffer content becomes more and more different from the file. If you are satisfied with the changes, you will write the altered buffer back out to the file, and end the session.

A window's Mode Line has an indicator immediately to the left of emacs: that shows the modification state of the buffer in the window. Its three states are -- (not modified), ** (modified), and **%%** (read only).

The **emacs** editor keeps a record of all the keys you have pressed (text and commands) since the beginning of the editing session, up to a limit currently set at 15,000 characters. If you are within the limit, it is possible to undo the entire session for this buffer, one change at a time. If you have multiple buffers (page 244) then each buffer will have its own undo record.

Undoing is considered so important that it is given a backup key sequence, just in case some keyboards cannot easily handle the primary sequence. The two sequences are (CONTROL)-_ (underscore, which on old ASR-33 TTY keyboards was used where ⊛ is used now) and (CONTROL)-**X u**. When you type (CONTROL)-_ **emacs** undoes the last command and moves the cursor to that position in the buffer, so you can see what happened. If you type (CONTROL)-_ a second time, then the next to the last command is undone, and so on. If you keep on typing (CONTROL)-_, eventually you will get the buffer back to its original unmodified state, and the ** Mode Line indicator will change to --. This is in contrast to **vi**, where undo works only on the most recent command.

When you break the string of undo commands with *anything* (text or any command except undo) then all the reverse changes you made during the string of undos become a part of the change record, and can themselves be undone. This offers a way to redo some or all of the undos. If you decide you backed up too far, type a command (something innocuous like (CONTROL)-**F** that does not change the buffer), and begin undoing in reverse. Some examples follow.

Commands	Effect
(CONTROL)-_	Undo the last change.
(CONTROL)-_ (CONTROL)-F (CONTROL)-_	Undo the last change, and change it back again.
(CONTROL)-_ (CONTROL)-_	Undo the last two changes.
(CONTROL)-_ (CONTROL)-_ (CONTROL)-F (CONTROL)-_ (CONTROL)-_	Undo two changes, and change them both back again.
(CONTROL)-_ (CONTROL)-_ (CONTROL)-F (CONTROL)-_	Undo two changes, and change one of them back again.

If you do not remember the last change you made, you can type (CONTROL)-_ and undo it. If it was a change that you wanted to make, type (CONTROL)-F (CONTROL)-_ and make it again. If you modified a buffer by accident, you can keep typing (CONTROL)-_ until the Mode Line indicator shows -- once more.

If the buffer is completely ruined and you want to start over, issue the command (META)-x revert-buffer to discard the current buffer contents and reread from the associated file—**emacs** will ask you to confirm.

OPTIONAL

Mark and Region

In a buffer, Point is the current editing position, which you can move anywhere in the buffer by moving the cursor. It is also possible to set a Mark in the buffer. The contiguous characters between Point and Mark (either one may come first) are called the *Region*. There are many commands that operate on a buffer's current Region and not just on the characters near Point.

The Mark is not easily movable like Point. Once it is set, it can be moved only by setting it somewhere else. Each buffer has only one Mark. The (CONTROL)-@ command explicitly sets the Mark at the current cursor (and Point) position. Some keyboards generate (CONTROL)-@ when you type (CONTROL)-(SPACE). While this is not really a backup key binding, it is occasionally a convenient alternative. You can use (CONTROL)-X (CONTROL)-X to exchange Point and Mark.

To establish a Region, you usually position Point at one end of the desired Region, set Mark with (CONTROL)-@, and then move Point to the other end of the Region. If you forget where you left the Mark, you can move the cursor back to it again with (CONTROL)-X (CONTROL)-X, or hop back and forth with repeated (CONTROL)-X (CONTROL)-X to show the Region more clearly.

If one Region boundary or the other is not to your liking, swap Point and Mark with (CONTROL)-X (CONTROL)-X to move the cursor from one end of the Region to the other, and move Point. Continue until you are satisfied with the Region.

There are many possibilities for operating on a Region. Some examples follow.

(META)-**W**

Copy the Region between Point and Mark nondestructively (without killing it) to the Kill Ring.

(CONTROL)-**W**

Kill the Region.

(META)-**x** *print-region*

Send the Region between Point and Mark to the print spooler.

(CONTROL)-**X a**

Prompt for a buffer and append Region between Point and Mark to that buffer.

(META)-**x** *append-to-file*

Prompt for a filename and append Region between Point and Mark to that file.

(CONTROL)-**X** (CONTROL)-**U**

Convert Region between Point and Mark to uppercase.

(CONTROL)-**X** (CONTROL)-**L**

Convert Region between Point and Mark to lowercase.

Each time you set the Mark in a buffer, you are also pushing the Mark's former location onto the buffer's *Mark Ring*. The Mark Ring is organized as a FIFO (First In First Out) list and holds the 16 most recent locations where the Mark was set. Each buffer has its own Mark Ring.

This record of recent Mark history is useful because it often holds locations that you want to jump back to quickly. Jumping to a location pointed to by the Mark Ring can be faster and easier than scrolling or searching your way through the buffer to find the site of a previous change.

To work your way backward along the trail of former Mark locations, give the command (CONTROL)-**U** (CONTROL)-**@** one or more times. Each time you give the command, **emacs** will

- move Point (and the cursor) to the current Mark location,
- save the current Mark location at the *oldest* end of the Mark Ring, and
- pop off the *youngest* (most recent) Mark Ring entry and set Mark.

Each additional (CONTROL)-**U** (CONTROL)-**@** command will cause **emacs** to move Point and the cursor to the previous entry on the Mark Ring.

Although this process may seem complex, it is really just a safe jump to a previous Mark location. It is safe because each jump's starting point is recirculated back through the Mark Ring where it is easy to find again. You can jump to all the previous locations on the Mark

Ring (it may be fewer than 16) by giving the command (CONTROL)-**U** (CONTROL)-**@** again and again. You can go around the ring as many times as you like, and stop whenever you want to.

Some commands set Mark automatically: the idea is to leave a book-mark before moving Point a long distance. One example is (META)->, which sets Mark before jumping to the end of the buffer. You can then go back to your starting position with (CONTROL)-**U** (CONTROL)-**@**. Searches be-have similarly. To avoid surprises, the message `Mark Set` appears in the Echo Area whenever the Mark is set, either explicitly or implicitly.

Cutting and Pasting: Yanking Killed Text

Recall that Killed text is not actually discarded, but kept in the Kill Ring. The Kill Ring holds the last 30 pieces of killed text, and it is visible from all buffers.

Retrieving text from the Kill Ring is called *yanking*. This terminology is opposite from **vi**'s; in **vi** *yanking* pulls text from the buffer, and *putting* puts text into the buffer. Killing and yanking are roughly analogous to cutting and pasting, and are **emacs**' primary mechanism for moving and copying text.

The following are the most common kill and yank commands:

(META)-**d**

>Kill forward to the end of current word.

(META)-(DELETE)

>Kill backward to beginning of previous word.

(CONTROL)-**K**

>Kill to end of line, not including (LINEFEED).

(CONTROL)-**U** 1 (CONTROL)-**K**

>Kill to end of line, including (LINEFEED).

(CONTROL)-**U** 0 (CONTROL)-**K**

>Kill back to beginning of current line.

(META)-**w**

>Copy Region between Point and Mark to Kill Ring, but do *not* erase from the buffer.

(CONTROL)-**W**

>Kill Region from Point to Mark.

(META)-**z char**

>Kill up to but not including the next occurrence of **char**.

(CONTROL)-**Y**

>Yank most recently killed text into current buffer at Point. Set Mark at beginning of this text, and position Point and cursor at the end.

(META)-**y**

> Erase the just-yanked text, rotate the Kill Ring, and yank the next item (only after (CONTROL)-**Y** or (META)-**y**).

To move two lines of text, move Point to the beginning of the first line, and enter (CONTROL)-**U 2** (CONTROL)-**K** to kill two lines. Then move Point to the destination position, and enter (CONTROL)-**Y**.

To copy two lines of text, move Point to the beginning of the first line, and type (CONTROL)-**U 2** (CONTROL)-**K** (CONTROL)-**Y** to kill and then yank back immediately. Then move Point to the destination position, and type (CONTROL)-**Y**.

To copy a larger piece, set the Region to cover this piece and then type (CONTROL)-**W** (CONTROL)-**Y** to kill and then yank back at once. Then move Point to the destination, and type (CONTROL)-**Y**. You can also set the Region and use (META)-**w** to copy the Region to the Kill Ring.

OPTIONAL

The Kill Ring is organized as a fixed length FIFO (First In First Out) list, with each new entry causing the eldest (once you build up to 30 entries in the Kill Ring) to be discarded. Simple cut and paste operations generally use only the newest entry. The older entries are kept to give you time to change your mind about a deletion. If you do change your mind, it is possible to "mine" the kill ring like an archaeological dig, working backward through time and down through the strata of killed material to copy a specific item back into your buffer.

To view every entry in the Kill Ring, begin a yanking session with (CONTROL)-**Y**. This copies the youngest entry to your buffer at the current cursor position. If this is not the item you want, continue the yanking session by typing (META)-**y**. This will erase the previous yank and copy the next youngest entry to the buffer at the current cursor position. If this still is not the item you wanted back, type (META)-**y** again to erase it and retrieve a copy of the next entry, and so on. You can continue this all the way back to the very oldest entry. If you continue to type (META)-**y**, you wrap back to the youngest again. In this manner you can examine each entry as many times as you wish.

The sequence is (CONTROL)-**Y** followed by any mixture of (CONTROL)-**Y** and (META)-**y**. If you type any other command after (META)-**y**, the sequence is broken, and you must give the (CONTROL)-**Y** command again to start another yank session. This new yank session does *not* restart the dig from the youngest entry.

As you work backward in the Kill Ring, it is useful to think of advancing a Last Yank pointer back through history to older and older entries. This pointer is *not* reset to the youngest entry until you give a new kill command. Using this technique, you can work backward part way through the Kill Ring with (CONTROL)-**Y** and a few (META)-**y**'s, then give some commands that do not kill, and then pick up where you left off with another (CONTROL)-**Y** and a succession of (META)-**y**'s.

It is also possible to position the Last Yank pointer with positive or negative numeric arguments to (META)-**y**. Refer to the on-line documentation for more information.

Inserting Special Characters

As stated earlier, **emacs** inserts everything that is not a command into the buffer at the current cursor position. To insert characters that would ordinarily be **emacs** commands, you can use the **emacs** escape character, (CONTROL)-**Q**. There are two ways of using this escape character:

- (CONTROL)-**Q** followed by any other character inserts that character in the buffer, no matter what command interpretation it was supposed to have.

- (CONTROL)-**Q** followed by three octal digits inserts a byte with that value in the buffer.

> **CAUTION**
>
> Depending on the way your terminal is set up, (CONTROL)-**Q** may clash with software flow control. If (CONTROL)-**Q** seems to have no effect, it is most likely being used for flow control. You must bind another key to insert special characters (page 262).

Global Buffer Commands

The **vi** editor and its predecessors had global commands for buffer-wide search and replacement. Their default operating Region was the entire buffer. The **emacs** editor has a similar family of commands. Their operating Region begins at Point and extends to the end of the buffer. If you wish to operate on the complete buffer, use (META)-**<** to set Point at the beginning of the buffer before issuing the command.

Line Oriented Operations

These commands all take a regular expression and apply it to the lines between Point and the end of the buffer.

(META)-**x** *occur*

> Prompts for a regular expression and lists each line with a match for the expression in a buffer named *Occur*.

(META)-**x** *delete-matching-lines*

> Prompts for a regular expression, and then deletes each line with a match for the expression.

(META)-**x** *delete-non-matching-lines*

> Prompts for a regular expression, and deletes each line that does *not* have a match for that expression.

The (META)-**x** *occur* command puts its output in a special buffer named *Occur*, which you can peruse and discard or use as a jump menu to reach each line quickly. To use the *Occur* buffer as a jump menu, switch to it (page 244), get the cursor on the copy of the desired destination line, and type (CONTROL)-**C** (CONTROL)-**C**. This switches to the buffer that was searched and positions the cursor on the line that the regular expression originally matched.

As with any buffer change, you can undo the deletion commands.

Unconditional and Interactive Replacement

These commands operate on the Region between Point and the end of the buffer, changing every string match or regular expression match. An unconditional replacement makes all replacements without question. An interactive replacement gives you the opportunity to see and approve each replacement before it is made.

(META)-x *replace-string* ·

> Prompts for **string** and **newstring**. Then replaces every instance of **string** with **newstring**. Point is left at the site of the last replacement, but the Mark was automatically set at the time you gave the command, and you can return to it with (CONTROL)-**U** (CONTROL)-**@**.

(META)-x *replace-regexp*

> Behaves similarly, replacing every **regexp** with **newstring**.

(META)-% string

or

(META)-x *query-replace*

> Behaves similarly, replacing some of the matches of **string** with **newstring**.

(META)-x *query-replace-regexp*

> Behaves similarly, replacing some of the matches for **regexp**.

If you choose to do an interactive replacement, each instance of **string** or match of **regexp** is displayed, and you are prompted for what action to take for this case. These are some of the commands you can give at this time:

(ESCAPE)

> Do not do any more replacements; quit now.

(SPACE)

> Make this replacement and go on.

(DELETE)

> Do *not* make this replacement. Skip over it and go on.

,

(comma) Make this replacement, display the result, and ask for another command. Any command is legal except that (DELETE) is treated like (SPACE) and does not undo the change.

.

(period) Make this replacement and quit searching.

!

(exclamation point) Replace this, and all remaining instances, without asking any more questions.

Working with Files

When you *visit* (**emacs** terminology for calling up) a file, **emacs** reads it into an internal buffer (page 244), edits the buffer contents, and eventually saves the buffer back into the file. The commands discussed here relate to visiting and saving files.

Each **emacs** buffer keeps a record of its default directory (the directory the file was read from or the working directory if it is a new file) that is prepended to any relative pathname you give it. This is a convenience to save some typing. Enter (META)-x *pwd* to print the default directory for the current buffer or (META)-x *cd* to prompt for a new default directory, and assign it to this buffer.

Visiting Files

These are the commands for visiting files:

(CONTROL)-X (CONTROL)-F

Prompt for a filename and read its contents into a freshly created buffer. Assign the file's final pathname component as the buffer name. Other buffers are unaffected. It is common and often useful to have several files simultaneously open for editing.

(CONTROL)-X (CONTROL)-V

Prompt for a filename and read its contents into the current buffer (overwriting the contents of the current buffer). If the current buffer is modified, **emacs** gives you a chance to write its contents out to a file. Use this command when you are *sure* you will not want to use this buffer later in the editing session, perhaps after you have tried to visit a wrong or nonexistent filename.

(CONTROL)-X 4 (CONTROL)-F

Prompt for a filename and read its contents into a freshly created buffer. Assign the file's final pathname component as the buffer name. Create a new window for this buffer, and select that window. The window selected before the command still shows the buffer it was showing before, although the new window may cover up part of the old window.

The **emacs** editor deals well with visiting a file that has been already called up and whose image is now in a buffer. After a check of modification time to be sure the file has not been changed since it was last called up, **emacs** simply switches you to that buffer.

To create a nonexistent file, simply call it up. An empty buffer will be created and properly named, so you can eventually save it. The message (New File) appears in the Echo Area, reflecting **emacs**'s understanding of the situation. Of course if this "new file" grew out of a typographical error, you probably will want to issue (CONTROL)-X (CONTROL)-V with the correct name.

Saving Files

You save a buffer by copying its contents back to the original file you called up. These are the relevant commands:

(CONTROL)-X (CONTROL)-S

> This is the workhorse file saving command. It saves the current buffer into its original file. If the current buffer is not modified, you will get the message (No changes need to be written).

(CONTROL)-X s

> For each modified buffer, you are asked if you wish to save it. Answer **y** or **n**. This command is given automatically as you exit **emacs**, to save any buffers that have been modified but not yet written out. However, if you want to save intermediate copies of your work, you can give it at any time.

CAUTION

It is usually during (CONTROL)-X s that you discover files whose buffers were modified by mistake, and now **emacs** wants to save the wrong changes back to the file. *Do not* answer **y** if you are not sure. First get done with the (CONTROL)-X s dialog by typing **n** to any saves you are not clear about. Then you have several options:

- Save the suspicious buffer into a temporary file with (CONTROL)-X (CONTROL)-W, and analyze it later.

- Undo the changes with a string of (CONTROL)-_ until the ∗∗ indicator disappears from the buffer's Mode Line.

- If you are sure all the changes are wrong, use (META)-x *revert-buffer* to get a fresh copy of the file.

- Kill the buffer outright. Since it is modified, you will be asked if you are sure.

- Give the (META)-~ (tilde) command to clear the modified condition and ∗∗ indicator. A subsequent (CONTROL)-X s will then believe that the buffer does not need to be written.

(META)-x *set-visited-file-name*

> Prompt for a filename, and set this name as the current buffer's "original" name.

(CONTROL)-X (CONTROL)-W

> Prompt for a filename, set this name as the "original" file for the current buffer, and save the current buffer into that file. This is equivalent to (META)-x *set-visited-file-name* followed by (CONTROL)-X (CONTROL)-S.

(META)-~

> (tilde) Clear modified flag from the current buffer. If you have mistakenly typed (META)-~ against a buffer with changes you want to keep, you need to make sure the modified condition and its ** indicator are turned back on before leaving **emacs**, or all the changes will be lost. One easy way to do this is to insert a (SPACE) into the buffer and then remove it again with (DELETE).

CAUTION

Clearing the modified flag ((META)-~) will allow you to exit without saving a modified buffer without any warning.

Working with Buffers

An **emacs** buffer is a storage object that you can edit. It often holds the contents of a file, but can also exist without being associated with any file. You can only select one buffer at a time, designated as the *current buffer*. Most commands operate only on the current buffer, even when multiple windows show two or more buffers on the screen. For the most part, each buffer is its own world: it has its own name, its own modes, its own file associations, its own modified state, and indeed may have its own special keybindings. Following are some commands you can use to create, select, list, and manipulate buffers.

(CONTROL)-X b

> Prompt for a buffer name, and select it. If it does not exist, create it first.

(CONTROL)-X 4 b

> Prompt for a buffer name, and select it in another window. The existing window is not disturbed, although the new window may overlap it.

(CONTROL)-X (CONTROL)-B

> Create a buffer named *Buffer List* and display it in another window. The existing window is not disturbed, although the new window may overlap it. The new buffer is not selected. In the *Buffer List* buffer, each buffer's data is shown, with name, size, mode(s) and original filename. A **%** appears for a read-only buffer, a * indicates a modified buffer, and . appears for the selected buffer.

(META)-x *rename-buffer*

> Prompt for a new buffer name, and give this new name to the current buffer.

(CONTROL)-X (CONTROL)-Q

> Toggle the current buffer's read-only status and the associated **%%** Mode Line indicator. This can be useful to prevent accidental buffer modification or to allow modification of a buffer when visiting a read-only file.

(CONTROL)-X a

> Prompt for a buffer name, and append the current Region between Point and Mark to the end of that buffer.

(META)-x *prepend-to-buffer*

> Prompt for a buffer name, and append the current Region between Point and Mark to the end of that buffer.

(META)-x *copy-to-buffer*

> Prompt for a buffer name, and delete the contents of the buffer before copying the current Region between Point and Mark into that buffer.

(META)-x *insert-buffer*

> Prompt for a buffer name, and insert the entire contents of that buffer into the current buffer at Point.

(CONTROL)-X k

> Prompt for a buffer name, and delete that buffer. If the buffer is modified but unsaved, you will be asked to confirm.

(META)-x *kill-some-buffers*

> Go through the entire buffer list, and offer the chance to delete each buffer. As with (CONTROL)-X k, you will be asked to confirm the kill order if a modified buffer is not yet saved.

Working with Windows

An **emacs** *window* is a viewport that looks into a buffer. The **emacs** screen begins by displaying a single window, but this screen space can later be divided among two or more windows. On the screen, the *current window* holds the cursor and views the *current buffer*.

A window views one buffer at a time. You can switch the buffer that a window views by giving the command (CONTROL)-X b **buffer-name** in the current window. Multiple windows can view one buffer, each window may view different parts of the same buffer, and each window carries its own value of Point. Any change to a buffer will be reflected in all the windows viewing that buffer. Also, a buffer can exist without a window open on it.

Window Creation by Splitting

One way to divide up the screen is to explicitly split the starting window into two or more pieces. The command (CONTROL)-X 2 splits the current window in two, with one new window above the other. A numeric argument is taken as the size of the upper window in lines. The command (CONTROL)-X 5 splits the current window in two, with the new windows arranged side by side. A numeric argument is taken as the number of columns to give the left window.

While these commands split the current window, both windows continue to view the same buffer. You can select a new buffer in either or both new windows, or you can scale each window to show different positions in the same buffer.

For example, (CONTROL)-U (CONTROL)-X 2 splits the current window in two, and because of the special "times 4" interpretation of (CONTROL)-U standing alone, the upper window is to be given 4 lines (barely enough to be useful).

Manipulating Windows

You can use (CONTROL)-X o (the letter oh) to select the other window. If more than two windows are on the screen, a sequence of (CONTROL)-X o commands will cycle through them all in top-to-bottom, left-to-right order. The (META)-(CONTROL)-V command scrolls the other window. If there are more than two, the command will scroll the window that (CONTROL)-X o would select next. You may use a positive or negative scrolling argument, just as with (CONTROL)-V scrolling in the current window.

Other-Window Display

In normal **emacs** operation, explicit window splitting is not nearly so common as the implicit splitting done by the family of (CONTROL)-X 4 commands. One of these commands is (CONTROL)-X 4 b, which prompts for a buffer name and selects it in the other window. If there is no other window, it begins with a half-and-half split that arranges the windows one above the other. Another command, (CONTROL)-X 4 f, prompts for a filename, calls it up in the other window, and selects the other window. If there is no other window, it begins with a half-and-half split that arranges the windows one above the other.

Adjusting and Deleting Windows

Windows may be destroyed when they get in the way; no data is lost in the window's associated buffer, and another window can be made at will. The (CONTROL)-X 0 (zero) command deletes the current window and give its space to its neighbors, while (CONTROL)-X 1 deletes all windows except the current window.

It is also possible to adjust the dimensions of the current window, once again at the expense of its neighbors. You can make a window shorter with (META)-x *shrink-window*. Use (CONTROL)-X ^ to increase the height of a window, (CONTROL)-X } to make the window wider, and (CONTROL)-X { to make the window narrower. Each of these commands adds or subtracts one line or column to or from the window, unless you precede the command with a numeric argument.

The **emacs** editor has its own guidelines for a window's minimum useful size, and may destroy a window before you force one of its dimensions all the way down to zero. Although the window is gone, the buffer remains intact.

Foreground Shell Commands

The **emacs** editor can run a subshell (a shell that is a child of the shell that is running **emacs**—see "Processes," page 283) to execute a single command line, optionally with input from a Region of the current buffer and optionally with command output replacing the Region contents. This is analogous to executing a shell command from **vi** and having the input come from the file and the output go back into the file (page 207).

(META)-!

> (exclamation) Prompt for a shell command, execute it, and display the output.

(CONTROL)-U (META)-!

> (exclamation) Prompt for a shell command, execute it, and insert the output at Point.

(META)-|

> (vertical bar) Prompt for a shell command, give the Region contents as input, filter it through the command, and display the output.

(CONTROL)-U (META)-|

> (vertical bar) Prompt for a shell command, give the Region contents as input, filter it through the command, delete the old Region contents, and insert the output in that position.

The **emacs** editor can also start an interactive subshell, running continuously in its own buffer. This is discussed later in Shell Mode.

Background Shell Commands

The **emacs** editor can run processes in the background, with output fed into a growing **emacs** buffer that does not have to remain in view. You can continue editing while the background process runs, and look at its output later. Any shell command can be run, without any restrictions.

The growing output buffer is always named *compilation*, and you can read it, copy from it, or edit it in any way, without waiting for the background process to finish. Most commonly, this buffer is used to see the output of program compilation, and then to correct any syntax errors found by the compiler.

To run a process in the background, give the command (META)-x *compile* to prompt for a shell command and begin executing it as a background process. The screen splits in half to show the *compilation* buffer.

You can switch to the *compilation* buffer and watch the execution if you wish. To make the display scroll as you watch, position the cursor at the very end of the text with a (META)-> command. If you are not interested, just remove the window (with (CONTROL)-X 0 if you are in it, (CONTROL)-X 1 otherwise) and keep working. You can switch back to the *compilation* buffer later with (CONTROL)-X b.

You can kill the background process with (META)-x *kill-compilation*; **emacs** will ask for confirmation, then kill the background process.

If standard format error messages appear in *compilation*, you can automatically visit the line in the file where each one occurred. Give the command (CONTROL)-X ` (backquote or accent grave) to split the screen into two windows and visit the file and line of the next error message. Scroll the *compilation* buffer so that this error message appears at the top of its window. Use (CONTROL)-U (CONTROL)-X ` to start over with the first error message and visit that file and line.

Language-Sensitive Editing

The **emacs** editor has a large collection of feature sets specific to a certain variety of text. The feature sets are called *Major Modes,* and a buffer may have only one Major Mode at a time.

A buffer's Major Mode is private to the buffer, and does not affect editing in any other buffer. If you switch to a new buffer having a different mode, rules for the new mode are immediately in effect. To avoid confusion, the name of a buffer's major mode appears in the Mode Line of any window viewing that buffer.

There are three classes of major modes:

- for editing human languages (e.g., text, **nroff**, TeX);
- for editing programming languages (e.g. C, Fortran, Lisp); and
- for special purposes (e.g., shell, **mail**, dired, **ftp**).

In addition, there is a major mode that does nothing special at all: Fundamental Mode. A major mode usually sets up the following:

- Special commands unique to the mode, possibly with their own key bindings. There may be just a few for languages, but special purpose modes may have dozens.
- Mode specific character syntax and regular expressions defining word constituent characters, delimiters, comments, whitespace, and so on. This conditions the behavior of commands oriented to syntactic units such as words, sentences, comments, or parenthesized expressions.

Selecting a Major Mode

The **emacs** editor chooses and sets a mode when a file is called up by matching the filename against a set of regular expression patterns describing the filename and filename extension. The explicit command to enter a Major Mode is (META)-x *modename-mode*. This command is rarely used except to correct wrong guesses.

A file can define its own mode by having the text -*- modename -*- somewhere in the first nonblank line, possibly buried inside a comment suitable for that programming language.

Human-Language Modes

A *human* language is meant to be eventually used by humans, possibly after being formatted by some text-formatting program. Human languages share many conventions about the structure of words, sentences, and paragraphs; with regard to these textual units, the major human language modes all behave the same.

Beyond the common region, each mode offers additional functionality oriented to a specific text formatter such as TeX, LaTeX or **nroff**. Text-formatter extensions are beyond the scope of this presentation; the focus here is on the commands relating to human textual units (e.g., words, sentences, and paragraphs).

Working with Words

As a mnemonic aid, the bindings are defined parallel to the character-oriented bindings (CONTROL)-**F**, (CONTROL)-**B**, (CONTROL)-**D**, (DELETE), and (CONTROL)-**T**.

As discussed earlier, (META)-**f** and (META)-**b** move forward and backward over words, just as (CONTROL)-**F** and (CONTROL)-**B** move forward and backward over characters. They may start from a position inside or outside the word to be traversed, but in all cases Point finishes just beyond the word, adjacent to the last character skipped over. They will accept a numeric argument specifying the number of words to be traversed.

The keys (META)-**d** and (META)-(DELETE) kill words forward and backward, just as (CONTROL)-**D** and (DELETE) delete characters forward and backward. They leave Point in exactly the same finishing position as (META)-**f** and (META)-**b**, but they kill the words they pass over. They will also accept a numeric argument.

(META)-**t** transposes the word before Point with the word after Point.

Working with Sentences

As a mnemonic aid, three of the bindings are defined parallel to the line oriented bindings: (CONTROL)-**A**, (CONTROL)-**E**, and (CONTROL)-**K**.

As discussed earlier, (META)-**a** moves back to the beginning of a sentence and (META)-**e** moves forward to the end. In addition, (CONTROL)-**X** (DELETE) kills backward to the beginning of a sentence while (META)-**k** kills forward to the end of a sentence.

The **emacs** editor recognizes sentence ends with a regular expression kept in a variable named **sentence-end**. (If you are curious, give the command (CONTROL)-**H** v sentence-end (RETURN) to view this variable.) Briefly, it looks for the characters ., ?, or ! followed by two (SPACE)s or an end-of-line marker, possibly with close quotation marks or close braces.

The (META)-**a** and (META)-**e** commands leave Point adjacent to the first or last nonblank character in the sentence. They will accept a numeric argument specifying the number of sentences to traverse, and a negative argument will run them in reverse.

The (META)-**k** and (CONTROL)-**X** (DELETE) commands kill sentences forward and backward, in a manner analogous to (CONTROL)-**K** line kill. They leave Point in exactly the same finishing position as (META)-**a** and (META)-**e**, but kill the sentences they pass over. They too will accept a numeric argument. (CONTROL)-**X** (DELETE) is useful for quickly backing out of a half-finished sentence.

Working with Paragraphs

As discussed earlier, (META)-**[** moves back to the most recent paragraph beginning, and (META)-**]** moves forward to the next paragraph ending. The (META)-**h** command marks the paragraph (i.e., puts Point at the beginning and Mark at the end) that the cursor is currently on, or the next paragraph if it is in between.

The (META)-**]** and (META)-**[** commands leave Point at the beginning of a line, adjacent to the first character or last character of the paragraph. They will accept a numeric argument specifying the number of paragraphs to traverse, and will run in reverse if given a negative argument.

In human language modes, paragraphs are separated by blank lines and text formatter command lines, and an indented line starts a paragraph. Recognition is based on the regular expressions stored in the variables **paragraph-separate** and **paragraph-start**. A paragraph is composed of complete lines, including the final line terminator. If a paragraph starts following one or more blank lines, then the last blank line before the paragraph belongs to the paragraph.

Filling

The **emacs** editor can *fill* a paragraph to fit a specified width. It will break lines and rearrange them as necessary. Breaking takes place only between words, and there is no hyphenation. Filling can be done automatically as you type or in response to your explicit command.

(META)-**x** *auto-fill-mode* turns Auto Fill Mode on or off. Turn it off or on by giving the same command again. When Auto Fill Mode is on, emacs automatically breaks lines when you type (SPACE) or (RETURN) and are currently beyond the specified line width. This feature is useful when you are entering new text.

Auto Fill Mode does not automatically refill the entire paragraph you are currently working on. If you add new text in the middle of a paragraph, Auto Fill Mode will break your new text as you type, but will not refill the complete paragraph. To refill a complete paragraph or Region of paragraphs, either use (META)-**q** to refill the current paragraph or (META)-**g** to refill each paragraph in the region between Point and Mark.

As before, paragraph boundaries are defined by the regular expressions **paragraph-separate** and **paragraph-start**.

You can change the filling width from its default value of 70 by setting the variable fill-column with either (CONTROL)-**X f** to set fill-column to the current cursor position, or (CONTROL)-**U nnn** (CONTROL)-**X f** to set fill-column to **nnn**, where 0 is the left margin.

Case Conversion

The **emacs** editor can force words or Regions to all uppercase, to all lowercase, or initial caps (i.e., first letter uppercase, balance lowercase). The commands follow:

(META)-l

> (lowercase ell) Convert word to the right of Point to lowercase.

(META)-u

> Convert word to the right of Point to uppercase.

(META)-c

> Convert word to the right of Point to initial caps.

(CONTROL)-X (CONTROL)-L

> Convert Region between Point and Mark to lowercase.

(CONTROL)-X (CONTROL)-U

> Convert Region between Point and Mark to uppercase.

The word-oriented conversions move Point over the word just converted, the same as (META)-f, allowing you to walk through text, converting each word with (META)-l, (META)-u, or (META)-c, and skipping over words to be left alone with (META)-f.

A positive numeric argument converts that many words to the right of Point, moving Point as it goes. A negative numeric argument converts that many words to the left of Point, but leaves Point stationary. This is useful for quickly changing the case of words you have just typed. Some examples appear below.

These characters and commands	Produce these results
HELLO(META)--(META)-l	hello
hello(META)--(META)-u	HELLO
hello(META)--(META)-c	Hello

The word conversions are not picky about beginning in the middle of a word; in all cases they consider the first word constituent character to the right of Point as the beginning of the word to be converted.

Text Mode

With very few exceptions, the commands for human-language text units such as words and sentences are always left turned on and available, even in the programming language modes. Text Mode adds very little to these basic commands, but is still worth turning on just to get the (TAB) key. Use the command (META)-x *text-mode*.

In Text Mode, (TAB) runs the function ***tab-to-tab-stop***. By default, (TAB) stops are set every 8 columns. You can adjust them with (META)**-x *edit-tab-stops***, which switches to a special *Tab Stops* buffer, where the current stops are laid out on a scale for you to edit. The new stops are installed when/if you type (CONTROL)**-C** (CONTROL)**-C**, but you are free to kill this buffer ((CONTROL)**-X k**) or switch away from it ((CONTROL)**-X b**) without ever changing the stops.

The tab stops you set here affect *only* the interpretation of (TAB) characters arriving from the keyboard. The emacs editor automatically inserts enough spaces to reach the (TAB) stop. This does *not* affect the interpretation of (TAB) characters already in the buffer or the underlying file. If you edit the (TAB) stops and then use them, you can still print your file, and the hard copy will look the same as the text on the screen.

C Mode

Programming languages are read by humans but are interpreted by machines. Besides continuing to handle some of the human language text units (e.g., words and sentences), the major programming language modes address the additional problems of

- dealing with "balanced expressions" enclosed by parentheses, brackets, or braces as textual units

- dealing with comments as textual units

- dealing with indention

In **emacs**, there are major modes to support C, Fortran, and several variants of Lisp. In these modes the commands for human textual units are still available, with occasional redefinitions: for example, a paragraph is bounded only by blank lines, and indention does not signal a paragraph start. In addition, each mode has custom coding to handle the language-specific conventions for balanced expressions, comments, and indention. This presentation discusses only C mode.

Working with Expressions

The **emacs** Major Modes are limited to lexical analysis. They can recognize most tokens (e.g., symbols, strings, numbers) and all matched sets of parentheses, brackets, and braces. This is enough for Lisp, but not for C. The C mode lacks a full-function syntax analyzer, and is not prepared to recognize all of C's possible expressions.

(In the **emacs** documentation, the recurring term *sexp* refers to the historic Lisp term *S-expression*. Unfortunately, it is sometimes used interchangeably with *expression*, even though the language might not be Lisp at all.)

Following are the **emacs** commands applicable to parenthesized expressions and some tokens. By design, the bindings run parallel to the (CONTROL) commands for characters and the (META) commands for words. All of these commands will accept a numeric argument, and will run in reverse if that argument is negative.

(CONTROL)-(META)-**f**

> Move forward over an expression.

(CONTROL)-(META)-**b**

> Move backward over an expression. The exact behavior for (CONTROL)-(META)-**f** depends on what character lies to the right of Point (or left of Point—depending on which direction you are moving Mark):
>
> - If the first non-whitespace is an opening delimiter (parenthesis, bracket, or brace) then Point is moved just past the matching closing delimiter.
>
> - If the first non-whitespace is a token, then Point is moved just past the end of this token.

(CONTROL)-(META)-**k**

> Kill an expression forward. It leaves Point at the same finishing position as (CONTROL)-(META)-**f**, but kills the expression it traverses.

(CONTROL)-(META)-**@**

> Set Mark at the position (CONTROL)-(META)-**f** would move to, without changing Point. To see the marked region clearly, you can look at both ends with a pair of (CONTROL)-**X** (CONTROL)-**X** commands to interchange Point and Mark.

Function Definitions

In **emacs**, a balanced expression at the outermost level is considered to be a function definition, and is often called a *defun* even though that term is specific to Lisp alone. Most generally, it is understood to be a function definition in the language at hand.

In C mode, a function definition is understood to include the return data type, the function name, and the argument declarations appearing before the { character.

These are the commands for operating on function definitions:

(CONTROL)-(META)-**a**

> Move to the beginning of the most recent function definition. You can use this command to scan forward through a buffer one function at a time.

(CONTROL)-(META)-**e**

> Move to the end of the next function definition. You can use this command to scan backward through a buffer one function at a time.

(CONTROL)-(META)-h

> Put Point at the beginning and Mark at the end of the current (or next, if between) function definition. This command sets up an entire function definition for a Region oriented operation such as kill.

> **CAUTION**
>
> The **emacs** editor now believes that an opening brace at the left margin is part of a function definition. This is a heuristic to speed up the reverse scan for a definition's leading edge. If your code has an indention style that puts that opening brace elsewhere, you may get unexpected results.

Indention

The **emacs** C mode has extensive logic to control the indention of C programs. Furthermore, you can adjust the logic for many different styles of C indention.

Indention is called into action by these commands:

(TAB)

> Adjust the indention of the current line. (TAB) inserts or deletes whitespace at the beginning of the line until the indention conforms to the current context and rules in effect. Point is not moved at all unless it lies in the whitespace area; in that case it is moved to the end of that whitespace. (TAB) does not insert anything except leading whitespace, so you can hit it at any time and at any position in the line. If you really want to insert a tab in the text, you can use (META)-i or (CONTROL)-Q (TAB).

(LINEFEED)

> Shorthand for (RETURN) followed by (TAB). The (LINEFEED) key is a convenience for entering new code, giving you an autoindent as you begin each line.

To indent multiple lines with a single command, there are two possibilities:

(CONTROL)-(META)-q

> Re-indent all the lines inside the next pair of matched braces. (CONTROL)-(META)-q assumes the left brace is correctly indented, and drives the indention from there. If the left brace itself needs help, type (TAB) on its line before giving this command. All the lines up to the matching brace will be indented as if you had typed (TAB) on each one.

(CONTROL)-(META)-\

> Re-indent all the lines in the current Region between Point and Mark. Put Point just to the left of a left brace and then give the command. All the lines up to the matching brace will be indented as if you had typed (TAB) on each one.

OPTIONAL

Customizing Indention

Many styles of C programming have evolved, and **emacs** makes an effort to support automatic indention for all of them. The indention coding is controlled by six numeric and two Boolean variables, all of which you can set.

In this presentation, the variables are briefly described, and several style sheets are given. Those wishing the long story are referred to the indention section of the online **emacs** manual.

The numeric variables follow:

c-indent-level

> Controls indention of C statements within the surrounding block. The surrounding block's indention is the indention of the line containing the open brace.

c-continued-statement-offset

> Controls extra indention for a statement within a statement, such as a **then** clause, that is not within braces.

c-brace-offset

> Controls extra indention for a line starting with an open brace.

c-brace-imaginary-offset

> An open brace following other text is treated as if it were this far to the right of the start of its line.

c-argdecl-indent

> Controls indention level of declarations of C function arguments.

c-label-offset

> Controls extra indention for a line that is a label, case, or default.

The Boolean variables follow:

c-auto-newline

> Normally set to **nil** (false). If set to **t** (true), then newlines are automatically inserted after colons and semicolons, and before and after left and right braces. This is sometimes called *Electric C Mode*. However, many consider it too busy, and it does not mesh with the Berkeley-style end-of-line open brace.

c-tab-always-indent

> Normally set to **t** (true). When set to **nil** (false), then the ⟨TAB⟩ key indents only when Point lies in the line's initial whitespace. Anywhere to the right of a printing character, ⟨TAB⟩ does no indenting and only inserts itself.

OPTIONAL Continued

The style sheets defining indention (in characters) for the common K&R (Kernighan and Ritchie), Berkeley, and GNU styles appear below:

Variable	K&R	Berkeley	GNU
c-indent-level	5	8	2
c-continued-statement-offset	5	8	2
c-brace-offset	–5	–8	0
c-brace-imaginary-offset	0	0	0
c-argdecl-indent	0	8	5
c-label-offset	–5	–8	–2

Comment Handling

These are the commands that facilitate working with comments:

(META)-;

> (semicolon) Insert a comment on this line, or align an existing comment. This command inserts or aligns a comment. Its behavior differs according to the current situation on this line:
>
> - If there is no comment on this line, an empty one is created at the value of comment-column.
>
> - If text already on this line overlaps the position of comment-column, a comment is placed one space after the end of the text.
>
> - If there is already a comment on this line but not at the current value of comment-column, the command realigns the comment at that column. If text is in the way, it places the comment one space after the end of the text.
>
> Now that an aligned (possibly empty) comment exists on the line, move Point to the start of the comment text.

(CONTROL)-**X** ;

> Set comment column to the column after Point. The left margin is column 0.

(CONTROL)-**U** – (CONTROL)-**X** ;

> Kill the comment on the current line. The command (CONTROL)-**U** (CONTROL)-**X**; sets comment-column from the first comment found above this line, then performs a (META)-; command to insert or align a comment at that position.

(CONTROL)-**U** (CONTROL)-**X** ;

> Set comment column to the position of the first comment found above this line, then execute a (META)-; command to insert or align a comment on this line.

Each buffer has its own **comment-column** variable, which you can view with the (CONTROL)-**H** v *comment-column* (RETURN) help command.

Special-Purpose Modes

The **emacs** editor has a third family of Major Modes that are not oriented toward a particular language and not even oriented toward ordinary editing. Instead, they perform some special function. They may define their own key bindings and commands to accomplish that function. Some examples follow:

- Rmail: Read, archive, and compose email.
- Dired: Move around in an **ls –l** display and operate on files.
- VIP: Simulate a complete **vi** environment.
- Shell: Run an interactive subshell from inside an **emacs** buffer.

Only Shell mode is discussed in this book.

Shell Mode

One-time shell commands and region filtering have been discussed earlier. Shell mode differs: each **emacs** buffer in Shell mode has an underlying interactive shell permanently associated with it. This shell takes its input from the last line of the buffer and sends its output back to the buffer, advancing Point as it goes. The buffer, if not edited, is a record of the complete shell session.

The shell runs asynchronously, whether you have its buffer in view or not. The **emacs** editor uses idle time to read the shell's output and add it to the buffer.

Type (META)-**x** *shell* to create a buffer named *shell* and start a subshell. If a buffer named *shell* exists already, **emacs** just switches to that buffer.

The shell name to run is taken from one of these sources:

- the Lisp variable **explicit-shell-file-name**
- the environment variable **ESHELL**
- the environment variable **SHELL**

If you really want to start a second shell, then first use (META)-**x** *rename-buffer* to change the name of the existing shell's buffer. This process can be continued to create as many subshells and buffers as you want, all running in parallel.

In Shell mode, a special set of commands is defined. They are mostly bound to two-key sequences starting with (CONTROL)-**C**. Each sequence is meant to be similar to the ordinary control characters found in UNIX, but with a leading (CONTROL)-**C**. These are some of the Shell mode commands:

(RETURN)

> If Point is at the end of the buffer, **emacs** inserts the (RETURN) and sends this (the last) line to the shell. If Point is elsewhere, it copies this line to the end of the buffer, peeling off the old shell prompt (see the regular expression **shell-prompt-pattern**) if one existed. Then this copied line, now the last in the buffer, is sent to the shell.

(CONTROL)-**C** (CONTROL)-**D**

> Send (CONTROL)-**D** to shell or its subjob.

(CONTROL)-C (CONTROL)-C

> Send (CONTROL)-C to shell or its subjob.

(CONTROL)-C (CONTROL)-\

> Send quit signal to shell or its subjob.

(CONTROL)-C (CONTROL)-U

> Kill the text on the current line not yet completed.

(CONTROL)-C (CONTROL)-R

> Scroll back to beginning of last shell output, putting the first line of output at the top of the window.

(CONTROL)-C (CONTROL)-O

> Delete the last batch of shell output.

OPTIONAL

Customizing emacs

At the center of **emacs** is a Lisp interpreter written in C. This version of Lisp is significantly extended with many special commands specifically oriented to editing. The interpreter's main task is to execute the Lisp-coded system that actually implements the "look and feel" of **emacs**.

Reduced to essentials, this system implements a continuous loop that watches keystrokes arrive, parses them into commands, executes those commands, and updates the screen.

There are a number of ways to customize this behavior.

- As single keystrokes come in, they are mapped immediately through a keyboard translation table. By changing the entries in this table, it is possible to swap keys. If you are used to **vi**, you can swap (DELETE) and (CONTROL)-**H**. Then (CONTROL)-**H** will backspace as it does in **vi**, and (DELETE), which is not used by **vi**, will be the Help key. Of course if you use (DELETE) as an interrupt key, you may want to choose another key to swap with (CONTROL)-**H**.

- The mapped keystrokes are then gathered into small groups called *key sequences*. A key sequence may be only a single key, such as (CONTROL)-**N**, or may have two or more keys, such as (CONTROL)-**X** (CONTROL)-**F**. Once gathered, the key sequences are used to select a particular procedure to be executed. The rules for gathering each key sequence and the specific procedure name to be executed when that sequence comes in are all codified in a series of tables called *keymaps*. By altering the keymaps, you can change the gathering rules, or change which procedure is associated with which sequence. If you are used to **vi**'s use of (CONTROL)-**W** to back up over the word you are entering, you may want to change **emacs'** (CONTROL)-**W** binding from its standard **kill-region** to **delete-word-backward**.

- The command behavior is often conditioned by one or more global variables or options. It may be possible to get the behavior you want by setting some of these variables.

- The command itself is usually a Lisp program that can be reprogrammed to make it behave as desired. While this is not for beginners, the Lisp source to nearly all commands is available, and the internal Lisp system is fully documented. As mentioned before, it is common to load customized Lisp code at startup time even if you did not write it yourself.

Most **emacs** documentation glosses over all the translation, gathering, and procedure selection, and talks about keystrokes as though they were the actual commands. However, it is still important to know that the underlying machinery exists, and to understand that its behavior can be changed.

The .emacs **Startup File**

Each time you start **emacs**, it loads the file of Lisp code named .emacs from your home directory. This is the most common way to customize **emacs** for yourself. There are two command-line options controlling this:

–q

Ignore the .emacs file; just start up without it. This is one way to get past a bad .emacs file.

–u **userid**

Use the .emacs file from the home directory of **userid**.

This startup file is generally concerned only with key binding and option setting, and it is possible to write the Lisp statements in a fairly straightforward style.

Each parenthesized Lisp statement is a Lisp function call. Inside the parentheses, the first symbol is the function name, and the rest of the (SPACE)-separated tokens are arguments to that function. The most common function in the .emacs file is simple assignment to a global variable, and it is named **setq**. The first argument is the name of a variable to be set, and the second argument is its new value. For example:

```
(setq c-indent-level 8)
```

sets the variable named **c-indent-level** to 8.

To set the default value for a variable that is buffer-private, use the function **name setq-default**.

To set a specific element of a vector, use the function **name aset**. The first argument is the name of the vector, the second is the target offset, and the third is the new value of the target entry.

In the startup file, the new value is usually a constant. Briefly, the formats of these constants are as follows:

OPTIONAL Continued

Numbers

Decimal integers, with an optional minus sign.

Strings

Similar to C strings, but with extensions for (CONTROL) and (META) characters: \C-s yields (CONTROL)-**S**, \M-s yields (META)-**s**, and \M-\C-s yields (CONTROL)-(META)-**s**.

Characters

Not like C characters; start with **?** and continue with a printing character or with a backslash escape sequence (e.g., ?a, ?\C-i, ?\033).

Booleans

Not 1 and 0; use instead **t** for *true* and **nil** for *false*.

Other Lisp objects

Begin with a single quotation mark, and continue with the object's name.

Remapping Keys

The **emacs** command loop begins each cycle by translating incoming keystrokes into the name of the command to be executed. The basic translation operation uses the ASCII value of the current incoming character to index a 128-element vector called a *keymap*.

Sometimes a character's eighth bit is interpreted as the (META) *case,* but this can't always be relied upon. At the point of translation, all (META) characters appear with the (ESCAPE) prefix, whether they were actually typed that way or not.

Each position in this vector is one of the following:

- Not defined at all. No translation possible in this map.

- The name of another keymap—switches to that keymap and waits for the next character to arrive.

- The name of a Lisp function to be called. Translation process is done; call this command.

Since keymaps can reference other keymaps, an arbitrarily complex recognition tree can be set up. However, the mainstream **emacs** bindings use at most three keys, with a very small group of well-known *prefix keys*, each with its well-known keymap name.

Each buffer may have a *local keymap* that, if present, will be used first for any keystrokes arriving while a window into that buffer is selected. This allows the regular mapping to be extended or overridden on a per-buffer basis, and is most often used to add bindings for a major mode.

OPTIONAL Continued

The basic translation flow runs as follows:

- Map the first character through the buffer's local keymap; if it is defined as a Lisp function name, then translation is done, and **emacs** executes that function. If not defined, then use this same character to index the global top level keymap.

- Map the first character through the top-level global keymap **global-map**. At this stage and each following stage, the following conditions hold:

- If the entry for this character is not defined, it is an error. Send a bell to the terminal, and discard all the characters entered in this key sequence.

- If the entry for this character is defined as a Lisp function name, translation is done, and the function is executed.

- If the entry for this character is defined as the name of another keymap, then switch to that keymap and wait for another character to select one of its elements.

Everything must be a command or an error. Ordinary characters that are to be inserted in the buffer are usually bound to the command **self-insert-command**. The well-known prefix characters are each associated with a keymap. Some of these keymaps follow:

ctl-x-map

For characters following (CONTROL)-**X**

ctl-x-4-map

For characters following (CONTROL)-**X 4**

help-map

For characters following (CONTROL)-**H**

esc-map

For characters following (ESCAPE) (including (META) characters)

mode-specific-map

For characters following (CONTROL)-**C**

To see the current state of the keymaps, you may type (CONTROL)-**H b** at any time. They appear in the following order: first local, then global, and finally the shorter maps for each prefix key. Each line has the name of the Lisp function to be called; the documentation for that function can be retrieved with the commands (CONTROL)-**H f function-name** or (CONTROL)-**H k key-sequence**.

OPTIONAL Continued

The most common sort of keymap customization is making small changes to the global command assignments without creating any new keymaps or commands. This is most easily done in the **.emacs** file, using the Lisp function **define-key**.

The **define-key** takes three arguments:

- keymap name
- single character defining a position in that map
- command to be executed when this character appears

For instance, to bind the command **backward-kill-word** to (CONTROL)-**W**, use the statement

```
(define-key global-map "\C-w" 'backward-kill-word)
```

or to bind the command kill-region to (CONTROL)-**X** (CONTROL)-**K**, use the statement

```
(define-key ctl-x-map "\C-k" 'kill-region)
```

The \ character causes **C-w** to be interpreted as (CONTROL)-**W** instead of three letters (equivalent to \^w also). The unmatched single quotation mark in front of the command name is correct. It is a Lisp escape character to keep the name from being evaluated too soon.

A Sample .emacs File

If executed, the following **.emacs** file produces a plain editing environment that minimizes surprises for **vi** users. Of course if any section or any line is inapplicable or not to your liking, you can edit it out or comment it with one or more ; comment characters beginning in column 1. If your system does not use (CONTROL)-**S** (CONTROL)-**Q** flow control, take out the section labeled Flow Control below.

```
; Preference Variables

(setq make-backup-files nil)        ;Don't make backup files
(setq backup-by-copying t)          ;If you do, at least don't destroy links
(setq delete-auto-save-files t)     ;Delete autosave files when writing orig
(setq blink-matching-paren nil)     ;Don't blink opening delimiter
(setq-default case-fold-search nil) ;Don't fold cases in search
(setq require-final-newline 'ask)   ;Ask about missing final newline

;; Keyboard Remapping

;; Set up keyboard-translate-table as a 128-byte string,
;; and initialize this string for 1-1 mapping.  Later, we
;; can easily remap a key without wondering if its entry exists.
;; This preliminary step is needed for swapping C-h and DEL,
;; and also for reassigning
;; C-s and C-q to fall in line with someone's flow control.
;
(setq keyboard-translate-table (make-string 128 0))
(let ((i 0))
  (while (< i 128)
    (aset keyboard-translate-table i i)
    (setq i (1+ i))))
```

```
;; Now swap mappings for C-h and DEL.
(aset keyboard-translate-table ?\C-h ?\177)
(aset keyboard-translate-table ?\177 ?\C-h)

;; End of Keyboard Remapping


;; Flow Control

;; If in your system C-s and C-q are taken for the purposes of
;; flow control, follow the advice in GNU Emacs Lisp Reference
;; Manual, Sections 33.4 and
;; 33.6. First tell Emacs that C-s and C-q have a flow-control role,
;; and then remap two other keys as C-s and C-q.
(set-input-mode nil t)   ;cbreak mode - C-s, C-q are flow control

;; Remap C-\ to C-s and C-^ to C-q.
(aset keyboard-translate-table ?\C-\\ ?\C-s)
(aset keyboard-translate-table ?\C-^  ?\C-q)

;; End of Flow Control

;; Reassigning C-w to keep on deleting words backward

;; C-w is supposed to be kill-region, but this is a great burden
;; for vi-trained fingers.  Bind it instead to backward-kill-word
;; for more familiar, friendly behavior.
(define-key global-map "\^w" 'backward-kill-word)

;; For kill-region we use instead a two-key sequence C-x C-k.
(define-key ctl-x-map "\^k" 'kill-region)

;; End of C-w reassignment


;; C-mode Berkeley setup

;; For C-mode, set up the indention state variables for Berkeley-style
;; indention.  The default GNU settings are also shown here, but
;; commented out.

;; Tune C indention variables to Berkeley settings.
(setq c-indent-level  8)
(setq c-continued-statement-offset  8)
(setq c-brace-offset  -8)
(setq c-argdecl-indent  8)
(setq c-label-offset  -8)

;; Tune C indention variables to GNU settings.
;;(setq c-indent-level  2)
;;(setq c-continued-statement-offset  2)
;;(setq c-brace-offset  0)
;;(setq c-argdecl-indent  5)
;;(setq c-label-offset  -2)

;; End of C-mode Berkeley setup
```

Resources for emacs

If you would like to try out **emacs**, but it is not available at your site, or after spending time with **emacs**, you want to try out more of its features and capabilities and wish to see more documentation, there is more material available in both paper and electronic form. GNU **emacs** itself is available in source form.

Usenet emacs FAQ (Frequently Asked Questions)

If you have access to Usenet, many newsgroups now maintain a file of frequently asked questions and their answers. An excellent **emacs** FAQ file is available that addresses more than 125 common questions; copies of it can be found in the newsgroups **gnu.emacs.help**, **comp.emacs**, and **news.answers**. It has the most up-to-date information and is strongly recommended as a starting point.

Access to emacs

If you have Internet access, you can use anonymous ftp to copy the current distribution from host **prep.ai.mit.edu**. There is no charge. It is probably best to begin by retrieving the file **/pub/gnu/GNUinfo/FTP** for the most current instructions and list of alternative archive sites.

This same ftp file has some information about getting **emacs** via **uucp**, reproduced here for readers without **ftp**:

```
OSU is distributing via UUCP: most GNU software, MIT C Scheme,
Compress, News, RN, NNTP, Patch, some Appletalk stuff, some of the
Internet Requests For Comment (RFC) et al..  See their periodic
postings on the Usenet newsgroup comp.sources.d for informational
updates.  Current details from <staff@cis.ohio-state.edu> or
<...!osu-cis!staff>.

Information on how to uucp some GNU programs is available via
electronic mail from: uunet!hutch!barber, hqda-ai!merlin, acornrc!bob,
hao!scicom!qetzal!upba!ugn!nepa!denny, ncar!noao!asuvax!hrc!dan,
bigtex!james (aka james@bigtex.cactus.org), oli-stl!root,
src@contrib.de (Germany), toku@dit.co.jp (Japan) and info@ftp.uu.net.
```

If you have no electronic access to Internet or uucp, you can order **emacs** on tape directly from the Free Software Foundation for about $200. Many different media and tape formats are available, and you can also buy typeset copies of the **emacs** user manual, the **emacs** Lisp Manual, and an **emacs** Reference Card.

The Free Software Foundation can be reached at these addresses:

Mail:

> Free Software Foundation, Inc.
> 675 Massachusetts Avenue
> Cambridge, MA 02139
> USA

Email:

> gnu@prep.ai.mit.edu

Phone:

> 617-876-3296

SUMMARY

You can precede many of the following commands with a numeric argument to make the command repeat the number of times specified by the argument. Precede a numeric argument with (CONTROL)-**U** to keep **emacs** from entering the argument as text.

Moving the Cursor

Key	Action—Move Cursor
(CONTROL)-**F**	Forward by characters
(CONTROL)-**B**	Backward by characters
(META)-**f**	Forward by words
(META)-**b**	Backward by words
(META)-**e**	To end of sentence
(META)-**a**	To beginning of sentence
(META)-**[**	To end of paragraph
(META)-**]**	To beginning of paragraph
(META)-**>**	Forward to end of buffer
(META)-**<**	Backward to beginning of buffer
(CONTROL)-**E**	To end of line
(CONTROL)-**A**	To beginning of line
(CONTROL)-**N**	Down by lines
(CONTROL)-**P**	Up by lines
(CONTROL)-**V**	Forward (scroll) by windows
(META)-**v**	Backward (scroll) by windows
(CONTROL)-**L**	Clear and repaint screen, and scroll current line to center of window.
(META)-**r**	To beginning of middle line
(CONTROL)-**U** num (META)-**r**	To beginning of line number **num** (**0**=top, –=bottom)

Killing and Deleting

Key	Action
(CONTROL)-**D**	Delete the characters under and to the right of cursor.
(DELETE)	Delete the characters to the left of cursor.
(META)-**d**	Kill from cursor forward to the end of current word.
(META)-(DELETE)	Kill from cursor backward to beginning of previous word.
(META)-**k**	Kill forward to the end of a sentence.
(CONTROL)-**X** (DELETE)	Kill backward to the beginning of a sentence.

(Continued)

Key	Action
(CONTROL)-K	Kill the text from the cursor forward to (but not including) the line ending (LINEFEED). If there is no text between the cursor and the (LINEFEED), kill the (LINEFEED) itself.
(CONTROL)-U 1 (CONTROL)-K	Kill from cursor forward to and including (LINEFEED).
(CONTROL)-U 0 (CONTROL)-K	Kill from cursor backward to beginning of this line.
(META)-z char	Kill up to but not including the next occurrence of char.
(META)-w	Copy Region to Kill Ring; do not erase from the buffer.
(CONTROL)-W	Kill Region.
(CONTROL)-Y	Yank most recently killed text into current buffer at Point. Set Mark at beginning of this text, Point and cursor at the end.
(META)-y	Erase the just-yanked text, rotate the Kill Ring, and yank the next item (only after (CONTROL)-Y or (META)-y).

Searching

Key	Action
(CONTROL)-S	Incrementally prompt for a string, and search forward for a match.
(CONTROL)-S (ESCAPE)	Prompt for a complete string, and search forward for a match.
(CONTROL)-R	Incrementally prompt for a string, and search backward for a match.
(CONTROL)-R (ESCAPE)	Prompt for a complete string, and search backward for a match.
(META)-(CONTROL)-S	Incrementally prompt for a regular expression, and search forward for a match.
(META)-(CONTROL)-S (ESCAPE)	Prompt for a complete regular expression, and search forward for a match.
(META)-x isearch-backward-regexp	Incrementally prompt for a regular expression, and search backward for a match.
(META)-x isearch-backward-regexp (ESCAPE)	Prompt for a complete regular expression, and search backward for a match.

Online Help

Key	Action
(CONTROL)-H a	Prompt for **string**, then show a list of commands whose names contain **string**.
(CONTROL)-H b	Show a table (it will be long) of all the key bindings now in effect.
(CONTROL)-H c key-sequence	Print the name of the command bound to this **key-sequence**.
(CONTROL)-H k key-sequence	Print the name and documentation of the command bound to this **key-sequence**.
(CONTROL)-H f	Prompt for the name of a Lisp **function**, and print the documentation for that Lisp function.
(CONTROL)-H i	(eye) Takes you to the top menu of Info, a documentation browser.
(CONTROL)-H l	(ell) Show the last 100 characters typed.
(CONTROL)-H m	Show the documentation and special key bindings for the current major mode.
(CONTROL)-H n	Show the **emacs** news file.
(CONTROL)-H t	Runs an **emacs** tutorial session.
(CONTROL)-H v	Prompts for a Lisp variable name, and gives the documentation for that variable.
(CONTROL)-H w	Prompts for a **command-name**, and gives the key sequence, if any, bound to that command.

Region

Key	Action
(META)-W	Copy the Region nondestructively to the Kill Ring.
(CONTROL)-W	Kill the Region.
(META)-x *print-region*	Send the Region to the print spooler.
(CONTROL)-X a	Prompt for buffer name, and append Region to that buffer.
(META)-x *append-to-file*	Prompt for filename, and append region to that file.
(CONTROL)-X (CONTROL)-U	Convert Region to uppercase.
(CONTROL)-X (CONTROL)-L	Convert Region to lowercase.

Working with Lines

Key	Action
(META)-x *occur*	Prompt for a regular expression, and list each line with a match for the expression in a buffer named *Occur*.
(META)-x *delete-matching -lines*	Prompt for a regular expression, and delete each line with a match for that expression.
(META)-x *delete-non-matching-lines*	Prompt for a regular expression, and delete each line that does *not* match that expression.

Unconditional and Interactive Replacement

Key	Action
(META)-x *replace-string*	Prompt for **string** and **newstring**. Replaces every instance of **string** with **newstring**. Mark is set at the start of the command.
(META)-% *or* (META)-x *query-replace*	As above, but query for replacement of each instance of **string**. See table of responses below.
(META)-x *replace-regexp*	Prompt for a **regular expression** and **newstring**. Replaces every instance of the **regular expression** with **newstring**. Mark is set at the start of the command.
(META)-x *query-replace-regexp*	As above, but query for replacement of each instance of the **regular expression**. See table of responses below.

Responses to Replacement Queries

Key	Action
(ESCAPE)	Do not do any more replacements; quit now.
(SPACE)	Make this replacement and go on.
(DELETE)	Do *not* make this replacement. Skip over it and go on.
,	(comma) Make this replacement, display the result, and ask for another command.
.	(period) Make this replacement and quit searching.
!	(exclamation point) Replace this, and all remaining instances, without asking any more questions.

Working with Windows

Key	Action
(CONTROL)-X b	Switch buffer that window views.
(CONTROL)-X 2	Split current window into 2 vertically.
(CONTROL)-X 5	Split current window into 2 horizontally.
(CONTROL)-X o	(lowercase oh) Select other window.
(META)-(CONTROL)-V	Scroll other window.
(CONTROL)-X 4 b	Prompt for buffer name, and select it in other window
(CONTROL)-X 4 f	Prompt for filename, and select it in other window.
(CONTROL)-X 0	(zero) Delete current window.
(CONTROL)-X 1	Delete all but current window.
(META)-x *shrink-window*	Make current window one line shorter.
(CONTROL)-X ^	Make current window one line taller.
(CONTROL)-X }	Make current window one character wider.
(CONTROL)-X {	Make current window one character narrower.

Working with Files

Key	Action
(CONTROL)-X (CONTROL)-F	Prompt for a filename and read its contents into a freshly created buffer. Assign the file's final pathname component as the buffer name.
(CONTROL)-X (CONTROL)-V	Prompt for a filename, and read its contents into the current buffer (overwriting the contents of the current buffer).
(CONTROL)-X 4 (CONTROL)-F	Prompt for a filename, and read its contents into a freshly created buffer. Assign the file's final pathname component as the buffer name. Create a new window for this buffer, and select that window. This splits the screen in half if you begin with only one window.
(CONTROL)-X (CONTROL)-S	Save the current buffer to the original file.
(CONTROL)-X S	Prompt for whether or not to save each modified buffer (y/n).
(META)-x *set-visited-file-name*	Prompt for a filename, and set this name as the current buffer's "original" name.
(CONTROL)-X (CONTROL)-W	Prompt for a filename, set this name as the "original" file for the current buffer, and save the current buffer into that file.
(META)-~	(tilde) Clear modified flag from the current buffer. Use with caution.

Working with Buffers

Key	Action
(CONTROL)-X (CONTROL)-S	Save the current buffer into its associated file.
(CONTROL)-X (CONTROL)-F	Prompt for a filename and visit that file.
(CONTROL)-X b	Prompt for a buffer name and select it. If it does not exist, create it first.
(CONTROL)-X 4 b	Prompt for a buffer name, and select it in another window. The existing window is not disturbed, although the new window may overlap it.
(CONTROL)-X (CONTROL)-B	Create a buffer named *Buffer List*, and display it in another window. The existing window is not disturbed, although the new window may overlap it. The new buffer is not selected. In the *Buffer List* buffer, each buffer's data is shown, with name, size, mode(s), and original filename.
(META)-x *rename-buffer*	Prompt for a new buffer name, and give this new name to the current buffer.
(CONTROL)-X (CONTROL)-Q	Toggle the current buffer's read-only status and the associated **%%** Mode Line indicator.
(CONTROL)-X a	Prompt for buffer name, and append the current Region to the end of that buffer.
(META)-x *prepend-to-buffer*	Prompt for buffer name, and append the current Region to the end of that buffer.
(META)-x *copy-to-buffer*	Prompt for buffer name, and delete the contents of the buffer before copying the current Region into that buffer.
(META)-x *insert-buffer*	Prompt for buffer name, and insert the entire contents of that buffer into the current buffer at Point.
(CONTROL)-X k	Prompt for buffer name, and delete that buffer.
(META)-x *kill-some-buffers*	Go through the entire buffer list, and offer the chance to delete each buffer.

Foreground Shell Commands

Key	Action
(META)-!	(exclamation) Prompt for a shell command, execute it, and display the output.
(CONTROL)-U (META)-!	(exclamation) Prompt for a shell command, execute it, and insert the output at Point.
(META)-|	(vertical bar) Prompt for a shell command, give the Region contents as input, filter it through the command, and display the output.
(CONTROL)-U (META)-|	(vertical bar) Prompt for a shell command, give the Region contents as input, filter it through the command, delete the old Region contents, and insert the output in that position.

Background Shell Commands

Key	Action
(META)-x *compile*	Prompt for a shell command and run it in the background, with output going to a buffer named *compilation*.
(META)-x *kill-compilation*	Kill the background process.

Case Conversion

Key	Action
(META)-l	(lowercase ell) Convert word to the right of Point to lowercase.
(META)-u	Convert word to the right of Point to uppercase.
(META)-c	Convert word to the right of Point to initial caps.
(CONTROL)-X (CONTROL)-L	Convert Region between Point and Mark to lowercase.
(CONTROL)-X (CONTROL)-U	Convert Region between Point and Mark to uppercase.

C Mode

Key	Action
(CONTROL)-(META)-**f**	Move forward over an expression.
(CONTROL)-(META)-**b**	Move backward over an expression.
(CONTROL)-(META)-**k**	Kill an expression forward. It leaves Point at the same finishing position as (CONTROL)-(META)-**f**, but kills the expression it traverses.
(CONTROL)-(META)-**@**	Set Mark at the position (CONTROL)-(META)-**f** would move to, without changing Point.
(CONTROL)-(META)-**a**	Move to the beginning of the most recent function definition.
(CONTROL)-(META)-**e**	Move to the end of the next function definition.
(CONTROL)-(META)-**h**	Put Point at the beginning and Mark at the end of the current (or next, if between) function definition.

Shell Mode

Key	Action
(RETURN)	Sends the current line to the shell.
(CONTROL)-**C** (CONTROL)-**D**	Send (CONTROL)-**D** to shell or its subjob.
(CONTROL)-**C** (CONTROL)-**C**	Send (CONTROL)-**C** to shell or its subjob.
(CONTROL)-**C** (CONTROL)-****	Send quit signal to shell or its subjob.
(CONTROL)-**C** (CONTROL)-**U**	Kill the text on the current line not yet completed.
(CONTROL)-**C** (CONTROL)-**R**	Scroll back to beginning of last shell output, putting the first line of output at the top of the window.
(CONTROL)-**C** (CONTROL)-**O**	Delete the last batch of shell output.

REVIEW EXERCISES

1. Given a buffer full of English text, answer the following questions.

   a. How would you change every instance of *his* to *their*?

   b. How would you do this only in the final paragraph?

   c. Is there a way to look at every usage in context before it gets changed?

   d. How would you deal with the possibility that *His* might begin a sentence?

2. What command moves the cursor to the end of the current paragraph? Can you use this command to skip through the buffer in one-paragraph steps?

3. Suppose you are typing a long sentence and get lost in the middle.

    a. Is there an easy way to kill the botched sentence and start over?

    b. What if it is just one word that is incorrect? Is there an alternative to backspacing one letter at a time?

4. After you have been working on a paragraph for a while, most likely some lines have become too short and others are too long. Is there a command to "neaten up" the paragraph without rebreaking all the lines by hand?

5. Suppose you want to impersonate an Apple2 hacker. Is there a way to change the whole buffer to capital letters? Can you think of a way to change just one paragraph?

6. How would you reverse the order of two paragraphs?

7. How would you reverse two words?

8. Imagine that you saw a Usenet posting with something particularly funny in it and saved the posting to a file. How would you incorporate this file into your own buffer? What if you only wanted a couple of paragraphs? How would you add > to the beginning of each included line?

ADVANCED REVIEW EXERCISES

9. Assume your buffer contains the C code shown here, with the major mode set for C, and the cursor positioned at the end of the while line as shown.

```
/*
 * Copy string s2 to s1.  s1 must be large enough
 * return s1
 */
char *
strcpy(s1, s2)
register char *s1, *s2;
{
      register char *os1;

      os1 = s1;
      while (*s1++ = *s2++)
      ;
return(os1);
}

/* Copy source into dest, stopping after '\0' is copied, and
    return a pointer to the '\0' at the end of dest.  Then our caller
    can concatenate to the dest string without another strlen call. */
char *
stpcpy (dest, source)
      char *dest;
      char *source;
{
  while ((*dest++ = *source++) != '\0') ■
    ; /* void loop body */
  return (dest - 1);
}
```

a. What command moves the cursor to the opening brace of strcpy? What command moves the cursor past the closing brace? Can you use them to skip through the buffer in one-procedure steps?

b. Assume the cursor is just past the closing parenthesis of the while condition. How do you move to the matching opening parenthesis? How do you move back to the matching close parenthesis again? Does the same command set work for matched [] and {}? How does this differ from the **vi** % command?

c. One procedure is indented in the Berkeley indention style; the other is indented in the GNU style. What command re-indents a line in accordance with the current indentation style you have set up? How would you re-indent an entire procedure?

d. Suppose you want to write five string procedures and intend to use strcpy as a starting point for further editing. How would you make five duplicate copies of the strcpy procedure?

e. How would you compile the code without leaving **emacs**?

CHAPTER 10

The Bourne Shell

The Bourne Shell is both a command interpreter and a high-level programming language. As a command interpreter, it processes commands that you enter in response to its prompt. When you use the Bourne Shell as a programming language, it processes groups of commands stored in files called shell scripts. This chapter expands on the interactive features introduced in Chapter 5, explains how to create and run shell scripts, and explores aspects of shell programming, such as variables and control flow commands. Although this chapter is primarily about the Bourne Shell, most of it also applies to the Korn Shell. The theoretical portions of this chapter and the sections "Creating a Simple Shell Script" and "Command Separation and Grouping" apply to the C Shell as well as the Korn Shell. Chapters 11 and 12 describe the C Shell and Korn Shell.

Background

This chapter starts by describing some fundamentals of using the shell. The first section, "Creating a Simple Shell Script," describes the basics of writing and running simple shell scripts. The following two sections—"Command Separation and Grouping" and "Redirecting the Standard Error"—provide information that you will find useful whether you are writing shell scripts or just using the shell interactively. The rest of the chapter explains concepts and commands, such as subshells, variables, and control structures, that you will need to write more sophisticated shell scripts.

Because many users prefer the Bourne Shell's programming language to the C Shell's, and because it is the basis of the Korn Shell programming language, this chapter describes Bourne Shell programming in detail. In the section on control flow commands, simple examples that illustrate the concepts are followed by more complicated examples in sections marked **OPTIONAL**. The more complex scripts illustrate traditional shell programming practices and introduce some UNIX utilities often used in scripts. If shell programming is new to you, you may want to skip these sections the first time you read the chapter. Return to them later when you feel comfortable with the basic concepts.

If you are not interested in mastering shell programming right now, you may want to skip the "Processes," "Variables," and "Control Flow Commands" sections of the chapter. However, you should read the "Keyword Shell Variables" section (page 292). The keyword shell variables control important characteristics of the shell environment when you are using the shell either interactively as a command interpreter or as a programming language.

Creating a Simple Shell Script

A *shell script* is a file that contains commands to be executed by the shell. The commands in a shell script can be any commands you can enter in response to a shell prompt. For example, a command in a shell script might invoke a UNIX utility, a compiled program you have written, or another shell script. Like commands you give on the command line, a command in a shell script can use ambiguous file references and can have its input or output redirected from a file or sent through a pipe. (You can also use pipes and redirection with the input and output of the script itself.) In addition to the commands you would ordinarily use on the command line, there are a group of commands, the *control flow commands*, that were designed specifically for use in shell scripts. The control flow commands enable you to alter the order of execution of commands in a script as you would alter the order of execution of statements in a typical structured programming language.

The easiest way to run a shell script is to give its filename on the command line. The shell then interprets and executes the commands in the script, one after another. Thus, by using a shell script you can simply and quickly initiate a complex series of tasks or a repetitive procedure.

Making a File Executable

In order to execute a shell script by giving its name as a command, you must have permission to read and execute the file that contains the script. Execute permission tells the shell and the system that the owner, group, or public has permission to execute the file. It also implies that the content of the file is executable.

When you initially create a shell script using an editor such as **vi**, the file will typically not have its execute permission set. The example below shows a file, **whoson**, that is a shell script containing three command lines. When you initially create a file like **whoson**, you cannot execute it by giving its name as a command because you do not have execute permission.

```
$ cat whoson
date
echo Users Currently Logged In
who

$ whoson
whoson: execute permission denied
```

The shell does not recognize **whoson** as an executable file and issues an error message when you try to execute it.

As shown in Chapter 4, the **chmod** utility changes the access privileges associated with a file. Below, **ls** with the **–lg** options displays the access permissions of **whoson** before and after **chmod** gives the owner execute permission.

```
$ ls -lg whoson
-rw-r--r-- 1 alex    pubs      42  Jun 17 10:55 whoson
$ chmod u+x whoson
$ ls -lg whoson
-rwxr--r-- 1 alex    pubs      42  Jun 17 10:55 whoson
```
Execute permission for the owner
```
$ whoson
Fri Jun 17 10:59:40 PDT 1994
Users Currently Logged In
alex      console Jun 17 08:26
jenny     tty02   Jun 17 10:04
hls       tty06   Jun 17 08:51
```

The first **ls** displays a hyphen as the fourth character, indicating that the owner does not have permission to execute the file. Then **chmod** uses two arguments to give the owner execute access permission. The **u+x** causes **chmod** to add (+) execute access permission (**x**) for the owner (**u**). (The **u** stands for *user*, although it actually refers to the owner of the file, who may or may not be the user of the file at any given time.) The second argument is the name of the file. The second **ls** shows an **x** in the fourth position, indicating that the owner now has execute permission.

If other users are going to execute the file, you must also change group and/or public access privileges. For more information on access permissions, refer to "Access Permissions" in Chapter 4 and to **ls** and **chmod** in Part II.

Finally, the shell executes the file when its name is given as a command. If you try typing **whoson** in response to a shell prompt and you get an error message such as whoson: Command not found., your login shell is not set up to search for executable files in the working directory. Try giving the command below.

```
$ ./whoson
```

The ./ explicitly tells the shell to look for an executable file in the working directory. To change your environment so that the shell will search the working directory, refer to the **PATH** variable on page 293.

Now you know how to write and execute your own simple shell scripts. Shell scripts are convenient tools for running complex commands and series of commands that are run frequently. The next two sections of the chapter, "Command Separation and Grouping" and "Redirecting the Standard Error," describe features that are useful when you are running commands either on a command line or from within a script. The following section, "Processes," explains the relationships between commands, shell scripts, and UNIX system processes. It describes how a shell script is invoked and run, and describes the environment in which it is run.

Command Separation and Grouping

When you give the shell commands interactively or write a shell script, you must separate commands from one another. This section reviews the ways you can do this that were covered in Chapter 5 and introduces a few new ones.

The (NEWLINE) and ; Characters

The (NEWLINE) character is a unique command separator because it initiates execution of the command preceding it. You have seen this throughout this book each time you press the (RETURN) key at the end of a command line.

The semicolon (;) is a command separator that *does not* initiate execution of a command and *does not* change any aspect of how the command functions. You can execute a series of commands sequentially by entering them on a single command line and separating each from the next by a ;. To initiate execution of the sequence of commands, you must terminate the command line with a (RETURN).

```
$ a ; b ; c
```

If **a**, **b**, and **c** are commands, the preceding command line yields the same results as the following three command lines:

```
$ a
$ b
$ c
```

Although the white space around the semicolons in the example above makes the command line easier to read, it is not necessary. None of the command separators needs to be surrounded by (SPACE)s or (TAB)s.

The \ Character

When you are entering a very long command line and you reach the right side of your display screen, you can use a backslash (\) character to continue the command on the next line. The backslash quotes the (NEWLINE) character that follows it so that the shell does not treat it as a command terminator.

The | and & Characters

Other command separators are the pipe symbol (|) and the background task symbol (&). These command separators *do not* start execution of a command but *do* change some aspect of how the command functions. They alter where the input or output comes from or goes to, or they determine whether the shell executes the task in the background or in the foreground.

The following command line initiates a job that comprises three tasks. The shell directs the output from task **a** to task **b** and directs **b**'s output to **c**. Because the shell runs the entire job in the foreground, you do not get a prompt back until task **c** runs to completion.

```
$ a | b | c
```

The next command line executes tasks **a** and **b** in the background and task **c** in the foreground. The shell displays the process identification numbers (PIDs) for the processes running in the background. You get a prompt back as soon as **c** finishes.

```
$ a & b & c
14271
14272
```

The following command line executes all three tasks as background jobs. You get a prompt immediately.

```
$ a & b & c &
14290
14291
14292
```

You can use a pipe to send the output from one subtask to the next and run the whole job as a background task. Again, the prompt comes back immediately.

```
$ a | b | c &
14302
```

OPTIONAL

You can see a demonstration of sequential and concurrent processes run in both the foreground and background. Create a group of executable files named **a**, **b**, **c**, and **d**. Have each file echo its name over and over as file **a** (below) does. The \c causes **echo** to suppress the (NEWLINE) it ordinarily prints.

```
$ cat a
echo "aaaaaaaaaaaaaaaaaaaaaaaaae\c"
echo "aaaaaaaaaaaaaaaaaaaaaaaaae\c"
echo "aaaaaaaaaaaaaaaaaaaaaaaaae\c"
echo "aaaaaaaaaaaaaaaaaaaaaaaaae\c"
echo "aaaaaaaaaaaaaaaaaaaaaaaaae\c"
```

Your version of **echo** may use an option, **-n**, instead of \c.

```
$ echo -n "no newline here"
no newline here$
```

Execute the files sequentially and concurrently, using the example command lines from this section. When you execute two of these shell scripts sequentially, their outputs follow each other. When you execute two of them concurrently, their output is interspersed as control is passed back and forth between the tasks. The results will not always be identical because the UNIX system schedules jobs slightly differently each time they run. Two sample runs are shown here:

```
$ a&b&c&
14717
14718
14719
$ aaaaaaaaaaaaaaaaaaaaaaaaaaaaccccccccccccccccccccccccccccccccccc
ccccccccccccccccccccccccccccccccccccccccccccccccccccccccccccccccc
cccccccccccccccccccccccccccccccaaaaaaaaaaaaaaaaaaaaaaaaaaaaaaaaaa
aaaaaaaaaaaaaaaaaaaaaaaaaaaaaaaaaaaaaaaaaaaaaaaaaaaaaaaaaaaaaaaaa
aaaaaaaaaaaabbbbbbbbbbbbbbbbbbbbbbbbbbbbbbbbbbbbbbbbbbbbbbbbbbbbbb
bbbbbbbbbbbbbbbbbbbbbbbbbbbbbbbbbbbbbbbbbbbbbbbbbbbbbbbbbbbbbbbbbb
bbbbbbbbbbbbbbbbbbb
```

```
$ a&b&c&
14738
14739
14740
$ ccccccccccccccccccccccccccccccccccccccccccccccccccccccccccccccc
ccccccccccccccccccccccccccccccccccccccccccccccccccccccccccccccccc
ccccccbbbbbbbbbbbbbbbbbbbbbbbbbbbbbbbbbbbbbbbbbbbbbbbbbbbbbbbbbaaa
aaaaaaaaaaaaaaaaaaaaaaaaaaaaaaaaaaaaaaaaaaaaaaaaaaaaaaaaaaaaaaaaa
aaaaaaaaaaaaaaaaaaaaaaaaaaaaaaaaaaaaaaaaaaaaaaaaaaaaaaaaaaaaaaaaa
aabbbbbbbbbbbbbbbbbbbbbbbbbbbbbbbbbbbbbbbbbbbbbbbbbbbbbbbbbbbbbbbb
bbbbbbbbbbbbbbbbbbb
```

Command Grouping

You can use parentheses to group commands. The shell creates a new shell, a *subshell*, for each group, treating each group of commands as a job and forking processes as needed to execute the commands.

The command line below executes commands **a** and **b** sequentially in the background while executing **c** in the foreground. The shell prompt returns when **c** finishes execution.

```
$ (a ; b) & c
15007
```

This example differs from the earlier example **a & b & c** because tasks **a** and **b** are initiated not concurrently but sequentially.

Similarly, the following command line executes **a** and **b** sequentially in the background and, at the same time, executes **c** and **d** sequentially in the background. The prompt returns immediately.

```
$ (a ; b) & (c ; d) &
15020
15021
```

In the following shell script, the second pair of parentheses creates a subshell to run the commands following the pipe. Because of the parentheses, the output of the first **tar** command is available for the second **tar** command, despite the intervening **cd** command. Without the parentheses, the output of the first **tar** would be sent to **cd** and lost, because **cd** does not accept input from its standard input. The **$1** and **$2** are shell variables that represent the first and second command line arguments (page 296). The first pair of parentheses, which create a subshell to run the first two commands, are necessary so that users can call **cpdir** with relative pathnames. Without these parentheses, the first **cd** command would change the working directory of the script (and, consequently, the working directory of the second **cd** command), whereas with the parentheses only the working directory of the subshell changes.

```
$ cat cpdir
(cd $1 ; tar cf - . ) | (cd $2 ; tar xvf - )
$ cpdir /home/alex/sources /home/alex/memo/biblio
```

The preceding command line copies the files and subdirectories included in the /**home/alex/sources** directory to the directory named /**home/alex/memo/biblio** . This shell script is equivalent to using the –**r** option with **cp**. (Refer to **cp** in Part II. For information about the **tar** utility, see **tar** in Part II).

Refer to the "Processes" section on page 283 for more information about subshells.

Redirecting the Standard Error

Chapter 5 described the concept of standard output and explained how to redirect a command's standard output. In addition to the standard output, commands can send their output to another place: the *standard error*. A command can send error messages to standard error to keep them from getting mixed up with the information it sends to its standard output. Just as with the standard output, unless you redirect it, the shell sends a command's standard error output to the terminal. Unless you redirect one or the other, you will not know the difference between the output a command sends to its standard output and the output it sends to its standard error.

The following examples demonstrate how to redirect the standard output and the standard error to different files or to the same file. When you call **cat** with the name of a file that does not exist and the name of a file that does exist, it sends an error message to the standard error and copies the file to the standard output. Unless you redirect them, both messages appear on the terminal.

```
$ cat y
This is y.
$ cat x y
cat: x: No such file or directory
This is y.
```

When you redirect the standard output of a command using the "greater than" symbol, the error output is not affected—it still appears on the terminal.

```
$ cat x y > hold
cat: x: No such file or directory
$ cat hold
This is y.
```

Similarly, when you send the standard output through a pipe, the error output is not affected. In the example below, the standard output of **cat** is sent through a pipe to the **tr** (translate) command, which is used to convert lowercase characters to uppercase. The text that **cat** sends to the standard error is not translated, because it goes directly to the terminal rather than through the pipe.

```
$ cat x y | tr "[a-z]" "[A-Z]"
cat: x: No such file or directory
THIS IS Y.
```

The following example redirects the standard output and the error output to different files. The notation 2> tells the shell where to redirect the error output. The 1> is the same as > and tells the shell where to redirect the standard output. You can use > in place of 1>.

```
$ cat x y 1> hold1 2> hold2
$ cat hold1
This is y.
$ cat hold2
cat: x: No such file or directory
```

In the next example, 1> redirects the standard output to **hold**. Then 2>&1 declares file descriptor 2 to be a duplicate of file descriptor 1. The result is that both the standard output and the standard error are redirected to **hold**.

```
$ cat x y 1> hold 2>&1
$ cat hold
cat: x: No such file or directory
This is y.
```

In the above example, 1> **hold** precedes 2>&1. If they had been listed in the opposite order, the standard error would have been redirected to be a duplicate of the standard output before the standard output was redirected to **hold**. In that case only the standard output would have been redirected.

The next example declares file descriptor 2 to be a duplicate of file descriptor 1 and sends file descriptor 1 through a pipe to the **tr** command.

```
$ cat x y 2>&1 | tr "[a-z]" "[A-Z]"
CAT: X: NO SUCH FILE OR DIRECTORY
THIS IS Y.
```

You can also use **1>&2** to redirect the standard output of a command to the standard error. This technique is often used in shell scripts to send error messages to the standard error. In the following script, the standard output of the first **echo** command is redirected to the standard error:

```
$ cat message_demo
echo This is an error message. 1>&2
echo This is not an error message.
```

If you use **message_demo** and you do not redirect the standard output or the standard error of the script, the output of both **echo** commands will appear on your terminal. However, if you redirect the standard output, error messages like the one above will still go to your terminal. Refer to **links** on page 308 for an example of a script that uses **1>&2** to redirect the output of **echo** to the standard error to display error messages.

You can also use the **exec** command to redirect the standard input, standard output, and standard error of a shell script from within the script (page 329).

Processes

A *process* is the execution of a command by the UNIX system. The shell that starts up when you log in is a command, or a process, like any other. Whenever you give the name of a UNIX utility on the command line, a process is initiated. When you run a shell script, another shell process is started, and additional processes are created for each command in the script. Depending on how you invoke the shell script, the script will be run either by a new shell or by a subshell of the current shell.

Process Structure

Like the file structure, the process structure is hierarchical. It has parents, children, and even a *root*. A parent process *forks* a child process, which in turn can fork other processes. *Fork* is the name of an operating system routine that creates a new process. (You can also use the term *spawns;* the words are interchangeable.) One of the first things the UNIX operating system does to begin execution when a machine is started up is to start a single process— process identification (PID) number 1. This process holds the same position in the process structure as the root directory does in the file structure. It is the ancestor of all processes that each user works with. If there are terminals attached to the system, it forks a **getty** process for each terminal, which waits until a user starts to log in. The action of logging in transforms the **getty** process into a **login** process, and finally into the user's shell process.

Executing a Command

When you give the shell a command, it usually forks (or spawns) a child process to execute the command. While the child process is executing the command, the parent process *sleeps*. While a process is sleeping, it does not use any computer time; it remains inactive, waiting to wake up. When the child process finishes executing the command, it dies. The parent process (which is running the shell) wakes up and prompts you for another command.

When you request that the shell run a process in the background (by ending a command with an &), the shell forks a child process without going to sleep and without waiting for the child process to run to completion. The parent process, executing the shell, reports the PID number of the child and prompts you for another command. The child process runs in the background, independent of its parent.

Although the shell forks a process for most of the commands you give it, some commands are built into the shell, and consequently the shell does not need to fork a process to run them. For a complete list of the built-in commands refer to page 335.

Within a given process, such as your login shell or a subshell, you can declare, initialize, read, and change variables. By default however, a variable is local to a process. When a process forks a child process, the parent does not automatically pass the value of a variable to the child. You can make the value of a variable available to child processes by using the **export** command. Refer to page 289 for information about the **export** command.

Process Identification

The UNIX system assigns a unique process identification (PID) number at the inception of each process. As long as a process is in existence, it keeps the same PID number. During one session, the same process is always executing the login shell. When you fork a new process—for example, when you use an editor—the new (child) process has a different PID number from its parent process. When you return to the login shell, you will find it is still being executed by the same process and has the same PID number as when you logged in.

The interaction below shows that the process running the shell forked (is the parent of) the process running **ps**. When you call **ps** with the –l option, it displays a long listing of information about each process. The line of the **ps** display with **sh** in the COMMAND column refers to the process running the shell. The column headed by PID lists the process ID number. The column headed PPID lists the PID number of the *parent* of each of the processes. From the PID and PPID columns, you can see that the process running the shell (PID 11279) is the parent of the process running **ps** (PID 11285): The parent PID number of **ps** is the same as the PID number of the shell. (See **ps** in Part II (page 663) for a complete description of all the columns the –l option displays.)

```
$ ps -1
       F UID   PID  PPID CP PRI NI  SZ  RSS WCHAN       STAT TT  TIME COMMAND
20488201 114 11279 11278  0  15  0  72  416 kernelma    S    p2  0:00 -sh
20000001 114 11285 11279 19  29  0 212  448             R    p2  0:00 ps -1
```

When you give another **ps –l** command, you can see that the shell is still being run by the same process but that it forked another process to run **ps**.

```
$ ps -l
     F UID   PID  PPID  CP PRI NI SZ  RSS WCHAN       STAT TT  TIME COMMAND
20488201 114 11279 11278  0  15  0  72  420 kernelma     S    p2 0:00 -sh
20000001 114 11292 11279 18  29  0 212  448              R    p2 0:00 ps -l
```

The section "PID Numbers" (page 299) describes two shell variables, **$$** and **$!**, that report on process identification numbers.

Invoking a Shell Script

With the exception of the commands that are built into the shell, whenever you give the shell a command on the command line, the shell forks, which creates a duplicate of the shell process (that is, a subshell). The new process attempts to *exec*, or execute, the command. Like fork, exec is a routine executed by the operating system. If the command is an executable program (such as a C program), the exec will succeed, and the system will execute the command as part of the current process. If the command is a shell script, however, the exec will fail. When the exec fails, the command is assumed to be a shell script, and the subshell will run the commands in the script. Unlike your login shell, which expects input from the command line, the subshell takes its input from a file, the shell script.

You can save the shell the trouble of trying and failing with the initial exec by using the **sh** command to exec a shell to run the script directly. In the following example, **sh** creates a new shell that takes its input from the file called **whoson**:

$ sh whoson

Because the **sh** command expects to read a file containing commands, you do not need execute permission for **whoson**. (However, you do need read permission.) Note that although **sh** takes its input from a file, its standard input, standard output, and standard error are still connected to the terminal.

Although using **sh** to invoke a shell script is more direct from the operating system's point of view, users typically prefer to make the file executable and run the script by typing its name on the command line. It is easier just to type the name, and it is consistent with the way other kinds of programs are invoked (so users do not need to know whether they are running a shell script or another kind of program).

You can also put a special sequence of characters on the first line of a shell script to indicate to the operating system that it is a script. Because the operating system checks the initial characters of a program before attempting to **exec** it, these characters save the system from making an unsuccessful attempt. They also tell the system which utility to use (usually the Bourne, C, or Korn Shell).

If the first two characters of a script are **#!**, the system interprets the characters that follow as the pathname of the program that should execute the script. The following example specifies that the current script should be run by the Bourne Shell:

```
$ cat bourne_script
#!/bin/sh
echo This is a Bourne Shell script.
```

If the first character of a script is a pound sign and the second character is *not* an exclamation point, the system uses the C Shell to run the script.

Comments

When a pound sign occurs in a location in a script other than the first character position, the shell script interprets it as indicating the beginning of a comment. The shell ignores everything between a pound sign and the next (NEWLINE) character.

Variables

The shell has variables you create and assign values to, as well as variables that are set by the shell itself. In this chapter the variables you can name and assign values to are referred to as *user-created variables*. You can change the values of these variables at any time, and you can make them *readonly*, so that they cannot subsequently be changed. You can also *export* them, so that they will be accessible to shells you may fork during the current login session. All variables, even those whose values are numbers, are stored as strings of characters.

Those variables that are set by the shell are referred to as *shell variables*. Some of the shell variables are called *keyword variables*, or *keyword parameters*, because their short, mnemonic names have special meanings to the shell. When you start a shell (by logging in, for example), the shell inherits several keyword variables from the environment. Among these variables are **HOME**, which identifies your home directory, and **PATH**, which determines what directories the shell looks in when you give it a command. Other keyword variables are created by the shell and initialized with default values when it is started up, whereas others do not exist until you set them. Although the shell automatically assigns values to the keyword variables, you can change them at any time. Normally, you would set them in your **.profile** file if they need to be changed at all.

Another group of shell variables do not have distinct names and values. You can reference these variables with special, two-character labels (such as **$?** and **$#**). The values of these variables reflect different aspects of your ongoing interaction with the shell. For example, whenever a command is given on the command line, each argument on the command line becomes the value of one of these special shell variables. These variables enable you to create shell scripts that use command line arguments. Because you cannot assign values to these variables as you can to the others, they are referred to in this chapter as *readonly shell variables*. (However, you can change some of these variables using the **set** command—see page 298.)

The following sections describe user-created variables, keyword shell variables, and readonly shell variables.

User-Created Variables

You can declare any sequence of letters and digits as the name of a variable, as long as the first character is a letter. The first line in the example below declares the variable named **person** and initializes it with the value **alex**. When you assign a value to a variable, **you must not precede or follow the equal sign with a** (SPACE) **or** (TAB).

Since the **echo** command copies its arguments to the standard output, you can use it to display the values of variables.

```
$ person=alex
$ echo person
person
$ echo $person
alex
```

The second line shows that **person** does not represent **alex**. The string **person** is echoed as **person**. The shell only substitutes the value of a variable when you precede the name of the variable with a dollar sign ($). The command echo $person displays the value of the variable **person**. It does not display **$person** because the shell does not pass **$person** to **echo** as an argument. Because of the leading **$** the shell recognizes that **$person** is the name of a variable, *substitutes* the value of the variable, and passes that value to **echo**. The **echo** command displays the value of the variable, not its name, never knowing that you called it with a variable. The final command (above) displays the value of the variable **person**.

You can prevent the shell from substituting the value of a variable by quoting the leading **$**. Double quotation marks will not prevent the substitution; however, single quotation marks or the backslash (\) character will.

```
$ echo $person
alex
$ echo "$person"
alex
$ echo '$person'
$person
$ echo \$person
$person
```

Since double quotation marks do not prevent variable substitution but do turn off the special meanings of most other characters, they are useful both when you are assigning values to variables and when you use those values. In order to assign a value that contains (SPACE)s or (TAB)s to a variable, use double quotation marks around the value.

```
$ person="alex and jenny"
$ echo "$person"
alex and jenny
```

When you reference a variable that contains (TAB)s or multiple adjacent (SPACE)s, you should also use quotation marks to preserve the spacing. If you do not quote the variable, **echo** interprets each string of nonblank characters in the value as a separate argument, and it puts a single space between them when it copies them to the standard output.

```
$ person="alex    and    jenny"
$ echo "$person"
alex    and    jenny
$ echo $person
alex and jenny
```

Although the shell does not interpret special characters such as * and ? as special when they occur in the value of a variable, it does interpret them as special when you reference the variable. Consequently, they should also be quoted.

```
$ memo=alex*
$ echo "$memo"
alex*
$ echo $memo
alex.report alex.summary
$ ls
alex.report
alex.summary
```

The example above shows that when **$memo** is not quoted, the shell matches the value alex* to two files in the working directory, **alex.report** and **alex.summary**. When the variable is quoted, **echo** displays alex*.

Removing Variables   A variable exists as long as the shell in which it was created exists. To remove the value of a variable, set it to null.

```
$ person=
$ echo $person

$
```

You can remove a variable with the **unset** command. For example, to remove the **person** variable, you would give the following command:

```
$ unset person
```

The readonly Command   You can use the **readonly** command to ensure that the value of a variable cannot be changed. The next example declares the variable **person** to be readonly. You must assign a value to a variable *before* you declare it to be readonly; you cannot change its value after the declaration. When you attempt to change the value of a readonly variable, the shell displays an error message.

```
$ person=jenny
$ echo $person
jenny
$ readonly person
$ person=helen
person: is read only
```

If you use the **readonly** command without an argument, it displays a list of all user-created readonly variables. If the user had made any keyword shell variables readonly, they would also be displayed. The **readonly** command does not display the special readonly shell variables (e.g., **$?, $#**).

```
$ readonly
readonly person
```

The export Command   Variables are ordinarily local to the process in which they are declared. Consequently, a shell script does not have access to variables you declared in your login shell unless you take actions to make the variables available. The most commonly used method for making variables available to child processes is with the **export** command.

Once you use the **export** command with a variable name as an argument, the shell places the value of the variable in the calling environment of child processes. This *call by value* gives each child process a copy of the variable for its own use.

Below, the **extest1** shell script assigns a value of american to the variable named **cheese**. Then it displays its filename (**extest1**) and the value of **cheese**. The **extest1** script then calls **subtest**, which attempts to display the same information. Then **subtest** declares a **cheese** variable and displays its value. When **subtest** finishes, it returns control to the parent process executing **extest1**, which again displays the value of the original **cheese** variable.

```
$ cat extest1
cheese=american
echo "extest1 1: $cheese"
subtest
echo "extest1 2: $cheese"
$ cat subtest
echo "subtest 1: $cheese"
cheese=swiss
echo "subtest 2: $cheese"
$ extest1
extest1 1: american
subtest 1:
subtest 2: swiss
extest1 2: american
```

The **subtest** script never receives the value of **cheese** from **extest1**, and **extest1** never loses the value. When a process attempts to display the value of a variable that has not been declared, as is the case with **subtest**, it displays nothing—the value of an undeclared variable is that of a null string.

The following script, **extest2**, is the same as **extest1** except that it uses the **export** command to make **cheese** available to the **subtest** script:

```
$ cat extest2
export cheese
cheese=american
echo "extest2 1: $cheese"
subtest
echo "extest2 2: $cheese"
```

```
$ extest2
extest2 1: american
subtest 1: american
subtest 2: swiss
extest2 2: american
```

Here, the child process inherits the value of **cheese** as american and, after displaying this value, changes *its copy* to swiss. When control is returned to the parent, the parent's copy of **cheese** still retains its original value, american.

The read Command   As you begin writing shell scripts, you will soon realize that one of the most common uses of user-created variables is for storing information that the script prompts the user for. Using the **read** command, your scripts can accept input from the user and store the input in variables you create. The **read** command reads one line from the standard input and assigns the line to one or more variables. The following script shows how **read** works:

```
$ cat read1
echo "Go ahead: \c"
read firstline
echo "You entered: $firstline"
$ read1
Go ahead: This is a line.
You entered: This is a line.
```

The first line of the **read1** script uses **echo** to prompt you to enter a line of text. The \c suppresses the (NEWLINE) following the string that **echo** displays. When you use a character like \ that has a special meaning to both the shell and to the **echo** command, you must quote it so that the shell passes it along unchanged to **echo**. In the example above, the entire text string is quoted.

The second line in the example above reads the text into the variable **firstline**. The third line verifies the action of the **read** command by displaying the value of **firstline**. The variable is quoted (along with the text string) in this example because you, as the script writer, cannot anticipate what characters the user might answer in response to the prompt. For example, consider what would happen if the variable were not quoted and the user entered * in response to the prompt.

```
$ read1_no_quote
Go ahead: *
You entered: read1 read1_no_quote script.1
$ ls
read1    read1_no_quote    script.1
```

As the **ls** command demonstrates, the shell expanded the asterisk into a list of all the files in the working directory. When the variable **$filename** is surrounded by double quotation marks, the asterisk is not expanded by the shell. Thus, the **read1** script shown above behaves correctly.

```
$ read1
Go ahead: *
You entered: *
```

Of course, if you want the shell to use the special meanings of the special characters, you should not use quotation marks.

The **read2** script shown below prompts for a command line and reads it into the variable **command**. The script then executes the command line by placing **$command** on a line by itself. (Note that the **$** in front of **command** is *not* a shell prompt.) When the shell executes the script, it replaces the variable with its value and executes the command line as part of the script.

```
$ cat read2
echo "Enter a command: \c"
read command
$command
echo Thanks
```

Below, **read2** reads a command line that calls the **echo** command. The shell executes the command and then displays Thanks. In the next example, **read2** reads a command line that executes the **who** utility.

```
$ read2
Enter a command: echo Please display this message.
Please display this message.
Thanks
$ read2
Enter a command: who
alex       tty11          Jun 17 07:50
scott      tty07          Jun 17 11:54
Thanks
```

In the following example, the **read3** script reads values into three variables. The **read** command assigns one word (that is, one sequence of non-blank characters) to each variable.

```
$ cat read3
echo "Enter something: \c"
read word1 word2 word3
echo "Word 1 is: $word1"
echo "Word 2 is: $word2"
echo "Word 3 is: $word3"
$ read3
Enter something: this is something
Word 1 is: this
Word 2 is: is
Word 3 is: something
```

If you enter more words than **read** has variables, **read** assigns one word to each variable, with all the left-over words going to the last variable. Actually, **read1** and **read2** both assigned the first word and all the left-over words to the one variable they each had to work with.

Below, **read** accepts five words into three variables. It assigns the first word to the first variable, the second word to the second variable, and the third through fifth words to the third variable.

```
$ read3
Enter something: this is something else, really.
Word 1 is: this
Word 2 is: is
Word 3 is: something else, really.
```

Command Substitution   A second common use of user-created variables is to store the output of a command. When you enclose a command between two backquotes, or grave accent marks (`), the shell replaces the command, including the accent marks, with the output of the command. This process is referred to as *command substitution*.

The following shell script assigns the output of the **pwd** utility to the variable **dir** and displays a message containing this variable:

```
$ cat dir
dir=` pwd `
echo "You are using the $dir directory."
$ dir
You are using the /home/jenny directory.
```

Although this example illustrates how to use backquotes to assign the output of a command to a variable, it is not a realistic example. You can more easily display the output of **pwd** in the output of **echo** without using a variable.

```
$ cat dir2
echo You are using the ` pwd ` directory.
$ dir2
You are using the /home/jenny directory.
```

Refer to the **dataset** script (page 298), the **links** script (page 308), and the **safedit** script (page 324) for more examples of the use of backquotes to assign values to variables.

Keyword Shell Variables

Most of the keyword variables are either inherited by the shell when it is started up or declared and initialized by the shell at that time. You can assign new values to these variables from the command line or from the **.profile** file in your home directory.

Typically, users want these variables to apply to their login shell as well as to any other shells or subshells they might create. Consequently, these variables must be exported. They can be exported before or after they are set. Traditionally they are exported after they are set.

HOME   By default, your home directory is your working directory when you first log in. The system administrator determines your home directory when you establish your account and stores this information in the

/etc/passwd file. When you log in, the shell inherits the pathname of
your home directory and assigns it to the variable **HOME**.

When you give a **cd** command without an argument, **cd** makes the
directory whose name is stored in **HOME** the working directory.

```
$ pwd
/home/jenny/planning
$ echo $HOME
/home/jenny
$ cd
$ pwd
/home/jenny
```

The example above shows the value of the **HOME** variable and the effect
of the **cd** utility. After you execute **cd** without an argument, the pathname
of the working directory is the same as the value of **HOME**.

PATH   When you give the shell an absolute or relative pathname that is not
just a simple filename as a command, it looks in the specified directory for
an executable file with the appropriate filename. If the executable file does
not have the exact pathname that you specify, the shell reports that it cannot find (or execute) the program. Alternatively, if you give the shell a simple
filename as a command, it searches through certain directories for the program you want to execute. The shell looks in several directories for a file that
has the same name as the command and that you have execute permission
for. The **PATH** shell variable controls this search path.

When you log in, the shell assigns a default value to the **PATH** variable.
On SunOS, the default specifies that the shell search the **/usr/ucb**, **/bin**, and
/usr/bin directories. These are the standard directories for storing utilities. If
the shell does not find the file in any of these directories, it reports that it
cannot find (or execute) the command.

The **PATH** variable specifies the directories in the order the shell is to
search them. Each must be separated from the next by a colon. The following command causes the search for an executable file to start with **/usr/ucb**,
followed by **/bin** and **/usr/bin**. If the shell fails to find the file in those directories, it looks in **/home/jenny/bin** and then in the working directory
(specified by a trailing colon). For security reasons it is a good idea to search
the standard directories before the working directory. The **export** command
below makes the new value of **PATH** accessible to subshells and other shells
you may invoke during the login session.

```
$ PATH=/usr/ucb:/bin:/usr/bin:/home/jenny/bin:
$ export PATH
```

Since UNIX traditionally stores executable files in directories called **bin**,
users also typically put their executables in their own **bin** directories. If you
put your own **bin** directory in your **PATH** as Jenny has, the shell will look
there for any commands that it cannot find in the standard directories.

MAIL   The MAIL variable contains the name of the file that your mail is
stored in. Normally, the absolute pathname of this file is **/var/mail/name**,

or **/var/spool/mail/name**, where **name** is your login name. On older systems, mail files were stored in **/usr/mail** or **/usr/spool/mail**.

The **MAILPATH** variable contains a list of filenames separated by colons. If this variable is set, the shell informs you when any one of the files is modified (e.g., when mail arrives). You can follow any of the filenames in the list with a percent sign (%) followed by a message. The message will replace the **you have mail** message when you get mail while you are logged in.

The **MAILCHECK** variable specifies how often, in seconds, the shell checks for new mail. The default is 600 seconds (10 minutes). If you set this variable to zero, the shell will check before each prompt.

PS1   The shell prompt lets you know that the shell is waiting for you to give it a command. The Bourne Shell prompt used in the examples throughout this book is a **$** followed by a (SPACE). Your prompt may differ. The shell stores the prompt as a string in the **PS1** variable. When you change the value of this variable, the appearance of your prompt changes.

If you are working on more than one machine, it can be helpful to incorporate a machine name in your prompt. The following example shows how to change the prompt to the name of the machine you are using, followed by a colon and a (SPACE).

```
$ PS1="` hostname `: "
bravo: echo test
test
bravo:
```

Refer to page 334 for a shell function that causes the prompt to display the name of the working directory.

PS2   Prompt string 2 is a secondary prompt that the shell stores in **PS2**. On the first line of the following example, an unclosed quoted string follows an **echo** command. The shell assumes that the command is not finished and, on the second line, gives the default secondary prompt (>). This prompt indicates that the shell is waiting for the user to continue the command line. The shell waits until it receives the quotation mark that closes the string and then executes the command.

```
$ echo "demonstration of prompt string
> 2"
demonstration of prompt string
2
$ PS2="secondary prompt: "
$ echo "this demonstrates
secondary prompt: prompt string 2"
this demonstrates
prompt string 2
$
```

The second command above changes the secondary prompt to second-ary prompt: followed by a (SPACE). A multiline **echo** command demonstrates the new prompt.

IFS   You can always use a (SPACE) or (TAB) to separate fields on the command line. When you assign **IFS** (internal-field separator) the value of another character, you can also use this character to separate fields.

The following example demonstrates how setting IFS can affect interpretation of a command line:

```
$ cat a:b:c:d
cat: a:b:c:d: No such file or directory
$ IFS=:
$ cat a:b:c:d
cat: a: No such file or directory
cat: b: No such file or directory
cat: c: No such file or directory
cat: d: No such file or directory
```

The first time **cat** is called, the shell interprets the string a:b:c:d as a single argument, and **cat** reports that there is no such file as **a:b:c:d**. After IFS is set to : the shell interprets the same string as four separate arguments.

There are a variety of side effects of changing the **IFS** variable, so change it cautiously.

CDPATH   The CDPATH variable affects the operation of the **cd** command. It takes on the value of a list of absolute pathnames (similar to the PATH variable) and is usually set in the **.profile** file with command lines such as the following:

```
$ CDPATH=:$HOME:$HOME/literature
$ export CDPATH
```

If **CDPATH** is not set, when you specify a simple filename as an argument to **cd**, **cd** always searches the working directory for a subdirectory with the same name as the argument. If the subdirectory does not exist, **cd** issues an error message. If **CDPATH** is set, **cd** searches for an appropriately named subdirectory in one of the directories in the **CDPATH** list. If it finds one, that directory becomes the working directory. Since users typically want **cd** to search the working directory first, **CDPATH** usually starts with a colon.

TZ   The TZ variable describes what time zone your login session will operate in. It is usually set by the system administrator. The format for setting the TZ variable is shown below.

TZ=zzzX[ddd]

The **zzz** is the three-letter name of the local time zone, X is the number of hours that the local time zone differs from Coordinated Universal Time (UTC), also called Greenwich Mean Time (GMT), and **ddd** is the three-letter name of the local daylight saving time zone.

The following command sets the **TZ** variable for California:

```
$ TZ=PST8PDT
$ export TZ
```

Running .profile with the . Command   After you edit your **.profile** file to change the values of keyword shell variables, you do not have to wait until the next time you log in to put the changes into effect. You can run **.profile** with the . (dot) command. Using the . command is similar to running a shell script, except that the . command runs the script as part of the current process. Consequently, when you use . to run a script from your login shell, changes you make to the variables from within the script affect the login shell. If you ran **.profile** as a regular shell script, the new variables would be in effect only in the subshell running the script.

The **.profile** file below sets the **TERM**, **PATH**, **PS1**, and **CDPATH** variables as well as setting the line kill character to (CONTROL)-**U**. The . command puts the new values into effect.

```
$ cat .profile
TERM=vt100
PATH=/usr/ucb:/bin:/usr/bin:/home/alex/bin:
PS1="alex: "
CDPATH=:$HOME
export TERM PATH PS1 CDPATH
stty kill '^u'
$ . .profile
alex:
```

Readonly Shell Variables

Name of the Calling Program   The shell stores in the variable **$0** the name of the command that you use to call a program. It is variable number zero because it appears before the first argument on the command line.

```
$ cat abc
echo The name of the command used
echo to execute this shell script was $0
$ abc
The name of the command used
to execute this shell script was abc
```

This shell script uses **echo** to verify the name of the script you are executing. The **abc** file must be executable (use **chmod**), and your **PATH** must be set up to search the working directory in order for this example to work.

Command Line Arguments   The shell stores the first nine command line arguments in the variables **$1**, **$2**, ..., **$9** (often called *positional parameters*). Although the other arguments are not thrown away, they must be promoted to one of the first nine positions before you can access them using one of these variables (see the **shift** command on page 297). These variables appear in this, the "Readonly Shell Variables" section, because you cannot assign them values using an equal sign. You can, however, use the **set** command (page 298) to assign new values to them.

```
$ cat display_5args
echo The first five command line
echo arguments are $1 $2 $3 $4 $5
```

```
$ display_5args jenny alex helen
The first five command line
arguments are jenny alex helen
```

The **display_5args** script displays the first five command line arguments. The variables representing arguments that were not present on the command line, **$4** and **$5**, have a null value.

The variable **$*** represents all the command line arguments (not just the first nine), as the **display_all** program demonstrates:

```
$ cat display_all
echo $*
$ display_all a b c d e f g h i j k l m n o p
a b c d e f g h i j k l m n o p
```

The **$@** variable is the same as **$*** except when they are enclosed in double quotation marks. Using "**$***" puts a single pair of double quotation marks around the entire set of arguments; using "**$@**" quotes the arguments individually. This makes **$@** more useful than **$*** in shell scripts, as the **whos** script on page 313 demonstrates.

The variable **$#** contains the number of arguments on the command line. This string variable represents a decimal number. You can use the **expr** utility to perform computations involving this number, and you can use **test** to perform logical tests on it. There is more information on **expr** and **test** in the "Control Flow Commands" section of this chapter (page 301) and in Part II.

```
$ cat num_args
echo "This shell script was called
with $# arguments."
$ num_args helen alex jenny
This shell script was called
with 3 arguments
```

In the preceding example, the **echo** command echoes a quoted string that spans two lines. Because the newline is quoted, the shell passes the entire string that is between the quotation marks—including the newline—to **echo** as an argument.

The shift Command   The **shift** command promotes each of the command line arguments. The second argument (which was represented by **$2**) becomes the first (now represented by **$1**), the third becomes the second, the fourth becomes the third, and so forth.

Using the command line argument variables (**$1-$9**), you can access only the first nine command line arguments from a shell script. The **shift** command gives you access to the tenth command line argument by making it the ninth, and it makes the first unavailable. Successive **shift** commands make additional arguments available. There is, however, no "unshift" command to bring back arguments that are no longer available.

```
$ cat demo_shift
echo "arg1= $1      arg2= $2      arg3= $3"
shift
echo "arg1= $1      arg2= $2      arg3= $3"
shift
echo "arg1= $1      arg2= $2      arg3= $3"
shift
echo "arg1= $1      arg2= $2      arg3= $3"
shift
$ demo_shift alice helen jenny
arg1= alice      arg2= helen      arg3= jenny
arg1= helen      arg2= jenny      arg3=
arg1= jenny      arg2=      arg3=
arg1=      arg2=      arg3=
demo_shift: cannot shift
```

This example calls the **demo_shift** program with three arguments. Double quotation marks were used around the arguments to **echo** to preserve the spacing of the output display. The program displays the arguments and shifts them repeatedly, until there are no more arguments to shift. The shell displays an error message when the script executes **shift** after it has run out of variables.

The set Command   When you call **set** with one or more arguments, it sets the values of the command line argument variables (**$1-$9**) to its arguments. The following script uses **set** to set the first three command line argument variables:

```
$ cat set_it
set this is it
echo $3 $2 $1
$ set_it
it is this
```

You can use command substitution (page 292) with **set** to cause it to use the standard output of another command as its arguments.

The script below shows how to use the **date** utility and the **set** command to provide the date in a useful format. The first command shows the output from **date**. Then **cat** displays the **dataset** script. The first command in the script uses backquotes to set the command line argument variables to the output of **date.** Subsequent commands display the values of variables **$1, $2, $3,** and **$4.** The final command displays the date in a format that you can use in a letter or report. You can also use the **format** argument to **date** to modify the format of its output. Refer to **date** in Part II.

```
$ date
Fri Jun 17 23:04:09 PDT 1994
$ cat dataset
set `date`
echo $*
echo
echo "Argument 1: $1"
```

```
echo "Argument 2: $2"
echo "Argument 3: $3"
echo "Argument 4: $4"
echo
echo $2 $3, $6
$ dateset
Fri Jun 17 23:04:13 PDT 1994

Argument 1: Fri
Argument 2: Jun
Argument 3: 17
Argument 4: 23:04:13

Jun 17, 1994
```

Without any arguments, **set** displays a list of the variables that are set. Note that **set** displays user-created variables (e.g., **person=alex**) as well as shell keyword variables.

```
$ set
HOME=/home/alex
IFS=

LOGNAME=alex
MAIL=/var/spool/mail/alex
PATH=/usr/ucb:/bin:/usr/bin:/home/alex/bin:
PS1=$
PS2=>
SHELL=/bin/sh
TERM=vt100
person=alex
```

PID Numbers The shell stores the PID number of the process that is executing it in the $$ variable. In the following interaction, echo displays the value of this variable, and the **ps** utility confirms its value. Both commands show that the shell has a PID of 14137.

```
$ echo $$
14137
$ ps
   PID  TT STAT TIME COMMAND
  14137 14  S   0:06 sh
  14565 14  R   0:02 ps
```

On many systems, the **echo** command is built into the Bourne Shell and thus does not cause the shell to create another process. However, the results are the same whether **echo** is a built-in command or not, because the shell substitutes the value of **$$** *before* it forks a new process to run a command. The next example shows that the shell substitutes the value of **$$** *before* it forks a new process. The shell substitutes the value of **$$** and passes that value to **cp** as a prefix for a new filename. This technique is useful for creating

unique filenames when the meaningfulness of the names does not matter—
it is often used in shell scripts for creating names of temporary files.

```
$ echo $$
14137
$ cp memo $$.memo
$ ls
14137.memo memo
```

The example below demonstrates that the shell creates a new shell process when it runs a shell script. The example uses the **id2** script, which displays the PID of the process running the subshell that runs **id2**.

```
$ cat id2
echo $0 PID = $$
$ echo $$
14137
$ id2
id2 PID = 15253
$ echo $$
14137
```

The first **echo** in the example displays the PID of the login shell. Then **id2** displays its name (**$0**) and the PID of the subshell. Finally, the last **echo** shows that the current process is the login shell again.

The **$!** variable has the value of the PID number of the last process that you ran in the background. The following example executes **ps** as a background task and then uses **echo** to display the value of **$!**:

```
$ ps &
15309
    PID  TT STAT TIME COMMAND
  14137  14  S   0:07 sh
  14309  14  R   0:02 ps
echo $!
15309
$
```

Although the prompt in this example appears to be out of sequence, it is not. The shell displays a prompt after displaying the PID number of a background process. The output from the background process follows the prompt. The **echo** command is given in response to the prompt, although the command does not appear to follow the prompt immediately. You can press (RETURN) if you want to see another prompt before issuing a command.

Exit Status   When a process stops executing for any reason, it returns an *exit status* to its parent process. The exit status is also referred to as a *condition code* or *return code*. The shell stores the exit status of the last command in the **$?** variable.

By convention, a nonzero exit status represents a false value and means that the command failed. A zero is true and means that the command was successful.

You can specify the exit status that a shell script will return by using an **exit** command, followed by a number, to terminate the script. If you do not use **exit** with a number to terminate a script, the exit status of the script will be the exit status of the last command the script ran. The following example shows that the number specifies the exit status:

```
$ cat es
echo This program returns an exit
echo status of 7.
exit 7
$ es
This program returns an exit
status of 7.
$ echo $?
7
$ echo $?
0
```

The **es** shell script displays a message and then terminates execution with an **exit** command that returns an exit status of 7. Then **echo** displays the value of the exit status of **es**. The second **echo** displays the value of the exit status of the first **echo**. The value is zero because the first **echo** was successful.

Control Flow Commands

The *control flow commands* alter the order of execution of commands within a shell script. They include control structures—simple two-way branch If statements, multiple branch Case statements, and For, While, and Until statements. In addition, the shell provides Here documents, which redirect the standard input to a command in a script from within the script itself; the **exec** command, which transfers control to another command or script; and the **trap** command, which specifies commands to be executed when a script terminates prematurely.

If Then

The format of the If Then control structure follows. The **bold** words in the format description are the items you supply to cause the structure to have the desired effect. The other words are the keywords the shell uses to identify the control structure.

```
if test-command
    then
        commands
fi
```

As seen in Figure 10-1, the If statement tests the status returned by the **test-command** and transfers control based on this status. When you spell *if* backward, it's *fi;* the Fi statement marks the end of the If structure.

The following script prompts you and reads in two words. Then it uses an If structure to evaluate the result returned by the **test** command when it compares the two words. The **test** command returns a status of *true,* if the two words are the same, and *false,* if they are not. Double quotation marks

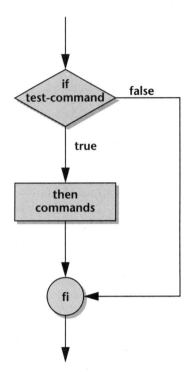

Figure 10-1   If Then Flowchart

are used around $word1 and $word2 so that **test** will work properly if the user enters a string that contains a (SPACE) or another special character.

```
$ cat if1
echo "word 1: \c"
read word1
echo "word 2: \c"
read word2

if test "$word1" = "$word2"
    then
        echo Match
fi
echo End of program.
$ if1
word1: peach
word2: peach
Match
End of program.
```

The If statement executes the statements immediately following it if *its* argument (that is, everything following the keyword If up to a (NEWLINE) or semicolon) returns a *true* exit status. The **test** utility returns a *true* status if its first and third arguments have the relationship specified by its second argument. If this command returns a *true* status (= 0), the shell executes the commands between the Then and Fi statements. If the command returns a *false* status (not = 0), the shell passes control to the statement after Fi without executing the statements between Then and Fi. The effect of this If statement is to display Match if the two words match. It always displays End of program.

The next program uses an If structure at the beginning of a script to check that the user supplied at least one argument on the command line. The effect of this If statement is to display a message and exit from the script if the user did not supply an argument.

```
$ cat chkargs
if test $# = 0
    then
            echo You must supply at least one argument.
            exit
fi
echo Program running.
$ chkargs
You must supply at least one argument.
$ chkargs abc
Program running.
```

A test like the one in **chkargs** is a key component of any script that requires arguments. To prevent the user from receiving meaningless or confusing information from the script, it should always check to see whether the user has supplied the appropriate arguments. Sometimes the script will simply test to see whether arguments exist (as in **chkargs**), whereas other scripts will need to test for a specific number of arguments or specific kinds of arguments (readable files, for example). Refer to **test** in Part II for more information on the kinds of tests the **test** command will perform.

The following example is another version of **chkargs** that checks for arguments in a way that is more traditional for UNIX shell scripts. First, the example uses the square bracket ([]) synonym for **test**. Rather than using the word **test** in your scripts, you can surround the arguments to **test** with square brackets, as shown. The square brackets must be surrounded by white space (that is, (SPACE)s or (TAB)s).

```
$ cat chkargs
if [ $# = 0 ]
    then
            echo Usage: chkargs argument... 1>&2
            exit 1
fi
echo Program running.
exit 0
$ chkargs
Usage: chkargs arguments
$ chkargs abc
Program running.
```

Second, the error message is a *usage message* that uses a standard notation to specify the arguments the script takes. Usage messages similar to the

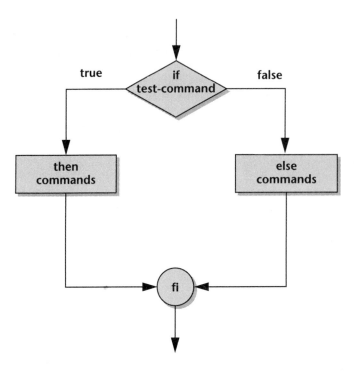

Figure 10-2   If Then Else Flowchart

one in **chkargs** are provided by many UNIX utilities. When you call a command with the wrong number or kinds of arguments, you will often see a usage message. (Try giving the **cp** command without any arguments.) The notation is similar to the notation used in the "Format" descriptions for the utilities in Part II. The ... following **argument** indicates that there may be more than one instance of **argument**.

Third, the usage message is redirected to the standard error.

Fourth, after presenting the usage message, **chkargs** exits with an exit status of 1, indicating that an error occurred. The **exit** command at the end of the script causes **chkargs** to exit with a 0 exit status.

If Then Else

The introduction of the Else statement turns the If structure into the two-way branch shown in Figure 10-2. The format of the If Then Else control structure follows:

```
if test-command
    then
        commands
    else
        commands
fi
```

If the **test-command** returns a *true* status, the If structure executes the commands between the Then and Else statements and then diverts control to Fi, and the shell continues with the next command in the script. If the **test-command** returns a *false* status, it executes the commands following the Else statement.

The following script builds on the **chkargs** script. When you call **out** with arguments that are names of files, it displays the files on the terminal. If the first argument is a –v, **out** uses **more** to display the files.

After determining that it was called with at least one argument, **out** tests its first argument to see if it is not –v. If the test is true (if the first argument is not –v), the script uses **cat** to display the files. If the test is false (if the first argument is –v), **out** shifts the arguments to get rid of the –v and displays the files using **more**. The SunOS versions of **cat** and **more** do not recognize the –– argument. You can omit this argument in the **out** script and it will still work properly in most cases. See "Optional" following the example.

```
$ cat out
if [ $# = 0 ]
    then
            echo "Usage: out [-v] filenames" 1>&2
            exit 1
fi
if [ "$1" != "-v" ]
    then
            cat -- "$@"
    else
            shift
            more -- "$@"
fi
```

OPTIONAL

In **out**, the –– argument to **cat** and **more** tells the utility that no more options follow on the command line. This argument prevents **cat** and **more** from interpreting a filename that begins with – as an option. Although many UNIX commands recognize the –– option, the **more** and **cat** utilities under SunOS do not, so there is no easy way to prevent them from interpreting a filename argument as an option under SunOS. Both commands recognize this option under BSD 4.4.

If Then Elif

The format of the If Then Elif control structure follows:

if **test-command**
    then
            commands
    elif **test-command**
        then
                commands
    else
            commands
fi

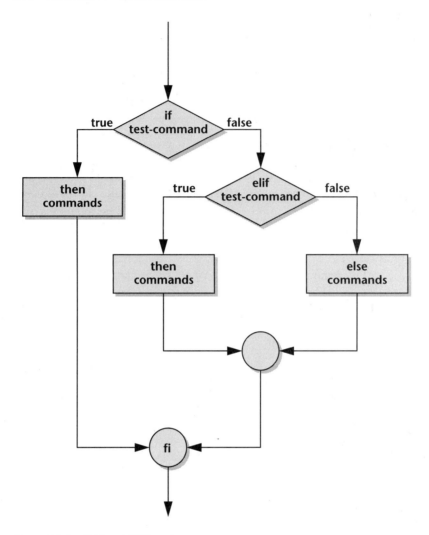

Figure 10-3   If Then Elif Flowchart

The Elif statement combines the Else and If statements and allows you to construct a nested set of If Then Else structures (Figure 10-3).

The example on the next page shows an If Then Elif control structure. This shell script compares three words. In the first If statement it uses an AND operator (–a) as an argument to **test**. The **test** command returns a *true* status only if the first and the second logical comparisons are true (that is, if **word1** matches **word2**, and **word2** matches **word3**). If **test** returns a *true* status, the program executes the command following the next Then statement and passes control to Fi, and the script terminates.

If the three words are not the same, the structure passes control to the first Elif, which begins a series of tests to see whether any pair of words is the same. As the nesting continues, if any one of the If statements is satisfied, the structure passes control to the next Then statement and subsequently to the statement after Fi. Each time an Elif statement is not satisfied, the structure passes control to the next Elif statement.

```
$ cat if3
echo "word 1: \c"
read word1
echo "word 2: \c"
read word2
echo "word 3: \c"
read word3
if [ "$word1" = "$word2" -a "$word2" = "$word3" ]
    then
        echo "Match: words 1, 2, & 3"
    elif [ "$word1" = "$word2" ]
        then
            echo "Match: words 1 & 2"
    elif [ "$word1" = "$word3" ]
        then
            echo "Match: words 1 & 3"
    elif [ "$word2" = "$word3" ]
        then
            echo "Match: words 2 & 3"
    else
        echo No match
fi
```

The **if3** script uses double quotation marks around the arguments to **echo** that contain & to prevent the shell from interpreting & as a special character.

OPTIONAL

The following script, **links**, demonstrates the If Then and If Then Elif control structures. The **links** script finds links to a file specified as the first argument to **links**. When you run **links**, you can specify a second argument, which is the directory in which **links** will begin searching for links. The **links** script searches that directory and all of its subdirectories. If you do not specify a directory on the command line, **links** begins its search at the working directory.

OPTIONAL Continued

```
$ cat links
:
# identify links to a file

# Usage: links file [directory]

if [ $# = 0 ]
    then
        echo "Usage: links file [directory]"  1>&2
        exit 1
fi
if [ -d "$1" ]
    then
        echo "Usage: links file [directory]" 1>&2
        exit 1
    else
        file="$1"
fi
if [ $# = 1 ]
    then
        directory= "."
    elif [ -d "$2" ]
        then
            directory="$2"
    else
        echo "Usage: links file [directory]" 1>&2
        exit 1
fi

# Check for existence of file:
ls "$file" 2> /dev/null | grep "$file" > /dev/null
if [ $? != 0 ]
    then
        echo "links: $file not found" 1>&2
        exit 1
fi

# Check link count on file:
set -- ` ls -l "$file"`
linkcnt=$2
if [ $linkcnt = 1 ]
    then
        echo "links: no other links to $file" 1>&2
        exit 0
fi

# Get the inode of the given file:
set ` ls -i "$file"`
inode=$1

# Find and print the files with that inode number:
echo "links: using find to search for links..." 1>&2
find "$directory" -inum $inode -print
```

In the example below, Alex uses **links** while he is in his home directory to search for links to a file called **letter** in the working directory. The **links** script reports **/home/alex/letter** and **/home/jenny/draft** are links to the same file.

```
$ links letter /home
links: using find to search for links...
/home/alex/letter
/home/jenny/draft
```

In addition to the If Then Elif control structure, **links** introduces other features that are commonly used by experienced shell programmers. The following discussion describes **links** section by section.

The second and third lines of **links** are comments—the shell ignores the text that follows pound signs up to the next (NEWLINE) character. The first two comments in **links** briefly identify what the file does and how to use it. The square brackets around the **directory** argument in the usage statement indicate that the **directory** argument is optional. Because a pound sign as the first character of a script has a special status on some systems (page 285), the comments do not begin on the first line. The first line contains only a colon (:), which is the null command. (All it does is return a 0 exit status.) In this script, the colon is just a place holder—it occupies the first character position so that a pound sign does not occur there.

The first If statement in **links** tests to see whether **links** was called with any arguments. If **links** was not called with any arguments, **links** sends a usage message to the standard error and exits with a status of 1. The double quotation marks around the usage message prevent the shell from interpreting the square brackets as special characters.

The second If statement verifies that **$1** is not a directory. If it is a directory, **links** presents a usage message and exits. If it is not a directory, **links** saves the value of **$1** in the **file** variable because later in the script the **set** command resets the command line arguments. If the value of **$1** were not saved before the **set** command, it would be lost.

The next section of **links** is an If Then Elif statement. The first **test-command** determines whether the user specified a single argument on the command line. If the **test-command** returns 0 (true), the user-created variable named **directory** is assigned the value of the working directory (.). If the **test-command** returns a false value, the Elif statement is executed. The Elif statement tests to see whether the second argument is a directory (the **-d** argument to **test** returns a *true* value if the file exists and is a directory). If it is a directory, the **directory** variable is set equal to the second command line argument, **$2**. If **$2** is not a directory, **links** displays a usage message to the standard error and exits with a status of 1.

The next section of **links** verifies that **$file** is the name of an existing file. This is an important section of the script because it would be pointless for **links** to spend time looking for links to a nonexistent file. Unfortunately, the **test** command on some versions of UNIX does not provide a simple way to determine that a file exists without also deter-

mining whether it has other characteristics that do not matter to **links**. Consequently, the **links** script uses a roundabout technique for verifying the existence of the file. The **links** script uses **ls** to list the name of **$file** and sends the standard output through a pipe to the **grep** command, which searches for the string $file. If $file exists, the standard output of **ls** contains the name of the file. If $file does not exist, **ls** sends a message to its standard error and nothing to its standard output. The standard error output of **ls** and the standard output of **grep** are redirected to **/dev/null**. The **/dev/null** file is a special file, the "bit bucket," which is guaranteed to be empty. Users commonly redirect unwanted output to **/dev/null**, effectively throwing the output away. In this case, the output of **grep** is redirected there because **links** only uses the exit status of **grep**. The exit status of **grep** is 0 if **grep** found the string it was searching for, and 1 otherwise. If **grep** returns a nonzero exit status, an error message is displayed. This message uses the standard format for error messages from shell scripts—the script name followed by a colon and the message.

Next **links** uses **set** and **ls –l** to check the number of links $file has. The **set** command uses command substitution to set the readonly shell variables **$1** to **$9** to the output of **ls –l**. In the output of **ls –l**, the second field is the link count, so the user-created variable **linkcnt** is set equal to **$2**. The **––** is used with the **set** command to prevent it from interpreting as an option the first argument **ls –l** produces (the first argument is the access permissions for the file, and it is likely to begin with –). The If statement checks whether **$linkcnt** is equal to 1; if it is, **links** presents a message and exits. Although this message is not, strictly speaking, an error message, it is redirected to the standard error. The way **links** has been written, all informational messages are sent to the standard error. Only the final product of **links**, the pathnames of links to the specified file, is sent to the standard output. Because the standard output contains only the pathnames of links, users can easily send it through a pipe to a filter.

If the link count is greater than one, **links** goes on to identify the inode for **$file**. As Chapter 4 explained (page 82), comparing the inodes associated with filenames is a good way to determine whether the filenames are links to the same file. The **links** script uses **set** again to set the readonly shell variables to the output of **ls –i**. The first argument to **set** will be the inode number for the file, so the user-created variable named **inode** is set to the value of **$1**.

Finally, **links** uses the **find** utility to search for filenames having inodes that match $inode. The **find** utility searches for files that meet the criteria specified by its arguments. The **find** utility begins its search with the directory specified by its first argument (**$directory**, in this case), and it searches all subdirectories. The other arguments to **find** specify that files having inodes matching $inode should be printed on the standard output. Because files in different filesystems may have the same inode number (yet they are not linked), **$directory** should be in the same filesystem as **$file** for accurate results. Refer to page 80 and page 503 for more information about filesystems and links. Refer to Part II for more information about **find**.

The **echo** above the **find** command in **links**, which tells the user that **find** is running, is included because **find** is slow. Because **links** does not include a final exit statement, the exit status of **links** will be that of the last command it runs, **find**.

When you are writing a script like **links**, it is easy to make mistakes. While you are debugging it, you can use the shell's –x option, which causes the shell to echo each command it runs. This trace of a script's execution can give you a lot of information about where bugs are. To run a script with the –x option, use a command such as the following:

```
$ sh -x links
```

You can also set the shell's –x option by putting the following **set** command at the top of the script.

```
set -x
```

For In

The For In structure has the following format:

```
for loop-index in argument-list
do
      commands
done
```

This structure (Figure 10-4) assigns the value of the first argument in the **argument-list** to the **loop-index** and executes the **commands** between the Do and Done statements. The Do and Done statements mark the beginning and end of the For loop.

After the structure passes control to the Done statement, it assigns the value of the second argument in the **argument-list** to the **loop-index** and repeats the **commands**. The structure repeats the **commands** between the Do and Done statements—once for each of the arguments in the **argument-list**. When the structure exhausts the **argument-list**, it passes control to the Done statement, and the shell continues with the next command in the script.

The For In structure shown below assigns **apples** to the user-created variable **fruit** and then displays the value of **fruit**, which is **apples**. Next, it assigns **oranges** to **fruit** and repeats the process. When it exhausts the argument list, the structure transfers control to the statement following Done, which displays a message.

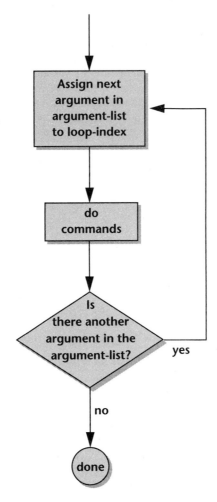

Figure 10-4   For In Flowchart

```
$ cat fruit
for fruit in apples oranges pears bananas
do
     echo $fruit
done
echo Task complete.


$ fruit
apples
oranges
pears
bananas
Task complete.
```

For

The For structure has the following format:

for **loop-index**
do
    commands
done

In the For structure, the **loop-index** automatically takes on the value of each of the command line parameters, one at a time. It performs a series of commands involving each parameter in turn.

The shell script below shows a For structure displaying each of the command line arguments. The first line of the shell script, for args, implies for args in "$@", where the shell expands "$@" into a quoted list of command line arguments. The balance of the script corresponds to the For In structure.

```
$ cat for_test
for args
do
      echo $args
done

$ for_test candy gum chocolate
candy
gum
chocolate
```

OPTIONAL

The script below, **whos**, demonstrates the usefulness of the implied **$@** in the For structure. You can give **whos** one or more **ids** for users as arguments (e.g., a user's name or login), and **whos** will display information about the users. The information **whos** displays is taken from the first and fifth fields in the **/etc/passwd** file. The first field always contains a user's login, and the fifth field typically contains the user's name. You can use a login as an argument to **whos** to identify the user's name or use a name as an argument in order to identify the login. The **whos** script is similar to the **finger** utility, although **whos** provides less information.

```
$ cat whos
:
# adapted from finger.sh by Lee Sailer
# UNIX/WORLD, III:11, p. 67, Fig. 2

if [ $# = 0 ]
    then
         echo "Usage: whos id..." 1>&2
         exit 1
fi

for i
do
    awk -F: '{print $1, $5}' /etc/passwd |
    grep -i "$i"
done
```

Following, **whos** identifies the user whose login is chas and the user whose name is Marilou Smith.

```
$ whos chas "Marilou Smith"
chas Charles Casey
msmith Marilou Smith
```

The **whos** script uses a For statement to loop through the command line arguments. The implied use of **$@** in the For loop has particular utility in this script because it causes the For loop to treat an argument containing a space as a single argument. For instance, in the example above, the user quoted **Marilou Smith**, which causes the shell to pass it to the script as a single argument. Then the implied **$@** in the For statement causes the shell to regenerate the quoted argument **Marilou Smith** so that it is again treated as a single argument.

For each command line argument, **whos** searches for the **id** in the /etc/passwd file. Inside the For loop, the **awk** utility extracts the first (**$1**) and fifth (**$5**) fields from the lines in /etc/passwd (which contain the user's login and information about the user, respectively). The **$1** and **$5** are arguments that the **awk** command sets and uses—they are included within single quotes and are not interpreted at all by the shell. (Do not confuse them with the readonly shell variables that correspond to the command line arguments.) The first and fifth fields are piped to the **grep** utility. The **grep** utility searches for **$i**, (which has taken on the value of a command line argument) in its input. The –i option causes **grep** to ignore case as it searches. It prints out each line in its input that contains the current argument.

Because the **whos** script gets its information from the /etc/passwd file, the information it displays will only be as informative as the information in /etc/passwd. For more information about **awk** and **grep**, refer to **awk** and **grep** in Part II. For more information about /etc/passwd, refer to Chapter 14.

While

The While structure (Figure 10-5) has the following format:

while **test-command**
do
    commands
done

As long as the **test-command** returns a *true* exit status, the structure continues to execute the series of **commands** delimited by the Do and Done statements. Before each loop through the **commands**, the structure executes the **test-command**. When the exit status of the **test-command** is *false,* the structure passes control to the Done statement, and the shell continues with the next command in the script.

The shell script shown below first initializes the variable **number** to the character value of zero—shell variables can take on only values of character strings. The **test** utility, represented by [and], then determines if the value

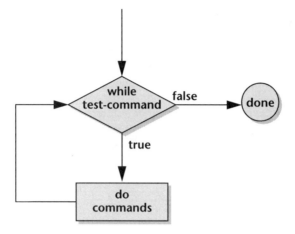

Figure 10-5   While Flowchart

of the variable **number** is less than 10. The **count** script calls **test**, using –**lt** to perform a *numerical* test. [You must use –**ne** (not equal), –**eq** (equal), –**gt** (greater than), –**ge** (greater than or equal), –**lt** (less than), or –**le** (less than or equal) for numerical comparisons, and = (equal) or != (not equal) for string comparisons.] The **test** utility has an exit status of *true* as long as **number** is less than 10. As long as **test** returns *true*, the structure executes the commands between the Do and Done statements.

The first command following Do displays the string represented by **number**. The next command uses the **expr** utility to increment the value of **number** by one. Here, **expr** converts its arguments to numbers, adds them, converts the result to characters, and echoes them to the standard output. The backquotes cause the command that they enclose to be replaced by the output of the command. This value is then assigned to the variable **number**. The first time through the loop, **number** has a value of zero, so **expr** converts the strings **0** and **1** to numbers, adds them, and converts the result back to a string (**1**). The shell then assigns this value to the **number** variable. The Done statement closes the loop and returns control to the While statement to start the loop over again. The final **echo** command causes **count** to send a (NEWLINE) to the standard output, so that the next prompt occurs in the leftmost column on the display (rather than immediately following **9**).

```
$ cat count
number=0
while [ "$number" -lt 10 ]
do
    echo "$number\c"
    number=` expr $number + 1 `
done
echo
$ count
0123456789
$
```

OPTIONAL

The next shell script, **spell_check**, shows another use of a While structure. You can use **spell_check** to find the incorrect spellings in a file. It uses the **spell** utility, which checks your file against a dictionary of correctly spelled words. The **spell** utility sends a list of the words that are not in its dictionary to the standard output. This script goes a step further, enabling you to identify a list of words that should be considered correct spellings and removing those words from the output of **spell**. This script is useful for removing words that you use frequently, such as names and technical terms, that are not in a standard dictionary.

The **spell** utility also provides an option that enables you to do what the spell_check script does.

The **spell_check** script requires two filename arguments: the first file contains your list of correctly spelled words, and the second file is the file that is to be checked. The first If statement verifies that the user specified two arguments, and the next two If statements verify that both arguments are readable files. (With the –r operator, **test** determines whether a file is readable, and the exclamation point negates the sense of the following operator.)

```
$ cat spell_check
:
# remove correct spellings from spell output

if [ $# != 2 ]
    then
        echo "Usage: spell_check file1 file2" 1>&2
        echo "file1: list of correct spellings" 1>&2
        echo "file2: file to be checked" 1>&2
        exit 1
fi

if [ ! -r "$1" ]
    then
        echo "spell_check: $1 is not readable" 1>&2
        exit 1
fi

if [ ! -r "$2" ]
    then
        echo "spell_check: $2 is not readable" 1>&2
        exit 1
fi

spell "$2" |
while read line
do
    grep "^$line\$" "$1" > /dev/null
    if [ $? != 0 ]
        then
            echo $line
    fi
done
```

The **spell_check** script sends the output from **spell** through a pipe to the standard input of the While command, and the While structure reads one line at a time from its standard input. The **test-command** (that is, **read line**) returns a *true* exit status as long as it receives a line from the standard input. Inside the While loop, **grep** determines whether the line that was read is in the list of correctly spelled words. The pattern **grep** searches for (the value of the **line** variable) is preceded and followed by special characters that specify the beginning and end of a line (^ and $, respectively). These special characters are used so that **grep** will find a match only if the **$line** variable matches an entire line in the file of correctly spelled words. (Otherwise, **grep** would match a string such as **tomo** in the output of **spell** if the file of correctly spelled words contained the word **tomorrow**.) The output of **grep** is redirected to /dev/null, because it is not needed (output that is redirected to /dev/null disappears). Then the If statement checks the exit status of **grep**, which is 0 only if a matching line was found. If the exit status is *not* 0, the word was *not* in the file of correctly spelled words, and **echo** displays it on the standard output. Once the While structure detects the End Of File, the **test-command** returns a *false* exit status, control is passed out of the While structure, and the script terminates.

Before you use **spell_check**, you should create a file of correct spellings containing words that you use frequently but that are not in a standard dictionary. For example, if you work for a company named **Blankenship and Klimowski, Attorneys**, you would put Blankenship and Klimowski into the file. The following example shows how **spell_check** checks the spelling in a file called **memo** and removes Blankenship and Klimowski from the output list of incorrectly spelled words.

```
$ spell memo
Blankenship
Klimowski
targat
hte
$ cat word_list
Blankenship
Klimowski
$ spell_check word_list memo
targat
hte
```

Refer to Part II for more information about **spell**.

Until

The Until and While structures are very similar. They differ only in the sense of the test at the top of the loop. Figure 10-6 shows that Until continues to loop *until* the **test-command** returns a *true* exit status. The While structure loops *while* the **test-command** continues to return a *true* or nonerror contion. The Until structure is shown following.

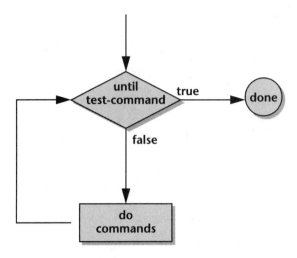

Figure 10-6   Until Flowchart

until **test-command**
do
    commands
done

The following script demonstrates an Until structure that includes a **read** command. When the user enters the correct string of characters, the **test-command** is satisfied, and the structure passes control out of the loop.

```
$ cat until1
secretname=jenny
name=noname
echo Try to guess the secret name!
echo
until [ "$name" = "$secretname" ]
do
    echo "Your guess: \c"
    read name
done
echo Very good.
$ until1
Try to guess the secret name!

Your guess: helen
Your guess: barbara
Your guess: jenny
Very good
```

The **locktty** script below is similar to the **lock** command on Berkeley UNIX. It prompts the user for a key (or password), and then it uses an Until control structure to "lock" the terminal. The Until statement causes the system to ignore any characters typed at the keyboard until the user types in the original key, which unlocks the terminal. The **locktty** script can keep people from using your terminal while you are away from it for short periods of time. It saves you from having to log out if you are concerned about other users using your login.

```
$ cat locktty
:
# adapted from lock.sh by Howard G. Port and
# Evelyn Siwakowsky
# UNIX/WORLD, III:4, p. 74, Fig. 3

trap '' 1 2 3 18
stty -echo
echo "Key: \c"
read key_1
echo
echo "Again: \c"
read key_2
echo
key_3=
if [ "$key_1" = "$key_2" ]
    then
            tput clear
            until [ "$key_3" = "$key_2" ]
            do
                    read key_3
            done
    else
            echo "locktty: keys do not match" 1>&2
fi
stty echo
```

The **trap** command at the beginning of the **locktty** script stops a user from being able to terminate the script by sending it a signal (e.g., by pressing the interrupt key, which is usually (DELETE) or (CONTROL)-C). Trapping signal 18 means that no one can use (CONTROL)-Z (job control, a stop from a tty) to defeat the lock. The **stty –echo** command causes the terminal not to echo characters typed at the keyboard to the screen. This prevents the keys (or passwords) the user types in from appearing on the screen. After turning off echoing, the script prompts the user for a key, reads the key into the user-created variable **key_1**, and then prompts the user to enter the same key again and saves it in the user-created variable **key_2**. The statement **key_3=** creates a variable with a null value. If **key_1** and **key_2** match, **locktty** clears the screen (with the **tput** command) and starts an Until loop. The Until loop keeps attempting to read from the terminal and assigning the input to the **key_3** variable. Once the user types in a string that matches one of the original keys (**key_2**), the Until loop terminates, and echoing is turned back on.

For more information about **stty**, refer to **stty** in Part II. The **trap** command is described on page 330.

The Break and Continue Commands

You can interrupt a For, While, or Until loop with a Break or Continue command. The Break command transfers control to the statement after the Done statement, terminating execution of the loop. The Continue command transfers control to the Done statement, which continues execution of the loop.

Case

The Case structure is shown below.

```
case test-string in
    pattern-1)
        commands-1
        ;;
    pattern-2)
        commands-2
        ;;
    pattern-3)
        commands-3
        ;;
    .
    .
    .
esac
```

Figure 10-7 shows that the Case structure provides a multiple branch decision mechanism. The path that the structure chooses depends on a match or lack of a match between the **test-string** and one of the **patterns**.

The following Case structure uses the value of the character that the user enters as the **test-string**. This value is represented by the variable **letter**. If the test string has a value of **A**, the structure executes the command following **A)**. If the test string has a value of **B** or **C**, the structure executes the appropriate command. The asterisk indicates *any string of characters*

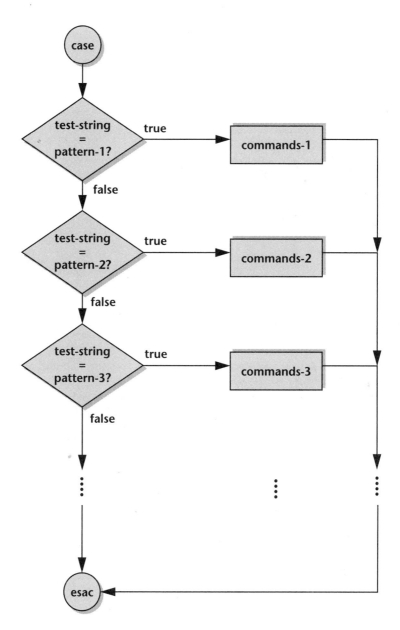

Figure 10-7   Case Flowchart

and serves as a catchall, in case there is no match. The second sample execution of **case1** shows the user entering a lowercase **b**. Because **b** does not match the uppercase **B** in the Case statement, the program tells you there is no match.

```
$ cat case1
echo "Enter A, B, or C: \c"
read letter
case "$letter" in
    A)
        echo You entered A
        ;;
    B)
        echo You entered B
        ;;
    C)
        echo You entered C
        ;;
    *)
        echo You did not enter A, B, or C
        ;;
esac

$ case1
Enter A, B, or C: B
You entered B
$ case1
Enter A, B, or C: b
You did not enter A, B, or C
```

The pattern in the Case structure is analogous to that of an ambiguous file reference. You can use the special characters and strings shown below:

Pattern	Matches
*	An asterisk matches any string of characters. You can use it for the default case.
?	A question mark matches any single character.
[...]	Square brackets define a character class. Any characters enclosed within square brackets are tried, one at a time, in an attempt to match a single character. A hyphen between two characters specifies a range of characters.
|	A vertical bar separates alternate choices that will satisfy a particular branch of the Case structure.

The next program is a variation of the previous one. This script accepts uppercase and lowercase letters.

```
$ cat case2
echo "Enter A, B, or C: \c"
read letter
case "$letter" in
    a|A)
        echo You entered A
        ;;
    b|B)
```

```
             echo You entered B
             ;;
        c|C)
             echo You entered C
             ;;
        *)
             echo You did not enter A, B, or C
             ;;
esac
$ case2
Enter A, B, or C: b
You entered B
$
```

The following example shows how the Case structure can be used to
create a menu. The menu in the script **command_menu** uses the **echo**
command to present menu items and prompt the user for a selection.
The Case structure executes the appropriate utility, depending on the
user's selection.

```
$ cat command_menu
:
# menu interface to simple commands

echo "\n        COMMAND MENU\n"
echo " a.  Current date and time"
echo " b.  Users currently logged in"
echo " c.  Name of the working directory"
echo " d.  Contents of the working directory\n"
echo "Enter a, b, c, or d:  \c"
read answer
echo
case "$answer" in
    a)
        date
        ;;
    b)
        who
        ;;
    c)
        pwd
        ;;
    d)
        ls -C
        ;;
    *)
        echo "There is no selection: $answer"
        ;;
esac
echo
```

```
$ command_menu

        COMMAND MENU

    a.  Current date and time
    b.  Users currently logged in
    c.  Name of the working directory
    d.  Contents of the working directory

Enter a, b, c, or d: a

Fri Jun 17 14:11:57 PDT 1994
```

The Case control structure is also frequently used in scripts for taking different actions, depending on how many command line arguments the script was called with. The script below, **safedit**, uses a Case structure that branches based on the number of command line arguments (**$#**). The **safedit** script saves a backup copy of a file you are editing with **vi**.

```
$ cat safedit
:
# adapted from safedit.sh by Evan Kaminer
# UNIX/WORLD, IV:11, p. 129, Listing 2

PATH=/usr/ucb:/bin:/usr/bin
script=`basename $0`
case $# in
    0)
        vi
        exit 0
        ;;
    1)
        if [ ! -f "$1" ]
            then
                vi "$1"
                exit 0
        fi
        if [ ! -r "$1" -o ! -w "$1" ]
            then
                echo "$script: check permissions "\
"on $1" 1>&2
                exit 1
            else
                editfile=$1
        fi
        if [ ! -w "." ]
            then
                echo "$script: backup cannot be " \
"created in the working directory" 1>&2
                exit 1
        fi
        ;;
```

```
    *)
                echo "Usage: $script [file-to-edit]" 1>&2
                exit 1
                ;;
    esac
    tempfile=/tmp/$$.$script
    cp $editfile $tempfile
    if vi $editfile
        then
                mv $tempfile bak.`basename $editfile`
                echo "$script: backup file created"
        else
                mv $tempfile editerr
                echo "$script: edit error--copy of " \
    "original file is in editerr" 1>&2
    fi
```

If the user calls **safedit** without any arguments, the Case structure executes its first branch and calls **vi** without a filename argument. Because an existing file is not being edited, **safedit** does not create a backup file. (See the :w command on page 201 for an explanation of how to exit from **vi** when you have called it without a filename.) If the user calls **safedit** with one argument, the commands in the second branch of the Case structure are run, and **safedit** verifies that **$1** is the name of a file for which the user has read and write permission or that the file specified by **$1** does not yet exist. The **safedit** script also verifies that the user has write permission for the working directory. If the user calls **safedit** with more than one argument, the third branch of the Case structure presents a usage message and exits with a status of 1.

In addition to the use of a Case structure for branching based on the number of command line arguments, the **safedit** script introduces several other features that are commonly used in shell scripts. First, at the beginning of the script the **PATH** variable is set to search **/usr/ucb**, **/bin**, and **/usr/bin**. This ensures that the commands executed by the script will be the standard utilities (which are kept in those directories). By setting **PATH** inside a script, you can avoid the problems that might occur if users have set up **PATH** to search their own directories first and they have scripts or programs with the same names as utilities the script uses.

If it is installed on your SunOS system, the **/usr/5bin** directory contains commands from the System V compatibility package. A command in this directory with the same name as a SunOS command (e.g., **echo**) usually has some different options or features. If you prefer to use the commands provided in a compatibility package, set the **PATH** variable to search **/usr/5bin** first.

Second, the following line creates a variable named **script** and assigns the simple filename of the script to it.

```
    script=`basename $0`
```

The **basename** command sends the simple filename component of its argument to the standard output, which is assigned to the variable called **script** using command substitution. If Alex calls the script with any one of the following commands, the output of **basename** will always be the simple filename **safedit**:

```
$ /home/alex/bin/safedit memo

$ ./safedit memo

$ safedit memo
```

After the **script** variable is set to the simple filename of the script, the **script** variable is used in place of the filename in usage and error messages. By using a variable that is derived from the command that invoked the script rather than a filename that has been typed directly into the script, you can create links to the script or rename it, and the usage and error messages will still provide accurate information.

A third significant feature of **safedit** is the use of the **$$** variable in a temporary filename. The statement below the Esac statement creates and assigns a value to the **tempfile** variable. This variable contains the name of a temporary file that is stored in the **/tmp** directory (as are many temporary files). The temporary filename begins with the PID of the current shell and ends with the name of the script. The PID is used because it ensures that the filename will be unique, and **safedit** will not attempt to overwrite an existing file (as might happen if two people were using **safedit** at the same time and not using unique filenames). The name of the script is appended so that, should the file be left in **/tmp** for some reason, you or the system administrator will be able to figure out where it came from. The PID is used in front of **$script** in the filename, rather than after it, because of the 14-character limit on filenames on some filesystems on older versions of UNIX. Since the PID is what ensures the uniqueness of the filename, it is placed first so that it will not be truncated. (If the **$script** component is truncated, the filename will still be unique.) For the same reason, when a backup file is created inside the If control structure a few lines down in the script, the filename is composed of the string **bak.** followed by the name of the file being edited. If **bak** were used as a suffix rather than a prefix and the original filename were 14 characters, the **.bak** might be lost, and the original file would be overwritten. The **basename** command extracts the simple filename of **$editfile** before it is prefixed with **bak.**.

Fourth, **safedit** uses an unusual **test-command** in the If structure, **vi $editfile**. The **test-command** calls **vi** to edit **$editfile**. When the user finishes editing the file and exits from **vi**, **vi** returns an exit code that is the basis for branching by the If control structure. If the editing session completed successfully, **vi** returns a 0, and the statements following the Then statement are executed. If **vi** does not terminate normally (as would occur if the user used a **kill** command from another terminal to kill the **vi** process), **vi** returns a nonzero exit status, and the statements following Else are executed.

The Here Document

A Here document allows you to redirect input to a shell script from within the shell script itself. It is called a Here document because it is *here,* immediately accessible in the shell script, instead of *there,* in another file.

The following script, **birthday**, contains a Here document. The two *less than* symbols on the first line indicate to the shell that a Here document follows. One or more characters that delimit the Here document follow the *less than* symbols—this example uses plus signs. Whereas the first delimiter can occur adjacent to the *less than* symbols, the second delimiter must occur on a line by itself. The shell sends everything between the two delimiters to the process as its standard input. In the following example, it is as though you had redirected the standard input to **grep** from a file, except that the file is embedded in the shell script. Just as the shell does not treat special characters that occur in the standard input of a shell script as special, so also the special characters that occur between the delimiters in a Here document are not considered special.

```
$ cat birthday
grep -i "$1" <<+
Alex      June 22
Barbara  February 3
Darlene  May 8
Helen    March 13
Jenny    January 23
Nancy    June 26
+
$ birthday Jenny
Jenny    January 23
$ birthday June
Alex      June 22
Nancy    June 26
```

When you run **birthday**, it lists all the lines in the Here document that contain the argument you called it with. In the preceding example, the first time **birthday** is run, it displays Jenny's birthday because it is called with an argument of **Jenny**. The second run displays all the birthdays in June.

OPTIONAL

The next script, **bundle**, includes a clever use of a Here document.* The **bundle** script is an elegant example of a type of script that is often called **shar** (for *sh*ell *ar*chive). The **bundle** script creates a file that contains several other files that can easily be recreated.

Creating a single file like this is useful when you want to send several files through electronic mail. Although the **tar** utility can also be used to combine files, **tar** puts (CONTROL) and null characters into the resulting file that **mail** cannot handle. (See Part II for more information about **tar**.) If your system makes a special interpretation of the first character of a script (page 285), add a top line to **bundle** containing a colon (:).

---

*Brian W. Kernighan and Rob Pike,
The UNIX Programming Environment, (c) 1984,
Reprinted by permission of Prentice Hall, Inc., Englewood Cliffs, NJ

```
$ cat bundle
# bundle:  group files into distribution package

echo '# To unbundle, sh this file'
for i
do
    echo "echo $i 1>&2"
    echo "cat >$i <<'End of $i'"
    cat $i
    echo "End of $i"
done
```

As the example below shows, the output that **bundle** creates is a shell script, which is redirected to a file called **bothfiles**. It contains the contents of each file given as an argument to **bundle** (**file1** and **file2** in this case) inside a Here document. To extract the original files from **bothfiles**, the user simply runs it. Before each Here document is a **cat** command that causes the Here document to be written to a new file when **bothfiles** is run.

```
$ cat file1
This is a file.
It contains two lines.
$ cat file2
This is another file.
It contains
three lines.
$ bundle file1 file2 > bothfiles
$ cat bothfiles
# To unbundle, sh this file
echo file1 1>&2
cat >file1 <<'End of file1'
This is a file.
It contains two lines.
End of file1
echo file2 1>&2
cat >file2 <<'End of file2'
This is another file.
It contains
three lines.
End of file2
```

Below, **file1** and **file2** are removed before **bothfiles** is run. The **bothfiles** script echoes the names of the files it creates as it creates them. Finally, the **ls** command shows that **bothfiles** has recreated **file1** and **file2**.

```
$ rm file1 file2
$ sh bothfiles
file1
file2
$ ls
bothfiles
file1
file2
```

The exec Command

The **exec** command is a shell built-in command that has two primary purposes: to run a command without creating a new process and to redirect the standard input, standard output, or standard error of a shell script from within the script.

When the shell executes a command that is not built into the shell, it typically creates a new process. The new process inherits environment variables from its parent process, but not the local variables of its parent. In contrast, when you run a command using **exec**, **exec** executes the new command in place of (overlays) the current process. Consequently, the environment, including local variables, of the original process is available to the new command.

Insofar as **exec** runs a command in the environment of the original process, it is similar to the . (dot) command (page 295). However, unlike the . command, which can only run scripts, **exec** can run both scripts and compiled programs. Also, whereas the . command returns control to the original script when it finishes running, **exec** does not.

The format of the **exec** command follows:

exec **command arguments**

Because no new process is created when you run a command using **exec**, the command runs more quickly. However, since **exec** does not return control to the original program, the **exec** command can be used only with the last command that you want to run in a script. The following script shows that control is not returned to the script:

```
$ cat exec_demo
who
exec date
echo This echo command is never executed.
$ exec_demo
barbara   console Jun 16 07:15
chas      tty05 . Jun 16 06:33
Thu Jun 16 08:20:51 PDT 1994
```

The next example is a modified version of the **out** script (page 305). It uses **exec** to execute the final command the script runs. Since the original **out** script runs either **cat** or **more** and then terminates, the new version of **out** uses **exec** with both **cat** and **more**.

```
$ cat out
if [ $# = 0 ]
    then
        echo "Usage: out [-v] filenames" 1>&2
        exit 1
fi
if [ "$1" != "-v" ]
    then
        exec cat -- "$@"
    else
        shift
        exec more "$@"
fi
```

The second major use of **exec** is to redirect the standard input, standard output, or standard error of a script. From inside a shell script, you can use **exec** to redirect the input to or output from the script. After a command such as the following, all the input to a script is redirected to come from the file called **infile**:

```
exec < infile
```

Similarly, the following command redirects the standard output and the standard error to **outfile** and **errfile**, respectively:

```
exec > outfile 2> errfile
```

When a script prompts the user for input, it is useful to redirect the output from within the script to go to the terminal, in cases when the user is likely to have redirected the output from the script. When redirecting the output in a script, you can use **/dev/tty** as a synonym for the user's terminal. The **/dev/tty** device is a pseudonym the system maintains for the terminal the user is logged in on. The pseudonym enables you to refer to the user's terminal without knowing which device it is. (The actual device appears in the second column of the output of **who**.) By redirecting the output from a script to **/dev/tty**, you can ensure that prompts will go to the user's terminal, regardless of whether the user redirected the output from the script. The following command redirects to the terminal the output from a script that contains it:

```
exec > /dev/tty
```

Using **exec** to redirect the output to **/dev/tty** has one disadvantage—all subsequent output is redirected, unless you use **exec** again in the script. If you do not want to redirect the output from all subsequent commands in a script, you can redirect the individual **echo** commands that display prompts.

```
echo "Please enter your name:\c " > /dev/tty
```

Some versions of UNIX, including SunOS, allow you also to redirect the input to **read** to come from **/dev/tty**.

```
read name < /dev/tty
```

On older versions of UNIX, you cannot redirect the input to the **read** command.

The trap Command

You can use the **trap** command to trap a *signal*. A signal is a report to a process about a condition. The UNIX system uses signals to report interrupts generated by the user (e.g., by pressing the interrupt key) as well as bad system calls, broken pipes, illegal instructions, and other conditions. Using the **trap** command you can direct the actions a script will take when it receives a signal.

This discussion covers the six signals that are significant when you work with shell scripts. The following table lists the signals, the signal numbers that systems often ascribe to them, and the conditions that usually generate each signal. The signal numbers may be different on your system—check the file named **/usr/include/sys/signal.h**, or ask your system administrator.

Signal	No.	Generating Condition
hang up	1	Disconnect phone line
terminal interrupt	2	Pressing the interrupt key (usually (DELETE) or (CONTROL)-C)
quit	3	Pressing (CONTROL)-| or (CONTROL)-\
kill	9	The **kill** command with the –9 option (cannot be trapped)
software termination	15	Default of the kill command
stop	18	Pressing the job control stop key (usually (CONTROL)-Z)

When a script traps a signal, it takes whatever action you specify. It can remove files or finish any other processing as needed, display a message, terminate execution immediately, or ignore the signal. If you do not use a **trap** command in a script, any of the above signals can terminate it while it is running in the foreground. Because the kill signal cannot be trapped, you can always use **kill –9** to terminate a script (or any other process). Refer to **kill** in Part II.

The format of a **trap** command is shown below.

trap ['commands'] signal-numbers

The **signal-numbers** are the numbers of the signals that the **trap** command will catch. One or more **signal-numbers** must be present. The **commands** part is optional. If it is not present, the command resets the trap to its initial condition, which is to exit from the script. If the **commands** part is present, the shell executes the **commands** when it catches one of the signals. After executing the **commands**, the shell resumes executing the script where it left off. If you want **trap** to prevent a script from exiting when it receives a signal, but not to explicitly run any commands, you can use **trap** with a null (empty) **command**. The following command traps signal number 15, and the script continues:

```
$ trap '' 15
```

The following script demonstrates the use of the **trap** command to trap signal number 2. It returns an exit status of 1.

```
$ cat inter
trap 'echo PROGRAM INTERRUPTED; exit 1' 2
while :
do
    echo Program running.
done
```

The first line of **inter** sets up a trap for signal number 2. When the signal is caught, the shell executes the two commands between the single quotation marks in the **trap** command. The **echo** command displays the message PROGRAM INTERRUPTED. Then **exit** terminates this shell, and the parent shell displays a prompt. If the **exit** command were not there, the shell would return control to the While loop after displaying the message. The While loop repeats continuously until the script receives a signal, because the : command always returns a *true* exit status.

The **trap** command is frequently used in shell scripts to remove temporary files when a script is terminated prematurely. If a script has created temporary files and then is terminated before it removes them, they will be left around, cluttering up the /**tmp** filesystem.

The following shell script, **addbanner**, uses two **trap** commands to remove a temporary file. Together, the two **trap** commands remove a temporary file when the script terminates normally or due to a hangup, software interrupt, quit, or software termination signal.

```
$ cat addbanner
:
script=` basename $0 `

if [ ! -r "$HOME/banner" ]
    then
        echo "$script: need readable $HOME/banner" \
        "file" 1>&2
        exit 1
fi

trap 'exit 1' 1 2 3 15
trap 'rm /tmp/$$.$script 2> /dev/null' 0

for file
do
    if [ -r "$file" -a -w "$file" ]
        then
            cat $HOME/banner $file > /tmp/$$.$script
            cp /tmp/$$.$script $file
            echo "$script: banner added to $file" 1>&2
        else
            echo "$script: need read and write" \
            "permission for $file" 1>&2
    fi
done
```

When it is called with one or more filename arguments, **addbanner** loops through the files, adding a header to the top of each. This script is useful when you use a standard format at the top of your documents, such as a standard layout for memos, or when you want to add a standard header to shell scripts. The header is kept in a file called **banner** in the user's home directory. The HOME shell variable is used to indicate the user's home directory, so that **addbanner** can be used by several users without modification. If Alex uses /**home/alex** in place of $HOME and he then gives the script to Jenny, she will either have to change it, or **addbanner** will use Alex's **banner** file when Jenny runs **addbanner**.

The first **trap** command in **addbanner** causes it to exit with a status of 1 when it receives a hangup, software interrupt, or software termination signal. The second **trap** command uses a 0 in place of **signal-number**, which causes **trap** to execute its command argument *whenever* the script exits due to an **exit** command or due to reaching its end. Together, these two **trap** commands remove a temporary file whether the script terminates either normally or prematurely. The standard error output of the second **trap** command is sent to **/dev/null** for cases in which the **trap** attempts to remove a nonexistent temporary file. In those cases, **rm** sends an error message to the standard error output. Because the standard error output is redirected to **/dev/null**, the user will not see the message.

Functions

UNIX System V Release 2 introduced *shell functions*; later versions of UNIX, such as SunOS, also support shell functions. A shell function is similar to a shell script, in that it stores a series of commands for execution at a later time. However, because the shell stores a function in the computer's main memory instead of in a file, you can access it more quickly than you can a script. Also, the shell preprocesses (parses) a function so that it starts up more quickly than a script. Finally, the shell executes a shell function in the same shell that called it.

Users typically declare shell functions either in their **.profile** file or in scripts they want to use the functions in; or they enter the functions directly from the command line. You can remove functions with the **unset** command. The shell will not keep functions once you log out.

The format you use to declare a shell function is shown below.

```
function-name ()
{
    commands
}
```

The **function-name** is the name you use to call the function. The **commands** comprise the list of commands the function executes when you call it. These **commands** can include anything you can include in a shell script.

The next example shows how to create a simple function that displays the date, a header, and a list of the people who are using the system. This function runs the same commands as the **whoson** script described on page 277.

```
$ whoson ()
{
    date
    echo Users Currently Logged In
    who
}
$ whoson
Thu Jun 16 09:51:09 PDT 1994
Users Currently Logged In
hls       console Jun 16 08:59
alex      tty20   Jun 16 09:33
jenny     tty24   Jun 16 09:23
```

If you want to have the **whoson** function always available without having to enter it each time you log in, put its definition in your **.profile** file. After adding **whoson** to your .profile file, run **.profile** using the . (dot) command to put the changes into effect immediately. For more information about .profile, see page 71.

```
$ cat .profile
TERM=vt100
export TERM
stty kill '^u'
whoson ()
{
    date
    echo Users Currently Logged In
    who
}
$ . .profile
```

The next function changes your prompt to include the name of the new working directory when you change directories. After you define this function in your **.profile** file and run **.profile**, you can change directories using the go command, and the new directory will be displayed as part of your prompt.

```
$ cat .profile
.

.
# adapted from go by S. D. Andarmani
# UNIX/WORLD, III:5, p. 77, Fig. 6


go ()
{
    cd $1
    PS1="[ ` pwd `] "
}

$ . .profile
$ pwd
/home/alex
$ go literature
[/home/alex/literature] go
[/home/alex]
```

SUMMARY

The shell is both a *command interpreter* and a *programming language*. As a command interpreter, the shell executes commands you enter in response to its prompt. When you use it as a programming language, the shell executes commands from files called *shell scripts*.

You can declare shell scripts to be functions, so that they are immediately available and the shell can execute them more quickly.

The shell executes commands by means of processes. Each process has a unique process identification (PID) number. When you give the shell a command, it generally *forks* a new process that executes the command. The shell has some commands that are built in. It does not fork a new process to execute these commands.

Built-in Command	Action
:	Null command.
.	Execute a program or shell script as part of the current process.
` pgm `	Replace with the output of the **pgm** command.
break	Exit from For, While, or Until loop.
cd	Change working directory.
continue	Start with next iteration of For, While, or Until loop.
echo	Display arguments.
eval	Scan and evaluate the command line.
exec	Execute a program in place of the current process.
exit	Exit from current shell (usually the same as (CONTROL)-**D**).
export	Place the value of a variable in the calling environment.
getopts	Parse arguments to a shell script.
hash	Remember the location of a command in the search path.
newgrp	Change the user's group.
pwd	Print the name of the working directory.
read	Read a line from the standard input.
readonly	Declare a variable to be readonly.
return	Exit from a function.
set	Set shell flags or command line argument variables; without an argument, display a list of all variables.
shift	Promote each command line argument.
test	Compare arguments.
times	Display times for the current shell and its children.
trap	Trap a signal.
type	Display how each argument would be interpreted as a command.
umask	File-creation mask.
unset	Remove a variable or function.
wait	Wait for a background process to terminate.

You can execute a shell script (or a compiled program) by giving yourself execute permission for the file (using **chmod**) and using the name of the file as a command. If you precede the filename of a shell script with an **sh** command, you do not need execute permission.

The shell allows you to define *variables*. When you give the shell a command, it examines the command line for words that begin with unquoted dollar signs. It assumes that these words are variables and substitutes a value for each of them. You can declare and initialize a variable by assigning a value to it; you can remove a variable declaration by using the **unset** command.

The shell also defines some variables. The readonly variables are preceded by dollar signs because you can only reference them in this manner—you cannot assign values to them.

Variable	Contents
CDPATH	List of directories for the shell to check when you give a **cd** command
HOME	Pathname of your home directory
IFS	Internal-field separator
MAIL	File where the system stores your mail
MAILCHECK	Specifies how often the shell checks your mailbox for new mail
MAILPATH	List of other potential mailboxes
PATH	Search path for commands
PS1	Prompt string 1
PS2	Prompt string 2
SHELL	Identifies the name of the invoked shell
$0	Name of the calling program
$n	Value of the nth command line argument (can be changed by **set**)
$*	All of the command line arguments (can be changed by **set**)
$@	All of the command line arguments (can be changed by **set**)
$#	Count of the command line arguments
$$	PID number of the current process
$!	PID number of the most recent background task
$?	Exit status of the last task that was executed

The shell provides the following *control structures* so you can alter the flow of control within a shell script:

- If Then Fi
- If Then Else Fi
- If Then Elif Else Fi
- For In Do Done
- For Do Done
- While Do Done
- Until Do Done
- Case In Esac

A list of the special characters the shell recognizes follow:

Special Character	Function
NEWLINE	Initiates execution of a command
;	Separates commands
( )	Groups commands for execution by a subshell or identifies a function
&	Executes a command in the background
|	Pipe
>	Redirects standard output
>>	Appends standard output
<	Redirects standard input
<<	Here document
*	Any string of characters in an ambiguous file reference
?	Any single character in an ambiguous file reference
\	Quotes the following character
'	Quotes a string, preventing all substitutions
"	Quotes a string, allowing variable and command substitution
`	Performs command substitution
[ ]	Character class in an ambiguous file reference
$	References a variable
.	Executes a command (only at the beginning of a line)
#	Begins a comment
{ }	Command grouping (used to surround the contents of a function)
:	Null command, returns true exit status

REVIEW EXERCISES

1. Set up your **PATH** variable so that it searches the following directories in order:

   a. **/usr/ucb**

   b. **/bin**

   c. **/usr/lbin**

   d. **/usr/bin**

   e. your own **bin** directory

   f. the working directory

   If there is a file called **whereis** in **/usr/ucb** and also one in your own **bin**, which one will be executed when you type **whereis** on the command line? (Assume you have execute permission for both of the files.)

2. If your **PATH** variable is not set to search the working directory, how can you execute a program located there?

3. Explain what happens when you give the following commands:

   ```
   $ person=jenny
   $ echo $'person'
   $ echo $\person
   ```

   What does this imply about the order in which the shell processes the command line?

4. Write a shell script that displays the first 12 command line arguments, one argument per line.

5. Name two ways you can identify the PID of your login shell.

6. The following shell script adds entries to a file called **journal** in your home directory. It can help you keep track of phone conversations and meetings.

   ```
   $ cat journal
   :
   # journal: add journal entries to the file
   # $HOME/journal

   file=$HOME/journal
   date >> $file
   echo "Enter name of person or group:  \c"
   read person
   echo "$person" >> $file
   echo >> $file
   cat >> $file
   echo "----------------------------------" >> $file
   echo >> $file
   ```

   Add commands to **journal** to verify that the user has write permission for a file called **journal** in the user's home directory, if such a file exists. The script should take appropriate actions if a **journal** file exists and the user does not have write permission. Verify that the modified script works.

What did you have to do to the script in order to be able to execute it? Why does it use **read** the first time it accepts input from the terminal and the **cat** utility the second time?

7. What are the two ways you can execute a shell script when you do not have execute access permission? Can you execute a shell script if you do not have read access permission?

ADVANCED REVIEW EXERCISES

8. Type in the following shell scripts and run them:

```
$ cat report_dir
old_dir=`pwd`
echo "Current working directory:   " $old_dir
go_home
echo "Current working directory:   " `pwd`

$ cat go_home
cd
echo "New working directory:   " `pwd`
echo "Last working directory:   " $old_dir
```

What is wrong? Change them so that they work correctly.

9. Explain the behavior of the following shell script:

```
$ cat quote_demo
twoliner="This is line 1.
This is line 2."
echo "$twoliner\n"
echo $twoliner
```

10. Enhance the **spell_check** script (page 316) so that you can specify a list of words that you want to add to the output of **spell**. You can use a list of words like this to cull usages you do not want in your documents. For example, if you decide you want to use **disk** rather than **disc** in your documents, you can add **disc** to the list of words, and **spell_check** will complain if you use **disc** in a document.

11. Modify the **locktty** script (page 319) to accept an optional argument, **banner**. The **locktty** script should display the string **banner** on the user's screen while the terminal is locked. Use the **banner** command to display the string. The **banner** command displays its arguments to the standard output.

You can use the **banner** argument to display a message such as "back at 1," "see Jenny," or "at lunch" while the terminal is locked.

12. Write a shell function that defines **ls** to be the same as /bin/ls –F. Once you have the **ls** function defined, how can you run the **ls** utility without the –F option?

It is typically not a good idea to redefine the names of standard UNIX utilities such as **ls**. Why not? List all the reasons you can think of.

13. It is typically not a good idea to redefine the names of standard UNIX utilities such as **ls**. Why not? List all the reasons you can think of. Run the following two command lines:

```
$ whereis mail
$ whereis Mail
```

Which one of the commands reported runs if you enter **mail** on the command line? Are the programs listed by these two **whereis** commands the same or different? If you would rather use a different **mail** program, what changes can you make so the Shell finds the right one?

CHAPTER 11

The C Shell

The C Shell performs the same function as the Bourne and Korn Shells—it provides an interface between you and the UNIX operating system. It is an interactive command interpreter as well as a high-level programming language. At any one time you will be using either the Bourne Shell, the Korn Shell, or the C Shell, although it is possible to switch back and forth between them. This chapter contrasts the C Shell with the Bourne Shell, paying particular attention to those facets of the C Shell that are absent from the Bourne Shell. Although Chapter 10 is not specifically about the C Shell, it discusses many important concepts that are common to both shells and provides a good background for this chapter. The unique features of the Korn Shell are described in Chapter 12.

Background

The C Shell originated on Berkeley UNIX, although many manufacturers have provided the C Shell in their implementations of System V. You can customize the C Shell to make it more tolerant of mistakes and easier to use. By setting the proper shell variables, you can have the C Shell warn you when you appear to be accidentally logging out or overwriting a file. The alias mechanism makes it easy to change the names of existing commands and create new ones. The history mechanism allows you to edit and rerun previous command lines. Also, C Shell variables are much more versatile than those of the Bourne Shell. The C Shell processes arrays of numbers and strings and evaluates logical and numerical expressions.

Because of aliases, history, and other features, you may want to use the C Shell as your login shell. At the same time, you may find the Bourne Shell easier to use as a programming language.

Entering and Leaving the C Shell

If your version of UNIX has the C Shell and you are not already using it, you can execute the C Shell by giving the command **csh**. If you are not sure which shell you are using, use the **ps** utility to find out. It will show that you are running **csh** (the C Shell), **sh** (the Bourne Shell), or **ksh** (the Korn Shell).

If you want to use the C Shell as a matter of course, the system administrator can set up the **/etc/passwd** file so that you are using the C Shell immediately when you log in. On Berkeley-based systems (such as SunOS), you can make this change yourself by giving a **chsh csh** (change to C Shell) command. Use **chsh sh** if you want to go back to using the Bourne Shell.

You can run Bourne, C, and Korn Shell scripts while using any one of the shells as a command interpreter. Several methods have been provided for selecting the shell that will run a script. Refer to page 365, "C Shell Scripts."

There are several ways to leave a C Shell. The way that you use is dependent on two factors: whether the shell variable **ignoreeof** is set and whether you are using the shell that you logged in on or another shell that you created after you logged in. If you are not sure how to exit from a C Shell, press (CONTROL)-D. You will either exit or receive instructions on how to exit. If you have not set **ignoreeof** and it has not been set for you in one of your startup files (page 365), you can exit from any shell using (CONTROL)-D (the same procedure you use to exit from the Bourne Shell).

If **ignoreeof** is set, (CONTROL)-D will not work. The **ignoreeof** variable causes the shell to display a message telling you how to exit. You can always exit from a C Shell by giving an **exit** command. A **logout** command allows you to exit only from the login shell. More information on **ignoreeof** can be found on page 363.

History

The history mechanism maintains a list of recently used command lines, also called *events,* and it provides a shorthand for reexecuting any of the events in the list. The shorthand also enables you to execute variations on previous commands and to reuse arguments from them. The shorthand makes it easy to replicate complicated commands and arguments that you used earlier in the login session and to enter a series of commands that differ from one another in minor ways. The history list is also useful as a record of what you have done. It can be helpful when you have made mistakes and are not sure what you did or when you want to keep a record of a procedure that involved a series of commands.

The **history** variable (page 362) determines the number of events preserved in this list. Typically, you will want to preserve about 100 events. If you attempt to preserve too many events, you may run out of memory.

The C Shell assigns a sequential *event number* to each of your command lines. If you wish, the C Shell can display this number as part of its prompt (page 362). Many of the examples in this chapter show numbered prompts. The history mechanism preserves events whether or not you use a numbered prompt.

Give the following command manually, or place it in your .cshrc start-up file, to establish a history list of the 100 most recent events:

```
% set history = 100
```

The following command causes the C Shell to save the 20 most recent events across login sessions:

```
% set savehist = 20
```

After you set **savehist,** you can log out and log in again, and the events from the previous login session will still be available in your history list.

Give the command **history** to display the events in the history list. When you first set the **history** variable, the history list will just record the events back to the comand line you used to set it.

```
32 % history
   22 set history = 100
   23 ls -lg
   24 cat temp
   25 rm temp
   26 vi memo
   27 lpr memo
   28 vi memo
   29 lpr memo
   30 mail jenny < memo
   31 rm memo
   32 history
```

As you run commands and your history list becomes longer, it will run off the top of the screen when you use the **history** command. Pipe the output of **history** through **more** to browse through it, or use the **tail** command to look at the end of it. (Refer to **tail** on page 57 or in Part II).

Reexecuting Events

You can reexecute any event in the history list. Even if there is no history list, you can always reexecute the previous event. There are three ways to reference an event: by its absolute event number, by its number relative to the current event, or by the text it contains.

All references to events begin with an exclamation point. One or more characters follow the exclamation point to specify an event.

Reexecuting the Previous Event

You can always reexecute the previous event by giving the command !!. In the following example, event 4 reexecutes event 3.

```
3 % ls -lg text
-rw-rw-r-- 1 alex   pubs       5  Jun 14 12:51 text
4 % !!
ls -lg text
-rw-rw-r-- 1 alex   pubs       5  Jun 14 12:51 text
```

When you use the history mechanism to reexecute an event, the C Shell displays the command it is executing, as the example above shows.

Using Event Numbers

A number following an exclamation point refers to an event. If that event is in the history list, the C Shell executes it. A negative number following an exclamation point references an event relative to the current event (e.g., !–3 refers to the third preceding event). Both of the following commands reexecute event 3:

```
7 % !3
ls -lg text
-rw-rw-r-- 1 alex   pubs       5  Jun 14 12:51 text
8 % !-5
ls -lg text
-rw-rw-r-- 1 alex   pubs       5  Jun 14 12:51 text
```

Using Event Text

When a string of text follows an exclamation point, the C Shell searches for and executes the most recent event that *began* with that string. If you enclose the string between question marks, the C Shell executes the most recent event *containing* that string. The final question mark is optional if a (RETURN) would immediately follow it.

```
53 % history
      48 cat letter
      49 cat memo
      50 lpr memo
      51 mail jenny < memo
      52 ls -lg
      53 history
```

```
54 % !l
ls -lg
  .

  .
55 % !lpr
lpr memo
56 % !?letter?
cat letter
  .

  .
```

Words Within Events

You can select any word or series of words from an event. The words are numbered starting with 0, representing the first command on the line, and continuing with 1, representing the first word following the command, through *n*, representing the last word on the line.

To specify a particular word from a previous event, follow the event specification (such as **!14**) with a colon and the number of the word in the previous event. (Use **!14:3** to specify the third word from event 14.) You can specify a range of words by separating two word numbers with a hyphen. The first word following the command (word number one) can be specified by a caret (^), and the last word, by a dollar sign.

```
72 % echo apple grape orange pear
apple grape orange pear
73 % echo !72:2
echo grape
grape
74 % echo !72:^
echo apple
apple
75 % !72:0 !72:$
echo pear
pear
76 % echo !72:2-4
echo grape orange pear
grape orange pear
77 % !72:0-$
echo apple grape orange pear
apple grape orange pear
```

As the next example shows, **!$** refers to the last word of the previous event. You can use this shorthand to edit, for example, a file you just displayed with **cat**.

```
% cat report.718
  .
% vi !$
vi report.718
  .
```

If an event contains a single command, the word numbers correspond to the argument numbers. If an event contains more than one command, this correspondence is not true for commands after the first. Event 78, below, contains two commands, separated by a semicolon so that the shell executes them sequentially. The semicolon is word number five.

```
78 % !72 ; echo helen jenny barbara
echo apple grape orange pear ; echo helen jenny barbara
apple grape orange pear
helen jenny barbara
79 % echo !78:7
echo helen
helen
80 % echo !78:4-7
echo pear ; echo helen
pear
helen
```

Modifying Previous Events

On occasion, you may want to reexecute an event, changing some aspect of it. Perhaps you entered a complex command line with a typo or incorrect pathname. Or you may want to reexecute a command, specifying a different argument. You can modify an event, or a word of an event, by following the event or word specifier with a colon and a modifier. The following example shows the substitute modifier correcting a typo in the previous event.

```
145 % car /home/jenny/memo.0507 /home/alex/letter.0507
car: Command not found.
146 % !!:s/car/cat
cat /home/jenny/memo.0507 /home/alex/letter.0507
   .
   .
```

As a special case, you can use an abbreviated form of the substitute modifier, shown here, to change the most recent event.

```
% ^old^new
```

produces the same results as

```
% !!:s/old/new
```

Thus, event 146 could have been entered as

```
146 % ^car^cat
cat /home/jenny/memo.0507 /home/alex/letter.0507
   .
   .
```

Following is a list of modifiers.

Modifier	Mnemonic	Effect
h	head	Remove the last element of a pathname.
r	root	Remove the filename extension.
t	tail	Remove all elements of a pathname except the last.
&	repeat	Repeat the previous substitution.
p	print	Do not execute the modified event.
q	quote	Quote the modifications so that no further modifications take place.
[g]s/**old**/**new**/	substitute	Substitute **new** for **old**.

OPTIONAL Continued

The **s** modifier substitutes the first occurrence of the old string with the new one. Placing a **g** before the **s** (**g**s/old/new/) causes a global substitution, replacing all occurrences of the old string. The / is the delimiter in these examples, but you can use any character that is not in either the **old** or the **new** string. The final delimiter is optional if a (RETURN) would immediately follow it. Like the **vi** Substitute command, the history mechanism replaces an ampersand (&) in the new string with the old string. The shell replaces a null old string (s//**new**/) with the previous old string or string within a command that you searched for with ?string?.

The following examples demonstrate the use of history modifiers:

```
66 % echo /home/jenny/letter.0406 /home/jenny/memo.prv
/home/jenny/letter.0406 /home/jenny/memo.prv
67 % !!:h
echo /home/jenny /home/jenny/memo.prv
/home/jenny /home/jenny/memo.prv
68 % echo !66:2:h
echo /home/jenny
/home/jenny
69 % echo !66:2:t
echo memo.prv
memo.prv
70 % echo !66:1:r
echo /home/jenny/letter
/home/jenny/letter
71 % echo !66:1:p
echo /home/jenny/letter.0406
```

Event 66 displays two filenames. Event 67 recalls the previous event, modified by **h**. Because the command did not specify a word from the event, it modified word 1 and recalled the entire previous event. Events 68 through 70 recall and modify specific words from event 66. In these cases, only the specified words are recalled. Event 71 uses the **p** modifier to display, but not execute, the resulting command.

Alias

The **alias** command performs a string substitution on the command line according to your specifications. The C Shell alias mechanism allows you to define new commands. The format of an **alias** command is shown below.

alias [**entered-command** [**executed-command**]]

The **entered-command** is the command that you enter in response to the C Shell prompt. The **executed-command** is the string that **alias** substitutes for the **entered-command**.

The following example shows how to use **alias**. The **alias** command in event 6 causes the C Shell to substitute **ls –lg** every time you give an **ll** command. Event 7 demonstrates this substitution.

```
5 % ls
one      three   two
6 % alias ll ls -lg
7 % ll
total 3
-rwxrw-r-- 1 jenny pubs      17  Mar   5 11:36 one
-rw-rw-r-- 1 jenny pubs      42  Mar   5 11:14 three
-rwxrw-r-- 1 jenny pubs      11  Mar   5 11:35 two
```

Instead of using **ll** as an alias, you can use **ls**; however, this is not recommended. If you do use it, scripts that you run will also use the alias, which may cause them to malfunction. However, if you do use **ls** rather than **ll**, you can avoid the alias substitution (on the command line only) by placing \ in front of **ls**.

```
8 % alias ls ls -lg
9 % ls three
-rw-rw-r-- 1 jenny  pubs  42 Mar   5 11:14 three
10 % \ls three
three
```

You can use **alias** to create short names for commands that you use often. For example, if you use the **more** utility frequently, you could use **alias** to substitute **more** when you give the command **m**.

```
10 % alias m more
11 % m aldus.brief
  .
  .
```

You can also use **alias** to protect yourself from mistakes. The example below uses an alias to substitute the interactive version of the **mv** utility when you give the command **mi**. The interactive option to **mv** causes it to prompt you for verification when the move would overwrite an existing file.

```
12 % alias mi mv -i
13 % mi aldus.brief.2 aldus.brief
remove aldus.brief? y
```

Finally, you can use **alias** to create new commands. If your system does not have the **head** utility, you can use the alias below to create your own. The **sed** command below prints out ten lines of a file and quits. This is similar to what the **head** utility does. Refer to Chapter 3 for more information about **head**, and to Part II for information about **sed**.

```
14 % alias head sed 10q
15 % head aldus.brief
 .
 .
 .
```

When you give an **alias** command without any arguments (event 16), the C Shell displays a list of all the aliases. When given with one argument (event 17), the alias for that argument is displayed. An **unalias** command (event 18) removes an alias from the list of aliases.

```
16 % alias
head    sed 10q
ll      ls -lg
m       more
mi      mv -i
17 % alias head
sed 10q
18 % unalias head
19 % alias
ll      ls -ig
m       more
mi      mv -i
```

OPTIONAL

Implementation of alias

When you enter a command line, the C Shell breaks it into commands. Next, the C Shell substitutes an alias for each command that has an alias. After it makes these substitutions, the C Shell substitutes aliases over and over again until there are no aliases left. The **alias** command flags a self-referencing alias to prevent an infinite loop.

```
82 % alias a b
83 % alias b c
84 % alias c echo finished
85 % alias
a       b
b       c
c       (echo finished)
86 % a
finished
```

Events 82, 83, and 84 define a series of aliases that reference each other; event 85 uses **alias** without any arguments to display all the aliases. The C Shell executes event 86 as follows:

OPTIONAL Continued

- **a** is replaced by its alias **b**.
- **b** is replaced by its alias **c**.
- **c** is replaced by its alias **echo finished**.

There are no further aliases, so the shell executes the **echo** command.

Argument Substitution

The **alias** command substitutes command line arguments using the same scheme as the history mechanism, with a single exclamation point representing the current event. Modifiers are the same as those used by **history** (page 347). The exclamation points are quoted in the following example, so that the shell does not interpret them but passes them on to **alias**:

```
21 % alias last echo \!:$
22 % last this is just a test
test
23 % alias fn2 echo \!:2:t
24 % fn2 /home/jenny/test /home/alex/temp
/home/barbara/new
temp
```

Event 21 defines an alias for **last** that echoes the last argument. Event 23 defines an alias for **fn2** that echoes the simple filename, or tail, of the second argument on the command line.

Job Control

Using the C Shell's job control, you can move commands from the foreground to the background and vice versa, stop commands temporarily, and get a list of the current jobs.

When you give a command to the C Shell, it assigns the command a job number. You can then use the job number to work with the command. In the following example, the C Shell lists the job number and PID number of each command run in the background. The **jobs** command lists the current jobs.

```
86 % spell glossary > glossary.out &
[1] 26025
87 % date &
[2] 26028
Fri Jun 17 16:56:11 PDT 1994
[2]    Done                    date
88 % find /usr -name ace -print > findout &
[2] 26041
89 % jobs
[1]    - Running      spell glossary > glossary.out
[2]    + Running      find /usr -name ace -print > findout
```

In this example, the **jobs** command lists the first job, a **spell** command, as job 1. The **date** command does not appear in the **jobs** list because it completed before **jobs** was run. Since the **date** command also completed before **find** was run, the **find** command became job 2.

To move a job that is running in the background into the foreground, use the **fg** command with the job number as an argument. When specifying the job, precede the job number with a percent sign. The following example moves job 2 into the foreground:

```
90 % fg %2
```

You can also refer to a job by following the percent sign with a unique string that identifies the first few characters of the command. Instead of the above command, for example, you could have used **fg %find** or **fg %f** since either one uniquely identifies job 2. If you precede the string with a question mark, it will match a job that contains the string anywhere within the command. If there is only one job running in the background, an **fg** command without any arguments will bring it to the foreground.

To put the job into the background, press (CONTROL)-**Z** to stop the job. Then use the **bg** command to resume the job running in the background.

```
91 % bg
```

When a job is running in the background, you can use the **stop** command to stop it. Then use **bg** or **fg** to restart it.

If a background job attempts to read from the terminal, the C Shell will stop it. When this happens you must move the job into the foreground, so that it can read from the terminal.

Although background jobs are ordinarily allowed to send output to the terminal, you can cause the C Shell to stop a job if it attempts to write to the terminal. Give the command **stty tostop** if you want background commands to stop when they attempt to write to the terminal.

The C Shell notifies you whenever a job *changes state*. Specifically, it notifies you when a job starts, stops, completes, or moves from the foreground to the background, or vice versa. By default, the C Shell displays the notice after your next prompt so that the notice does not disrupt your work. If you set the **notify** variable, the C Shell will notify you immediately about any job that changes state (see "Shell Variables That Act As Switches," page 363). If you do not set the **notify** variable, you can still cause the C Shell to notify you immediately about specific commands. The **notify** command causes the C Shell to display a notice about a specific job immediately after a change in state. Without an argument, **notify** reports on the current job. With a job as an argument, it reports on the specified job. Both of the following commands will cause the shell to notify you when job 2 changes state:

```
92 % notify %2
```

```
93 % notify %find
```

The C Shell also warns you if you try to leave a shell while there are stopped jobs. After the warning, if you then use the **jobs** command to review the list of jobs, or if you immediately try to leave the C Shell again, you will be allowed to leave, and your jobs will be terminated.

Redirecting the Standard Error

Under the C Shell, you can combine and redirect the standard output and the standard error (page 281) using a *greater than* symbol followed by an ampersand.

```
14 % cat x
cat: x: No such file or directory
15 % cat y
This is y.
16 % cat x y >& hold
17 % cat hold
cat: x: No such file or directory
This is y.
```

It is useful to combine and redirect output when you want to run a slow command in the background and do not want its output cluttering up your terminal screen. For example, because the **find** utility often takes a while to complete, it is a good idea to run it in the background.

The next command finds all the files anywhere in the filesystem hierarchy that are called **bibliography**. It runs in the background and sends its output to a file called **findout**. Because the **find** utility sends to its error output a report of directories that you do not have permission to search, you will have a record in the **findout** file of any files called **bibliography** that are found, as well as a record of the directories that could not be searched.

```
18 % find / -name bibliography -print >& findout &
```

In the above example, if you did not combine the standard error output with the standard output, the error messages would appear on your screen (and the **findout** file would contain only the list of files that were found).

While you are running a command in the background that has its output redirected to a file, you can look at the output by using the **tail** utility with the –**f** option. The –**f** option causes **tail** to display new lines as they are written to the file.

```
19 % tail -f findout
```

To terminate the **tail** command, press the interrupt key (usually (DELETE) or (CONTROL)-**C**). Refer to Part II for more information about **find** and **tail**.

Filename Generation

The C Shell generates filenames the same way the Bourne Shell does, with an added feature. Refer to Chapter 5 for an introduction to filename generation.

The C Shell uses the tilde (~) as a special character for filename generation. By itself, ~ expands into the pathname of your home directory. When you follow the tilde with the login name of a user, the C Shell expands it into the pathname of the home directory of that user. The following example shows how to copy the file named **idea.txt** into Helen's home directory (Helen's login name is hls):

```
152 % cp idea.txt ~hls
```

You can turn off the filename-expansion feature of the C Shell by setting the **noglob** variable. When **noglob** is set, the shell treats *, ?, [], and ~ as regular characters.

Filename Completion

Some versions of the C Shell complete filenames and user names after you specify unique prefixes. Filename completion is similar to filename generation, but the goal of filename completion is always to select a single file. Together, they make it practical to use long, descriptive filenames.

To enable the filename completion feature, set the **filec** variable. Refer to the "Variables" section for more information about the **set** command and **filec**.

```
41 % set filec
```

To use filename completion when you are typing in a filename on the command line, type in enough of the name to uniquely identify the file in the directory, and then press (ESCAPE). The C Shell will fill in the name. The following example shows the user typing the command **cat trig1A**, pressing (ESCAPE), and the system filling in the rest of the filename of the file that begins with the string **trig1A**:

```
42 % cat trig1A → (ESCAPE) → cat trig1A.302488
```

If two or more filenames match the prefix, the C Shell fills in the filenames to the point where the ambiguity occurs and causes the terminal to beep. (Some terminals flash instead of beeping.)

```
43 % ls h*
help.hist      help.text      help.trig01
44 % cat h → (ESCAPE) → cat help.  (BEEP)
```

You can fill in enough characters to resolve the ambiguity and then press (ESCAPE) again. Alternatively, you can press (CONTROL)-**D**, and the C Shell will present a list of matching filenames.

```
45 % cat help → (CONTROL)-D → cat help
                              help.text
                              help.hist
                              help.trig01
```

The C Shell will then redraw the command line you have typed, so that you can disambiguate the filename (and press (ESCAPE) again) or finish typing the rest of the name.

The (ESCAPE) and (CONTROL)-**D** keys can also be used with the tilde (~) to expand user names. If you type in ~ and a unique prefix for a user name, you can then press (ESCAPE), and the shell will complete it. If you press (CONTROL)-**D**, the shell presents a list of alternatives.

```
46 % mail ~all → (ESCAPE) → mail allen
47 % mail ~al → (CONTROL)-D → mail ~al  (BEEP)
                             alex
                             allen
```

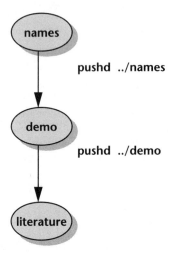

Figure 11-1 Creating a Directory Stack

Directory Stack Manipulation

The C Shell has the ability to store a list of directories you are using, and it enables you to move among them simply and easily. The list is referred to as a *stack*. You can think of it as a stack of dinner plates, where you typically add plates to and remove plates from the top of the stack.

You can display the contents of the stack using the **dirs** command. If you call **dirs** when the stack is empty, **dirs** puts the working directory on the top of the stack.

```
53 % dirs
~/literature
```

The **dirs** command uses the tilde to represent the user's home directory. In this and the following examples, the directory structure shown in Figure 4-6 is assumed.

To change directories and add the new directory to the top of the stack, use the **pushd** (push directory) command. The **pushd** command also displays the contents of the stack. The following example is illustrated in Figure 11-1:

```
54 % pushd ../demo
~/demo ~/literature
55 % pwd
/home/alex/demo
56 % pushd ../names
~/names ~/demo ~/literature
57 % pwd
/home/alex/names
```

When you use **pushd** without an argument, it changes the working directory to the second directory on the stack and makes it the top directory on the stack. This action is shown in Figure 11-2.

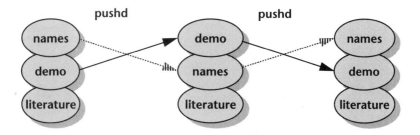

*Figure 11-2 Using **pushd** to Change Directories*

```
58 % pushd
~/demo ~/names ~/literature
59 % pwd
/home/alex/demo
```

Using **pushd** in this way, you can easily move back and forth between two directories. To access another directory in the stack, call **pushd** with a numeric argument (preceded by a plus sign). The directories in the stack are numbered starting with the top directory, which is number 0. The following **pushd** command changes the working directory to **literature** and moves it to the top of the stack:

```
60 % pushd +2
~/literature ~/demo ~/names
61 % pwd
/home/alex/literature
```

To remove a directory from the stack, use the **popd** (pop directory) command. As Figure 11-3 shows, without an argument, **popd** removes the top directory from the stack and changes the working directory to the new top directory.

```
64 % popd
~/demo ~/names
65 % pwd
/home/alex/demo
```

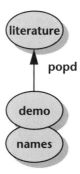

*Figure 11-3 Using **popd** to Remove a Directory from the Stack*

To remove a directory other than the top one from the stack, use **popd** with a numeric argument, preceded by a plus sign. If you remove a directory other than directory number 0 on the stack, this command does not change the working directory.

```
66 % popd +1
~/demo
67 % pwd
/home/alex/demo
```

Variables

The C Shell, like the Bourne Shell, uses only string variables. The C Shell can, however, work with these variables as numbers. You must use the **expr** command to perform arithmetic operations on numbers in the Bourne Shell. The arithmetic functions of **expr**, and more, are built into the C Shell.

This section uses the term *numeric variable* to describe a string variable that contains a number that the C Shell uses in arithmetic or logical-arithmetic computations. However, no true numeric variables exist.

A C Shell variable name consists of 1 to 20 characters, which can be letters, digits, and underscores (_). The first character of a variable name cannot be a digit.

Variable Substitution

Three commands declare and manipulate variables: **set**, **@**, and **setenv**. The **set** command assumes that a variable is a nonnumeric string variable. The **@** command works only with numeric variables. Both **set** and **@** declare local variables. The **setenv** command declares a variable *and* places it in the calling environment of all child processes. Using **setenv** is similar to using **export** in the Bourne Shell (see page 289 for a discussion of local and environment variables).

Once the value—or merely the existence—of a variable has been established, the C Shell substitutes the value of that variable when it sees the variable on a command line or in a shell script. The C Shell, like the Bourne Shell, recognizes a word that begins with a dollar sign as a variable. If you quote the dollar sign by preceding it with a backslash (\$), the shell will not perform the substitution. When a variable is within double quotation marks, the substitution occurs even if you quote the dollar sign. If the variable is within single quotation marks, the substitution will not occur, regardless of whether or not you quote the dollar sign.

String Variables

The C Shell treats string variables similarly to the way the Bourne Shell does. The major difference is in their declaration and assignment. The C Shell uses an explicit command, **set** (or **setenv**), to declare and/or assign a value to a string variable.

```
1 % set name = fred
2 % echo $name
fred
3 % set
argv    ()
home    /home/jenny
name    fred
shell   /bin/csh
status  0
```

Event 1 declares the variable **name** and assigns the string **fred** to it. Unlike the Bourne Shell, the C Shell allows (SPACE)s around the equal sign. (They are not required with **set**; however, they are required with **setenv**.) Event 2 displays this value. When you give a **set** command without any arguments, it displays a list of all the declared variables and their values. When you give a **set** command with only the name of a variable and no value, it sets the variable to a null string. Refer to events 4 and 5, below. Events 6 and 7 show that the **unset** command removes a variable from the list of declared variables.

```
4 % set name
5 % echo $name
6 % unset name
7 % set
argv    ()
home    /home/jenny
shell   /bin/csh
status  0
```

Arrays of String Variables

Before you can access individual elements of an array, you must declare the entire array. To declare an array, you need to assign a value to each element of the array.

```
8 % set colors = (red green blue orange yellow)
9 % echo $colors
red green blue orange yellow
10 % echo $colors[3]
blue
11 % echo $colors[2-4]
green blue orange

12 % set shapes = ('' '' '' '' '')
13 % echo $shapes
14 % set shapes[4] = square
15 % echo $shapes[4]
square
```

Event 8 declares the array of string variables named **colors** to have five elements and assigns values to each of these elements. If you do not know the values of the elements at the time you declare an array, you can declare an array containing the necessary number of null elements. See event 12.

You can reference an entire array by preceding its name with a dollar sign (event 9). A number in square brackets following a reference to the array refers to an element of the array (events 10, 14, and 15). Two numbers in square brackets, separated by a hyphen, refer to two or more adjacent elements of the array (event 11). See "Special Forms of User Variables," page 361, for more information on arrays.

Numeric Variables

The **@** command assigns a value to a numeric variable. You can declare single numeric variables with the **@** command, just as you can use the **set** command to declare nonnumeric variables. If you give **@** a nonnumeric argument, it displays an **Expression syntax.** error message.

Many of the expressions that the **@** command can evaluate and the operators it recognizes are derived from the C programming language. The format of a declaration or assignment using the **@** command is shown below.

> @ **variable-name operator expression**

The **variable-name** is the name of the variable that you are declaring or assigning a value to. The **operator** is one of the C assignment operators: =, +=, −=, *=, /=, or %=. (See page 534 for an explanation of these operators.) The **expression** is an arithmetic expression that can include most C operators; refer to "Expressions," the subsection that follows. You can use parentheses within the expression for clarity or to change the order of evaluation. Parentheses must surround parts of the expression that contain any of the following characters: <, >, &, or |.

Expressions

An expression can be composed of constants, variables, and the following operators (listed in order of decreasing precedence):

Operators		Function
Parentheses		
	()	change the order of evaluation
Unary Operators		
	−	unary minus
	~	one's complement
	!	logical negation
Arithmetic Operators		
	%	remainder
	/	divide
	*	multiply
	−	subtract
	+	add

(Continued)

Operators	Function
Shift Operators	
>>	right shift
<<	left shift
Relational Operators	
>	greater than
<	less than
>=	greater than or equal to
<=	less than or equal to
!=	not equal to (compare strings)
==	equal to (compare strings)
Bitwise Operators	
&	AND
^	exclusive OR
I	inclusive OR
Logical Operators	
&&	AND
II	OR

Expressions follow these rules:

- The shell considers a number that begins with a 0 (zero) to be an octal number.

- The shell evaluates a missing or null argument as 0.

- All results are decimal numbers.

- Except for != and ==, the operators act on numeric arguments.

- You must separate each element of an expression from adjacent elements by a (SPACE), unless the adjacent element is an &, I, <, >, (, or).

There is also a group of expressions that involve files rather than numeric variables or strings. These expressions are described on page 367.

```
216 % @ count = 0
217 % echo $count
0
218 % @ count = ( 5 + 2 )
219 % echo $count
7
220 % @ result = ( $count < 5 )
221 % echo $result
0
```

```
222 % @ count += 5
223 % echo $count
12
224 % @ count++
225 % echo $count
13
```

Event 216 declares the variable **count** and assigns a value of 0 to it. Event 218 shows the result of an arithmetic operation being assigned to a variable. Event 220 uses **@** to assign the result of a logical operation involving a constant and a variable to **result**. The value of the operation is false (=0) because the variable **count** is not less than 5. Event 222 is a compressed form of the following assignment statement:

```
% @ count = ( $count + 5 )
```

Event 224 uses a postfix operator to increment **count** by 1.

Arrays of Numeric Variables

You must use the **set** command to declare an array of numeric variables before you can use the **@** command to assign values to the elements of the array. The **set** command can assign any values to the elements of a numeric array, including zeros, other numbers, and null strings.

Assigning a value to an element of a numeric array is similar to assigning a value to a simple numeric variable. The only difference is that you must specify the element, or index, of the array. The format is shown below.

@ **variable-name[index] operator expression**

The **index** specifies the element of the array that is being addressed. The first element has an index of 1. The **index** must be either a numeric constant or a variable. It cannot be an expression. In the preceding format, the square brackets around **index** are part of the format and do not indicate that **index** is optional.

```
226 % set ages = (0 0 0 0 0)
227 % @ ages[2] = 15
228 % @ ages[3] = ($ages[2] + 4)
229 % echo $ages[3]
19
230 % echo $ages
0 15 19 0 0
```

Elements of a numeric array behave as though they were simple numeric variables. The difference is that you must use **set** to declare a numeric array. Event 226 above declares an array with five elements, each having a value of 0. Events 227 and 228 assign values to elements of the array, and event 229 displays the value of one of the elements. Event 230 displays all the elements of the array.

Braces

You can use braces to distinguish a variable from surrounding text without the use of a separator (e.g., a (SPACE)).

```
100 % set prefix = Alex
101 % echo $prefix is short for $prefix{ander}.
Alex is short for Alexander.
```

Without braces in this example, **prefix** would have to be separated from ander with a (SPACE) so that the shell would recognize **prefix** as a variable. This change would cause Alexander to become Alex ander.

Special Forms of User Variables

A special variable in the following format stores the number of elements in an array:

    $#variable-name

You can determine whether a variable has been declared or not by testing a variable of the next format:

    $?variable-name

This variable has a value of 1 if **variable-name** has been declared. Otherwise it has a value of 0.

```
205 % set days = (mon tues wed thurs fri)
206 % echo $#days
5
207 % echo $?days
1
208 % unset days
209 % echo $?days
0
```

Event 206 displays the number of elements in the **days** array that was set in event 205. Event 207 shows that **days** has been declared because **$?days** echoes as 1 (= true). Events 208 and 209 show what happens when **days** is unset.

Shell Variables

This section lists the shell variables that are either set by the shell, inherited by the shell from the environment, or set by the user and used by the shell. The section is divided into two parts. The first contains variables that take on significant values (e.g., the PID number of a background process). The second part lists variables that act as switches—*on* if they are declared, *off* if they are not.

Many of these variables are most often set from within one of the C Shell's two startup files: **.login** or **.cshrc**. Refer to pages 365 and 366 for more information about **.login** and **.cshrc**.

Shell Variables That Take On Values

$argv   This shell variable contains the command line arguments from the command that the shell invoked. For example, **argv[0]** contains the name of the calling program, and **argv[1]** contains the first command line argument. You can change any element of this array except **argv[0]**. Use **argv[*]** to reference all the arguments together. You can abbreviate references to argv as **$*** (short for **$argv[*]**) and **$n** (short for **$argv[n]**).

$#argv   The shell sets this variable to the number of elements in **argv**, excluding the element **argv[]**.

$cdpath   The **cdpath** variable affects the operation of **cd** in the same way the Bourne Shell's **CDPATH** variable does (page 295). It takes on the value of a list of absolute pathnames (similar to the **PATH** variable) and is usually set in the **.login** file with a command line such as the following:

```
set cdpath = (/home/jenny /home/jenny/letters)
```

When you call **cd** with a simple filename, it searches the working directory for a subdirectory with that name. If one is not found, **cd** searches the directories listed in **cdpath** for the subdirectory.

$cwd   The shell sets this variable to the name of the working directory. When you access a directory through a symbolic link, the C Shell sets **cwd** to the name of the symbolic link. Refer to page 83 for more information about symbolic links.

$history   This variable controls the size of your history list. As a rule of thumb, its value should be kept around 100. If you assign too large a value, the shell can run out of memory. Refer to "History," page 343.

$HOME   This variable is the same as the **HOME** variable in the Bourne Shell. It has the value of the pathname of the home directory of the user. The **cd** command refers to this variable, as does the filename expansion of ~ (see "Filename Generation," page 352).

$PATH   This variable is the same as the **PATH** variable in the Bourne Shell. If it is not set, you can execute a file only if you specify its full pathname. You can set your **PATH** variable with a command such as the following:

```
% setenv PATH (/usr/bin /usr/ucb /bin ~/bin .)
```

$prompt   This variable is similar to the **PS1** variable in the Bourne Shell. If it is not set, the prompt will be %, or # for the system administrator (Superuser). The shell expands an exclamation point in the prompt string to the current event number. (Just as the shell replaces a variable in a shell script with its value, the shell replaces an exclamation point in the prompt string with the current event number.) Following is a typical command line from a **.cshrc** file that sets the value of **prompt**:

```
set prompt = '! % '
```

You must quote the exclamation point so the shell does not expand it before assigning it to the variable **prompt**.

$savehist   This variable specifies the number of commands that will be saved from the history list when you log out. These events are saved in a file called **.history** in your home directory. The shell uses them as the initial history list when you log in again, so that your history continues across login sessions.

$shell   This variable contains the pathname of the shell.

$status   This variable contains the exit status returned by the last command.

$$ As in the Bourne Shell, this variable contains the PID number of the current shell.

Shell Variables That Act As Switches

The following shell variables act as switches; their values are not significant. If the variable has been declared, the shell takes the specified action. If not, the action is not taken or is negated. You can set these variables in your .cshrc file, in a shell script, or from the command line.

$echo   When you call the C Shell with the –x option, it sets the **echo** variable. You can also set **echo** using a **set** command. In either case, when you declare **echo**, the C Shell displays each command before it executes that command.

$filec   The **filec** variable enables the filename completion feature. Filename completion is a new feature of the C Shell that complements the filename generation facility. When **filec** is set, you can a enter a partial filename on the command line and then press (ESCAPE) to cause the shell to complete it, or press (CONTROL)-**D** to list all the filenames that match the prefix you entered. Refer to page 353 for more information about filename completion.

$ignoreeof   When you set the **ignoreeof** variable, you cannot exit from the shell using (CONTROL)-**D**, so you cannot accidentally log out. When this variable is declared, you must use **exit** or **logout** to leave a shell.

$noclobber   The **noclobber** variable prevents you from accidentally overwriting a file when you redirect output. It also prevents you from creating a file when you attempt to append output to a nonexistent file. To override **noclobber**, add an exclamation point to the symbol you use for redirecting or appending output (that is, >! and >>!).

When you do *not* declare **noclobber**, these command lines have the following effects.

Command Line	Effect
x > fileout	Redirects the standard output from process x to **fileout**. Overwrites **fileout** if it exists.
x >> fileout	Redirects the standard output from process x to **fileout**. Appends new output to the end of **fileout** if it exists. Creates **fileout** if it does not exist.

When you declare **noclobber**, the command lines have the following effects.

Command Line	Effect
x > fileout	Redirects the standard output from process x to **fileout**. The C Shell displays an error message if **fileout** exists and it does not overwrite the file.
x >> fileout	Redirects the standard output from process x to **fileout**. Appends new output to the end of **fileout** if it exists. The C Shell displays an error message if **fileout** does not exist. It does not create the file.

$noglob   When you declare **noglob**, the C Shell will not expand ambiguous filenames. You can use ∗, ?, ~, and [] on the command line or in a shell script without quoting them.

$nonomatch   When you declare **nonomatch**, the C Shell passes an ambiguous file reference that does not match a filename to the command that is being called. The shell does not expand the file reference. When you do not declare **nonomatch**, the C Shell generates a No match. error message and does not execute the command.

```
35 % cat questions?
No match.
36 % set nonomatch
37 % cat questions?
cat: questions?: No such file or directory
```

$notify   When the **notify** variable is set, the C Shell will send a message to your terminal whenever one of your background commands completes. Ordinarily, the C Shell will notify you about a job completion immediately before the next prompt. Refer to "Job Control," page 350.

$verbose   The C Shell declares the **verbose** variable when you call it with the –v option. You can also declare it using the **set** command. In either case, **verbose** causes the C Shell to display each command after a history substitution. (Refer to "History," page 343.)

C Shell Scripts

Just as the Bourne Shell can execute a file of Bourne Shell commands, so also the C Shell can execute a file of C Shell commands. The concepts of writing and executing scripts in the two shells are similar. However, the methods of declaring and assigning values to variables and the syntax of control structures are different.

Executing a C Shell Script

You can run Bourne, C, and Korn Shell scripts while using any one of the shells as a command interpreter. There are several different methods for selecting the shell that will run a script. On some implementations of the UNIX system, one way you can cause a script to be run by the C Shell is to put a pound sign (#) as the first character of the first line. However, if the first character of the script is a pound sign and the second character is an exclamation point, some systems interpret the following characters as the name of a shell to be used to run the script. If the line below is used as the first line of a script, the script will be run under the C Shell.

```
#!/bin/csh
```

If you run a script by explicitly invoking a particular shell, it will be run by that shell regardless of what is on its first line. In the following example, the script **reminder** will be run by the C Shell.

```
75 % csh reminder
```

Refer to "Invoking a Shell Script" on page 285 for more information about ways to select a shell to run a script.

Automatically Executed Shell Scripts

The Bourne Shell automatically executes one file (the **.profile** file in your home directory) when you log in. The C Shell executes three files at different times during a session.

.login   When you log in and start a session, the C Shell executes the contents of the **.login** file that is located in your home directory. This file should contain commands that you want to execute once, at the beginning of each session. The environment is established from this shell script. You can use **setenv** to declare environment variables here. You can also declare the type of terminal that you are using in your **.login** file. A sample **.login** file follows:

```
76 % cat .login
setenv TERM vt100
stty erase '^X' kill '^U' -lcase -tabs
echo "This is who's on the machine:"
who
```

This file establishes the type of terminal that you are using by setting the **TERM** variable. In this case, the Termcap name for the terminal is vt100. The sample **.login** file then executes the **stty** utility, displays a message, and executes the **who** utility so that you know who else is using the machine. More information about the **setenv** command can be found in "Variables," starting on page 356.

.cshrc   The C Shell executes the **.cshrc** file that is located in your home directory each time you invoke a new C Shell, such as when you log in or execute a C Shell script. You can use this file to establish variables and parameters that are local to a specific shell. Each time you create a new shell, the C Shell reinitializes these variables for the new shell. A sample **.cshrc** file follows:

```
77 % cat .cshrc
set noclobber
set ignoreeof
set history = 100
set prompt = "! % "
set PATH = (/usr/bin /usr/ucb /bin ~/bin .)
alias h history
alias ll ls -lg
```

This sample **.cshrc** file sets several shell variables and establishes two aliases.

.logout   The C Shell executes the **.logout** file in your home directory when you log off the system—normally when you finish your session.

Below is a sample **.logout** file that displays a reminder. The **sleep** command ensures that **echo** has time to display the message before the system logs you out (for dial-up lines).

```
78 % cat .logout
echo Remember to turn on call
echo forwarding before you go home.
sleep 10
```

Control Structures

The C Shell uses many of the same control structures as the Bourne Shell. In each case the syntax is different, but the effects are the same. This section summarizes the differences between the control structures in the two shells. A more complete discussion of control structures can be found in Chapter 10.

If

The format of the If control structure is as follows:

if (**expression**) **simple-command**

The If control structure works only with simple commands, not pipes or lists of commands. You can use the If Then control structure (page 368) to execute more complex commands.

```
79 % cat if_1
# routine to show the use of a simple If
# control structure
#
if ($#argv == 0) echo "if_1: there are no arguments"
```

This program checks to see if it was called without any arguments. If the expression (enclosed in parentheses) evaluates to *true*—that is, if there were zero arguments on the command line—the If structure displays a message to that effect.

In addition to the logical expressions listed on page 358, you can use expressions that return a value based on the status of a file. The format of this type of expression is shown below:

–n filename

where **n** is from the following list.

n	Meaning
d	The file is a directory file.
e	The file exists.
f	The file is an ordinary file.
o	The user owns the file.
r	The user has read access to the file.
w	The user has write access to the file.
x	The user has execute access to the file.
z	The file is 0 bytes long.

If the specified file does not exist or is not accessible, the C Shell evaluates the expression as 0. Otherwise, if the result of the test is true, the expression has a value of 1; if it is false, the expression has a value of 0.

Goto

The format of a Goto statement is as follows:

goto **label**

A Goto statement transfers control to the statement beginning with **label:**. The following example demonstrates the use of Goto:

```
80 % cat goto_1
#
# test for 2 arguments
#
if ($#argv == 2) goto goodargs
echo "Usage: goto_1 arg1 arg2"
exit 1
goodargs:
  .
  .
```

The message the **goto_1** script presents is a standard usage message. Refer to page 303 for more information about usage messages.

Interrupt Handling

The Onintr statement transfers control when you interrupt a shell script. The format of an Onintr statement is shown below.

onintr **label**

When you press the interrupt key during execution of a shell script, the shell transfers control to the statement beginning with **label:**.

This statement allows you to terminate a script gracefully when it is interrupted. You can use it to ensure that, when it is interrupted, a shell script removes temporary files before returning control to the shell.

The following script demonstrates Onintr. It loops continuously until you press the interrupt key, at which time it displays a message and returns control to the shell.

```
81 % cat onintr_1
# demonstration of onintr
onintr close
while (1 == 1)
    echo Program is running.
    sleep 2
end
close:
echo End of program.
```

If the script created temporary files, it might use Onintr to remove them.

```
close:
rm -f /tmp/$$*
```

The ambiguous file reference **/tmp/$$*** matches all files in **/tmp** that begin with the PID of the current shell. Refer to page 299 for a description of this technique for naming temporary files.

If Then Else

The three forms of the If Then Else control structure are as follows:

Form 1:

if (**expression**) then
    commands
endif

Form 2:

if (**expression**) then
    commands
else
    commands
endif

Form 3:

```
if (expression) then
        commands
else if (expression) then
        commands
     .
     .
     .
else
        commands
endif
```

The first form is an extension of the simple If structure; it executes more complex **commands** or a series of **commands** if the **expression** is true. This form is still a one-way branch.

The second form is a two-way branch. If the **expression** is true, the structure executes the first set of **commands**. If it is false, the set of **commands** following Else is executed.

The third form is similar to the If Then Elif structure of the Bourne Shell. It performs tests until it finds an **expression** that is true and then executes the corresponding **commands**.

```
82 % cat if_else_1
# routine to categorize the first
# command line argument
#
set class
set number = $argv[1]
#
if ($number < 0) then
    @ class = 0
else if (0 <= $number && $number < 100) then
    @ class = 1
else if (100 <= $number && $number < 200) then
    @ class = 2
else
    @ class = 3
endif
#
echo The number $number is in class ${class}.
```

This example program assigns a value of 0, 1, 2, or 3 to the variable **class**, based on the value of the first command line argument. The variable **class** is declared at the beginning of the program for clarity; you do not need to declare it before its first use. Again, for clarity, the script assigns the value of the first command line argument to **number**. The first If statement tests to see if **number** is less than 0. If it is, the script assigns 0 to **class**. If it is not, the second If tests to see if the number is between 0 and 100. The && is a logical AND, yielding a value of *true* if the expression on each side is true. If the number is between 0 and 100, 1 is assigned to **class**. A similar test determines whether the number is between 100 and 200. If it is not, the final Else assigns 3 to **class**. Endif closes the If control structure.

The final statement uses braces ({}) to isolate the variable **class** from the following period. Again, the braces isolate the period for clarity; the shell does not consider a punctuation mark as part of a variable name. The braces would be required if you wanted other characters to follow immediately after the variable.

Foreach

The Foreach structure parallels the For In structure of the Bourne Shell. Its format is as follows:

    foreach **loop-index (argument-list)**
         commands
    end

This structure loops through the **commands**. The first time through the loop, the structure assigns the value of the first argument in the **argument-list** to the **loop-index**. When control reaches the End statement, the shell assigns the value of the next argument from the **argument-list** to the **loop-index** and executes the commands again. The shell repeats this procedure until it exhausts the **argument-list**.

The following C Shell script uses a Foreach structure to loop through the files in the working directory containing a specified string of characters in their filename and to change the string. For example, it can be used to change the string **memo** in filenames to **letter**. The filenames **memo.1**, **dailymemo**, and **memories** would be changed to **letter.1**, **dailyletter**, and **letterries**. This script requires two arguments: the string to be changed and the new string. The **argument-list** of the Foreach structure uses a regular expression to loop through all filenames that contain the first argument. For each filename that matches the regular expression, the **mv** utility changes the filename. The **sed** utility substitutes the first argument for the second argument in the filename. The **$1** and **$2** are abbreviated forms of **$argv[1]** and **$argv[2]**. (Refer to Part II for more information about **sed**.)

```
83 % cat rename
# Usage: rename arg1 arg2
#          changes the string arg1 in the names of files
#          in the working directory to the string arg2
#
if ($#argv != 2) goto usage

foreach i ( *$1* )
    mv $i ` echo $i | sed -n s/$1/$2/p `
end

usage:
echo "Usage: rename arg1 arg2"
exit 1
```

The next script uses a Foreach loop to assign the command line arguments to the elements of an array.

```
84 % cat foreach_1
# routine to zero-fill argv to 20 arguments
#
set buffer = (0 0 0 0 0 0 0 0 0 0 0 0 0 0 0 0 0 0 0 0)
set count = 1
#
if ($#argv > 20) goto toomany
#
    foreach argument ($argv[*])
        set buffer[$count] = $argument
        @ count++
    end

#
# REPLACE argtest ON THE NEXT LINE WITH
# THE PROGRAM YOU WANT TO CALL.
exec argtest $buffer[*]
exit 0
#
toomany:
echo "Usage: foreach_1 [up to 20 arguments]"
exit 1
```

This script calls another program named **argtest** with a command line guaranteed to contain 20 arguments. If **foreach_1** is called with fewer than 20 arguments, it fills the command line with zeros to complete the 20 arguments for **argtest**. More than 20 arguments cause it to display a usage message.

The Foreach structure loops through the commands one time for each of the command line arguments. Each time through the loop, it assigns the value of the next argument from the command line to the variable **argument**. Then it assigns each of these values to an element of the array **buffer**. The variable **count** maintains the index for the **buffer** array. A postfix operator increments **count** using the **@** command (@ count++). An **exec** command (page 329), calls **argtest** so that a new process is not initiated. (Once **argtest** is called, the process running this routine is no longer needed, so there is no need for a new process.)

Break and Continue

You can interrupt a Foreach loop with a Break or Continue statement. These statements execute the remaining commands on the line before they transfer control. Break transfers control to the statement after the End statement, terminating execution of the loop. Continue transfers control to the End statement, which continues execution of the loop.

While

The format of the While structure follows.

> while (**expression**)
>   **commands**
> end

This structure continues to loop through the **commands** *while* the expression is true. If the **expression** is false the first time it is evaluated, the structure never executes the **commands**. You can use Break and Continue statements in a While structure; refer to the previous discussion.

```
85 % cat while_1
# Demonstration of a While control structure.
# This routine sums the numbers between 1 and
# n, n being the first argument on the command
# line.
#
set limit = $argv[1]
set index = 1
set sum = 0
#
    while ($index <= $limit)
        @ sum += $index
        @ index++
    end
#
echo The sum is $sum
```

This program computes the sum of all the integers up to and including n, where n is the first argument on the command line. The += operator assigns the value of **sum + index** to **sum**.

Switch

The Switch structure is analogous to the Case structure of the Bourne Shell.

> switch (**test-string**)
>
>   case **pattern:**
>   **commands**
>   breaksw
>
>   case **pattern:**
>   **commands**
>   breaksw
>
>   .
>   .
>
>   default:
>   **commands**
>   breaksw
>
> endsw

The **breaksw** statement causes execution to continue after the **endsw** statement. Refer to the discussion of the Case statement in Chapter 10 (page 320) for a discussion of special characters you can use within the patterns.

```
86 % cat switch_1
# Demonstration of a Switch control structure.
# This routine tests the first command line argument
# for yes or no, any combination of upper and lower-
# case characters.
#
# test that argv[1] exists
if ($#argv == 0) then
    echo "Usage: switch_1 [yes|no]"
    exit 1
else
# argv[1] exists, set up switch based on its value
    switch ($argv[1])
    #
    # case of YES
        case [yY][eE][sS]:
        echo Argument one is yes.
        breaksw
    #
    # case of NO
        case [nN][oO]:
        echo Argument one is no.
        breaksw
    #
    # default case
        default:
        echo Argument one is neither yes nor no.
        breaksw
    endsw
endif
```

Reading User Input

Some implementations of the C Shell use a **set** command to read a line from the terminal and assign it to a variable.

The following portion of a shell script prompts the user and reads a line of input into the variable **input_line**:

```
echo "Input the next condition:"
set input_line = $<
```

If your version does not have this feature, you can use the **head** utility to read user input.

```
echo "Input the next condition:"
set input_line = ` head -1 `
```

Here, **head –1** displays the first line it receives from its standard input. The backquotes cause the shell to execute the command in place, replacing the command they enclose with the output from the command. See page 292 for more information on command substitution.

Built-in Commands

Built-in commands are part of (built into) the C Shell.

When you give a simple filename as a command, the shell searches the directory structure for the program you want, using the **PATH** variable as a guide. When it finds the program, the shell forks a new process to execute it.

The shell executes a built-in command as part of the calling process. It does not fork a new process to execute the command. It does not need to search the directory structure for the command program because the program is immediately available to the shell. The following list describes many of the built-in commands.

@   This command is similar to the **set** command, but it can evaluate expressions. See "Numeric Variables," page 358.

alias   This command creates and displays aliases. See "Alias," page 348.

alloc   This command displays a report of the amount of used and free memory.

bg   This command moves jobs into the background. See "Job Control," page 350.

cd (or chdir)   This command changes working directories. Refer to the **cd** utility in Part II for more information.

dirs   This command displays the directory stack. See "Directory Stack Manipulation," page 354.

echo   This command displays its arguments. Refer to **echo** in Part II for more information.

eval   This command scans and evaluates the command line. When you put **eval** in front of a command, the command is scanned twice by the shell before it is executed. This is useful when you have a command that is generated as a result of command or variable substitution. Because of the order in which the shell processes a command line, it is sometimes necessary to repeat the scan in order to achieve the desired result.

exec   This command is similar to the **exec** command of the Bourne Shell. The **exec** command overlays the program that is currently being executed with another program in the same shell. The original program is lost. Refer to the **exec** command in Chapter 10 (page 329) for more information; also refer to **source** later in this section.

exit   You can use this command to exit from a C Shell. When you follow it with an argument that is a number, the number is the exit status that the shell returns to its parent process. Refer to the **status** variable, page 363.

fg   This command moves jobs into the foreground. See "Job Control," page 350.

glob   This command is like the **echo** command, except it does not display spaces between its arguments and does not follow its display with a (NEWLINE).

hashstat   This command reports on the efficiency of the C Shell's *hash* mechanism. The C Shell uses the hash mechanism to speed the process of searching through the directories in your search path.

history   This command displays the history list of commands. See "History," page 343.

jobs   This command identifies the current jobs, or commands. See "Job Control," page 350.

kill   This command terminates jobs or processes. See **kill** in Part II.

limit   This command limits the computer resources that can be used by the current process and any processes it creates. You can put limits on the number of seconds the process can use the central processing unit (CPU), the size of files that can be created, and so forth.

login   This command, which you can follow with a user name, logs in a user.

logout   This command ends a session if you are using your original (login) shell.

nice   This command can be used to lower the processing priority of a command or a shell. It is useful if you want to run a command that makes large demands on the central processing unit of the computer but you do not need the output of the command right away. If you are the Superuser, you can use **nice** to raise the processing priority of a command.

nohup   This command allows you to log off while processes are running in the background without terminating the processes. Some systems are set up to do this automatically. Refer to **nohup** in Part II.

notify   This command causes the shell to notify you immediately when the status of one of your jobs changes. Refer to "Job Control," page 350.

OPTIONAL Continued

popd   This command removes a directory from the directory stack. See "Directory Stack Manipulation," page 354.

pushd   This command changes the current working directory and places the new directory at the top of the directory stack. See "Directory Stack Manipulation," page 354.

rehash   This command is used to recreate the internal tables used by the C Shell's hash mechanism. Whenever a new C Shell is invoked, the hash mechanism creates a sorted list of all commands available to the user. You should use the **rehash** command after you add a command to one of the directories in the search path to cause the shell to recreate the sorted list of commands. If you do not, the C Shell may not be able to find the new command.

repeat   This command takes two arguments: a count and simple command (no pipes or lists of commands). It repeats the command the number of times specified by the count.

set   This command declares, initializes, and displays the values of local variables. See "Variables," page 356.

setenv   This command declares and initializes the values of environment variables. See "Variables," page 356. Many systems include a **printenv** or **env** command that displays the values of environment variables.

shift   This command is analogous to the Bourne Shell **shift** command, page 297. Without an argument, **shift** promotes the indexes of the **argv[*]** array. You can use it with an argument to perform the same operation on another array.

source   The **source** command causes the current C Shell to execute a shell script given as its argument. It is similar to the . command in the Bourne Shell. The **source** command expects a C Shell script, so no leading pound sign is required in the script. The current shell executes **source** so that the script can contain commands, such as **set**, that affect the current shell. After you make changes to the .cshrc or .login file, you can use **source** to execute it from within the login shell in order to put the changes into effect.

stop   This command stops a job that is running in the background. See "Job Control," page 350.

suspend   This command stops the current shell. It is similar to (CONTROL)-**Z**, which stops jobs running in the foreground.

time   The **time** command executes the command that you give it as an argument. It displays the elapsed time, the system time, and the execution time for the command. Without an argument, **time** displays the times for the current shell and its children.

umask   This command can be used to identify or change the access permissions that are assigned to files you create. Refer to **umask** in Part II for more information.

unalias   This command removes an alias. See "Alias," page 348.

unhash   This command turns off the hash mechanism. Refer to the **hashstat** and **rehash** built-ins.

unlimit   This command removes limits on the current process. See **limit**, page 375.

unset   This command removes a variable declaration. See "Variables," page 356.

unsetenv   This command removes an environment variable declaration. See "Variables," page 356.

wait   This command causes the shell to wait for all child processes to terminate, as does the Bourne Shell's **wait** command. When you give a **wait** command in response to a C Shell prompt, the C Shell will not display a prompt and will not accept a command until all background processes have finished execution. If you interrupt it with the interrupt key, **wait** displays a list of outstanding processes before returning control to the shell.

Control Structures

The control structures listed below are also built-in commands. They allow you to alter the flow of control in C Shell scripts. Refer to "Control Structures," beginning on page 366.

- Break
- Continue
- Foreach End
- Goto
- If
- If Then Endif
- If Then Else Endif
- Onintr
- Switch Case Breaksw Default Endsw
- While End

SUMMARY

The C Shell, like the Bourne Shell, is both a command interpreter and a programming language. It was developed at the University of California at Berkeley and has most of the facilities of the Bourne Shell, plus some others.

Among its most important features, the C Shell

- Protects against overwriting files and accidentally logging off
- Maintains a history of recent commands
- Provides an alias mechanism for altering commands
- Provides job control
- Provides filename completion
- Provides directory stack manipulation
- Executes specific files when you log in, log out, and fork a new shell
- Evaluates logical and numerical expressions
- Processes arrays of variables representing numbers and strings
- Uses control structures to control execution within a shell script

REVIEW EXERCISES

1. How can you review a list of the commands you executed recently? How can you reexecute the last event?

2. Assume the following is your history list:

```
37   mail alex
38   cd /home/jenny/correspondence/business/cheese_co
39   more letter.0321
40   vi letter.0321
41   cp letter.0321 letter.0325
42   grep hansen letter.0325
43   vi letter.0325
44   lpr letter*
45   cd ../milk_co
46   pwd
47   vi wilson.0321 wilson.0329
```

Using the history mechanism, what commands can you use to

a. send mail to Alex

b. use **vi** to edit a file called **wilson.0329**

c. print a hard copy of **wilson.0329**

d. rename **wilson.0321** to **wilson.0322**

3. How can you identify all the aliases currently in effect?

4. What statement can you put in your **.cshrc** file to prevent yourself from accidentally overwriting a file when you redirect output? How can you

override this feature? What statement can you put in your **.cshrc** file to prevent the C Shell from expanding ambiguous filenames?

5. Assume the working directory contains the following files:

```
adams.ltr.03
adams.brief
adams.ltr.07
abelson.09
abelson.brief
anthony.073
anthony.brief
azevedo.99
```

What will happen if you press (ESCAPE) after typing the following commands?

a. **more adams.l**

b. **cat a**

c. **ls ant**

d. **file az**

What will happen if you press (CONTROL)-**D** after typing these commands?

e. **ls ab**

f. **more A**

6. What does the following command do?

137 % **pushd ~/literature**

7. If you start a command in the foreground and later decide that it should run in the background, what should you do? How can you prevent a command from sending output to the terminal once you have moved it into the background?

ADVANCED REVIEW EXERCISES

8. What lines do you need to change in the Bourne Shell script **command_menu** in Chapter 10 (page 323) to make it a C Shell script? Make the changes and verify that it works.

9. Put the following line in your **.login** file. If there is another line in your **.login** file that sets the **prompt** variable, put a # in front of it to make it into a comment for the time being.

set prompt = "! ` pwd ` > "

Put the next line into your **.cshrc** file.

alias go 'chdir \!:1; set prompt = "! ` pwd ` >"'

Together these two lines in your **.login** and **.cshrc** files will include the name of the working directory in your prompt if you use the command

go to change directories. For example, if Alex is in his **letter** directory and the current event number is 27, his prompt will be

```
27 /home/alex/letter>
```

Verify that these statements work. Why do you need a statement in your **.login** file as well as one in your **.cshrc** file? (This exercise assumes that the C Shell is your login shell.)

10. Users often find **rm** (and even **rm –i**) too unforgiving because it removes files irrevocably. Create an alias that will move your files into a temporary directory (such as **$HOME/.trash**) when you give the command **delete**. Create a second alias called **undelete** that will move a file from the temporary directory into the working directory. Finally, put the following lines in your **.logout** file to remove any files that you deleted during the login session:

```
/bin/rm –f $HOME/.trash/* >& /dev/null
```

What happens if there are no files in the **.trash** directory?

CHAPTER 12

The Korn Shell and Advanced Shell Programming

The Korn Shell includes features of both the Bourne Shell and the C Shell. It provides many of the interactive features of the C Shell, including those hallmark features of the C Shell that make it popular as an interactive command interpreter: aliases, job control, and the history mechanism. It also introduces several new user interface features, including command line editing. This chapter covers these features as well as those that make the Korn Shell a first class programming language.

Background

Because it is designed so that scripts written for the Bourne Shell will run under it without modification, the Korn Shell includes nearly all the features of the Bourne Shell. In addition, the Korn Shell provides report formatting capabilities, built-in arithmetic, data types, control flow, and other features that greatly improve its usefulness as a programming language. This chapter uses the terms *program* and *script* interchangeably.

The design philosophy of the Korn Shell maximizes execution speed of scripts. Many features that need to be run as separate processes under other shells are built into the Korn Shell. An example is the **expr** utility that is used to perform arithmetic functions under the other shells. When **expr** is called from a script, most of the time is spent forking a process to run **expr** and converting character variables to numeric ones and then converting them back again. With the functionality of **expr** built into it, and with the availability of numeric variables, the Korn Shell can run a script that performs arithmetic more quickly than the Bourne Shell. Contrast the **count** Bourne Shell script on page 315 with the Korn Shell function on page 389.

This chapter describes the unique characteristics of the Korn Shell. It supplements Chapter 10, "The Bourne Shell," and Chapter 11, "The C Shell." Because job control under the Korn Shell is virtually identical to job control under the C Shell, this chapter only mentions it briefly (refer to "Job Control" page 350).

The Korn Shell underwent a major revision in 1988, and another revision in 1993. This chapter describes the 1988 version, and indicates the new features and changed semantics in the 1993 version, referred to as Korn Shell 93. The first part of this chapter discusses the Korn Shell as an interactive environment. The second part describes the Korn Shell programming language.

Korn Shell Basics

If you want to use the Korn Shell as your login shell, your system administrator can set up the **/etc/passwd** file so that you will be using the Korn Shell whenever you log in. If you do not want to log directly into the Korn Shell, use the command **ksh** to start a Korn Shell after you log in.

The basic behavior of the Korn Shell mimics that of the other shells: you type a command that names an executable program or script, optionally followed by arguments that are interpreted by the command. You can correct mistakes as described on page 27 before you press the (RETURN) key. You can also use the Korn Shell's powerful command line editing and history editing facilities to create and modify command lines.

Like the Bourne and C Shells, the Korn Shell evaluates variables, searches for aliases or functions, expands pathname wild cards, and handles file redirection before the command is executed. It is important to understand the precise sequence in which these steps are carried out, because it affects the meaning of the command line. Before describing the steps in command processing in detail, this chapter describes the various Korn Shell constructs that are involved in these steps, including aliases, functions, I/O redirection, variable expansion and evaluation, tilde expansion, and command substitution.

Startup Files

The Korn Shell uses all the environment variables used by the Bourne Shell as well as several others. These variables establish the characteristics of your environment, such as what editor you will use for command-line editing and history manipulation and editing. Set up these variables, along with commands that establish other characteristics of the Korn Shell environment, in one of the Korn Shell startup files.

Like the Bourne Shell, the Korn Shell reads and executes /etc/**profile** and the .**profile** file in your home directory when you log in. If you set the **ENV** variable to the filename of a readable file, the Korn Shell can also execute another file whenever a new shell begins execution. Users typically name this file .**kshrc** because it is analogous to the C Shell's .cshrc file.

In Korn Shell 93, command substitution and arithmetic evaluation are performed as part of the evaluation of **ENV** before its value is used. Thus your .**profile** file could have a line of the form

```
ENV=$(find . -name .kshrc -print)
```

to set **ENV** to the pathname of a .**kshrc** file anywhere in your home directory hierarchy. Of course, this particular command could cause trouble if you have more than one file named .**kshrc** in this hierarchy, and would also slow the startup of the shell.

How you use the startup files depends on whether the Korn Shell is your login shell. If it is your login shell, you can use the .**profile** file to set up Korn Shell variables. Be sure to use the **export** command for those variables that you want to be available to child processes. In your .**profile** file you should also establish your erase and line kill keys and set up the same variables you would set up for the Bourne Shell (**CDPATH, PATH, PS1, PS2, TERM**, and so on), unless these are set in /etc/**profile**. The Korn Shell uses **COLUMNS** rather than **TERM** to determine the width of the terminal screen. By default, **COLUMNS** is set to 80—set it if the number of columns on your screen is not 80. Even though the Korn Shell does not use **TERM**, you should still set it, because it is used by **vi** and other utilities.

Set options with the **set** command and define aliases and functions in the file specified by **ENV**. You can also export functions, just as you can export aliases, to make them accessible to child processes. Use **typeset** with the –x option to export a function (See "Variable Attributes," page 391).

If the Korn Shell is not your login shell, set the variables that are specific to the Korn Shell in the file specified by **ENV** rather than in .**profile**, since the Korn Shell will not execute .**profile** when you invoke it. The **ENV** variable tells the Korn Shell what file to execute whenever a Korn Shell is started. Use the file specified by **ENV** to set the rest of the Korn Shell variables and define aliases, functions, and options to the **set** command. You can set **ENV** in the **.login** or **.profile** file, so it is ready any time you start a Korn Shell.

When you start up the Korn Shell, it inherits the environment variables that were set by the previous shell. You need to reset variables that should have different values, such as **SHELL** and **PS1**, while you are using the Korn Shell. Set and export them in the file specified by **ENV**.

Sample **.profile** and **.kshrc** files follow. The **trackall** option in the **.kshrc** file makes all aliases tracked so they can be recalled more quickly. The –x option to **alias** exports the alias so it can be accessed by subshells.

```
$ cat .profile
CDPATH=:$HOME
ENV=$HOME/.kshrc
FCEDIT=/usr/bin/vi
HISTFILE=$HOME/.ksh_hist
HISTSIZE=100
PATH=/usr/ucb:/bin:/usr/bin:$HOME/bin:
PS1='! $PWD> '
SHELL=/usr/bin/ksh
TERM=vt100
VISUAL=/usr/bin/vi
export CDPATH ENV FCEDIT HISTSIZE HISTFILE
export PATH PS1 SHELL TERM VISUAL
stty erase ^H kill ^U

$ cat .kshrc
set -o trackall
alias -x m=more
alias -x h=history
```

Running Korn Shell Scripts

To execute a Korn Shell script, use the script name as an argument to the **ksh** command:

```
3 $ ksh script_name
```

This command will work whether or not your interactive shell is the Korn Shell when you execute it. If you are currently using the Korn Shell as your command interpreter, and you have execute permission for the file in which the script is kept, then you can simply use the filename as a command:

```
4 $ script_name
```

On some systems, you can use a #! line at the start of the script to ensure that the script is run by the Korn Shell (page 286):

```
#!/usr/bin/ksh
```

There are two drawbacks to this method. First, there is no guarantee that your system's Korn Shell is in **/usr/bin**. If the Korn Shell on your system is located in a directory other than **/usr/bin**, you will need to use the appropriate pathname in place of **/usr/bin/ksh**. Second, if you move your script to another system that does not support the #! feature, or on which the location of the Korn Shell is different, then this method will also fail.

Customizing Your Environment

The Korn Shell allows you to customize your environment by turning various options on or off, creating aliases for commands, and choosing values for certain built-in variables. Typically you put your choices in startup files, which the Korn Shell automatically reads when you log in.

Korn Shell Options

One way that you can control the interactive behavior of the Korn Shell is by setting or unsetting options. Use the **set −o** command to set an option, and the **set +o** command to unset it:

```
$ set -o ignoreeof
$ set +o markdirs
```

This turns on the **ignoreeof** option, and turns off the **markdirs** option (**markdirs** causes the shell to display a slash following directory names generated by wildcard characters). These options are useful when you use the Korn Shell interactively. Some options have shorthand option letters that allow you to set or unset them quickly. For example, the **xtrace** option has the option letter x, so that instead of typing

```
$ set -o xtrace
```

you can type

```
$ set -x
```

This is the command, familiar from the Bourne Shell, for turning on the debugging trace feature. A table at the end of this chapter shows a list of the Korn Shell options, associated option letters if any, and their meanings.

You can set and unset several options with the same command. The following command turns on **xtrace** (−x) and **vi** while turning off **ignoreeof** and **nounset** (+u). A complete list of options appears on page 449.

```
$ set -x -o vi +o ignoreeof +u
```

Controlling the Prompt

A dollar sign ($) is the default prompt for the Korn Shell. To change your prompt, set the **PS1** variable as in the Bourne Shell. Like the C Shell, the Korn Shell keeps track of the current command number, and as in the C shell it is represented by an !. An exclamation point in the value of the **PS1** variable will cause the Korn Shell to include the current command number in the prompt. Because the Korn Shell has a history mechanism and you can access previous commands by event number, it is useful to display the event number in the prompt.

```
$ PS1="! $ "
2 $
```

The Korn Shell automatically sets the **PWD** variable to the pathname of the working directory. If you **cd** to a directory through a symbolic link, this variable is set to the path that you used to get there, not necessarily the pathname of the hard link. The Korn Shell evaluates shell variables in the **PS1** string each time it presents the prompt, so if you include **PWD** in the prompt, it will identify the working directory.

Give the following command to set your prompt to display the pathname of the working directory as well as the event number:

```
$ PS1='! $PWD> '
2 /home/alex/literature>
```

The Korn Shell follows Bourne Shell rules for evaluating variables inside quotation marks: single quotation marks suppress immediate evaluation, while double quotation marks do not (page 287). You must surround the value of **PS1** with single quotation marks to prevent the Korn Shell from substituting the value of the **PWD** variable when you initially set **PS1**. If you use double quotation marks instead, the Korn Shell will evaluate **$PWD** with its value when it initially sets the prompt, and the prompt will not change when you change directories.

The 1993 Korn Shell also performs command substitution and evaluates arithmetic expressions for **PS1** before displaying the prompt. For example, using Korn Shell 93, you can display the date and time, current directory, and command number in your prompt like this:

```
$ PS1=' ` date `: $PWD: ! > '
Tue Oct 05 20:51:45 1993: /home/alex/literature: 2 >
```

This example will not work with the 1988 Korn Shell; `date` would literally be in the prompt.

Korn Shell Aliases

The Korn Shell provides aliases that are similar to C Shell aliases, although Korn Shell aliases have a different syntax, some additional features, and do not allow arguments. Use a Korn Shell function if you need to use arguments. Korn Shell functions are very similar to Bourne Shell functions.

The format of the command used for establishing an alias is shown below.

alias [–x] **name=command**

The **x** option causes **alias** to export the alias, so that it will be accessible to child processes. Even exported aliases are not available after you log out and then log in again, so users typically establish aliases in one of the Korn Shell startup files (page 383).

The next example creates and then uses an exported alias for a **chmod** command:

```
$ alias -x xp='chmod +x'
$ xp script_name
```

You can use the –t option to alias to create a tracked alias, as shown here:

alias –t **name**

You must have defined the alias **name** with a prevous invocation of **alias**; you cannot use the –t option and define the alias at the same time. Tracked aliases play a role in the Korn Shell similar to that of the hashing mechanism in the C Shell. When you set up a tracked alias for a command, **alias** uses the absolute pathname for the command in its definition of the alias. On subsequent executions of the command, the shell uses this pathname, which is more efficient since it avoids a path search. Later, if you change the **PATH** variable, all tracked aliases will become undefined. The next time you use each alias, the Korn Shell will reestablish its pathname.

The Korn Shell has an option, **trackall**, that causes the Korn Shell to create a tracked alias for each command that you enter. Users typically use this option rather than setting up tracked aliases for individual commands.

```
$ set -o trackall
```

When you call it with no arguments, **alias** lists all the aliases that are currently set, as does the C Shell **alias** command. Also, you can use the first of the following commands to list all exported aliases, and the second to list all tracked aliases:

```
$ alias -x
$ alias -t
```

To remove an alias, use the **unalias** command followed by the alias name. The following example removes the alias **delete**:

```
$ unalias delete
```

Korn Shell Functions

There are two different syntaxes for function definition. One uses Bourne Shell syntax:

func_name()
{
commands
}

In some versions of the Bourne Shell you can omit the braces ({}) if the function definition is only a single command. In the Korn Shell the braces are always necessary. The first brace ({) can appear on the same line as the parentheses.

The second syntax uses the **function** keyword:

function **func_name**
{
commands
}

In the 1988 version of the Korn Shell these two forms are equivalent. In the 1993 version they are not; the definition using the **function** keyword preserves existing function semantics, while the version using the C-like () notation gives the function the slightly different POSIX.2 semantics. POSIX functions are executed in the same environment as the current shell or as dot-scripts (scripts invoked with the dot [.] command—page 295). In Korn Shell 93, functions defined with the **function** keyword have traditional Korn Shell semantics.

You can delete a function definition with the –f option to unset:

```
$ unset -f func_name
```

The Korn Shell stores functions in memory, so that they run more efficiently than scripts. The Korn Shell allows you to store a function in a file and have it loaded into memory only when it is first referenced. If you define many functions in your $ENV file, they are immediately available whenever you log on. However, the $ENV file is also read each time you start a subshell. If this file gets too large, the overhead of starting a subshell that will need few or none of these functions becomes unacceptable. You can give a function the **autoload** attribute by issuing the following command.

```
$ autoload func_name
```

The autoload attribute causes a function to be undefined. However, the Korn Shell "remembers" that there is a function with that name. When it is referenced, the Korn Shell looks for the function, doing a path search similar to that done for regular commands, but using the **FPATH** environment variable rather than **PATH**. The syntax of **FPATH** is identical to that of **PATH**: a colon-separated list of absolute pathnames of directories. When you invoke an autoloaded function, the Korn Shell looks for a file with the same name as the function in each directory in **FPATH**. If it finds such a file, it reads the file to find a definition of that function. It is your responsibility to ensure that the function definition and the file in which it is stored have the same name. Typically, you will have one directory in which you keep many small files, each of which contains a single function definition. If you are working on several projects that make use of different shell functions, then you might have several such directories. These are the directories whose pathnames you would put in **FPATH**.

The Korn Shell allows you to create local variables in functions. A variable is local to a function if it is only recognized inside the function. Ordinarily, a variable that is assigned a value anywhere in a shell script will be recognized throughout the shell session. Such a variable is referred to as a global variable, and by default all Korn Shell variables are global. If a function has a local variable whose name is the same as the name of a global variable, then inside the function all references to that name refer to the function's local version, and outside the function all references to that name refer to the global variable.

You make a variable local to a function with the built-in **typeset** command. The syntax **typeset varname** inside a function definition makes **varname** a local variable. (You can use **typeset** much more generally to set variable attributes; see "Variable Attributes," page 391.) The following example shows the use of local variables in an interactive session. (This is a function, not a shell script—do not put it in a file and attempt to execute it. A function is like a built-in you can write yourself.)

```
$ count=10
$ function count_down
> {
> typeset count
> count=$1
> while [[ $count > 0 ]]
> do
> echo $count ...
> count=` expr $count - 1`
> done
> echo Blast Off!
> return
> }
$ echo $count
10
$ count_down 6
6 ...
5 ...
4 ...
3 ...
2 ...
1 ...
Blast Off!
$ echo $count
10
```

The principal use for local variables is in a function written for general use. You may need to use some variables in this function, and you do not want the names of these variables to cause accidental interactions with variables of the same name in the programs that call this function. Therefore, you should make the variables of your function local.

OPTIONAL

Functions in Korn Shell 93

In Korn Shell 93 a new facility allows you to associate two functions, called *discipline functions,* with each shell variable. One of these functions must be named **var_name.get**, and the other **var_name.set**, where **var_name** is the name of the variable. If a variable has associated discipline functions, then the **.get** function is automatically called each time the variable is referenced, and the **.set** function is called each time the variable has a value assigned to it.

Korn Shell 93 also has new variables associated with discipline functions. If a variable that has a **.get** function is referenced, or if a variable that has a **.set** function has a value assigned to it, the predefined variable **.sh.name** is automatically assigned the name of the variable. If the variable being set or referenced is a member of an array, then the predefined variable **.sh.subscript** is set to the subscript of that array member. When a variable is assigned a value, but not when it is referenced, the predefined variable **.sh.value** is assigned the same value.

There are many ways that discipline functions can be useful. One way is in debugging scripts. Suppose that you have written a shell program in which a variable named **TARGET** is being assigned a mysterious value, and you cannot figure out why or where. This is a common and frustrating type of problem in all programming languages. Rather than using the built-in debugging facility (**set –x**) which produces a lot of output, you can create a function named **TARGET.set** as part of your script:

```
TARGET.set()
{
echo "At $LINENO: $.sh.name assigned $.sh.value" >> /tmp/trace
}
```

Then the file named **/tmp/trace** will keep a record of the values assigned to **TARGET**.

Using Korn Shell Variables

Like the Bourne Shell and the C Shell, the Korn Shell allows you to create and use variables. The rules for naming and referring to variables are similar in all the shells. A variable name consists of letters, digits, and the underscore character, and cannot start with a digit. Thus **A76**, **MY_CAT**, and **___X___** are valid variable names, while **69TH_STREET** and **MY–NAME** are not. In Korn Shell 93, an ordinary variable's name may start with a period. A widely (but not universally) adopted convention is to use only uppercase letters for variable names that are exported (*environment variables*), and to use mixed case or lowercase letters for other variables. Korn Shell 93 supports compound variables, which resemble data structures in other programming languages, and have a period as part of their names. See page 402 for a further discussion of compound variables.

You assign values to variables as in the Bourne Shell, by typing statements of the form

VARIABLE=value

There must be no white space on either side of the = sign. If you want to include spaces in the value of the variable, you must put quotation marks around the value.

$ VARIABLE=" value with spaces in and around it "

You can use either single or double quotation marks, but they are not always equivalent.

In the Korn Shell, as in the Bourne and C Shells, a variable's value is referenced by preceding the variable name with a $ sign, as in **$VARIABLE**. This is actually a special case of the more general syntax **${VARIABLE}**, in which the variable name is enclosed by **${}**. This syntax is sometimes necessary. For example, the Korn Shell refers to the arguments on its command line by position, using the special variables **$1**, **$2**, **$3** and so forth. This works up to **$9**. If you wish to refer to arguments past the ninth, you must use braces, as in **${10}**.

Another context where the braces are necessary is catenation of a variable value with another string. Here is one sequence of commands you might type, with its output:

```
$ SUFF=ization
$ POL=polar$SUFF
$ ORG=organ$SUFF
$ echo $POL $ORG
polarization organization
```

You might like to do the same thing with a prefix:

```
$ PREF=counter
$ WAY=$PREFclockwise
$ FAKE=$PREFfeit
$ echo $WAY $FAKE
```

This does not work; there is no output except for a blank line. The reason is that the symbols **PREFclockwise** and **PREFfeit** are valid variable names, which are not set. By default the Korn Shell evaluates the value of an unset variable as an empty string, and displays this value. To achieve the intent of these statements, you should refer to the **PREF** variable using braces:

```
$ PREF=counter
$ WAY=${PREF}clockwise
$ FAKE=${PREF}feit
$ echo $WAY $FAKE
counterclockwise counterfeit
```

You can unset a variable with the **unset** built-in command:

```
$ unset PREF SUFF
```

This removes the variable's value and attributes.

Variable Attributes

A significant difference between the Bourne and Korn Shells is that you can associate attributes with a Korn Shell variable that control the values it can have. Use the built-in **typeset** command to set an attribute for a variable. For example, you can assign a variable the **uppercase** attribute with **typeset –u**. A variable with this attribute will translate all letters in its value to uppercase.

```
$ typeset -u NAME
$ NAME="Barbara Jackson"
$ echo $NAME
BARBARA JACKSON
```

Similarly, you can assign a variable the **lowercase** attribute with **typeset –l**.

One of the most useful of variable attributes is the integer attribute. By default, the values of Korn Shell variables are stored as strings. If you want to do arithmetic on a variable, the string variable is internally converted into a number, manipulated, and then turned back into a string. A variable with the integer attribute is stored as an integer. This makes arithmetic much faster. You assign the integer attribute with **typeset –i**:

```
$ typeset -i COUNT
```

The Korn Shell allows you to assign a base other than 10 to an integer variable. The Korn Shell will then use this base to display the variable. The syntax is **typeset –ibase**, where **base** is the base you want to use to display the variable's value. If the base is not 10, the value is displayed as **base#value**:

```
$ COUNT=20
$ typeset -i2 BCOUNT
$ BCOUNT=$COUNT
$ echo $COUNT $BCOUNT
20 2#10100
```

(In base 2, the value 20 is written as 10100.)

One of the most important attributes of a variable is the **export** attribute, which is familiar from the **export** command of the Bourne Shell. If a variable has this attribute then a copy of it is inherited by child processes. The Korn Shell supports the **export** command, and also provides the **typeset –x** command to set the export attribute. You can set the export attribute for functions as well as variables; an exported function will be available in subshells.

The Korn Shell supports several variable attributes that are useful for formatting output. A variable can be assigned a particular width (number of columns), and can be left- or right-justified within that width. Leading zeroes can be added or suppressed. The corresponding options to **typeset** are shown below.

Option	Effect
–L**width**	Left-justify within a width of **width**.
–R**width**	Right-justify within a width of **width**.
–LZ**width**	Left-justify within a width of **width**, stripping any leading zeroes.
–RZ**width**	Right-justify within a width of **width**, filling in leading zeroes if the variable's value starts with a digit.
–Z**width**	Same as –RZ**width**

If the width is omitted, then the width of the first value assigned to the variable is used. Here are some examples of the use of these attributes:

```
$ typeset -L8 FRUIT1 FRUIT2
$ FRUIT1=apple
$ FRUIT2=watermelon
$ echo $FRUIT1$FRUIT2
apple    watermel
$ echo $FRUIT2$FRUIT1
watermelapple
$ typeset -RZ2 DAY
$ DAY=2; echo $DAY
02
$ typeset -LZ MONTH
$ MONTH=11; echo $MONTH/$DAY/95
11/02/95
$ MONTH=8; echo $MONTH/$DAY/95
8 /02/95
```

A variable can be given the **readonly** attribute. Variables with this attribute cannot be set. Thus you should set them before or at the same time that you give them this attribute:

```
$ PATH=/usr/ucb:/bin:/usr/bin:/usr/local/bin:/usr/games
$ typeset -r PATH FPATH=/usr/local/funcs
```

In this example **PATH** and **FPATH** are given the **readonly** attribute. You can set the variable's value within the **typeset** command, as shown with **FPATH**.

You can use the **readonly** built-in command in place of **typeset –r**:

```
$ readonly PATH FPATH=/usr/local/funcs
```

Built-in Variables

The Korn Shell automatically defines a number of variables when you start a session. They are referred to as *built-in* variables. These include most of the Bourne Shell's Keyword Shell Variables (page 292), and a number of others. Some of these variables have values set by the Korn Shell, which also changes their values automatically during your session. Do not assign values to these variables. Others are variables you can assign values to, and that have special meaning for the Korn Shell.

The variables shown in the following table have the same meanings as in the Bourne Shell; refer to page 292 for a discussion of their values and meaning:

Variable	Meaning
HOME	The pathname of your home directory.
PATH	The list of directories the shell searches for commands.
MAIL	The file where your mail is stored.
PS1	The shell prompt string.
PS2	The secondary shell prompt.
IFS	The internal field separator.
CDPATH	The list of absolute pathnames searched by **cd** for subdirectories.
TZ	The time zone.
@	All the command line arguments, as individual arguments.
*	All the command line arguments, as a single argument.
#	The number of command line arguments.

The following Korn Shell variables are not supported by the Bourne Shell.

EDITOR, FCEDIT   These two variables have special meaning for the Korn Shell's command line editing feature (page 428), and are discussed in the section describing that feature.

_ (underscore)   This variable is set by the Korn Shell. Its value is the last argument of the previous simple command in this instance of the Korn Shell. This is similar, but not identical, to the C Shell's !$ expression.

```
$ cat file1 file2 file3 > all3files
$ echo $_
file3
```

If you had issued these commands in the C Shell, using !$ instead of $_, the output would have been all3files. The Korn Shell underscore argument specifically refers to arguments, not arbitrary symbols on the command line. There is no way to refer to the last symbol on the command line from the Korn Shell.

ENV   If this variable is set, its value is interpreted as the name of a file that is read when the Korn Shell is invoked. See "Startup Files," page 383.

FPATH   You can set this variable, whose syntax is like that of **PATH** (page 293). It is used to find files in which shell functions can be located and loaded. See the discussion of Shell Functions and the built-in **autoload** command (page 388).

HISTFILE, HISTSIZE   The Korn Shell uses the **HISTFILE** variable to store the name of its history file, which stores the most recently executed commands. The value of **HISTSIZE** is the number of commands kept in **HISTFILE**. See the discussion of "History" on page 425.

LINENO   Before the Korn Shell executes a command from a script or function, it sets the value of **LINENO** to the line number of the command about to be executed. Here is an example using a function:

```
$ showline ()
> {
> date
> echo Function $0: at line $LINENO
> }
$ showline
Thu Oct 07 20:18:32 1993
Function showline: at line 3
```

If you use the **LINENO** variable in an interactive session, its value is always 1. In this respect the Korn Shell behaves as if each command you type is a one-line script.

LINES, COLUMNS, PS3   You can set the values of these variables to control the format of output generated by the built-in Select command. This multi-line command is designed for use in shell programs rather than for interactive use. See the section on Built-in Commands, page 405.

PWD, OLDPWD   The Korn Shell automatically stores the absolute pathname of the current working directory, as set by the most recent **cd** command, in **PWD**, and it stores the pathname of the previous working directory in **OLDPWD**. You can toggle back and forth between directories by giving the command **cd $OLDPWD**.

The value of **$PWD** is not necessarily the same as the value returned by the **/bin/pwd** command, because the **PWD** variable keeps track of the traversal of symbolic links. In a sense, it knows not only where you are, but how you got there. Consider the following sequence of commands:

```
$ cd $HOME
$ mkdir top top/level2 top/level2/level3
$ ln -s top/level2 symdir
$ cd symdir
$ /bin/pwd
/home/alex/top/level2
$ echo $PWD
/home/alex/symdir
```

In the Korn Shell, the **pwd** command is a predefined alias (essentially for **echo $PWD**), so it keeps track of symbolic links.

OPTARG, OPTIND These variables are set by the Korn Shell's built-in **getopts** command, and are discussed in the section on "Built-in Commands" (page 405).

PPID At its invocation, the Korn Shell sets this variable to the process ID of its parent process. It does not change throughout the lifetime of the Korn Shell session. Do not attempt to set its value.

PS4 This is the prompt string that the Korn Shell uses in debugging mode. The Bourne Shell has a trace facility that you turn on with the command **set –x**. The Korn Shell supports the same feature. However, in the Bourne Shell each line of trace output is always preceded by a + sign. The Korn Shell precedes each line of trace output by **PS4**, which is + by default. For example:

```
$ MYNAME=` who am i `
$ set -x
$ echo $MYNAME
+ echo alex
alex
$ PS4='At Line $LINENO: '
+ PS4=At Line $LINENO:
$ echo $MYNAME
At Line 1: echo alex
alex
```

Using **set –x** interactively is of little value. However, when you are debugging scripts, it can be useful to have the line number appear as part of the trace output.

In Korn Shell 93, command substitution and arithmetic expression evaluation will be performed each time PS4 is evaluated. Thus you can type

```
$ PS4='` date `: Line $LINENO: '
```

and the trace output will then include the date and time of each traced command, as well as the line number. This feature is useful for debugging scripts that run overnight or that take a long time to execute.

RANDOM   This variable is set by the Korn Shell. Each time it is referenced, it is assigned an integer value randomly chosen between 0 and 32767, inclusive. It is useful in several programming contexts, including test programs, quizzes, and games.

SECONDS   This variable is an integer and is set by the Korn Shell. At the time it is referenced, its value is the number of seconds that have elapsed since the start of the Korn Shell session. You can include it in your prompt, but it is more useful for timing events in scripts:

```
$ cat quiz
echo "What is the smallest prime number that is larger than 50?"
START=$SECONDS
read ANSWER
FINISH=$SECONDS
echo "You took $(($FINISH - $START)) seconds to answer"
if [ $ANSWER -ne 53 ]
then
echo "and you were incorrect; the answer is 53."
fi
```

The expression **$(($FINISH – $START))** is an example of the Korn Shell's built-in arithmetic capability.

In the 1993 Korn Shell, **SECONDS** is a floating point variable that keeps track of time in milliseconds and is displayed with three digits to the right of the decimal point.

TMOUT   If **TMOUT** is set, and if **TMOUT** seconds elapse after a prompt is issued with no input, the shell exits. This variable is usually set by the system administrator in a global startup file. If you unset it, you do not disable the timeout. You could try to set it to a large value, but the global startup file typically sets the readonly attribute for **TMOUT**. If it is not a readonly variable, you can set it to 0 to disable it.

OPTIONAL

Expanding Shell Variables

The Korn Shell expression **$name** expands to the value of the variable **name**. If **$name** is null, or if **name** is not set and you have not set the **nounset** option, then **$name** expands to a null string. Often this is what you want, but sometimes, particularly in shell programs, you may want to take some other action when you evaluate a null or unset variable. The Korn Shell provides the following alternatives:

- Use a default value for the variable.
- Use a default value, and assign that value to the variable.
- Display an error.

You can choose these alternatives by using modifiers to the variable name.

To use a default variable for a null or unset variable, you use the :– modifier. Write the variable as follows:

${name:–default}

The Korn Shell interprets the :– to mean that if **name** is null or unset, then **default** is expanded, and the expanded value is used instead. The value of **name** does not change. For example, to list the contents of directory **$LIT** using a default, you might write

```
ls ${LIT:-/home/alex/literature}
```

The default can itself have variable references that are expanded, as in

```
ls ${LIT:-$HOME/literature}
```

You can choose to supply defaults for unset variables, but let variables set to null expand as null, by omitting the colon:

```
ls ${LIT-$HOME/literature}
```

The :– modifier does not set the value of a null or unset variable. In a script you may want to detect that you are using a default at the first reference to the variable, and then assign that default to the variable, so that the variable has that value until it is changed. You can do this with the := modifier:

${name:=default}

The Korn Shell expands the expression **${name:=default}** in the same manner as **${name:–default}**, but has the side effect of setting the value of **name** to the expanded value of **default**. Thus, if your script contains a line such as the following

```
ls ${LIT:=/home/alex/literature}
```

and **LIT** is unset or null at the point where this line is executed, it will be assigned the value **/home/alex/literature**. A common feature of Korn Shell scripts is to use this expansion modifier with the colon (:) command at the start of scripts to set any variables that may be unset. As in the Bourne Shell, the Korn Shell's colon command has the effect of evaluating each token in the remainder of the command line, but does not otherwise execute any commands. Thus, to set a default for a null or unset variable, you can use this syntax:

: ${name:=default}

Without the leading colon, the shell would evaluate and then attempt to execute the "command" that resulted from the evaluation. In the Korn Shell, the order of evaluation is such that if a variable is a command and you name that variable, then it is executed. If it is not a valid command, you will get an error. For example, suppose that your script needs a directory to create temporary files and uses the value of **$TEMP-DIR** for this directory. The following line will default **TEMPDIR** to **/tmp**:

OPTIONAL Continued

```
: ${TEMPDIR:=/tmp}
```

Again, if you omit the : from the :=, the Korn Shell will assign values for unset variables but not for null ones.

Sometimes a script needs the value of a variable, and there is no reasonable default that you can supply at the time that you write the script. In this case you can force the script to write an error message, and terminate with status 1 if the variable is null or unset. The modifier for this purpose is :?:

```
cd ${TESTDIR:?mesg}
```

If **TESTDIR** is null or unset, then the Korn Shell will display the expanded value of **mesg** on standard error and terminate the script. If you omit **mesg**, then a default error message (`parameter null or not set`) is written to standard error. If you omit the :, then an error occurs only if the variable is unset; a null variable will expand to a null string. Interactive shells do not exit when you use :?.

In addition to these modifiers, the Korn Shell also provides a powerful set of string pattern matching operations that make it very useful as a string processing language. These operations take strings and delete prefixes or suffixes that match patterns. There are four operations:

removes minimal matching prefixes.

removes maximal matching prefixes.

%   removes minimal matching suffixes.

%%   removes maximal matching suffixes.

The syntax for using these is similar to that for the modifiers listed above:

${**varname** op **pattern**}

where **op** is one of the operators shown above, and **pattern** is a match pattern similar to that used with filename wild cards. These operators are most commonly used to manipulate pathnames to extract or remove components, or to change suffixes.

```
$ SOURCEFILE=/usr/local/src/prog.c
$ echo ${SOURCEFILE#/*/}
local/src/prog.c
$ echo ${SOURCEFILE##/*/}
prog.c
$ echo ${SOURCEFILE%/*}
/usr/local/src
$ echo ${SOURCEFILE%%/*}

$ echo ${SOURCEFILE%.c}
/usr/local/src/prog
$ CHOPFIRST=${SOURCEFILE#/*}
$ NEXT=${CHOPFIRST%%/*}
$ echo $NEXT
local
```

OPTIONAL Continued

Although these operators are often used on pathnames, they can be applied to any string.

Because substring operators are evaluated as part of variable expansion, you can use them in the **PS1** prompt. An earlier example showed how to include the current working directory in your prompt (page 386). If this prompt string is too long, you can include only the last component. Often this is enough to tell you where you are:

```
$ PS1='${PWD##/*/} !> '
literature 23>
```

Another useful prompt string matches and removes any pathname prefix from $PWD that matches $HOME/:

```
$ PS1='${PWD##$HOME/} !> '
/home/alex 23> cd literature
literature 24> cd stories
literature/stories 25> cd /usr/local/bin
/usr/local/bin 26>
```

When you are in a subdirectory of your home directory, the prompt shows only the path relative to **$HOME**. If you are anywhere else, it shows the absolute pathname.

A related operator, which does not do pattern matching, is the string length operator. The expression **${#name}** evaluates to the length of the string **name**.

```
$ MYNAME="John Q. Public"
$ echo ${#MYNAME}
14
```

Extended Pattern Matching Operators

The Korn Shell provides more pattern matching operators than the Bourne or C shells; it provides a complete regular expression pattern matching language. Regular expressions are used in a number of UNIX system utilities such as **awk**, **grep**, and **vi**, and are explained in Appendix A. However, the Korn Shell has its own, slightly different syntax for regular expression patterns.

You can match zero or more instances of any pattern with the syntax *(pattern). This works both for filename expansion and for shell variable operations. For example, suppose you have a directory with the following files:

```
$ ls
a           abcbcbcx   abx       xaabby    xaby      xcy
ab          abcx       acx       xabaay    xbbaay    xy
```

You can list all files starting with **ab** in the usual way:

```
$ ls ab*
ab          abcbcbcx   abcx      abx
```

Suppose, however, that you want to list all files whose names consist of **x**, followed by zero or more occurrences of the string **ab**, followed by **y**. No Bourne Shell filename pattern will work. The Korn Shell allows you to type

```
$ ls x*(ab)y
xababy  xaby     xy
```

You can match one or more instances of a pattern with the construct **+(pattern)**:

```
$ ls x+(ab)y
xababy  xaby
```

The pattern can itself be a regular expression. For example, to list all the files whose names consist of **x**, followed by any combination of **a**'s and **b**'s, followed by **y**, you can use this pattern:

```
$ ls x+([ab])y
xaabby xababy xaby xbbaay
```

The construct **?(pattern)** matches zero or one occurrences of a string matching **pattern**. **!(pattern)** matches anything that does not match **pattern**. And **@(pattern1|pattern2|...)** matches anything that matches either **pattern1** or **pattern2** or ....

```
$ ls x?([abc])y
xcy xy
$ ls x!(*(ab))y
xaabby xbbaay xcy
$ ls x@(+(a)+(b)|+(b)+(a))y
xaabby xaby xbbaay
```

The 1993 Korn Shell has greatly expanded the number and power of string operations on variables. There are a number of position-dependent substring operations:

${name:startpos}**   expands to the substring of **$name, starting from character position **startpos**. You can use any Korn Shell arithmetic expression for **startpos** and for the other symbols that represent character positions in these constructs. For example:

```
$ NAME=McGonigle; POS=3
$ echo ${NAME:$POS}
Gonigle
```

${name:startpos:len}**   expands to the substring of **$name, starting at **startpos** and consisting of **len** characters (or fewer, if **$name** is not sufficiently long).

${name/pattern/replace}**   expands to the value of **$name, with the first occurrence of **pattern** (which can include any of the regular expression operators above) replaced by **replace**.

```
$ MAGIC=abracadabra
$ echo ${MAGIC/abr/o}
oacadabra
```

${name/#pattern/replace}   is the same, except that the pattern must match the beginning of the string. This is sometimes referred to as an *anchored pattern*.

${name/%pattern/replace}   is the same, except that the pattern must match the end of the string.

${name//pattern/replace}**   expands to the value of **$name, with each occurrence of pattern replaced by **replace**, as in this example:

```
$ MAGIC=abracadabra
$ echo ${MAGIC//abr/o}
oacadoa
```

Arrays and Compound Variables

The Korn Shell supports one-dimensional array variables. In versions of the Korn Shell prior to Korn Shell 93, the array subscripts must be integers in the range 0 through 511. You do not have to declare array variables. If you use any variable name with a subscript, then that variable is treated as an array. Subscripts are enclosed within square brackets:

```
$ PRES[0]=Washington
$ PRES[1]="Adams, J"
$ PRES[2]=Jefferson
```

You can assign values to an entire array at once by using the **set** command with the –A option:

```
$ set -A PRES Washington "Adams, J" Jefferson Madison Monroe "Adams, JQ"
```

Typically this syntax is used to initialize an array. You can use **typeset** to assign attributes to arrays as you do to simple variables. You can also specify the size of an array with **typeset** if you know its size in advance.

```
$ typeset -L20 REPRESENTATIVES[435] SENATORS[100] JUSTICES[9]
```

To reference an array variable, use the **${}** notation. Enclose the subscripted array name within the braces:

```
$ echo The third president was ${PRES[2]}.
The third president was Jefferson.
```

You can use any valid shell arithmetic expression as a subscript. You can also use the symbol *, which stands for all the array entries:

```
$ echo $PRES[*]
Washington Adams, J Jefferson Madison Monroe Adams, JQ
```

If you use the symbol @ instead of * in a subscript, the effect is the same. The difference is the same as the difference between $* and $@ (page 297), and only occurs if the array reference is within double quotation marks. In that case, an expression "${PRES[*]}" expands to a single string that contains embedded spaces, while "$PRES[@]" expands to separate strings, one for each array element.

In Korn Shell 93, there are a significant number of additions to the syntax for array processing. One simple addition is an alternate way to initialize an array. You can write

```
$ PRES=(Washington "Adams, J" Jefferson Madison Monroe ...)
```

instead of using **set** –A. The strings inside the parentheses become the values of the variable, which becomes an array of as many elements as there are strings.

Associative Arrays

A more complex addition is support for associative arrays. An associative array is one whose subscripts are arbitrary symbols. The name comes from the fact that an associative array is simply a sequence of associations between a subscript and the corresponding value. In Korn Shell 93, associative arrays can have arbitrary strings as subscripts. The following example will create an array in which the subscripts are presidents' names and the corresponding values are the names of their vice presidents (some presidents had more than one vice president):

```
$ VICEPRES=([Washington]="Adams, J" ["Adams, J"]=Jefferson \
[Jefferson]="Burr, Clinton" [Madison]="Clinton, Gerry")
```

You can then refer to **${VICEPRES[Washington]}**, which expands to the string Adams, J.

Compound Variables

Korn Shell 93 also supports compound variables, which are similar to C structures or Pascal records. A compound variable has component variables. The components are referred to using the variable's name, followed by a period, followed by the component name. Thus you can create a compound variable called **name** with components **first**, **middle**, and **last**. Before you can create components of a compound variable, the base variable name must exist. Here is an example:

```
$ name=""
$ name.first=Robert
$ name.middle=Louis
$ name.last=Stevenson
```

There is a shorthand for this, similar to the shorthand for initializing arrays:

```
name=(first=Robert middle=Louis last=Stevenson)
```

Compound variables are useful for keeping related data items together and for copying, assigning, or displaying them in a group.

Korn Shell Arithmetic

The Korn Shell has the ability to evaluate a broad class of arithmetic expressions. In the 1988 Korn Shell, all arithmetic is done on integer quantities. The 1993 version has added the ability to do floating point arithmetic as well. There are a number of contexts in which the shell does arithmetic. One is with arguments of the Let built-in command:

```
$ let COUNT=COUNT+1 VALUE=VALUE*10+NEW
```

In this example, the variables **COUNT**, **VALUE**, and **NEW** should have integer numeric values. Each argument to Let is evaluated as a separate expression. You must quote arguments that contain spaces.

You can use Korn Shell arithmetic in many other contexts besides the Let statement. The Korn Shell evaluates an arithmetic expression enclosed between $((and)) to produce a value that can be used anywhere that a numeric value can be used. For example:

```
$ echo There are $((60*60*24*365)) seconds in a non-leap year
There are 31536000 seconds in a non-leap year
```

You can use variables inside the double parentheses. If you do, the $ sign that precedes the variable references is optional inside the parentheses:

```
$ x=23
$ y=37
$ echo $((2*x + 3*y))
157
$ echo $((2*$x + 3*$y))
157
```

The POSIX shell requires that the $ sign precede all variable references inside arithmetic expressions, so it only supports the second of the two usages above. The POSIX shell does not support the Let form of arithmetic.

The Korn Shell supports logical as well as arithmetic operators. The following table shows the operators that the Korn Shell supports, and the meaning of each.

Operator	Description
+	Addition
−	Subtraction
*	Multiplication
/	Division
%	Remainder
<<	Left shift (bit operation)
>>	Right shift (bit operation)
&	and (bit operation)
&&	and (logical)
|	inclusive or (bit operation)
||	inclusive or (logical)
~	not (bit operation)
!	not (logical)
^	exclusive or (bitwise)
<	Less than
>	Greater than
<=	Less than or equal to
>=	Greater than or equal to
==	Equals
!=	Not equal to

If you are familiar with the C programming language, you will recognize these operators, all of which are present in C.

The 1993 Korn Shell adds some new operators, also taken from C: the increment (++) and decrement (--) operators, in both prefix and postfix form, the comma operator (,), and the arithmetic conditional operator (?:). Their semantics coincides with their semantics in C.

The remainder operator (%) gives the remainder when its first operand is divided by its second. Thus the expression $((16%7)) has the value 2.

OPTIONAL

The result of a logical operation is always either zero or one. Consider the following sequence:

```
$ Var1=5
$ Var2=6
$ Var3=$(( $Var1 & $Var2 ))
$ Var4=$(( $Var1 && $Var2 ))
$ echo $Var3 $Var4
4 1
$ Var5=$(( $Var1 | $Var2 ))
$ Var6=$(( $Var1 || $Var2 ))
$ Var7=$(( $Var1 ^ $Var2 ))
$ echo $Var5 $Var6 $Var7
7 1 3
$ Var8=$(( !$Var1 ))
$ echo $Var8
0
$ Var9=$(( $Var1 < $Var2 ))
$ Var10=$(( $Var1 > $Var2 ))
$ echo $Var9 $Var10
1 0
```

The bitwise and operator (&) selects the bits that are on in both 5 (0101 in binary) and 6 (0110 in binary); the result is binary 0100, which is 4. The logical operator (&&)produces a result of one if both of its operands are nonzero, and zero otherwise. The bitwise inclusive or operator (|) selects the bits that are on in either of 0101 and 0110, resulting in 0111, which is 8. The logical or operator produces a result of one if either of its operands are nonzero, and zero otherwise. The bitwise exclusive or operator (^) selects the bits that are on in either, but not both, of the operands 0101 and 0110, giving 0011, which is 3. The logical not operator (!) produces a result of one if its operand is zero, and zero otherwise. The comparison operators all produce a result of one if the comparison is true, and zero otherwise.

The 1993 Korn Shell has also made a significant addition to arithmetic: it supports floating point variables. You can declare a variable to be of floating type with **typeset –F** or **typeset –E**. They are not equivalent; the –E type's values are displayed in scientific notation:

```
$ typeset -F X
$ typeset -E Y
$ X=123.456
$ Y=$((X + 1.0))
$ echo $X $Y
123.456 1.24456e02
```

The symbol **e02** means "times 10 to the second power." Korn Shell 93 has also added built-in support for the math library (trigonometric and exponential) functions.

Built-in Commands

The Korn Shell provides a much richer set of built-in commands than either the Bourne or C Shells. They include commands for option processing, I/O, control flow, and control of the user's environment. Some of these commands have been mentioned previously; this section focuses on the built-in commands that differ significantly from the Bourne Shell's commands.

Control Flow Commands

The control flow commands are primarily useful for shell programming, although they can occasionally be useful in interactive work. The Korn Shell's built-in commands that control the process flow are If, For, While, Case, Until, and Select. All of these except Select are also present in the Bourne Shell, and the For (page 313) and Case (page 320) commands are essentially identical to their Bourne Shell variants.

The If (page 301), While (page 314), and Until (page 317) commands have in common the use of a test command. You can use the same syntax for Korn Shell test commands that you use in the Bourne Shell. However, you can also use the built-in command **[[** (two consecutive left brackets). This command has the syntax

[[**conditions**]]

The result of executing this command, like the **test** command, is simply a return status. The **conditions** allowed within the brackets are almost a superset of those accepted by **test** (page 719). While the **test** utility uses **–n** to test for a symbolic link, the Korn Shell uses **–L**. The Korn Shell adds these new tests for file attributes:

–a file

is true if **file** exists.

–O file

is true if **file** exists and its owner ID is the effective user ID of the shell (i.e., your effective user ID if the shell is interactive).

–G file

is true if **file** exists and its group ID is the effective group ID of the shell (i.e., your effective group ID if the shell is interactive).

–S file

is true if **file** exists and is a socket.

file1 –nt file2

is true if **file1**'s modification time is newer (more recent) than **file2**'s.

file1 –ot **file2**

> is true if **file1**'s modification time is older than **file2**'s.

file1 –ef **file2**

> is true if **file1** and **file2** are links to the same file.

The **test** utility's numeric relational operators **–gt**, **–ge**, **–lt**, **–le**, **–eq** and **–ne** can be used with **[[**. However, the Korn Shell allows you to use arithmetic expressions, not just constants, as the operands.

```
$ [[ $(( ${#HOME} + 14 )) -lt ${#PWD} ]]
$ echo $?
1
```

In this example, the condition is false (=1). The condition would be true (=0) if the length of the string $HOME plus 14 was less than the length of the string $PWD. See the **es** script on page 301 for more about $?.

The **test** utility allows you to test if strings are equal or unequal. The Korn Shell **[[** command adds comparison tests for string operators: The > and < operators compare strings for order (so that, for example, "aa" < "bbb"). The = operator tests for pattern match, not just equality: `[[ string = pattern ]]` is true if string matches pattern. This operator is not symmetrical; the pattern must appear on the right side of the = sign. For example, `[[ artist = a* ]]` is true, while `[[ a* = artist ]]` is not true.

OPTIONAL

You can use the **&&** (logical and) and **||** (logical or) operators to combine conditions. The meaning of these in combining conditions is the same as their meaning in command lists. (See "Token Splitting" in the section on "Command Processing," page 430.)

```
$ [[ -d bin && -f src/myscript.sh ]] && cp src/myscript.sh \
bin/myscript && chmod +x bin/myscript || echo "Cannot make \
executable version of myscript"
```

This example has a command list that is started by a compound condition. The condition tests that the directory **bin** and the file **src/myscript.sh** exist. If this is true, then **cp** copies **src/myscript.sh** to **bin/myscript**. If the copy succeeds, then **chmod** makes **myscript** executable. If any of these steps fails, then **echo** displays a message.

The **[[** command is useful by itself, but you will probably use it most as the test command for control flow commands. This command also allows an arithmetic test. This test appears inside double parentheses `(( ))` instead of square brackets. These double parentheses are not preceded by a **$** sign, and the value of this test is not a numeric value, only a true or false exit status. You can use all of the logical arithmetic operators shown on page 403. You can write either

```
if [[ $(( ${#HOME} + 14 )) -lt ${#PWD} ]]
then ...
```

or

```
if (( $(( ${#HOME} + 14 )) < ${#PWD} ))
then ...
```

The second version uses comparison operators that are familiar from arithmetic and thus may be more natural for you to use.

Note that [[is a command. Therefore you must precede and follow it with (SPACE)s. Suppose that you write a line without the (SPACE), like this:

```
if [[-d "$dirname"]]
    ...
```

When the Korn Shell encounters the sequence [[-d, it treats this as a single token, and tries to find a command with that name.

On the other hand, the Korn Shell recognizes the token ((, and treats it as a special symbol, not a command. Thus you need not follow ((with a (SPACE).

Select

The Korn Shell's Select control structure (Figure 12-1) is a new construct, not based on anything in previous shells. It displays a menu, assigns a value to a variable based on the user's choice of items, and executes a series of commands. The syntax of Select, which is a multiline command, follows.

select **varname** [in **arg** ...]
do
    commands
done

First, Select generates and displays a menu of the **arg** items. The menu is formatted with numbers before each item. For example, a Select structure that begins with

```
select fruit in apple banana blueberry kiwi orange watermelon
```

would display the following menu:

```
1) apple
2) banana
3) blueberry
4) kiwi
5) orange
6) watermelon
```

You can have many items in the list of **args**. The Select structure uses the values of the **LINES** and **COLUMNS** variables to determine the size of the display. If the number of items to be displayed is more than about **$LINES** $* 2/3$, then Select will display the menu in multiple columns. (**LINES** has a default value of 24, and **COLUMNS** a default of 80.)

After displaying the menu, Select displays the value **$PS3**, the special Select prompt. The default value of **PS3** is the characters #?, but typically you would set **PS3** to a meaningful prompt string for the particular situation.

If the user enters a valid number (one in the menu range), then Select sets the value of **varname** to the argument corresponding to the entered number, and executes the commands between Do and Done. Select then reissues the **PS3** prompt and waits for a user choice. It does this repeatedly un-

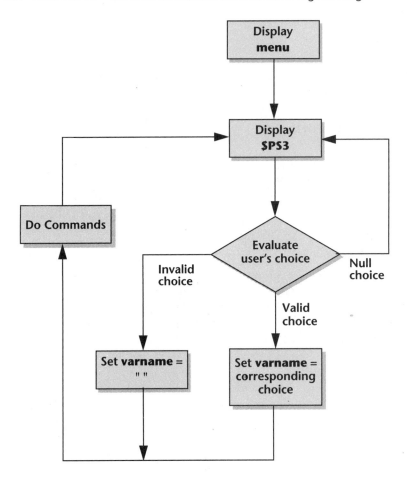

Figure 12-1   Select Flowchart

til something causes it to exit the statements between Do and Done. Typically that something is a Break, Return, or Exit statement. Break has the effect
of exiting from the loop. Return is useful if Select is inside a function, and
causes the function to return. Exit will exit the current shell. Following is a
script fragment that illustrates the use of Select:

```
$ cat fruit
PS3="Choose your favorite fruit from these possibilities: "
select FRUIT in apple banana blueberry kiwi orange watermelon
do
 if [[ -z "$FRUIT" ]]
 then
 echo "You better not have any fruit salad."
 else
 echo "You chose $FRUIT as your favorite."
 fi
 break
done
```

```
$ fruit
1) apple
2) banana
3) blueberry
4) kiwi
5) orange
6) watermelon
Choose your favorite fruit from these possibilities: 3
You chose blueberry as your favorite.
```

If the user enters an invalid menu choice, then **varname** is set to a null string and the commands between Do and Done are executed. It is a good idea to test for a null string in the commands in case the user enters an invalid value. If the user simply presses (RETURN), the Korn Shell redisplays the menu and the **PS3** prompt. The Korn Shell stores the user's response in the built-in variable **REPLY**.

As the syntax indicates, you can omit the word **in** and the list of arguments. If you do, then Select uses the current values of the positional parameters **$@**.

Option Processing

The way that a UNIX utility interprets its command line is up to the specific utility. However, there are conventions that most UNIX utilities conform to. (See "The Command Line" page 90.) In particular, if the utility takes options, then they are indicated by using letters preceded by a hyphen, as in

$ **ls -l -r -t**

(See pages 633 and 634 for descriptions of these arguments.) The options usually must precede other arguments such as filenames. Many utilities allow you to combine options behind a single hyphen. The previous command can also be written like this:

$ **ls -lrt**

Some utilities have options that themselves require arguments. The **cc** utility has a –o option that must be followed by the filename of the executable file. (See **cc**, page 558.) Typically, option arguments are separated from their option letters by a space:

$ **cc -o prog prog.c**

A final argument convention allows you to deal with filenames that start with a hyphen. If you have a file whose name happens to be –l, then the command

$ **ls -l**

is ambiguous: it could mean a long listing of all files in the current directory or a listing of the file named –l. It is interpreted as the former. You should avoid creating files whose names begin with hyphens, but if you do create them, many UNIX utilities follow the convention that a –– argument (two consecutive hyphens) indicates the end of options. Thus you could type

$ **ls -- -l**

or

$ **ls ./-1**

to list the file.

These are conventions, not hard-and-fast rules, and there are a number of UNIX utilities that do not follow them (such as **tar** and **find**), but following such conventions is a good idea; it makes it much easier for users to learn to use your program. When you write shell programs that require options, you should follow the UNIX option conventions unless you have a compelling reason to do otherwise.

The Korn Shell's **getopts** built-in command is designed to make it easy for you to write programs that follow the UNIX argument conventions. The syntax for **getopts** is shown below:

getopts **optstring varname** [arg ...]

The **opstring** argument is a list of the valid option letters. If an option takes an argument, you indicate that fact by following the corresponding letter with a colon (:). Thus the option string **dxo:lt:r** indicates that **getopts** should search for –**d**, –**x**, –**o**, –**l**, –**t**, or –**r** options, and that the –**o** and –**t** options take arguments. A leading colon on **optstring** has a special meaning that is described below.

The **getopts** command checks an argument list for options in optstring. The **varname** argument names a Korn Shell variable in which any option letter found by **getopts** is stored. By default, **getopts** uses the command line arguments, but if you supply a list of arguments after the **varname**, they will be used instead.

The built-in variables **OPTIND** and **OPTARG** play a special role in conjunction with **getopts**. When a Korn Shell program starts to execute, the value of **OPTIND** is 1. Each time **getopts** locates an argument it increments **OPTIND** to be the index of the next argument to be processed. If the option takes an argument, then the value of the argument is assigned to **OPTARG**.

To understand the use of **getopts**, first consider the following problem: you have to write a program that can take three options.

- If the user uses the –**b** flag, then your program should ignore white space at the start of input lines.

- If the user uses the –**t** flag followed by the name of a directory, then your program should use that directory for temporary files. Otherwise it should use /**tmp**.

- If the user uses the –**u** flag, then your program should translate all its output to uppercase.

An argument of –– should end option processing. If the user supplies any option other than –**b**, –**t** or –**u**, that option should be ignored. The problem is to write the portion of the program that determines which options the user has supplied. Here is one possible way that does not use **getopts**:

```
SKIPBLANKS=
TMPDIR=/tmp
CASE=lower

while [[ "$1" = "-*" ]] # Remember, [[ = ]] does pattern match
do
        case $1 in
        -b)     SKIPBLANKS=TRUE ;;
        -t)     if [ -d "$2" ]
                then
                        TMPDIR=$2
                        shift
                else
                        print "$0: -t takes a directory argument." >&2
                        exit 1
                fi ;;
        -u)     CASE=upper ;;
        --)     break   ;;          # Stop processing options
        *)      print "$0: Invalid option $1 ignored." >&2 ;;
        esac
        shift
done
```

This program fragment has a While loop that checks that the first argument
starts with a –. While this is true, the program loops through a case statement
that checks all the possible options. Note that the case has a –– case label,
whose action is to break out of the while loop, and a * case label, which will
recognize any unknown option and whose action is to print an error message but to let processing continue. On each pass through the loop, the program does a Shift to get to the next argument. If an option takes an
argument, the program does an extra Shift to get past that argument. Here is
a program fragment that processes the same options, but uses **getopts**:

```
SKIPBLANKS=
TMPDIR=/tmp
CASE=lower

while getopts :bt:u arg
do
        case $arg in
        b)      SKIPBLANKS=TRUE ;;
        t)      if [ -d "$OPTARG" ]
                then
                        TMPDIR=$OPTARG
                else
                        print "$0: $OPTARG is not a directory." >&2
                        exit 1
                fi ;;
        u)      CASE=upper ;;
        :)      print "$0: Must supply an argument to $OPTARG." >&2
                exit 1 ;;
        \?)     print "Invalid option $OPTARG ignored." >&2 ;;
        esac
done
shift $((OPTIND-1))
```

There are a number of important differences between these examples.
One is that the second version has only a single call to shift, at the end. Because **getopts** uses **OPTIND** to find the next item to process, it does not need
to shift the arguments. Another difference is in the case labels. The labels in
the second case do not start with a hyphen, because the value of **$arg** is just
the option letter. Also, getopts recognizes –– as the end of the options so you

do not have to explicitly specify it in the Case statement. But the most important difference has to do with the way that errors are handled.

Because **getopts** knows which options are valid and which options require arguments, it can detect errors in the command line. There are two ways that **getopts** can handle these errors, and you choose one by placing or omitting a colon before the **optstring** argument. Notice that the example uses a leading colon in **optstring**. When you use this colon, if **getopts** finds an invalid option it sets its varname argument to the string ?, and sets **OPTARG** to the option letter. This explains the \?) case label in the second example. When you use the leading colon and omit an argument for an option that requires one, **getopts** assigns the string : to **varname** and also stores the option letter in **OPTARG**. This explains the :) case label. In both cases, **getopts** does not write any error message; it leaves that task to you.

If you omit the leading colon from **optstring**, the error detection behavior of **getopts** changes. In this case both an invalid option and a missing option argument will cause **varname** to be assigned the string ?. OPTARG is not set, and **getopts** writes its own diagnostic message to standard error. Generally this method is less desirable, since you have less control over what the user sees when he or she makes an error.

Using **getopts** will not necessarily make your programs shorter. Its principal advantages are that it provides a uniform programming interface, and that it enforces conventional handling of options.

Input and Output

A programming language needs commands for input and output. In the Korn Shell, the input command is **read**, and the output command is **print**.

The read command

The syntax of **read** is similar to the Bourne Shell's **read**, but the Korn Shell **read** provides additional functionality. The syntax of **read** follows:

    read [–prs] [–un] [varname...]

The variable names are optional. The command

    read

by itself is valid, and reads an entire input line from standard input into the variable **REPLY**. If you do supply **varname** arguments, then **read** splits the input line into fields using the characters in **$IFS** as field separators. Each variable is assigned a single field. If there are not enough variables, the last variable is assigned a string value equal to the remainder of the input line. If there are not enough fields, the leftover variables are set to null strings (page 291).

The Korn Shell allows you to specify an input prompt by using the syntax **varname?prompt** for the first input variable name. For example, if your script has a line of the form

```
read MON?"Enter month, day and year separated by spaces: " DAY YR
```

then execution of this command will cause the script to issue the prompt

```
Enter month, day and year separated by spaces:
```

and then pause while you type an input line. If you type three values, they will be assigned to **MON**, **DAY** and **YR**.

The Korn Shell **read** supports four options:

–p

> This option is explained in the description of the Korn Shell coprocess (page 434). The command
>
> ```
> read -p...
> ```
>
> reads its input line from the standard output of the coprocess.

–r raw

> This option requests raw input. Ordinarily, if the input line ends in a backslash character (\), the \ and the (NEWLINE) are discarded, and the next line is treated as a continuation of the input. If you specify **read –r**, then a trailing backslash is not treated specially. You might find this useful if you are reading an input file that is itself a shell script, and you want to reproduce it faithfully.

–s

> This option causes **read** to copy its input line to the history file. This option is useful if you want to write a shell script that keeps a history of its own input in the same way that the Korn Shell does.

–un

> This option takes an integer argument, **n**, which is a file descriptor, and causes **read** to take its input from that file descriptor. Thus
>
> ```
> read -u4 arg1 arg2
> ```
>
> is equivalent to
>
> ```
> read arg1 arg2 <&4
> ```
>
> See "File Descriptors," page 416, for a discussion of redirection and file descriptors.

The **read** command has exit status zero if it successfully reads any data. It has nonzero exit status when it reaches the end of the file. This allows you to use **read** as a test command in a multiline command. An example follows.

```
$ cat names
Alice Jones
Robert Smith
John Q. Public
```

```
$ while read First Rest
> do
>         print $Rest, $First
> done < names
Jones, Alice
Smith, Robert
Q. Public, John
```

OPTIONAL

Notice the redirection of input for the compound While structure. It is important that you only do the redirection here, and not in the call to **read**. The reason is that each time you redirect input, the input file is opened and repositioned at the start. Look at the difference between these examples:

```
$ read line1 < names; print $line1; read line2 < names; print $line2
Alice Jones
Alice Jones
$ (read line1; print $line1; read line2; print $line2) < names
Alice Jones
Robert Smith
```

In the first example, each **read** opens **names** and starts at the beginning. In the second example, the **names** file is opened once, as standard input of the subshell created by the parentheses. Each **read** then reads successive lines of standard input.

Another way to get the same effect is to open the input file with **exec** and hold it open as shown below. (More on opening files on page 416).

```
$ exec 3< names
$ read -u3 line1; print $line1; read -u3 line2; print $line2
Alice Jones
Robert Smith
$ exec 3<&-
```

The print Command

The **print** command is a replacement for **echo**. Although **echo** is still supported, it has a significant disadvantage: there are two versions of **echo** in wide use, and they are incompatible. The System V **echo** uses escape characters, such as \c (which suppresses the trailing (NEWLINE)). The BSD **echo** does not recognize (and therefore echoes) these escapes; instead it treats the –n option as special. The Korn Shell **print** has a uniform syntax on all UNIX systems, and you should use it in any programs that you expect to be ported to multiple environments. The syntax of **print** is

print [–nprRs] [–un] [**string**...]

By default, **print** writes the strings to standard output, recognizes the escape characters of System V **echo**, and recognizes the –n option of BSD **echo**.

Remember that the \ character is a special character to the shell, and you must quote it to use it in any of the print escapes. Here is an example of the use of **print** escapes:

Escape	Meaning
\a	The alert character (typically makes the display beep or flash).
\b	The backspace character.
\c	Does not print, and suppresses a trailing (NEWLINE).
\f	Form feed. This puts a (CONTROL)-L character in the output stream.
\n	(NEWLINE). This allows a single call to **print** to write multiple lines.
\r	(RETURN). This puts a (CONTROL)-M (carriage return) character in the output stream.
\t	(TAB) character.
\\	Backslash.
\0nnn	The ASCII character whose octal value is **nnn**. You can use 1 to 3 octal digits.

```
$ print "Columbus had three ships:\n\tThe Nina\n\tThe Pinta\n\tThe Santa Maria"
Columbus had three ships:
        The Nina
        The Pinta
        The Santa Maria
```

Some of the options to **print** have the same meaning as the corresponding options for **read**.

−p

This option causes the output of **print** to be directed to the coprocess.

−s

This option directs the output of **print** to the history file.

−un

This option directs the output of **print** to file descriptor **n**.

−n

This option suppresses the trailing (NEWLINE).

−r

This option causes **print** to ignore the special meaning of the escapes, so that they are printed as ordinary characters.

−R

This option does the same as −**r**, and also causes **print** to treat any following fields as string arguments, even if they start with a hyphen. An exception is made for −**n**.

An example of the use of some **print** options follows.

```
$ print -R -n -p "This NEWLINE \nwill not be recognized"
-p This NEWLINE \nwill not be recognized$
```

The shell prompt for the next command appears at the end of the output line, because the −**n** option suppresses the trailing (NEWLINE).

416 CHAPTER 12   The Korn Shell and Advanced Shell Programming

File Descriptors

When a process wants to use a file, it must first open that file. When it does so, the UNIX system associates a number with the file, called a *file descriptor*. Each process has its own set of open files and its own file descriptors. After a process opens a file, it can do I/O on that file by referring to it with the file descriptor. When the process no longer needs the file, it closes it, freeing the file descriptor.

A typical UNIX process starts with three files open: standard input, which has file descriptor zero; standard output, with file descriptor 1; and standard error, with file descriptor 2. Often those are all the files the process needs. The Korn Shell allows you to redirect standard input, standard output, and standard error of all the commands that you invoke, just as the Bourne Shell does. Recall that you can redirect standard output with the symbol > or the symbol 1>, and that you redirect standard error with the symbol 2> (page 281).The numbers preceding the >'s are the file descriptors of standard input and output respectively. In principle, you can redirect other file descriptors, but since file descriptors other than 0, 1, and 2 do not have any special conventional meaning, it's rarely useful for you to do this. The principal exception is in programs that you write yourself. In this case, you control the meaning of all the files your program uses, and you can use redirection usefully.

The Korn Shell allows you to open files using the built-in **exec** command. You can use **exec** with or without a command argument, and when you supply a command argument, **exec** has very different semantics (page 329). However, you can also do something like this:

```
$ exec 3> outfile
$ exec 4< infile
$ exec 5<> inoutfile
```

The first of these commands opens file **outfile** for output and holds it open, associating it with file descriptor 3. The second opens file **infile** for input, associating it with file descriptor 4. The third opens file **inoutfile** for input and output, associating it with file descriptor 5.

You need not know a file's name to open it; you can duplicate a file descriptor by making it refer to the same file as another open file descriptor, such as standard input or output. The command

```
exec n<&m
```

means open or redirect file descriptor **n** as a duplicate of file descriptor **m**. Note that you use the token <& regardless of whether the file descriptor you are duplicating is used for input, output, or both.

Once you have opened a file, you can use it for input and output in two different ways. You can use I/O redirection in any command line, redirecting standard output to another file descriptor with >&n, or redirecting standard input from another file descriptor with **<&n**. You can also use the built-in **read** and **print** commands. (See "Input and Output," page 412.) If you invoke other commands, including functions, they inherit these open files and file descriptors. When you have finished using a file, you can close it with

```
exec n<&-
```

An example illustrating the use of file descriptors is shown below. The shell function **mycp**, when invoked as

```
mycp source dest
```

copies **source** to **dest**. If only one argument is supplied, it is interpreted as a source, and

```
mycp source
```

copies **source** to standard output. If **mycp** is invoked with no arguments, then it just copies standard input to standard output.

```
function mycp
{
 case $# in
 0)       exec 3<&0 4<&1 ;;
 1)       exec 3< $1 4<&1 ;;
 2)       exec 3< $1 4> $2 ;;
 *)       print "Usage: mycp [source [dest]]"
          exit 1 ;;
 esac

 cat <&3 >&4
 exec 3<&- 4<&-
}
```

The real work of this function is done in the second-to-last line, in the call to **cat**. The rest just arranges for file descriptors 3 and 4, which are the input and output of the **cat** command, to be associated with the right file.

Following is a short program that illustrates the use of Korn Shell file descriptors. This program takes two filenames on the command line and sorts both to temporary files. It then merges the sorted files to standard output, preceding each line by a number that indicates which file it came from.

The Korn Shell does not have string comparison operators for "less than or equal to" or "greater than or equal to." You can use "not greater than," as in this example ([[! "$Line1" > "$Line2"]] in the If statement), as an equivalent for "less than or equal to."

OPTIONAL Continued

```
# Function to check argument count
usage ()
{
        if [[ $# -ne 2 ]]
        then
                print -u2 "Usage: $0 file1 file2"
                exit 1
        fi
}
# Default temporary directory
: ${TEMPDIR:=/tmp}
# Check argument count
usage "$@"
# Set up temporary files for sorting
file1=$TEMPDIR/file1.$$
file2=$TEMPDIR/file2.$$
# Sort
sort $1 > $file1
sort $2 > $file2
# Open files $file1 and $file2 for reading.  Use FD's 3 and 4.
exec 3<$file1
exec 4<$file2
# Read the first line of each file to figure out how to start.
read -u3 Line1
Status1=$?
read -u4 Line2
Status2=$?
# Strategy: while there's still input left in both files:
#       Output the lesser line.
#       Read a new line from the file that line came from.
while [[ $Status1 -eq 0 && $Status2 -eq 0 ]]
do
        if [[ ! "$Line1" > "$Line2" ]]
        then
                print "1.\t$Line1"
                read -u3 Line1
                Status1=$?
        else
                print "2.\t$Line2"
                read -u4 Line2
                Status2=$?
        fi
done
# Now one of the files is at end-of-file.
# Read from each file until the end.
# First file1:
while [[ $Status1 -eq 0 ]]
do
        print "1.\t$Line1"
        read -u3 Line1
        Status1=$?
done
# Next file2:
while [[ $Status2 -eq 0 ]]
do
        print "2.\t$Line2"
        read -u4 Line2
        Status2=$?
done
# Close and remove both input files
exec 3<&- 4<&-
rm -f $file1 $file2
exit 0
```

Job Control

A job is a command pipeline. You can create several jobs on a single command line:

```
$ find . -print | wc -l > /tmp/fc & grep -l alex /tmp/* > alexfiles &
[1] 18839
[2] 20191
$
```

The portion of the command line up to the first & is one job. It consists of two processes (running **find** and **wc**) connected by a pipe. The second job is a single process, running **grep**. Both jobs have been put into the background by the trailing & characters, so the Korn Shell does not wait for them to complete before it gives you another prompt. Before the prompt, the shell displays two pieces of information about each background job: its job number in square brackets and its process ID. Job control under the Korn Shell is identical to that of the C Shell, refer to page 350 for more information on Job control.

The Korn Shell's **kill** command has the same purpose as the Bourne Shell's: to send a signal to a process, or to a job. You can use the usual Bourne Shell syntax:

kill –n PID

where **n** is the signal number, and **PID** is the process ID of the process that gets the signal.

The Korn Shell also supports named signals. To send a signal to a job, you can refer to the signal by name.

```
$ kill -QUIT %1
```

This command sends the QUIT signal to job number 1. Unfortunately, the names of supported signals vary from system to system, which makes portable use of **kill** difficult. (See page 331 for a table of commonly used signal numbers.) The following signals are supported on most UNIX systems:

Signal	Description
INT	The Interrupt signal. You send the foreground job an INT signal when you type your interrupt character.
QUIT	The Quit signal.
TERM	The Terminate signal. This is the default signal sent by **kill** if you do not specify a signal.
KILL	The Kill signal.
HUP	The Hangup signal.

Generally, any of these will terminate a process. A program that is interrupted often has things in an unpredictable state: temporary files may be open, or permissions may be changed. A well-written application will trap, or detect, the arrival of signals and clean up before exiting. Most carefully written applications will trap the INT, QUIT, and TERM signals. Try one of these first, typically INT. Because an application can be written to ignore these signals, you may need to use KILL. The KILL signal cannot be trapped or ignored; it is a "sure kill."

Other Built-in Commands

The **whence** command tells you the absolute pathname of a utility:

```
$ whence grep
/bin/grep
```

In this form, **whence** will only report the pathnames of utilities that actually have a pathname; it will not tell you about aliases, functions, or built-ins. With the –v option, **whence** will tell you the type of any command or reserved word that you can use in the Korn Shell:

```
$ whence pwd
pwd
$ whence -v pwd
pwd is a shell built-in
$ whence -v func
func is a function
$ whence -v if
if is a keyword
```

The command **type** is a predefined alias for **whence –v**.

You can use the **trap** command to cause a shell script to execute a command when it receives an error or signal or upon exiting from a function or script. The syntax of **trap** is similar to the Bourne Shell's **trap** (page 330), but you can use signal names rather than numbers:

trap ['command'] [event]

You should quote the command, because it must be passed to **trap** as a single argument. The **event** arguments are either names of signals (e.g., INT, TERM) or one of the following:

DEBUG

This event occurs after every simple command. Thus the command

```
trap 'echo $PWD >> /tmp/dir_trace' DEBUG
```

will cause your script to append its current directory pathname to the file **/tmp/dir_trace** after each simple command.

ERR

This event occurs whenever a command completes with nonzero exit status. The command

```
trap 'cleanup ; exit 1' ERR
```

will cause your script to execute **cleanup** (typically a user-defined function) and then exit the script with status 1.

EXIT

> This event occurs whenever the script exits. Prior to Korn Shell 93, functions can have their own traps, and the EXIT event for a function occurs when the function returns. This provision violates the requirements of the POSIX.2 Standard (page 753), and Korn Shell 93 has changed the semantics as follows. For functions defined with the **funcname()** notation, the POSIX.2 **trap** semantics will prevail. Exiting such a function will not cause an EXIT event. For functions defined with the **function** keyword, the historical **trap** semantics will prevail.

0

> The same as EXIT.

If action is a null string, then the corresponding signal or event is ignored. Remember, you cannot ignore or set a trap for the KILL signal. Any attempt to do so is itself ignored. If you have set the action for a signal or event using **trap** and you want to reset it to its default behavior, you can do so by using the string '–' (a hyphen) as the action. The **trap** command by itself lists all current traps in a form that can be saved and reread later by the shell.

Command Line Editing

The Korn Shell allows you to edit the current command line. If you make a mistake, you do not need to back up to the point of the mistake and reenter the command from there or press the line kill key and start over. You can use one of the built-in editors to edit the command line. You can also access and edit previous command lines stored in your history file (page 426).

The Korn Shell provides two built-in editors, one similar to **vi** (Chapter 8), and the other similar to **emacs** (Chapter 9). Although **emacs** is not a standard editor and is not usually provided as part of a UNIX system, it is widely available. Depending on how the Korn Shell is set up on your system, you may be able to use one, both, or neither of the editors.

Use the following **set** command to set up your environment so that you can use the built-in **vi** editor.

```
9 $ set -o vi
```

Alternatively, you can set the **VISUAL** or the **EDITOR** variable to the pathname of **vi**. If you set both variables, **VISUAL** will take precedence over **EDITOR**.

```
10 $ VISUAL=/usr/bin/vi
11 $ EDITOR=/usr/bin/vi
```

Use one of the following command lines if you want to use the **emacs** editor for command-line editing.

```
12 $ set -o emacs
13 $ VISUAL=/usr/local/bin/emacs
14 $ EDITOR=/usr/local/bin/emacs
```

The pathname describing the location of **emacs** varies from system to system. However, this does not matter; you can set the **VISUAL** or **EDITOR** variable to any pathname that ends in either **vi** or **emacs**. The Korn Shell takes the last component as an indication of the built-in editor that you want to use, and does not actually look in that path for an editor. If you set **VISUAL** or **EDITOR** to a pathname that ends in **gmacs**, then the Korn Shell uses the **emacs** built-in editor with very slightly different semantics, based on the Gnu version of **emacs**. Korn Shell 93 uses the **gmacs** version only. Although you do not have to set these variables to complete pathnames, it is a good idea to do so as other utilities may make use of these variables and may require a full pathname.

Using the Built-in vi Editor

When you are entering Korn Shell commands with **vi** as your command-line editor, you will be in Input Mode while you type commands. This is the opposite of **vi**'s initial mode when you start to edit a file. The shell's behavior is no different from what occurs when you enter commands with the Bourne Shell. When you press (RETURN) to end a command line, the Korn Shell executes the command as usual.

If you discover an error before you press (RETURN), you can press (ESCAPE) to enter Command Mode. You can then use many **vi** commands to edit the command line. It is as though you have a one-line window to edit a one-line file. You can use **vi** cursor positioning commands, such as **h** and **l**, or **w** and **b**, optionally preceded by a repeat factor (page 210). However, you cannot use the arrow keys to position the cursor. And you cannot use the Search Forward (/) or Search Backward commands (?), as they have other meanings (page 426). You can modify the command line using **vi** Command Mode editing commands such as **x** (delete character), **r** (replace character), ~ (change case), and . (repeat last change). To return to Input Mode, use an Insert (**i**, **I**), Append (**a**, **A**), Replace command (**R**), or Change (**c**, **C**). You do not have to return to Input Mode to run the command; just press (RETURN), even if you are in the middle of the command line.

If you want to edit the command line using the full power of **vi**, you can press (ESCAPE) to enter Command Mode and type **v**. The Korn Shell will then call the *real* **vi** editor (not the Korn Shell's built-in **vi**) with a file consisting of a single line, the command line in its current state. When you leave **vi**, the Korn Shell will execute the command or commands you edited. You can create a multiline sequence of commands in this manner.

Pathname Operations

In Command Mode you can also use several commands that are not included in the **vi** editor. These commands manipulate filenames and are called *Pathname Listing, Pathname Completion,* and *Pathname Expansion.*

Pathname Listing

While the cursor is on a word, enter Command Mode (if you are not already in it) and type an equal sign (=). The built-in **vi** editor will respond by listing all the pathnames that would match the current word if an asterisk were appended to it. For example, suppose that the directory **films** contains the files **casablanca**, **city_lights**, **dark_passage**, **dark_victory**, and **modern_times**. You want to use **cat** to display one of the files, and you type

```
11 $ cat films/dar
```

At this point (before you have pressed (RETURN)) you realize that you are not sure what the full name of the file is. If you press (ESCAPE) and then =, the Korn Shell's built-in **vi** editor will list the files and then re-echo the partial command, including the prompt, like this:

```
1) dark_passage
2) dark_victory
11 $ cat films/dar
```

The cursor will be on the letter **r**, where you left it, and you will be in Command Mode. To finish typing a pathname, you must first type **a** to append.

Pathname Completion

This facility allows you to type a portion of a pathname and have the built-in **vi** editor supply the rest. You invoke Pathname Completion by pressing (ESCAPE) followed by a backslash (\). If the portion of the pathname that you have typed so far is sufficient to determine the entire pathname uniquely, then that pathname is displayed. If more than one pathname would match, then the built-in **vi** completes the pathname up to the point where there are choices, and leaves you in Input Mode to type more. If you enter

```
12 $ cat films/dar
```

and, at this point, press (ESCAPE)\ the Korn Shell will extend the command line like this:

```
12 $ cat films/dark_
```

because every file in films that starts with **dar** has **k_** as the next characters. You will be left in Input Mode, with the cursor just past the _ character. If you add enough information to distinguish between the two possible files, you can invoke Pathname Completion again. Suppose that you now enter **p** and then press (ESCAPE)\. The Korn Shell will complete the command line:

```
12 $ cat films/dark_passage
```

Since there is no further ambiguity, the shell appends a space and leaves you in Input Mode to finish typing the command line.

Pathname Expansion

This facility is like an interactive version of ordinary wildcard expansion. You invoke Pathname Expansion by pressing (ESCAPE) followed by an asterisk (*), which causes the word under the cursor to be replaced by all pathnames that would be matched by that word if it were followed by an asterisk. If you enter

12 $ `cat films/dar`

and then press (ESCAPE)*, the command line is expanded to

12 $ `cat films/dark_passage films/dark_victory`

After it fills in the filenames, the built-in **vi** editor leaves you in Input Mode, with the cursor past the last character in the line. At this point you can make any corrections that you like to the line (using the other commands of built-in **vi**) and press (RETURN) to execute the command. If no filenames match, the built-in **vi** editor will cause your terminal to beep. (Some terminals flash rather than beep.)

The built-in **vi** editor commands are listed on page 451.

CAUTION

Remember that pressing (RETURN) causes the Korn Shell to execute the command regardless of whether you are in Command Mode or Input Mode and regardless of where the cursor is on the command line. At the next prompt, you will be back in Input Mode.

Using the Built-in emacs Editor

The **emacs** editor differs from **vi** in that it is modeless. Thus you do not move back and forth between Command Mode and Input Mode, as in **vi**. Like **vi**, the built-in **emacs** editor provides commands for moving around in the command line and for modifying part or all of the text. It also supports Pathname Listing, Pathname Completion, and Pathname Expansion.

In **emacs**, most commands are control characters. This allows **emacs** to distinguish between input and commands, and thus to dispense with modes. The (ESCAPE) key also plays a special role in **emacs**, as do the erase and kill characters (page 227).

The commands in the Korn Shell's built-in **emacs** editor differ in a few cases from the commands in the stand-alone **emacs** editor. This discussion covers only the Korn Shell built-in **emacs**.

In **emacs**, you perform cursor movement using both (CONTROL) and (ESCAPE) commands. To move the cursor one character backward in the command line, type (CONTROL)-**B**. Typing (CONTROL)-**F** moves it one character forward (page 222). As with **vi**, it is possible to precede these movements with counts. However, to use a count you must first press (ESCAPE); otherwise the numbers you type will be entered on the command line.

Like **vi**, **emacs** also provides word motions and line motions. To move backward or forward one word in the command line, type (ESCAPE) **b** or (ESCAPE) **f** (page 222). To move several words, use a count by pressing (ESCAPE) followed by the number. You can get to the beginning of the line by pressing (CONTROL)-**A**, to the end by pressing (CONTROL)-**E**, and to the next instance of the character **c** by pressing (CONTROL)-**]** followed by **c**.

You can add text to the command line by just moving the cursor to the correct place and typing the desired text. To delete text, move the cursor just to the right of the characters that you want to delete, and then press the Erase character once for each character that you want to delete.

> **CAUTION**
>
> If you want to delete the character directly under the cursor, press (CONTROL)–**D**. If you enter (CONTROL)–**D** on an empty line or at the beginning of the line, it may terminate your shell session.

If you want to delete the entire command line, type the line kill character. This has the usual effect, except that you can type it while the cursor is anywhere in the command line. If you want to delete from the cursor to the end of the line, use (CONTROL)-**K**.

The built-in **emacs** editor allows you to mark positions in the line and then refer to the mark with other commands. You can mark the cursor position by typing (ESCAPE) followed by (SPACE). If a position has been marked, then typing (CONTROL)-**W** will delete from the mark to the current cursor position (forward or backward). The character at the current cursor position is not deleted.

The built-in **emacs** editor commands are listed on page 453.

Pathname Listing, Completion, and Expansion using the built-in **emacs** editor are performed almost the same as in **vi**. The sequence (ESCAPE) = in **emacs** does Pathname Listing just as it does in **vi**. Pathname Expansion is also the same in both editors: the (ESCAPE) ∗ sequence works in **emacs** just as in **vi**. Pathname Completion is different: you request it by typing two successive (ESCAPE) characters, rather than (ESCAPE) \.

History

The Korn Shell keeps a history of recently executed commands in a file, which means that the history can persist from one shell session to the next. You can select, edit, and reexecute any command in the history list from the current or a previous login session. A significant advantage of Korn Shell history over C Shell history is that the Korn Shell remembers multiline commands in their entirety, and allows you to edit them. The C Shell only remembers the first line of multiline commands.

If it is set, the **HISTSIZE** variable determines the number of commands that are saved in the history list. If it is not set, 128 commands are saved. The **HISTFILE** variable identifies the file the list is stored in. If **HISTFILE** is not set, the history file will be kept in a file named **.sh_history** in your home directory.

Some versions of the Korn Shell keep incrementing the event number from one login session to the next. Consequently, the event numbers eventually become very large. To cause the history mechanism to start over with number 1, remove the history file. The next time you log in, the first prompt will be event 1, and events from previous sessions will not be available.

To access and edit any of the commands in the history file, you can use either the built-in **vi** editor, the built-in **emacs** editor, or the built-in command **fc**.

Using the Built-in vi Editor on Previous Commands

When you are using the built-in **vi** editor and are in Command Mode, you can access previous commands using several **vi** commands that move the cursor up and down. It is as if you are using **vi** to edit a copy of the history file, with a screen that has only one line on it. If you use the **k** command to move up one line, you will access the previous command. Then, if you use the **j** command to move down one line, you will be back to the original command.

You can search through the history list using **vi**'s Search Forward and Search Backward commands to find the most recent command that contains a specific string of text. Press the forward slash (/) key followed by a Search String to find the most recent command containing a string that matches the Search String. Use a question mark (?) in place of the forward slash to access the next command containing the string. The forward slash and question mark search in the opposite directions of the corresponding commands in the **vi** utility. (Or you can think of the history file as being built and stored upside down, with the most recent commands at the top.) Also, unlike the Search Strings the **vi** utility uses, these Search Strings cannot contain regular expressions.

To access an event in the history list by event number, enter the number followed by a **G**. Using **G** without a number will access the oldest command available in the history list. This is the opposite of what **G** does in the **vi** utility.

When you initially move to the command, you are in Command Mode, not Input Mode. Once the command you want to reexecute is on the command line, you can edit it as you like or press (RETURN) to execute it.

Using the fc Command

The built-in command **fc** (*fix* command) enables you to display the history file as well as to edit and reexecute previous commands. It provides many of the same capabilities as the built-in editors.

Viewing the History List

When called with the –l option, **fc** displays commands from the history file on the standard output. By default, **fc** –l lists the 16 most recent commands in a numbered list.

```
28 $ fc -l
13 vi memo.0490
14 lpr memo.0490
15 mv memo.0490 memo.041190
16 cd
17 view calendar
18 cd correspondence
19 vi letter.adams01
```

```
20 spell letter.adams01
21 nroff letter.adams01 > adams.out
22 more adams.out
23 lpr adams.out
24 rm adams.out
25 cd ../memos
26 ls
27 rm *0486
28 fc -l
```

Because the Korn Shell sets up an alias, **history**, for the **fc –l** command, you can also use the **history** command to print the history list.

The **fc** command can take one or two arguments when it is used with the –l option. The arguments specify a part of the history list to be displayed. The format of this command is shown below.

fc –l **first** [**last**]

The **fc** command lists commands beginning with the most recent event that matches the first argument. The argument can be either the number of the event, the first few characters of the command line, or a negative number (which is taken to be the **n**th previous command). The next command displays the history list beginning with event 17.

```
29 $ fc -l 17
17 view calendar
18 cd correspondence
19 vi letter.adams01
20 spell letter.adams01
21 nroff letter.adams01 > adams.out
22 more adams.out
23 lpr adams.out
24 rm adams.out
25 cd ../memos
26 ls
27 rm *0486
28 fc -l
29 fc -l 17
```

If you give **fc** a second argument, it prints out all commands from the most recent event that matches the first argument to the most recent event that matches the second. The following command lists the most recent event that began with the string view through the most recent command line that began with the letters sp:

```
30 $ fc -l view sp
17 view calendar
18 cd correspondence
19 vi letter.adams01
20 spell letter.adams01
```

To list a single command from the history file, use the same identifier for the first and second arguments. The following command lists event 17:

```
31 $ fc -l 17 17
17 view calendar
```

In Korn Shell 93, the **fc** command has been renamed **hist**. You can still use **fc**, however, because it is an alias for **hist**.

Editing and Reexecuting Previous Commands

You can use **fc** to edit and reexecute previous commands.

fc [–e **editor**] [**first** [**last**]]

When you call **fc** with the –e option followed by the name of an editor, **fc** will call up the editor with commands in the Work Buffer. Without first and last, **fc** defaults to the most recent command. The next example invokes the **vi** editor to edit the most recent command:

```
32 $ fc -e vi
```

The **fc** command does not use the Korn Shell's built-in **vi** editor. It uses the stand alone **vi** utility. If you set the **FCEDIT** variable, you do not need to use the –e option to specify an editor on the command line.

```
33 $ FCEDIT=/usr/bin/vi
34 $ export FCEDIT
35 $ fc
```

In Korn Shell 93, the variable **HISTEDIT** is used in place of **FCEDIT**. More precisely, the variable expression ${HISTEDIT:–$FCEDIT} is used. This stands for the value of **HISTEDIT** if it is set, and the value of **FCEDIT** otherwise.

If you call **fc** with a single argument, it will invoke the editor to allow you to work on the specified command. The next example starts **vi** with command 21 in the Work Buffer. When you exit from **vi**, the Korn Shell automatically executes the command.

```
36 $ fc 21
```

Again, you can identify commands with numbers or by specifying the first few characters of the command name. The next example calls the editor to work on the most recent event that begins with the letters vi through event number 22:

```
37 $ fc vi 22
```

When you use the editor to change a series of commands, or when you call the editor to work on one command and then add other commands, the Korn Shell treats the entire set of commands as one event. That is, if you edit a series of commands (as shown above) and execute them, they will be listed as a single new event in the history list.

Reexecuting Previous Commands Without Calling the Editor

You can reexecute previous commands without going into the editor. If you call **fc** with – as the name of the editor, it skips the editing phase and reexecutes the command. The following example reexecutes event 23:

```
38 $ fc -e - 23
lpr adams.out
```

The Korn Shell sets up an alias, **r**, that you can use instead of the above command. The following example has the same effect as the one above:

```
39 $ r 23
lpr adams.out
```

When you use either one of the two previous examples, you can tell **fc** to substitute one string for another. The next example substitutes the string john for the string adams in event 20:

```
40 $ r adams=john 20
spell letter.john01
```

You can use a positive or negative number or a string as an event identifier. Without the event identifier, **r** performs the substitution on the previous event.

In Korn Shell 93, the new option –s is equivalent to –e –, which is considered obsolete (but still supported).

Command Processing

The Korn Shell always reads at least one line before processing a command. Some of the Korn Shell's built-in commands, such as If and Case, span multiple lines. Such commands are referred to as *compound* or *multiline* commands. When the Korn Shell recognizes a compound command, it will read the entire command before processing it. This can include many lines. In interactive sessions, the Korn Shell will prompt you with the secondary prompt, **$PS2**, after you have typed the first line of a multiline command until it recognizes the command end. The default value for **PS2** is > , as in the Bourne Shell.

The basic steps that the Korn Shell carries out to process a command are these:

- token splitting: dividing the stream of input characters into symbols, and recognizing of I/O redirection operators

- alias substitution: recognizing when the first token of the command is an alias, and expanding it

- tilde substitution: replacing the special symbols that start with ~ by their expanded values

- command substitution: evaluating commands inside backquotes (` `) or command substitution brackets (**$()**) and replacing them by their standard output

- parameter expansion: expansion of all the shell variable expressions that are not protected by quoting

- wildcard expansion: replacing wildcarded pathnames by their expanded lists of pathnames

- quote processing: removal of most quotes from the command line

- I/O redirection: redirection of standard input, standard output, standard error or other file descriptors

- execution of the command

OPTIONAL Continued

The order in which these steps are carried out affects the meaning of the commands that you type. For example, suppose that you set a variable to a value that looks like the instruction for output redirection:

$ SENDIT="> /tmp/saveit"

Then you type a command, using the variable's value to do the redirection:

$ date $SENDIT

You might think that the Korn Shell will expand this line to

date > /tmp/saveit

and execute the **date** command, storing the output in **/tmp/saveit**. But this will not work. As the list above indicates, the Korn Shell recognizes input and output redirection before it tries to evaluate variables. What happens instead is that the **date** command executes with an argument of **$SENDIT**, which in this case will cause it to return an error.

Following is a more detailed description of each of these steps.

Token Splitting

The Korn Shell first processes a command by splitting it into tokens (separate words or symbols). At this point the Korn Shell can determine whether the command is simple or compound, and recognizes I/O re-direction operators, although it does not yet perform the redirection. Korn Shell I/O redirection includes the familiar Bourne Shell operators for standard input (<), standard output (>), appending standard output (>>), standard error (2>), pipes (|), and here documents (<<). In addition, the Korn Shell can duplicate or redirect any file descriptor, if you precede the redirection operator with the file descriptor number. Thus the following command executes program **prog** with file descriptor 3 open for reading file **infile**, and file descriptor 4 open for writing file **outfile**:

$ prog 3< infile 4> outfile

When the Korn Shell has divided a command line into tokens, it looks at tokens starting from the left to determine what type of com-mand it is. If the first token is a left parenthesis, then the remainder of the input up to a matching right parenthesis is treated as a compound command (regardless of how many lines it spans) and executed in a subshell. If the first token is a double right parenthesis, then the input up to a matching double right parenthesis is treated as a single argu-ment to a Let command. Any other token that is not part of an I/O re-direction or the start of a built-in compound command (e.g., For, Case) is taken to be the first token of a simple command. The remainder of the input up to a simple command terminator makes up the rest of the command. The terminators are the familiar ones from the Bourne Shell (semicolon, pipe symbol, (NEWLINE), &&, ||) plus the special token |&. This latter token creates a coprocess. The notion of a coprocess, which does not exist in either the Bourne or C shells, is discussed on page 434.

The command separators && and || provide a convenient form of conditional execution. They stand for *and* and *or* respectively. You can combine commands into command lists separated by the && and || operators.

The && separator causes the Korn Shell to test the exit status of the command preceding it. If the command succeeded, then the next command is executed; otherwise it is skipped. You can use this construct to conditionally execute commands:

```
$ mkdir backup && cp -r source backup
```

This creates the directory **backup**. If the **mkdir** succeeds, then the contents of directory **source** are copied recursively to **backup**.

The || separator also causes the Korn Shell to test the exit status of the first command, but has the opposite effect: the remaining command(s) are executed only if the first one failed (i.e., exited with non-zero status):

```
$ mkdir backup || echo "mkdir of backup failed" >> /tmp/log
```

The exit status of a command list is the exit status of the last command executed. You can group lists with parentheses. For example, you could combine the previous two examples:

```
$ (mkdir backup && cp -r source backup) || echo "mkdir of backup \
failed" >> /tmp/log
```

In the absence of parentheses, && and || have equal precedence and are grouped left to right. This means that the command line

```
$ true || false && false
```

is treated as equivalent to

```
$ (true || false) && false
```

and has exit status 1, while the command line

```
$ false && false || true
```

is treated equivalently to

```
$ (false && false) || true
```

and has exit status 0. You can use pipes anywhere in a list that you can use simple commands, and the pipe symbol has highest precedence of all. This means that the command line

```
$ cmd1 | cmd2 || cmd3 | cmd4 && cmd5 | cmd6
```

is interpreted as if you had typed

```
$ (cmd1 | cmd2) || ( (cmd3 | cmd4) && (cmd5 | cmd6) )
```

Do not rely on the precedence rules if you have to use such complex commands. Rather, use parentheses to indicate the way you want the shell to group the commands.

You can put variable assignments on a command line. These assignments apply to the command only. The command

```
$ TEMPDIR=~/temp my_script
```

runs **my_script** with the value of **TEMPDIR** set to **~/temp**. The **TEMP-DIR** variable is not set, or if already set is not changed, except for the execution of the command. In the Bourne Shell, you can place these assignments anywhere on the command line, not just at the beginning. The Korn Shell does not normally allow this placement.

Alias Substitution

The Korn Shell next processes all of the command line except for I/O redirection and variable assignments by going through a series of expansions. The first expansion is alias substitution, in which the shell determines whether or not the first token is an alias. The Korn Shell will not replace an alias while processing the same alias. This prevents infinite recursion in handling an alias such as

```
$ alias ls='ls -F'
```

Tilde Substitution

Next, the Korn Shell performs tilde substitution. The Korn Shell provides the tilde expansion feature of the C Shell, but with some added capabilities. As with the C Shell, you can use the tilde (~) by itself on the command line to represent your home directory. Also, you can use ~ followed by a user's login name to represent the home directory of that user. The additional capabilities are provided by ~+ and ~~, which are synonyms for **$PWD** and **$OLDPWD** respectively. Any other token that starts with a tilde is left unchanged.

Command Substitution

After tilde substitution, the Korn Shell performs command substitution. This is familiar from the Bourne Shell. A string within backquotes is treated as a command, which is executed within a subshell, and the text within and including the backquotes is replaced by the standard output of the command. Although the Korn Shell supports this syntax, it is obsolete. The Korn Shell also provides a new syntax: **$(command)**.

```
$ ls -l $(find . -name README -print)
```

This command uses **find** to find files under the current directory with the name **README**. The list of such files is the standard output of **find**, and becomes the list of arguments to **ls**. It is equivalent to

```
$ ls -l `find . -name README -print`
```

One advantage of the new syntax is that it avoids the rather arcane rules for token handling, quote handling, and escaped backquotes within the old syntax. Another advantage of the new syntax is that it can be nested, where the old syntax cannot. For example, you can do a long listing of all the **README** files whose size exceeds the size of **./README** with the following command:

```
$ ls -l $(find . -name README -size +$(echo $(cat ./README | wc -c)c ) -print )
```

Try giving this command after **set –x** to see how it is expanded. If there is no **README** file, you will just get the output of **ls –l**. The symbols $((constitute a separate token; they introduce an arithmetic expression, not a command substitution. Thus if you want to use a parenthesized sub-shell within $(), you must have a space between the $(and the next (.

Parameter Expansion

After the Korn Shell has performed command substitutions in the command line, it performs all of the parameter expansions that are discussed in the section titled "Expanding Shell Variables" (page 399). Variables are not expanded if they are enclosed within single quotation marks. If they are enclosed in double quotation marks, they are expanded, but the resulting text is not subject to pathname wildcard expansion. At this point the command consists of a sequence of words, which are parts of the command line separated by the field separators in the **IFS** variable. Variables that were expanded within double quotation marks are not split into words. The following example illustrates this distinction:

```
$ sillyarg=xxx%yyy
$ IFS="% "
$ set $sillyarg "$sillyarg"
$ echo "$1"
xxx
$ echo "$2"
yyy
$ echo "$3"
xxx%yyy
```

The second line tells the Korn Shell that the characters (SPACE) and % should be treated as field separators. The next line sets the positional parameters. The expression **$sillyarg** is expanded as two arguments, xxx and yyy, with the embedded % treated as a field separator. The expression **"$sillyarg"** is expanded as a single argument, and its embedded % is treated as part of the argument's value.

Wildcard Expansion

After variables are expanded and split into words where necessary, the wildcard characters in each word are expanded if you have not used the **noglob** option to disable wildcard expansion. These characters are the same as in the Bourne Shell: ?, * and ranges in []. As in the Bourne Shell, path components that start with a period must be matched explicitly or specified by an option such as **ls –a**. In Korn Shell 93, you can change the character or characters that have to be matched explicitly and are displayed with the **–a** option to **ls**. The variable **FIGNORE** defines a regular expression that specifies all the pathnames that must be matched explicitly. For example, if you set **FIGNORE** to [a-z]q, then **ls** would not display filenames beginning with a lowercase letter followed by a q, unless you explicitly specified that a filename begin with these letters (**ls** [a–z]q*) or used the **–a** option.

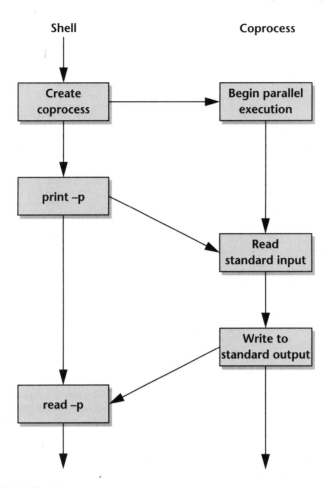

Figure 12-2   The Coprocess

Processing Quotation Marks

With two exceptions, the Korn Shell next removes all single and double quotation marks. Escaped quotes and quotes that are the result of expanding variables are not removed. These remain as part of the command line.

I/O Redirection and the Coprocess

Most typed commands are executed in a new process, although this is not true of the Korn Shell's built-in commands. When an ordinary command is executed, any I/O redirection is performed on the new process before the command starts to run. If I/O redirection is applied to a built-in command, the Korn Shell arranges that the redirection only applies to that command, even though it executes in the same process as the shell. Shell functions also execute in the current process, although they have private sets of positional parameters, traps, and options. For example, the command **set –x** within a function will not turn on the **xtrace** option for the parent shell.

The Korn Shell supports a feature known as *the coprocess*, which allows you to start a process that runs in the background and communicates directly with its parent shell (Figure 12-2). You invoke a process as the coprocess by ending its command line with the token |&.

The command must be a filter (reads from standard input and writes to standard output) and it must flush its output whenever it has accumulated a line, rather than saving several lines for output at once. When the command is invoked as the coprocess, it is connected via a two-way pipe to the current shell. You can read its standard output by using the –p option to the Korn Shell's **read** command. You can write to the coprocess's standard input by using the –p option with the **print** command. These commands are described in the section on "Input and Output," page 412.

These requirements limit the usefulness of the coprocess. It serves best as a tool to put a new interface on an interactive program. You can, however, easily construct scripts with the required properties:

```
$ cat to_upper
while read arg ; do
    echo "$arg" | tr '[a-z]' '[A-Z]'
done
```

The UNIX **tr** utility does not flush its output after each line, but this "wrapper" script does. For each line read, it writes to standard output the line translated to uppercase. Following is a script that invokes **to_upper** as the coprocess:

```
$ cat coproc_script
to_upper |&
line_count=0
while read pathname ; do
    line_count=$(( $line_count + 1 ))
    print -p "$pathname"
    read -p newpath
    print $line_count: "$newpath" | tr '/' '\\'
done
$ echo $PWD
/home/alex/literature
$ echo $PWD | coproc_script
1: \HOME\ALEX\LITERATURE
```

The coprocess is most useful when it is a frequently used tool and the invoking script transforms the tool's input or output.

Korn Shell Programs

As an interactive shell, the Korn Shell's great advantages lie in its aliasing capacity and its command line and history editing mechanisms. As a programming language, it has many features, some of which are not available in other shells:

- powerful control flow constructs: For, If, While, Case, Select and Until

- recursive functions

- local variables

- built-in integer arithmetic and integer data types

- extended trap handling

- input (**read**) and Output (**print**) facilities

- file control and I/O redirection for any file descriptor, including file descriptor duplication

- array variables and string manipulation operators

Earlier sections of this chapter discussed most of these features, many of which are useful both interactively and for shell programming. This section develops a complete shell program to show you how to combine some of these features effectively.

Program Structures

The structures that the Korn Shell provides are not a random assortment. They have been carefully chosen to provide most of the structural features that you will find in other procedural languages such as C or Pascal. A procedural language must provide you with these capabilities:

- The ability to declare, assign, and manipulate variables and constant data. The Korn Shell provides string variables, together with powerful string operations, and integer variables, with a complete set of arithmetic operations.

- The ability to break large problems into small ones by creating subprograms. The Korn Shell allows you to create functions and to call scripts from other scripts. Korn Shell functions can be called recursively; that is, a Korn Shell function can call itself. You may not need to use recursion often, but occasionally it allows you to solve apparently difficult problems with ease.

- The ability to execute statements conditionally, using statements like the Korn Shell's If.

- The ability to execute statements iteratively, using statements like While and For.

- The ability to transfer data to and from the program, communicating both with data files and with users.

Programming languages implement these capabilities in different ways, but with the same ideas in mind. When you want to solve a problem using a program, you must first figure out a procedure that will lead you to a solution. Such a procedure is called an *algorithm*. Typically, you can implement the same algorithm in roughly the same way in different programming languages, and you will find yourself using the same kinds of constructs in each language. Earlier in this chapter you saw examples of the use of all the Korn

Shell programming structures except recursion. An example of a recursive Korn Shell function that will prove useful is shown in the next section.

Recursion

A recursive construct is one that is defined in terms of itself. This may seem circular, but need not be. To avoid circularity, a recursive definition must have a special case that is not self-referential. Recursive ideas occur in every-day life. For example, you can define an ancestor as either your mother, or your father, or one of their ancestors. This definition is not circular; it specifies unambiguously who your ancestors are (your mother or your father or your mother's mother or father or your father's mother or father, etc.).

A number of UNIX system utilities can operate recursively. Look at the –R option to the **chmod** and **chown** utilities in Part II for an example.

Solve the following problem using a recursive shell function:

> *Write a shell function **makepath** that, given a pathname, creates all the components in that pathname as directories. For example, the command **makepath a/b/c/d** should create directories a, a/b, a/b/c, and a/b/c/d.*

(The **mkdir** utility on many UNIX systems supports a –p option that does exactly this. Solve the problem without using **mkdir –p**.)

One algorithm for a recursive solution is this:

- Examine this path argument. If it is a null string, or if it names an already existing directory, do nothing and return.

- If it is a simple path component, create it (using **mkdir**) and return.

- Otherwise, call **makepath** using the path prefix of the original argu-ment. This will (eventually) create all the directories up to the last component, which you can then create with **mkdir**.

In general, a recursive function must invoke itself with a simpler version of the problem than it was given, until finally it gets called with a simple case that does not need to call itself.

Here is one possible solution based on this algorithm:

```
makepath()
{
        if [[ ${#1} -eq 0 || -d $1 ]]
        then
                return 0         # Do nothing
        fi
        # Check if arg is a simple path component:
        if [[ "${1%/*}" = "$1" ]]
        then
                mkdir $1
                return $?
        fi
        makepath ${1%/*} || return 1
        mkdir $1
        return $?
}
```

In the test for a simple component (If statement, eighth line), the left expression is the argument after the shortest suffix that starts with a / character has been stripped away (page 398). If there is no such character (for example, if $1 is alex) then nothing gets stripped off, and the two sides are equal. Suppose the argument is a simple filename preceded by a slash, such as /usr. In that case, the expression ${1%/*} evaluates to a null string. To make the function work in this case, you must take two precautions: put the left expression within quotation marks as shown, and ensure that your recursive function behaves sensibly when passed a null string as an argument. In general, good programs are robust; they are prepared for borderline, invalid, or meaningless input and behave appropriately.

By putting a **set –x** command at the first line of the function, you can turn on tracing and watch the recursion work.

```
$ makepath a/b/c
+ [[ 5 -eq 0 ]]
+ [[ -d a/b/c ]]
+ [[ a/b = a/b/c ]]
+ makepath a/b
+ [[ 3 -eq 0 ]]
+ [[ -d a/b ]]
+ [[ a = a/b ]]
+ makepath a
+ [[ 1 -eq 0 ]]
+ [[ -d a ]]
+ [[ a = a ]]
+ mkdir a
+ return 0
+ mkdir a/b
+ return 0
+ mkdir a/b/c
+ return 0
```

You can see the function work its way down the recursive path and back up again. It is instructive to invoke **makepath** with an invalid path, and see what happens. The example below shows what happens when you try to create the path **/a/b/c**, which requires that you create directory **a** in the root directory. Unless you have privileges, you are not permitted to do that.

```
$ makepath /a/b/c
+ [[ 6 -eq 0 ]]
+ [[ -d /a/b/c ]]
+ [[ /a/b = /a/b/c ]]
+ makepath /a/b
+ [[ 4 -eq 0 ]]
+ [[ -d /a/b ]]
+ [[ /a = /a/b ]]
+ makepath /a
+ [[ 2 -eq 0 ]]
+ [[ -d /a ]]
+ [[ = /a ]]
+ makepath
```

```
+ [[ 0 -eq 0 ]]
+ return 0
+ mkdir /a
mkdir: Cannot make directory "/a"; Permission denied
(error 13)
+ return 1
+ return 1
+ return 1
```

The recursion stops only when **makepath** is passed a null argument and the error return is passed all the way back, so the original **makepath** exits with nonzero status.

CAUTION

The example has glossed over a potential problem that you may encounter when you use recursive functions. The problem is due to the fact that, by default, Korn Shell variables are global. During the execution of a recursive function, many separate instances of that function may be simultaneously active. All but one of them are waiting for their "child" invocation to complete. If a recursive Korn Shell function uses variables, then unless you make the variables local, these functions will all share a single copy of each variable. This can give rise to side effects that are rarely what you want. As a rule, you should use **typeset** (page 391) to make all the variables of recursive functions local.

A Programming Problem: makesccs

This section combines some of the Korn Shell programming constructs into a complete program. The example uses **admin**, one of the UNIX system's Source Code Control System (SCCS) commands. If you are not familiar with SCCS, refer to page 475 for a description. The example also makes use of **find** (page 600).

The specification for the program follows.

> *Write a program, **makesccs**, that takes two directory names as arguments, **source** and **target**. The program should create a copy of the hierarchy rooted at **source** in **target**, except that each regular file under **source** should be checked in to a corresponding SCCS file under **target** using the **admin** command. If **target** does not exist, it should be created. The program should ensure that the pathname **source** is not a prefix of the pathname **target**, and vice versa. It should skip any file in **source** that is not a directory or regular file (such as a FIFO or socket).*

The command

```
makesccs srcdir sccsdir
```

should create a hierarchy under **sccsdir** identical to the hierarchy under **srcdir**, except that if (for example) **srcdir/functions/func1.sh** is a regular file, then the command should create **sccsdir/functions/s.func1.sh**.

There are as many ways to solve a problem like this as there are programmers, so your **makesccs** program probably will not look like the one developed in this section.

Here is an algorithm for solving the problem:

- Check the command line for the correct number and type of arguments. If invalid, say so and exit.

- Traverse the source tree, using the **find** command to produce pathnames. For each pathname that **find** returns:

  —If the pathname refers to a directory, then make the corresponding path under the target.

  —If the pathname refers to a regular file, then

    —Construct the name of the SCCS file that would correspond to it.

    —Create that SCCS file using admin.

  —If the pathname refers to any other type of file, then write a message to a report file and skip the file.

- At each stage, if an error occurs, write an appropriate message to an error file.

A few functions to manipulate pathnames will be useful in solving the problem. The UNIX utility **dirname**, given a pathname, writes the path prefix to standard output. Such a utility is easily implemented as a Korn Shell function, and this is left to you as an exercise. The **basename** utility does the opposite: **basename path** writes the last component of **path** to standard output.

If you have a file whose pathname is **a/b/c/d**, you want to create the pathname **a/b/c/s.d** as the corresponding SCCS filename.

```
sccsname()
{
        _dir=$(dirname $1)
        _base=$(basename $1)
        echo $_dir/s.$_base
}
```

The **sccsname** function picks the pathname apart and glues it back together again, inserting an **s.** at the appropriate place. The answer is written to standard output to enable you to use **sccsname** inside a command substitution statement such as

```
newname=$(sccsname oldname)
```

One function needs to check the command line arguments for validity. This function should ensure that exactly two arguments have been passed, that **$1** names an existing directory, that **$2** either does not exist or names an existing directory, and that neither argument is a prefix of the other.

```
checkargs()
{
        # Check argument count
        if [[ $# != 2 ]]
        then
                print -u2 "usage: checkin source dest"
                exit 1
        fi
        # Check first argument
        if [[ ! -d $1 ]]
        then
                print -u2 "$1: Not a directory"
                exit 1
        fi
        # Check second argument
        if [[ -a $2 && ! -d $2 ]]
        then
                print -u2 "$2: Not a directory"
                exit 1
        fi
        # Check that neither argument is a prefix of the other
        if [[ $1 = $2* || $2 = $1* ]]
        then
                print -u2 "Cannot create one hierarchy below \
or above the other"
                exit 1
        fi

        return 0
}
```

You can invoke this function with a command such as **checkargs** "$@",
which passes the command line arguments directly to **checkargs**.

The main part of the program will use **find** to locate the files and directories. The command **find** $source –**print** will write the pathname of each
file in the hierarchy rooted at **$source**, one per line, to standard output. If
the script pipes this output into a loop and reads each pathname into a shell
variable, it can manipulate that variable as follows:

- Determine whether the pathname names a directory, a regular file, or
  something else.

- Construct a corresponding pathname rooted in the target directory.

- Use **admin** to create the SCCS file at that pathname.

Thus, the main body of the program can have the following structure:

find **$source** -print |
while read **pathname**
do
    commands
done

The program has to deal sensibly with errors and special conditions. It
opens two files, one to report errors and one to log the names of files that
were skipped.

Putting the various pieces together, and filling in the missing ones, here
is a complete program to solve the problem:

```
makepath()
{
        if [[ ${#1} -eq 0 || -d $1 ]]
        then
                return 0
        fi
        if [[ "${1%/*}" = "$1" ]]
        then
                mkdir $1
                return $?
        fi
        makepath ${1%/*} || return 1
        mkdir $1
        return $?
}
sccsname()
{
        _dir=$(dirname $1)
        _base=$(basename $1)
        echo $_dir/s.$_base
}
checkargs()
{
        if [[ $# != 2 ]]
        then
                print -u2 "usage: checkin <source> <dest>"
                exit 1
        fi
        if [[ ! -d $1 ]]
        then
                print -u2 "$1: Not a directory"
                exit 1
        fi
        # Check second argument
        if [[ -a $2 && ! -d $2 ]]
        then
                print -u2 "$2: Not a directory"
                exit 1
        fi
        # Check that neither argument is a prefix of the other
        if [[ $1 = $2* || $2 = $1* ]]
        then
                print -u2 "Cannot create one hierarchy below or above the other"
                exit 1
        fi
        return 0
}
ERRS=./err_file
REPORT=./report
checkargs "$@"
# Open error and report files
exec 3>$ERRS
exec 4>$REPORT
source=$1
dest=$2
find $source -print |
while read pathname
do
        target=$dest${pathname#$source}
        if [[ -d $pathname ]]
        then
                makepath $target || print -u3 "Cannot create $target"
        elif [[ -f $pathname ]]
        then
                target=$(sccsname $target)
                admin -i$pathname $target >&4 2>&3 || \
                        print -u3 "Cannot create $target"
        else
                print -u4 "$pathname not directory or regular file: skipped"
        fi
done
exec 3<&-
exec 4<&-
exit 0
```

There are a number of ways to improve this program. For example, its exit status does not always reflect what happened. The exercises at the end of this chapter ask you to modify the program in various ways.

Another Programming Problem: quiz

Here is another problem that you can solve with a Korn Shell program. This problem calls for interaction with the user, and consequently the solution will require different shell programming features.

Following is the problem statement in general terms:

> *Write a generic multiple choice quiz program. The program should get its questions from data files, and present them to the user. It should keep track of the number of correct and incorrect answers. The user must be able to exit the program at any time, with a summary of results to that point.*

The detailed design of this program, and even the detailed description of the problem, depends on a number of choices: How will the program know which subjects are available for quizzes? How will the user choose a subject? How will the program know when the quiz is over? Should the program present the same questions (for a given subject) in the same order each time, or should it scramble them?

Of course, there are many perfectly good choices that you can make in the specification of the problem. The following details make the problem specification more specific:

- Each subject will correspond to a subdirectory of a master quiz directory. This directory will be named in the environment variable **QUIZDIR**, whose default will be **/usr/lib/quiz**.

- Each question in a particular subject corresponds to a file in the subject directory.

- The representation of the question is as follows. The first line of the file is the text of the question. If it takes more than one line, the (NEWLINE) must be escaped with a backslash. (This choice makes it easy to read a single question with the built-in read command.) The second line of the file is an integer that is the number of choices. The next several lines are the choices themselves. The last line is the correct answer. For example, here is a sample question file:

```
Who discovered the principle of the lever?
4
Euclid
Archimedes
Thomas Edison
The Lever Brothers
Archimedes
```

- The program will present all the questions in a subject directory. At any point, the user can interrupt the quiz with (DELETE), at which point the program will summarize the results so far and exit. If the user does not interrupt, then when the program has asked all the questions, it will summarize the results and exit.

- The program should scramble the questions in a subject before presenting them.

Following is a top-level design for this program:

1. Initialize. This involves a number of steps, such as setting counts of the number of questions asked so far, and the number correct and wrong, to zero.
2. Present the user with a choice of subject, and get the user's response.
3. Change to the corresponding subject directory.
4. Determine the questions to be asked (i.e., the filenames in that directory). Rearrange them in random order.
5. Repeatedly present questions and ask for answers until the quiz is over or is interrupted by the user.
6. Present the results and exit.

Clearly some of these steps (such as step 3) are simple, while others (such as step 4) are complex and worthy of analysis on their own. Use shell functions for any complex step, and use the built-in **trap** command to handle a user interrupt.

Here is a skeleton version of the program, with empty shell functions:

```
function initialize
{
# To be filled in.
}

function choose_subj
{
# To be filled in.  Will write choice to standard output.
}

function scramble
{
# To be filled in.  Will store names of question files, scrambled,
# in an array variable named questions.
}

function ask
{
# To be filled in.  Reads a question file, asks it, and checks the
# answer. Returns 1 if the answer was correct, 0 otherwise.  If it
# encounters an invalid question file, exit with status 2.
}

function summarize
{
# To be filled in.  Presents the user's score.
}

# Main program
initialize                      # Step 1 in top level design
trap 'summarize ; exit 0' INT   # To handle user interrupt

subject=$(choose_subj)          # Step 2
[[ $? -eq 0 ]] || exit 2        # If no valid choice, exit

cd $subject || exit 2           # Step 3

scramble                        # Step 4

for ques in questions           # Step 5
```

```
do
        ask $ques
        result=$?
        num_ques=$(( $num_ques + 1 ))
        if (( $result == 1 ))
        then
                num_correct=$(( $num_correct + 1 ))
        fi
        echo       # skip a line before next question
sleep ${QUIZDELAY:=1}
done

summarize                       # Step 6
exit 0
```

To make reading the results a bit easier for the user, there is a **sleep** call inside the question loop. It delays **$QUIZDELAY** seconds (default = 1) between questions.

Now the task is to fill in the missing pieces of the program. In a sense, this program is being written backwards. The details (the shell functions) come first in the file, but come last in the development process. This is a common programming practice. In this case it is an instance of top-down design. Fill in the broad outline of the program first and supply the details later. In this way you break the problem up into smaller problems, each of which you can work on independently. Shell functions are a great help in using the top-down approach.

One way to write the initialize function follows:

```
function initialize
{
        num_ques=0      # Number of questions asked so far
        num_correct=0   # Number answered correctly so far
        cd ${QUIZDIR:=/usr/lib/quiz} || exit 2
}
```

Although it is logically part of initialization, the **trap** statement belongs in the main program. In the Korn Shell (prior to Korn Shell 93), traps inside of functions are local to the function (page 420) they appear in. In this case a **trap** statement in the initialize function would only abort the program if the user hit the (DELETE) key at the moment the initialize function was being executed.

The next function, **choose_subj**, is a bit more complicated and is implemented using a Select statement.

```
function choose_subj
{
        subjects=$(\ls)
        PS3="Choose a subject for the quiz from the following:   "
        select Subject in $subjects
        do
                if [[ -z "$Subject" ]]
                then
                        echo "No subject chosen.   Bye." >&2
                        exit 1
                fi
                echo $Subject
                return 0
        done
}
```

The function starts by getting a list of subject directories, using the **ls** command. The call to **ls** is escaped (by preceding the **ls** with a \) to ensure that if there is an alias or function named **ls** it will not be used. Next the Select command presents the user with a list of subjects (the directories found by **ls**) and places the chosen directory name in **Subject**. See page 407 for a description of Select. Finally the function writes the subject directory to standard output, where (as shown in the skeleton program) it will be captured in a variable.

You must be prepared for the **cd** command to fail. The directory may be unsearchable, or conceivably another user may have removed the directory in between the **ls** command and the **cd** command.

The **scramble** function presents a number of difficulties. It uses an array variable to hold the names of the questions. You need an algorithm that can randomly scramble the various entries in an array and can make use of the Korn Shell's built-in **RANDOM** variable. Here is an implementation of the **scramble** function.

```
function scramble
{
        set -A questions $(\ls)
        quescount=${#questions[*]}        # Number of array elements
        index=$(($quescount - 1))
        while (( $index > 0 ))
        do
                target=$(($RANDOM % $index))
                exchange $target $index
                        # exchange is another function; see below
                index=$(($index - 1))
        done
}
```

This function initializes the array variable **questions** to the list of filenames (questions) in the current directory. The variable **quescount** is set to the number of such files. Then the following algorithm is used: Let the variable index count down from **quescount − 1** (the index of the last entry in the array variable). For each value of **index**, the function chooses a random value target between 0 and **index**, inclusive. The command

```
target=$(($RANDOM % $index))
```

produces a random value between **0** and **index − 1** by taking the remainder (the % operator) when **$RANDOM** is divided by index. The function then exchanges the elements of **questions** at positions **target** and **index**. It is convenient to do this in another function, named exchange.

```
function exchange
{
        temp_value=${questions[$1]}
        questions[$1]=${questions[$2]}
        questions[$2]=$temp_value
}
```

Function **ask** also makes use of the Select command. It must read the question file named in its argument and use the contents of that file to present the question, accept the answer, and see if it is right—see the code that follows.

This function makes use of file descriptor 3 to read successive lines from the question file, whose name was passed as an argument to the function. It reads the question into the variable named **ques**. It constructs the variable **choices** by initializing it to the null string, and then successively appending a colon followed by the next choice. (The purpose of this rather obscure code is discussed below.) Then it sets PS3 to the value of **ques**, and uses the Select command, which has the effect of prompting the user with **ques**. The Select command places the user's answer in **answer**, and the function then checks it against the correct answer from the file. If the user has not made a valid choice, then Select will continue to issue the prompt and wait for a response.

The construction of the **choices** variable is done with an eye to avoiding a potential problem. Suppose that one of the answers has some white space in it. Then it might appear as two or more arguments in **choices**. To avoid this, change the built-in **IFS** variable to recognize only the colon character as a separator, and set the function arguments to **$choices**. Be careful to remove the leading colon in **choices**. The Select statement's default feature of using the positional arguments does the rest of the work.

```
function initialize
{
        num_ques=0                  # Number of questions asked so far
        num_correct=0               # Number answered correctly so far
        cd ${QUIZDIR:=/usr/lib/quiz} || exit 2
}

function choose_subj
{
        subjects=$(\ls)
        PS3="Choose a subject for the quiz from the following:  "
        select Subject in $subjects
        do
                if [[ -z "$Subject" ]]
                then
                        echo "No subject chosen.  Bye." >&2
                        exit 1
                fi
                echo $Subject
                return 0
        done
}

function exchange
{
        temp_value=${questions[$1]}
        questions[$1]=${questions[$2]}
        questions[$2]=$temp_value
}

function scramble
{
        set -A questions $(\ls)
        quescount=${#questions[*]}        # Number of elements
        index=$(($quescount-1))
        while (( $index > 0 ))
        do
                target=$(($RANDOM % $index))
                exchange $target $index
                index=$(($index - 1))
        done
}

function ask
{
        exec 3<$1
        read -u3 ques || exit 2
        read -u3 num_opts || exit 2
```

```
                index=0
                choices=""
                while (( $index < $num_opts ))
                do
                        read -u3 next_choice || exit 2
                        choices="$choices:$next_choice"
                        index=$(( $index + 1 ))
                done

                read -u3 correct_answer || exit 2
                exec 3<&-

                SaveIFS="$IFS"
                IFS=":"
                choices=${choices#:}
                set $choices

                echo "You may press the Interrupt Key at any time to quit."
                PS3=$ques"  "        # Make $ques the prompt for select, but...
                                     # ...add some spaces for legibility.
                select answer
                        do
                        IFS="$SaveIFS"
                        if [[ -z "$answer" ]]
                        then
                                echo  Not a valid choice. Please choose again.
                        elif [[ "$answer" = "$correct_answer" ]]
                        then
                                echo Correct!
                                return 1
                        else
                                echo No, the answer is $correct_answer.
                                return 0
                        fi
                done
}

function summarize
{
        if (( $num_ques == 0 ))
        then
                echo "You did not answer any questions"
                exit 0
        fi

        percent=$(( $num_correct*100/$num_ques ))
        print "You answered $num_correct questions correctly, out of \
$num_ques total questions."
        print "Your score is $percent percent."
}

# Main program
initialize
trap 'summarize ; exit 0' INT

subject=$(choose_subj)
[[ $? -eq 0 ]] || exit 2

cd $subject || exit 2

echo            # Skip a line
scramble

for ques in ${questions[*]}
do
        ask $ques
        result=$?
```

```
              num_ques=$(( $num_ques + 1 ))
              if (( $result == 1 ))
              then
                          num_correct=$(( $num_correct + 1 ))
              fi
              echo                 # skip a line between questions
       sleep ${QUIZDELAY:=1}
       done

       summarize
       exit 0
```

Korn Shell Options

The following list presents the Korn Shell options. The letter in parentheses following some of the options can be used to abbreviate the option (see "Korn Shell Options," page 385).

Option	Description
allexport (a)	Set the export attribute for every shell variable at the time that it is assigned a value.
bgnice	Run all background jobs at a lower priority.
emacs	Use the **emacs** built-in editor for history and command-line editing.
errexit (e)	Execute the ERR trap and then exit immediately if any command fails (returns nonzero status).
gmacs	Like **emacs**, but uses the GNU **emacs** version of the built-in editor. In Korn Shell 93, **gmacs** and **emacs** have identical behavior, similar to the **gmacs** behavior of earlier versions of the Korn Shell.
ignoreeof	Do not exit when the user types EOF (usually (CONTROL)-**D**). If this option is set, you must type **exit** or an alias for **exit** to end a Korn Shell session.
keyword (k)	Use Bourne Shell syntax for assignments on the command line.
markdirs	Append a trailing slash character (/) to directory names that are created by wildcard expansion.
monitor (m)	Run background jobs in a separate process group. When such jobs complete, report this fact. This is the default behavior on systems with job control (i.e., on virtually all UNIX systems.)
noclobber	Do not allow I/O redirection with > to overwrite an existing file. You can force overwriting with >|, which looks like but is not the same as the C Shell's >! operator for forcing overwriting.
noexec (n)	Read commands, check them for syntactic correctness, but do not execute them. Useful for scripts, this option is ignored in interactive shells.

(Continued)

Option	Description
noglob (f)	Do not expand pathname wildcards.
nolog	Do not put function definitions in the history file.
notify (b)	Korn Shell 93 only. Display an announcement that a background job has completed immediately, instead of waiting for the next shell prompt.
nounset (u)	Treat unset variable names as errors. If the Korn Shell attempts to expand an unset variable and the **nounset** option is turned off, the variable expands to a null string.
physical (P)	Cause the built-in **cd** and **pwd** commands to use physical mode—they will not track symbolic links (page 83).
privileged (p)	Disable reading of $HOME/.profile. (See "Startup Files," page 383.) Instead, use /etc/suid_profile. If this option is turned off, then the Korn Shell's effective user and group IDs are set to the real user and group IDs. The idea of the privileged option is to defeat attempts by users to gain privileges by writing shell scripts with the set-user-ID bit on. See the description of the **chmod** command in Part II for a description of this bit.
trackall (h)	Track each alias.
verbose (v)	Copy standard input to standard error.
vi	Use the **vi** built-in editor for history and command-line editing.
viraw	Like **vi**, but with character-at-a-time rather than line-at-a-time input.
xtrace (x)	Turn on the debugging trace.

The **bgnice** option is on by default, as is the **monitor** option on all systems that support job control.

SUMMARY

The Korn Shell implements nearly all of the features of the Bourne Shell as well as versions of many of the most useful interactive features of the C Shell. The Korn Shell is highly customizable: by choosing settings for options and values for some built-in variables, and by defining aliases and functions, you can create a personal interactive environment.

You can assign attributes to Korn Shell variables with the **typeset** command. The Korn Shell provides operators to do pattern matching on variables, to provide default values for variables, and to evaluate the length of variable values. The Korn Shell also supports array variables and local variables for functions. The Korn Shell provides built-in integer arithmetic capabilities, using the Let command and expression syntax similar to C-language expressions. The 1993 version of the Korn Shell provides floating point arithmetic and additional arithmetic operators.

Condition testing in the Korn Shell is similar to that of the **test** utility, but the Korn Shell provides more testing primitives, including string ordering and string pattern matching. The Korn Shell provides special syntax to allow you to use arithmetic and logical expressions as conditions.

The Korn Shell provides a rich set of control structures for conditional and iterative execution. The Select statement provides a simple method for creating menus in shell scripts and repeatedly prompting the user for responses. The While, Until, and If statements have the same syntax as their Bourne Shell counterparts but can take advantage of the Korn Shell's more powerful logical and arithmetic condition testing.

The Korn Shell provides the ability to manipulate file descriptors. Coupled with powerful built-in **read** and **print** commands, this allows shell scripts to have as much control over input and output as programs written in lower level languages. The Korn Shell provides all the I/O redirection capabilities familiar from the Bourne and C shells, and others besides. A unique feature of the Korn Shell is its ability to launch a coprocess, a process that executes in parallel with the Korn Shell and whose standard input and output are connected via a two-way pipe to the parent shell's **print –p** and **read –p** commands.

You can edit your command line and commands from the history file using either of the Korn Shell's built-in **vi** or **emacs** editors. If you use the built-in **vi** editor, you start in Input Mode, unlike the way you normally enter **vi**. You can switch between Command and Input Mode. The **emacs** editor is modeless, and distinguishes commands from editor input by recognizing control characters as commands.

Commands for Built-in vi Editor

Cursor Movement Commands (vi)

Command	Action
l or (SPACE)	(ell) Move 1 character to the right.
h	Move 1 character to the left.
w	Move 1 word to the right.
b	Move 1 word to the left.
W	Move 1 space-delimited word to the right.
B	Move 1 space-delimited word to the left.
0	Move to beginning of line.
$	Move to end of line.
e	Move to end of word.
E	Move to end of space-delimited word.
^	Move to first nonblank position on line.
fx	Move to next (right) occurrence of **x**.

(Continued)

Command	Action
Fx	Move to previous (left) occurrence of **x**.
;	(semicolon) Repeat last f or F command.
,	(comma) Repeat last f or F command, but in opposite direction.

Changing Text (vi)

Command	Action
i	Enter insert mode before current character.
a	Enter insert mode after current character.
I	Enter insert mode before first nonblank character.
A	Enter insert mode at end of line.
rx	Replace current character with **x**.
R	Overwrite, starting at current character, until (ESCAPE).
nx	Delete **n** characters, starting at the current character.
nX	Delete **n** characters, starting just past the current character.
D	Delete from the current character to the end of line.
dd	Delete the entire command.
C	Change from the current character to the end of line.

History Editing Commands (vi)

Command	Action
j	Move back one command in history.
k	Move forward one command in history.
/string (RETURN)	Search backward for command with **string**.
?string (RETURN)	Search forward for command with **string**.
n	Repeat previous search.
N	Repeat previous search in opposite direction.
nv	Enter full screen **vi** to edit command number **n**, or the current command if **n** is omitted.
#	Insert the current command as a comment in the history file.

Miscellaneous Commands (vi)

Command	Action
(ESCAPE)=	List pathnames that match the current word.
(ESCAPE)\	Complete current word to a unique pathname or partial pathname.
(ESCAPE)*	Expand current word to all matching pathnames.
u	Undo previous change.
~	Change the case of the current character.
n.	Repeat, **n** times, the most recent command that caused a change. If **n** is omitted, it defaults to 1.

Commands for Built-in emacs Editor

Cursor Movement Commands (emacs)

Command	Action
(CONTROL)-F	Move 1 character to the right.
(CONTROL)-B	Move 1 character to the left.
(ESCAPE)f	Move 1 word to the right.
(ESCAPE)b	Move 1 word to the left.
(CONTROL)-A	Move to beginning of line.
(CONTROL)-E	Move to end of line.
(CONTROL)-] x	Move to next instance of **x**.

Changing Text (emacs)

Command	Action
Erase	Delete the character to the right of the current character.
(CONTROL)-D	Delete the current character.
(CONTROL)-K	Delete to end of line.
Kill	Delete the entire line.
(CONTROL)-T	Transpose the current and next (to right) character.
(CONTROL)-W	Delete all characters from the current character to the Mark.
(ESCAPE)D	Delete one word to right.
(ESCAPE)h	Delete one word to left.

(Continued)

Command	Action
(ESCAPE)l	Change next word to all lowercase.
(ESCAPE)c	Change next word to all uppercase.
(ESCAPE)-.	Insert last word from previous command line before the current character.

History Editing Commands (emacs)

Command	Action
(CONTROL)-P	Move to previous line in history file.
(CONTROL)-N	Move to next line in history file.
(ESCAPE)<	Move to first line in history file.
(ESCAPE)>	Move to last line in history file.
(CONTROL)-R **string**	Search backward for **string**.

Miscellaneous Commands (emacs)

Command	Action
(ESCAPE)=	List pathnames that match the current word.
(ESCAPE) (ESCAPE)	Complete current word to a unique pathname or partial pathname.
(ESCAPE)✳fs	Expand current word to all matching pathnames.
(CONTROL)-U	Repeat the next command four times.
(CONTROL)-V	Display the current version of the Korn Shell.
(CONTROL)-L	Redisplay the current line.

REVIEW EXERCISES

1. The command **dirname path** treats **path** as a pathname and writes to standard output the path prefix, that is, everything up to but not including the last component. Thus,

```
dirname a/b/c/d
```

writes a/b/c to standard output. If path is a simple filename (has no / characters), then **dirname** writes a . to standard output.

Implement **dirname** as a Korn Shell function. Make sure that it behaves sensibly when given values of path such as /.

2. Implement the **basename** utility, which writes the last component of its pathname argument to standard output, as a Korn Shell function. For example,

    ```
    basename a/b/c/d
    ```

    writes **d** to standard output.

3. The UNIX **basename** utility has an optional third argument. If you type

    basename **path suffix**

    then, after removing the **path** prefix from **path**, **basename** removes any suffix of **path** that is identical to **suffix**. For example:

    ```
    $ basename src/shellfiles/prog.sh .sh
    prog
    $ basename src/shellfiles/prog.sh .c
    prog.sh
    ```

    Add this feature to the function you wrote for Problem 2.

ADVANCED REVIEW EXERCISES

4. Write a Korn Shell function that takes a directory name as an argument and writes to standard output the maximum of the lengths of all file-names in that directory. If the function's argument is not a directory name, then your function should write an error message to standard output and exit with nonzero status.

5. Modify the function you wrote in answer to Problem 4 to recursively descend all subdirectories of the named directory and find the maximum length of any filename in that hierarchy.

6. Write a Korn Shell function that lists the number of regular files, directories, block special files, character special files, FIFOs, and symbolic links in the current directory. Do this in two different ways:

    a. Use the first letter of the output of **ls -l** to determine a file's type.

    b. Use the file type condition tests of the **[[** command to determine a file's type.

7. The **makesccs** program on page 439 depends on the fact that **find** will write the pathname of a directory before it writes the pathname of any files in that directory. Suppose that this were not reliably true. Fix **makesccs**.

8. Change **makesccs** so that if any call to **admin** fails, the program continues (as it does now) but eventually exits with nonzero status.

9. In the **makesccs** program, file descriptors 3 and 4 are opened, and then during the loop, output is directed to these descriptors. An alternate method would be to simply append the output each time it occurs, using, for example

```
print "Cannot create $target" >> $ERRS
```

rather than

```
print -u3 "Cannot create $target"
```

What is the difference, and why does it matter?

10. In principle, recursion is never necessary. It can always be replaced by an iterative construct such as While or Until. Rewrite the **makepath** function as a nonrecursive function. Which version do you prefer?

CHAPTER 13

Programming Tools

The UNIX system provides an exceptional programming environment. Because the operating system was written mostly in C by highly talented programmers who had their own needs in mind, UNIX provides an ideal environment for programming in C. Operating system services are readily accessible to the C programmer in the form of function libraries and system calls. In addition, there are a variety of tools for making the development and maintenance of programs easier.

457

Background

This chapter describes how to use the C compiler as well as two of the most useful software development tools, the **make** utility and two source code management systems, the Source Code Control System (SCCS) and the Revision Control System (RCS). The **make** utility helps you keep track of which modules of a program have been updated, and it helps to ensure that when you compile a program you use the latest versions of all program modules. Source code management systems track the versions of files involved in a project.

Programming In C

One of the main reasons the UNIX system provides an excellent C programming environment is that C programs can easily access the services of the operating system. The system calls—the routines that make operating system services available to programmers—are written in C, like most of the rest of the operating system. The system calls provide services such as creating files, reading from and writing to files, collecting information about files, allocating memory, and sending signals to processes. When you write a C program, you can use the system calls in the same way you use ordinary C program modules, or *functions,* that you have written.

A variety of *libraries* of functions have been developed to support programming in C on UNIX. The libraries are collections of related functions that you can use just as you use your own functions and the system calls. Many of the library functions access basic operating system services through the system calls, providing the services in ways that are more suited to typical programming tasks. Other library functions serve special purposes (e.g., the math library functions).

This chapter describes the processes of writing and compiling a C program. However, it will not teach you to program in C. If you want to learn C, consult one of the many available texts.

Writing a C Program

You must use an editor, such as **vi**, to write a C program. When you create a C program file, add .c as an extension to the filename. The C compiler expects C source files to end in .c.

Typing in the source code for a program is similar to typing in a memo or shell script—the editor does not know whether your file is a C program, a shell script, or an ordinary text document. You are responsible for making the contents of the file structurally and syntactically suitable for the C compiler to process.

Figure 13-1 illustrates the structure of a simple C program. The first two lines of the program are comments that describe what the program does. The string /* identifies the beginning of the comment, and the string */ identifies the end—the C compiler ignores all the characters between them. Because a comment can span two or more lines, the */ at the end of the first

```
$ cat tabs.c
/* convert tabs in standard input to spaces in */    ─ Comment
/* standard output while maintaining columns */

#include    <stdio.h>                                 Preprocessor
#define     TABSIZE     8                              Directives

main()
{
int c;          /* character read from stdin   */
int posn = 0;   /* column position of character */
int inc;        /* column increment to tab stop */

while ((c = getchar()) != EOF)
    switch(c)
        {
        case '\t':                  /* c is a tab */
            inc = findstop(posn);
            posn += inc;
            for ( ; inc > 0; inc--)                    Main
                putchar(' ');                          Function
            break;
        case '\n':                  /* c is a newline */
            putchar(c);
            posn = 0;
            break;
        default:            /* c is anything else */
            putchar(c);
            posn++;
            break;
        }
}

/* compute size of increment to next tab stop */

findstop(col)                                          ─ Function
int col;   /* column position of tab character */
{
return (TABSIZE - (col % TABSIZE));
}
```

Figure 13-1   A Simple C Program

line and the /* at the beginning of the second are not necessary—they were included in **tabs.c** for clarity. As the comment explains, the program reads its standard input, converts TAB characters into the appropriate number of spaces, and writes the transformed input to the standard output. Like many UNIX utilities, this program is a filter.

   Preprocessor directives follow the comments at the top of the program; these are instructions for the C preprocessor. During the initial phase of compilation, the C preprocessor expands the directives, making the program ready for the later stages of the compilation process.

You can use the **#define** preprocessor directive to define *symbolic constants* and *macros*. Symbolic constants are names that you can use in your programs in place of constant values. For example, **tabs.c** uses a **#define** preprocessor directive to associate the symbolic constant, **TABSIZE**, with the constant 8. **TABSIZE** is used in the program in place of the constant 8 as the distance between TAB stops. By convention, the names of symbolic constants are composed of all uppercase letters.

By defining symbolic names for constant values, you can make your program easier to read and easier to modify. If you later decide to change a constant, you need only change the preprocessor directive rather than changing the value everywhere it occurs in your program. If you replace the **#define** directive for **TABSIZE** in Figure 13-1 with the following directive, the program will place TAB stops every four columns rather than every eight:

```
#define    TABSIZE    4
```

You can also use **#define** statements to define macros, which are similar to short functions. The following macro determines whether a character is a digit:

```
#define    numeric(n)    (n >= '0' && n <= '9')
```

You can use the macro **numeric(n)** in your code in the same way you use functions. However, macros are not really functions—the C preprocessor replaces macros with C code rather than with function calls.

When several symbolic constant and macro definitions are used in different modules of a program, they are typically collected together in a single file called a *header file* (or an *include file*). Although the C compiler does not put constraints on the names of header files, by convention they end in .h. The name of the header file is then listed in an **#include** preprocessor directive in each program source file that uses any of the symbolic constants or macros. The program in Figure 13-1 uses **getchar** and **putchar**, which are macros defined in **stdio.h** on many systems. The **stdio.h** header file defines a variety of general-purpose macros and is used by many system calls and C library functions.

The angle brackets (< and >) that surround **stdio.h** in **tabs.c** instruct the C preprocessor to look for the header file in a standard directory (/**usr/include** on most systems). If you want to include a header file from another directory, use double quotes and specify the absolute pathname of the file. The following example includes a header file from one of Alex's directories:

```
#include "/home/alex/cprogs/ledg.h"
```

Although you can call most C functions anything you want, each program must have exactly one function named **main**. The main function is the control module—your program begins execution with the main function. Typically, **main** will call other functions in turn, which may call yet other functions, and so forth. By putting different operations into separate functions, you can make a program easier to read and maintain. The program in

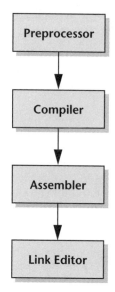

Figure 13-2   Components of the Compilation Process

Figure 13-1 uses a function **findstop** to compute the distance to the next
(TAB) stop. Although this single statement could easily have been included
in the main function, isolating it in a separate function draws attention to a
key computation.

Functions can also make both development and maintenance of the
program more efficient. By putting a frequently used code segment into a
function, you avoid entering the same code over and over again into the program. Later when you want to make changes to the code, you only need to
change it once.

If your program is long and involves several functions, you may want to
split it into two or more files. A C program can be split into any number of
different files; however, each function must be wholly contained within a
file. You should put **#define** preprocessor directives into a header file and include the header file in any source file that uses the directives. Each source
filename must have a .c extension.

Compiling a Program

To compile **tabs.c**, give the following command:

```
$ cc tabs.c
```

The **cc** utility calls the C preprocessor, the C compiler, the assembler,
and the link editor. The four components of the compilation process are
shown in Figure 13-2. The C preprocessor expands symbolic constant and
macro definitions and also includes header files. The compilation phase creates assembly language code corresponding to the instructions in the source
file. Then the assembler creates machine-readable object code. One object

file is created for each source file. Each object file has the same name as the source file, with the exception that the .c extension is replaced with a .o. In the previous example, a single object file would be created, **tabs.o**. However, after the C compiler successfully completes all phases of the compilation process for a program contained in a single source file, it creates the executable file and then removes the .o file. If you successfully compile **tabs.c**, you will not see the .o file.

During the final phase of the compilation process, the link editor searches specified libraries for functions your program uses and combines object modules for those functions with your program's object modules. By default, the C compiler searches the standard C library, **libc.a**, which contains functions that handle input and output and provides many other general-purpose capabilities. If you want the link editor to search other libraries, you must use the –l option to specify the libraries on the command line. Unlike most options to UNIX system utilities, the –l option does not come before all filenames on the command line—it comes after all the filenames of all modules that it applies to. In the next example, the C compiler searches the math library, **libm.a**:

```
$ cc calc.c -lm
```

As you can see from the example, the –l option uses abbreviations for library names, appending the letter following –l to **lib** and adding a .a extension. The **m** in the example above stands for **libm.a**.

As the last step of the compilation process, by default the link editor creates an executable file named **a.out**. If there is only one object file, **cc** removes the object file after it successfully creates the executable. In the next example, there are several object files, and **cc** does not remove them. The –O option causes **cc** to use the C compiler optimizer. The optimizer makes object code more efficient so that the executable program runs more quickly.

```
$ cc -O ledger.c acctspay.c acctsrec.c
$ ls
a.out        acctspay.o   acctsrec.o   ledger.o
acctspay.c   acctsrec.c   ledger.c
```

You can use the executable **a.out** in the same way you use shell scripts and other programs—by typing its name on the command line. The program in Figure 13-1 expects to read from its standard input, so once you have created the executable, **a.out**, you can use a command such as the following to run it:

```
$ a.out < mymemo
```

If you want to save the **a.out** file, you should change the name to a more descriptive one. Otherwise, you might accidentally overwrite it during a later compilation.

```
$ mv a.out tabs
```

To save the trouble of renaming **a.out** files, you can specify the name of the executable file when you use **cc**. If you use the –o option, the C compiler will give the executable the name of your choice rather than **a.out**. In the next example, the executable is called **accounting**:

```
$ cc -o accounting ledger.c acctspay.c acctsrec.c
```

Assuming the executable file does not read from its standard input or require arguments, you can run it with the following command:

```
$ accounting
```

If you want to compile some but not all of the modules of a program, you can use the –c option to **cc**, which suppresses the link editing phase. The –c option is useful because it does not treat unresolved external references as errors; this capability enables you to compile and debug the syntax of the modules of a program as you create them. Once you have compiled and debugged all the modules, you can run **cc** again with the object files as arguments to produce an executable program. In the next example, **cc** produces three object files but no executable:

```
$ cc -c ledger.c acctspay.c acctsrec.c
$ ls
acctspay.c acctspay.o acctsrec.c acctsrec.o ledger.c    ledger.o
```

If you then run **cc** again using the object files, **cc** will produce the executable. Because the C compiler recognizes the filename extension .o, it recognizes that the files only need to be linked. You can also include both .c and .o files on a single command line, as in this example:

```
$ cc -o accounting ledger.o acctspay.c acctsrec.o
```

The C compiler recognizes that the .c file needs to be preprocessed and compiled, whereas the .o files do not. The C compiler also accepts assembly language files ending in .s, and it treats them appropriately (that is, **cc** assembles and links them). This feature makes it easy to modify and recompile a program.

With large programs that have many different modules, the ability to compile modules separately and link them with previously compiled modules can save time. The **make** utility provides an automated method for figuring out what program modules need to be recompiled (page 469). For more information about the C compiler, refer to **cc** in Part II.

Debugging C Programs

The C compiler is liberal about the kinds of constructs it allows in programs. Like many other UNIX utilities, **cc** seems to be based on the philosophy that the user *means* what he or she says (or types) and that no news is good news. The C compiler allows almost anything that is logically possible according to the definition of the language. Although this approach gives the programmer a great deal of flexibility and control, it can make debugging difficult.

One way to debug a C program is to insert print statements at critical points throughout the source code. For example, if there were a bug in the

464 CHAPTER 13 Programming Tools

tabs.c program presented earlier in this chapter, you might add the following calls to the **fprintf()** function to learn more about the behavior of the
program when it runs:

```
case '\t':                    /* c is a tab */
    fprintf(stderr, "before call to findstop, posn is %d\n", posn);
    inc = findstop(posn);
    fprintf(stderr, "after call to findstop, posn is %d\n", posn);
    posn += inc;
    for ( ; inc > 0; inc--)
        putchar(' ');
    break;
case '\n':                    /* c is a newline */
    fprintf(stderr, "got a newline\n");
    putchar(c);
    posn = 0;
    break;
default:                         /* c is anything else */
    fprintf(stderr, "got another character\n");
    putchar(c);
    posn++;
    break;
```

The **fprintf** statements in the example above send their messages to the
standard error, so if you redirect the output of this program you can separate
them from the standard output. Here is an example that demonstrates the
operation of this program on a short input file:

```
$ cat testtabs
xyz TAB abc
$ tabs < testtabs > testspaces
got another character
got another character
got another character
before call to findstop, posn is 3
after call to findstop, posn is 3
got another character
got another character
got another character
got a newline
$ cat testspaces
xyz       abc
$
```

Using lint to Find Errors in a Program

For simple programs, or in cases where you may have some idea of what is
wrong with your program, adding print statements that help you trace the
execution of the code can often help you debug the problem quickly. The
UNIX system also provides several tools to help you debug programs.

The C program verifier, **lint**, is one of the most useful debugging tools. It
checks programs for potential bugs and portability problems. Unlike the C
compiler, **lint** is very strict. It detects and reports on a wide variety of problems and potential problems, including variables that are used before they
are set, arguments to functions that are not used, and functions that use return values that were never returned.

The **lint** utility uncovers two problems with the sample program, **tabs.c**:

```
$ lint tabs.c
tabs.c(27): warning: main() returns random value to invocation
environment
putc returns value which is always ignored
```

By convention, if a program runs successfully it should return a zero value; if it does not, the exit code is undefined. If you add the following statement at the end of the **main()** function in **tabs.c**, the first warning from **lint** will disappear:

```
return 0;
```

The second warning from **lint** may seem puzzling, since the program does not include any calls to **putc**. The message refers to **putc** because **putchar** is a macro that calls **putc**; the problem with **tabs.c** is that the return codes from the calls to **putchar** are never checked. If **putchar** fails, the error will not be detected and the output of the **tabs** program will be incorrect.

Although you are free to ignore **lint**'s warnings and go ahead and compile your program, a warning typically means that the program has a bug or a nonportable construct, or that you have violated a standard of good programming. Paying attention to **lint**'s warnings is a good way to debug your programs and to hone your programming skills.

Using the **dbx** Symbolic Debugger

UNIX systems also provide debuggers for tackling problems that evade **lint** and the C compiler. These debuggers include **adb**, **sdb**, and **dbx**. The **dbx** utility is a popular high-level (symbolic) debugger—it enables you to analyze the execution of a program in terms of C language statements. It also provides a lower-level view for analyzing the execution of a program in terms of the machine instructions.

The **dbx** utility enables you to monitor and control the execution of a program. You can step through a program on a line-by-line basis while you examine the state of the execution environment. It also allows you to examine *core* files. When a serious error occurs during the execution of a program, the operating system displays Segmentation violation -- Core dumped or a similar message and creates a **core** file containing information about the state of the program and the system when the failure occurred. Using **dbx** you can identify the line in the program where the error occurred, the values of variables at that point, and so forth. Because **core** files tend to be large and take up valuable disk space, be sure to remove them after you are done.

If you want to use the debugger with a program, you should use the –**g** option when you compile the program. The –**g** option causes **cc** to generate additional information that is used by the debugger, as shown in the example that follows.

If you try to debug a program that does not include the symbol table information **dbx** expects, you will see a warning message (as in the following example). Recompile the program with the appropriate options and start **dbx** again.

```
$ dbx tabs
Reading symbolic information...
Read 12 symbols
warning: main routine not compiled with the -g option
    .
    .
    .
$ cc -g tabs.c -o tabs
```

To run the debugger on the sample executable, specify the name of the file on the command line when you run **dbx**. After **dbx** reads in the file, it prompts for input with the string **(dbx)**. The **list** command prints the first ten lines of the source code (comments, **#include**, and **#define** lines are not included; they were processed by the C preprocessor before the program was compiled into executable form).

```
$ dbx tabs
Reading symbolic information...
Read 63 symbols
(dbx) list
 7 int posn = 0;
 8 int inc;
 9
10  while ((c=getchar()) != EOF)
11      switch(c)
12          {
13 case '\t':
14      inc = findstop(posn);
15      posn += inc;
16      for ( ; inc > 0; inc--)
```

The next few commands check on particular values. The **where** command reports which function is currently active, along with its address (a hexadecimal number). You can use the **whatis** command to find out the declaration that applies to a particular variable (in this case, the variable **col** is an integer). Finally, you can use **whereis** to locate a variable; in this example, the variable col was found in the **findstop** function in the **tabs** program.

```
(dbx) where
main() at 0x2290
(dbx) whatis col
int col;
(dbx) whereis col
variable: 'tabs'findstop'col
```

One of the most important features of a debugger is the ability to run a program under controlled circumstances; you can stop the running process whenever you would like to check on the state of some variables, for example. The next statement tells **dbx** to stop the process whenever the function **findstop** is called. Having made that request, the following statement runs the current program (**tabs**, as specified on the command line when **dbx** was started) and uses the file **testtabs** for input. When the process stops, you can use **print** to check the value of a variable at that point (**posn**, in this case) and also use the **where** command to learn which function is active and how it was called. In this example, the process was stopped in the function **findstop**, as requested; **findstop** had been called by **main**.

```
(dbx) stop in findstop
(2) stop in findstop
(dbx) run < testtabs
Running: tabs < testtabs
stopped in findstop at line 38 in file
"/home/alex/cprogs/tabs.c"
    38                  return (TABSIZE - (col % TABSIZE));
(dbx) print posn
posn = 3
(dbx) where
findstop(col = 3), line 38 in "/home/alex/cprogs/tabs.c"
main(), line 17 in "/home/alex/cprogs/tabs.c"
```

Having examined the variables of interest, the next command (**cont**) causes the process to continue running. The **testtabs** file contained only one line; the process finishes executing, and the results appear on the screen, since the run command line did not redirect the output. The debugger reports that execution completed and reports the exit code values. To end the session, use the **quit** command.

```
(dbx) cont
xyz     abc
execution completed, exit code is 33627
program exited with 91
(dbx) quit
```

The **dbx** utility supports many commands that are designed to make debugging easier. If you are not sure which commands are available, you can ask **dbx** to list them by using the **help** command, as shown below. You can also request more detailed help on specific commands.

```
$ dbx
(dbx) help
      Command Summary
Execution and Tracing
  catch   clear   cont    delete   ignore   next    rerun
  run     status  step    stop     trace    when
  .
  .

The command 'help <cmdname>' provides additional help for each command
(dbx)
```

For a complete description of the **dbx** utility, see the documentation supplied with your computer system.

System Calls

The three fundamental responsibilities of the UNIX kernel are to control processes, to manage the filesystem, and to operate peripheral devices. As a programmer, you have access to these kernel operations through system calls and library functions. This section discusses system calls at a general level; a detailed treatment is beyond the scope of this book.

A system call, as the name implies, instructs the system (kernel) to carry out an operation directly on your behalf. A library routine is indirect; it issues system calls for you. The advantages of a library routine are that it may insulate you from the low level details of kernel operations and that it has been written carefully, to make sure it performs efficiently.

For example, it is straightforward to use the Standard I/O library function **fprintf()** to send text to the standard output or standard error. Without this function, you would need to issue several system calls to achieve the same result. The calls to the library routines **putchar()** and **getchar()** in Figure 13-1 ultimately use the **write()** and **read()** system calls to perform the I/O operations.

Controlling Processes

When you enter a command line at a Shell prompt, the Shell process calls the fork system call to create a copy of itself (spawn a child) and then uses an exec system call to overlay that copy in memory with a different program (the command you asked it to run). You can use fork and exec in your own programs to perform the same task. Some of the other system calls that affect processes include:

- **wait()**   cause the parent process to wait for the child to finish running before it resumes execution

- **exit()**   cause a process to exit

- **nice()**   change the priority of a process

- **kill()**   send a signal to a process

Accessing the Filesystem

Many operations take place when a program reads or writes to a file. The program needs to know where the file is located; the filename must be converted to an inode number on the correct filesystem on a particular disk. Your access permissions must be checked, not only for the file itself but also for all the intervening directories in the path to the file. The file is not stored in one continuous piece on the disk; all the disk blocks that contain pieces of the file must be located. The appropriate kernel device driver must be called to control the actual operation of the disk. Finally, once the file has been found, the program may need to find a particular location within the file, rather than working with it sequentially from beginning to end.

Some of the most common system calls in filesystem operations include:

- **stat()**   get status information from an inode, such as the inode number, the device on which it is located, owner and group information, and the size of the file.
- **access()**   check file access permissions
- **creat()**   create a new file
- **open()**   open an existing file
- **read()**   read a file
- **write()**   write a file
- **close()**   close a file
- **unlink()**   unlink a file (delete a name reference to the inode)
- **chmod()**   change file access permissions
- **chown()**   change file ownership

Access to peripheral devices on a UNIX system is handled through the file-system interface. Each peripheral device is represented by one or more special files, usually located in **/dev**. When you read or write to one of these special files, the kernel passes your requests to the appropriate kernel device driver. As a result, you can use the standard system calls and library routines to interact with these devices—you do not need to learn a new set of specialized functions. This is one of the most powerful features of the UNIX system because it allows users to use the same basic utilities on a wide range of devices.

The availability of standard system calls and library routines is the key to the portability of UNIX tools. For example, as an applications programmer, you can rely on the read and write system calls working the same way on different versions of the UNIX system and on different types of computers. The systems programmer who writes a device driver or ports the kernel to run on a new computer, however, must understand the details at their lowest level.

The make **Utility**

When you have a large program with many source and header files, the files typically depend on one another in complex ways. When you change a file that other files depend on, you *must* recompile all dependent files. For example, you might have several source files, all of which use a single header file. When you make a change to the header file, each of the source files must be recompiled. The header file might depend on other header files, and so forth. These sorts of dependency relationships are shown in Figure 13-3. (Each arrow in Figure 13-3 points from a file to another file that depends on it.)

When you are working on a large program, it can be difficult, time consuming, and tedious to determine which modules need to be recompiled due to their dependency relationships. The **make** utility automates this process.

In its simplest use, **make** looks at *dependency lines* in a file named **makefile** in the working directory. The dependency lines indicate relationships among files, specifying a *target file* that depends on one or more *prerequisite* files. If you have modified any of the prerequisite files more recently than its target file, **make** updates the target file based on *construction commands* that follow the dependency line. The **make** utility normally stops if it encounters an error during the construction process.

A simple **makefile** has the following format:

target: prerequisite-list
<u>TAB</u> **construction-commands**

The dependency line is composed of the **target** and the **prerequisite-list**, separated by a colon. The **construction-commands** line must start with a <u>TAB</u> and must follow the dependency line.

The **target** is the name of the file that depends on the files in the **prerequisite-list**. The **construction-commands** are regular commands to the shell that construct (usually compile and/or link) the target file. The **make** utility executes the **construction-commands** when the modification time of one or more of the files in the **prerequisite-list** is more recent than that of the target file.

The example below shows the dependency line and construction commands for the file called **form** in Figure 13-3. It depends on its prerequisites, **size.o** and **length.o**. An appropriate **cc** command constructs the **target**.

```
form:    size.o length.o
         cc -o form size.o length.o
```

Each of the prerequisites on one dependency line can be a target on another dependency line. For example, both **size.o** and **length.o** are targets on other dependency lines. Although the example in Figure 13-3 is simple, the nesting of dependency specifications can create a complex hierarchy that specifies relationships among many files.

The following **makefile** corresponds to the complete dependency graph shown in Figure 13-3. The executable file **form** depends on two object files, and the object files each depend on their respective source files and a header file, **form.h**. In turn, **form.h** depends on two other header files.

```
$ cat makefile
form:    size.o length.o
         cc -o form size.o length.o

size.o:   size.c form.h
          cc -c size.c

length.o: length.c form.h
          cc -c length.c

form.h:   num.h table.h
          cat num.h table.h > form.h
```

The last line illustrates the fact that you can put any Bourne Shell command on a construction line. (However, creating a header file by catenating two other header files is not something you see done often.) Because **makefiles** are processed by the Bourne Shell, the command line should be one that you could input in response to a Bourne Shell prompt.

Implied Dependencies

You can rely on *implied* dependencies and construction commands to make your job of writing a **makefile** easier. If you do not include a dependency line

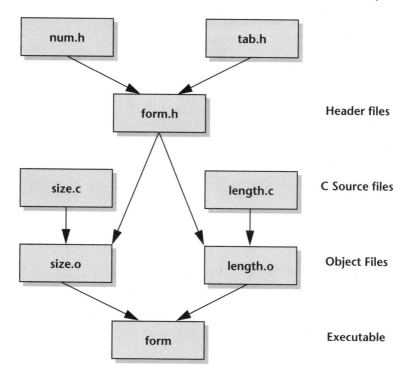

Figure 13-3   Dependency Graph for the Target **form**

for an object file, **make** assumes that it depends on a compiler or assembler source code file. Thus, if a prerequisite for a target file is **xxx.o**, and there is no construction command following a dependency line for the **xxx.o** target, **make** looks for one of the following files in the working directory. If it finds an appropriate source file, **make** provides a default construction command line that calls the proper compiler or the assembler to create the object file.

Filename	Type of File
xxx.c	C source code
xxx.r	RATFOR source code
xxx.f	FORTRAN77 source code
xxx.y	YACC source code
xxx.l	Lex source code
xxx.s	assembler code
xxx.mod	Modula 2 source code
xxx.p	Pascal source code
xxx.sh	Shell scripts

RATFOR, Modula 2, Pascal, and FORTRAN77 are standard programming languages, and YACC and Lex are UNIX tools for creating command languages.

The next example shows a **makefile** that keeps a file named **compute** up-to-date. The first three lines (each beginning with a pound sign, #) are comment lines. Because **make** ignores lines that begin with pound signs, you can use pound signs to set off comments. The first dependency line shows that **compute** depends on two object files: **compute.o** and **calc.o**. The corresponding construction line gives the command **make** needs to produce **compute**. The next dependency line shows that **compute.o** not only depends on its C source file but also on a header file, **compute.h**. The construction line for **compute.o** uses the C compiler optimizer (–O option). The third set of dependency and construction lines is not required. In their absence, **make** would infer that **calc.o** was dependent on **calc.c** and would produce the command line needed for the compilation.

```
$ cat makefile
#
# makefile for compute
#

compute:        compute.o calc.o
                cc -o compute compute.o calc.o

compute.o:      compute.c compute.h
                cc -c -O compute.c

calc.o:         calc.c
                cc -c calc.c

clean:          rm *.o
```

There are no prerequisites for the last target, **clean**, in the **makefile** above. This target is commonly used to get rid of extraneous files that may be out of date or no longer needed, such as .o files.

Following are some sample executions of **make**, based on the previous **makefile**. As the **ls** command below shows, **compute.o**, **calc.o**, and **compute** are not up-to-date. Consequently, the **make** command runs the construction commands that recreate them.

```
$ ls -l
total 22
-rw-rw----  1 alex       179 Jun 21 18:20 calc.c
-rw-rw----  1 alex       354 Jun 21 16:02 calc.o
-rwxrwx---  1 alex      6337 Jun 21 16:04 compute
-rw-rw----  1 alex       780 Jun 21 18:20 compute.c
-rw-rw----  1 alex        49 Jun 21 16:04 compute.h
-rw-rw----  1 alex       880 Jun 21 16:04 compute.o
-rw-rw----  1 alex       311 Jun 21 15:56 makefile
$ make
        cc -c -O compute.c
        cc -c calc.c
        cc -o compute compute.o calc.o
```

If you run **make** once and then run it again without making any changes to the prerequisite files, **make** indicates that the program is up-to-date by not executing any commands.

```
$ make
'compute' is up to date.
```

The following example uses the **touch** utility to change the modification time of a prerequisite file. This simulation shows what would happen if you were to make a change to the file. The **make** utility executes only the commands necessary to make the out-of-date targets up-to-date.

```
$ touch calc.c
$ make
          cc -c calc.c
          cc -o compute compute.o calc.o
```

In the next example, **touch** changes the modification time of **compute.h**. The **make** utility recreates **compute.o** because it depends on **compute.h**, and **make** recreates the executable because it depends on **compute.o**.

```
$ touch compute.h
$ make
          cc -c -O compute.c
          cc -o compute compute.o calc.o
```

As these examples illustrate, **touch** is useful when you want to fool **make** into recompiling programs or into *not* recompiling them. You can use it to update the modification times of all the source files so that **make** considers that nothing is up-to-date. The **make** utility will then recompile everything. Alternatively, you can use **touch** or the **–t** option to **make** to touch all relevant files so that **make** considers everything to be up-to-date. This is useful if the modification times of files have changed, yet the files are all up-to-date. (For example, this situation occurs when you copy a complete set of files from one directory to another.) If you want to see what **make** *would* do if you ran it, run **make** with the **–n** option.

Once you are satisfied with the program you have created, you can use the **makefile** to clean out the files you no longer need. It is useful to keep intermediate files around while you are writing and debugging your program, so that you only need to rebuild the ones that need to change. If you will not be working on the program again for a while, though, you should release the disk space. The advantage of using a **clean** target in your **makefile** is that you do not have to remember all the little pieces that can safely be deleted. The example below simply removes all the object (**.o**) files.

```
$ make clean
rm *.o
$
```

Macros

The **make** utility has a macro facility that enables you to create and use macros within a **makefile**. The format of a macro definition is shown below.

ID = list

Replace **ID** with an identifying name, and replace **list** with a list of filenames. After this macro definition, **$(ID)** represents **list** in the **makefile**.

By default, **make** invokes the C compiler without any options (except the –c option when it is appropriate to compile but not to link a file). You can use the **CFLAGS** macro definition, as shown below, to cause **make** to call the C compiler with specific options. Replace **options** with the options you want to use.

CFLAGS = **options**

The following **makefile** uses macros, implied dependencies, and constructions:

```
#
# makefile: report, print, printf, printh
#

CFLAGS  = -O
FILES = in.c out.c ratio.c process.c tally.c
OBJECTS = in.o out.o ratio.o process.o tally.o
HEADERS = names.h companies.h conventions.h

report:    $(OBJECTS)
           cc -o report $(OBJECTS)

ratio.o:   $(HEADERS)

process.o: $(HEADERS)

tally.o:   $(HEADERS)

print:
       pr $(FILES) $(HEADERS) | lpr

printf:
       pr $(FILES) | lpr

printh:
       pr $(HEADERS) | lpr
```

Following the comment lines, the **makefile** uses **CFLAGS** to make sure that **make** always selects the C optimizer (–O option) when it invokes the C compiler as the result of an implied construction. (Whenever you put a construction line in a **makefile**, the construction line overrides **CFLAGS** and any other implied construction lines.) Following **CFLAGS**, the **makefile** defines the **FILES**, **OBJECTS**, and **HEADERS** macros. Each of these macros defines a list of files.

The first dependency line shows that **report** depends on the list of files that **OBJECTS** defines. The corresponding construction line links the **OBJECTS** and creates an executable file named **report**.

The next three dependency lines show that three object files depend on the list of files that **HEADERS** defines. There are no construction lines, so when it is necessary, **make** looks for a source code file corresponding to each of the object files and compiles it. These three dependency lines ensure that the object files are recompiled if any of the header files is changed.

You can combine several targets on one dependency line, so these three dependency lines could have been combined into one line, as follows:

```
ratio.o process.o tally.o: $(HEADERS)
```

The final three dependency lines send source and header files to the printer. They have nothing to do with compiling the **report** file. None of these targets (**print, printf,** and **printh**) depends on anything. When you call one of these targets from the command line, **make** executes the construction line following it. As an example, the following command prints all the source files that **FILES** defines:

```
$ make printf
```

Source Code Management

When you work on a project involving many files that evolve over long periods of time, it can be hard to keep track of the versions of the files, especially if several people are making updates. This problem occurs particularly in large software development projects. Source code and documentation files change frequently as you fix bugs, enhance programs, and release new versions of the software. It becomes even more complex when there is more than one active version of each file. Frequently, customers are using one version of a file while a newer version is being modified. You can easily lose track of the versions and accidentally undo changes that were already made or duplicate earlier work.

To help avoid these kinds of problems, the UNIX system includes utilities for managing and tracking changes to files. These utilities comprise two separate source code management systems: SCCS, the Source Code Control System and RCS, the Revision Control System. Although they can be used on any text file, these tools are most often used to manage source code and software documentation.

Both systems can control who is allowed to update files. For each update, they record who made the changes and include notes about why the

Figure 13-4   The History of an SCCS File

changes were made. Because they store the original version of a file as well as changes to the file as they are made, it is possible to regenerate any version of a file. Saving the changes that are made to a file rather than a complete new version conserves disk space; however, the SCCS or RCS files themselves consume a lot of space because of all the information they store about each update. Whether these tools actually save disk space or not depends on the sizes of the files and the nature of the changes that are made to them.

The following sections provide overviews of SCCS and RCS. The utilities for both systems are described in more detail in Part II, where they are listed under their individual names. The underlying file formats for the two systems are different and incompatible, so you should choose to work with one system or the other. Which one you choose may depend on personal preference, what is available on your system, or what your colleagues prefer (should you need to share your files with others).

Evolution of an SCCS File

When you change an SCCS file and record the changes in SCCS, the set of changes is referred to as a *delta*. Each delta has an associated version number, or SCCS Identification String (called SID), consisting of either two or four components. The first two, which are always used, are the *release* and *level* numbers. When an SCCS file is initially created, by default SCCS assigns a release number of 1 and a level number of 1, which corresponds to Version 1.1 (or delta 1.1). Also by default, SCCS assigns subsequent version numbers of 1.2, 1.3, and so on. However, you have control over the version numbers and can skip level numbers or change the release number. You should ordinarily only change the release number when the file has undergone a major revision.

Usually, files undergo a sequential development, where each delta includes all previous deltas. This kind of development is depicted in Figure 13-4. However, there are cases when changes are made to an intermediate version of a file. For example, if you were working on the source code file shown in Figure 13-4, and you had to make an emergency bug fix to Version 2.1 to deliver to customers prior to delivering Version 2.2, you would want to record a delta that reflected that fix but that excluded the changes involved in Version 2.2. In that case you would create the *branch* delta shown in Figure 13-5.

It is possible that you would work on the two deltas to Version 2.1 concurrently or that you would work on one while someone else worked on the other. However, because SCCS was designed to avoid the problems of coordination that occur when changes are made independently on the same file, SCCS normally prohibits concurrent deltas to the same version. Although you ordinarily would not want to, you can override this restriction if necessary.

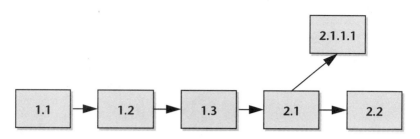

Figure 13-5   A Branch in the Evolution of an SCCS File

Unlike the earlier, sequentially applied deltas, the branch delta in Figure 13-5 has four components to its version number: *release, level, branch,* and *sequence number.* Version 2.1.1.1 is the first delta to the first branch on Release 2, Level 1. Successive deltas on that branch would be 2.1.1.2, 2.1.1.3, and so forth. Successive branches on Version 2.1 would start with deltas 2.1.2.1, 2.1.3.1, and so forth.

The evolution of an SCCS file can become complicated when there are many branch deltas. When you record changes to a file, try to keep the evolution of the versions as simple as you can. You should make a delta to a file only when you are sure that the changes you have made are complete. For example, when you are fixing a collection of bugs in a file, you should fix each one and completely test it before recording the changes in a delta. This technique saves you from having deltas that reflect incomplete, transitional stages in the history of a file.

Creating an SCCS File

The **admin** utility is one of the most important SCCS utilities—you can use it to create SCCS files as well as to change characteristics of existing SCCS files. If you have a Bourne Shell script called **blitz**, you can use **admin** to create an SCCS encoded version.

The **admin** command in Figure 13-6 creates the initial version of the SCCS encoded file **s.blitz**, Version 1.1. This file includes the contents of the file **blitz** as well as the control information SCCS adds. The statement **admin** presents, **No id keywords (cm7)**, is a warning message. The string in parentheses, **cm7**, is a code for a help message. If you give the command **help** followed by the code, the **help** utility will produce an explanation of the message.

```
$ help cm7
cm7:
'No id keywords'
No SCCS identification keywords were substituted for.
You may not have any keywords in the file,
in which case you can ignore this warning.
.
.
```

As the **help** utility explains, the message in Figure 13-6 indicates that there are no SCCS keywords in the encoded file. Keywords are SCCS codes you can use to insert information about the SCCS file into the text retrieved from the

```
$ cat blitz
:
# A script that noisily but cautiously
# empties the working directory

echo "The working directory is ` pwd ` "
echo "Delete all files in ` pwd ` ? \c"
read answer
case $answer in
        y|Y|[yY]es)
                    echo "OUCH!!!   BANG!!!   SPLAT!!!"
                    rm *
                    echo "We got 'em boss!"
                    ;;
        *)          echo "Files remain untouched"
                    ;;
esac
$ admin -iblitz s.blitz
No id keywords (cm7)
```

Figure 13-6   Contents of the **blitz** *File*

encoded file. For example, you can use keywords to identify the SCCS file-name, the version number, and the date and time the text was retrieved from the encoded file.

On some systems, you need to run the SCCS commands indirectly using another utility called **sccs**. If the examples do not work as shown, or if your search path does not seem to include the directory where the SCCS utilities are stored, try prefacing each command line with **sccs**. You would give the preceding command as **sccs help cm7**.

One SCCS keyword inserts a string @(#) in a file that the **what** command recognizes. The **what** command is an SCCS utility that sends to the standard output the text that follows the string @(#). Many standard UNIX utilities include these strings to identify the version number of the program. For example, you can use **what** to identify the version of the Korn Shell on a system.

```
$ what /bin/ksh
/bin/ksh:
        Version 11/16/88d
```

Because keywords are not used in the examples in this book, you can ignore the warning message when it occurs in the examples.

Although you can call the **admin** utility with many other arguments, in the form shown in Figure 13-6 its format is:

admin –i*name* **filename**

The **name** is the name of the file SCCS will encode. The **filename** is the name of the SCCS encoded file, and it must start with an **s.** prefix.

After you use **admin** to create an SCCS encoded file, you should move the original file to a backup directory. If you leave the original file in the working directory, SCCS will not allow you to retrieve the file from the encoded version while you are in that directory.

If you will use SCCS to manage many files, you may want to keep the **s.** files in a subdirectory named SCCS, rather than cluttering up your current directory. Otherwise, your directory will become crowded with two versions of every file: the SCCS encoded file and its latest version. On many systems, the **sccs** utility will look for the SCCS files in an SCCS subdirectory automatically. For example, if the file **SCCS/s.blitz** exists, the following two commands will have the same result.

```
$ sccs get SCCS/s.blitz
$ sccs get blitz
```

In the second form above, the **sccs** command not only looks for the file in the subdirectory SCCS, it does not require you to use the standard **s.** prefix with the filename.

Retrieving an SCCS File

You should not edit an SCCS encoded file such as **s.blitz**—editing the file would defeat the purpose of using SCCS. Use the **get** utility with the –e option to create an unencoded, writable version of the file. The –e option indicates to SCCS that you intend to edit the file and make a delta. In other words, it indicates to SCCS that you plan to make changes and record the changes in SCCS. If you call the **get** utility without the –e option, SCCS will create an unencoded version of the file that is not writable. The following command recreates the file **blitz** for editing:

```
$ get -e s.blitz
1.1
new delta 1.2
16 lines
```

The **get** command displays the version number of the retrieved delta, the version number that will be applied when the new changes are recorded in SCCS, and the number of lines in the file. If you forget to move the original **blitz** file to another directory after you create **s.blitz**, **get** will display the following error message. (Again, you can give the command **help ge4** to find out more about the error message.)

```
ERROR [s.blitz]: writable 'blitz' exists (ge4)
```

By default, the **get** command retrieves the most recent delta to the file. In the case of the file **s.blitz**, that delta is Version 1.1. You can also use **get** with the –r option to retrieve a specific delta or to change the number of the new delta.

```
$ get -e -r2 s.blitz
1.1
new delta 2.1
16 lines
```

Because there are no existing versions with a release number of 2, this command retrieves the latest delta prior to Release 2, and it changes the new version number to 2.1. If versions with a release number of 2 already existed, this command would have retrieved the most recent one.

If you retrieve a version that is earlier than the most recent version, SCCS will create a branch delta. For example, if a version number higher than 1.2 exists for **s.blitz**, retrieving Version 1.2 creates a branch delta.

```
$ get -e -r1.2 s.blitz
1.2
new delta 1.2.1.1
16 lines
```

It is easiest to keep track of the evolution of your SCCS files if only one **get** is active for a specific file at a time. However, SCCS allows you to simultaneously update different versions of a file as long as you put the retrieved files in different directories. If you try to retrieve a version while the working directory contains a previously retrieved version that is editable, SCCS displays an error message.

By default, SCCS prevents you from simultaneously working on two deltas to the same version of a file. If you want to have more than one **get** active against a single version of a file, you must use the **admin** utility to add the **j** flag to the SCCS file (SCCS distinguishes between *options,* which are used on the command line, and *flags,* which are added to a file as control information). Refer to **admin** in Part II for more information.

Recording Changes to an SCCS File

After you have edited the retrieved file and are ready to record the changes in SCCS, use the **delta** utility to record your changes. The user who retrieves a file must be the one who gives the **delta** command. Consequently, you can use **delta** only if you were the one who executed the corresponding **get**.

```
$ delta s.blitz
comments?
```

The **delta** utility prompts you for comments. In response, enter the reason for the changes. Assuming you had changed the **echo** commands inside the Case control structure in **blitz** as shown in Figure 13-7, you might enter the comment shown. Most versions of SCCS use a (NEWLINE) to terminate a comment, so to continue a comment from one line to the next, you must escape the (NEWLINE) character (that is, precede the (NEWLINE) with a backslash). Other versions of SCCS expect comments to span multiple lines, and they terminate a comment when you use (CONTROL)-**D** on a line by itself. If your version of SCCS uses (CONTROL)-**D** to terminate a comment, do not escape the (NEWLINE)s that occur within comments.

```
$ cat blitz
:
# A script that cautiously
# empties the working directory

echo "The working directory is ` pwd` "
echo "Delete all files in ` pwd` ? \c"
read answer
case "$answer" in
      y|Y|[yY]es)
                  echo "Files being removed"
                  rm *
                  echo "Done"
                  ;;
      *)          echo "Files remain untouched"
                  ;;
esac
$ delta s.blitz
comments? frivolous statements replaced \
with serious ones
No id keywords (cm7)
1.2
3 inserted
3 deleted
13 unchanged
```

Figure 13-7   Modified **blitz** *File*

In the example in Figure 13-7, **delta** displays a warning message followed by the version number and a summary of the changes that were made to the file after you enter your comments.

If you make a delta and later decide to remove it, you can use the **rmdel** utility to delete it. The following command removes Version 1.2 of **s.blitz**:

```
$ rmdel -r1.2 s.blitz
```

The **rmdel** utility removes only the latest version, or the latest version on a branch. After using **rmdel** to remove the latest version, you can remove the next most recent version, and so forth.

Although you would not want to edit it, you can look at an SCCS encoded file to get a better idea of how SCCS works. The file **s.blitz** is shown in Figure 13-8. To look at an encoded file, use **cat** with the –v option and pipe the output through **more**. The –v option causes **cat** to display visible representations of nonprinting characters. The characters ^A at the start of some lines represent (CONTROL)-**A**, which SCCS uses to identify lines that contain control information.

```
$ cat -v s.blitz | more
^Ah48993
^As 00003/00003/00013
^Ad D 1.2 94/06/21 10:38:25 alex 2 1
^Ac frivolous statements replaced
^Ac with serious ones
^Ae
^As 00016/00000/00000
^Ad D 1.1 94/06/21 10:35:34 alex 1 0
^Ac date and time created 94/06/21 10:35:34 by alex
^Ae
^Au
^AU
^At
^AT
^AI 1
:
^AD 2
# A script that noisily but cautiously
^AE 2
^AI 2
# A script that cautiously
^AE 2
# empties the working directory

echo "The working directory is ` pwd ` "
echo "Delete all files in ` pwd ` ? \c"
read answer
case $answer in
        y|Y|[yY]es)
^AD 2
                echo "OUCH!!  BANG!!  SPLAT!!"
^AE 2
^AI 2
                echo "Files being removed"
^AE 2
                rm *
^AD 2
                echo "We got 'em boss!"
^AE 2
^AI 2
                echo "Done"
^AE 2
                ;;
        *)      echo "Files remain untouched"
                ;;
esac
^AE 1
```

Figure 13-8   Contents of an Encoded SCCS File

```
$ prs s.blitz
s.blitz:

D 1.2 94/06/21 10:38:25 alex 2 1
00003/00003/00013
MRs:
COMMENTS:
frivolous statements replaced
with serious ones

D 1.1 94/06/21 10:35:34 alex 1 0
00016/00000/00000
MRs:
COMMENTS:
date and time created 94/06/21 10:35:34 by alex
```

Figure 13-9   The **prs** *Utility*

Obtaining the History of an SCCS File

The **prs** utility prints information about the history of an SCCS file. Although you can call **prs** with a variety of arguments that specify what information it reports and the format of the report, when it is called without any arguments, **prs** prints summary information about all deltas.

Figure 13-9 shows the following information about each delta: the date and time of creation, the user who made the delta, the sequence number of the delta and its predecessor, and the number of lines inserted, deleted, and unchanged. After the **MRs:** label would be a list of any modification request (MR) numbers for the delta. A *modification request* is a bug report against a program or software document. There is no information after the modification request label in Figure 13-9 because the examples do not use MR numbers. If you use the **v** flag and the **–m** option with **admin**, **delta** prompts you for MR numbers each time you use it. See **admin** in Part II for more information.

Restricting Access to SCCS Files

You can use the **admin** utility to establish a list of users who are allowed to make deltas to an SCCS file. By default, the list of users who can make changes to a file is empty, which means that anyone can make a delta. The following command gives permission to Alex and Jenny and implicitly denies permission to everyone else. After this command is executed, only Alex and Jenny will be able to make deltas:

```
$ admin -aalex -ajenny s.blitz
```

The **-e** (erase) option removes a user from the list, denying him or her permission to make deltas. The following command removes Jenny from the list of authorized users.

```
$ admin -ejenny s.blitz
```

In addition to allowing you to restrict access to a list of users, SCCS allows you to *lock* releases of a file so that no one can change them. The following command uses the **-f** option to set the l flag to lock Release 1 of **s.blitz**:

```
$ admin -fl1 s.blitz
```

After executing this command, if you try to retrieve a Release 1 delta for editing, **get** will give you an error message. Use the following command to lock all releases of the **s.blitz** file:

```
$ admin -fla s.blitz
```

The Revision Control System (RCS)

The Revision Control System (RCS) has many of the same features as SCCS. Like SCCS, each RCS file can have four components to its version number (release, level, branch, and sequence number). For the most common case, RCS was designed to be simpler to use than SCCS. SCCS and RCS also differ in the method they use to reconstruct a file when you request a particular version: SCCS starts with the original (version 1.1) file and applies all the changes leading up to the version you have requested. RCS starts with the latest version; if you have requested an earlier version of the file, RCS works backward, taking out the changes that were applied after the version you seek. Since most people work forward, making changes based on the latest copy of a file, it is usually faster to retrieve a file from RCS than from SCCS.

The examples in this section correspond to the examples presented in the section of this chapter on SCCS. Each example will be explained briefly, to avoid repeating material that has already been covered in detail in the earlier section.

If your current directory includes a subdirectory called RCS, the RCS commands will place the encoded files in that subdirectory. Like SCCS encoded files, RCS encoded files have special names. Each RCS encoded file ends with the two-character suffix **,v**.

Creating an RCS File

To create an RCS file, use the **ci** (check in) command. In the following example, the **ci** command reports that it is creating the file **RCS/blitz,v** from the input file **blitz** (note the direction of the arrow) and prompts you to enter a description of the file. Finally, **ci** reports the applicable revision number and confirms that it has finished running (done).

```
$ ci blitz
RCS/blitz,v <-- blitz
enter description, terminated with a single '.' or end of file:
```

```
NOTE: This is NOT the log message!
>> A script that empties the working directory
>> .
initial revision: 1.1
done
$
```

Retrieving and Recording Changes to an RCS File

To retrieve an RCS file, use the **co** (check out) command. If you plan to edit the file, you need to request a lock (so that no one else will retrieve the same file for editing). The following command puts a writable copy of the file **blitz** in your directory:

```
$ co -l blitz
RCS/blitz,v --> junk
revision 1.1 (locked)
done
$
```

The **co** utility will not overwrite a writable copy of the file, if one exists, in your current directory. In that case, you will see a message such as the following:

```
writable blitz exists; remove it? [ny](n):
```

If you press (RETURN), the default response to the question is *no* (**n**); the existing **blitz** will not be overwritten, and the current version of **blitz** will not be retrieved. If you do want to overwrite the file, respond with a **y**.

To retrieve a particular version of a file, use **co** with the -r option. Unlike SCCS, this command is only used to retrieve a file at a version level that already exists; you need to use the **ci** command to create new version levels. In this example, you decide to check in your changes to **blitz** at release version 2; **ci** prompts you to enter some comments about what you have done for the file's change log. After checking in the file, you need to make additional changes to version 1 of the file, so you use the -r option to retrieve the file at revision level 1.

```
$ ci -r2 blitz
RCS/blitz,v <-- blitz
new revision: 2.1; previous revision: 1.1
enter log message, terminated with single '.' or end of file:
>> major changes
>> .
done
$ co -l -r1 blitz
RCS/blitz,v --> blitz
revision 1.1 (locked)
done
$ vi blitz
.
.
.
$ ci blitz
RCS/blitz,v <-- blitz
new revision: 1.1.1.1; previous revision 1.1
enter log message, terminated with single '.' or end of file:
>> minor changes
>> .
done
$
```

486   CHAPTER 13   Programming Tools

Because a higher revision level exists for this file, **ci** created a new branch at the lower level (1.1.1.1).

Like SCCS, RCS recognizes certain keyword strings in a file. The command that looks for keywords is **ident**. There are no RCS keywords in the file blitz, as **ident** reports below.

```
$ ident blitz
blitz:
ident warning: no id keywords in blitz.
```

To remove a change to the file, use the -o option with the **rcs** command. In the following example, revision 2.1 is removed from the file **blitz**. Although SCCS allows you to remove only the latest version of a file on a particular branch, RCS allows you to remove intermediate versions. If the latest revision of blitz is version 2.3, the following command will remove version 2.2. Version 2.3, however, is not renumbered (it does not become version 2.2); the next **co** or **ci** command sequence will create version 2.4.

```
$ rcs -o2.2 blitz
RCS file: RCS/blitz,v
deleting revision 2.2
done
$
```

Like an SCCS-encoded file, there is no reason for you to work with an RCS-encoded file directly (that is, with non-RCS commands). If you look at an RCS file, you may learn a little about how it works and how it differs from the format of an SCCS file. Figure 13-10 shows the contents of the **RCS/blitz,v** file.

Obtaining the History of an RCS File

You can use the **rlog** command to display the history of an RCS file. Without additional options, **rlog** prints information about all the deltas that have been made to the file, as the following example demonstrates:

```
$ rlog blitz
RCS file: RCS/blitz,v
Working file: blitz
head: 1.2
branch:
locks: strict
access list:
symbolic names:
comment leader: "# "
keyword substitution: kv
total revisions: 2; selected revisions: 2
description:
----------------------------
revision 1.2
date: 1994/06/21 15:38:25; author: alex; state: Exp;
lines: +2 -2
frivolous statements replaced
```

```
with serious ones
----------------------------
revision 1.1
date: 1994/06/21 15:35:34; author: alex; state: Exp;
Initial revision
=========================================================
```

```
$ cat RCS/blitz,v
head 1.2;
access;
symbols;
locks; strict;
comment @# @;


1.2
date 94.06.21.15.38.25;        author alex;        state Exp;
branches;
next 1.1;


1.1
date 94.06.21.15.35.34;        author alex;        state Exp;
branches;
next ;

desc
@@


1.2
log
@frivolous statements replaced
with serious ones
@
text
@:
# A script that noisily but cautiously
# empties the working directory.
echo "The working directory is ` pwd` "
echo "Delete all files in ` pwd` ? \c"
read answer
case $answer in
     y|Y|[yY]es)
             echo "Files being removed"
             rm *
             echo "Done"
             ;;
     *) echo ""Files remain untouched"
     ;;
esac
@


1.1
log
@Initial revision
@
text
@d10 1
a10 1
             echo "OUCH!! BANG!! SPLAT!!"
d12 1
a12 1
             echo "We got 'em, boss!"
@
```

Figure 13-10   The **blitz** *File with RCS Encoding*

Restricting Access to RCS Files

The **rcs** command recognizes the same options as the SCCS **admin** command for adding and removing users from the list allowed to make deltas to a file, but uses a slightly different format. As with SCCS, by default anyone can check in a delta. The following command gives permission only to Alex and Jenny (excluding everyone else):

```
$ rcs -aalex,jenny blitz
```

The -e (erase) option removes a user from the list, denying permission to check in deltas. The following command removes Jenny from the list of authorized users:

```
$ rcs -ejenny blitz
```

SUMMARY

The operating system interface to C programs and a variety of software development tools make the UNIX system well suited to programming in C. The C libraries provide general-purpose C functions that make operating system services and other functionality available to C programmers. The standard C library, **libc**, is always accessible to C programs, and you can use other libraries by including them in an option to the **cc** command.

You can write a C program using a text editor, such as **vi**. C programs always have a function called **main** and often have several other functions. You can use preprocessor directives to define symbolic constants and macros and to instruct the preprocessor to include header files.

When you use the **cc** command, it first calls the C preprocessor, followed by the C compiler and the assembler. The compiler creates assembly language code, which the assembler uses to create object modules. Finally, the link editor combines the object modules into an executable file. You can use the C program verifier, **lint**, and a debugger (such as **dbx**) to aid in the process of debugging a program.

The **make** utility uses a file named **makefile** that documents the relationships among files. You can use it to keep track of which modules of a program are out-of-date and to compile files in order to keep all modules up-to-date.

Several utility programs comprise the Source Code Control System, SCCS, used to track changes to files involved in large software projects. SCCS stores the original files as well as each set of changes that was made to the originals so that you can regenerate any version of a file at any time. SCCS also documents the history of a file by recording who made each delta and when and why they made it. The Revision Control System, RCS, is another popular set of utilities for managing sourcce code.

1. How would you instruct the C preprocessor to include the header file **/usr/include/math.h** in your C program? How would you instruct it to include **/home/alex/headers/declar.h**?

2. What function does every C program have? Why should you split large programs into several functions?

3. What command could you use to compile **prog.c** and **func.c** into an executable called **cprog**?

4. In the **makefile** below, identify:

   a. targets

   b. construction commands

   c. prerequisites

   d. macros

   ```
   $ cat makefile
   COBJECTS = menu.o users.o resellers.o prospects.o
   HFILES = menu.h

   leads: $(COBJECTS)
           cc -o leads $(COBJECTS)

   menu.o users.o resellers.o prospects.o: $(HFILES)
   ```

5. If you are using the **makefile** in the previous exercise, what will happen if you give the following command?

   ```
   $ make
   ```

6. After compiling **leads** (refer to the **makefile** in exercise 4), if you change **users.c** and run **make** again, what will **make** do?

7. Write a **makefile** that reflects the following relationships:

   a. The C source files **transactions.c** and **reports.c** are compiled to produce an executable **accts**.

   b. **transactions.c** and **reports.c** include a header file **accts.h**.

   c. The header file **accts.h** is composed of two other header files: **trans.h** and **reps.h**.

8. What command can you use to create an SCCS encoded version of a file called **answers**? What command can you use to retrieve an editable version of **answers**?

9. How can you restrict the SCCS encoded file **s.answers** so that

   a. only barbara and hls can make changes

   b. no one can make changes to Release 2

10. If you retrieve Version 4.1 of the file **s.answers** for editing and then attempt to retrieve the same version again, what will SCCS do? Why is SCCS set up this way?

11. Modify the **tabs.c** program so that it exits cleanly (with a specific return value). Compile the program and run it using **dbx**. What values does **dbx** report when execution completes?

12. Suppose the file named **answers** includes revisions at levels 1.1 through 1.4 and you need to delete revision 1.2. How can you accomplish this if:

   a. the file is managed by SCCS (**s.answers**)?

   b. the file is managed by RCS (**answers,v**)?

CHAPTER 14

System Administration

The system administrator is responsible for setting up new users, installing and removing terminals and workstations, making sure there is enough space on the disk, backing up files, installing and upgrading software, bringing up and shutting down the system, monitoring system and network activity, helping users when they have problems, and many other computer housekeeping tasks.

Background

Because UNIX is so flexible, and because it runs on so many different machines, this chapter cannot discuss every system configuration or every action you will have to take as a system administrator. This chapter complements the administration sections of the manuals that came with your computer. The chapter assumes you are familiar with the following terms. Refer to the Glossary, page 767, for definitions.

block	daemon	device filename	device
environment	filesystem	fork	kernel
login shell	mount (a device)	process	restricted shell
root filesystem	signal	spawn	system console

SunOS pioneered a filesystem structure that was very different from earlier releases of UNIX. The new organization made it easier for other computers running compatible software to share certain files that are identical on many systems, such as utilities and manual pages. At the same time, each system must maintain private areas for files that are different on all systems, such as databases, system log files, and spooling areas. SunOS introduced the /var filesystem to hold those files.

This chapter describes the typical location of files, utilities, and directories on SunOS. The /var directory does not exist on typical Berkeley systems or other older versions of UNIX. Instead, subdirectories of /var were located in the /usr directory.

The System Administrator and the Superuser

One person is often designated as the system administrator. On large systems this can be a full-time job. On smaller systems, a user of the system may be assigned to do system administration in addition to his or her other work.

The system administrator has access to certain system-wide powers that are beyond those of ordinary users.

- Some commands, such as commands that halt the system, can be executed only by the system administrator.

- Read, write, and execute file access permissions do not affect the system administrator.

- The system administrator can search any directory and create a file in or remove a file from any directory. The system administrator can also read from, write to, or execute any file.

- Some restrictions and safeguards that are built into some commands do not apply to the system administrator. For example, the system administrator can change any user's password without knowing the old password.

Because these powers affect the security of all users' files as well as the security of the entire system, there is a special login name and password for the user who can log in on the system to perform these functions. The login name is generally *root*. Although you can set up a UNIX system with any name in place of root, it is not advisable to do so. Many programs depend on this name being *root*. There is also a special term for the user who has logged in as *root;* this user is called the *Superuser.*

Because of the extensive powers of destruction you have when you are the Superuser, it is a good idea to become the Superuser only when necessary. If you are just doing your ordinary day-to-day work, log in as yourself. That way you will not erase someone else's files or bring down the machine by mistake.

There are three ways to become the Superuser:

1. When you bring up the system, if it comes up in single-user mode (page 495), you are automatically logged in as the Superuser.

2. Once the system is up and running in multiuser mode (page 496), you can log in as *root,* and if you supply the proper password, you will be the Superuser.

3. You can give an **su** (substitute user) command while you are logged in as yourself, and, with the proper password, you will have the privileges of the Superuser. To be sure that you are using the system's official version of **su** (and not one planted on your system by someone trying to break in), you should always specify **su**'s absolute pathname (that is, **/usr/bin/su**) when you use it. You must also be a member of the group whose group id is 0 (this group is often named *wheel)* to be permitted to **su** to root. See page 499 for a description of the **/etc/group** file.

Once you have given an **su** command to become the Superuser, you return to your normal status by terminating the shell (by pressing (CONTROL)**-D** or giving an **exit** command). To remind you of your special powers, the shell normally displays a different prompt (usually #) while you are logged in as the Superuser.

System Administration Tools

Many of the commands you will use as the Superuser are typically kept in the **/usr/etc** directory. They are kept there (rather than in **/usr/bin**) to lessen the chance that a user other than the Superuser will try to use one by mistake. You can execute these commands by giving their full pathnames on the command line (e.g., **/usr/etc/newfs**) *or* by including the **/usr/etc** directory in your **PATH** when you are logged in as the Superuser. The following line in the **/.profile** file will put **/usr/etc** in your **PATH** when you log in as *root* using either the Bourne or Korn Shell:

```
PATH=/usr/etc:$PATH
```

If your Superuser login uses the C Shell, also put the next line in the /.**login** file. You need to set the **PATH** variable in both **.login** and **.profile** because in certain cases (such as when you initially start up the system) the Superuser login uses the Bourne Shell, regardless of whether it is set up to use the C Shell.

```
set path = (/usr/etc $path)
```

Detailed Description of System Operation

This section covers the following topics:

- booting the system
- single-user mode and maintenance
- the transition from single-user to multiuser mode
- multiuser mode
- logging in
- bringing the system down
- crashes

It covers these topics so that you understand the basics of how the system functions and can make intelligent decisions as a system administrator. It does not cover every aspect of system administration to the depth necessary to set up or modify all system functions. It provides a guide to bringing a system up and keeping it running on a day-to-day basis. Refer to your system manual for procedures specific to your machine.

Subsequent sections of this chapter and Part II of this book describe many of the system administration files and utilities in detail.

Bringing Up (Booting) the System

Booting a system is the process of reading the UNIX system kernel into the system memory and starting it running. (The kernel is the heart of the UNIX system and is usually stored in /**vmunix** on Berkeley-derived systems, such as SunOS.)

Most systems come up automatically, whereas others may require you to enter information at the system console before they get started. As the last step of the boot procedure, the UNIX operating system runs the **init** program as process number 1. The **init** program is the first genuine process to run after booting, and it becomes the parent of all the login shells that will eventually run on the system.

When you bring the system up, it may either go into single-user mode or multiuser mode, depending on how your boot program is set up and depending on how you start the booting process (many systems have different commands that bring the system up into either single-user or multiuser mode). If your system goes into single-user mode, you can terminate that mode and enter multiuser mode by pressing (CONTROL)-**D**.

On most Berkeley UNIX systems there are two run command scripts: /etc/rc and /etc/rc.local. SunOS uses an additional script, /etc/rc.boot. The /etc/rc.boot script checks the integrity of the filesystems, if it exists; otherwise, that task is handled by /etc/rc. The second part of the /etc/rc script runs at the time that the multiuser state begins. The /etc/rc script calls the /etc/rc.local script, which is intended to be customized to carry out tasks that are unique to your site. As the system administrator, you should edit /etc/rc.local rather than /etc/rc in order to lessen the chance of making serious errors that could interrupt the system startup process.

Single-User Mode

When your system is in single-user mode, only the system console is enabled; however, you can still run programs from the console as you would from any terminal in multiuser mode. The only difference is that not all filesystems may be mounted. You will not be able to access files on filesystems that are not mounted.

When you change a file while in single-user mode, the modified file is not written out automatically to the hard disk. To cause the system to write out any changes you have made, type the **sync** command periodically while in single-user mode as well as right before going into multiuser mode.

Maintenance

With the system in single-user mode, you can perform maintenance that requires filesystems unmounted or just a quiet system (no one except you using it, so that no user programs interfere with disk maintenance and backup programs).

Backing Up Files

Although you can back up files while other people are using the system, it is better if you back them up while users are not using the files; the files will not be changing, and you will be assured of accurate copies of all the files.

Checking Filesystem Integrity

The **fsck** (filesystem check) utility verifies the integrity of a filesystem and, if possible, repairs any problems it finds. A filesystem (except the root) must not be mounted while **fsck** is checking it.

If you do not specify a device when you run **fsck**, **fsck** will check all devices listed in the /etc/fstab file.

Because many filesystem repairs destroy data, **fsck** asks you before making each repair. Two options cause **fsck** to run without asking you questions. The –y option assumes a *yes* response to all questions, and a –n assumes *no*.

Always run **fsck** on a filesystem before it is mounted. The **fsck** utility should be run on *all* filesystems before the UNIX system is brought up in multiuser mode after it has been down for any reason. Many **rc** scripts run **fsck** on all filesystems that will be mounted (frequently with the –y option and using **fstab** to specify the files to be checked). Refer to **fsck** in Part II for more information.

Going Multiuser

After you have determined that all is well with all filesystems, you can bring the operating system up to multiuser mode.

Pressing (CONTROL)-D in response to the Superuser prompt (when the system is in single-user mode) brings the system up to the multiuser mode. The **init** utility reads a file named **/etc/ttytab** to determine which terminal and dial-in lines to activate. It also runs the **/etc/rc** script, which mounts the filesystems and starts many system services.

Multiuser Mode

Multiuser mode is the normal state for a UNIX system. All appropriate filesystems are mounted, and users can log in from all connected terminals and dial-in lines.

Logging In

When you bring a system up in multiuser mode, **init** forks a series of **getty** processes, each associated with a line users can log in on. Each **getty** process displays a login: prompt on a terminal and waits for someone to try to log in. When you enter your login name, **getty** establishes the characteristics of your terminal and then overlays itself with a **login** process and passes it whatever you entered in response to the login: prompt. The **login** program consults the **/etc/passwd** file to see if there is a password associated with the login name you entered. If there is, **login** prompts you for a password; if not, it continues without requiring a password. If your login name requires a password, **login** verifies the password you enter by checking the **/etc/passwd** file. If either your login name or password are not correct, **login** displays Login incorrect, and prompts you to log in again.

If the login name and password are correct, **login** consults the **/etc/passwd** file to initialize your user and group IDs, establish your home directory, and determine which shell you will be working with.

The **login** command looks in the **/etc/group** file to identify all the groups the user belongs to (refer to the discussion on page 499 for more information). It also assigns values to **HOME**, **SHELL**, and **USER**, which the user's login shell inherits, and displays the contents of the **/etc/motd** file. Finally, the login process overlays itself with the program specified in the user's **/etc/passwd** file entry (usually a shell, which reads and executes the commands in the user's **.profile** or **.login** and **.cshrc** files).

Running a Program and Logging Out

When you see a shell prompt, you can execute a program or log off the system. When you log out, the process running the shell dies, and the operating system signals **init** that one of its children has died. When **init** receives one of these signals, it updates two filesystems files that track logins (**/etc/utmp** and **/var/adm/wtmp**) and starts a new **getty** process for that terminal line.

Bringing the System Down

A program named **/etc/shutdown** performs all the tasks involved in bringing the system down. Use this script to bring the system down; refer to your system manual for more information. The next section describes the steps you can use to perform the key steps of **shutdown** manually, if necessary.

Going to Single-User Mode

Because going from multiuser to single-user mode can affect other users, you must be the Superuser to make this change. Make sure you give other users enough warning before going to single-user mode; otherwise they may lose whatever they were working on.

Although it is not recommended, you can use the following procedure in place of **shutdown**:

1. Log in as *root* or use **su** to become the Superuser.

2. Use **wall** (write all) to warn everyone who is using the system to log off.

3. Give the command **sync** three times in a row. The **sync** utility forces the system to write out the contents of all disk buffers, thereby ensuring that the data on the disk is up-to-date. Because **sync** returns a prompt *before* it has completed, giving the command three times or more is one way you can be confident that at least the first one has time to complete.

4. Use **umount** to unmount all mounted devices. (You can use **mount** without an argument to see what devices are mounted.)

5. Give the command **kill –TERM 1** to bring the system down to single-user mode.

Turning the Power Off

Once the system is in single-user mode, shutting it down is quite straightforward. If you have run any programs since you brought it down to single-user mode, you must run **sync** again (do it several times) before turning the power off or resetting the system. Consult your system manual for details on your system.

The only time you will not use **sync** before turning the power off or resetting the system is after using **fsck** to repair the root filesystem. Refer to **fsck** in Part II for details.

Crashes

A *crash* is the system stopping when you do not intend it to. After a crash, the operating system must be brought up carefully to minimize possible damage to the filesystems. Frequently, there will be no damage or minimal damage to the filesystems.

Although the filesystems are frequently checked automatically during the boot process, you may have to check them manually, depending on how your system is set up and how you initiated the boot process. To check the filesystems manually after a crash, boot the system into single-user mode.

DO NOT mount any devices other than the root (which the UNIX system mounts automatically). Run **fsck** on the root immediately, repairing the root as suggested by **fsck**. If you repair the root filesystem, reboot the system immediately *without* running **sync**. Then run **fsck** on all the other filesystems *before* mounting them. Repair them as needed. Make note of any ordinary files or directories that you repair (and can identify), and inform their owners that they may not be complete or correct. Look in the **lost+found** directory in each filesystem for missing files. Refer to **fsck** in Part II for more information.

If files are not correct or are missing altogether, you may have to recreate them from a backup copy of the filesystem. Refer to "Backing Up Files," page 506, for more information.

When the system crashes, it attempts to save information on its state that you can use to debug the problem. If there is enough disk space, the system will save a complete copy of the data in the computer's memory in a temporary, *scratch* directory. When the system reboots, it will look for this crash dump and transfer it to a file under **/var/crash** (or **/usr/adm/crash**). For each crash, two files will be stored: a copy of the version of **/vmunix** that was running at the time of the crash and a copy of the contents of the system's memory. These files will be named **vmunix.N** and **vmcore.N**, where N represents a sequence number (so you know which files are related). Debugging the UNIX kernel is an advanced topic that is beyond the scope of this book.

OPTIONAL

Important Files and Directories

Many files are important to the administration of the system. This section details the most common files, listed in alphabetical order. Refer also to page 76, "Important Standard Directories and Files." On SunOS and many other systems, some of these files are shared across multiple hosts using the Network Information Service (NIS–page 163).

/dev/null   Any output you redirect to this file will disappear. You can send error messages from shell scripts here when you do not want the user to see them.

If you redirect input from this file, it will appear as a null (empty) file. You can create an empty file named **nothing** by giving the following command. You can also use this technique to truncate an existing file to zero length without changing its permissions.

```
$ cat /dev/null > nothing
```

/var/spool/cron   By default, users cannot use the **at** or **crontab** utilities to schedule jobs in advance. The **/var/spool/cron** directory includes files named **at.allow** and **cron.allow** that list the login names of users who are permitted to use these utilities. Files called **at.deny** and **cron.deny** in this directory specify users who are not permitted to use the corresponding utilities. If you wish to allow everyone to use them, create empty **at.deny** and **cron.deny** files (and do not create **at.allow** or **cron.allow** files).

OPTIONAL Continued

/etc/group Groups allow users to share files or programs without allowing all system users access to them. This scheme is useful if several users are working with files that are not public information.

An entry in the **/etc/group** file has the four fields shown below. If an entry is too long to fit on one line, end the line with a backslash (\), which will quote the following (RETURN), and continue the entry on the next line.

group-name:password:group-ID:login-name-list

The **group-name** is from one to six characters, the first being alphabetic and none being uppercase. The **password** is an optional encrypted password. Because there is no good way to enter a password into the **group** file, group passwords are not very useful and should be avoided. The **group-ID** is a number between 0 and 65,535, with 0-99 being reserved. The **login-name-list** is a comma-separated list of users who belong to that group. A sample entry in a **group** file is shown below. The group is named **pubs**, has no password, and has a group ID of 100.

```
pubs::100:alex,jenny,scott,hls,barbara
```

The /etc/group file does not define groups. Groups come into existence when a user is assigned a group ID number in the **/etc/passwd** file. The /etc/group file associates a name with each group.

Each user has a primary group, which is the group that user is assigned in the **/etc/passwd** file. In addition, you may belong to other groups, depending on what **login-name-lists** you are included on in the /etc/group file. In effect, you simultaneously belong to both your primary group and to any groups you are assigned to in /etc/group. When you attempt to access a file you do not own, the operating system checks to see whether you are a member of the group that has access to the file. If you are, your access permissions are controlled by the group access permissions for the file. If you are not a member of the group that has access to the file, you are subject to the public access permissions for the file.

When you create a new file, it is assigned to the group that is associated with the directory the file is being written into, assuming that you belong to the group. If you do not belong to the group that has access to the directory, the file is assigned to your primary group.

On older releases of the UNIX System, you need to use the **newgrp** command to change your group ID number to another group, assuming you are listed in the **login-name-list** of that group. The **newgrp** command takes an argument, which is the name of the group you want to change to. (You can always use **newgrp** without an argument to change your group ID back to what it was when you first logged in.)

/etc/mtab The *mount table* file contains a list of all currently mounted devices and is called **/etc/mtab**. When you call **mount** without any arguments, **mount** consults this table and displays a list of mounted devices. On most systems, this file is not an ASCII text file—you cannot edit it with a text editor. (In any case, you *should not* edit it.)

OPTIONAL Continued

The operating system maintains its own internal mount table, which may, on occasion, differ from this file. The surest way to bring the **mtab** file in line with the operating system's mount table is to bring the system down and reboot it. Each time you (or an **rc** script) call **mount** or **umount**, these programs make the necessary changes to **mtab**.

/etc/motd   The **/etc/motd** file contains the message of the day, which is displayed each time someone logs in. The file should be kept short because users tend to see the message many times. Being subjected to a long message of the day can also be tedious for users who communicate with the system over slow dial-up lines.

/etc/passwd   Each entry in the **passwd** file occupies a line, has seven fields, and describes one user to the system. Colons separate each field from the adjacent fields.

login-name:password:user-ID:group-ID:info:directory:program

The **login-name** is the user's login name—the name the user enters in response to the `login:` prompt. The **password** is an encrypted version of the user's password. Although it is optional, for security reasons every account should have a password.

The **user-ID** is a user ID number from 0 to 65,535, with 0 indicating the Superuser, and 0-99 reserved by convention. The **group-ID** identifies the user as a member of a group. It is a number between 0 and 65,535, with 0-99 being reserved. The **info** is information that various programs, such as accounting programs, use to further identify the user. Normally, it contains at least the user's name.

The **directory** is the absolute pathname of the user's home directory. The **program** is the program that will run after the user logs in. If **program** is not present, **/bin/sh** is assumed. You can put **/bin/csh** here to log in to the C Shell, or **/bin/ksh** to log in to the Korn Shell.

A brief sample **passwd** file is shown below. The **info** field stores names.

```
# cat /etc/passwd                              /
root:Urv8ynuDi2U:0:1::/:/bin/sh
bill:GE9tC647f01:102:100:Bill Hanley:/home/bill:/bin/csh
roy:QpIR2E.zANA:104:100:Roy Wong:/home/roy:/bin/ksh
alex:.NhVehQ04s:106:100:Alex Watson:/home/alex:/bin/sh
jenny:gKnL.DLFami:107:100:Jenny Chen:/home/jenny:/bin/sh
```

The program specified in the right-hand field of each line in the **passwd** file is usually a shell, but as shown below, it can be any program. The following line in the **passwd** file will create a "user" whose only purpose is to execute the **who** utility:

```
who::1000:1000:execute who:/usr:/bin/who
```

Using **who** as a login name causes the system to log you in, execute the **who** utility, and log you out. This entry in the **passwd** file does not provide a shell—there is no way for you to stay logged in after **who** is finished executing.

.profile   The Bourne and Korn Shells execute the commands in this file in the same environment as the shell each time a user logs in.

This file *must* be located in a user's home directory. (Each user has a different .profile file.) It usually specifies a terminal type (for **vi** and other programs), runs **stty** to establish terminal characteristics desired by the user, and performs other housekeeping functions when a user logs in.

A typical .profile file specifying a vt100 terminal and (CONTROL)-H as the erase key is as follows:

```
$ cat .profile
TERM=vt100
export TERM
stty erase '^h'
```

If you log in from more than one type of terminal, you may want to construct a more elaborate routine, such as the following one, that asks you for the terminal type each time you log in:

```
$ cat .profile
echo 'Terminal type: \c'
read TERM
export TERM
stty erase '^h'
```

.login   This file performs the same function as the .profile file in the user's home directory, but it is used by the C Shell.

The Run Command (rc) Files   The **init** program executes a series of run command, or **rc**, files during the boot process. The run command scripts perform tasks such as checking and mounting filesystems (when the system goes multiuser), removing temporary files (after the filesystems are mounted) and starting daemons to handle system services. On SunOS, the files **/etc/rc.boot**, **/etc/rc**, and **/etc/rc.local** are run (in that order). Changes and additions for your site should be confined to **/etc/rc.local**.

/etc/fstab   The file that contains a list of device filenames that **fsck** checks by default is called **/etc/fstab** on systems derived from Berkeley UNIX, such as SunOS. This list should be the same as the list of devices that the run command (**rc**) script mounts when you bring the system up to multiuser mode. A sample file follows.

```
# cat /etc/fstab
/dev/sd6a      /              4.2      rw            1 1
/dev/sd6b      swap           swap     rw            0 0
/dev/sd6d      /usr           4.2      rw            1 2
/dev/sr0       /cdrom         4.2      ro,noauto  0 0
sobell:/home   /sobell/home   nfs      rw,bg,hard 0 0
```

OPTIONAL Continued

The **/etc/fstab** file includes six fields separated by spaces. They specify:

- the block device name (page 505)
- the mount directory of the filesystem
- the filesystem type
- options, such as whether the filesystem is mounted for reading and writing (default) or just for reading. If there is no entry for a particular field, a hyphen serves as a placeholder
- a number indicating how often the filesystem is backed up
- a number used by **fsck** to determine the sequence in which the filesystem should be checked

/vmunix   This file contains the UNIX system kernel that is loaded when you boot the system.

/etc/shutdown   Use this program to bring the system down properly—refer to your system manual for more information. On some systems the **/etc/shutdown** file is a shell script; on others it is a C program. If you do not have this program, refer to the section of this chapter called "Bringing the System Down" on page 497.

Types of Files

The UNIX System supports several types of files: ordinary, directory, block special, character special, fifo special, sockets, and symbolic links. Ordinary files hold user data; directories hold directory information. Special files represent routines in the kernel that provide access to some feature of the operating system. Block and character special files represent device drivers that let you communicate with peripheral devices such as terminals, printers, and disk drives. Fifo (*first in, first out*) special files, also called *named pipes*, allow unrelated programs to exchange information. Sockets allow unrelated processes on the same or different computers to exchange information. One type of socket, the UNIX domain socket, is a special file. Symbolic links allow you to link files that are in different filesystems. (Plain links, or *hard links*, work only within a single filesystem.)

Ordinary Versus Directory Files

An *ordinary* file stores user data, such as textual information and programs.

A *directory* is a disk file with a standard format that stores a list of names of ordinary files and other directories. It relates each of these filenames to an *inode number*. An inode number identifies the *inode* for a file, which is a data structure that defines the file's existence. Inodes contain critical information such as who the owner of the file is and where it is located on disk.

When you move (**mv**) a file, you change the filename portion of the directory entry that is associated with the inode that describes the file. You do not create a new inode.

When you make an additional hard link (**ln**) to a file, you create another reference (an additional filename) to the inode that describes the file. You do not create a new inode.

When you remove (**rm**) a file, you remove the entry in the directory that describes the file. When you remove the last link to a file (the inode keeps track of the number of links), the operating system puts all the blocks the inode pointed to back in the *free list* (the list of blocks on the disk that are available for use).

Every directory always has at least two entries (**.** and **..**). The **.** entry is a link to the directory itself. The **..** entry is a link to the parent directory. In the case of the root directory, where there is no parent, the **..** entry is a link to the root directory itself. Ordinary users cannot create hard links to directories.

Symbolic Links

Because each filesystem has a separate set of inodes, you can create hard links to a file only from within the filesystem in which the file resides. To get around this limitation, the UNIX system has symbolic links. Files that are linked by a symbolic link do not share an inode, so you can create a symbolic link to a file from within any filesystem. You can also create a symbolic link to a directory. Refer to Chapter 4 for more information about symbolic links.

Special Files

By convention, special files appear in the /**dev** directory. Each special file represents a device: You read from and write to the file to read from and write to the device it represents. (Fifo special files represent pipes: You read from and write to the file to read from and write to the pipe. Similarly, you read from and write to a socket special file to read from and write to the socket.) Although you will not normally read directly from or write directly to device files, the kernel and many UNIX system utilities do.

The following example shows a sampling of the display an **ls –l** command produces for the /**dev** directory on a system running SunOS:

```
# ls -l /dev
crw-rw-rw-  1 root     37,  69 Mar 15  1994 audio
crw--w--w-  1 root      0,   0 Oct 20 08:10 console
crw-------  1 root     29,   0 Mar 15  1994 klog
crw-r-----  1 root      3,   1 Mar 15  1994 kmem
srw-rw-rw-  1 root      0,   0 Sep 30 08:53 log
crw-rw-rw-  1 root      3,   2 Oct 20 09:32 null
crw-r-----  1 root     17,  48 Mar 15  1994 rsd6a
brw-r-----  1 root      7,  48 Mar 15  1994 sd6a
crw-rw-rw-  1 root      2,   0 Oct 20 13:49 tty
crw--w----  1 jenny    12,   0 Oct 20 15:13 ttya
crw-rw-rw-  1 root     12,   1 Oct 19 10:42 ttyb
```

The first character of each line is always **b**, **c**, **d**, **l**, **p**, or **s** for block, character, directory, symbolic link, pipe, or socket (see below). The next nine characters represent the permissions for the file, followed by the number of hard links and the names of the owner and group. Where the number of bytes in a file would appear for an ordinary or directory file, a device file shows its *major* and *minor device numbers* separated by a comma (see below). The rest of the line is the same as any other **ls –l** listing.

Fifo Special Files

Unless you are writing sophisticated programs, you will not be working with fifo special files (called *named pipes*).

The term *fifo* stands for *first in, first out*—the way any pipe works. The first information that you put in one end is the first information that comes out the other end. When you use a pipe on a command line to send the output of a program to the printer, the printer prints the information in the same order that the program produced it.

The UNIX system has had pipes for many generations. Without named pipes, only processes that were children of the same ancestor could exchange information using pipes. Using named pipes, *any* two processes can exchange information. One program writes to a fifo special file. Another program reads from the same file. The programs do not have to run at the same time or be aware of each other's activity. The operating system handles all buffering and information storage.

Sockets

Like fifo special files, sockets allow processes that are not running at the same time and that are not the children of the same ancestor to exchange information. Sockets are the central mechanism of the interprocess communication facility that is the basis of the networking facility. When you use networking utilities, pairs of cooperating sockets manage the communication between the processes on your computer and the remote computer. Sockets form the basis of utilities such as **rlogin** (remote login) and **rcp** (remote copy).

Major and Minor Device Numbers

A *major device number* represents a class of hardware devices: a terminal, printer, tape drive, disk drive, and so on. In the preceding list of the /**dev** directory, all the terminals have a major device number of 12.

A *minor device number* represents a particular piece of hardware within a class. Although all the terminals are grouped together by their major device number (12), each has a different minor device number (ttya is 0, ttyb is 1, and so on). This setup allows one piece of software (the device driver) to service all similar hardware while being able to distinguish among different physical units.

Block and Character Devices

This section makes distinctions based on typical device drivers. Because the distinctions are based on device drivers, and because device drivers can be changed to suit a particular purpose, the distinctions in this section will not pertain to every system.

A *block device* is an I/O (input/output) device that is characterized by

- the ability to perform random access reads
- a specific block size
- handling only single blocks of data at a time
- accepting only transactions that involve whole blocks of data
- being able to have a filesystem mounted on it
- having the kernel buffer its input and output
- appearing to the operating system as a series of blocks numbered from 0 through $n-1$, where n is the number of blocks on the device

The standard block devices on a UNIX system are disk and tape drives.

A *character device* is any device that is not a block device. Some examples of character devices are printers, terminals, and modems.

The device driver for a character device determines how a program reads from and writes to the device. For example, the device driver for a terminal allows a program to read the information you type on the terminal in two ways. A program can read single characters from a terminal in *raw* mode (that is, without the driver doing any interpretation of the characters). This mode has nothing to do with the *raw device* described in the following section. Alternatively, a program can read a line at a time. When a program reads a line at a time, the driver handles the erase and kill characters, so that the program never sees typing mistakes and corrections. In this case the program reads everything from the beginning of a line to the (RETURN) that ends a line; the number of characters in a line can vary.

Raw Devices

Device driver programs for block devices usually have two entry points so that they can be used in two ways: as block devices *or* as character devices. The character device form of a block device is called a *raw* device. A raw device is characterized by

- direct I/O (no buffering through the kernel)
- a one-to-one correspondence between system calls and hardware requests
- device-dependent restrictions on I/O

An example of a utility that uses a raw device is **fsck**. It is more efficient for **fsck** to operate on the disk as a raw device, not restricted by the fixed size of blocks in the block device interface. Because **fsck** has full knowledge of the underlying filesystem structure, it can operate on the raw device using the largest possible units. When a filesystem is mounted, processes normally access the disk through the block device interface. This explains why it is important to allow **fsck** only to modify an unmounted filesystem. Otherwise, there would be the danger that another process would change a disk block using the block device while **fsck** was rearranging the underlying structure through the raw device. The result would be a corrupted filesystem.

Day-to-Day System Administration Functions

In addition to bringing up and shutting down the system, you have other responsibilities as the system administrator. This section covers the most important of these responsibilities.

Backing Up Files

One of the most neglected tasks of the system administrator is making backup copies of files on a regular basis. The backup copies are vital in two instances: when the system malfunctions and files are lost, and when a user (or the system administrator) deletes a file by accident.

You must back up the filesystems on a regular basis. Backup files are usually kept on floppy disks or magnetic tape, as determined by your system. Exactly how often you should back up which files depends on your system and needs. The criterion is, "If the system crashes, how much work are you willing to lose?" Ideally, you would back up all the files on the system every few minutes so that you would never lose more than a few minutes of work.

The trade-off is, "How often are you willing to back up the files?" The backup procedure typically slows down the machine for other users, takes a certain amount of your time, and requires that you have and store the media (tape or disk) that you keep the backup on.

The more people using the machine, the more often you should back up the filesystems. A common schedule might have you perform a partial backup one or two times a day and a full backup one or two times a week.

A *partial* backup makes copies of the files that have been created or modified since the last backup. A *full* backup makes copies of all files, regardless of when they were created or accessed.

Using the dump and restore Utilities

You can use the **dump** utility either to back up an entire filesystem, or to back up only those files that have changed since the last **dump**. The **restore** utility can be used either to restore an entire filesystem or an individual file or piece of the filesystem hierarchy.

The **dump** utility will make a backup at any of ten *levels*, numbered 0 through 9. A level 0 dump is a dump of an entire filesystem. Dumps at levels 1 through 9 back up any files that have changed since the most recent dump at a lower level. For example, if you do a level 0 dump and then a level 5 dump, the level 5 dump will include any files that changed since the level 0 dump. If you then do a level 7 dump, it will include all files that changed since the level 5 dump. Then if you do another level 5 dump, it will include all the files that changed since the original level 0 dump, and so on.

Because level 0 dumps are slow, it is typical to do several higher-level dumps between level 0 dumps. A common strategy is to do a level 0 dump weekly and partial dumps daily. Whether all your partial dumps are at a single level, or whether you use an ascending or descending sequence of levels (or another scheme) depends on your needs.

For the best results, you should always run **dump** when the filesystem you are dumping is unmounted and the system is in single-user mode. The following command performs a level 0 dump of **/usr**:

```
# /etc/dump 0uf /dev/rmt0 /usr
```

The **u** option specifies that the file **/etc/dumpdates** should be updated. The **/etc/dumpdates** file keeps a record of the dumps that have been performed. If **/etc/dumpdates** is not updated, the next time you do a dump, **dump** will not recognize this dump in the process of identifying files to be dumped. In the above command, the **f** option followed by **/dev/rmt0** specifies that **/dev/rmt0** is the device to be dumped to. If the device you are using corresponds to the default dump device for your system, you do not need to use the **f** option.

To restore an entire filesystem from a dump tape, you should first restore the most recent level 0 dump. This should be done carefully, since **restore** will overwrite the existing filesystem. When you are logged in as Superuser and the system is in single-user mode, change directory to the directory the filesystem is mounted on and give the following command:

```
# /etc/restore rf /dev/rmt0
```

Following this command, you should give the same command to restore from any partial backups. Restore the oldest one first and continue through the most recent one.

You can also use **restore** to extract individual files from a tape. The **i** option to **restore** enables you to interactively select files. Using a shell-like interface and commands similar to **ls**, **cd**, and **pwd**, you can move around the directory hierarchy selecting files to extract. The **restore** utility builds a list of files to extract, and then when you give it the **extract** command, it extracts all the files in the list.

If there is no tape device on your system and your system is connected to a network, you may be able to use **rdump** and **rrestore** to access a tape drive on another system over the network. Consult the documentation that was supplied with your system for more information on **dump**, **rdump**, **restore** and **rrestore**. You should find detailed examples in your system manual that will include the names for the tape devices on your system as well as the parameters you should specify to make the most efficient use of your system resources.

Adding and Removing Users

More than a login name is required for a user to be able to log in and use the system. A user must have the necessary files, directories, permissions, and, optionally, a password in order to log in. Minimally, a user must have an entry in the /etc/passwd file and a home directory. If you choose to run the Network Information Service (NIS) to manage the passwd database, refer to your system manuals for information on configuring and managing NIS.

Adding a New User

Some manufacturers have shell scripts (such as /etc/adduser) for adding new users. If your system has one of these scripts, use it. Otherwise, the following description explains how to add a new user to the system.

The first item a new user requires is an entry in the /etc/passwd file. Use **vipw** to edit the **passwd** file. The **vipw** utility locks the file so that no one else can edit it while you are editing it, and then it calls **vi**. Below is a sample entry in the /etc/passwd file; refer to page 500 for more information. Do *not* use a group or user ID less than 100.

```
alex::106:100:Alex Watson:/home/alex:/bin/sh
```

If you want to give the user a password, use the **passwd** utility with the user's login name as an argument. Because you are logged in as the Superuser, **passwd** does not ask you for the old password, even if there is one. Because of this special treatment, you can give users a new password when they forget their old one.

```
# passwd alex
Changing password for alex.
New password:
Type new password again:
```

Now use **mkdir** to create the user's home directory you specified in the passwd file and **chown** to make the user the owner of the new directory. Use **chgrp** to associate the new directory with the owner's primary group. Finally, use **chmod** to establish the desired access privileges. The following example sets up the directory so that anyone besides the owner can scan through and read files in the home directory, but they cannot change files or write to the directory:

```
# mkdir /home/alex
# chown alex /home/alex
# chgrp pubs /home/alex
# chmod 755 /home/alex
```

To test the new setup, log in as the new user and create an appropriate .profile or .login file in the new user's home directory. (You may have to manually assign a value to and export the **TERM** shell variable if you want to use **vi** to create this file—see page 29.) It is a common practice to have a default .login or .profile file that is copied into each new user's home directory.

Removing a User

Remove a user by removing the user's entry in the **passwd** file and removing all the user's files and directories. If appropriate, make a backup copy of all the files belonging to the user before deleting them.

If you just want to prevent a user from logging in temporarily and the system is not on a network, you can put an **x** in the user's password field in the **passwd** file. You will need to give the user a new password when you want to allow the user to log in again. In some networked environments, just changing a user's password will not prevent the user from logging in—you need to remove the user's entry in the **passwd** file.

Checking Your Mail and Log Files

If you do not forward root's mail to yourself, remember to check periodically to see if there is any mail for the system administrator. Users frequently use electronic mail to communicate with the system administrator.

You will not receive reminders about mail that arrives for *root* if you always use the **su** command to perform system administration tasks. However, after using **su** to become *root,* you can give the **Mail –u root** command to look at the Superuser's mail. You should also look at the system log files regularly for evidence of problems. Two important files are **/var/adm/messages**, where the operating system and some applications record errors, and the files in the **/var/log** directory, which include errors from the mail system (syslog files).

Scheduling Routine Tasks

It is a good practice to schedule certain routine tasks to run automatically. For example, you may want to remove old core files once a week, summarize accounting data daily, and rotate system log files monthly. The **cron** utility is designed to run commands at regularly scheduled times. Using the **crontab** utility, a user may submit a list of commands in a format that can be read and executed by **cron**. Refer to **crontab** in Part II for more information.

Installing New Software and Upgrades

Most manufacturers provide detailed instructions to guide you through the process of installing new software or system upgrades; some even provide special tools or menu-driven user interfaces to simplify the task. As you acquire local software, especially free (public domain) software, you should install it on your system in a consistent, predictable manner. For example, you might create a directory tree under **/usr/local** for binaries (**/usr/local/bin**), manual pages (**/usr/local/man**), and so forth. You should avoid installing nonstandard software in the standard system directories (such as **/bin** and **/usr/bin**) to prevent confusion later and to avoid overwriting or losing the software when you install standard software upgrades in the future. Make sure that the users on your system know where to find the local software, and remember to make an announcement whenever you install, change, or remove local tools.

Problems

It is your responsibility as the system administrator to keep the system secure and running smoothly. If a user is having a problem, it usually falls to the administrator to help the user get back on the right track. This section presents some suggestions on ways to keep users happy and the system functioning at its peak.

When a User Cannot Log In

When a user has trouble logging in on the system, the problem may be a user error, or a problem with the system software or hardware. These steps may help you determine where the problem is.

- Determine if just that one user has a problem, just that one user's terminal has a problem, or if the problem is more widespread.

- If just that user has a problem, it may be that the user does not know how to log in. The user's terminal will respond when you press (RETURN), and you will be able to log in as yourself. Make sure the user has a valid login name and password; then show the user how to log in.

- Make sure the user's home directory exists and corresponds to the entry in the **/etc/passwd** file. Check the user's startup files (**.profile** or **.login** and **.cshrc**) for errors. Verify that the user owns his or her home directory and startup files, and that they are readable (and, in the case of the home directory, executable). Confirm that the entry for the user's login shell in the **/etc/passwd** file is valid (i.e., that the entry is accurate and that the shell exists exactly as specified).

- Change the user's password, if there is a chance that he or she has forgotten the correct password.

- If just that one user's terminal has a problem, other users will be using the system, but that user's terminal will not respond when you press (RETURN). Try pressing the (BREAK) and (RETURN) keys alternately to reestablish the proper baud rate. Make sure the terminal is set for a legal baud rate. Try pressing the keys listed below:

Keys	What they do
(CONTROL)-Q	This key "unsticks" the terminal if someone pressed (CONTROL)-S.
interrupt	This key stops a runaway process that has hung up the terminal. The interrupt key is usually (DELETE) or (CONTROL)-C.
(ESCAPE)	This key can help if the user is in Input Mode in **vi**.
(CONTROL)-L	This key redraws the screen if the user was using **vi**.
(CONTROL)-R	This key is an alternate for (CONTROL)-L.
:q! (RETURN)	This sequence will get the user out of **ex**.

- Check the terminal cable from where it plugs into the terminal to where it plugs into the computer. Check the **/etc/ttytab** entry for that line. Finally, try turning the terminal off and then turning it back on again.

- If the problem appears to be widespread, check to see if you can log in from the system console. If you can, make sure the system is in multiuser mode. If you cannot, the system may have crashed—reboot it.

Keeping a Machine Log

A machine log that includes the following information may be helpful in finding and fixing problems with the system. Note the time and date for each entry in the log. Avoid the temptation of keeping the log *only* on the computer, because it will be most useful to you at times when the machine is down.

Condition	Action
Hardware modifications	Keep track of all modifications to the hardware—even those installed by factory representatives.
System software modifications	Keep track of any modification that anyone makes to the operating system software, whether it is a patch or a new version of a program.
Hardware malfunctions	Keep as accurate a list as possible of any problems with the system. Make note of any error messages or numbers that the system displays on the system console and what users were doing when the problem occurred.
User complaints	Make a list of all reasonable complaints made by knowledgeable users (e.g., machine is abnormally slow).

Keeping the System Secure

No system with dial-in lines or public access to terminals is absolutely secure. You can make your system as secure as possible by changing the Superuser password frequently and choosing passwords that are hard to guess. Do not tell anyone who does not *absolutely* need to know what the Superuser password is. You can also encourage system users to choose difficult passwords and to change them periodically.

A password that is hard to guess is one that someone else would not be likely to think that you would have chosen. Do not use words from the dictionary, names of relatives, pets, or friends, or backward spellings of words. A good strategy is to choose a couple of short words, include some punctuation (e.g., put a (SPACE) between them), and replace a couple of the letters in the words with numbers. Remember that only the first eight characters of a password are significant.

Make sure that no one (except the Superuser) can write to files containing programs that are owned by root and run in the set user ID mode (e.g., **Mail** and **su**). Also make sure that users do not transfer programs that run in the set user ID mode and are owned by root onto the system by means of mounting tapes or disks. These programs can be used to circumvent system security. Refer to **chmod** in Part II for more information about the set user ID mode.

Monitoring Disk Usage

Disk space is usually a precious commodity. Sooner or later, you will probably start to run out of it. Do not fill up a disk—the UNIX operating system runs best with at least 5 to 30 percent of the disk space free in each filesystem. The minimum amount of free space you should maintain on each filesystem is machine-dependent. Using more than the maximum optimal disk space in a filesystem degrades system performance. If there is no space on a filesystem, you cannot write to it at all.

The UNIX System provides several programs that you can use to determine who is using how much disk space on what filesystems. Refer to the **du** and **df** utilities and the **–size** option of the **find** utility in Part II. In addition to these utilities, you can use the disk quota system to manage disk space, as described below.

The *only* ways to increase the amount of free space on a filesystem are to delete files and condense directories. This section contains some ideas on ways to maintain a filesystem so that it does not get overloaded.

Growing Files

Some files, such as log files and temporary files, grow automatically over time. Core dump files take up space and are rarely needed. Also, users occasionally create processes that accidentally generate huge files. As the system administrator, you must review these files periodically so that they do not get out of hand.

If a filesystem is running out of space quickly (e.g., over the period of an hour rather than weeks or months), the first thing to do is to figure out why it is running out of space. Use the **ps –aux** command to determine whether a user has created a runaway process that is creating a huge file. In evaluating the output of **ps**, look for a process that has used a large amount of CPU time. If such a process is running and creating a large file, the file will continue to grow as you free up space. If you remove the huge file, the space it occupied will not be freed until the process terminates, so you need to kill the process. Try to contact the user running the process and ask the user to kill it. If you cannot contact the user, log in as root and kill the process. Refer to **kill** in Part II for more information.

If no single process is consuming the disk space, but rather it has been used up gradually, you should locate unneeded files and delete them. You can archive them using **cpio** or **tar** before you delete them.

You can safely remove any files named **core** that have not been accessed for several days. The following command performs this function:

```
# find / -name core -atime +3 -exec rm {} \;
```

Look through the /**tmp** and /**var/tmp** directories for old temporary files and remove them. The /**usr/lib/spell/spellhist** file keeps track of all the misspelled words that **spell** finds—make sure it does not get too big. Keep track of disk usage in /**var/spool**, /**var/adm**, /**var/log**, and /**var/crash**.

OPTIONAL

Disk Quota System

Berkeley-based systems, such as SunOS, include a disk quota system for limiting the disk space and number of files owned by individual users. You can choose to limit each user's disk space or the number of files each user can own or both. For each resource that is limited, there are actually two limits. The lower limit, or *quota*, can be exceeded by the user although a warning is presented each time the user logs in when he or she is above the quota. After a certain number of warnings (set by the system administrator), the system will behave as if the user has reached the upper limit. Once the upper limit is reached or the user has received the specified number of warnings, the user will not be allowed to create any more files or use any more disk space. The user's only recourse at that point is to remove some files.

Users can review their usage and limits with the **quota** command. The Superuser can use **quota** to obtain information about any user.

To set up the disk quota system, you may have to reconfigure the system. The system configuration process is beyond the scope of this book. Refer to the system administration manuals that came with your system.

Once you have reconfigured the system, you must decide which filesystems to limit and how to allocate space among users. Typically, only filesystems that contain users' home directories, such as /**home**, are limited. Use the **edquota** command to set the quotas, and then **quotaon** to start the quota system. You will probably want to put the **quotaon** command into the appropriate run command script, so that the quota system will be enabled when you bring the system up (page 501). The quota system is automatically disabled when the filesystems are unmounted.

Getting Information to Users

As the system administrator, one of your primary responsibilities is communicating with the system users. You need to make announcements such as when the system will be down for maintenance, when a class on some new software will be held, and how users can access the new system printer. You can even start to fill the role of a small local newspaper, letting users know about new employees, births, the company picnic, and so on.

Different items you want to communicate will have different priorities. Information about the company picnic in two months is not as time-sensitive as the fact that you are bringing the system down in five minutes. To meet these differing needs, the UNIX operating system provides different ways of communicating. The most common methods are described and contrasted below. All of these methods are generally available to everyone, except for **motd** (the message of the day), which is typically reserved for the Superuser.

wall   The **wall** (write all) utility is most effective for communicating immediately with everyone who is logged in. It works in the same way as **write**, but it sends a message to everyone who is logged in. Use it if you are about to bring the system down or you are in another crisis situation. Users who are not logged in will not get the message.

Use **wall** while you are the Superuser *only* in crisis situations—it will interrupt anything anyone is doing.

write   Use the **write** utility to communicate with any individual user who is logged in. You might use it to ask a user to stop running a program that is bogging down the system. Users can also use **write** to ask you, for example, to mount a tape or restore a file.

mail   The **mail** utility is useful for communicating less urgent information to one or more system users. When you send mail, you have to be willing to wait for each user to read the mail. The mail utilities are useful for reminding users that they are forgetting to log out, bills are past due, or they are using too much disk space.

Users can easily make permanent records of messages they receive via **mail**, as opposed to messages received via **write**, so that they can keep track of important details. It would be appropriate to use **mail** to inform users about a new, complex procedure—each user could keep a copy of the information for reference.

Message of the Day   All users see the message of the day each time they log in. You can edit the **/etc/motd** file to change the message. The message of the day can alert users to upcoming periodic maintenance, new system features, or a change in procedures.

msgs   On some systems the **msgs** utility displays news: meeting announcements, new hardware or software on the system, new employees, parties, and so on.

SUMMARY

The system administrator is responsible for backing up files, adding and removing users, helping users who have problems logging in, and keeping track of disk usage and system security.

This chapter explains many of the files and programs you will have to work with to maintain a UNIX system. Much of the work you do as the system administrator requires you to log in as the Superuser. The login name for the Superuser is *root*. When you are logged in as the Superuser, you have extensive system-wide powers that you do not normally have. You can read from and write to any file and execute programs that ordinary users are not permitted to execute.

A series of programs and files control how the system appears at any given time. Many of the files you work with as the system administrator are located in the **/usr/etc** directory.

When you bring up the system, it is frequently in single-user mode. In this mode, only the system console is functional, and not all the filesystems are mounted. When the system is in single-user mode, you can back up files and use **fsck** to check the integrity of filesystems before you mount them. The **init** utility brings the system to its normal multiuser state.

With the system running in multiuser mode, you can still perform many administration tasks, such as adding users and terminals.

REVIEW EXERCISES

1. What option should you use with **fsck** if you just want to review the status of your filesystems without making any changes to them? How does **fsck** determine what devices to check if you do not specify one on the command line?

2. How does single-user mode differ from multiuser mode?

3. If Alex belongs to five groups—inhouse, pubs, sys, other, and supers— how would his group memberships be represented? Assume that inhouse is his primary group. How would Alex create a file that belongs to the group pubs?

4. How can you identify the user ID of another user on your system? What is the user ID of root?

5. How can you redirect the output of the **find** command so that whatever it sends to the standard error disappears?

6. How many inodes does a file have? What happens when you add a hard link to a file? What happens when you add a symbolic link?

7. What are the differences between a raw device and a block device?

8. Develop a strategy for coming up with a password that an intruder would not be likely to guess but that you will be able to remember.

9. How would you communicate each of the following messages?

   a. The system is coming down tomorrow at 6:00 in the evening for periodic maintenance.

   b. The system is coming down in five minutes.

   c. Jenny's jobs are slowing the system down drastically, and she should postpone them.

   d. Alex's wife just had a baby girl.

10. How would you restrict access to a tape drive on your system so that only certain users could read and write tapes?

11. When **fsck** puts files in a **lost+found** directory, it has lost the directory information for the files (and thus has lost the names of the files). Each file is given a new name, which is the same as the inode number for the file:

    ```
    $ ls -l lost+found
    -rw-r--r-- 1 alex      110 Jun 10 10:55 51262
    ```

    What can you do to identify these files and restore them?

PART II

The UNIX Utility Programs

Following is a list of the utilities grouped by function. Although most of these are true utilities (that is, programs), others are commands that are built into the shells.

Utilities That Display and Manipulate Files

Utility	Function
awk	search for and process patterns in a file (page 530)
cat	join or display files (page 556)
comm	compare sorted files (page 571)
cp	copy files (page 573)
cpio	store and retrieve files in an archival format (page 575)
diff	display the differences between two files (page 585)
find	find files (page 600)
grep	search for a pattern in files (page 619)
head	display the beginning of a file (page 623)
ln	make a link to a file (page 626)
lpr	print files (page 628)
ls	display information about files (page 631)
mkdir	make a directory (page 648)
more	display a file, one screenful at a time (page 649)
mv	move (rename) a file (page 652)
od	dump a file (page 656)
pr	paginate a file (page 658)
rcp	copy files to or from a remote computer (page 666)
rm	remove a file (page 674)
rmdir	remove a directory (page 677)
sed	stream editor (noninteractive) (page 680)
sort	sort and/or merge files (page 693)
spell	check a file for spelling errors (page 703)
tail	display the last part of a file (page 709)
tar	store or retrieve files from an archival file (page 712)
uniq	display lines of a file that are unique (page 727)
wc	display counts of lines, words, and characters (page 731)

Communication Utilities

Utility	Function
ftp	transfer files over a network connection (page 612)
mail	send or receive electronic mail (page 638)
mesg	enable/disable reception of messages (page 647)
telnet	connect to a remote computer over a network (page 717)
write	send a message to another user (page 733)

Utilities That Display and Alter Status

Utility	Function
cd	change to another working directory (page 560)
chgrp	change the group that is associated with a file (page 561)
chmod	change the access mode of a file (page 562)
chown	change the owner of a file (page 566)
date	display or set the time and date (page 580)
df	display the amount of available disk space (page 584)
du	display information on disk usage (page 592)
file	display file classification (page 599)
finger	display detailed information on users (page 606)
kill	terminate a process (page 624)
nice	change the priority of a command (page 654)
nohup	run a command that will keep running after you log out (page 655)
ps	display process status (page 663)
ruptime	display status of computers attached to a network (page 678)
rwho	display names of users on computers attached to a network (page 679)
sleep	process that sleeps for a specified interval (page 692)
stty	display or set terminal parameters (page 705)
umask	set file-creation permissions mask (page 726)
w	display information on system users (page 729)
who	display names of users (page 732)

Utilities That Are Programming Tools

Utility	Function
cc	C compiler (page 558)
make	keep a set of programs current (page 645)
touch	update a file's modification time (page 722)

Source Code Management (SCCS, RCS) Utilities

Utility	Function
admin	create or change the characteristics of an SCCS file (page 523)
ci	create or record changes in an RCS file (page 567)
co	retrieve an unencoded version of an RCS file (page 569)
delta	record changes in an SCCS file (page 582)
get	create an unencoded version of an SCCS file (page 615)
prs	print the history of an SCCS file (page 660)
rcs	Create or change the characteristics of an RCS file (page 668)
rlog	print a summary of the history of an RCS file (page 671)
rmdel	remove a delta from an SCCS file (page 676)

Miscellaneous Utilities

Utility	Function
at	execute a shell script at a specified time (page 527)
cal	display a calendar (page 554)
calendar	present reminders (page 555)
crontab	schedule a command to run at a regularly specified time (page 578)
echo	display a message (page 593)
expr	evaluate an expression (page 595)
fsck	check and repair a filesystem (page 609)
rlogin	log in on a remote computer (page 673)
tee	copy the standard input to the standard output and to one or more files (page 716)
test	evaluate an expression (page 719)
tr	replace specified characters (page 723)
tty	display the terminal pathname (page 725)

The following sample command shows the format that is used throughout Part II. These descriptions of the commands are similar to the descriptions in the user's reference manual that comes with your UNIX system; however, most users find the descriptions in this book easier to read and understand. These descriptions emphasize the most useful features of the commands and often leave out the more obscure features. For information about the less commonly used features, refer to the manuals that come with your system. Some of the features described here for a particular command may not be available to you if you are running an older version of SunOS or Berkeley UNIX.

522   Part II   The UNIX Utility Programs

sample command

This section gives the name of the command and a brief description.

Format

sample_command [options] arguments

This section includes syntax descriptions like the one above that show you how to run the command. Options and arguments enclosed in square brackets ([]) are not required.

Hyphenated words listed as arguments to a command identify single arguments (e.g., **source-file**) or groups of similar arguments (e.g., **directory-list**). As an example, **file-list** means a list of one or more files.

Summary

Unless stated otherwise, the output from a command goes to its standard output. The "Standard Input and Standard Output" section on page 94 explains how to redirect output so that it goes to a file other than the terminal.

The statement that a command "takes its input from files you specify on the command line or from its standard input" indicates that the command is a member of the class of UNIX commands that takes input from files specified on the command line or, if you do not specify a filename, from its standard input. It also means that the command can receive input redirected from a file or sent through a pipe (page 101).

Arguments

This section describes the arguments that you use when you run the command. The argument itself, as shown in the preceding "Format" section, is printed in **bold type**.

Options

This section lists the common options that you can use with the command. Unless specified otherwise, you must precede all options with a hyphen. Most commands accept a single hyphen before multiple options (page 91).

Notes

You will find miscellaneous notes, some important and others merely interesting, in this section.

Examples

This section contains examples of how to use the command. It is tutorial and is more casual than the preceding sections of the command description.

admin

Create an SCCS file or change the characteristics of an SCCS file.

Format

admin [options] –iname filename
admin [options] –n file-list
admin [options] file-list

Summary

The **admin** utility is part of SCCS (Source Code Control System—page 476). The **admin** utility creates and changes characteristics of SCCS files.

Use the first format shown above to create an SCCS-encoded version of an existing file, or use the second format to create one or more new SCCS-encoded files that are not based on existing files. The third format changes the characteristics of SCCS files.

Arguments

In the first format, **filename** is the name that will be given to the newly encoded SCCS file. Like the names of all SCCS files, the **filename** must begin with the characters **s.**. In the second format, **file-list** is a list of SCCS filenames to be assigned to the newly created files. Each of the files in the **file-list** must also begin with **s.**. The first format creates a single SCCS-encoded file based on an existing file. The second format creates any number of new SCCS-encoded files based on null deltas.

The **file-list** in the third format is a list of existing SCCS files. If you include a directory in **file-list**, **admin** includes in **file-list** all of the SCCS-encoded files in the directory.

Options

–iname

> **initialize**   The **admin** utility uses the file called **name** as the initial delta for a new SCCS file.

–n

> **new**   This option causes SCCS to create a new SCCS-encoded file. When it is used without the **–i** option, **admin** creates a new SCCS file based on a null delta (an empty file). When you use the **–i** option, you do not need to use **–n**, as it is redundant.

–rx

> **release**   This option identifies the version number **admin** will associate with an initial delta. Replace **x** with the version number

(page 476). If you specify only the release component of the version number, SCCS inserts the delta into the first level of the release. For example, if you use –r3, SCCS inserts the delta into Version 3.1. If the release is not specified on the command line, **admin** inserts the initial delta into Version 1.1. The –r option can be used only when –i is also used.

–fflag[value]

This option inserts a **flag** in the SCCS file. Flags override default characteristics of SCCS files. Any number of flags may be specified on a single command line. See the next section for information about flags and their values.

–dflag

delete   This option removes a **flag** from an SCCS file. Multiple –d options can be used on a single command line to remove multiple flags. See the next section for information about flags.

–ycomment

The –y option causes **admin** to insert **comment** as the comment for the initial delta in a new SCCS file. Replace **comment** with the text of your comment. You must surround your comment with quotation marks if it contains spaces. If you do not use –y when creating an initial delta, SCCS inserts a standard comment, including the date and time of creation and the login of the user who created it. You can use –y only when creating an initial delta. Otherwise, **admin** ignores it.

–mmrlist

The **mrlist** is a list of the modification requests that are the reason for an initial delta. Replace **mrlist** with a comma-separated list of modification request numbers. The –m option can be used only if the **v** flag is set, and only on an initial delta. Refer to the next section for an explanation of flags.

–alogin

authorize   This option adds **login** to the list of users who are allowed to make deltas to the files. Replace **login** with the user's login name. Before any users are added to the list of authorized users, the list is assumed to be empty, and any user can make a delta. You can use any number of –a options on a command line. If a numerical group ID is used in place of **login**, all the users belonging to the group can make deltas to the file. If a **login** is preceded by an exclamation point, **!login**, the user will be denied permission to make deltas.

–elogin

> **erase**   Once you have used the –a option to add a user to the list of authorized users, you can remove that user with –e. Like the –a option, you can use –e with a numerical group ID in place of **login**, and you can use –e several times on a command line.

Flags

The **admin** utility can insert flags in SCCS files to change default characteristics of the files. Each **flag** must be preceded by the –f option on the command line.

llist

> **lock** (starts with the letter ell)   This flag identifies releases that users are not allowed to make deltas against. The **list** may include a single release number, several release numbers separated by commas, or **a**, which locks all releases.

v

> **verbose**   This flag causes the **delta** utility to prompt you for modification request numbers in addition to comments.

b

> **branch**   This flag allows you to create branch deltas for the highest-numbered trunk delta. To make these branches, you must use the –b option with the **get** utility. You can always make branch deltas for trunk deltas that have successors on the trunk (that is, regardless of whether the **b** flag is set).

j

> **joint edit**   This flag allows multiple concurrent updates to the same version of an SCCS file. This flag is rarely used, because one of the purposes of SCCS is to prevent different people from making changes to the same file at the same time. If this flag is not set, once you have used **get** with the –e option on a version of an SCCS file, you must use **delta** to record the changes before anyone can again use **get** with the –e option on that version.

Examples

The following command creates a new SCCS-encoded file called **s.menu1** that includes the file **menu1** as its first delta.

```
$ admin -imenu1 s.menu1
No id keywords (cm7)
```

The **admin** utility displays the message No id keywords, indicating that there are no SCCS keywords in the new file. When keywords are included in an SCCS file, information about the SCCS file is inserted in the corresponding text file retrieved by **get**. Keywords are beyond the scope of this book— you can ignore the warning message when it occurs in the examples.

The next command creates three new SCCS-encoded files. These files are not created from existing files, and, consequently, the initial version of each is empty.

```
$ admin -n s.menu_mon s.menu_tues s.menu_wed
```

The next example locks Release 2 of **s.menus_march**, the SCCS-encoded file. It also adds Alex and Barbara to the list of users who are authorized to make deltas. Of course, Alex and Barbara cannot make deltas to Release 2.

```
$ admin -fl2 -aalex -abarbara s.menus_march
```

Any time after you execute the above command, you can remove Barbara from the list with the following command. This command also uses the **–d** option to remove the lock on Release 2.

```
$ admin -dl2 -ebarbara s.menus_march
```

at

Execute a shell script at a time you specify.

Format

at [–csm] **time** [date] [+ **increment**]
at [–l | –r] [**job-list**]
atq

Summary

The **at** utility causes the operating system to execute commands it receives from its standard input. It executes them as a shell script in the working directory at the time you specify.

When the operating system executes commands using **at**, it uses electronic mail to send you the standard output and standard error output of the resulting process. You can redirect the output to avoid getting mail.

The **atq** utility provides a list of **at** jobs you have queued. It is similar to **at** with the –l option.

Arguments

In the first format shown above, **time** is the time of day you want **at** to execute the job. You can specify the **time** as a one-, two-, or four-digit number. One- and two-digit numbers specify an hour, and four-digit numbers specify an hour and minute. The **at** utility assumes a 24-hour clock unless you place **am**, **pm**, **midnight**, or **noon** immediately after the number, in which case, **at** uses a 12-hour clock. You can use the word **now** in place of **time**; however, if you do, you must also specify a **date** or an **increment** (that is, the command **at now** is not valid, but the command **at now saturday** is).

The **date** is the day of the week or date of the month on which you want **at** to execute the job. If you do not specify a day, **at** executes the job today if the hour you specify in **time** is greater than the current hour. If the hour is less than the current hour, **at** executes the job tomorrow.

To specify a day of the week, you can spell it out or abbreviate it to three letters. You can also use the days **today** and **tomorrow**.

Use the name of a month followed by the number of the day in the month to specify a date. You can follow the month and day number with a year.

The **increment** is a number followed by one of the following (plural or singular is allowed): **minutes, hours, days, weeks, months**, or **years**. The **at** utility adds the **increment** to the **time** (and **date**) you specify. In place of **increment**, you can use the word **next** (e.g., to specify **next week, next month**, or **next year**).

In the second format shown above, **job-list** is a list of one or more job numbers for **at** jobs. You can identify job numbers using the –l option to **at**.

Options

By default, **at** uses the shell specified by the **SHELL** variable in your environment. To override that, use the –c or –s options. The –l and –r options are not for use when you initiate a job with **at**. You can use them only to determine the status of a job or to cancel a job.

–c

> Use the C Shell to run your job.

–l

> **list**   This option displays a list of all jobs that you have submitted with **at**. The **job-list** is a list of one or more job numbers of the jobs you want **at** to list. If you do not include a **job-list**, **at** lists all your jobs.

–m

> **mail**   If you use this option, **at** sends you mail after the job is run. The mail contains the standard error output if there was any; otherwise, it contains a short message informing you that no errors occurred. Without this option, **at** does not provide any confirmation that the job was run (except for mailing you any output that is not redirected to a file).

–r

> **remove**   This option cancels jobs that you previously submitted with **at**. The **job-list** argument is a list of one or more job numbers of the jobs you want to cancel. If you do not remember the job number, use the –l option to list your jobs and their numbers.

–s

> Use the Bourne Shell to run your job.

Notes

The shell saves the environment variables and the working directory that are in effect at the time you submit an **at** job, so that they are available when it executes the commands.

The system administrator must put your login name in the file named /etc/cron.d/at.allow for you to be able to use **at**.

Examples

You can use either of the following techniques to paginate and print **long_file** at two o'clock tomorrow morning. The first example executes the command directly from the command line, and the second example uses a file containing the necessary command (**pr_tonight**) and executes it using **at**. If you execute the command directly from the command line, you must signal the end of the list of commands by pressing (CONTROL)-**D** at the beginning of a line. The line that begins with job contains the job number and the time **at** will execute the job.

```
$ at 2am
at> pr long_file | lpr
at> (CONTROL)-D
job 5600 at Fri Jul 8 02:00:00  1994
$ cat pr_tonight
pr long_file | lpr
$ at 2am < pr_tonight
job 5601 at Fri Jul 8 02:00:00  1994
```

If you give an **at** –l command following the two preceding commands, **at** displays a list of jobs in its queue.

```
$ at -l
5600 a      Fri Jul 8 02:00:00  1994
5601 a      Fri Jul 8 02:00:00  1994
```

The following command removes one of the jobs from the queue.

```
$ at -r 5600
$ at -l
5601 a      Fri Jul 8 02:00:00  1994
```

The next example executes **cmdfile** at 3:30 P.M. (1530 hours) one week from next Wednesday.

```
$ at 1530 wed +1 week < cmdfile
job 2600 at Wed Jul 20 15:30:00 1994
```

The final example executes a job at 7 P.M. on Friday that finds core dumps under your home directory. It creates an intermediate file, redirects the error output, and prints the file.

```
$ at 7pm Friday
at> find $HOME -name core -print > report.out 2> report.err
at> lpr report.out
at> (CONTROL)-D
job 6800 at Fri Jul 8 19:00:00 1994
```

awk

Search for and process a pattern in a file.

Format

awk [–Fc] –f **program-file** [**file-list**]
awk **program** [**file-list**]

Summary

The **awk** utility is a pattern-scanning and processing language. It searches one or more files to see if they contain lines that match specified patterns and then performs actions, such as writing the line to the standard output or incrementing a counter, each time it finds a match.

You can use **awk** to generate reports or filter text. It works equally well with numbers and text; when you mix the two, **awk** will almost always come up with the right answer.

The authors of **awk** (Alfred V. Aho, Peter J. Weinberger, and Brian W. Kernighan) designed it to be easy to use and, to this end, they sacrificed execution speed.

The **awk** utility takes many of its constructs from the C programming language. It includes the following features:

- flexible format
- conditional execution
- looping statements
- numeric variables
- string variables
- regular expressions
- C's printf

The **awk** utility takes its input from files you specify on the command line or from its standard input.

Arguments

The first format uses a **program-file**, which is the pathname of a file containing an **awk** program. See "Description," on the next page.

The second format uses a **program**, which is an **awk** program included on the command line. This format allows you to write simple, short **awk** programs without having to create a separate **program-file**. To prevent the shell from interpreting the **awk** commands as shell commands, it is a good idea to enclose the **program** in single quotation marks.

The **file-list** contains pathnames of the ordinary files that **awk** processes. These are the input files.

Options

If you do not use the –f option, **awk** uses the first command line argument as its program.

–fprogram-file

> **file**   This option causes **awk** to read its program from the **program-file** given as the first command line argument.

–Fc

> **field**   This option specifies an input field separator, **c**, to be used in place of the default separators (⟨SPACE⟩ and ⟨TAB⟩). The field separator can be any single character.

Notes

See page 552 for examples of **awk** error messages.

Description

An **awk** program consists of one or more program lines containing a **pattern** and/or **action** in the following format:

> pattern { action }

The **pattern** selects lines from the input file. The **awk** utility performs the **action** on all lines that the **pattern** selects. You must enclose the **action** within braces so that **awk** can differentiate it from the **pattern**. If a program line does not contain a **pattern**, **awk** selects all lines in the input file. If a program line does not contain an **action**, **awk** copies the selected lines to its standard output.

To start, **awk** compares the first line in the input file (from the **file-list**) with each **pattern** in the **program-file** or **program**. If a **pattern** selects the line (if there is a match), **awk** takes the **action** associated with the **pattern**. If the line is not selected, **awk** takes no action. When **awk** has completed its comparisons for the first line of the input file, it repeats the process for the next line of input. It continues this process, comparing subsequent lines in the input file, until it has read the entire **file-list**.

If several **patterns** select the same line, **awk** takes the **actions** associated with each of the **patterns** in the order in which they appear. It is therefore possible for **awk** to send a single line from the input file to its standard output more than once.

Patterns

You can use a regular expression (refer to Appendix A), enclosed within slashes, as a pattern. The ~ operator tests to see if a field or variable matches a regular expression. The !~ operator tests for no match.

You can process arithmetic and character relational expressions with the following relational operators.

Operator	Meaning
<	less than
<=	less than or equal to
==	equal to
!=	not equal to
>=	greater than or equal to
>	greater than

You can combine any of the patterns described above using the Boolean operators || (OR) or && (AND).

The comma is the range operator. If you separate two patterns with a comma on a single **awk** program line, **awk** selects a range of lines beginning with the first line that contains the first pattern. The last line **awk** selects is the next subsequent line that contains the second pattern. After **awk** finds the second pattern, it starts the process over by looking for the first pattern again.

Two unique patterns, **BEGIN** and **END**, allow you to execute commands before **awk** starts its processing and after it finishes. The **awk** utility executes the actions associated with the **BEGIN** pattern before, and with the **END** pattern after, it processes all the files in the **file-list**.

Actions

The action portion of an **awk** command causes **awk** to take action when it matches a pattern. If you do not specify an action, **awk** performs the default action, which is the Print command (explicitly represented as {print}). This action copies the record (normally a line—see "Variables" on the next page) from the input file to **awk**'s standard output.

You can follow a Print command with arguments, causing **awk** to print just the arguments you specify. The arguments can be variables or string constants. Using **awk**, you can send the output from a Print command to a file (>), append it to a file (>>), or pipe it to the input of another program (|).

Unless you separate items in a Print command with commas, **awk** catenates them. Commas cause **awk** to separate the items with the output field separator (normally a (SPACE)—see "Variables" on the next page).

You can include several actions on one line within a set of braces by separating them with semicolons.

Comments

The **awk** utility disregards anything on a program line following a pound sign (#). You can document an **awk** program by preceding comments with this symbol.

Variables

You declare and initialize user variables when you use them (that is, you do not have to declare them *before* you use them). In addition, **awk** maintains program variables for your use. You can use both user and program variables in the pattern *and* in the action portion of an **awk** program. Following is a list of program variables.

Variable	Represents
NR	record number of current record
$0	the current record (as a single variable)
NF	number of fields in the current record
$1-$n	fields in the current record
FS	input field separator (default: (SPACE) or (TAB))
OFS	output field separator (default: (SPACE))
RS	input record separator (default: (NEWLINE))
ORS	output record separator (default: (NEWLINE))
FILENAME	name of the current input file

The input and output record separators are, by default, (NEWLINE) characters. Thus, **awk** takes each line in the input file to be a separate record and appends a (NEWLINE) to the end of each record that it sends to its standard output. The input field separators are, by default, (SPACE)s and (TAB)s. The output field separator is a (SPACE). You can change the value of any of the separators at any time by assigning a new value to its associated variable. Also, the input field separator can be set on the command line using the –F option.

Functions

The functions that **awk** provides for manipulating numbers and strings follow.

Name	Function
length(**str**)	returns the number of characters in **str**; if you do not supply an argument, it returns the number of characters in the current input record
int(**num**)	returns the integer portion of **num**
index(**str1**,**str2**)	returns the index of **str2** in **str1** or 0 if **str2** is not present
split(**str**,**arr**,**del**)	places elements of **str**, delimited by **del**, in the array **arr**[1]...**arr**[n]; returns the number of elements in the array
sprintf(**fmt**,**args**)	formats **args** according to **fmt** and returns the formatted string; mimics the C programming language function of the same name
substr(**str**,**pos**,**len**)	returns a substring of **str** that begins at **pos** and is **len** characters long

Operators

The following **awk** arithmetic operators are from the C programming language.

Operator	Function
*	multiplies the expression preceding the operator by the expression following it
/	divides the expression preceding the operator by the expression following it
%	takes the remainder after dividing the expression preceding the operator by the expression following it
+	adds the expression preceding the operator and the expression following it
−	subtracts the expression following the operator from the expression preceding it
=	assigns the value of the expression following the operator to the variable preceding it
++	increments the variable preceding the operator
−−	decrements the variable preceding the operator
+=	adds the expression following the operator to the variable preceding it and assigns the result to the variable preceding the operator
−=	subtracts the expression following the operator from the variable preceding it and assigns the result to the variable preceding the operator
*=	multiplies the variable preceding the operator by the expression following it and assigns the result to the variable preceding the operator
/=	divides the variable preceding the operator by the expression following it and assigns the result to the variable preceding the operator
%=	takes the remainder, after dividing the variable preceding the operator by the expression following it, and assigns the result to the variable preceding the operator

Associative Arrays

An associative array is one of **awk**'s most powerful features. An associative array uses strings as its indexes. Using an associative array, you can mimic a traditional array by using numeric strings as indexes.

You assign a value to an element of an associative array just as you would assign a value to any other **awk** variable. The format is shown below.

array[string] = value

The **array** is the name of the array, **string** is the index of the element of the array you are assigning a value to, and **value** is the value you are assigning to the element of the array.

There is a special For structure you can use with an **awk** array. The format is:

for (**elem** in **array**) **action**

The **elem** is a variable that takes on the values of each of the elements in the array as the For structure loops through them, **array** is the name of the array, and **action** is the action that **awk** takes for each element in the array. You can use the **elem** variable in this **action**.

The "Examples" section contains programs that use associative arrays.

Printf

You can use the Printf command in place of Print to control the format of the output that **awk** generates. The **awk** version of Printf is similar to that of the C language. A Printf command takes the following format:

printf "**control-string**" **arg1, arg2, ..., argn**

The **control-string** determines how Printf will format **arg1-n**. The **arg1-n** can be variables or other expressions. Within the **control-string**, you can use \n to indicate a (NEWLINE) and \t to indicate a (TAB).

The **control-string** contains conversion specifications, one for each argument (**arg1-n**). A conversion specification has the following format:

%[–][x[.y]]**conv**

The – causes Printf to left justify the argument. The x is the minimum field width, and the **.y** is the number of places to the right of a decimal point in a number. The **conv** is a letter from the following list.

conv	Conversion
d	decimal
e	exponential notation
f	floating-point number
g	use f or e, whichever is shorter
o	unsigned octal
s	string of characters
x	unsigned hexadecimal

Refer to the following "Examples" section for examples of how to use Printf.

Examples

A simple **awk** program is shown on the following page.

```
{ print }
```

This program consists of one program line that is an action. It uses no pattern. Because the pattern is missing, **awk** selects all lines in the input file. Without any arguments, the Print command prints each selected line in its entirety. This program copies the input file to its standard output.

The following program has a pattern part without an explicit action.

```
/jenny/
```

In this case, **awk** selects all lines from the input file that contain the string **jenny**. When you do not specify an action, **awk** assumes the action to be Print. This program copies all the lines in the input file that contain **jenny** to its standard output.

The following examples work with the **cars** data file. From left to right, the columns in the file contain each car's make, model, year of manufacture, mileage, and price. All white space in this file is composed of single ⬛TAB⬛s (there are no ⬛SPACE⬛s in the file).

```
$ cat cars
plym    fury    77    73    2500
chevy   nova    79    60    3000
ford    mustang 65    45    10000
volvo   gl      78    102   9850
ford    ltd     83    15    10500
chevy   nova    80    50    3500
fiat    600     65    115   450
honda   accord  81    30    6000
ford    thundbd 84    10    17000
toyota  tercel  82    180   750
chevy   impala  65    85    1550
ford    bronco  83    25    9500
```

The first example below selects all lines that contain the string chevy. The slashes indicate that chevy is a regular expression. This example has no action part.

Although neither **awk** nor shell syntax requires single quotation marks on the command line, it is a good idea to use them, because they prevent many problems. If the **awk** program you create on the command line includes ⬛SPACE⬛s or any special characters that the shell will interpret, you must quote them. Always enclosing the program in single quotation marks is the easiest way of making sure you have quoted any characters that need to be quoted.

```
$ awk '/chevy/' cars
chevy   nova    79    60    3000
chevy   nova    80    50    3500
chevy   impala  65    85    1550
```

The next example selects all lines from the file (it has no pattern part). The braces enclose the action part—you must always use braces to delimit the action part, so that **awk** can distinguish the pattern part from the action part. This example prints the third field (**$3**), a (SPACE) (indicated by the comma), and the first field (**$1**) of each selected line.

```
$ awk '{print $3, $1}' cars
77 plym
79 chevy
65 ford
78 volvo
83 ford
80 chevy
65 fiat
81 honda
84 ford
82 toyota
65 chevy
83 ford
```

The next example includes both a pattern and an action part. It selects all lines that contain the string chevy and prints the third and first fields from the lines it selects.

```
$ awk '/chevy/ {print $3, $1}' cars
79 chevy
80 chevy
65 chevy
```

The next example selects lines that contain a match for the regular expression h. Because there is no explicit action, it prints all the lines it selects.

```
$ awk '/h/' cars
chevy    nova     79     60     3000
chevy    nova     80     50     3500
honda    accord   81     30     6000
ford     thundbd  84     10     17000
chevy    impala   65     85     1550
```

The next pattern uses the matches operator (~) to select all lines that contain the letter h in the first field.

```
$ awk '$1 ~ /h/' cars
chevy    nova     79     60     3000
chevy    nova     80     50     3500
honda    accord   81     30     6000
chevy    impala   65     85     1550
```

The caret (^) in a regular expression forces a match at the beginning of the line or, in this case, the beginning of the first field.

```
$ awk '$1 ~ /^h/' cars
honda    accord   81     30     6000
```

A pair of brackets surrounds a character class definition (refer to Appendix A, "Regular Expressions"). Below, **awk** selects all lines that have a second field that begins with t or m. Then it prints the third and second fields, a dollar sign, and the fifth field.

```
$ awk '$2 ~ /^[tm]/ {print $3, $2, "$"  $5}' cars
65 mustang $10000
84 thundbd $17000
82 tercel $750
```

The next example shows three roles that a dollar sign can play in an **awk** program. A dollar sign followed by a number forms the name of a field. Within a regular expression, a dollar sign forces a match at the end of a line or field (5$). Within a string, you can use a dollar sign as itself.

```
$ awk '$3 ~ /5$/ {print $3, $1, "$"  $5}' cars
65 ford $10000
65 fiat $450
65 chevy $1550
```

Below, the equals relational operator (==) causes **awk** to perform a numeric comparison between the third field in each line and the number 65. The **awk** command takes the default action, Print, on each line that matches.

```
$ awk '$3 == 65' cars
ford    mustang 65     45       10000
fiat    600     65     115      450
chevy   impala  65     85       1550
```

The next example finds all cars priced at or under $3000.

```
$ awk '$5 <= 3000' cars
plym    fury    77     73       2500
chevy   nova    79     60       3000
fiat    600     65     115      450
toyota  tercel  82     180      750
chevy   impala  65     85       1550
```

When you use double quotation marks, **awk** performs textual comparisons, using the ASCII collating sequence as the basis of the comparison. Below, **awk** shows that the *strings* 450 and 750 fall in the range that lies between the *strings* 2000 and 9000.

```
$ awk '$5 >= "2000" && $5 < "9000"' cars
plym    fury    77     73       2500
chevy   nova    79     60       3000
chevy   nova    80     50       3500
fiat    600     65     115      450
honda   accord  81     30       6000
toyota  tercel  82     180      750
```

When you need a numeric comparison, do not use quotation marks. The next example gives the correct results. It is the same as the previous example but omits the double quotation marks.

```
$ awk '$5 >= 2000 && $5 < 9000' cars
plym     fury     77        73        2500
chevy    nova     79        60        3000
chevy    nova     80        50        3500
honda    accord   81        30        6000
```

Next, the range operator (,) selects a group of lines. The first line it selects is the one specified by the pattern before the comma. The last line is the one selected by the pattern after the comma. If there is no line that matches the pattern after the comma, **awk** selects every line up to the end of the file. The example selects all lines starting with the line that contains volvo and concluding with the line that contains fiat.

```
$ awk '/volvo/ , /fiat/' cars
volvo    gl       78        102       9850
ford     ltd      83        15        10500
chevy    nova     80        50        3500
fiat     600      65        115       450
```

After the range operator finds its first group of lines, it starts the process over, looking for a line that matches the pattern before the comma. In the following example, **awk** finds three groups of lines that fall between chevy and ford. Although the fifth line in the file contains ford, **awk** does not select it because, at the time it is processing the fifth line, it is searching for chevy.

```
$ awk '/chevy/ , /ford/' cars
chevy    nova     79        60        3000
ford     mustang  65        45        10000
chevy    nova     80        50        3500
fiat     600      65        115       450
honda    accord   81        30        6000
ford     thundbd  84        10        17000
chevy    impala   65        85        1550
ford     bronco   83        25        9500
```

When you are writing a longer **awk** program, it is convenient to put the program in a file and reference the file on the command line. Use the –f option, followed by the name of the file containing the **awk** program.

Following is an **awk** program that has two actions and uses the BEGIN pattern. The **awk** utility performs the action associated with BEGIN before it processes any of the lines of the data file. The **pr_header awk** program uses BEGIN to print a header.

The second action, {**print**}, has no pattern part and prints all the lines in the file.

```
$ cat pr_header
BEGIN   {print "Make    Model    Year    Miles    Price"}
        {print}
```

```
$ awk -f pr_header cars
Make    Model    Year    Miles    Price
plym    fury     77      73       2500
chevy   nova     79      60       3000
ford    mustang 65       45       10000
volvo   gl       78      102      9850
ford    ltd      83      15       10500
chevy   nova     80      50       3500
fiat    600      65      115      450
honda   accord   81      30       6000
ford    thundbd 84       10       17000
toyota  tercel   82      180      750
chevy   impala   65      85       1550
ford    bronco   83      25       9500
```

In the previous and following examples, the white space in the headers is composed of single (TAB)s, so that the titles line up with the columns of data.

```
$ cat pr_header2
BEGIN   {
print "Make      Model    Year    Miles    Price"
print "--------------------------------------------"
}
          {print}
```

```
$ awk -f pr_header2 cars
Make    Model    Year    Miles    Price
--------------------------------------------
plym    fury     77      73       2500
chevy   nova     79      60       3000
ford    mustang 65       45       10000
volvo   gl       78      102      9850
ford    ltd      83      15       10500
chevy   nova     80      50       3500
fiat    600      65      115      450
honda   accord   81      30       6000
ford    thundbd 84       10       17000
toyota  tercel   82      180      750
chevy   impala   65      85       1550
ford    bronco   83      25       9500
```

When you call the **length** function without an argument, it returns the number of characters in the current line, including field separators. The $0 variable always contains the value of the current line. In the next example, **awk** prepends the length to each line, and then a pipe sends the output from **awk** to **sort**, so that the lines of the **cars** file appear in order of length. Because the formatting of the report depends on (TAB)s, including three extra characters at the beginning of each line throws off the format of the last line. A remedy for this situation will be covered shortly.

```
$ awk '{print length, $0}' cars | sort
19 fiat 600      65       115      450
20 ford ltd      83       15       10500
20 plym fury     77       73       2500
20 volvo         gl       78       102      9850
21 chevy         nova     79       60       3000
21 chevy         nova     80       50       3500
22 ford bronco   83       25       9500
23 chevy         impala   65       85       1550
23 honda         accord   81       30       6000
24 ford mustang  65       45       10000
24 ford thundbd  84       10       17000
24 toyota        tercel   82       180      750
```

The **NR** variable contains the record (line) number of the current line. The following pattern selects all lines that contain more than 23 characters. The action prints the line number of all the selected lines.

```
$ awk 'length > 23 {print NR}' cars
3
9
10
```

You can combine the range operator (,) and the **NR** variable to display a group of lines of a file based on their line numbers. The next example displays lines 2 through 4.

```
$ awk 'NR == 2 , NR == 4' cars
chevy    nova      79       60       3000
ford     mustang 65        45       10000
volvo    gl        78       102      9850
```

The **END** pattern works in a manner similar to the **BEGIN** pattern, except **awk** takes the actions associated with it after it has processed the last of its input lines. The following report displays information only after it has processed the entire data file. The **NR** variable retains its value after **awk** has finished processing the data file, so that an action associated with an **END** pattern can use it.

```
$ awk 'END {print NR, "cars for sale." }' cars
12 cars for sale.
```

The next example uses If commands to change the values of some of the first fields. As long as **awk** does not make any changes to a record, it leaves the entire record, including separators, intact. Once it makes a change to a record, it changes all separators in that record to the default. The default output field separator is a (SPACE).

```
$ cat separ_demo
        {
        if ($1 ~ /ply/)  $1 = "plymouth"
        if ($1 ~ /chev/) $1 = "chevrolet"
        print
        }

$  awk -f separ_demo cars
plymouth fury 77 73 2500
chevrolet nova 79 60 3000
ford    mustang 65      45      10000
volvo   gl      78      102     9850
ford    ltd     83      15      10500
chevrolet nova 80 50 3500
fiat    600     65      115     450
honda   accord  81      30      6000
ford    thundbd 84      10      17000
toyota  tercel  82      180     750
chevrolet impala 65 85 1550
ford    bronco  83      25      9500
```

You can change the default value of the output field separator by assigning a value to the **OFS** variable. There is one ⌨TAB character between the quotation marks in the following example.

This fix improves the appearance of the report but does not properly line up the columns.

```
$ cat ofs_demo
BEGIN   {OFS = "⌨TAB"}
        {
        if ($1 ~ /ply/)  $1 = "plymouth"
        if ($1 ~ /chev/) $1 = "chevrolet"
        print
        }

$ awk -f ofs_demo cars
plymouth        fury    77      73      2500
chevrolet       nova    79      60      3000
ford    mustang 65      45      10000
volvo   gl      78      102     9850
ford    ltd     83      15      10500
chevrolet       nova    80      50      3500
fiat    600     65      115     450
honda   accord  81      30      6000
ford    thundbd 84      10      17000
toyota  tercel  82      180     750
chevrolet       impala  65      85      1550
ford    bronco  83      25      9500
```

You can use Printf to refine the output format (refer to page 535). The following example uses a backslash at the end of a program line to mask the following (NEWLINE) from **awk**. You can use this technique to continue a long line over one or more lines without affecting the outcome of the program.

```
$ cat printf_demo
BEGIN   {
  print "                                        Miles"
  print "Make         Model        Year    (000)      Price"
  print \
   "_____"
        }
        {
        if ($1 ~ /ply/)  $1 = "plymouth"
        if ($1 ~ /chev/) $1 = "chevrolet"
        printf "%-10s %-8s   19%2d    %5d      $ %8.2f\n",\
               $1, $2, $3, $4, $5
        }
```

```
$ awk -f printf_demo cars
                             Miles
Make         Model        Year    (000)         Price
-------------------------------------------------------
plymouth     fury         1977     73     $  2500.00
chevrolet    nova         1979     60     $  3000.00
ford         mustang      1965     45     $ 10000.00
volvo        gl           1978    102     $  9850.00
ford         ltd          1983     15     $ 10500.00
chevrolet    nova         1980     50     $  3500.00
fiat         600          1965    115     $   450.00
honda        accord       1981     30     $  6000.00
ford         thundbd      1984     10     $ 17000.00
toyota       tercel       1982    180     $   750.00
chevrolet    impala       1965     85     $  1550.00
ford         bronco       1983     25     $  9500.00
```

The next example creates two new files, one with all the lines that contain chevy and the other with lines containing ford.

```
$ cat redirect_out
/chevy/         {print > "chevfile"}
/ford/          {print > "fordfile"}
END             {print "done."}
$ awk -f redirect_out cars
done.
$ cat chevfile
chevy   nova    79      60      3000
chevy   nova    80      50      3500
chevy   impala  65      85      1550
```

The **summary** program produces a summary report on all cars and newer cars. The first two lines of declarations are not required; **awk** automatically declares and initializes variables as you use them. After **awk** reads all the input data, it computes and displays averages.

```
$ cat summary
BEGIN   {
        yearsum = 0 ; costsum = 0
        newcostsum = 0 ; newcount = 0
        }
        {
        yearsum += $3
        costsum += $5
        }
$3 > 80 {newcostsum += $5 ; newcount ++}
END     {
        printf "Average age of cars is %3.1f years\n",\
               90 - (yearsum/NR)
        printf "Average cost of cars is $%7.2f\n",\
               costsum/NR
      printf "Average cost of newer cars is $%7.2f\n",\
               newcostsum/newcount
        }
```

```
$ awk -f summary cars
Average age of cars is 13.2 years
Average cost of cars is $6216.67
Average cost of newer cars is $8750.00
```

Following, **grep** shows the format of a line from the **passwd** file that the next example uses.

```
$ grep 'mark' /etc/passwd
mark:4zvDGYGEbYHJg:107:100:ext 112:/home/mark:/bin/csh
```

The next example demonstrates a technique for finding the largest number in a field. Because it works with the **passwd** file, which delimits fields with colons (:), it changes the input field separator (**FS**) before reading any data. (Alternatively, the –**F** option could be used on the command line to change the input field separator.) This example reads the **passwd** file and determines the next available user ID number (field 3). The numbers do not have to be in order in the **passwd** file for this program to work.

The pattern causes **awk** to select records that contain a user ID number greater than any previous user ID number that it has processed. Each time it selects a record, it assigns the value of the new user ID number to the **saveit** variable. Then **awk** uses the new value of **saveit** to test the user ID of all subsequent records.

Finally, **awk** adds 1 to the value of **saveit** and displays the result.

```
$ cat find_uid
BEGIN          {FS = ":"
                saveit = 0}
$3 > saveit    {saveit = $3}
END            {print "Next available UID is " saveit + 1}
```

```
$ awk -f find_uid /etc/passwd
Next available UID is 192
```

The next example shows another report based on the **cars** file. This report uses nested If Else statements to substitute values based on the contents of the price field. The program has no pattern part—it processes every record.

```
$ cat price_range
{
if ($5 <= 5000) $5 = "inexpensive"
else if ($5 > 5000 && $5 < 10000) $5 = "please ask"
else if ($5 >= 10000) $5 = "expensive"
printf "%-10s %-8s    19%2d    %5d    %-12s\n",\
        $1, $2, $3, $4, $5
}
```

```
$ awk -f price_range cars
plym       fury       1977       73       inexpensive
chevy      nova       1979       60       inexpensive
ford       mustang    1965       45       expensive
volvo      gl         1978       102      please ask
ford       ltd        1983       15       expensive
chevy      nova       1980       50       inexpensive
fiat       600        1965       115      inexpensive
honda      accord     1981       30       please ask
ford       thundbd    1984       10       expensive
toyota     tercel     1982       180      inexpensive
chevy      impala     1965       85       inexpensive
ford       bronco     1983       25       please ask
```

Below, the **manuf** associative array uses the contents of the first field of each record in the **cars** file as an index. The array is composed of the elements **manuf[plym]**, **manuf[chevy]**, **manuf[ford]**, and so on. The ++ C language operator increments the variable that it follows.

The action following the **END** pattern is the special For structure that loops through the elements of an associative array. A pipe sends the output through **sort** to produce an alphabetical list of cars and the quantities in stock.

```
$ cat manuf
awk '    {manuf[$1]++}
END      {for (name in manuf) print name, manuf[name]}
' cars |
sort
```

```
$ manuf
chevy 3
fiat 1
ford 4
honda 1
plym 1
toyota 1
volvo 1
```

The **manuf.sh** program is a more complete shell script that includes error checking. This script lists and counts the contents of a column in a file, with both the column number and the name of the file specified on the command line.

The first **awk** action (the one that starts with {count) uses the shell variable **$1** in the middle of the **awk** program to specify an array index. The single quotation marks cause the shell to substitute the value of the first command line argument in place of **$1**, so that **$1** is interpreted before the **awk** command is invoked. The leading dollar sign (the one before the first single quotation mark) causes **awk** to interpret what the shell substitutes as a field number. Refer to Chapter 10 for more information on shell scripts.

```
$ cat manuf.sh
if [ $# != 2 ]
    then
        echo "Usage: manuf.sh field file"
        exit 1
fi
awk < $2 '
        {count[$'$1']++}
END     {for (item in count) printf "%-20s%-20s\n",\
            item, count[item]}' |
sort

$  manuf.sh
Usage: manuf.sh field file
$  manuf.sh 1 cars
chevy               3
fiat                1
ford                4
honda               1
plym                1
toyota              1
volvo               1

$  manuf.sh 3 cars
65                  3
77                  1
78                  1
79                  1
80                  1
81                  1
82                  1
83                  2
84                  1
```

The **word_usage** script displays a word usage list for a file you specify on the command line. The **deroff** utility removes **nroff** and **troff** commands from a file and, with the –w option, lists the words one to a line. The **sort** utility orders the file with the most frequently used words at the top of the list. It sorts groups of words that are used the same number of times in alphabetical order. Refer to **sort** in Part II for more information.

```
$ cat word_usage
deroff -w $* |
awk        '
          {count[$1]++}
END       {for (item in count) printf "%-15s%3s\n", item, count[item]}' |
sort +1nr +0f -1

$ word_usage textfile
the            42
file           29
fsck           27
system         22
you            22
to             21
it             17
SIZE           14
and            13
MODE           13
.
.
.
```

Below is a similar program in a different format. The style mimics that of a C program and may be easier to read and work with for more complex **awk** programs.

```
$ cat word_count
deroff -w $* |
awk '    {
          count[$1]++
}
END       {
          for (item in count)
                {
                if (count[item] > 4)
                     {
                     printf "%-15s%3s\n", item, count[item]
                     }
                }
} ' |
sort +1nr +0f -1
```

The **tail** utility displays the last ten lines of output, illustrating that words occurring fewer than five times are not listed.

```
$ word_count textfile | tail
directories    5
if             5
information    5
INODE          5
more           5
no             5
on             5
response       5
this           5
will           5
```

The next example shows one way to put a date on a report. The first line of input to the **awk** program comes from **date**. The **awk** program reads this line as record number 1 (NR == 1) and processes it accordingly. It processes all subsequent records with the action associated with the next pattern (NR > 1).

```
$ cat report
if (test $# = 0) then
            echo "You must supply a filename."
            exit
fi
(date; cat $*) |
awk '
NR == 1             {print "Report for", $1, $2, $3 ", " $6}
NR >  1             {print $5 "        " $1}'
$ report cars
Report for Mon Jul 11, 1994
2500       plym
3000       chevy
10000      ford
9850       volvo
10500      ford
3500       chevy
450        fiat
6000       honda
17000      ford
750        toyota
1550       chevy
9500       ford
```

The next example uses the **numbers** file and sums each of the columns in a file you specify on the command line. It performs error checking, discarding fields that contain nonnumeric entries. It also displays a grand total for the file.

```
$ cat numbers
10        20        30.3      40.5
20        30        45.7      66.1
30        xyz       50        70
40        75        107.2     55.6
50        20        30.3      40.5
60        30        45.0      66.1
70        1134.7    50        70
80        75        107.2     55.6
90        176       30.3      40.5
100       1027.45   45.7      66.1
110       123       50        57a.5
120       75        107.2     55.6
```

```
$ cat tally
awk '   BEGIN    {
                 ORS = ""
                 }

NR == 1 {
        nfields = NF
        }
        {
        if ($0 ~ /[^0-9. \t]/)
                {
                print "\nRecord " NR " skipped:\n\t"
                print $0 "\n"
                next
                }
        else
                {
                for (count = 1; count <= nfields; count++)
                        {
                        printf "%10.2f", $count > "tally.out"
                        sum[count] += $count
                        gtotal += $count
                        }
                print "\n" > "tally.out"
                }
        }

END     {
        for (count = 1; count <= nfields; count++)
                {
                print "  -------" > "tally.out"
                }
        print "\n" > "tally.out"
        for (count = 1; count <= nfields; count++)
                {
                printf "%10.2f", sum[count] > "tally.out"
                }
        print "\n\n        Grand Total " gtotal "\n" > "tally.out"
} ' < numbers


$ tally
Record 3 skipped:
        30      xyz     50      70

Record 6 skipped:
        60      30      45.0    66.1

Record 11 skipped:
        110     123     50      57a.5
```

```
$ cat tally.out
        10.00      20.00      30.30      40.50
        20.00      30.00      45.70      66.10
        40.00      75.00     107.20      55.60
        50.00      20.00      30.30      40.50
        70.00    1134.70      50.00      70.00
        80.00      75.00     107.20      55.60
        90.00     176.00      30.30      40.50
       100.00    1027.45      45.70      66.10
       120.00      75.00     107.20      55.60
       -------    -------    -------    -------
       580.00    2633.15     553.90     490.50

        Grand Total 4257.55
```

The next **awk** example reads the **passwd** file. It lists users who do not have passwords and users who have duplicate user ID numbers. (The **pwck** utility will also perform these checks, as well as a few more.)

```
$ cat /etc/passwd
bill::102:100:ext 123:/home/bill:/bin/sh
roy:QpMB2EaP.zANA:104:100:ext 475:/home/roy:/bin/sh
tom:QBaUycsXmi9mk:105:100:ext 476:/home/tom:/bin/sh
lynn:.BhVeaghQ045s:166:100:ext 500:/home/lynn:/bin/sh
mark:gKBLaE8DLFamM:107:100:ext 112:/home/mark:/bin/sh
sales:zBKaNBGoJ.29o:108:100:ext 102:/m/market:/bin/sh
anne:71BNXqWaSWgOk:109:100:ext 355:/home/anne:/bin/sh
toni::164:100:ext 357:/home/toni:/bin/sh
ginny:tBitPlajFWa.I:115:100:ext 109:/home/ginny:/bin/sh
chuck:JBwaFE/5XJYrE:116:100:ext 146:/home/chuck:/bin/sh
neil:7TBaVtLZarhS6:164:100:ext 159:/home/neil:/bin/sh
rmi:T3aBxazCvnqz2:118:100:ext 178:/home/rmi:/bin/sh
vern:aBIncbxAa9eDs:119:100:ext 201:/home/vern:/bin/sh
bob:nsjBgab1dvsmQ:120:100:ext 227:/home/bob:/bin/sh
janet:TBQ65yZYaOqjI:122:100:ext 229:/home/janet:/bin/sh
maggie:BWabz/pGLkb6g:124:100:ext 244:/home/maggie:/bin/sh
dan::126:100::/home/dan:/bin/sh
dave:5JBELKmauB4/s:108:100:ext 427:/home/dave:/bin/sh
mary:rIBYnLS/LD9B6:129:100:ext 303:/home/mary:/bin/sh
```

```
$ cat passwd_check
awk < /etc/passwd '       BEGIN    {
              uid[void] = ""   # tell awk that uid is an array
              }
              {                # no pattern indicates process all records
              dup = 0          # initialize duplicate flag
              split($0, field, ":") # split into fields delimited by ":"
              if (field[2] == "")     # check for null password field
                    {
                    if (field[5] == "")      # check for null info field
                          {
                          print field[1] " has no password."
                          }
                    else
                          {
                          print field[1] " ("field[5]") has no password."
                          }
                    }
```

```
            for (name in uid)        # loop through uid array
                   {
                   if (uid[name] == field[3])      # check for 2nd use of UID
                          {
                          print field[1] " has the same UID as "\
                                        name " : UID = " uid[name]
               dup = 1  # set duplicate flag
                          }
                   }
            if (!dup)         # same as: if (dup == 0)
                          # assign UID and login name to uid array
                   {
                   uid[field[1]] = field[3]
                   }
}'
```

$ passwd_check
bill (ext 123) has no password.
toni (ext 357) has no password.
neil has the same UID as toni : UID = 164
dan has no password.
dave has the same UID as sales : UID = 108

The final example shows a complete interactive shell script that uses **awk**
to generate a report.

```
$ cat list_cars
trap 'rm -f $$.tem > /dev/null;echo $0 aborted.;exit 1' 1 2 15
echo "Price range (e.g., 5000 7500): \c"
read lowrange hirange

echo '
                              Miles
Make        Model       Year  (000)      Price
--------------------------------------------------' > $$.tem
awk < cars '
$5 >= '$lowrange' && $5 <= '$hirange' {
        if ($1 ~ /ply/)  $1 = "plymouth"
        if ($1 ~ /chev/) $1 = "chevrolet"
        printf "%-10s %-8s   19%2d   %5d   $ %8.2f\n", $1, $2, $3, $4, $5
        }' | sort -n +5 >> $$.tem
cat $$.tem
rm $$.tem
```

$ list_cars
Price range (e.g., 5000 7500): 3000 8000

```
                              Miles
Make        Model       Year  (000)       Price
--------------------------------------------------
chevrolet   nova        1979    60     $ 3000.00
chevrolet   nova        1980    50     $ 3500.00
honda       accord      1981    30     $ 6000.00
```

```
$ list_cars
Price range (e.g., 5000 7500): 0 2000


Make        Model       Year      (000)         Price
---------------------------------------------------------
fiat        600         1965      115      $     450.00
toyota      tercel      1982      180      $     750.00
chevrolet   impala      1965       85      $    1550.00

$ list_cars
Price range (e.g., 5000 7500): 15000 100000

                                  Miles
Make        Model       Year      (000)         Price
---------------------------------------------------------
ford        thundbd     1984       10      $ 17000.00
```

Error Messages

The following examples show some of the more common causes of **awk**'s infamous error messages (and nonmessages).

The first example leaves the single quotation marks off the command line, so the shell interprets **$3** and **$1** as shell variables. Another problem is that because there are no single quotation marks, the shell passes **awk** four arguments instead of two.

```
$ awk {print $3, $1} cars
awk: syntax error near line 1
awk: illegal statement near line 1
```

The next command line includes a typo that **awk** does not catch (prinnt). Instead of issuing an error message, **awk** just does not do anything useful.

```
$ awk '$3 >= 83 {prinnt $1}' cars
```

The next example has no braces around the action.

```
$ awk '/chevy/ print $3, $1' cars
awk: syntax error near line 1
awk: bailing out near line 1
```

There is no problem with the next example—**awk** did just what you asked it to. (None of the lines in the file contained a z).

```
$ awk '/z/' cars
```

The following program contains a useless action (the Print command is probably missing).

```
$ awk '{$3}' cars
awk: illegal statement 56250
 record number 1
```

The next example shows another improper action, but this time **awk** did not issue an error message.

```
$ awk '{$3  " made by "  $1}' cars
```

Following is a format that **awk** did not particularly care for. This example needs a backslash after the first Print command to quote the following (NEWLINE).

```
$ cat print_cars
BEGIN           {print
"Make    Model    Year    Miles    Price"}
                {print}
```

```
$ awk -f print_cars cars
awk: illegal statement 57422
```

You must use double quotation marks, not single quotation marks, to delimit strings.

```
$ awk '$3 ~ /5$/ {print $3, $1, '$' $5}' cars
awk: trying to access field 10000
 record number 3
```

cal

Display a calendar.

Format

cal [month] year
cal

Summary

The **cal** utility displays a calendar for a month or year.

Arguments

The arguments specify the month and year for which **cal** displays a calendar. The **month** is a decimal integer from 1 to 12, and the **year** is a decimal integer. If you do not specify any arguments, **cal** displays a calendar for the current month.

Notes

Do not abbreviate the year. The year 94 does not represent the same year as 1994.

Examples

The following command displays a calendar for August 1994.

```
$ cal 8 1994
      August 1994
 S   M  Tu   W  Th   F   S
     1   2   3   4   5   6
 7   8   9  10  11  12  13
14  15  16  17  18  19  20
21  22  23  24  25  26  27
28  29  30  31
```

The next command displays a calendar for all of 1949.

```
$ cal 1949

                                    1949

         Jan                      Feb                      Mar
 S  M Tu  W Th  F  S      S  M Tu  W Th  F  S      S  M Tu  W Th  F  S
                   1                  1  2  3  4  5             1  2  3  4  5
 2  3  4  5  6  7  8      6  7  8  9 10 11 12      6  7  8  9 10 11 12
 9 10 11 12 13 14 15     13 14 15 16 17 18 19     13 14 15 16 17 18 19
16 17 18 19 20 21 22     20 21 22 23 24 25 26     20 21 22 23 24 25 26
23 24 25 26 27 28 29     27 28                    27 28 29 30 31
30 31
         Apr                      May                      Jun
 S  M Tu  W Th  F  S      S  M Tu  W Th  F  S      S  M Tu  W Th  F  S
                1  2      1  2  3  4  5  6  7                1  2  3  4
 3  4  5  6  7  8  9      8  9 10 11 12 13 14      5  6  7  8  9 10 11
10 11 12 13 14 15 16     15 16 17 18 19 20 21     12 13 14 15 16 17 18
17 18 19 20 21 22 23     22 23 24 25 26 27 28     19 20 21 22 23 24 25
24 25 26 27 28 29 30     29 30 31                 26 27 28 29 30
```

calendar

Present reminders.

Format

calendar

Summary

The UNIX system provides **calendar** as a service. If your system is set up to run **calendar** automatically, it will send you mail (typically once a day). The mail will contain lines from a file called **calendar** in your home directory that contain that day's or the next day's date. You can also use the **calendar** command to display these lines from your **calendar** file.

Notes

During the weekend, the *next day* goes through Monday.

The **calendar** file *must* be in your home directory and must have read access permission for everyone. The dates can appear anywhere on the line in the file, in various formats, but must show the month preceding the day of the month.

When you execute **calendar**, or have your **.profile** or .login file execute it, **calendar** displays any lines in the **calendar** file that contain that day's or the next day's date.

The **calendar** utility ignores a year as part of the date.

Examples

The following example of a **calendar** file shows some of the ways you can express the date. If you place this file in your home directory, each of the three lines will be sent to you by **mail** on the date you specify and one day previous to it.

```
$ cat calendar
This line will be displayed on 7/20
Jul 28: remember to call Frank
On July 30 five years ago...
```

You can also include other calendar files in your personal calendar, without copying the entries or working to keep them up to date. In the following example, Alex will receive mail about any notices posted to the system's public calendar, as well as birthday reminders from his own birthday file.

```
$ cat calendar
# include "/usr/pub/calendar"
# include "/home/alex/personal/birthdays"
10/20:  9 am -- project meeting, room 101
.
.
```

cat

Join or display files.

Format

cat [options] [file-list]

Summary

The **cat** utility joins files end to end. It takes its input from files you specify on the command line or from its standard input. You can use **cat** to display the contents of one or more text files on the terminal.

Arguments

The **file-list** is composed of pathnames of one or more files that **cat** displays. You can use a hyphen in place of a filename to cause **cat** to read its standard input (e.g., **cat a – b** gets its input from file **a**, its standard input [terminated by a (CONTROL)-**D** if you enter it at the keyboard], and then file **b**).

Options

–b

blank   When used with the **–n** option, **–b** causes **cat** to omit line numbers on blank lines.

–e

end of line   This option marks the ends of lines with dollar signs. In order for this option to work, you must use it with the **–v** option.

–n

number   This option causes **cat** to display line numbers at the left of each line.

–s

single space   With this option, when there are multiple adjacent empty lines in a file, **cat** displays a single blank line.

–t

tabs   This option marks (TAB)s with ^Is. In order for this option to work, you must use it with the **–v** option.

–u

unbuffered   This option causes **cat** not to buffer output.

–v

visual   This option causes **cat** to display nonprinting characters other than (TAB)s, (NEWLINE)s, and **FORMFEED**s. It also allows the **–t** and **–e** options to function.

Notes

Use the **od** utility (page 656) to display the contents of a file that does not contain text (e.g., an executable program file).

The name **cat** is derived from one of the functions of this utility, *catenate*, which means to join together sequentially, or end to end.

> **CAUTION**
>
> Despite **cat**'s warning message, the shell destroys the input file (**letter**) before invoking **cat** in the following example.
>
> ```
> $ cat memo letter > letter
> cat: input letter is output
> ```
>
> If you are using the C Shell or the Korn Shell, you can prevent problems of this sort by setting the **noclobber** variable (pages 363 and 449).

Examples

The following command line displays on the terminal the contents of the text file named **memo**.

```
$ cat memo
.
.
```

The next example catenates three files and redirects the output to a file named **all**.

```
$ cat page1 letter memo > all
```

You can use **cat** to create short text files without using an editor. Enter the command line shown below, type the text that you want in the file, and then press (CONTROL)-**D** on a line by itself. The **cat** utility takes its input from its standard input (the terminal), and the shell redirects its standard output (a copy of the input) to the file you specify. The (CONTROL)-**D** signals the end of file and causes **cat** to return control to the shell. (See also page 95.)

```
$ cat > new_file
.
.
(text)
.
.
(CONTROL)-D
```

Below, a pipe sends the output from **who** to the standard input of **cat**. The **cat** utility creates the **output** file that contains the contents of the **header** file, the output of **who**, and finally, **footer**. The hyphen on the command line causes **cat** to read its standard input after reading **header** and be   ·· ·· **footer**.

```
$ who | cat header - footer > output
```

cc

C compiler

Format

cc [options] file-list [–larg]

Summary

Based on the command line options, **cc** compiles, assembles, and loads C language source files. It can also assemble and load assembly language source files or merely load object files.

The **cc** utility uses the following naming conventions:

- A filename extension of **.c** indicates a C language source program.

- A filename extension of **.s** indicates an assembly language source program.

- A filename extension of **.o** indicates an object program.

The **cc** utility takes its input from files you specify on the command line. Unless you use the **–o** option, **cc** stores the executable program it produces in **a.out**.

Arguments

The **file-list** contains the pathnames of the files that **cc** is to compile, assemble, and/or load.

Options

Without any options, **cc** accepts C language source files, assembly language source files, and object files that follow the naming conventions outlined above. It compiles, assembles, and loads these files as appropriate, producing an executable file named **a.out**. The **cc** utility puts the object code in files with the same base filename as their source but with a filename extension of **.o**. If you compile, assemble, and load a single C source file with one **cc** command, **cc** deletes the object file. Some of the options that are most commonly used are:

–c

compile This option causes **cc** not to load object files. The **cc** utility compiles and/or assembles source files and leaves the corresponding object code in files with filename extensions of **.o**.

–o file

output   This option causes **cc** to place the executable program in **file** instead of **a.out**. You can use any filename in place of **file**.

–O

> **optimize**   This option optimizes the object code produced by the compiler (usually for best performance).

–S

> **compile only**   With this option, **cc** compiles C files and leaves the corresponding assembly language source code in files with file-name extensions of **.s**.

–g

> This option causes **cc** to include additional information that is used by the debugger.

–larg

> **search library**   With this option, **cc** searches both the **/lib/libarg.a** and the **/usr/lib/libarg.a** libraries and loads any required functions. You must replace **arg** with the name of the library you want to search. For example, the **–lm** option normally loads the standard math library.
>
> The position of this option is significant; it generally needs to go at the end of the command line. The loader uses the library only to resolve undefined symbols from modules that *precede* the library option on the command line.

Examples

The first example compiles, assembles, and loads a single C program, **compute.c**. The executable output is put in **a.out**. The **cc** utility deletes the object file.

```
$ cc compute.c
```

The next example compiles the same program, using the C optimizer (**–O** option). It assembles and then loads the optimized code. The **–o** option causes **cc** to put the executable output in **compute**.

```
$ cc -O -o compute compute.c
```

Next, a C source file, an assembly language file, and an object file are compiled, assembled, and loaded. The executable output goes to **progo**.

```
$ cc -o progo procom.c profast.s proout.o
```

Finally, **cc** searches the standard math library stored in **/lib/libm.a** when it is loading the **himath** program. It places the executable output in **a.out**.

```
$ cc himath.c -lm
```

cd

Change to another working directory.

Format

cd [**directory**]

Summary

When you call **cd** and specify a directory, that directory becomes the working directory. If you do not specify a directory on the command line, **cd** makes your home directory the working directory.

Argument

The **directory** is the pathname of the directory that you want to become the working directory.

Notes

The **cd** program is not really a utility but a built-in command in the Bourne Shell, the C Shell, and the Korn Shell. Refer to the discussion of the **HOME** shell variable on pages 286, 362, and 393. Chapter 4 contains a discussion of **cd**.

Each of the three shells has a variable, **CDPATH** (**cdpath** in the C Shell), that affects the operation of **cd**. The **CDPATH** variable contains a list of directories **cd** will search in addition to the working directory. If **CDPATH** is not set, **cd** searches only the working directory. If it is set, **cd** searches each of the directories in **CDPATH**'s directory list. Refer to page 295 for more information about **CDPATH**, or page 362 for more information about **cdpath**.

The Korn Shell built-in **cd** command has some features in addition to those common to all three shells.

Examples

The following command makes your home directory become the working directory.

```
$ cd
```

The next command makes the **/home/alex/literature** directory the working directory. The **pwd** utility verifies the change.

```
$ cd /home/alex/literature
$ pwd
/home/alex/literature
```

Next, **cd** makes a subdirectory of the working directory the new working directory.

```
$ cd memos
$ pwd
/home/alex/literature/memos
```

Finally, **cd** uses the .. reference to the parent of the working directory to make the parent the new working directory.

```
$ cd ..
```

chgrp

Change the group that is associated with a file.

Format

chgrp [options] group file-list

Summary

The **chgrp** utility changes the group that is associated with a file.

Arguments

The **group** is the name or numeric group ID of the new group. The **file-list** is a list of pathnames of the files whose group association you want to change.

Options

–f

> **force**   This option causes **chgrp** not to display any error messages.

–R

> **recursive**   When you include directories in **file-list**, this option causes **chgrp** to descend the directory hierarchy, setting the specified group ID on all files encountered.

Notes

Only the owner of a file or the Superuser can change the group association of a file. You must belong to the specified group as well as be the owner of the file (unless you are the Superuser).

Example

The following command changes the group that the **manuals** file is associated with. The new group is pubs.

```
$ chgrp pubs manuals
```

chmod

chmod

Change the access mode of a file.

Format

chmod [options] who[operation][permission] file-list
chmod [options] mode file-list

Summary

The **chmod** utility changes the ways in which a file can be accessed by the owner of the file, the group to which the file belongs, and/or all other users. Only the owner of a file or the Superuser can change the access mode, or permissions, of a file.

You can specify the new access mode absolutely or symbolically.

Arguments

Arguments give **chmod** information about which files are to have their modes changed in what ways.

Symbolic

The **chmod** utility changes the access permission for the class of user specified by **who**. The class of user is designated by one or more of the following letters:

Letter	Meaning	
u	user	owner of the file
g	group	group to which the owner belongs
o	other	all other users
a	all	can be used in place of **u, g,** and o above

The **operation** to be performed is defined by the following list:

Operator	Meaning
+	add permission for the specified user class
–	remove permission for the specified user class
=	set permission for the specified user—reset all other permissions for that user class

The access **permission** is defined by the following list:

Letter	Meaning
r	read permission
w	write permission
x	execute permission
s	set user ID or set group ID (depending on the **who** argument) to that of the owner of the file while the file is being executed
t	set the sticky bit (only the Superuser can set the sticky bit, and it can only be used with **u**)—see page 780

Absolute

In place of the symbolic method of changing the access permissions for a file, you can use an octal number to represent the mode. Construct the number by ORing the appropriate values from the following table. (To OR two octal numbers from the following table, you can just add them. Refer to the second table following for examples.)

Number	Meaning
4000	Set user ID when the program is executed.
2000	Set group ID when the program is executed.
1000	Sticky bit.
0400	Owner can read the file.
0200	Owner can write to the file.
0100	Owner can execute the file.
0040	Group can read the file.
0020	Group can write to the file.
0010	Group can execute the file.
0004	Others can read the file.
0002	Others can write to the file.
0001	Others can execute the file.

The following table lists some typical modes.

Mode	Meaning
0777	Owner, group, and public can read, write, and execute file.
0755	Owner can read, write, and execute; group and public can read and execute file.
0644	Owner can read and write; group and public can read file.
0711	Owner can read, write, and execute; group and public can execute file.

Options

–f

> **force**   This option causes **chmod** not to display any error messages.

–R

> **recursive**   When you include directories in the **file-list**, this option causes **chmod** to descend the directory hierarchy, setting the specified modes on all files encountered.

Notes

You can use the **ls** utility (with the **–lg** options) to display file access privileges (page 633).

When you are using symbolic arguments, the only time you can omit the **permission** from the command line is when the **operation** is =. This omission takes away all permissions.

Examples

The following examples show how to use the **chmod** utility to change permissions on a file named **temp**. The initial access mode of **temp** is shown by **ls**.

```
$ ls -lg temp
-rw-rw-r-- 1 alex  pubs     57  Jul 12 16:47 temp
```

The command line below removes all access permissions for the group and all other users, so that only the owner has access to the file. When you do not follow an equal sign with a permission, **chmod** removes all permissions for the specified user class. The **ls** utility verifies the change.

```
$ chmod go= temp
$ ls -lg temp
-rw------- 1 alex  pubs     57  Jul 12 16:47 temp
```

The next command changes the access modes for all users (owner, group, and all others) to read and write. Now anyone can read from or write to the file. Again, **ls** verifies the change.

```
$ chmod a=rw temp
$ ls -lg temp
-rw-rw-rw- 1 alex  pubs     57  Jul 12 16:47 temp
```

Using an absolute argument, the **a=rw** becomes **666**. The next command performs the same function as the previous **chmod** command.

```
$ chmod 666 temp
```

The following command removes the write access privilege for all other users. This change means that members of the pubs group can still read from and write to the file, but other users can only read from the file.

```
$ chmod o-w temp
$ ls -lg temp
-rw-rw-r-- 1 alex   pubs      57  Jul 12 16:47 temp
```

The command that yields the same result using an absolute argument is shown below.

```
$ chmod 664 temp
```

The final command adds execute access privilege for all users. If **temp** is a shell script or other executable file, all users can now execute it.

```
$ chmod a+x temp
$ ls -lg temp
-rwxrwxr-x 1 alex   pubs      57  Jul 12 16:47 temp
```

Again, the absolute command that yields the same result follows:

```
$ chmod 775 temp
```

chown

Change the owner of a file.

Format

chown [options] owner [.group] file-list

Summary

The **chown** utility changes the owner of a file.

Arguments

The **owner** is the name or numeric user ID of the new owner. The **group** is the name or numeric group ID of the new group. The **file-list** is a list of path-names of the files whose ownership you want to change.

Options

–f

> **force** This option causes the **chmod** utility not to display any error messages.

–R

> **recursive** When you include directories in the **file-list**, this option causes **chown** to descend the directory hierarchy, setting the specified ownership on all files encountered.

Notes

Only the Superuser can change the ownership of a file on Berkeley-based systems such as SunOS.

Examples

The following command changes the owner of the **chapter1** file in the **manuals** directory. The new owner is Jenny.

```
# chown jenny manuals/chapter1
```

The command below makes alex the owner of all files in the /home/alex/literature directory and in all of its subdirectories. It also changes the group associated with the files to **pubs**.

```
# chown -R alex.pubs /home/alex/literature
```

ci

Create or record changes in an RCS file

Format

ci [options] file-list

Summary

The **ci** utility is part of RCS (Revision Control System—page 484). The **ci** utility creates or records changes in RCS-encoded files.

Arguments

The **file-list** is a list of filenames. If you do not specify the directory as part of the filename, the **ci** utility will create or change the file in a subdirectory named **RCS**. If there is no **RCS** directory, it will use the current directory. The options control the attributes of the file.

Options

–l[version-number]

> **lock**   After checking in the revision, retrieve a locked (editable) copy at the next revision level. This is a one-step equivalent to running **ci** followed by **co –l**.

–m[comments]

> **messages**   This option allows you to enter text that will be used as the reason for checking in a revision to the file. If you do not use the **–m** option and the standard input is a terminal, **ci** will prompt you for comments. To create a null comment, do not enter anything after the **–m** option, or enter a period (.) in response to the prompt for comments.

–r[version-number]

> **revision**   This option identifies the version number of the RCS-encoded file that is being checked in. This option is needed only if you do not want to use the default **version-number.**

–u[version-number]

> **unlock**   After checking in the revision, retrieve an unlocked (unwritable) copy at the current revision level. This is a one-step equivalent to running **ci** followed by **co.**

Notes

The name of an RCS-encoded file is the same as the name of the unencoded file with the two characters ,v added to the end. When working with RCS commands, you can omit the trailing ,v in a filename on the command line; the RCS commands will look for the encoded versions automatically (as **filename,v**).

Each version number may include up to four components: release, level, branch, and sequence number.

Examples

The first example demonstrates the use of the **ci** utility to create a new RCS file.

```
$ ci thesis
RCS/thesis,v  <--  thesis
enter description, terminated with a single '.' or end
of file:
NOTE: This is NOT the log message!
>> Master copy of my thesis.
>> .
initial revision: 1.1
done
$
```

The following examples illustrate the use of the **ci** utility after **co** has been used with the –l option to retrieve the highest revision on the trunk. In this example, the user enters comments directly on the command line with the –m option and uses the –l option to retrieve the next revision for editing.

```
$ ci -l -m"first pass at chapter one" thesis
RCS/thesis,v  <--  thesis
new revision: 1.2; previous revision: 1.1
done
```

The next example starts a new revision level, using the –r option.

```
$ ci -r2 thesis
RCS/thesis,v  <--  thesis
new revision: 2.1; previous revision: 1.2
enter log message:
(terminate with ^D or single '.')
>> major reorganization
>> .
done
```

co

Retrieve an unencoded version of an RCS file.

Format

co [options] file-list

Summary

The **co** utility is part of RCS (Revision Control System—page 484). The **co** utility retrieves files from their RCS-encoded versions. The options determine the characteristics of the retrieved files.

Arguments

The **file-list** is a list of filenames. If you do not specify the directory as part of the filename, the **co** utility will look for the file in a subdirectory named **RCS**. If there is no **RCS** directory, it will use the current directory.

Options

–ddate

> **date**   Retrieve the latest revision of the file made at or before the specified time.

–l[version-number]

> **lock**   Retrieve a locked (editable) copy of the file. If you do not specify a **version-number**, **co** retrieves the latest revision; otherwise, it retrieves the specified revision.

–p[version-number]

> **print**   This option causes **co** to send a copy of the file to the standard output. If you do not specify a **version-number**, **co** uses the latest revision.

–r[version-number]

> **revision**   This option identifies the **version-number** of the RCS-encoded file that is being checked out. This option is needed only if you do not want to retrieve the latest version. If you specify the **–r** option without a version number, **co** retrieves the latest revision.

–u[version-number]

> **unlock**   After checking in the revision, retrieve an unlocked (unwritable) copy at the current revision level. This is a one-step equivalent to running **ci** followed by **co**.

Notes

The name of an RCS-encoded file is the same as the name of the unencoded file with the two characters ,v added to the end. When working with RCS commands, you can omit the trailing ,v in a filename on the command line; the RCS commands will look for the encoded versions automatically (as filename,v).

Each version number may include up to four components: release, level, branch, and sequence number.

When specifying a date, the default time zone is Coordinated Universal Time (UTC), also known as Greenwich Mean Time (GMT). The RCS commands recognize dates in a variety of formats, such as

```
5:00 PM LT
1:00am, Jul. 15, 1994
Fri Jul 15 17:00:00 PDT 1994
```

In the example above, LT represents the local time (which is PDT, Pacific Daylight Time, in this case).

Examples

The first command retrieves the latest revision, but not for editing.

```
$ co thesis
RCS/thesis,v  -->  thesis
revision 1.4
done
```

The next command retrieves a writable copy of the file, setting a lock that prevents other users from retrieving a writable copy of the same file at this revision level.

```
$ co -l thesis
RCS/thesis,v  -->  thesis
revision 1.4 (locked)
done
```

The next command displays version 1.3 of **thesis** (without storing it in a new file).

```
$ co -r1.3 -p thesis
RCS/thesis,v  -->  stdout
revision 1.3
    .
    .
```

The last command retrieves the latest version of **thesis** that was checked in at or before the specified time.

```
$ co -d'Thu Jul 14 2 pm lt' thesis
    .
    .
```

comm

Compare sorted files.

Format

comm [options] file1 file2

Summary

The **comm** utility displays a line-by-line comparison of two sorted files. (If the files have not been sorted, **comm** will not work properly.) The display is in three columns. The first column lists all lines found only in **file1**, the second column lists lines found only in **file2**, and the third lists those common to both files. Lines in the second column are preceded by one (TAB), and those in the third column are preceded by two (TAB)s.

Input comes from the files you specify on the command line. (Refer to "Arguments" below for an exception.)

Arguments

The **file1** and **file2** are pathnames of the files that **comm** compares. You can use a hyphen in place of either **file1** or **file2** (but not both) to cause **comm** to use its standard input.

Options

You can use the options **–1**, **–2**, and **–3** individually or in combination.

–1

   comm does not display column 1 (does not display lines it finds only in **file1**).

–2

   comm does not display column 2 (does not display lines it finds only in **file2**).

–3

   comm does not display column 3 (does not display lines it finds in both files).

Examples

The following examples use two files, **c** and **d**, that are in the working directory. The contents of these files are shown below. As with all input to **comm**, the files are in sorted order. Refer to the **sort** utility for information on sorting files.

File c	File d
bbbbb	aaaaa
ccccc	ddddd
ddddd	eeeee
eeeee	ggggg
fffff	hhhhh

The first command (below) calls **comm** without any options, so it displays three columns. The first column lists those lines found only in file **c**, the second column lists those found in **d**, and the third lists the lines found in both **c** and **d**.

```
$ comm c d
        aaaaa
bbbbb
ccccc
                ddddd
                eeeee
fffff
        ggggg
        hhhhh
```

The next example shows the use of options to prevent **comm** from displaying columns 1 and 2. The result is column 3, a list of the lines common to files **c** and **d**.

```
$ comm -12 c d
ddddd
eeeee
```

cp

Copy one or more files.

Format

cp [options] source-file destination-file
cp [options] source-file-list destination-directory

Summary

The **cp** utility copies one or more ordinary files, including text and executable program files. It has two modes of operation: The first copies one file to another, and the second copies one or more files to a directory.

Arguments

The **source-file** is the pathname of the ordinary file that **cp** is going to copy. The **destination-file** is the pathname that **cp** will assign to the resulting copy of the file.

The **source-file-list** is one or more pathnames of ordinary files that **cp** is going to copy. When you use the **–r** option, the **source-file-list** can also contain directories. The **destination-directory** is the pathname of the directory in which **cp** places the resulting copied files.

When you specify a **destination-directory**, **cp** gives each of the copied files the same simple filename as its **source-file**. If, for example, you copy the text file **/home/jenny/memo.416** to the **/home/jenny/archives** directory, the copy will also have the simple filename **memo.416**, but the new pathname that **cp** gives it will be **/home/jenny/archives/memo.416**.

Options

–i

> **interactive**   This option causes **cp** to prompt the user whenever the copy will overwrite an existing file. After you enter **y**, **cp** will continue. If you enter anything other than **y**, **cp** will not make the copy.

–p

> **preserve**   This option causes **cp** to set the modification times and file access permissions of each copy to match those of the source-file. Without the **–p** option, **cp** uses the current file creation mask to modify the access permissions (Refer to **umask** on page 726 for a description of the file creation mask).

−r

recursive Use this option when the destination is a directory. If any of the files in the **source-file-list** is a directory, the **−r** option will cause **cp** to copy the contents of that directory and any of its subdirectories into the **destination-directory**. The subdirectories themselves are copied as well as the files they contain.

Notes

If the **destination-file** exists before you execute **cp**, **cp** overwrites the file, destroying the contents but leaving the access privileges and owner associated with the file as they were.

If the **destination-file** does not exist, **cp** uses the access privileges for the **source-file**. The user becomes the owner of the **destination-file**, and the user's group becomes the group associated with the **destination-file**.

Examples

The first command makes a copy of the file **letter** in the working directory. The name of the copy is **letter.sav**.

```
$ cp letter letter.sav
```

The next command copies all the files with filenames ending in .c into the **archives** directory, a subdirectory of the working directory. Each copied file retains its simple filename but has a new absolute pathname.

```
$ cp *.c archives
```

The next example copies **memo** from the **/home/jenny** directory to the working directory.

```
$ cp /home/jenny/memo .
```

The final command copies two files named **memo** and **letter** into another directory. The copies have the same simple filenames as the source files (**memo** and **letter**) but have different absolute pathnames. The absolute pathnames of the copied files are **/home/jenny/memo** and **/home/jenny/letter**.

```
$ cp memo letter /home/jenny
```

cpio

Store and retrieve files in an archive format.

Format

cpio –o[options]
cpio –i[options] [patterns]
cpio –p[options] directory

Summary

The **cpio** utility has three functions. It copies one or more files into a single archive file, retrieves specified files from an archive file it previously created, and copies directories. If you specify a tape or other removable media file, you can use **cpio** to create backup copies of files, to transport files to other, compatible systems, and to create archives.

Arguments

The **patterns** specify the files you want to retrieve with the –i option. The patterns take the same form as ambiguous file references for the shell, with ?, *, and [ ] matching the slash that separates files in a pathname. If you do not specify a pattern, **cpio** copies all the files.

The **directory** specifies the directory that is to receive the files that the –p option copies.

Options

The **cpio** utility has three major options and several other options that you can use with the major options. You can use only one major option at a time.

Major Options

–o

> **out**   This option causes **cpio** to read its standard input to obtain a list of pathnames of ordinary files. It combines these files, together with header information, into a single archive file that it copies to its standard output.

–i

> **in**   This option causes **cpio** to read its standard input, which **cpio** must have previously produced with the –o option. It selectively extracts files from its input, based on the patterns you give as arguments. Files that you stored using relative pathnames will appear in the working directory or a subdirectory. Files stored with absolute pathnames will appear as specified by their absolute pathnames.

–p

> **pass** This option causes **cpio** to read its standard input to obtain a list of pathnames of ordinary files. It copies these files to the directory you give as an argument. This option is useful for copying directories and their contents.

Other Options

–a

> **access time** **cpio** resets the access times of input files after copying them.

–B

> **block** This option blocks data written to or read from a raw magnetic tape device at 5120 bytes/record (do not use with the –p option). Without –B, the data blocks are 512 bytes each.

–c

> **compatible** This option causes **cpio** to write header information in ASCII, so that other (incompatible) machines can read the file. Without –c, only machines of the same type can read the archive properly.

–d

> **directory** **cpio** creates directories when needed as it is copying files (do not use with the –o option).

–f

> **files** This option copies all files not specified by the patterns (–i option only).

–l

> **link** When possible, this option links files instead of copying them (for use only with the –p option).

–m

> **modification time** This option keeps the original modification times of ordinary files. If you use **find** with the –**depth** option to send files to **cpio**, **cpio** also preserves the original modification times of directories.

–r

> **rename** This option allows you to rename files as **cpio** copies them. Before it copies each file, **cpio** prompts you with the name of the file—you respond with the new name. If you just press (RETURN), **cpio** will not copy the file.

−t

table of contents   This option displays a list of filenames without copying them. When you use this option with the −v option, **cpio** displays file access permissions, ownership, and access time along with the name of each file.

−u

unconditional   This option copies older files over newer ones with the same name—without this option, **cpio** will not overwrite these newer files.

−v

verbose   This option displays a list of files that **cpio** is copying.

Examples

The following example copies all the files in the working directory to the tape on /**dev/mt0**. It does not copy the contents of subdirectories, because **ls** does not supply the pathnames of files in subdirectories. When it finishes, **cpio** displays the number of 512 byte blocks it copied.

```
$ ls | cpio -o > /dev/mt0
7 blocks
```

The next example copies all the files in the working directory *and* all subdirectories. The −**depth** argument causes **find** to list all entries in a directory before listing the directory itself. The −**m** option causes **cpio** to preserve the original modification times of files. Because the −**depth** argument to **find** is used, **cpio** can also preserve the original modification times of directories. The −**B** option blocks the tape at 5120 bytes/record.

```
$ find . -depth -print | cpio -oB > /dev/mt0
30 blocks
```

Next, **cpio** copies all of Alex's home directory and all subdirectories to the floppy disk on device /**dev/fd0** (do not use the −**B** option on any media other than tape).

```
$ find /home/alex -print | cpio -o > /dev/fd0
293 blocks
```

The next command reads back the files that the previous command wrote to the disk. Because **cpio** will not overwrite newer files with older ones, the following command will not overwrite any files that have been updated since the previous **cpio** command. You can use the −**u** option to overwrite newer files.

```
$ cpio -i < /dev/fd0
```

The final example displays the table of contents for an archive file.

```
$ cpio -itv < /dev/fd0
```

crontab

Specify jobs to run at regularly scheduled times.

Format

crontab [filename]
crontab [options] [user-name]

Summary

The **crontab** utility allows you to submit a list of jobs that the system will run for you at the times you specify. The commands are stored in files that are referred to as **crontab** files. The system utility called **cron** reads the **crontab** files and runs the commands. If a command line in your **crontab** file does not redirect its output, the standard output and error output will be mailed to you.

Arguments

In the first format, **filename** is the name of a file that contains the **crontab** commands. If you do not specify a filename for **crontab** to read, it will read commands from the standard input as you type them; end with (CONTROL)-**D**.

The **user-name** in the second format can be specified by the Superuser to change the **crontab** file for a particular user.

Options

−e

> **edit**   This option runs a text editor on your **crontab** file, enabling you to add, change, or delete entries.

−l

> **list**   This option displays the contents of your **crontab** file.

−r

> **remove**   This option removes your **crontab** file.

Notes

Each **crontab** entry begins with five fields that specify when the command should run (minute, hour, day of the month, month of the year, and day of the week). If an asterisk appears in a field instead of a number, **cron** interprets that as a wild card for all possible values.

The system administrator determines which users should be allowed to use the **crontab** utility. By default, users cannot use the **crontab** utility to schedule jobs in advance. The **/var/spool/cron** directory includes a file named **cron.allow** that lists the login names of users who are permitted to use **crontab**. A file called **cron.deny** in this directory specifies users who are not permitted to use **crontab**. To allow everyone to use **crontab**, create an empty **cron.deny** file (and do not create a **cron.allow** file).

Examples

In the example below, the root user sets up a command to be run by **cron** every Saturday (day 6) morning at 2:05 A.M. that will remove all **core** files on the system that have not been accessed in the previous five days.

```
# crontab
5 2 ** 6      /usr/bin/find / -name core -atime +5 -exec rm {} \;
(CONTROL)-D
```

To add an entry to your **crontab** file, run the **crontab** utility with the –e (edit) option. If the **crontab** utility available on your system does not support the –e option, you need to make a copy of your existing **crontab** file, edit it, and then resubmit it as in the example below. The –l (list) option displays a copy of your **crontab** file.

```
# crontab -l > newcron
# cat newcron
5 2 ** 6      /usr/bin/find / -name core -atime +5 -exec rm {} \;
# vi newcron
 .
 .
 .
# crontab newcron
# crontab -l
05 2 ** 6  /usr/bin/find / -name core -atime +5 -exec rm {} \;
17 4 ***  /usr/etc/pwck
```

In this example, the root user added an entry to run the **pwck** utility (which checks the password file for errors) every morning at 4:17 A.M. Since the output of **pwck** was not redirected, it will be mailed to the root user automatically.

date

Display or set the time and date.

Format

date [option] [+format]
date [option] newdate

Summary

The **date** utility displays the time and date. The Superuser can use it to change the time and date.

Arguments

When the Superuser specifies a **newdate**, the system changes the system clock to reflect the new date. The **newdate** argument has the following format:

[yy[nn[dd]]]hhmm[.ss]

The optional **yy** specifies the last two digits of the year, the **nn** is the number of the month (01-12), **dd** is the day of the month (01-31), **hh** is the hour based on a 24-hour clock (00-23), and **mm** is the minutes (00-59). If you specify only the hour and minutes, **date** assumes that the month, day, and year have not changed. The **.ss** represents seconds, and is also optional.

Field Descriptor	Meaning
a	abbreviated weekday—Sun to Sat
d	day of the month—01 to 31
D	date in mm/dd/yy format
h	abbreviated month—Jan to Dec
H	hour—00 to 23
j	day of the year—001 to 366
m	month of the year—01 to 12
M	minutes—00 to 59
r	time in A.M./P.M. notation
y	last two digits of the year—00 to 99
S	seconds—00 to 59
T	time in HH:MM:SS format
w	day of the week—0 to 7 (Sunday = 0)
n	(NEWLINE) character
t	(TAB) character

You can use the +**format** argument to specify the format of the output of **date**. Following the + sign, you can specify a format string consisting of **field descriptors** and text. The **field descriptors** are preceded by percent signs, and each one is replaced by its value in the output. See the preceding page for a list of the **field descriptors**.

Any character in a format string that is not either a percent sign (%) or a field descriptor is assumed to be ordinary text and is copied to the output. You can use ordinary text to add punctuation to the date and to add labels (e.g., you can put the word DATE: in front of the date). You should surround the format argument with single quotation marks if it contains ⟨SPACE⟩s or other characters that have a special meaning to the shell.

Options

−u

> **universal**   This option displays or sets the date in Greenwich Mean Time (universal time). The system operates in GMT, and **date** converts it to and from the local standard time and daylight saving time.

Examples

The first example below shows how to set the date for 3:36 P.M. on July 12.

```
# date 07121536
Tue Jul 12 15:36 PDT 1994
```

The next example shows the **format** argument. It causes **date** to display the date in a commonly used format.

```
$ date '+%h %d, 19%y'
Jul 12, 1994
```

delta

delta

Record changes in an SCCS-encoded file.

Format

delta [options] file-list

Summary

The **delta** utility is part of SCCS (the Source Code Control System; see page 475 for more information). The **delta** utility records in SCCS the changes made to a file previously retrieved by using the **get** utility with the –e option.

Arguments

The **file-list** is a list of SCCS-encoded files, which all start with **s.**. If the list includes directory names, all files that begin with **s.** in the named directory are added to **file-list**. Any files in **file-list** that do not begin with **s.** or that are unreadable are ignored.

Options

–p

> **print**   This option causes **delta** to run the **diff** command to compare the versions of the file before and after the delta is performed. The results of the **diff** are displayed on the standard output.

–m[**mrlist**]

> **modification requests**   If the **v** flag has been set with the **admin** utility, this option can be used to input a list of modification requests. They will be used as the reason for the delta. You cannot use this option if the **v** flag has not been set. If the –m option is not used and the **v** flag has been set, the prompt MRs? will appear on the user's terminal if it is the standard input. Any input that precedes an unescaped (RETURN) will be used as modification request numbers. You can enter a null list of modification requests either by using the –m option with no **mrlist**, or by pressing (RETURN) after the MRs? prompt.

–y[**comments**]

> This option allows you to enter text that will be used as the reason for making the delta. If you do not use the –y option and the standard input is a terminal, **delta** will prompt you for comments. Whether you use the –y option or **delta** presents the comments? prompt, you can have a null comment. To create a null comment, do not enter anything after the –y option, or press (RETURN) after the comments? prompt.

–rversion-number

> **release**   This option is used only when the same person has two or
> more outstanding **get**s on the same SCCS file. The **–r** option identi-
> fies the **get** that the current **delta** corresponds to. You can specify
> the version number that was used for the **get** or the version num-
> ber that will be used for the **delta**.

Examples

These examples illustrate the use of the **delta** utility after **get** has been used
with the **–e** option to retrieve the highest trunk delta.

In the first example, the **v** flag is set on **s.memo**. In the subsequent **delta**,
the user is prompted for a list of modification requests. The user inputs a list
of numbers followed by (RETURN).

```
$ admin -fv s.memo
$ delta s.memo
MRs? 19539 74A 13704
comments?
    .
    .
```

In the next example, the **–m** option is used to enter the same list of modification requests.

```
$ delta -m"19539 74A 13704" s.memo
comments? changes based on reviews
    .
    .
```

Below, the user enters comments directly on the command line following the **–y** option.

```
$ delta -y"changes based on reviews" s.memo
MRs?
    .
    .
```

The final example illustrates what happens when you have multiple **get**s
outstanding on different versions of a file.

```
$ delta s.memo
    .
    .
ERROR [s.memo]: missing -r argument (de1)
```

You must use the **–r** option to identify the version associated with the delta.

```
$ delta -r2.2 s.memo
    .
    .
```

df

Display the amount of available disk space.

Format

df [options] [filesystem-list]

Summary

The **df** (disk free) utility reports how much free space is left on any mounted device or directory in terms of blocks. There is usually 1 kilobyte, or 1024 bytes, per block.

Arguments

When you call **df** without an argument, it reports on the free space on each of the currently mounted devices.

The **filesystem-list** is an optional list of one or more pathnames that specify the filesystems you want a report on. The **df** utility permits you to refer to a mounted filesystem by its device pathname *or* by the pathname of the directory it is mounted on.

Options

–i

    inodes   This option causes **df** to report on the number of inodes that are used and free.

–t

    type   This option causes **df** to report information about the filesystems of the specified type, such as **4.2** or **nfs**.

Examples

Below, **df** displays information about the two mounted filesystems on a machine.

```
$ df
Filesystem    kbytes    used    avail    capacity   Mounted on
/dev/sd6a     14983     4963    8522     37%        /
/dev/sd6d     139823 102348    23493    81%        /usr

$ df -t nfs
Filesystem    kbytes    used    avail    capacity   Mounted on
kudos:/home   845086 613857   146991    81%        /kudos/home
sobell:/home 273754 217385    28994    88%        /sobell/home
```

diff

Display the differences between two files.

Format

    diff [options] file1 file2
    diff [options] file1 directory
    diff [options] directory file2
    diff [options] directory1 directory2

Summary

The **diff** utility displays the differences between two files on a line-by-line basis. It displays the differences as instructions that you can use to edit one of the files to make it the same as the other.

When the arguments to **diff** are two filenames, **diff** compares the specified files. When the arguments are a file and a directory, **diff** compares the file with a file in the specified directory that has the same filename. When the arguments to **diff** are two directories, **diff** compares all the pairs of files in the two directories that have the same filenames.

Arguments

The **file1** and **file2** are pathnames of the files that **diff** works on. When the **directory** argument is used in place of **file2**, **diff** looks for a file in **directory** with the same name as **file1**. Similarly, when the directory argument is used in place of **file1**, **diff** looks for a file in **directory** with the same name as **file2**. You can use a hyphen in place of **file1** or **file2** to cause **diff** to use its standard input. When two directory arguments are specified, **diff** compares all files in **directory1** with files in **directory2** that have the same names.

Options

–b

> **blanks**   This option causes **diff** to ignore blanks ((SPACE)s and (TAB)s) at the ends of lines and to consider other strings of blanks equal.

–c[n]

> **context**   This option causes **diff** to display the sections of the two files that differ. If you do not specify **n**, **diff** displays the three lines before and the three lines following each line that differs. If you specify **n**, **n** is the number of lines of context that **diff** displays. Each line that is missing from **file2** is preceded by –; each line that is added to **file2** is preceded by +; and lines that have different versions in the two files are marked with !. When lines that differ are

within **n** lines of each other (or if **n** is not specified), they are grouped together in the output.

–e

ed   This option creates a script for the **ed** editor that will edit **file1** to make it the same as **file2**, and displays it on the standard output. You must add **w** (write) and **q** (quit) instructions to the end of the script if you are going to redirect input to **ed** from the script. When you use –e, **diff** displays the changes in reverse order—changes to the end of the file are listed before changes to the top. This prevents early changes from affecting later changes when the script is used as input to **ed**. If **ed** made changes to the top of the file first, the changes might affect later changes to the end of the file. For example, if a line near the top were deleted, subsequent line numbers in the script would be wrong.

Description

When you use **diff** without any options, it produces a series of lines containing Add (**a**), Delete (**d**), and Change (**c**) instructions. Each of these lines is followed by the lines from the file that you need to add, delete, or change. A *less than* symbol (<) precedes lines from **file1**. A *greater than* symbol (>) precedes lines from **file2**. The **diff** output is in the format shown below. A pair of line numbers separated by a comma represents a range of lines; **diff** uses a single line number to represent a single line.

Instruction	Meaning (to change file1 to file2)
line1 a line2,line3 > lines from file2	append lines from **file2** after line1 in **file1**
line1,line2 d line3 < lines from file1	delete line1 through line2 from **file1**
line1,line2 c line3,line4 < lines from file1 --- > lines from file 2	change line1 through line2 in **file1** to lines from **file2**

The **diff** utility assumes that you are going to convert **file1** to **file2**. The line numbers to the left of each of the **a**, **c**, or **d** instructions always pertain to **file1**; numbers to the right of the instructions apply to **file2**. To convert **file1** to **file2**, ignore the line numbers to the right of the instructions. (To convert **file2** to **file1**, run **diff** again, reversing the order of the arguments.)

Examples

The first example shows how **diff** displays the differences between two short, similar files.

```
$ cat m
aaaaa
bbbbb
ccccc
$ cat n
aaaaa
ccccc
$ diff m n
2d1
< bbbbb
```

The difference between files **m** and **n** is that the second line from file **m** (bbbbb) is missing from file **n**. The first line that **diff** displays (2d1) indicates that you need to delete the second line from file 1 (**m**) to make it the same as file 2 (**n**). Ignore the numbers following the letters on the instruction lines. (They would apply if you were converting **file2** to **file1**.) The next line **diff** displays starts with a *less than* symbol (<), indicating that this line of text is from **file1**. In this example you do not need this information—all you need to know is the line number so that you can delete the line.

The next example uses the same **m** file and a new file, **p**, to demonstrate **diff** issuing an **a** (append) instruction.

```
$ cat p
aaaaa
bbbbb
rrrrr
ccccc
$ diff m p
2a3
> rrrrr
```

In the preceding example, **diff** issued the instruction 2a3 to indicate that you must append a line to file **m**, after line 2, to make it the same as file **p**. The second line that **diff** displayed indicates that the line is from file **p** (the line begins with >, indicating **file2**). In this example you need the information on this line; the appended line must contain the text rrrrr.

The next example uses **m** again, this time with file **r**, to show how **diff** indicates a line that needs to be changed.

```
$ cat r
aaaaa
-q
ccccc
$ diff m r
2c2
< bbbbb
---
> -q
```

The difference between the two files is in line 2: File **m** contains bbbbb, and file **r** contains –q. Above, **diff** displays 2c2 to indicate that you need to change line 2. After indicating that a change is needed, **diff** shows that you must change line 2 in file **m** (bbbbb) to line 2 in file **r** (-q) to make the files the same. The three hyphens indicate the end of the text in file **m** that needs to be changed and the start of the text in file **r** that is to replace it.

Next, a *group* of lines in file **m** needs to be changed to make it the same as file **t**.

```
$ cat t
aaaaa
11111
hhhhh
nnnnn
$ diff m t
2,3c2,4
< bbbbb
< ccccc
---
> 11111
> hhhhh
> nnnnn
```

Above, **diff** indicates that you need to change lines 2 through 3 (2,3) in file **m** from bbbbb and ccccc to 11111, hhhhh, and nnnnn.

The next set of examples demonstrates how to use **diff** to keep track of versions of a file that is repeatedly updated, without maintaining a library of each version in its entirety. This is similar in concept to what SCCS does. With the –e option, **diff** creates a script for the **ed** editor that can recreate the second file from the first. If you keep a copy of the original file and the **ed** script that **diff** creates each time you update the file, you can recreate any version of the file. Because these scripts are usually shorter than the files they are relating, the scripts can help conserve disk space.

In these examples, **menu1** is the original file. When it needs to be updated, it is copied to **menu2** and the changes are made to the copy of the file. The resulting files are shown below.

```
$ cat menu1
BREAKFAST
        scrambled eggs
        toast
        orange juice

LUNCH
        hamburger on roll
        small salad
        milk shake

DINNER
        sirloin steak
        peas
        potato
        vanilla ice cream
```

```
$ cat menu2
BREAKFAST
        poached eggs
        toast
        orange juice

LUNCH
        hamburger on roll
        French fries
        milk shake

DINNER
        chef's salad
        fruit
        cheese
```

Below, **diff** with the −e option produces an **ed** script that details the changes between the two versions of the file. The first command line redirects the output from **diff** to **2changes**; **cat** displays the resulting file. The **ed** Change Mode is invoked by the **c** command. In this mode, the lines that you specify in the command are replaced by the text that you enter following the command. A period instructs **ed** to terminate the Change Mode and return to the Command Mode.

```
$ diff −e menu1 menu2 > 2changes
$ cat 2changes
12,15c
        chef's salad
        fruit
        cheese
.
8c
        French fries
.
2c
        poached eggs
.
```

The only commands missing from the **ed** script that **diff** creates are Write (**w**) and Quit (**q**). In the following example, **cat** appends these to **2changes**. (You can also use an editor to add the commands to the file.)

```
$ cat >> 2changes
w
q
CONTROL-D
```

The next example repeats the process when the file is updated for the second time. The file is copied (to **menu3**), the changes are made to the copy, and the original (**menu2** in this case) and the edited copy are processed by **diff**. The **cat** utility displays the **ed** script after the necessary commands have been added to it.

```
$ cat menu3
BREAKFAST
        poached eggs
        toast
        grapefruit juice

LUNCH
        tuna sandwich
        French fries

DINNER
        pot luck



$ diff -e menu2 menu3 > 3changes
$ cat >> 3changes
w
q
```
(CONTROL)-D

```
$ cat 3changes
12,14c
        pot luck

.
9d
7c
        tuna sandwich

.
4c

        grapefruit juice

.
w
q
```

The **menu2** and **menu3** files are no longer needed; **diff** can recreate them from **menu1**, **2changes**, and **3changes**. The process of recreating a file follows. First, copy the original file to a file that will become the updated file. (If you make changes to the original file, you may not be able to go back and recreate one of the intermediate files.)

```
$ cp menu1 recreate
```

Next, use **ed** to edit the copy of the original file (**recreate**) with input from **2changes**. The **ed** editor displays the number of characters it reads and writes. After it has been edited with **2changes**, the file is the same as the original **menu2**.

```
$ ed recreate < 2changes
214
189
$ cat recreate
BREAKFAST
        poached eggs
        toast
        orange juice

LUNCH
        hamburger on roll
        French fries
        milk shake

DINNER
        chef's salad
        fruit
        cheese
```

If you just want **menu2**, you can stop at this point. By editing the rec-reated **menu2** (now **recreate**) with input from **3changes**, the example below recreates **menu3**.

```
$ ed recreate < 3changes
189
139
$ cat recreate
BREAKFAST
        poached eggs
        toast
        grapefruit juice

LUNCH
        tuna sandwich
        French fries

DINNER
        pot luck
```

du

Display information on disk usage.

Format

du [options] [directory-list] [file-list]

Summary

The **du** (disk usage) utility reports how much space is used by a directory (along with all its subdirectories and files) or a file. It displays the number of blocks (usually 1024 bytes each) that are occupied by the directory or file.

Arguments

Without an argument, **du** displays information only about the working directory and its subdirectories. The **directory-list** specifies the directories you want information about. If you use the –a or –s option, you can also include the names of ordinary files in **file-list**.

Options

Without any options, **du** displays information only for each directory you specify, or about the working directory and its subdirectories if you do not specify any arguments.

–a

all This option displays information for each file in **file-list** and for each file in the directories in **directory-list**.

–s

summary This option displays summary information for each of the directories and files you specify.

Examples

Below, **du** displays size information about subdirectories in the working directory. The last line contains the grand total for the working directory and its subdirectories.

```
$ du
127       ./brown
5         ./memo
.
1493    .
```

Next, **du** displays only the grand total for the working directory.

```
$ du -s
1493    .
```

The last example displays the total size of all the files in **/usr** that the user can read (**du** skips files that are not readable).

```
$ du -s /usr
93647 /usr
```

echo

Display a message.

Format

echo [option] message

Summary

The **echo** command copies its arguments, followed by a (NEWLINE), to its standard output.

Arguments

The **message** is one or more arguments. These arguments can include quoted strings, ambiguous file references, and shell variables. A (SPACE) separates each argument from the others. The shell recognizes unquoted special characters in the arguments (e.g., the shell expands an asterisk into a list of filenames in the working directory).

On some systems, you can terminate the **message** with a \c to prevent **echo** from displaying the (NEWLINE) that normally ends a **message**. To prevent the shell from interpreting the backslash as a special character, you must quote it. The examples below show the three ways you can quote the \c. If that does not work on your system, use the **–n** option described below.

Options

–n

> newline   This option prevents **echo** from displaying a (NEWLINE) at the end of the message.

Notes

You can use **echo** to send messages to the terminal from a shell script (refer to Chapter 10). For other uses of **echo**, refer to the discussion of **echo** starting on page 106.

On some versions of the UNIX system, **echo** is built into the Bourne Shell. The Korn Shell provides both **echo** and the **print** command, which is similar to **echo** but has more features.

Examples

The second through fourth examples following show three ways to quote a \c and prevent **echo** from appending a (NEWLINE) to the end of the message.

```
$ echo 'Today is Friday.'
Today is Friday.
```

```
$ echo -n 'There is no newline after this.'
There is no newline after this.$

$ echo 'There is no newline after this.\c'
There is no newline after this.$

$ echo "There is no newline after this.\c"
There is no newline after this.$

$ echo There is no newline after this.\\c
There is no newline after this.$

$ echo 'This is a
> multiline
> echo command.'
This is a
multiline
echo command.
```

expr

Evaluate an expression.

Format

expr **expression**

Summary

The **expr** utility evaluates an expression and displays the result. It evaluates character strings that represent either numeric or nonnumeric values. Operators are used with the strings to form expressions.

Arguments

The **expression** is composed of strings with operators in between. Each string and operator constitute a distinct argument that you must separate from other arguments with a (SPACE). Operators that have special meanings to the shell (e.g., the multiplication operator, *) must be quoted.

The following list of **expr** operators is in order of decreasing precedence. You can change the order of evaluation by using parentheses.

: comparison

> This operator compares two strings, starting with the first character in each string and ending with the last character in the second string. The second string is a regular expression. If there is a match, it displays the number of characters in the second string. If there is no match, it displays a zero.

*	multiplication
/	division
%	remainder

> These operators work only on strings that contain the numerals 0 through 9 and optionally a leading minus sign. They convert the strings to integer numbers, perform the specified arithmetic operation on numbers, and convert the result back to a string before displaying it.

+	addition
–	subtraction

> These operators function in the same manner as those described above.

<	less than
<=	less than or equal to
=	equal to
!=	not equal to
>=	greater than or equal to
>	greater than

These relational operators work on both numeric and nonnumeric arguments. If one or both of the arguments is nonnumeric, the comparison is nonnumeric, using the machine collating sequence (usually ASCII). If both arguments are numeric, the comparison is numeric. The **expr** utility displays a 1 (one) if the comparison is true and a 0 (zero) if it is false.

&   AND

The AND operator evaluates both of its arguments. If neither is 0 or a null string, it displays the value of the first argument. Otherwise, it displays a 0. You must quote this operator.

| OR

This operator evaluates the first argument. If it is neither 0 nor a null string, it displays the value of the first argument. Otherwise, it displays the value of the second argument. You must quote this operator.

Notes

The **expr** utility returns an exit status of 0 (zero) if the expression is neither a null string nor the number 0, a status of 1 if the expression is null or 0, and a status of 2 if the expression is invalid.

The **expr** utility is useful in Bourne Shell scripts. Because the C and Korn Shells have the equivalent of **expr** built in, C and Korn Shell scripts do not normally use **expr**.

Although **expr** and this discussion distinguish between numeric and nonnumeric arguments, all arguments to **expr** are actually nonnumeric (character strings). When applicable, **expr** attempts to convert an argument to a number (e.g., when using the + operator). If a string contains characters other than 0 through 9 with an optional leading minus sign, **expr** cannot convert it. Specifically, if a string contains a plus sign or a decimal point, **expr** considers it to be nonnumeric.

Examples

The following examples show command lines that call **expr** to evaluate constants. You can also use **expr** to evaluate variables in a shell script. In the fourth example, **expr** displays an error message because of the illegal decimal point in 5.3.

```
$ expr 17 + 40
57
$ expr 10 - 24
-14
$ expr -17 + 20
3
$ expr 5.3 \* 4
expr: non-numeric argument
```

The multiplication (∗), division (/), and remainder (%) operators provide additional arithmetic power, as the examples below show. You must quote the multiplication operator (precede it with a backslash) so that the shell does not treat it as a special character (an ambiguous file reference). Note that you cannot put quotation marks around the entire expression, because each string and operator must be a separate argument.

```
$ expr 5 \* 4
20
$ expr 21 / 7
3
$ expr 23 % 7
2
```

The next two examples show how you can use parentheses to change the order of evaluation. You must quote each parenthesis and surround the backslash/parenthesis combination with (SPACE)s.

```
$ expr 2 \* 3 + 4
10
$ expr 2 \* \( 3 + 4 \)
14
```

You can use relational operators to determine the relationship between numeric or nonnumeric arguments. The command below uses **expr** to compare two strings to see if they are equal. The **expr** utility displays a 0 when the relationship is false, and a 1 when it is true.

```
$ expr fred = mark
0
$ expr mark = mark
1
```

Relational operators, which you must also quote, can establish order between numeric or nonnumeric arguments. Again, if a relationship is true, **expr** displays a 1.

```
$ expr fred \> mark
0
$ expr fred \< mark
1
$ expr 5 \< 7
1
```

The next command compares **5** with **m**. When one of the arguments **expr** is comparing with a relational operator is nonnumeric, **expr** considers the other to be nonnumeric. In this case, because **m** is nonnumeric, **expr** treats **5** as a nonnumeric argument. The comparison is between the ASCII (on most machines) values of **m** and **5**. The ASCII value of **m** is 109, and 5 is 53, so **expr** evaluates the relationship as true.

```
$ expr 5 \< m
1
```

The next example shows the matching operator determining that the four characters in the second string match four characters in the first string. The **expr** utility displays a 4.

```
$ expr abcdefghijkl : abcd
4
```

The & operator displays a 0 if one or both of its arguments are 0 or a null string. Otherwise, it displays the first argument.

```
$ expr '' \& book
0
$ expr magazine \& book
magazine
$ expr 5 \& 0
0
$ expr 5 \& 6
5
```

The | operator displays the first argument if it is not 0 or a null string. Otherwise, it displays the second argument.

```
$ expr '' \| book
book
$ expr magazine \| book
magazine
$ expr 5 \| 0
5
$ expr 0 \| 5
5
$ expr 5 \| 6
5
```

file

Display file classification.

Format

file [option] [file-list]

Summary

The **file** utility classifies files according to their contents.

Arguments

The **file-list** contains the pathnames of one or more files that **file** classifies. You can specify any kind of file, including ordinary, directory, and special files, in the **file-list**.

Options

–f file

> file   This option causes **file** to take the names of files to be examined from **file** rather than from the command line.

–L

> link   If the **file-list** includes a pathname that is a symbolic link, this option causes **file** to report on the file it points to.

Notes

The **file** utility works by examining the first part of a file, looking for keywords and special numbers (referred to as *magic numbers*) that the linker and other programs use. It also examines the access permissions associated with the file. The results of **file** are not always correct.

Examples

Some examples of file identification follow.

```
$ file memo proc new
memo:              English text
proc:              commands text
new:               empty
$ file /tmp/memo
/tmp/memo: symbolic link to memo3
$ file -L /tmp/memo
/tmp/memo: English text
```

A few of the classifications that **file** displays follow.

```
English text      directory    ascii text
c program text    empty        executable
commands text     sccs         data
```

find

find

Find files.

Format

find **directory-list expression**

Summary

The **find** utility selects files that are located in specified directories and are described by an expression. It does not generate any output without an explicit instruction to do so.

Arguments

The **directory-list** contains the pathnames of one or more directories that **find** is to search. When **find** searches a directory, it searches all subdirectories, to all levels.

The **expression** contains one or more criteria, as described in "Criteria," below. The **find** utility tests each of the files in each of the directories in the **directory-list** to see if it meets the criteria described by the **expression**.

A (SPACE) separating two criteria is a logical AND operator: The file must meet *both* criteria to be selected. A **–o** separating the criteria is a logical OR operator: The file must meet one or the other (or both) of the criteria to be selected.

You can negate any criterion by preceding it with an exclamation point. The **find** utility evaluates criteria from left to right unless you group them using parentheses.

Within the **expression** you must quote special characters so that the shell does not interpret them but passes them to the **find** utility. Special characters that you may frequently use with **find** are parentheses, square brackets, question marks, and asterisks.

Each element within the **expression** is a separate argument. You must separate arguments from each other with (SPACE)s. There must be a (SPACE) on both sides of each parenthesis, exclamation point, criterion, or other element. When you use a backslash to quote a special character, the (SPACE)s go on each side of the pair of characters (e.g., " \[").

Criteria

Following is a list of criteria that you can use within the **expression**. As used in this list, (±**n** is a decimal integer that can be expressed as +**n** (meaning more than **n**), –**n** (meaning less than **n**), or **n** (meaning exactly **n**).

–name **filename**

> The file being evaluated meets this criterion if **filename** matches its name. You can use ambiguous file references but must quote them.

–type filetype

> The file being evaluated meets this criterion if its file type is the specified **filetype**. You can select a file type from the following list.

filetype	Description
b	block special file
c	character special file
d	directory file
f	ordinary file
p	fifo (named pipe)
l	symbolic link
s	socket

–links ±n

> The file being evaluated meets this criterion if it has the number of links specified by ±**n**.

–user name

> The file being evaluated meets this criterion if it belongs to the user with the login name, **name**. You can use a numeric user ID in place of **name**.

–group name

> The file being evaluated meets this criterion if it belongs to the group with the group name, **name**. You can use a numeric group ID in place of **name**.

–inum n

> The file being evaluated meets this criterion if its inode number is **n**.

–size ±n[c]

> The file being evaluated meets this criterion if it is the size specified by ±**n**, measured in blocks. Follow **n** with the letter **c** to measure files in characters.

–atime ±n

> The file being evaluated meets this criterion if it was last accessed the number of days ago specified by ±**n**. When you use this option, **find** changes the access times of directories it searches.

–mtime ±n

> The file being evaluated meets this criterion if it was last modified the number of days ago specified by ±**n**.

–newer filename

> The file being evaluated meets this criterion if it was modified more recently than **filename**.

–print

> The file being evaluated always meets this action criterion. When evaluation of the **expression** reaches this criterion, **find** displays the pathname of the file it is evaluating. If this is the only criterion in the **expression**, **find** displays the names of all the files in the **directory-list**. If this criterion appears with other criteria, **find** displays the name only if the preceding criteria are met. Refer to "Discussion" and "Notes," following.

–ls

> The file being evaluated always meets this criterion. The **–ls** criterion is similar to **–print**, but reports more information about the file, including the inode number, size in blocks, permissions, number of lines, owner, group, size in characters, most recent modification date, and filename.

–exec command \;

> The file being evaluated meets this action criterion if the **command** returns a zero (true value) as an exit status. You must terminate the **command** with a quoted semicolon. A pair of braces ({}) within the **command** represents the filename of the file being evaluated. You can use the **–exec** action criterion at the end of a group of other criteria to execute the **command** if the preceding criteria are met. Refer to the following "Discussion."

–ok command \;

> This action criterion is the same as **–exec**, except that it displays each of the **command**s to be executed, enclosed in angle brackets, and executes the **command** only if it receives a **y** from its standard input.

–depth

> The file being evaluated always meets this action criterion. It causes **find** to take action on entries in a directory before it acts on the directory itself. When you use **find** to send files to the **cpio** utility, the **–depth** criterion enables **cpio** to preserve modification times of directories (assuming you use the **–m** option to **cpio).**

–mount

> The file being evaluated always meets this action criterion. It causes **find** not to search directories in filesystems other than the one in which the current **directory** (from the **directory-list** argument) resides.

–nouser

> The file being evaluated meets this criterion if it belongs to a user who is not in the **/etc/passwd** file (that is, the user ID associated with the file does not correspond to a known user of the system).

–nogroup

> The file being evaluated meets this criterion if it belongs to a group that is not listed in the **/etc/group** file.

–follow

> When this criterion is specified and **find** encounters a symbolic link pointing to a directory file, it will follow the link.

Discussion

Assume that **x** and **y** are criteria. The following command line never tests to see if the file meets criterion **y** if it does not meet criterion **x**. Because the criteria are separated by a (SPACE) (the logical AND operator), once **find** determines that criterion **x** is not met, the file cannot meet the criteria, so **find** does not continue testing. You can read the expression as "(test to see) if the file meets criterion **x** *and* ((SPACE) means *and*) criterion **y**."

> `$ find dir x y`

The next command line tests the file against criterion **y** if criterion **x** is not met. The file can still meet the criteria, so **find** continues the evaluation. It is read as "(test to see) if criterion **x** *or* criterion **y** is met." If the file meets criterion **x**, **find** does not evaluate criterion **y**, as there is no need.

> `$ find dir x -o y`

Certain "criteria" do not select files but cause **find** to take action. The action is triggered when **find** evaluates one of these *action criteria*. Therefore, the position of an action criterion on the command line, and not the result of its evaluation, determines whether **find** takes the action.

The **–print** action criterion causes **find** to display the pathname of the file it is testing. The following command line displays the names of all files in the **dir** directory (and all subdirectories) that meet criterion **x**.

> `$ find dir x -print`

The following command line displays the names of *all* the files in the **dir** directory (whether they meet criterion **x** or not).

> `$ find dir -print x`

Notes

You must explicitly instruct **find** to display filenames if you want it to do so. Unless you include the **–print** criterion or its equivalent on the command line, **find** does its work silently. Refer to the first example on the next page.

You can use the **–a** operator between criteria for clarity. This operator is a logical AND operator, just as the (SPACE) is.

Examples

The following command line finds all the files in the working directory, and all subdirectories, that have filenames that begin with **a**. The command uses a period to designate the working directory and quotes the ambiguous file reference. The command does not instruct **find** to do anything with these files—not even display their names. This is not a useful example, but it demonstrates a common problem when using **find**.

```
$ find . -name 'a*'
```

The next command line finds *and displays the filenames of* all the files in the working directory, and all subdirectories, that have filenames that begin with a.

```
$ find . -name 'a*' -print
.
.
```

The following command line sends a list of selected filenames to the **cpio** utility, which writes them to tape. The first part of the command line ends with a pipe symbol, so the shell expects another command to follow and prints a secondary prompt (>) before accepting the rest of the command line. You can read this **find** command as, "find, in the root directory and all subdirectories (/), all files that are ordinary files (**–type f**) that have been modified within the past day (**–mtime –1**), with the exception of files whose names are suffixed with .o (**! –name '*.o'**). (An object file carries a .o suffix and usually does not need to be preserved, as it can be recreated from the corresponding program source code.)

```
$ find / -type f -mtime -1 ! -name '*.o' -print |
> cpio -oB > /dev/rmt0
```

The command line below finds, displays the filenames of, and deletes all the files in the working directory, and all subdirectories, that are named **core** and **junk**. The parentheses, and the semicolon following **–exec**, are quoted so that the shell does not treat them as special characters. (SPACE)s separate the quoted parentheses from other elements on the command line. You can read this **find** command as, "find, in the working directory and all subdirectories (.), all files that are named **core** (**–name core**) *or* (**–o**) are named **junk** (**–name junk**) [if a file meets these criteria, continue with] *and* ((SPACE)) print (**–print**) the name of the file *and* ((SPACE)) delete the file (**–exec rm {}**)".

```
$ find . \( -name core -o -name junk \) -print -exec rm {} \;
.
.
```

The shell script below uses **find** with the **grep** command to identify the names of files that contain a particular string. This script enables you to look for a file when you remember its contents but cannot remember what its filename is. The **finder** script below locates files in the current directory and all subdirectories that contain the string specified on the command line.

```
$ cat finder
find . -exec grep -l "$1" {} \;
$ finder "Executive Meeting"
./january/memo.0102
./april/memo.0415
```

When **finder** is called with the string Executive Meeting, it locates two files containing that string, **./january/memo.0102** and **./april/memo.0415**. The period (.) in the pathnames represents the current directory (that is, **january** and **april** are subdirectories of the current directory).

The next command finds all files in two user directories that are larger than 100 blocks (**–size +100**) and have only been accessed more than five days ago—that is, have not been accessed within the past five days (**–atime +5**). This **find** command then asks whether you want to delete the file (**–ok rm {}**). You must respond to each of these queries with a **y** (for *yes*) or **n** (for *no*). The **rm** command works only if you have execute and write access permission to the directory.

```
$ find /home/alex /home/barbara -size +100 -atime +5 -ok rm {} \;
< rm ... /home/alex/notes >? y
< rm ... /home/alex/letter >? n
.
.
```

In this example, **/home/alex/memos** is a symbolic link to the directory named **/home/jenny/memos**. When the **–follow** option is used with **find**, the symbolic link is followed, and the contents of that directory are found.

```
$ ls -lg /home/alex
lrwxrwxrwx  1 alex    pubs      17 Aug 19 17:07 memos -> /home/jenny/memos
-rw-r--r--  1 alex    pubs    5119 Aug 19 17:08 report
$ find /home/alex -print
/home/alex
/home/alex/memos
/home/alex/report
/home/alex/.profile

$ find /home/alex -follow -print
/home/alex
/home/alex/memos
/home/alex/memos/memo.817
/home/alex/memos/memo.710
/home/alex/report
/home/alex/.profile
```

finger

Displays detailed information on users.

Format

finger [options] [user-list]

Summary

The **finger** utility displays the login names of users, together with their full names, terminal device numbers, the times they logged in, and other information. The options control how much information **finger** displays, and **user-list** consists of login names.

If you name a particular user on the command line, **finger** displays detailed information about that individual. If you do not specify a user, **finger** displays a short entry for every user that is currently logged in.

The **finger** utility understands network address notation. If your system is attached to a network, you can use **finger** to display information about users on remote systems that you can reach over the network.

Options

–l

long   This option causes **finger** to display detailed information about every user logged in on the system.

–m

match   If a **user-list** is specified, this option will cause the **finger** utility to display entries only for those users whose *login* names match the names given in **user-list**. Without this option, the **user-list** names will match *login* and *full* names.

–q

quick   This option causes **finger** to display only the login name, terminal device number, and the time the user logged in.

–s

short   This option causes the **finger** utility to provide a short report for each user.

Arguments

If you do not specify a **user-list**, the **finger** utility provides a short (–s) report on every user who is currently logged into the system. If you specify one or more user names, the **finger** utility provides a long (–l) report for each of the users you named.

If the name includes an at sign (@), the **finger** utility interprets the name following the @ sign as the name of a remote host to contact over the network. If there is also a name in front of the @ sign, **finger** provides information on that particular user on the remote system.

Description

The long report provided by the **finger** utility includes the user's login name, full name, home directory location, and login shell, followed by information about when the user last logged into the system and how long it has been since the user last typed on the keyboard or received and read electronic mail. After extracting this information from various system files, the **finger** utility then displays the contents of files named **.plan** and **.project** in the user's home directory. It is up to each user to create these files, which are usually used to provide more information about the user (such as telephone number, postal mail address, schedule, interests, etc.).

The short report generated by **finger** is similar to that provided by the **w** utility; it includes the user's login name, full name, the device number of the user's terminal, how much time has elapsed since the user last typed on the terminal keyboard, the time the user logged in, and the location of the user's terminal. If the user has logged in over the network, the name of the remote system is identified as the user's location.

Notes

When you specify a network address, the **finger** utility works by querying a standard network service that runs on the remote system. Although this service is supplied with most UNIX systems today, some sites choose not to run it (to minimize load on their systems, as well as possible security risks, or simply to maintain privacy). If you try to use **finger** to get information on someone at such a site, the result may be an error message or nothing at all. The remote system determines how much information to share with your system, and in what format. As a result, the report displayed for any given system may differ from the examples shown.

Examples

The first example displays information on all the users currently logged into the system.

```
$ finger
Login        Name           TTY  Idle      When      Where
hls          Helen Simpson  *p0     1   Wed  8:34   bravo
scott        Scott Adams    02 23:48   Tue 15:21   Room 307
jenny        Jenny Chen     03         Wed  9:07   Room 201
alex         Alex Watson    06         Wed  9:15   Room 219
```

In the example above, the asterisk (*) in front of the name of Helen's terminal (TTY) line indicates that she has blocked others from sending messages directly to her terminal (see **mesg**, pages 45 and 647).

Less information is presented in the next example, using the **–q** option.

```
$ finger -q jenny
Login    TTY      When
jenny    03   Wed  9:07
```

The next two examples cause **finger** to contact the remote system named **kudos** over the network for information.

```
$ finger @kudos
[kudos]
Login       Name          TTY  Idle    When      Where
alex        Alex Watson   01    21   Mon 10:54
roy         Roy Wong      p0         Wed 14:24  sobell.sro.com
```

```
$ finger watson@kudos
[kudos]
Login name: alex              In real life: Alex Watson
Directory: /home/alex         Shell: /bin/csh
On since Sep 19 10:54:49 on tty01
21 minutes Idle Time
Plan:
For appointments contact Jenny Chen, x1693.
.
```

fsck

Check and repair a filesystem.

Format

/etc/fsck [options] [filesystems-list]

Summary

The **fsck** utility verifies the integrity of a filesystem and reports on any problems it finds. For each problem it finds, **fsck** asks you if you want it to attempt to fix the problem or ignore it. If you repair the problem, you may lose some data; however, that is often the most reasonable alternative.

The **fsck** utility should be run only by the system administrator, who must be logged in as the Superuser. When **fsck** is run on a filesystem, the filesystem should not be mounted. The root filesystem, which cannot be unmounted, must be quiescent. The best way to ensure quiescence is to bring the system down to single-user mode.

Arguments

The **filesystems-list** is an optional list of filesystems you want **fsck** to check. If you do not specify a list, it checks the filesystems listed in the /etc/fstab file.

Except for the root, you should always check the raw device representing the filesystem. This device is usually the one whose simple filename begins with **r**.

Options

Without any options, **fsck** checks the filesystems in the **filesystems-list** (or in /etc/fstab). When a filesystem is consistent, you will see a report such as the following:

```
/dev/rsd6g
** /dev/rsd6g
** Last Mounted on /usr

** Phase 1 - Check Blocks and Sizes
** Phase 2 - Check Pathnames
** Phase 3 - Check Connectivity
** Phase 4 - Check Reference Count
** Phase 5 - Check Cylinder Groups
vvv files, www used, xxx free (yyy frags, zzz blocks, 0.n% fragmentation)
```

If **fsck** finds problems with a filesystem, it reports on each problem, giving you the choice of having it either repair or ignore it.

–y

>   **yes** The **fsck** utility assumes a *yes* response to all questions and makes any necessary repairs to the filesystem. If the filesystem is

corrupt, you can lose files by using –**y** to respond *yes* automatically to all of **fsck**'s questions.

–n

> **no**   The **fsck** utility assumes a *no* response to all questions and only reports on problems. It does not make any repairs.

–b**block#**

> This option causes **fsck** to use the block specified by **block#** as the superblock of the filesystem.

–p

> **preen**   This option causes **fsck** to supply a **y** response to questions about minor inconsistencies and an **n** response to all other questions. This option is often used when **fsck** is run by the run command scripts during the boot process.

Notes

If you are repairing a filesystem, you must run **fsck** on the unmounted filesystem. If you are repairing the root filesystem, run **fsck** while the system is in single-user mode and no other user processes are running. After repairing root, you must bring the system down immediately, without running **sync**, and reboot it.

Although it is technically feasible to repair files that are damaged and that **fsck** says you should remove, it is usually not practical. The best insurance against significant loss of data is frequent backups. Refer to page 506 for more information on backing up the system.

If you do not have write permission to the filesystem **fsck** is checking, **fsck** will report problems but not give you an opportunity to fix them.

When **fsck** encounters a file that has lost its link to its filename, **fsck** asks you whether you want to reconnect it. If you choose to reconnect it and fix the problem, the file is put in a directory called **lost+found**, and it is given its inode number as a name. In order for **fsck** to restore files in this way, there should be a **lost+found** directory in the root directory of each filesystem. For example, if your filesystems are /, **/usr**, and **/tmp**, you should have the following three **lost+found** directories: **/lost+found**, **/usr/lost+found**, and **/tmp/lost+found**.

Messages

This section explains **fsck**'s standard messages. It does not explain every message that **fsck** produces. In general, **fsck** suggests the most logical way of dealing with a problem in the file structure. Unless you have information that suggests another response, respond to its prompts with *yes*. Use the system backup tapes or disks to restore any data that is lost as a result of this process.

Phase	What is checked
Phase 1 – Check Blocks and Sizes	Phase 1 checks inode information.
Phase 1B – Rescan for More Dups	When **fsck** finds a duplicate block in Phase 1, it repeats its search. A *duplicate block* is a block that is claimed to be part of two different files.
Phase 2 – Check Pathnames	In Phase 2, **fsck** checks for directories that pointed to bad inodes it found in Phase 1.
Phase 3 – Check Connectivity	Phase 3 looks for unreferenced directories and a nonexistent or full **lost+found** directory.
Phase 4 – Check Reference Counts	Phase 4 checks for unreferenced files, a nonexistent or full **lost+found** directory, bad link counts, bad blocks, duplicate blocks, and incorrect inode counts.
Phase 5 – Check Cylinder Groups	Phase 5 checks the free block list and used inode list for allocated blocks, missing blocks, free inodes, missing inodes, and incorrect counts.

Cleanup

Once **fsck** has repaired the filesystem, it informs you about the status of the filesystem and tells you what you must do.

```
*****FILE SYSTEM WAS MODIFIED*****
```

The **fsck** utility displays the previous message if it has repaired the filesystem.

```
*****REBOOT UNIX*****
```

The **fsck** utility displays the previous message when it has modified the root filesystem. If you see this message, you must reboot the system immediately, without using **sync**. Refer to page 497 for more information.

```
vvv files, www used, xxx free (yyy frags, zzz blocks, 0.n fragmentation)
```

A filesystem block on a Berkeley filesystem can hold up to 8192 bytes of information. Each block is broken into *fragments,* or parts, so that when a file needs only a portion of a block, the remainder of the block can be made available for allocation to other files. This message lets you know how many files (**vvv**) are using how many fragment-sized blocks (**www**), and how many fragment-sized blocks are free in the filesystem. The numbers in parentheses break the free count into **yyy** free fragments and **zzz** free full-sized blocks, and the amount of fragmentation this represents.

ftp

Transfer files over a network connection.

Format

ftp [option] remote-computer

Summary

The **ftp** utility uses the standard File Transfer Protocol to transfer files between different systems that can communicate over a network. The **remote-computer** is the name or network address of the remote system. To use **ftp**, you must have an account (or access to a guest account) on the remote system.

Options

−n

> **no login**   Unless you specify this option, the **ftp** utility assumes that your login name on the remote system is the same as on the local system.

Arguments

If you specify a **remote-computer** on the command line, **ftp** will try to establish a connection to that system.

Description

The **ftp** utility is interactive; after you start it up, it prompts you to enter commands to transfer files or set parameters. In response to an ftp> prompt, you can use the following commands:

!

> Escape to a shell on your local system (use (CONTROL)-**D** to return to **ftp** when you are through).

binary

> Set the file transfer type so that you can transfer files that contain non-ASCII (unprintable) characters correctly.

cd **directory**

> Change to a different working directory on the remote system.

close

> Close the connection with the remote system without exiting from **ftp**.

dir [**directory**] [**file**]

> Display a directory listing from the remote system. If you do not specify a directory name, the current directory is displayed. If you specify a file name, the listing will be saved on the local system in that file; if not, it will appear on the standard output.

get **remote-file** [**local-file**]

> Pick up a copy of a single specified **remote-file** and store it on the local system. If you do not provide the name of a **local-file**, **ftp** will try to use the remote system's name for the file on the local system. You can provide a file's pathname as a valid **remote-file** or **local-file** name.

help

> Display a list of commands recognized by the **ftp** utility on the local system.

mget **remote-file-list**

> **multiple get** Unlike the **get** command, the **mget** command allows you to retrieve multiple files from the remote system. You can name the remote files literally or use wildcards.

mput **local-file-list**

> **multiple put** The **mput** command allows you to put multiple files from the local system onto the remote system. You can name the local files literally or use wildcards.

open

> If you did not specify a remote system on the command line, or if the attempt to connect to the system failed, you can specify the name of a remote system interactively with the **open** command.

put **local-file** [**remote-file**]

> Deposit a copy of a single **local-file** from the local system on the remote system. If you do not provide the name of a remote file, **ftp** will try to use the local system's name for the file on the remote system. You can provide a file's pathname as a valid **remote-file** or **local-file** name.

quit

> Quit the **ftp** session.

user **user-name**

> If the **ftp** utility did not log you in automatically, you can specify your account name interactively with the user command.

Notes

Many computers, including non-UNIX systems, support the File Transfer Protocol. The **ftp** command is an implementation of this protocol for UNIX systems, allowing you to exchange files with many different types of systems.

By convention, many sites offer archives of free information on a system named **ftp** (e.g., **ftp.uu.net**). You can use the guest account **anonymous** on many systems. When you log in as **anonymous**, you will be prompted to enter a password. Although any password will be accepted, by convention you should supply your login name and network address (e.g., **alex@sobell.sro.com**). This information helps the remote site to know who uses their services.

Examples

The **ftp** utility displays various messages to let you know how your requests are proceeding. To keep the example below clear and brief, the progress messages from **ftp** are not shown.

In the following example, the user connects to the remote system **bravo**. After listing the contents of the directory on the remote system, the user transfers a file from the current directory on the remote system to the **memos** directory on the local system. Next, the user lists the contents of the current directory on the local system, then changes the current directory on the remote system, and transfers all the C programs from the current directory on the local machine to the remote system.

```
$ ftp bravo
.
.
ftp> dir
.
.
ftp> get memo.921 memos/memo.921
.
.
ftp> !
$ ls
.
.
CONTROL-D
ftp> cd cprogs
ftp> mput *.c
.
.
ftp> quit
221 Goodbye.
```

See page 156 for additional information on using **ftp**.

get

Create an unencoded version of an SCCS file.

Format

get [options] file-list

Summary

The **get** utility is part of SCCS (the Source Code Control System; see page 475 for more information). The **get** utility retrieves files from their SCCS-encoded versions. The retrieved files are given the same names as their encoded counterparts, except the leading **s.** is removed. The options determine characteristics of the retrieved files.

Arguments

The **file-list** is a list of SCCS-encoded files, which all start with **s.**. If the list includes directory names, all files that begin with **s.** in the named directory are added to **file-list**. Any files in **file-list** that do not begin with **s.** or that are unreadable are ignored. The **get** utility will not create an unencoded version of a file if a file with the same name exists in the current directory.

Options

Without any options, **get** retrieves the most recent version of the SCCS file. The file will not be writable. To create an editable version of an SCCS file, you must use the −**e** option.

−e

> **edit**   Use this option to indicate to SCCS that you intend to edit the retrieved file and then to use **delta** to create a new SCCS-encoded version. The version of the encoded file that **get** will retrieve depends on the other options you use. If you do not use options to specify characteristics of the retrieved file, the most recent version of the encoded file will be retrieved. Once you have used **get** with the −**e** option on a particular version, you cannot use it again on the same version until after you have used **delta** to complete the first cycle of editing, unless you have set the **j** flag (see **admin** on page 523). You can always use **get** with the −**e** option on another version of the file; however, you must give the command from a different directory. If you try to use **get** with the −**e** option twice in the same directory, the second **get** will fail, because a writable file with the unencoded filename already exists in that directory.

–rversion-number

> **release** This option identifies a particular version of the SCCS-encoded file to be retrieved. If the **–e** option is used with **–r**, **–r** also determines the version number of the associated delta. The version number specified with the **–r** option may include up to four components: release, level, branch, and sequence number. The version retrieved depends on the version number components you specify with the **–r** option and on what versions already exist. Similarly, if you use **–e**, the version number of the created delta depends both on the number you specify and on what versions already exist. See "Version Numbers," below, for further information.

–b

> **branch** This option can be used with the **–e** option to create a branch delta for a trunk delta that has no successors on the trunk. To use the **–b** option, you must have set the **b** flag using the **admin** utility. If the **b** flag has not been set or if the retrieved delta has a successor delta, the **–b** option will be ignored.

–cdate-time

> **cutoff** This option causes deltas made after **date-time** to be excluded from the retrieved file. The **date-time** argument has the format:
>
> YY[MM[DD[HH[MM[SS]]]]]
>
> The brackets indicate that all components of **date-time** may be omitted except **YY**, starting from the right. The maximum possible values will be substituted for any omitted values (e.g., 59 is used if **SS** is omitted). The two-digit components may be separated by any number of nonnumeric characters. For example, a colon (:) may be used between the components (e.g., 94:02:25:03:36).

–k

> **keyword** You can use this option to recreate an editable file if you accidentally remove or ruin a file that you previously retrieved with **get**. The keywords in the new copy will be preserved, so they will not be lost when you finish editing the file and run **delta**.

Version Numbers

Following is a summary of how the **get** utility identifies what version to retrieve when you use the **–r** option and what version number to assign to the new delta. For each type of version number that you can specify with the **–r** option, and each set of conditions, the list describes the version that will be retrieved and the delta that will be created.

The summary on the next page describes the cases when the **–b** option is not in use. When you use the **–b** option, a new branch is always created.

The following descriptions refer to *trunk deltas* and *branch deltas*. Trunk deltas have two-component version numbers (release.level), whereas branch version numbers have four components (release.level.branch.sequence).

Component
Specified: Release

Condition: Release specified is the highest existing release.
Version retrieved: Highest existing level in the specified release.
Delta created: Next level for the specified release.

Condition: Release number is higher than the highest existing release.
Version retrieved: Highest existing level in the highest existing release.
Delta created: First level of the specified release number.

Condition: Release number is less than the highest existing release, and release number is nonexistent.
Version retrieved: Highest existing level in the highest release that is less than the specified release.
Delta created: A new branch for the retrieved delta.

Condition: Release number is less than the highest existing release, and release number exists.
Version retrieved: Highest existing trunk delta in the specified release.
Delta created: A new branch for the retrieved delta.

Component
Specified: Release.Level

Condition: No trunk successor exists.
Version retrieved: Specified trunk delta.
Delta created: Next trunk delta (that is, level + 1).

Condition: Trunk successor exists.
Version retrieved: Specified trunk delta (i.e., release.level).
Delta created: New branch for the retrieved trunk delta.

Component
Specified: Release.Level.Branch
Version retrieved: Highest sequence number on the specified branch.
Delta created: Next sequence number on the specified branch.

Component
Specified: Release.Level.Branch.Sequence

Condition: Branch corresponds to highest existing branch for the specified release.level.
Version retrieved: Specified release.level.branch.sequence.
Delta created: Next sequence number.

Condition: Branch number is less than the highest existing branch.
Version retrieved: Specified release.level.branch.sequence.
Delta created: New branch for the specified release.level.

Examples

The first command retrieves the highest numbered trunk delta. This file will not be editable.

```
$ get s.thesis
 3.1
 .
 .
```

The next command includes in the retrieved file only deltas created on or before 2 P.M. (1400 hours) on March 4, 1994.

```
$ get -c94:03:04:14:00:00 s.thesis
 .3.1
 .
 .
```

The following command retrieves the highest numbered trunk delta for editing. The new delta will have the same release number and the next level number.

```
$ get -e s.thesis
3.1
new delta 3.2
 .
 .
```

Below, the highest existing trunk delta will be retrieved (because the specified release, 4, is higher than any existing release). The new delta will be Version 4.1.

```
$ get -e -r4 s.thesis
3.1
new delta 4.1
 .
 .
```

grep

Search for a pattern in files.

Format

grep [options] pattern [file-list]

Summary

The **grep** utility searches one or more files, line by line, for a **pattern**. The **pattern** can be a simple string or another form of a regular expression (see Appendix A for more information on regular expressions). The **grep** utility takes various actions, specified by options, each time it finds a line that contains a match for the **pattern**.

The **grep** utility takes its input from files you specify on the command line or from its standard input.

Arguments

The **pattern** is a regular expression, as defined in Appendix A. You must quote regular expressions that contain special characters, (SPACE)s, or (TAB)s. An easy way to quote these characters is to enclose the entire expression within single quotation marks.

The **file-list** contains pathnames of ordinary text files that **grep** searches.

Options

If you do not specify any options, **grep** sends lines that contain a match for **pattern** to its standard output. If you specify more than one file on the command line, **grep** precedes each line that it displays with the name of the file that it came from and a colon.

−c

> **count**   This option causes **grep** to display only the number of lines in each file that contain a match.

−i

> **ignore case**   This option causes lowercase letters in the pattern to match uppercase letters in the file, and vice versa. Use this option when searching for a word that may be at the beginning of a sentence (that is, may or may not start with an uppercase letter).

−l

> **list**   The **grep** utility displays only the name of each file that contains one or more matches. It displays each filename only once, even if the file contains more than one match.

–n

number   The **grep** utility precedes each line by its line number in the file. The file does not need to contain line numbers. This number represents the number of lines in the file up to and including the displayed line.

–v

reverse sense of test   This option causes lines *not* containing a match to satisfy the search. When you use this option by itself, **grep** displays all lines that do not contain a match for the **pattern**.

Notes

The **grep** utility returns an exit status of 0 if it finds a match, 1 if it does not find a match, and 2 if the file is not accessible or there is a syntax error.

Two utilities perform functions similar to that of **grep**. The **egrep** utility can be faster than **grep** but may also use more memory. It allows you to use *full regular expressions,* which include a wider set of special characters than do ordinary regular expressions (page 741). The **fgrep** utility is fast and compact, but it can process only simple strings, not regular expressions.

Examples

The following examples assume that the working directory contains three files: **testa**, **testb**, and **testc**. The contents of each file are shown below.

File testa	File testb	File testc
aaabb	aaaaa	AAAAA
bbbcc	bbbbb	BBBBB
ff–ff	ccccc	CCCCC
cccdd	ddddd	DDDDD
dddaa		

The **grep** utility can search for a pattern that is a simple string of characters. The following command line searches **testa** for, and displays each line containing, the string bb.

```
$ grep bb testa
aaabb
bbbcc
```

The –v option reverses the sense of the test. The example below displays all the lines *without* bb.

```
$ grep -v bb testa
ff-ff
cccdd
dddaa
```

The **–n** option displays the line number of each displayed line.

```
$ grep -n bb testa
1:aaabb
2:bbbcc
```

The **grep** utility can search through more than one file. Below, **grep** searches through each file in the working directory. (The ambiguous file reference ∗ matches all filenames.) The name of the file containing the string precedes each line of output.

```
$ grep bb ∗
testa:aaabb
testa:bbbcc
testb:bbbbb
```

The search that **grep** performs is case-sensitive. Because the previous examples specified lowercase bb, **grep** did not find the uppercase string, BBBBB, in **testc**. The **–i** option causes both uppercase *and* lowercase letters to match either case of letter in the pattern.

```
$ grep -i bb ∗
testa:aaabb
testa:bbbcc
testb:bbbbb
testc:BBBBB
$ grep -i BB ∗
testa:aaabb
testa:bbbcc
testb:bbbbb
testc:BBBBB
```

The **–c** option displays the number of lines in the file that contain a match.

```
$ grep -c bb ∗
testa:2
testb:1
testc:0
```

The following command line displays lines from the file **text2** that contain a string of characters starting with st, followed by zero or more characters (.∗ represents zero or more characters in a regular expression—see Appendix A), and ending in ing.

```
$ grep 'st.∗ing' text2
.
.
.
```

The ^ regular expression can be used alone to match every line in a file. Together with the **–n** option, it can be used to display the lines in a file, preceded by their line numbers.

```
$ grep -n '^' testa
1:aaabb
2:bbbcc
3:ff-ff
4:cccdd
5:dddaa
```

The final command line calls the **vi** editor with a list of files in the working directory that contain the string Sampson. The backquotes (page 292) cause the shell to execute the **grep** command in place and supply **vi** with a list of filenames that you want to edit. (The single quotation marks are not necessary in this example, but they are required if the string you are searching for contains special characters or (SPACE)s. It is generally a good habit to quote the pattern, so that the shell does not interpret any special characters it may contain.)

```
$ vi `grep -l 'Sampson' * `
.
.
```

head

Display the beginning (head) of a file.

Format

head [–number] [file-list]

Summary

The **head** utility displays the beginning of a file. It takes its input from one or more files you specify on the command line or from its standard input.

Arguments

Without a **number**, **head** displays the first ten lines of a file. The **file-list** contains pathnames of the files that **head** displays. If you specify more than one file, **head** will print the filename of each file before it displays the first few lines. If you do not specify any files, **head** takes its input from its standard input.

Examples

The examples are based on the following **lines** file:

```
$ cat lines
line one
line two
line three
line four
line five
line six
line seven
line eight
line nine
line ten
line eleven
```

First, **head** displays the first ten lines of the **lines** file (no arguments).

```
$ head lines
line one
line two
line three
line four
line five
line six
line seven
line eight
line nine
line ten
```

The next example displays the first three lines (–3) of the file.

```
$ head -3 lines
line one
line two
line three
```

kill

Terminate a process.

Format

kill [option] PID-list

Summary

The **kill** utility terminates one or more processes by sending them signals. By default, **kill** sends software termination signals (signal number 15), although an option allows you to send a different signal. The process must belong to the user executing **kill**, unless the user is the Superuser. The **kill** utility displays a message when it terminates a process.

Arguments

The **PID-list** contains process identification (PID) numbers of processes **kill** is to terminate.

Options

You can specify a signal number, preceded by a hyphen, as an option before the **PID-list** to cause **kill** to send the signal you specify to the process.

Notes

The shell displays the PID number of a background process when you initiate the process. You can also use the **ps** utility to determine PID numbers.

If the software termination signal does not terminate the process, try using a kill signal (signal number 9). A process can choose to ignore any signal except signal number 9.

The **kill** command is built into both the C and Korn Shells. When you are using one of those shells, you can use job identifiers in place of the **PID-list**. Job identifiers consist of a percent sign (%) followed by either a job number or a string that uniquely identifies the job. The built-in versions of **kill** also allow you to specify signals by name rather than number. You can use the **kill** –1 command to list the signal names.

To terminate all processes that the current login process initiated and have the operating system log you out, give the command **kill** –9 0.

> **CAUTION**
>
> If you run the command **kill** –9 0 while you are logged in as Superuser, you will bring the system down.

If you do not specify a signal number when you give a **kill** command with process number 0, **kill** terminates all processes that you are running in the background.

Examples

The first example shows a command line executing the file **compute** as a background process and the **kill** utility terminating it.

```
$ compute &
17542
$ kill 17542
```

The next example shows the **ps** utility determining the PID number of the background process running a program named **xprog**, and the **kill** utility terminating **xprog** with signal number 9.

```
$ ps
  PID  TT  STAT   TIME COMMAND
22921  11    S   0:10 -sh
23714  11    S   0:00 xprog
23715  11    R   0:03 ps
$ kill -9 23714
23714 Killed
```

You can run the following command to terminate all your jobs and log yourself out:

```
$ kill -9 0
```

```
login:
```

You should not run this command if you are logged in as Superuser.

ln

Make a link to a file.

Format

ln [option] existing-file new-link
ln [option] existing-file-list directory

Summary

By default, **ln** makes *hard links*. A hard link to a file is indistinguishable from the original filename. You can refer to the file either by its original filename or by the name given to it by the **ln** command, and in either case the effects will be the same. All hard links to a file must be in the same filesystem as the original file.

When you are using **ln**, you can use the first format shown above to create a link between an existing file and a new filename. You can use the second format to link existing files into a different directory. The new links will have the same simple filenames as the original files but different full pathnames.

You can use **ln** to create *symbolic links* as well as hard links. Unlike a hard link, a symbolic link can exist in a different filesystem from the linked-to file. Also, a symbolic link can connect to a directory. Refer to page 83 for more information about symbolic links.

Arguments

The **existing-file** is the pathname of the file you want to make a link to. The **new-link** is the pathname of the new link. When you are making a symbolic link, the **existing-file** may be a directory; otherwise, it cannot be a directory.

Using the second format, the **existing-file-list** contains the pathnames of the ordinary files you want to make links to. The **ln** utility establishes the new links so that they appear in the **directory**. The simple filenames of the entries in the **directory** are the same as the simple filenames of the files in the **existing-file-list**.

Options

−s

symbolic link   This option causes **ln** to create a symbolic link. When you use this option, the **existing-file** and **new-link** may be directories.

Notes

A hard link is an entry in a directory that points to a file. The operating system makes the first link to a file when you create the file using an editor, a program, or redirected output. You can make additional links using **ln** and remove links with **rm**. The **ls** utility, with the –l option, shows you how many links a file has. Refer to page 80 for a discussion of links.

You can use symbolic links to link across filesystems and to create links to directories. When you use the **ls** –l command to list information about a symbolic link, **ls** displays –> and the name of the linked-to file after the name of the link.

Examples

The first command shown below makes a link between **memo2** in the /**home/alex/literature** directory and the working directory. The file appears as **memo2** (the simple filename of the existing file) in the working directory.

```
$ ln /home/alex/literature/memo2 .
```

The next command makes a link to the same file. This time, the file appears as **new_memo** in the working directory.

```
$ ln /home/alex/literature/memo2 new_memo
```

The command below makes a link that causes the file to appear in another user's directory. You must have write and execute access permission to the other user's directory for this command to work. If you own the file, you can use **chmod** to give the other user write access permission to the file.

```
$ ln /home/alex/literature/memo2 /home/jenny/new_memo
```

The next command makes a symbolic link to an existing file, **memo3**, in the directory /**home/alex/literature**. The symbolic link is in a different filesystem, /**tmp**. The **ls** –l command shows the linked-to filename.

```
$ pwd
/home/alex/literature
$ ln -s memo3 /tmp/memo
$ ls -l /tmp/memo
lrwxrwxrwx 1 alex  5  Jul 13 11:44 /tmp/memo -> memo3
```

lpr

Print files.

Format

lpr [options] [file-list]
lpq [–Pprinter] [job-number] [user]
lprm [–Pprinter] [job-number]

Summary

The **lpr** utility places one or more files in the printer queue. The **lpr** utility takes its input from files you specify on the command line or from its standard input. The output from **lpr** is placed in the queue.

The **lpq** utility provides status information about jobs currently in the printer queue. The **lprm** utility removes files from the queue.

Arguments

The **file-list** is a list of one or more pathnames of ordinary text files. The **job-number** argument to **lpq** and **lprm** is the identification number **lpr** assigns to a job. You can identify job numbers using **lpq**. The **user** argument to **lpq** is the login name of a user.

Options

Check with the system administrator about installation-dependent options.

–h

> **header**   This option causes **lpr** to skip printing a header page. If you do not use this option, **lpr** will print a page that identifies your login, the name of the first file in the print job, the system name, and the date and time you submitted the job.

–i[indention]

> This option causes **lpr** to indent the output. If you specify an **indention**, the output will be indented that number of spaces. Otherwise, it will be indented eight spaces.

–m

> **mail report**   The **lpr** utility uses **mail** to report when the file has finished printing.

–p

> **print**   The **lpr** utility uses **pr** to paginate the files.

–Pprinter

> This option causes **lpr** to send the output to the specified **printer**. If you do not use **–P**, **lpr** sends the output to a default printer. If you do not know what printer is the default one on your system, ask the system administrator.

–r

> **remove**   This option causes **lpr** to remove the file after it is put into the printer queue. If you use **–r** with the **–s** option, **lpr** waits until the file has been printed before removing it.

–s

> **symbolic link**   This option causes **lpr** to create a symbolic link to the file rather than copying it into the printer queue. Because of a limitation on the sizes of files **lpr** can place in the queue, it is sometimes necessary to use **–s** in order to print large files.

–wx

> **width**   When used with the **–p** option, x is used as the page width for **lpr**. Replace x with a number.

–#x

> The number x specifies the number of copies of each file in **file-list** that **lpr** will print.

Notes

If you do not use any options or arguments with **lpq**, **lpq** reports on all files in the queue for the default printer. You can use the **–P** option (as with **lpr**) to specify another printer; the **job-number** argument to specify a specific job; or the **user** argument to list all jobs submitted by a particular user.

The **lprm** utility, which removes files from the printer queue, can also take the **–P** option.

Examples

In the first example, **lpr** uses **pr** to paginate **memo.out** and prints it on the default printer.

```
% lpr -p memo.out
```

Below, **lpr** prints a file called **letter**. Because of the **–m** option, **lpr** will send a **mail** message to the user when the file has finished printing.

```
% lpr -m letter
```

The next example shows the jobs currently in the printer queue. The **lpq** utility lists the rank of each job in the queue as well as the user's name, the job identification number, the names of files in the job, and the total size of the job in bytes. The **lpq** command below shows that Alex has one job running and that both Alex and Jenny have jobs in the queue.

```
% lpq
alder is ready and printing
Rank    Owner    Job  Files              Total Size
active  alex     653  memo.out           134000 bytes
1st     alex     654  letter             13090 bytes
2nd     jenny    655  report.sts         18235 bytes
```

When you call **lpq** without a –**P** option, it lists all jobs in the queue for the default printer. In the example above, **lpq** listed jobs for the printer **alder**, which happens to be the default printer on the system. With a –**P** option, **lpq** lists jobs in the queue for the specified **printer**.

The **lprm** command will delete specified files from a printer's queue. Unless you are the Superuser, you can only remove files that you submitted yourself. To remove a specific job, use **lprm** with the job number (which is displayed by **lpq**) as an argument. The command below removes job number 654 from the printer queue.

```
% lprm 654
```

If you want to remove a job from a queue for a printer that is not the default printer, you must use the –**P** option with **lprm**. The final example removes job number 379 from the queue for a printer called **cedar**.

```
% lprm -Pcedar 379
```

ls

Display information about one or more files.

Format

ls [options] [file-list]

Summary

The **ls** utility displays information about one or more files. It lists the information alphabetically by filename unless you use an option to change the order.

Arguments

When you do not use an argument, **ls** displays the names of the files in the working directory. If you do not use the –a option, **ls** does not list files whose filenames begin with **.** .

The **file-list** contains one or more pathnames of files. You can use the pathname of any ordinary, directory, or device file. These pathnames can include ambiguous file references.

When you specify a directory, **ls** displays the contents of the directory. The **ls** utility displays the name of the directory only when it is needed to avoid ambiguity (that is, when **ls** is displaying the contents of more than one directory, it displays the names of the directories to indicate which files you can find in which directory). If you specify an ordinary file, **ls** displays information about just that file.

Options

The options determine the type of information **ls** displays, how it displays it, and the order in which it is displayed.

When you do not use an option, **ls** displays a short listing, containing only the names of files.

–a

all entries Without a **file-list** (no arguments on the command line), this option displays information about all the files in the working directory, including invisible files (those with filenames that begin with a period). When you do not use this option, **ls** does not list information about invisible files, unless you list the name of an invisible file in **file-list**.

In a similar manner, when you use this option with a **file-list** that includes an appropriate ambiguous file reference, **ls** displays information about invisible files. (The * ambiguous file reference does not match a leading period in a filename—see page 107.)

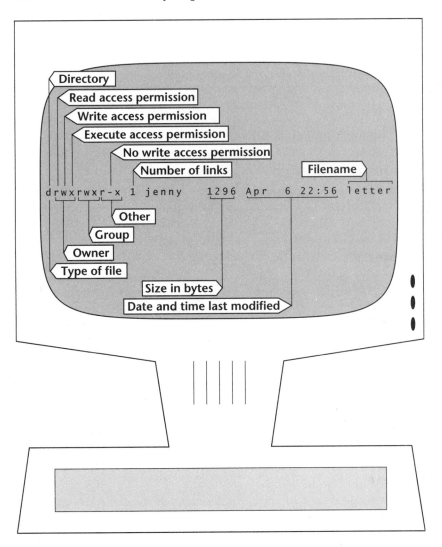

*Figure II-1   The Columns of the **ls –l** Command*

–c

change time   This option causes **ls** to sort files by the time the inode for the file was last changed.

–C

columns   This option lists files in vertically sorted columns. When output is going to the terminal, the –C option is the default.

-d

directory   This option displays the names of directories without displaying their contents. When you give this option without an argument, **ls** displays information about the working directory. This option displays ordinary files normally.

-F

This option displays a slash after each directory, an asterisk after each executable file, and an *at* sign (@) after symbolic links.

-g

group only   When used with the —l option, this option causes **ls** to include the group associated with the file(s), as an additional column (following the owner).

-i

inode   This option displays the inode number of each file. With the –l option, this option displays the inode number in column 1 and shifts each of the other items over one column to the right.

-l

long   This option displays several columns of information about each file. The –l option displays the six columns shown in Figure II-1. The first column, which contains 11 characters, is divided as follows. The first character describes the type of file:

First Character	Type of File
–	ordinary
b	block device
c	character device
d	directory
p	fifo (named pipe)
s	socket
l	symbolic link

Refer to pages 67 and 502 for more information on types of files.

The next nine characters represent all the access permissions associated with the file. These nine characters are divided into three sets of three characters each.

The first three characters represent the owner's access permissions. If the owner has read access permission to the file, an **r** appears in the first character position. If the owner is not permitted to read the file, a hyphen appears in this position. The next two positions represent the owner's write and execute access permissions. A **w** appears in the second position if the owner is permitted to write to the file, and an **x** appears in the third position if the owner is permitted to execute the file. An **s** in the third position indicates that the file has set user ID permission and execute permission. An **S** indicates set user ID without execute permission. A hyphen indicates the owner does not have the access permission associated with the character position.

In a similar manner, the second and third sets of three characters represent the access permissions of the user's group and other users. An **s** in the third position of the second set of characters indicates that the file has set group ID permission with execute permission, and an **S** indicates set group ID without execute permission.

The last character is **t** if the sticky bit is set with execute permission, and **T** if it is set without execute permission. Refer to **chmod** for information on changing access permissions.

The second column indicates the number of hard links to the file. Refer to page 80 for more information on links.

The third column displays the name of the owner of the file.

The fourth column indicates the size of the file in bytes or, if information about a device file is being displayed, the major and minor device numbers. In the case of a directory, this number is the size of the actual directory file, not the size of the files that are entries within the directory. (Use **du** to display the size of all the files in a directory.)

The last two columns display the date and time the file was last modified, and the filename.

–L

symbolic link   When you use this option, **ls** lists information about the file referenced by each symbolic link rather than information about the link itself.

–q

question marks   This option displays nonprinting characters in a filename as question marks. When output is going to a terminal, this is the default behavior.

–r

reverse   This option displays the list of filenames in reverse alphabetical order or, when you use it with the –t or –u options, in reverse time order (least recently modified or accessed first).

–R

recursive   This option recursively lists subdirectories.

−s

size   This option displays the size of each file in (usually 1024-byte) blocks. The size precedes the filename. With the −l option, this option displays the size in column 1 and shifts each of the other items over one column to the right.

−t

time modified   This option displays the list of filenames in order by the time of last modification. It displays first the files that were modified most recently.

−u

time accessed   When you use this option with the −t option, it sorts by the last time each file was accessed. When you use it with −l, it displays access times rather than modification times.

−1

one column   This option causes **ls** to list one filename per line. This is the default when output is not sent to the terminal.

Notes

Refer to page 105 for examples of using **ls** with ambiguous file references.

Examples

All the following examples assume that the user does not change to another working directory.

The first command line shows the **ls** utility with no arguments. You see an alphabetical list of the names of the files in the working directory.

```
$ ls
bin          calendar   letters
c            execute    shell
```

The –F option appends a slash (/) to files that are directories, an asterisk to files that are executable, and an *at* sign (@) after symbolic links.

```
$ ls -F
bin/         c/         calendar
execute*     letters/   shell@
```

Next, the –l (long) option displays a long list. The files are still in alphabetical order.

```
$ ls -l
total 8
drwxrwxr-x  2 jenny     80  May 20 09:17 bin
drwxrwxr-x  2 jenny    144  Mar 26 11:59 c
-rw-rw-r--  1 jenny    104  May 28 11:44 calendar
-rwxrw-r--  1 jenny     85  May  6 08:27 execute
drwxrwxr-x  2 jenny     32  Oct  6 22:56 letters
drwxrwxr-x 16 jenny   1296  Jun  6 17:33 shell
```

The –a (all) option lists all files, including invisible ones.

```
$ ls -a
.            .profile   c           execute    shell
..           bin        calendar    letters
```

Combining the –a and –l options displays a long listing of all the files, including invisible files, in the working directory. This list is still in alphabetical order.

```
$ ls -al
total 12
drwxrwxr-x  6 jenny    480 Jun  6 17:42 .
drwxrwx--- 26 root     816 Jun  6 14:45 ..
-rw-rw-r--  1 jenny    161 Jun  6 17:15 .profile
drwxrwxr-x  2 jenny     80 May 20 09:17 bin
drwxrwxr-x  2 jenny    144 Mar 26 11:59 c
-rw-rw-r--  1 jenny    104 May 28 11:44 calendar
-rwxrw-r--  1 jenny     85 May  6 08:27 execute
drwxrwxr-x  2 jenny     32 Oct  6 22:56 letters
drwxrwxr-x 16 jenny   1296 Jun  6 17:33 shell
```

If you add the –r (reverse order) option to the command line, **ls** produces a list in reverse alphabetical order.

```
$ ls -ral
total 12
drwxrwxr-x 16 jenny   1296 Jun  6 17:33 shell
drwxrwxr-x  2 jenny     32 Oct  6 22:56 letters
-rwxrw-r--  1 jenny     85 May  6 08:27 execute
-rw-rw-r--  1 jenny    104 May 28 11:44 calendar
drwxrwxr-x  2 jenny    144 Mar 26 11:59 c
drwxrwxr-x  2 jenny     80 May 20 09:17 bin
-rw-rw-r--  1 jenny    161 Jun  6 17:15 .profile
drwxrwx--- 26 root     816 Jun  6 14:45 ..
drwxrwxr-x  6 jenny    480 Jun  6 17:42 .
```

Use the –t and –l options to list files so that the most recently modified file appears at the top of the list.

```
$ ls -tl
total 8
drwxrwxr-x 16 jenny   1296 Jun  6 17:33 shell
-rw-rw-r--  1 jenny    104 May 28 11:44 calendar
drwxrwxr-x  2 jenny     80 May 20 09:17 bin
-rwxrw-r--  1 jenny     85 May  6 08:27 execute
drwxrwxr-x  2 jenny    144 Mar 26 11:59 c
drwxrwxr-x  2 jenny     32 Oct  6 22:56 letters
```

Together the **–r** and **–t** options cause **ls** to list files with the file you modified least recently at the top of the list.

```
$ ls -trl
total 8
drwxrwxr-x  2 jenny     32 Oct  6 22:56 letters
drwxrwxr-x  2 jenny    144 Mar 26 11:59 c
-rwxrw-r--  1 jenny     85 May  6 08:27 execute
drwxrwxr-x  2 jenny     80 May 20 09:17 bin
-rw-rw-r--  1 jenny    104 May 28 11:44 calendar
drwxrwxr-x 16 jenny   1296 Jun  6 17:33 shell
```

The next example shows **ls** with a directory filename as an argument. The **ls** utility lists the contents of the directory in alphabetical order.

```
$ ls bin
c        e        lsdir
```

The **–l** option gives a long listing of the contents of the directory; the **–g** option adds the group information.

```
$ ls -lg bin
total 3
-rwxrw-r-x 1 jenny pubs    48  Apr  6 21:38 c
-rwxrw-r-- 1 jenny pubs   156  Apr  6 21:40 e
-rwxrw-r-- 1 jenny pubs   136  May  7 16:48 lsdir
```

To display information about the directory file itself, use the **–d** (directory) option. This option causes **ls** to list information only about the directory.

```
$ ls -dl bin
drwxrwxr-x 2 jenny         80 May 20 09:17 bin
```

mail

Send or receive electronic mail.

Format

mail [–s **subject**] **user-list**
mail [**options**]

Summary

The **mail** utility sends and receives electronic mail. There may be more than one program called **mail** on your system. This book describes the Berkeley UNIX **mail** utility, also known as **Mail**. This utility is typically found in **/usr/ucb**, when **mail** and **Mail** are links to the same file containing the **mail** program.

When you use **mail** to send someone a message, the system puts the message in that user's mailbox, which is typically a file with the name **/var/spool/mail/login-name**, where **login-name** is the login name of the user you are sending the message to. When you use **mail** to read messages that other people have sent you, **mail** normally reads from your mailbox and then stores the messages after you read them in a file named **mbox** in your home directory.

The way **mail** appears and functions depends to a large extent on the **mail** *environment*. When you call **mail**, it establishes an environment that is based on variables that are set in two files: the **/usr/lib/Mail.rc** file and a **.mailrc** file in your home directory. The system administrator sets up the first file. You can change any aspects of your **mail** environment that the administrator has set up by setting variables in your **.mailrc** file. Or, if you are satisfied with the administrator's choices, you do not need to have a **.mailrc** file at all.

Options

–f [**filename**]

This option causes **mail** to read messages from **filename** instead of from your system mailbox. If you do not specify a filename, **mail** reads the **mbox** file in your home directory.

–H

headers   This option displays a list of message headers without giving you the opportunity to read the messages.

–s **subject**

When you are sending messages, this option sets the subject field to **subject**.

Arguments

Without any arguments, **mail** displays any messages that are waiting for you. With one or more arguments, **mail** sends messages. The **user-list** is a list of the users you are sending messages to.

Sending Messages

You send a message by giving the command **mail** followed by the login names of the people you want to send messages to. Depending on how its environment variables are set, **mail** may prompt you for a subject. If it does, enter a line of information in response to the prompt. This line will appear as the header when the recipients read the message. After entering the subject, **mail** is in the Input Mode, and you can enter the text of your message. The **mail** utility does not prompt you for the text.

You can run **mail** commands while **mail** is in the Input Mode. All Input Mode commands start with a tilde (~). They are called *tilde escapes* because they temporarily allow you to escape from the Input Mode so that you can give a command. The tilde must appear as the first character on a line.

The following list describes some of the more important tilde escapes.

~! command

Allows you to give a shell command while you are composing a message. Replace **command** with a shell command line.

~?

Displays a list of all tilde escapes.

~b name-list

blind   Sends blind carbon copies (Bcc) to the users who are in the **name-list**. The people who receive blind carbon copies are not listed on the copy of the message that goes to the addressee; the people who receive regular carbon copies (Cc) are listed—see ~c, following.

~c name-list

carbon copy   Sends carbon copies (Cc) to the users who are in the **name-list**.

~d

dead letter   Retrieves the **dead.letter** file from your home directory so you can continue or modify it. This file is created when you abort while sending mail.

~h

header   Causes **mail** to prompt you for the Subject, To, Cc, and Bcc fields. Each prompt includes the current entries for that field; you can use the erase and line kill keys to back up and edit the entries.

~m [msg-list]

> **message** Includes the messages specified by the **msg-list** in a message you are composing, placing a ⌜TAB⌝ at the beginning of each line. (Refer to "Reading Messages," following, for a description of **msg-list**.) You can use ~m only when you are sending a message while reading your messages (see the **m** and **r** commands, also in "Reading Messages").

~p

> **print** Displays the entire message you are currently composing.

~q

> **quit** Quits, saving the message you are composing in the file **dead.letter** in your home directory. See ~d for retrieving this file.

~r filename

> **read** Reads **filename** into the message you are composing.

~s subject

> **subject** Sets the subject field for the message you are composing to **subject**.

~t name-list

> **to** Adds the users in the **name-list** to the list of people who will receive the message.

~v

> **vi** Calls the **vi** editor so that you can edit the message you are composing.

~x

> **exit** Exits without saving the message you are composing.

Reading Messages

When you have mail you want to read, call **mail** without any arguments. The **mail** utility will display a list of headers of messages waiting for you. Each line of the display will have the following format:

> [>] **status message-# from-name date lines/characters [subject]**

The > indicates that the message is the current message. The **status** is N if the message is new, or **U** (for unread) if the message is not new (that is, you have seen its header before) but you have not read it yet. The **message-#** is the sequential number of the message in your mailbox. The **from-name** is the name of the person who sent you the message. The **date** and **lines/characters** are the date the message was sent and its size. The **subject** is the optional subject field for the message.

After the list of headers, **mail** displays its prompt, usually an ampersand (&). The **mail** utility is in Command Mode, waiting for you to give it a command. The easiest way to read your messages is to press (RETURN). After each message, **mail** will prompt you. Keep pressing (RETURN) to read each message in turn.

Pressing (RETURN) is a shorthand technique for printing the next message. Generally, you will give **mail** commands to manipulate and respond to your messages.

In the following summary of commands, **msg-list** is a message number, a range of message numbers (use a hyphen to indicate a range: a–b), or the login name of a user. If you do not specify a **msg-list** where one is called for, **mail** responds as though you had specified the current message. The *current message* is the message that is preceded by a > in the header list.

Most of the following commands can appear in your **.mailrc** file; however, it usually makes sense to use only **alias** and **set** there.

!command

Allows you to run a shell command while you are reading messages. Replace **command** with a shell command line.

| command

Pipe the current message through a shell **command** line.

?

Displays a list of all **mail** commands.

alias **a-name name-list**

Declares that **a-name** (alias name) represents all the login names in the **name-list**. When you want to send a message to everyone in the **name-list**, all you need to do is send a message to **a-name**. The **mail** utility automatically expands **a-name** into the **name-list**. This command usually appears in a **.mailrc** file.

d [msg-list]

delete   Deletes the messages in the **msg-list** from your mailbox.

x

exit   Exits from **mail** without changing your mailbox. If you deleted any messages during this session with **mail**, they are not removed from your mailbox.

h

header   Displays a list of headers. Refer to the z command if you want to scroll the list of headers.

m **name**

mail   Sends a message to **name**. Using this command is similar to calling **mail** with **name** from the command line.

p [msg-list]

> **print**   Displays the messages in the **msg-list**.

pr [msg-list]

> **preserve**   Preserves messages in the **msg-list** in your mailbox. Use this command after you have read a message but do not want to remove it from your mailbox. Refer to the **q** command.

q

> **quit**   Exits from **mail**, saving in your **mbox** file messages that you read and did not delete and leaving messages that you have not read in your mailbox. You can use the **pr** command to force **mail** to leave a message in your mailbox even though you have read it.

R [message]

> **reply**   Replies to a message. This command copies the subject line of the **message** and addresses a reply message to the person who sent you the **message**. Everyone who got a copy of the original **message** also gets a copy of the new message. The **R** command puts **mail** in Input Mode so you can compose a message.

r [message]

> **reply**   Replies to a message. This command is like the **R** command, except it sends a reply only to the person who sent you the message.

CAUTION

> **R** and **r** are not standard throughout the UNIX universe. You should verify what meanings apply to these commands on your system by testing **R** and **r** with an incoming **mail** message. If the result is not what you expected, use ~**q** to quit the message, and choose the other form of the reply command to send your response.

s [msg-list] [filename]

> **save**   Saves a message in a file. Without any arguments, this command saves the current message in your **mbox** file. If you specify only a **msg-list**, it saves in your **mbox** file the messages you specify. If you specify a **filename**, it saves your messages in that file. When you use the **q** command after saving a message, in a file, by default **mail** will not save the message in your mailbox or **mbox** file (unless you used the **s** command without a **filename**).

set

> See the introduction to the following section, "The **mail** Environment" for a description of this command. Although you can give the **set** command in response to a **mail** prompt, it is typically used in .mailrc files.

t [**msg-list**]

> Displays the messages in the **msg-list**.

top [**msg-list**]

> Displays the top few lines of the specified messages.

u [**msg-list**]

> **undelete** Restores the specified messages. You can restore a deleted message only if you have not quit from **mail** since you deleted the message.

v [**msg-list**]

> **vi** Edits the specified messages with **vi**.

z±

> Scrolls the list of headers (see the **h** command) forward (+) or backward (–).

The mail Environment

You can set up the **mail** environment by setting variables in the .**mailrc** file in your home directory, using the **mail set** command. The **set** command has the following format:

> set **name[=value]**

The **name** is the name of the **mail** variable that you are setting, and the **value** is the optional value you are assigning to the variable. The **value** may be either a string or a number. If you use **set** without a value, **mail** assigns the variable a null value (the values of some **mail** variables are not relevant; it is only important that they are set).

Following is a list of some of the more important **mail** variables:

askcc

> Set this variable if you want **mail** to prompt you for names of people to receive "carbon" copies of messages you send. By default, **mail** sets the **noaskcc** variable.

asksub

> Set this variable if you want **mail** to prompt you for a subject. By default, **mail** sets this variable.

crt=**number**

> Set this variable if you want **mail** to pipe long messages through **more**. Specify the number of lines on your screen with **number**. If you are using a standard ASCII terminal, set **number** to 24. The **mail** utility will use **more** by default.

ignore

> Set this variable if you want **mail** to ignore interrupts while you are composing and sending messages. Setting **ignore** can make your

job easier if you are working over a noisy telephone line. By default, **mail** sets the **noignore** variable.

record=**filename**

When you set this variable, **mail** puts a copy of all your outgoing messages in the file you specify with **filename**.

Notes

By default, the Bourne Shell checks every ten minutes for new mail. If mail has arrived, it presents a message before the next prompt. You can change the frequency of the checks by setting the **MAILCHECK** variable in your shell environment (page 293).

You can use the **vacation** utility to send a prerecorded response to anyone who sends you a message while you are on vacation (see your system documentation for more information on **vacation**).

Examples

The following example shows Alex reading his messages with **mail**. After calling **mail** and seeing that he has two messages, he gives the command **t 2** (just 2 is enough) followed by a (RETURN) to display the second message. After displaying the message, **mail** displays a prompt, and Alex deletes the message with a **d** command.

```
$ mail
Mail version SMI 4.1-OWV3 Mon Sep 23 07:17:24 PDT 1991
Type ? for help.
"/usr/spool/mail/alex": 2 messages 2 new
> N  1 jenny    Thu Jul 14 15:01 16/363 our meeting
  N  2 hls      Thu Jul 14 20:01 10/241 your trip
& t 2
(text of message 2)
.
.
.
& d
```

After reading his second message, Alex tries to read his first message by pressing (RETURN). The **mail** utility tells him he is at the end of his mailbox (At EOF), so he gives the command **t 1** (or just **1**) followed by a (RETURN) to view his first piece of mail. After reading it, he chooses to send a copy of it to the printer by typing **| lpr**. Finally, he decides he did not really want to delete his second message and that he wants to read both messages again later, so he exits from **mail** with an **x** command, leaving both messages in his mailbox.

```
& (RETURN)
At EOF
& t 1
(text of message 1)
.
.
.
& | lpr
& x
$
```

make

Keep a set of programs current.

Format

make [options] [target-files]

Summary

The **make** utility keeps a set of executable programs current, based on differences in the modification times of the programs and the source files that each is dependent on. The executable programs, or **target-files**, are dependent on one or more **prerequisite** files. The relationships between **target-files** and **prerequisites** are specified on *dependency lines* in a **makefile**. **Construction commands** follow the dependency line, specifying how **make** can update the **target-files**. Refer to page 469 for more information about makefiles.

Arguments

The **target-files** refer to targets on dependency lines in **makefile**. If you do not specify a **target-file**, **make** updates the target on the first dependency line in **makefile**.

Options

If you do not use the **–f** option, **make** takes its input from a file named **makefile** or **Makefile** in the working directory. Below, this file is referred to as **makefile**.

–f **file**

> **input file**   This option causes **make** to use **file** as input in place of **makefile**. You can use any filename in place of **file**.

–n

> **no execution**   This option causes **make** to display the commands it would execute to bring the **target-files** up to date, but not actually to execute the commands.

–t

> **touch**   This option updates modification times of target files but does not execute any construction commands. Refer to the **touch** utility.

Examples

The first example causes **make** to bring the **target-file** called **analysis** up to date by issuing the three **cc** commands shown below. It uses a file called **makefile** or **Makefile** in the working directory.

```
$ make analysis
cc -c analy.c
cc -c stats.c
cc -o analysis analy.o stats.o
```

The example below also updates **analysis**, but it uses a **makefile** called **analysis.mk** in the working directory.

```
$ make -f analysis.mk analysis
'analysis' is up to date.
```

The following example lists the commands **make** would execute to bring the **target-file** called **credit** up to date. It does not actually execute the commands.

```
$ make -n credit
cc -c -O credit.c
cc -c -O accounts.c
cc -c -O terms.c
cc -o credit credit.c accounts.c terms.c
```

The next example uses the **–t** option to update the modification time of the **target-file** called **credit**. After you use the **–t** option, **make** thinks that **credit** is up to date.

```
$ make -t credit
$ make credit
'credit' is up to date.
```

mesg

Enable/disable reception of messages.

Format

mesg [y|n]

Summary

The **mesg** utility enables or disables reception of messages sent by someone using the **write** or **talk** utilities. When you call **mesg** without an argument, it tells you whether messages are enabled or disabled.

Arguments

The **n** (no) disables reception of messages, and the **y** (yes) enables reception.

Options

There are no options.

Notes

On most systems, when you first log in, messages are enabled. Some utilities, such as **pr**, automatically disable messages while they are sending output to the terminal.

Examples

The following example demonstrates how to disable messages.

```
$ mesg n
```

The next example calls **mesg** without an option and verifies that you disabled messages.

```
$ mesg
is n
```

mkdir

Make a directory.

Format

mkdir [options] directory-list

Summary

The **mkdir** utility creates one or more directories.

Arguments

The **directory-list** contains one or more pathnames of directories that **mkdir** creates.

Options

–p

parent   If the parent directory of the directory you are creating does not already exist, it will be created by **mkdir** if you use the **–p** option.

Notes

You must have permission to write to and to search (execute permission) the parent directory of the directory you are creating. The **mkdir** utility creates directories that contain the standard invisible entries **.** (representing the directory itself) and **. .** (representing the parent directory).

Examples

The following command creates a directory named **accounts** as a subdirectory of the working directory, and a directory named **prospective** as a subdirectory of **accounts**.

```
$ mkdir -p accounts/prospective
```

Below, without changing working directories, the same user creates another subdirectory within the **accounts** directory.

```
$ mkdir accounts/existing
```

Finally, the user changes the working directory to the **accounts** directory and creates one more subdirectory.

```
$ cd accounts
$ mkdir closed
```

more

Display a file, one screenful at a time.

Format

more [options] [file-list]
page [options] [file-list]

Summary

The **more** utility allows you to view a text file at a terminal. It is similar to **cat** but pauses each time it fills the screen. In response to the **more** prompt, you can press (SPACE) to view another screenful, or use any of the other **more** commands to skip forward or backward in the file, display the current line number, invoke the **vi** editor, or display a list of the available commands. The **more** commands are described below. If you use the **page** command rather than **more**, the screen will be cleared before each screenful is printed, so that it will not appear to scroll.

The number followed by a percent sign that **more** displays as part of its prompt represents the portion of the file that has already been displayed.

This utility takes its input from files you specify on the command line or from its standard input.

Arguments

The **file-list** is the list of files that you want to view. If you do not specify any files in **file-list**, **more** reads from its standard input.

Options

–n

number of lines   This option specifies the number of lines **more** will display in a screenful. Replace **n** with the number of lines your terminal screen displays. If you do not use this option, **more** uses the **TERM** variable and the information in **/etc/termcap** to determine the size of the screen.

–d

display   This option causes **more** to display an explanatory message after each screenful (Press space to continue, 'q' to quit.) and to display a message after the user enters an illegal command (Press 'h' for instructions). This makes **more** easier for beginners to use.

–s

squeeze   This option causes **more** to present multiple, adjacent blank lines as a single blank line. When you use **more** to display paginated text, such as **nroff** output, this option cuts out page headers and footers.

+n

> This option causes **more** to start displaying the file at line number **n**.

+/pattern

> This option causes **more** to start displaying the file two lines above
> the line containing **pattern**.

Notes

You can set the options to **more** either from the command line when you call
more or by setting a variable called **MORE**. For example, to use **more** with the
–d option, you can use the following commands from the Bourne Shell.

> **$ MORE=-d; export MORE**

Bourne and Korn Shell users typically set **MORE** from their .profile file, and
C Shell users set it from their .cshrc file. Once you have set the **MORE** variable, **more** will be invoked with the specified option each time it is called.
The **MORE** variable applies whether you invoke **more** from the command
line or whether another utility (like **man** or **mail**) calls it.

Commands

Whenever **more** pauses, you may use any of the following commands. The
n is an optional numeric argument. It defaults to 1. You do not need to follow these commands with (RETURN).

Command	Effect
n(SPACE)	Displays n more lines; without n, it displays the next screenful.
d	Displays half a screenful.
nf	Skips **n** screenfuls and displays a screenful.
nb	Skips back **n** screenfuls and displays a screenful.
q or :q	Exits from more.
=	Displays the current line number.
v	Starts up the vi editor on the current file, at the current line.
h	Displays a list of all the more commands.
n/rexp	Searches for the nth occurrence of the regular expression **rexp**. The **n** is optional.
nn	Searches for the nth occurrence of the last regular expression entered.
!command	Invokes a shell and runs **command**.
n:n	Skips to the nth next file listed on the command line.
n:p	Skips to the nth previous file listed on the command line.
:f	Displays the current filename and line number.
.	Repeats the previous command.
(RETURN)	Displays the next line.

Examples

The following command line displays the file **letter**. To view more of **letter**, the user presses the (SPACE) bar in response to the **more** prompt.

```
$ more letter
    .
    .
(SPACE)--More--(71%)
    .
    .
$
```

Instead of pressing (SPACE), the user could have pressed **h** to display a list of the **more** commands, could have pressed **v** to cause **more** to invoke the **vi** editor on the current line, or could have given any one of the other **more** commands.

In the next example, **more** starts displaying **letter** two lines above the line containing the word **receive**.

```
$ more +/receive letter
...skipping
When we last spoke (January 14, 1994), I agreed that
we would ship your order within one week of
the date we receive it into our warehouse.
    .
    .
(SPACE)--More--(92%)
    .
    .
```

mv

Move (rename) a file.

Format

mv [options] existing-file new-filename
mv [options] existing-file-list directory
mv [options] existing-directory new-directory

Summary

The **mv** utility moves or renames one or more files. It has three formats. The first renames a single file with a new filename you supply. The second renames one or more files so that they appear in a specified directory. The third renames a directory.

The **mv** utility physically moves the file if it is not possible to rename it (that is, if you move it from one filesystem to another).

Options

–f

> **force**   This option causes **mv** to complete a move regardless of file access permissions. Refer to "Notes," on the next page.

–i

> **interactive**   This option causes **mv** to prompt you if a move would overwrite an existing file. If you respond **y** or **yes**, the move proceeds; otherwise, the file is not moved.

–

> The hyphen marks the end of the options and the beginning of the filenames on the command line. It keeps **mv** from interpreting a filename that begins with a hyphen as another option.

Arguments

In the first form of **mv**, the **existing-file** is a pathname that specifies the ordinary file that you want to rename. The **new-filename** is the new pathname of the file.

In the second form, the **existing-file-list** contains the pathnames of the files that you want to rename, and the **directory** specifies the new parent directory for the files. The files you rename will have the same simple filenames as the simple filenames of each of the files in the **existing-file-list** but new absolute pathnames.

The third form renames the **existing-directory** with the **new-directory** name. This form works only when the **new-directory** does not already exist.

Notes

The UNIX system implements **mv** as **ln** and **rm**. When you execute the **mv** utility, it first makes a link (**ln**) to the **new-file** and then deletes (**rm**) the **existing-file**. If the **new-file** already exists, **mv** deletes it before creating the link.

As with **rm**, you must have write and execute access permission to the parent directory of the **existing-file**, but you do not need read or write access permission to the file itself. If the move will overwrite an existing file that you do not have write permission for, **mv** displays the access permission and waits for a response. If you enter **y** or **yes**, **mv** renames the file; otherwise it does not. If you use the **–f** option, **mv** will not prompt you for a response— it will go ahead and overwrite the file.

If the **existing-file** and the **new-file** or **directory** are on different file-systems, the UNIX system implements **mv** as **cp** and **rm**. In this case, **mv** actually moves the file instead of just renaming it. After a file is moved, the user who moved the file becomes the owner of the file.

The **mv** utility will not move a file onto itself.

Examples

The first command line renames **letter**, a file in the working directory, as **letter.1201**.

```
$ mv letter letter.1201
```

The next command line renames the file so that it appears, with the same simple filename, in the **/usr/archives** directory.

```
$ mv letter.1201 /usr/archives
```

The next example renames all the files in the working directory whose names begin with **memo** so they appear in the **/usr/backup** directory.

```
$ mv memo* /usr/backup
```

nice

Change the priority of a command.

Format

nice [option] command-line

Summary

The **nice** utility executes a command line at a different priority than the command line would otherwise have. You can specify a decrement in the range of 1–19, which decreases the priority of the command. The Superuser can use **nice** to increase the priority of a command by using a negative decrement.

The C Shell has a built-in **nice** command that has a different syntax. Refer to "Notes," below.

Arguments

The **command-line** is the command line you want to execute at a different priority.

Options

Without any options, **nice** defaults to a decrement of 10 (the absence of an option is equivalent to a –10 option). You specify a decrement as a number preceded by a hyphen (to give a job the lowest priority possible, use an option of –19).

When you log in as the Superuser, you can specify a negative decrement as a number preceded by two hyphens (e.g., – –12). A negative decrement increases the priority of a command.

Notes

When you are using the C Shell's built-in **nice** command, a plus sign followed by a number decreases the priority of a process (e.g.,+12). The Superuser can increase the priority of a process by using a hyphen followed by a number (e.g.,–12).

Example

The following command executes **find** in the background at the lowest possible priority.

```
$ nice -19 find / -name core -print > corefiles.out &
24135
```

nohup

Run a command that will keep running after you log out.

Format

nohup **command-line**

Summary

The **nohup** utility executes a command line so that the command will keep running after you log out. Normally when you log out, the system kills all processes you have started.

The C Shell has a built-in **nohup** command. Refer to "Notes," below.

Arguments

The **command-line** is the command line you want to execute.

Options

There are no options.

Notes

If you do not redirect the output from a process that you execute with **nohup**, both the standard output *and* standard error output are sent to the file named **nohup.out** in the working directory. If you do not have write permission for the working directory, **nohup** opens a **nohup.out** file in your home directory.

Unlike the **nohup** utility, the C Shell's **nohup** command does not send output to the **nohup.out** file. The C Shell also automatically keeps commands that you run in the background running after you log out.

Example

The following command executes **find** in the background using **nohup**.

```
$ nohup find / -name core -print > corefiles.out &
14235
```

od

Dump the contents of a file.

Format

od [options] [file]

Summary

The **od** utility dumps the contents of a file. It is useful for viewing executable (object) files and text files with embedded nonprinting characters.

This utility takes its input from the file you specify on the command line or from its standard input.

Arguments

The **file** is the pathname of the file that **od** displays. If you do not specify a **file** argument, **od** reads from its standard input.

Options

If you do not specify an option, the dump is in octal.

−c

> **character**   This option produces a character dump. The **od** utility displays certain nonprinting characters as printing characters preceded by a backslash. It displays as three-digit octal numbers any nonprinting characters that are not in the following list.

Symbol	Character
\0	null
\b	(BACKSPACE)
\f	FORMFEED
\n	(NEWLINE)
\r	(RETURN)
\t	(TAB)

−d

> **decimal**   This option produces a decimal dump.

−o

> **octal**   This option produces an octal dump. This is the default.

−x

> **hexadecimal**   This option produces a hexadecimal dump.

Notes

The name **od** is short for octal dump.

Example

The example below shows the **sample** file displayed by **cat** and **od** with a –c option. The numbers to the left of the characters in the dump are the octal byte numbers of the first character on each line. The last number displayed is the octal byte number of the last byte in the file.

```
$ cat sample
This is a sample file.

It includes TABs:        , and NEWLINEs.
Here's what a dumped number looks like: 755.
$ od -c sample
0000000 T   h   i   s       i   s       a       s   a   m   p   l   e
0000020     f   i   l   e   . \n  \n  I   t       i   n   c   l   u
0000040 d   e   s       T   A   B   s   : \t  ,       a   n   d
0000060 N   E   W   L   I   N   E   s   . \n  H   e   r   e   '   s
0000100     w   h   a   t       a       d   u   m   p   e   d       n
0000120 u   m   b   e   r       l   o   o   k   s       l   i   k   e
0000140 :       7   5   5   . \n  \0
0000147
```

pr

Paginate a file for printing.

Format

pr [options] [file-list]

Summary

The **pr** utility breaks files into pages, usually in preparation for printing. Each page has a header with the name of the file, date, time, and page number.

The **pr** utility takes its input from files you specify on the command line or from its standard input. The output from **pr** goes to its standard output and is frequently redirected by a pipe to the **lpr** utility for printing.

Arguments

The **file-list** contains the pathnames of ordinary text files you want **pr** to paginate. If you do not specify any files, **pr** reads its standard input.

Options

You can embed options within the **file-list**. An embedded option affects only files following it on the command line.

+page

> This option causes **pr** to begin its output with the specified **page**. Note that this option begins with a *plus sign*, not a hyphen. Replace **page** with the page number you want to start with.

−columns

> This option causes **pr** to display its output in the number of **columns** specified. Replace **columns** with the number of columns you want.

−h header

> **header**   The **pr** utility displays the **header** at the top of each page in place of the filename. If the header contains (SPACE)s, you must enclose it within quotation marks. Replace **header** with the header you want **pr** to use.

−llines

> **length**   This option changes the page length from the standard 66 lines to **lines**. Replace **lines** with the number of lines per page you want.

−m

> **multiple columns**   This option displays all specified files simultaneously in multiple columns.

−s**x**

separate   This option separates columns with the single character x instead of (SPACE)s. Replace x with the delimiter you want to use. If you do not specify **x**, **pr** uses (TAB)s as separation characters.

−t

no header or trailer   This option causes **pr** not to display its five-line page header and trailer. The header that **pr** normally displays includes the name of the file, the date, time, and page number. The trailer is five blank lines.

−w**n**

width   This option changes the page width from its standard 72 columns to **n** columns. Replace **n** with the number of columns you want. This option is effective only with multicolumn output (that is, the −**m** and −**columns** options.)

Notes

When you use the −**columns** option to display the output in multiple columns, **pr** fills in an entire page of the first column before going to the second column, and so forth.

The **write** utility cannot send messages to your terminal while you are running **pr** with its output going to the terminal. Disabling messages prevents another user from sending you a message and disrupting **pr**'s output to your screen.

Examples

The first command line shows **pr** paginating a file named **memo** and sending its output through a pipe to **lpr** for printing.

```
$ pr memo | lpr
```

Next, **memo** is sent to the printer again, this time with a special heading at the top of each page. The job is run in the background.

```
$ pr -h 'MEMO RE: BOOK' memo | lpr &
23456
23457
```

Below, **pr** displays the **memo** file on the terminal, without any header, starting with page 3.

```
$ pr -t +3 memo
.
.
```

The final command displays the output from **ls** in six columns on the screen. This command line is useful on some older versions of the UNIX system that do not support the −C (column) option of **ls**.

```
$ ls | pr -6 -t
.
.
```

prs

Print a summary of the history of an SCCS file.

Format

prs [options] file-list

Summary

The **prs** utility is part of SCCS (Source Code Control System; see page 475 for more information). The **prs** utility prints a summary of one or more deltas to an SCCS file. If you do not give **prs** any options, it prints a standard summary of every delta in the history of a file. With options, **prs** prints a summary only of selected deltas. You can also use a data specification with the –**d** option to select the information that will be displayed about each delta and to select the format in which it will be displayed.

Arguments

The **file-list** is a list of SCCS-encoded files, which all start with **s.**. If the list includes directory names, all files that begin with **s.** in the named directory are added to **file-list**. The **prs** utility reports on all files listed in **file-list**. Any files in **file-list** that do not begin with **s.** or that are unreadable are ignored.

Options

–d

> **data-specification** This option specifies the data that will be included in the display and the format of the display. You can put labels into the display by including text in the data specification. Refer to "Data Specifications" for more information.

–r[**version-number**]

> **release** This option selects the delta you want information about. If you use –**r** without a version number, **prs** prints information about the most recent delta.

–c**date-time**

> **cutoff** This option can be used together with either –**e** or –**l** to select all the deltas made either before or after a cutoff date-time. The **date-time** argument has the format:
>
> YY[MM[DD[HH[MM[SS]]]]]
>
> The brackets indicate that all components of **date-time** may be omitted except **YY**, starting from the right. The maximum possible values will be substituted for any omitted values (e.g., 59 is used if **SS** is omitted). The two-digit components may be separated by any number of nonnumeric characters. For example, a colon (:) may be used between the components (e.g., 94:02:25:03:36). If the –**c** option is used, either –**e** or –**l** must also be used.

−e

earlier   When used with **−r**, this option causes **prs** to print information about all the deltas created earlier than the specified delta as well as about the specified delta. When used with **−c**, it causes **prs** to print information about all deltas created prior to the specified **date-time**.

−l

later   When used with **−r**, this option causes **prs** to print information about all the deltas created later than the specified delta, as well as about the specified delta. When used with **−c**, it causes **prs** to print information about all deltas created after the specified **date-time**.

−a

all   This option causes **prs** to print information about deltas that have been removed as well as about existing deltas. Without this option, only existing deltas are reported on.

Data Specifications

You can use the following keywords after the **−d** option to tell **prs** what information to display and how to display it. In the data specification following **−d**, you can use **\t** to specify a (TAB), or **\n** to specify a (NEWLINE). Text in the data specification that is not a keyword is printed in the output as it appears in the data specification. A typical data specification includes several keywords separated by (SPACE)s, (TAB)s, or (NEWLINE)s. The following specification is a default specification **prs** uses if you do not include a specification on the command line:

```
":Dt:\t:DL:\nMRs:\n:MR:COMMENTS:\n:C:"
```

The strings MRs: and COMMENTS: are labels, and the **\t** and **\n** represent (TAB) and (NEWLINE), respectively. All the other characters inside the double quotation marks are keywords. The following table lists the most useful keywords.

Keyword	Explanation
:DT:	Delta type (D for delta, R for removed delta)
:DL:	Number of lines inserted, deleted, and unchanged
:I:	Version number (SCCS Identification String)
:D:	Date delta was created
:T:	Time delta was created
:P:	Creator of the delta
:DS:	Sequence number of the delta
:DP:	Sequence number of the preceding delta
:MR:	Modification request numbers for the delta
:C:	Comments for the delta
:Dt:	The same as :DT :I: :D: :T: :P: :DS: :DP:

Examples

The first example prints standard information about every delta that has been made to the SCCS-encoded file **s.dissertation**.

```
$ prs s.dissertation
s.dissertation:

D 1.3 94/07/22 14:10:45 alex 3 2     00018/00005/04046
MRs:
COMMENTS:
edits

D 1.2 94/07/21 11:07:32 alex 2 1     00080/00000/04051
MRs:
COMMENTS:
added abstract for chapter 4

D 1.1 94/07/20 14:06:14 alex 1 0     04051/00000/00000
MRs:
COMMENTS:
date and time created 94/07/20 14:06:14 by alex
```

The next example prints information only about Version 1.3.

```
$ prs -r1.3 s.dissertation
s.dissertation:

D 1.3 94/07/22 14:10:45 alex 3 2     00018/00005/04046
MRs:
COMMENTS:
edits
```

Below, the comments are printed out for each delta that was created prior to 1:00 P.M. on July 22, 1994.

```
$ prs -d :C:  -c94:07:22:12 -e s.dissertation
added abstract for chapter 4

date and time created 94/07/20 14:06:14 by alex
```

The next command prints out the following information for the most recent delta: the type of the delta, the date and time of creation, and the creator of the delta. Spaces are used to separate the data items.

```
$ prs -d :DT: :D: :T: :P:  s.dissertation
D 94/07/22 14:10:45 alex
```

ps

Display process status.

Format

ps [options]

Summary

The **ps** utility displays status information about active processes.

When you run **ps** without any options, it displays the statuses of all active processes that your terminal controls. You will see five columns, each with one of the following headings:

Heading	Meaning
PID	**process ID** This column lists the process ID number of the process.
TT	**terminal** This column lists the number of the terminal that controls the process.
STAT	**state** This column includes up to four letters that specify the state of the process. The most common state designations are: S (sleeping for less than 20 seconds); I (idle, sleeping for more than 20 seconds); and R (runnable).
TIME	This column lists the number of minutes and seconds the process has been running.
COMMAND	This column lists the command name with which the process was called. Use the –w option to display the entire command line.

Options

–a

> **all**   This option displays status information for all processes that any terminal controls.

–e

> **environment**   This option prints the environment of the process as well as the command line.

–g

> **group**   This option prints the statuses of *process group* leaders in addition to other active processes. Your login shell is a process group leader, as are **getty** processes running on terminals no one is logged in on.

–l

> **long**   This option displays a complete status report comprising 14 columns. Each heading is listed on the next page.

Heading	Meaning
F	**flags** This column lists the flags associated with the process.
UID	**user ID** This is the user ID number of the owner of the process.
PID	**process ID** This column lists the process ID number of the process.
PPID	**parent PID** This is the process ID number of the parent process.
CP	**central processor utilization** The system uses this number for scheduling processes.
PRI	**priority** This is the priority of the process. The higher the number, the lower the priority of the process.
NI	**nice** This number is established by the nice utility and the operating system. It is used in computing the priority of the process.
SZ	**size** This number is the size, in blocks, of the core image of the process.
RSS	**resident set size** This is the real memory size of the process.
WCHAN	**wait channel** This column is blank for running processes. If the process is waiting or sleeping, this is the event it is waiting for.
STAT	**state** This column indicates the state of the process.
TT	**terminal** This column lists the number of the terminal that controls the process.
TIME	This column lists the number of minutes and seconds the process has been running.
COMMAND	This column lists the command name with which the process was called. Use the –w option to display the entire command line.

–u

user   This option causes **ps** to display user-oriented status information (additional columns, as well as the login name instead of the user's UID).

–w [w]

wide   The –w option causes **ps** to assume the width of your display is 132 columns instead of 80; as a result, **ps** truncates less of the command line information listed under COMMAND. The –ww causes **ps** to report the full command line, making no assumptions about the width of your display.

−x

> This option causes **ps** to include information about processes with
> no controlling terminal (e.g., daemons, **getty** processes).

Notes

The **ps** utility will not recognize options separated by (SPACE)s; options must
be run together, following a single hyphen. For example, **ps** –au is a valid
command line; **ps** –a –u produces an error message.

Because of the way **ps** obtains the command line, the COMMAND column may not be accurate.

Examples

The first example shows the **ps** utility, without any options, displaying the
user's active processes. The first process is the shell (**sh**), and the second is the
process executing the **ps** utility.

```
$ ps
  PID  TT  STAT   TIME  COMMAND
 24059 11  S      0:05  -sh (sh)
 24259 11  R      0:02  ps
```

With the –l (long) option, **ps** displays more information about each of
the processes.

```
$ ps -l
      F UID   PID  PPID CP PRI NI  SZ WCHAN    STAT TT  TIME  COMMAND
20488201 108 24059    1  0  15  0 108 kernelma S   11  0:05  -sh (sh)
20000001 108 24260 24059 78  30  0 248          R   11  0:00  ps -l
```

The next sequence of commands shows how to use **ps** to determine the
process number of a process running in the background and how to terminate that process using the **kill** command. In this case, it is not necessary to
use **ps**, because the shell displays the process number of the background processes. The **ps** utility verifies the PID number.

The first command executes **find** in the background. The shell displays
the PID number of the process, followed by a prompt.

```
$ find / -name memo -print > memo.out &
24264
$
```

Next, **ps** confirms the PID number of the background task. If you did not
already know this number, using **ps** would be the only way to find it out.

```
$ ps
  PID  TT STAT   TIME COMMAND
 24059 11 S      0:05 sh
 24264 11 R      0:05 find / -name memo -print
 24267 11 R      0:03 ps
```

Finally, the **kill** command terminates the process. Refer to the **kill** utility
for more information.

```
$ kill 24264
```

rcp

Copy one or more files to or from a remote computer.

Format

    rcp [options] source-file destination-file
    rcp [options] source-file-list destination-directory

Summary

The **rcp** utility copies one or more ordinary files, including text and execut-able program files, between two computers that can communicate over a network. Like the **cp** utility, it has two modes of operation: The first copies one file to another, and the second copies one or more files to a directory.

Arguments

The **source-file** is the pathname of the ordinary file that **rcp** is going to copy. To copy a file *from* a remote computer, precede the file's pathname with the name of the remote computer system followed by a colon (:). The **destination-file** is the pathname that **rcp** will assign to the resulting copy of the file. To copy a file *to* a remote computer, precede the file's pathname with the name of the remote computer system followed by a colon (:).

The **source-file-list** is one or more pathnames of ordinary files that **rcp** is going to copy. When you use the **–r** option, the **source-file-list** can also contain directories. To copy files *from* a remote computer, precede each file's pathname with the name of the remote computer system fol-lowed by a colon (:). The **destination-directory** is the pathname of the directory in which **rcp** places the resulting copied files. To copy files *to* a remote computer, precede the directory's pathname with the name of the remote computer system followed by a colon (:).

Options

–p

> **preserve**   This option causes **rcp** to set the modification times and file access permissions of each copy to match those of the **source-file**. Without the **–p** option, **rcp** uses the current file cre-ation mask to modify the access permissions. (Refer to **umask** on page 726 for a description of the file creation mask.)

–r

> **recursive**   You can use this option when the destination is a directory. If any of the files in the **source-file-list** is a directory, the **–r** option will cause **rcp** to copy the contents of that directory and any of its subdirectories into the **destination-directory**. The subdirectories themselves are copied, as well as the files they contain.

Notes

You must have a login account on the remote computer to be able to copy files to or from it using **rcp**. If the name of your local computer is specified in a file called **/etc/hosts.equiv** on the remote computer, the remote computer will not prompt you to enter your password. Computer systems listed in the **/etc/hosts.equiv** file are considered equally secure. An alternative way to specify a trusted relationship is on a per-user basis. Each user's home directory can contain a file called **.rhosts** that contains a list of trusted remote systems and users.

If you use a shell wildcard (such as ∗) in a remote filename, you must quote the pathname, so that the wildcard will be interpreted on the remote computer (and not by the local shell). As with **cp**, if the **destination-file** exists before you execute **rcp**, **rcp** overwrites the file.

Examples

The first example copies all the files with filenames ending in .c into the **archives** directory on the remote computer named **bravo**. Since the full pathname of the **archives** directory is not specified, **rcp** assumes that it is a subdirectory of the user's home directory on **bravo**. The copied files each retain their simple filenames.

```
$ rcp *.c bravo:archives
```

The next example copies **memo** from the **/home/jenny** directory on **bravo** to the working directory on the local computer.

```
$ rcp bravo:/home/jenny/memo .
```

The next command copies two files named **memo.new** and **letter** to jenny's home directory on the remote computer **bravo**. The absolute pathnames of the copied files on **bravo** are **/home/jenny/memo.new** and **/home/jenny/letter**.

```
$ rcp memo.new letter bravo:/home/jenny
```

The final command copies all the files in jenny's **reports** directory on **bravo** to the **oldreports** directory on the local computer, preserving the original modification dates and file access permissions on the copies.

```
$ rcp -p 'bravo:reports/*' oldreports
```

rcs

Create or change the characteristics of an RCS file.

Format

rcs [options] file-list

Summary

The **rcs** utility is part of RCS (Revision Control System—page 484). The **rcs** utility creates or changes the characteristics of RCS files. The options control the operations performed on the files.

Arguments

The **file-list** is a list of filenames. If you do not specify the directory as part of the filename, the **rcs** utility will look for the file in a subdirectory named RCS. If there is no RCS directory, it will use the current directory.

Options

–alogin[,login]

>**authorize**   This option adds **login** to the list of users who are allowed to make changes to an RCS file. Replace **login** with the user's login name. Before any users are added to the list of authorized users, the list is assumed to be empty, and any user can check in changes to the file. You can use this option to grant access to multiple users by following the –a option with a list of login names, separated by commas.

–elogin[,login]

>**erase**   This option removes **login** from the list of users who are allowed to make changes to an RCS file. Replace **login** with the user's login name. You can use this option to deny access to multiple users by following the –e option with a list of login names, separated by commas.

–i

>**initialize**   Create an empty (null) RCS file.

–l[version-number]

>**lock**   Set a lock for an RCS file. Normally, when you want to edit a revision of an RCS file you set the lock when you check out the file. If you forget to do so, you can use the –l option with the **rcs** command to set the lock retroactively. If you do not specify a **version-number rcs** locks the latest revision; otherwise, it sets the lock for the specified version.

–orevision-list

> **outdate** This option removes a revision, or range of revisions, from an RCS file. The **revision-list** can include one version number (e.g., **–r1.4**) or a pair of version numbers separated by a hyphen (e.g., **–r1.4–1.6**).

–r[version-number]

> **revision** This option identifies the version number of the RCS-encoded file that is being changed. This option is needed only if you do not want to change the latest version. If you do not specify a **version-number rcs** changes the latest revision; otherwise, it changes the specified version.

–u[version-number]

> **unlock** Unlock an RCS file. A lock on an RCS file is normally released when the file is checked in. Use this option to break the lock without checking in the file, or break a lock that was set by another user. If you do not specify a **version-number**, **rcs** unlocks the latest revision; otherwise, it removes the lock for the specified version.

Notes

The name of an RCS-encoded file is the same as the name of the unencoded file with the two characters **,v** added to the end. When working with RCS commands, you can omit the trailing **,v** in a filename on the command line; the RCS commands will look for the encoded versions automatically (as **file-name,v**).

Each version number may include up to four components: release, level, branch, and sequence number.

Examples

The following command creates a new RCS-encoded file with the name of RCS/menu1,v.

```
$ rcs -i menu1
RCS file: RCS/menu1,v
enter description, terminated with ^D or '.';
NOTE: This is NOT the log message!
>> basic menu
>> .
done
```

The next example adds Alex and Barbara to the list of users who are authorized to make changes to the file **menus_march**.

```
$ rcs -aalex,barbara menus_march
```

Having added barbara to the list, you can revoke her access with the following command.

```
$ rcs -ebarbara menus_march
```

The next command line removes revision 1.5 from the file **menu1**.

```
$ rcs -o1.5 menu1
RCS file: RCS/menu1,v
deleting revision 1.5
done
```

The last example deletes revision 1.5 through revision 1.8 from the file **menus_march**.

```
$ rcs -o1.5-1.8 menus_march
RCS file: RCS/menus_march,v
deleting revision 1.8
deleting revision 1.7
deleting revision 1.6
deleting revision 1.5
done
```

rlog

Print a summary of the history of an RCS file.

Format

rlog [options] file-list

Summary

The **rlog** utility is part of RCS (Revision Control System—page 484). The **rlog** utility displays a summary of the history of an RCS file. The options control how much information **rlog** displays.

Arguments

The **file-list** is a list of filenames. If you do not specify the directory as part of the filename, the **rlog** utility will look for the file in a subdirectory named RCS. If there is no **RCS** directory, it will use the current directory.

Options

–ddates[;dates]

> **date** This option uses file check-in dates to restrict the information displayed by **rlog**. You can select more than one range of dates by separating each range with a semicolon. Each range of dates is specified using greater than (>) and less than (<) symbols (and must be quoted to prevent the shell from interpreting those symbols as redirections). To see the history of a file during the month of October 1994, you would use

> **–d"Oct 1 1994 LT<Oct 31 1994 LT"**

–r[revision-list]

> **revision** This option restricts the information reported by **rlog** to the specified version numbers. If you specify the –**r** option without a version number, **rlog** reports on the latest revision. The revision list can include a range of version numbers by including a hyphen. For example, to see all the information on a file from version 1.2 to the current revision, use –**r1.2–**. For information on revisions prior to version 1.4, use –**r–1.4**. To restrict the display to revisions from 1.2 through 1.4, use –**r1.2–1.4**.

Notes

The name of an RCS-encoded file is the same as the name of the unencoded file with the two characters **,v** added to the end. When working with RCS commands, you can omit the trailing **,v** in a filename on the command line;

the RCS commands will look for the encoded versions automatically (as **filename,v**).

Each version number may include up to four components: release, level, branch, and sequence number.

When specifying a date, the default time zone is Coordinated Universal Time (UTC), also known as Greenwich Mean Time (GMT). The RCS commands recognize dates in a variety of formats, such as

```
5:00 PM LT
1:00am, Jul. 15, 1994
Fri Jul 15 17:00:00 PDT 1994
```

In the example above, LT represents the local time (which is PDT, Pacific Daylight Time, in this case).

Examples

The first example prints standard information about all the changes that have been made to the file **RCS/thesis,v**:

```
$ rlog thesis
RCS file: RCS/thesis,v:  Working file: thesis
head:          2.7
branch:
locks:     alex: 2.7;
access list:
symbolic names:
comment leader:     "# "
total revisions: 14;     selected revisions: 14
description:
-----------------------------
revision 2.7          locked by: alex;
date: 94/07/18 09:57:01; author: alex; state: Exp; lines
added/del: 11/7
add examples
-----------------------------
     .
     .
```

The next example prints information only about version 1.3.

```
$ rlog -r1.3 thesis
     .
     .
```

The final example displays information about the changes made during the last two weeks of July.

```
$ rlog -d'Jul 15 1994 PDT<Aug  1 1994 PDT' thesis
     .
     .
```

rlogin

Log in on a remote computer.

Format

rlogin [option] **remote-computer**

Summary

The **rlogin** utility establishes a login session on a remote computer, over a network.

Arguments

The **remote-computer** is the name of a computer that your system can reach over a network.

Options

–l user-name

> **login**   This option causes **rlogin** to log you in on the remote computer as the user specified by **user-name** rather than as yourself.

Notes

If the file named **/etc/hosts.equiv** on the remote computer specifies the name of your local computer, the remote computer will not prompt you to enter your password. Computer systems listed in the **/etc/hosts.equiv** file are considered equally secure.

An alternative way to specify a trusted relationship is on a per-user basis. Each user's home directory can contain a file called **.rhosts** that contains a list of trusted remote systems and users.

Examples

The following example illustrates the use of **rlogin**. On the local system, Alex's login name is **alex**, but on the remote computer **bravo**, his login name is **watson**. The remote system prompts alex to enter a password because he is logging in using a different user name than the one he uses on the local system.

```
$ who am i
alex         tty06         Sep 14 13:26
$ rlogin -l watson bravo
Password:
```

If the local computer is named **hurrah**, a **.rhosts** file on **bravo** like the one below will allow the user **alex** to log in as the user **watson** without entering a password.

```
$ cat /home/alex/.rhosts
hurrah alex
```

rm

Remove a file (delete a link).

Format

rm [options] file-list

Summary

The **rm** utility removes links to one or more files. It can be used to remove both hard links and symbolic links. When you remove the last hard link, you can no longer access the file, and the system releases the space the file occupied on the disk for use by another file (that is, the file is deleted). Refer to Chapter 4 for more information about hard links and symbolic links.

To delete a file, you must have execute and write access permission to the parent directory of the file, but you do not need read or write access permission to the file itself. If you are running **rm** from a terminal (that is, **rm**'s standard input is coming from a terminal) and you do not have write access permission to the file, **rm** displays your access permission and waits for you to respond. If you enter **y** or **yes**, **rm** deletes the file; otherwise it does not. If its standard input is not coming from the terminal, **rm** deletes the file without question.

Arguments

The **file-list** contains the list of files that **rm** deletes. The list can include ambiguous file references. Because you can remove a large number of files with a single command, use **rm** cautiously, especially when you are using an ambiguous file reference. If you are in doubt as to the effect of an **rm** command with an ambiguous file reference, use the **echo** utility with the same file reference first to evaluate the list of files the reference generates.

Options

–f

> **force**   This option causes **rm** to remove files for which you do not have write access permission, without asking for your consent.

–i

> **interactive**   This option causes **rm** to ask you before removing each file. If you use the –r option with this option, **rm** also asks you before examining each directory.

–r

> **recursive**   This option causes **rm** to delete the contents of the specified directory, including all its subdirectories, and the directory itself. Use this option cautiously.

Notes

The sections on the **ln** utility on pages 83 and 626 contain discussions about removing links.

Refer to the **rmdir** utility in Part II if you need to remove an empty directory.

When you want to remove a file that begins with a hyphen, you must prevent **rm** from interpreting the filename as an option. A good strategy is to use the full pathname of the file.

Examples

The following command lines delete files, both in the working directory and in another directory.

```
$ rm memo
$ rm letter memo1 memo2
$ rm /home/jenny/temp
```

The next example asks the user before removing each file in the working directory and its subdirectories. This command is useful for removing file-names that contain special characters, especially (SPACE)s, (TAB)s, and (NEWLINE)s. (You should never create filenames containing these characters on purpose, but it may happen accidentally.)

```
$ rm -ir .
```

rmdel

Remove a delta from an SCCS file.

Format

rmdel –rversion-number file-list

Summary

The **rmdel** utility is part of SCCS (Source Code Control System; see page 475 for more information). The **rmdel** utility removes changes that were previously recorded in an SCCS file using **delta**. The **rmdel** utility will not remove a delta if there is an outstanding **get** (that is, a **get** for which the corresponding **delta** has not been done) on the specified delta. Also, **rmdel** will not remove a delta if it has a successor (that is, **rmdel** will only remove the newest delta on the trunk or on a branch).

To use **rmdel** you must be the owner of the SCCS file and the directory it is in, or be the one who created the delta.

Arguments

The **file-list** is a list of SCCS-encoded files, which all start with **s.**. If the list includes directories, all files that begin with **s.** in the named directories are added to **file-list**. The **rmdel** utility removes the specified delta from all files in **file-list**. Any files in **file-list** that do not begin with **s.** or that are unreadable are ignored.

Options

–rversion-number

> release   This option is mandatory. Use it to specify the full version number of the delta you want to remove. If the delta is a trunk delta, the version number contains two components (release.level). If the delta is a branch delta, it contains four components (release.level.branch.sequence).

Examples

The following command is applied to an SCCS file called **s.memo**. These deltas to the **s.memo** file exist:

```
1.1
1.2
2.1
2.1.1.1
2.2
2.2.1.1
2.2.1.2
3.1
```

The only deltas that can be removed using **rmdel** are 3.1 (the only trunk delta with no successors), and 2.1.1.1, and 2.2.1.2. To use **rmdel** to remove branch delta 2.1.1.1, give the following command:

```
$ rmdel -r2.1.1.1 s.memo
```

rmdir

Remove a directory.

Format

rmdir **directory-list**

Summary

The **rmdir** utility deletes empty directories from the filesystem by removing links to those directories.

Arguments

The **directory-list** contains pathnames of empty directories that **rmdir** removes.

Notes

Refer to the **rm** utility with the **–r** option if you need to remove directories that are not empty, together with their contents.

Examples

The following command line deletes the empty **literature** directory from the working directory.

```
$ rmdir literature
```

The next command line removes the **letters** directory using an absolute pathname.

```
$ rmdir /home/jenny/letters
```

ruptime

Display status of computers attached to a network.

Format

ruptime [option]

Summary

The **ruptime** utility displays status information about computers attached to a network. By default, **ruptime** counts only those users who have used their terminals in the past hour.

Arguments

There are no arguments.

Options

−a

> **all**   This option causes **ruptime** to count all users who are currently logged in, even if they have been idle for more than one hour.

Notes

The information displayed by **ruptime** is broadcast on the network by the **rwhod** utility, which is typically started by a run command script when the system reboots. The **rwhod** utility can create a lot of traffic on the network and may not be running at your site. If **ruptime** displays a message such as no hosts!?!, **rwhod** is not running.

Examples

The following example illustrates the use of **ruptime**. The computer name appears in column 1. Column 2 reports the status of the system, followed by the amount of time the system has been up (or down). The number of users logged in on the system appears in the third column. The last column reports the load average for each machine. From left to right, the load averages indicate the number of processes that have been waiting to run in the past minute, 5 minutes, and 15 minutes. In this example, the computer **bravo** has been up and running for the past 21 days, 19 hours, and 40 minutes.

```
$ ruptime -a
bravo          up 21+19:40,    1 users,  load 0.12, 0.00, 0.03
hurrah         up 17+16:25,    2 users,  load 1.32, 1.93, 1.16
kudos        down  1+23:34
```

rwho

Display names of users on computers attached to a network.

Format

rwho [option]

Summary

The **rwho** utility displays the names of users currently logged in on computers attached to a network, together with their terminal device numbers, the times they logged in, and how much time has passed since they typed on their keyboards. By default, **rwho** displays only the names of users who have used their terminals in the past hour.

Arguments

There are no arguments.

Options

–a

all   This option causes **rwho** to display the names of all users who are currently logged in, even if they have been idle for more than one hour.

Notes

The information displayed by **rwho** is broadcast on the network by the **rwhod** utility, which is typically started by a run command script when the system reboots. The **rwhod** utility can create a lot of traffic on the network and may not be running at your site. If **rwho** displays no information, it is likely that **rwhod** is not running.

Examples

The following example illustrates the use of **rwho**. The user name appears in column 1, followed by the name of the computer and the terminal line, and the time at which the user logged in. If the fourth column is blank, the user is actively typing at the terminal; otherwise, the fourth column indicates how many hours and minutes have passed since the user last typed on the keyboard.

```
$ rwho -a
watson    bravo:tty01     Sep 14 10:19
barbara   hurrah:tty01    Sep 13 10:54   2:33
jenny     hurrah:tty02    Sep 14 14:24    :01
```

sed

Edit a file (noninteractively).

Format

sed [–n] –f **script-file** [**file-list**]
sed [–n] **script** [**file-list**]

Summary

The **sed** utility is a batch (noninteractive) editor. The **sed** commands are usually stored in a **script-file** (as in the first format shown above), although you can give simple **sed** commands from the command line (as in the second format). By default, **sed** copies lines from the **file-list** to its standard output, editing the lines in the process. It selects lines to be edited by position within the file (line number) or context (pattern matching).

The **sed** utility takes its input from files you specify on the command line or from its standard input. Unless you direct output from a **sed** script elsewhere, it goes to its standard output.

Arguments

The **script-file** is the pathname of a file containing a **sed** script (see "Description," on the next page).

The **script** is a **sed** script, included on the command line. This format allows you to write simple, short **sed** scripts without creating a separate script file.

The **file-list** contains pathnames of the ordinary files that **sed** processes. These are the input files. If you do not specify any files, **sed** takes its input from the standard input.

Options

If you do not use the **–f** option, **sed** uses the first command line argument as its script.

–f

> **file**   This option causes **sed** to read its script from the **script-file** given as the first command line argument.

–n

> **no print**   The **sed** utility does not copy lines to its standard output except as specified by the Print (**p**) instruction or flag.

Description

A **sed** script consists of one or more lines in the following format:

[address[, address]] instruction [argument-list]

The **address**es are optional. If you omit the **address**, **sed** processes all lines from the input file. The **address**es select the line(s) the **instruction** part of the command operates on. The **instruction** is the editing instruction that modifies the text. The number and kinds of arguments in the **argument-list** depend on the instruction.

The **sed** utility processes an input file as follows:

1. **sed** reads one line from the input file (**file-list**).

2. **sed** reads the first command from the **script-file** (or command line), and, if the address selects the input line, **sed** acts on the input line as the instruction specifies.

3. **sed** reads the next command from the **script-file**. If the address selects the input line, **sed** acts on the input line (as possibly modified by the previous instruction) as the new instruction specifies.

4. **sed** repeats step 3 until it has executed all of the commands in the **script-file**.

5. If there is another line in the input file, **sed** starts over again with step 1; otherwise it is finished.

Addresses

A line number is an address that selects a line. As a special case, the line number **$** represents the last line of the last file in the **file-list**.

A regular expression (refer to Appendix A) is an address that selects the lines that contain a string that the expression matches. Slashes must delimit a regular expression used as an address.

Except as noted, zero, one, or two addresses (either line numbers or regular expressions) can precede an instruction. If you do not use an address, **sed** selects all lines, causing the instruction to act on every input line. One address causes the instruction to act on each input line that the address selects. Two addresses cause the instruction to act on groups of lines. The first address selects the first line in the first group. The second address selects the next subsequent line that it matches; this line is the last line in the first group. After **sed** selects the last line in a group, it starts the selection process over again, looking for the next subsequent line that the first address matches. This line is the first line in the next group. The **sed** utility continues this process until it has finished going through the file.

Instructions

d

      delete   The Delete instruction causes **sed** not to write out the lines it selects. It also causes **sed** not to finish processing the lines. After

sed executes a Delete instruction, it reads the next input line from the **file-list** and begins over again with the first command in the **script-file**.

n

next   The Next instruction reads the next input line from the **file-list**. It writes out the currently selected line, if appropriate, and starts processing the new line with the *next* command in the **script-file**.

a

append   The Append instruction appends one or more lines to the currently selected line. If you do not precede the Append command with an address, it appends to each input line from the **file-list**. You cannot precede an Append instruction with two addresses. An Append command has the following format:

[**address**] a\
text \
text \
.
.
.
text

You must end each line of appended text, except the last, with a backslash. (The backslash quotes the following (NEWLINE).) The appended text concludes with a line that does not end with a backslash. The **sed** utility *always* writes out appended text, regardless of whether you set the **–n** flag on the command line. It even writes out the text if you delete the line to which you appended the text.

i

insert   The Insert instruction is identical to the Append instruction, except that it places the new text *before* the selected line.

c

change   The Change instruction is similar to Append and Insert, except that it changes the selected lines so that they contain the new text. You can use this command with two addresses. If you specify an address range, Change replaces the entire range of lines with a single occurrence of the new text.

s

substitute   The Substitute instruction is akin to that of **vi**. It has the following format:

[address[,address]] s/pattern/replacement-string/[g][p][w file]

The **pattern** is a regular expression that is delimited by any character (other than a (SPACE) or (NEWLINE)); however, slash (/) is traditionally used. The **replacement-string** starts immediately following the second delimiter and must be terminated by the same delimiter. The final (third) delimiter is required. The **replacement-string** can contain an ampersand (&), which **sed** replaces with the matched **pattern**. Unless you use the **g** flag, the Substitute instruction replaces only the first occurrence of the **pattern** on each selected line.

g

global flag   This flag causes the Substitute instruction to replace all nonoverlapping occurrences of the **pattern** on the selected lines.

p

print flag   This flag causes **sed** to send all lines on which it makes substitutions to its standard output. This flag overrides the –n option on the command line.

w

write flag   This flag is similar to the **p** flag, except that it sends the output to a specified file. A single (SPACE) and the name of a file must follow the Write flag.

p

print   The Print instruction writes the selected lines to the standard output. It writes the lines immediately and does not reflect the effects of subsequent instructions. This instruction overrides the –n option on the command line.

w

write   This instruction is similar to the **p** instruction, except that it sends the output to a specified file. A single (SPACE) and the name of a file must follow the Write instruction.

r

read   The Read instruction reads the contents of the specified file and appends it to the selected line. You cannot precede a Read instruction with two addresses. A single (SPACE) and the name of a file must follow a Read instruction.

q

quit   The Quit instruction causes **sed** to stop processing.

Control Structures

!

> **NOT**   The NOT structure causes **sed** to apply the following instruction, located on the same line, to each of the lines *not* selected by the address portion of the command.

{ }

> **group instructions**   When you enclose a group of instructions within a pair of braces, a single address (or address pair) selects the lines on which the group of instructions operates.

Notes

The name **sed** stands for *stream editor*.

Examples

The following examples use the input file **new**.

```
$ cat new
Line one.
The second line.
The third.
This is line four.
Five.
This is the sixth sentence.
This is line seven.
Eighth and last.
```

Unless you instruct it not to, **sed** copies all lines, selected or not, to its standard output. When you use the **–n** option on the command line, **sed** copies only specified lines.

The command line below displays all the lines in the **new** file that contain the word **line** (all lowercase). The command uses the address /line/, a regular expression. The **sed** utility selects each of the lines that contains a match for that pattern. The Print (**p**) instruction displays each of the selected lines.

```
$ sed '/line/ p' new
Line one.
The second line.
The second line.
The third.
This is line four.
This is line four.
Five.
This is the sixth sentence.
This is line seven.
This is line seven.
Eighth and last.
```

The preceding command does not use the **–n** option, so it displays all the lines in the input file at least once. It displays the selected lines an additional time because of the Print instruction.

The following command uses the **–n** option so that **sed** displays only the selected lines.

```
$ sed -n '/line/ p' new
The second line.
This is line four.
This is line seven.
```

Below, **sed** copies part of a file based on line numbers. The Print instruction selects and displays lines 3 through 6.

```
$ sed -n '3,6 p' new
The third.
This is line four.
Five.
This is the sixth sentence.
```

The command line below uses the Quit instruction to cause **sed** to display only the top of a file. This enables you to look at the top of a file in the same way the **head** command does. This **sed** command is a handy substitute for **head**, if you do not have **head** on your system. Below, **sed** displays the first five lines of **new**.

```
$ sed '5 q' new
Line one.
The second line.
The third.
This is line four.
Five.
```

When you need to give **sed** more complex or lengthy commands, you can use a script file. The following script file (**print3_6**) and command line perform the same function as the command line in the second preceding example.

```
$ cat print3_6
3,6 p
```

```
$ sed -n -f print3_6 new
The third.
This is line four.
Five.
This is the sixth sentence.
```

The **sed** script **append_demo** (below) demonstrates the Append instruction. The command in the script file selects line 2 and appends a (NEWLINE) and the text AFTER. to the selected line. Because the command line does not include the **–n** option, **sed** copies all the lines from the input file **new**.

```
$ cat append_demo
2 a\
AFTER.
```

```
$ sed -f append_demo new
Line one.
The second line.
AFTER.
The third.
This is line four.
Five.
This is the sixth sentence.
This is line seven.
Eighth and last.
```

The **insert_demo** script selects all the lines containing the string This and inserts a (NEWLINE) and the text BEFORE. before the selected lines.

```
$ cat insert_demo
/This/ i\
BEFORE.
```

```
$ sed -f insert_demo new
Line one.
The second line.
The third.
BEFORE.
This is line four.
Five.
BEFORE.
This is the sixth sentence.
BEFORE.
This is line seven.
Eighth and last.
```

The next example demonstrates a Change instruction with an address range. When you give a Change instruction a range of lines, it does not change each line within the range but changes the block of text to a single occurrence of the new text.

```
$ cat change_demo
2,4 c\
SED WILL INSERT THESE\
THREE LINES IN PLACE\
OF THE SELECTED LINES.
```

```
$ sed -f change_demo new
Line one.
SED WILL INSERT THESE
THREE LINES IN PLACE
OF THE SELECTED LINES.
Five.
This is the sixth sentence.
This is line seven.
Eighth and last.
```

The next example demonstrates a Substitute command. The **sed** utility selects all lines, because the command has no address. It replaces the first occurrence on each line of the string **line** with **sentence** and displays the resulting line. The **p** flag displays each line where a substitution occurs. The command line calls **sed** with the **–n** option, so that **sed** displays only the lines that the script explicitly requests it to display.

```
$ cat subs_demo
s/line/sentence/p

$ sed -n -f subs_demo new
The second sentence.
This is sentence four.
This is sentence seven.
```

The next example is similar to the preceding one, except a **w** flag and filename (**temp**) at the end of the Substitute command cause **sed** to create the file **temp**. The command line does not include the **–n** option, so it displays all lines, including those that **sed** changes. The **cat** utility displays the contents of the file **temp**. The word Line (starting with an uppercase L) is not changed.

```
$ cat write_demo1
s/line/sentence/gw temp

$ sed -f write_demo1 new
Line one.
The second sentence.
The third.
This is sentence four.
Five.
This is the sixth sentence.
This is sentence seven.
Eighth and last.

$ cat temp
The second sentence.
This is sentence four.
This is sentence seven.
```

Following is a Bourne Shell script named **sub** that will change all occurrences of REPORT to report, FILE to file, and PROCESS to process in a group of files. The For structure loops through the list of files supplied on the command line. (See page 311 for more information on the For structure.) As it processes each file, **sub** displays the filename before running **sed** on the file. This script uses a multiline embedded **sed** command—as long as the (NEWLINE) within the command are quoted (they are between single quotation marks), **sed** accepts the multiline command as though it appeared on a single command line. Each substitute command includes a **g** (global) flag to take care of the case where one of the strings occurs more than one time on a line.

```
$ cat sub
for file
do
        echo $file
        mv $file $$.subhld
        sed 's/REPORT/report/g
             s/FILE/file/g
             s/PROCESS/process/g' $$.subhld > $file
done
rm $$.subhld

$ sub file1 file2 file3
file1
file2
file3
```

Below, **sed** uses the Write command to copy part of a file to another file (**temp2**). The line numbers 2 and 4, separated by a comma, select the range of lines **sed** is to copy. This script does not alter the lines.

```
$ cat write_demo2
2,4 w temp2

$ sed -n -f write_demo2 new

$ cat temp2
The second line.
The third.
This is line four.
```

The script **write_demo3** is very similar to **write_demo2**, except that it precedes the Write command with the NOT operator (!), causing **sed** to write to the file the lines *not* selected by the address.

```
$ cat write_demo3
2,4 !w temp3

$ sed -n -f write_demo3 new

$ cat temp3
Line one.
Five.
This is the sixth sentence.
This is line seven.
Eighth and last.
```

Below, **next_demo1** demonstrates the Next instruction. When **sed** processes the selected line (line 3), it immediately starts processing the next line, without printing line 3. Thus, it does not display line 3.

```
$ cat next_demo1
3 n
p

$ sed -n -f next_demo1 new
Line one.
The second line.
This is line four.
Five.
This is the sixth sentence.
This is line seven.
Eighth and last.
```

The next example uses a textual address. The sixth line contains the string the, so the Next command causes **sed** not to display it.

```
$ cat next_demo2
/the/ n
p

$ sed -n -f next_demo2 new
Line one.
The second line.
The third.
This is line four.
Five.
This is line seven.
Eighth and last.
```

The next set of examples uses the file **compound.in** to demonstrate how **sed** instructions work together.

```
$ cat compound.in
1. The words on this page...
2. The words on this page...
3. The words on this page...
4. The words on this page...
```

The first example that uses **compound.in** instructs **sed** to substitute the string words with text on lines 1, 2, and 3, and the string text with TEXT on lines 2, 3, and 4. It also selects and deletes line 3. The result is **text** on line 1, TEXT on line 2, no line 3, and words on line 4. The **sed** utility made two substitutions on lines 2 and 3: It substituted text for words and TEXT for text. Then it deleted line 3.

```
$ cat compound
1,3 s/words/text/
2,4 s/text/TEXT/
3 d
```

```
$ sed -f compound compound.in
1. The text on this page...
2. The TEXT on this page...
4. The words on this page...
```

The next example shows that the ordering of instructions within a **sed** script is critical. After line 2 of the script substitutes the string TEXT in place of text, the third line displays all of the lines that contain TEXT. The Print instruction would have displayed no lines, or different lines, if it had been one line before or after its present location.

```
$ cat compound2
1,3 s/words/text/g
2,4 s/text/TEXT/g
/TEXT/ p
3 d
```

```
$ sed -f compound2 compound.in
1. The text on this page...
2. The TEXT on this page...
2. The TEXT on this page...
3. The TEXT on this page...
4. The words on this page...
```

Below, **compound3** appends two lines to line 2. The **sed** utility displays all the lines from the file once, because no **–n** option appears on the command line. The Print instruction at the end of the script file displays line 3 an additional time.

```
$ cat compound3
2 a\
This is line 2a.\
This is line 2b.
3 p
```

```
$ sed -f compound3 compound.in
1. The words on this page...
2. The words on this page...
This is line 2a.
This is line 2b.
3. The words on this page...
3. The words on this page...
4. The words on this page...
```

The next example shows that **sed** always displays appended text. Here line 2 is deleted, but the Append instruction still displays the two lines that were appended to it. Appended lines are displayed even if you use the **–n** option on the command line.

```
$ cat compound4
2 a\
This is line 2a.\
This is line 2b.
2 d

$ sed -f compound4 compound.in
1. The words on this page...
This is line 2a.
This is line 2b.
3. The words on this page...
4. The words on this page...
```

The final examples use regular expressions in addresses. The regular expression in the command below (^.) matches one character at the beginning of a line (that is, it matches every line that is not empty). The replacement string (between the second and third slashes) contains a (TAB) character followed by an ampersand (&). The ampersand takes on the value of whatever the regular expression matched. This type of substitution is useful for indenting a file to create a left margin. See Appendix A for more information on regular expressions.

```
$ sed 's/^./    &/' new
        Line one.
        The second line.
        The third.
    .
    .
```

You may want to put the above **sed** command into a shell script so that you will not have to remember it (and retype it) every time you want to indent a file.

```
$ cat indent
sed 's/^./    &/' $*
$ chmod u+x indent
$ indent new
        Line one.
        The second line.
        The third.
    .
    .
```

Generally, when you create a **sed** command that you think you may want to use again, it is a good idea to put it into a shell script or a **script-file** to save yourself the effort of trying to reconstruct it.

In the following shell script, the regular expression (two (SPACE)s followed by a *) matches one or more spaces at the end of a line. It removes trailing spaces at the end of a line, which is useful for cleaning up files that you created using **vi**. In **vi** it is easy to create lines that end in a space accidentally, and some **vi** commands do not work correctly on a line that ends in a (SPACE).

```
$ cat cleanup
sed 's/  *$//' $*
```

692 Part II The UNIX Utility Programs

sleep

Create a process that sleeps for a specified interval.

Format

sleep **time**

Summary

The **sleep** utility causes the process executing it to go to sleep for the time specified.

Arguments

The **time** is the length of time, in seconds, that the process will sleep.

Examples

You can use **sleep** from the command line to execute a command after a period of time. The example below executes a process in the background that reminds you to make a phone call in 20 minutes (1200 seconds).

```
$ (sleep 1200; echo 'Remember to make call.') &
2145
```

You can also use **sleep** within a shell script to execute a command at regular intervals. The following **per** shell script executes a program named **update** every 90 seconds.

```
$ cat per
while :
do
    update
    sleep 90
done
```

If you execute a shell script such as **per** in the background, you can only terminate it using the **kill** utility.

sort

Sort and/or merge files.

Format

sort [options] [field-specifier-list] [file-list]

Summary

The **sort** utility sorts and/or merges one or more text files in sequence. When you use the **–n** option, **sort** performs a numeric sort.

The **sort** utility takes its input from files you specify on the command line or from its standard input. Unless you use the **–o** option, output from **sort** goes to its standard output.

Arguments

The **field-specifier-list** specifies one or more sort fields within each line. The **sort** utility uses the sort fields to sort the lines from the **file-list**. The **file-list** contains pathnames of one or more ordinary files that contain the text to be sorted. The **sort** utility sorts and merges the files unless you use the **–m** option, in which case **sort** only merges the files.

Options

If you do not specify an option, **sort** orders the file in the machine collating (usually ASCII) sequence. You can embed options within the **field-specifier-list** by following a field specifier with an option without a leading hyphen—see "Description," later in this section.

–b

> **ignore leading blanks**   Blanks ((TAB) and (SPACE) characters) are normally field delimiters in the input file. Unless you use this option, **sort** *also* considers leading blanks to be part of the field they precede. This option causes **sort** to consider multiple blanks as single field delimiters with no intrinsic value, so **sort** does not consider these characters in sort comparisons.

–c

> **check only**   This option checks to see that the file is properly sorted. The **sort** utility does not display anything if everything is in order. It displays a message if the file is not in sorted order and returns an exit status of 1.

–d

> **dictionary order**   This option ignores all characters that are not alphanumeric characters or blanks. Specifically, **sort** does not consider punctuation and (CONTROL) characters.

–f

> **fold lowercase into uppercase**   This option considers all lower-
> case letters to be uppercase letters. Use this option when you are
> sorting a file that contains both uppercase and lowercase text.

–i

> **ignore**   This option ignores nonprinting characters when you per-
> form a nonnumeric sort.

–m

> **merge**   This option assumes that multiple input files are in sorted
> order and merges them without verifying that they are sorted.

–M

> **month**   This option compares fields that contain the names of
> months. It uses the first three nonblank characters in the field,
> shifts them to uppercase, and sorts in the order JAN, FEB, ..., DEC.
> It puts invalid entries first in the sorted list.

–n

> **numeric sort**   When you use this option, minus signs and deci-
> mal points take on their arithmetic meaning, and the **–b** option is
> implied. The **sort** utility does not order lines or order sort fields in
> the machine collating sequence but in arithmetic order.

–o filename

> **output filename**   The **filename** is the name of the output file.
> The **sort** utility sends its output to this file instead of to its standard
> output. Replace **filename** with a filename of your choice—it can be
> the same as one of the names in the **file-list**.

–r

> **reverse**   This option reverses the sense of the sort (for example,
> **z** precedes **a**).

–tx

> **set tab character**   When you use this option, replace the x with
> the character that is the field delimiter in the input file. This
> character replaces (SPACE)s, which become regular (nondelimiting)
> characters.

–u

> **unique**   This option outputs repeated lines only once. The **sort**
> utility outputs lines that are not repeated as it would without this
> option.

–ymem

>This option allows you to specify the amount of memory that **sort** will use, within system limits. Replace **mem** with the number of kilobytes of memory that you want **sort** to use. If you omit **mem**, **sort** will use the maximum amount of memory that the system allows. Replace **mem** with **0** to use the minimum amount of memory possible. When **sort** runs out of memory, it uses temporary files.

–zrec

>This option allows you to specify the maximum line length when you are merging files. Do not use it if you are sorting files. Replace **rec** with the number of bytes in the longest record you are merging. If you do not specify this option, **sort** may terminate abnormally if it encounters a long line.

Description

In the following description, a *line field* is a sequence of characters on a line in an input file. These sequences are bounded by blanks or by a blank and the beginning or end of the line. You use line fields to define a sort field.

A *sort field* is a sequence of characters that **sort** uses to put lines in order. The description of a sort field is based on line fields. A sort field can contain part or all of one or more line fields. Refer to Figure II-2.

The **field-specifier-list** contains pairs of pointers that define subsections of each line (sort fields) for comparison. If you omit the second pointer from a pair, **sort** assumes the end of the line. A pointer is in the form ±f.c. The first of each pair of pointers begins with a plus sign, and the second begins with a hyphen.

You can make a pointer (f.c) point to any character on a line. The **f** is the number of line fields you want to *skip*, counting from the beginning of the line. The **c** is the number of characters you want to *skip*, counting from the end of the last line field you skipped with **f**.

The **–b** option causes **sort** to count multiple leading blanks as a *single* line field delimiter character. If you do not use this option, **sort** considers each leading blank to be a character in the sort field and includes it in the sort comparison.

You can specify options that pertain only to a given sort field by immediately following the field specifier by one of the options **b**, **d**, **f**, **i**, **n**, or **r**. In this case, you must *not* precede the options with a hyphen.

If you specify more than one sort field, **sort** examines them in the order you specify them on the command line. If the first sort field of two lines is the same, **sort** examines the second sort field. If these are again the same, **sort** looks at the third field. This process continues for all the sort fields you specify. If all the sort fields are the same, **sort** examines the entire line.

If you do not use any options or arguments, the sort is based on entire lines.

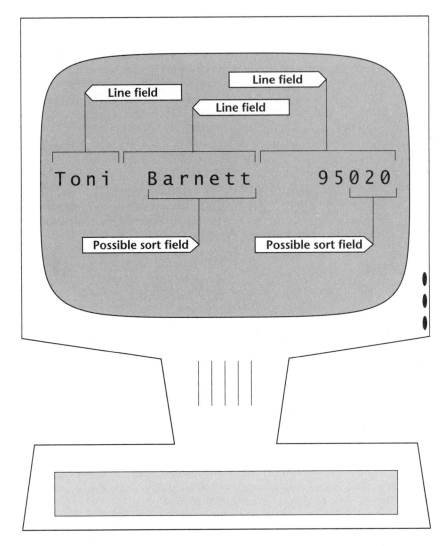

Figure II-2   Line Fields and Sort Fields

Examples

The examples on the following pages demonstrate some of the features and uses of the **sort** utility. The examples assume that a file named **list**, shown on the following page, is in the working directory. This file contains a list of names and ZIP codes. Each line of the file contains three fields: the first name field, the last name field, and the ZIP code field. In order for the examples to work, make sure all the blanks in the file are (SPACE)s, and not (TAB)s.

```
$ cat list
Tom Winstrom         94201
Janet Dempsey        94111
Alice MacLeod        94114
David Mack           94114
Toni Barnett         95020
Jack Cooper          94072
Richard MacDonald    95510
```

The first example demonstrates **sort** without any options or arguments other than a filename. Below, **sort** sorts the file on a line-by-line basis. If the first characters on two lines are the same, **sort** looks at the second characters to determine the proper sorted order. If the second characters are the same, **sort** looks at the third characters. This process continues until **sort** finds a character that differs between the lines. If the lines are identical, it does not matter which one **sort** puts first. The **sort** command in this example needs to examine only the first three letters (at most) of each line. The **sort** utility displays a list that is in alphabetical order by first name.

```
$ sort list
Alice MacLeod        94114
David Mack           94114
Jack Cooper          94072
Janet Dempsey        94111
Richard MacDonald    95510
Tom Winstrom         94201
Toni Barnett         95020
```

You can instruct **sort** to skip any number of line fields and characters on a line before beginning its comparison. Blanks normally separate one line field from another. The next example sorts the same list by last name, the second line field. The +1 argument indicates that **sort** is to *skip one line field* before beginning its comparison. It skips the first-name field. Because there is no second pointer, the sort field extends to the end of the line. Now the list is almost in last-name order, but there is a problem with Mac.

```
$ sort +1 list
Toni Barnett         95020
Jack Cooper          94072
Janet Dempsey        94111
Richard MacDonald    95510
Alice MacLeod        94114
David Mack           94114
Tom Winstrom         94201
```

In the example above, MacLeod comes before Mack. After finding that the sort fields of these two lines were the same through the third letter (Mac), **sort** put L before k, because it arranges lines in the order of ASCII character codes. In this ordering, uppercase letters come before lowercase, and therefore L comes before k.

The –**f** option makes **sort** treat uppercase and lowercase letters as equals and thus fixes the problem with MacLeod and Mack.

```
$ sort -f +1 list
Toni Barnett           95020
Jack Cooper            94072
Janet Dempsey          94111
Richard MacDonald      95510
David Mack             94114
Alice MacLeod          94114
Tom Winstrom           94201
```

The next example attempts to sort **list** on the third line field, the ZIP code. Below, **sort** does not put the numbers in order, but puts the shortest name first in the sorted list and the longest name last. With the argument of +2, **sort** *skips* two line fields and counts the (SPACE)s after the second line field (last name) as part of the sort field. The ASCII value of a (SPACE) character is less than that of any other printable character, so **sort** puts the ZIP code that is preceded by the greatest number of (SPACE)s first and the ZIP code that is preceded by the fewest (SPACE)s last.

```
$ sort +2 list
David Mack             94114
Jack Cooper            94072
Tom Winstrom           94201
Toni Barnett           95020
Janet Dempsey          94111
Alice MacLeod          94114
Richard MacDonald      95510
```

The –**b** option causes **sort** to ignore leading (SPACE)s. With the –**b** option, the ZIP codes come out in the proper order (below). When **sort** determines that MacLeod and Mack have the same ZIP codes, it compares the entire lines. The Mack/MacLeod problem crops up again because there is no –**f** option.

```
$ sort -b +2 list
Jack Cooper            94072
Janet Dempsey          94111
Alice MacLeod          94114
David Mack             94114
Tom Winstrom           94201
Toni Barnett           95020
Richard MacDonald      95510
```

The next example shows a **sort** command that not only skips line fields but skips characters as well. The +2.3 causes **sort** to skip two line fields and then skip three characters before starting its comparisons. The sort field is, and the following list is sorted in order of, the last two digits in the ZIP code.

The example takes advantage of the fact that if you use two options with **sort**, you can include them both after a single hyphen. The –**f** option does not fix the MacLeod and Mack problem, because **sort** never compares last names. When it determines that the last two digits of MacLeod and Mack's

ZIP codes are the same, it compares the entire lines, starting with the first names. These two lines are in first-name order. The issue of preventing **sort** from comparing entire lines is covered shortly.

```
$ sort -fb +2.3 list
Tom Winstrom          94201
Richard MacDonald     95510
Janet Dempsey         94111
Alice MacLeod         94114
David Mack            94114
Toni Barnett          95020
Jack Cooper           94072
```

The next set of examples uses the **cars** data file. From left to right, the columns in the file contain each car's make, model, year of manufacture, mileage, and price.

```
$ cat cars
plym     fury      77    73     2500
chevy    nova      79    60     3000
ford     mustang 65      45     10000
volvo    gl        78    102    9850
ford     ltd       83    15     10500
chevy    nova      80    50     3500
fiat     600       65    115    450
honda    accord    81    30     6000
ford     thundbd 84      10     17000
toyota   tercel    82    180    750
chevy    impala    65    85     1550
ford     bronco    83    25     9500
```

Without any options, **sort** displays a sorted copy of the file.

```
$ sort cars
chevy    impala    65    85     1550
chevy    nova      79    60     3000
chevy    nova      80    50     3500
fiat     600       65    115    450
ford     bronco    83    25     9500
ford     ltd       83    15     10500
ford     mustang 65      45     10000
ford     thundbd 84      10     17000
honda    accord    81    30     6000
plym     fury      77    73     2500
toyota   tercel    82    180    750
volvo    gl        78    102    9850
```

A +0 sort field specifier indicates a sort from the beginning of the line (skip zero fields). Unless you specify otherwise, a sort field extends to the end of the line.

The following example shows one problem to avoid when you are using **sort.** In this example, the objective is to sort by manufacturer and then by price within manufacturer. The command line instructs **sort** to sort on the entire line (+0) and then make a second pass, sorting on the fifth field all lines whose first-pass sort fields were the same (+4). Because no two lines are the same, **sort** makes only one pass, sorting on each entire line. (If two lines differed only in the fifth field, they would be sorted properly on the first pass anyway, so the second pass would be unnecessary.) Look at the lines with the ltd and mustang. They are sorted by the second field rather than the fifth, demonstrating that **sort** never made a second pass and never sorted by the fifth field.

```
$ sort +0 +4 cars
chevy    impala   65        85        1550
chevy    nova     79        60        3000
chevy    nova     80        50        3500
fiat     600      65        115       450
ford     bronco   83        25        9500
ford     ltd      83        15        10500
ford     mustang  65        45        10000
ford     thundbd  84        10        17000
honda    accord   81        30        6000
plym     fury     77        73        2500
toyota   tercel   82        180       750
volvo    gl       78        102       9850
```

The next example forces the first-pass sort to stop just before the second field by defining the end of the first sort field (–1). Now the ltd and mustang are properly sorted by price. But look at the bronco. It is less expensive than the other Fords, but **sort** has it positioned as the most expensive one. The **sort** utility put the list in ASCII collating sequence order, not numeric order: 9500 comes after 10000 because 9 comes after 1.

```
$ sort +0 -1 +4 cars
chevy    impala   65        85        1550
chevy    nova     79        60        3000
chevy    nova     80        50        3500
fiat     600      65        115       450
ford     mustang  65        45        10000
ford     ltd      83        15        10500
ford     thundbd  84        10        17000
ford     bronco   83        25        9500
honda    accord   81        30        6000
plym     fury     77        73        2500
toyota   tercel   82        180       750
volvo    gl       78        102       9850
```

The –**n** (numeric) option on the second pass puts the list in the proper order.

```
$ sort +0 -1 +4n cars
chevy    impala   65        85        1550
chevy    nova     79        60        3000
chevy    nova     80        50        3500
fiat     600      65        115       450
ford     bronco   83        25        9500
ford     mustang  65        45        10000
```

```
ford     ltd      83      15      10500
ford     thundbd 84      10      17000
honda    accord  81      30      6000
plym     fury    77      73      2500
toyota   tercel  82      180     750
volvo    gl      78      102     9850
```

The next example again shows that, unless you instruct it otherwise, **sort** orders a file starting with the field you specify and continuing to the end of the line. It does not make a second pass unless two of the first sort fields are the same. Although this example sorts the cars by years, it does not sort the cars by manufacturer within years.

```
$ sort +2 +0 cars
fiat     600     65      115     450
ford     mustang 65      45      10000
chevy    impala  65      85      1550
plym     fury    77      73      2500
volvo    gl      78      102     9850
chevy    nova    79      60      3000
chevy    nova    80      50      3500
honda    accord  81      30      6000
toyota   tercel  82      180     750
ford     ltd     83      15      10500
ford     bronco  83      25      9500
ford     thundbd 84      10      17000
```

Specifying an end to the sort field for the first pass allows **sort** to perform its secondary sort properly.

```
$ sort +2 -3 +0 cars
chevy    impala  65      85      1550
fiat     600     65      115     450
ford     mustang 65      45      10000
plym     fury    77      73      2500
volvo    gl      78      102     9850
chevy    nova    79      60      3000
chevy    nova    80      50      3500
honda    accord  81      30      6000
toyota   tercel  82      180     750
ford     bronco  83      25      9500
ford     ltd     83      15      10500
ford     thundbd 84      10      17000
```

The next examples demonstrate an important sorting technique: putting a list in alphabetical order, merging upper- and lowercase entries, and eliminating duplicates.

```
$ cat short
Pear
Pear
apple
pear
Apple
```

A plain sort:

```
$ sort short
Apple
Pear
Pear
apple
pear
```

A folded sort is a good start, but it does not eliminate duplicates.

```
$ sort -f short
Apple
apple
Pear
Pear
pear
```

The –u (unique) option eliminates duplicates but causes all the upper-case entries to come first.

```
$ sort -u short
Apple
Pear
apple
pear
```

When you attempt to use both –u and –f, the lowercase entries get lost.

```
$ sort -uf short
Apple
Pear
```

Two passes are the answer. Both passes are unique sorts, and the first folds uppercase letters onto lowercase ones.

```
$ sort -u +0f +0 short
Apple
apple
Pear
pear
```

spell

Check a file for spelling errors.

Format

spell [options] [+local-file] [file-list]

Summary

The **spell** utility checks the words in a file against a dictionary file. It displays a list of words that it cannot either find in the dictionary or derive from one of the words in the dictionary. This utility takes its input from files you list on the command line or from its standard input. You can also customize **spell**'s dictionary.

Arguments

The **file-list** is a list of files that **spell** checks. If you specify more than one file, **spell** generates one list of words for all the files.

The +**local-file** is a file containing a sorted list of words, one word per line. The **spell** utility removes the words in **local-file** from its output. The **local-file** supplements the standard dictionary with additional words that are correctly spelled. It is useful for removing proper names and technical terms from the output of **spell**.

Options

–v

This option displays all words that are not literally in the dictionary. As the example on the next page shows, it gives a proposed derivation for any word **spell** would normally accept.

–b

British   This option accepts British spellings.

Notes

The **spell** utility is not a foolproof way of finding spelling errors. It also does not check for misused but properly spelled words (e.g., *read* instead of *red*).

Examples

The following examples use **spell** to check the spelling in the **check** file. The –v option causes **spell** to display all words that are not actually in its dictionary.

```
$ cat check
Here's a sampel document that is tobe
used with th Spell utilitey.
It obviously needs proofing quite badly.

$ spell check
sampel
th
tobe
utilitey

$ spell -v check
sampel
th
tobe
utilitey
+ly     badly
+'s     Here's
+s      needs
+ly     obviously
+ing    proofing
+d      used
```

stty

Display or set terminal parameters.

Format

stty [options] [arguments]

Summary

Without any arguments, **stty** displays certain parameters affecting the operation of the terminal. For a list of some of these parameters and an explanation of each, see the following "Arguments" section. The arguments establish or change the parameter(s) you specify.

Options

Without an option or argument, **stty** displays a summary report that includes only a few of its parameters.

–a

    all   This option reports on all parameters.

–g

    generate   This option generates a report of the current settings in a format you can use as arguments to another **stty** command.

Arguments

The arguments to **stty** specify which terminal parameters **stty** is to alter. You can turn on each of the parameters that is preceded by an optional hyphen (indicated in the following list as [–]) by specifying the parameter without the hyphen. You can turn it off by specifying it with the hyphen. Unless specified otherwise, this section describes the parameters in their *on* states.

Special Keys and Characteristics

ek

    Set the erase and line kill keys to their default values: (DELETE) and (CONTROL)**-U**.

crt

    Set parameters appropriate for a crt (erase and kill wipe out the affected characters from the display).

erase **x**

    Set the erase key to **x**. To indicate a (CONTROL) character, precede the **x** with a caret and enclose both characters within single quotation marks (e.g., use '^H' for (CONTROL)**-H**). Use '^?' for (DELETE) and '^-' for undefined.

kill **x**

> Set the line kill key to **x**. See "erase," above, for conventions.

intr **x**

> Set the interrupt key to **x**. See "erase," above, for conventions.

sane

> Use this argument to set the terminal parameters to usually accept-
> able values. The **sane** argument is useful when several **stty** parame-
> ters have changed, making it difficult to use the terminal even to
> run **stty** to set things right. If **sane** does not appear to work, try
> entering (CONTROL)-**J** stty sane (CONTROL)-**J**.

size

> Display the size of the window (when run under a window system)
> in rows and columns.

werase **x**

> Set the word erase key to **x**. See "erase," above, for conventions.

Modes of Data Transmission

[–]raw

> The normal state is **–raw**. When the system reads input in its raw
> form, it does not interpret the following special characters: erase
> (usually (DELETE)), line kill (usually (CONTROL)-**U**), interrupt execution
> ((CONTROL)-**C**), and EOF ((CONTROL)-**D**). In addition, it does not use parity
> bits. With typical UNIX system humor, you can specify **–raw** as
> **cooked.**

[–]parenb

> Parity enable. When you specify **–parenb**, the system does not use
> or expect a parity bit when communicating with the terminal.

[–]parodd

> Select odd parity. (**–parodd** selects even parity.)

[–]cstopb

> Use two stop bits. (**–cstopb** specifies one stop bit.)

Treatment of Characters

[–]nl

> Only accept a (NEWLINE) character as a line terminator. With **–nl** in
> effect, the system accepts a (RETURN) character from the terminal as a
> (NEWLINE), while it sends a (RETURN) followed by a (LINEFEED) to the ter-
> minal in place of a (NEWLINE).

[–]echo

> Echo characters as they are typed (full duplex operation). If a terminal is half duplex and displays two characters for each one it should display, turn the echo parameter off (**–echo**).

[–]lcase

> For uppercase-only terminals, translate all uppercase characters into lowercase as they are entered. (Also [–]**LCASE**.)

[–]tabs

> Transmit each ⟨TAB⟩ character to the terminal as a ⟨TAB⟩ character. When **tabs** is turned off (**–tabs**), the system translates each ⟨TAB⟩ character into the appropriate number of ⟨SPACE⟩s and transmits these ⟨SPACE⟩s to the terminal. (Also [–]**tab3**.)
>
>   You can use the **tabs** utility to set the ⟨TAB⟩ stops on your terminal. By default, they occur every eight columns. Refer to the manuals that come with your system.

Data Line Specifications

[–]hup

> Disconnect telephone line when user logs out.

0

> Disconnect telephone line immediately.

110 300 600 1200 1800 2400
4800 9600 19200 38400

> Set the terminal baud rate to one of these numbers. The baud rate is set for you automatically as part of the login process; you should rarely, if ever, need to change it with **stty**.

Job Control Parameters

[–]tostop

> Stops background jobs if they attempt to send output to the terminal (**–tostop** allows background jobs to send output to the terminal).

Notes

The **stty** utility affects the terminal attached to its standard output. You can view or change the characteristics of a terminal other than the one you are using by redirecting the output from **stty**. Refer to the following command format.

    stty [**arguments**] > /dev/ttyxx

The **ttyxx** is the filename of the target terminal. You can change the characteristics of a terminal only if you own its device file or if you are the Superuser.

Examples

The first example shows **stty** without any arguments, displaying several terminal operation parameters. (Your system may display more or different parameters.) The character following the erase = is the erase key, and the one following kill = is the line kill key. The **stty** display always encloses these keys in single quotation marks. A ^ preceding a character indicates a (CONTROL) key. The example shows the erase key set to (CONTROL)-**H** and the line kill key set to (CONTROL)-**U**.

If **stty** does not display the erase character, it is set to its default, (DELETE) (on a Sun). If you do not see a kill character, it is set to its default, ^U (on a Sun).

```
$ stty
speed 1200 baud
erase = '^h'
-parenb -nl echo
```

Next, the **ek** argument returns the erase and line kill keys to their default values.

```
$ stty ek
```

The next display verifies the change. The **stty** utility does not display either the erase character or the line kill character, indicating that they are both set to their default values.

```
$ stty
speed 1200 baud
-parenb -nl echo
```

The next example sets the erase key to (CONTROL)-**H**. A ^ followed by an h represents the (CONTROL) character. You can enter either a lower- or uppercase letter.

```
$ stty erase '^h'
$ stty
speed 1200 baud
erase = '^H'
-parenb -nl echo
```

Below, **stty** sets the line kill key to (CONTROL)-**X**.

```
$ stty kill '^x'
$ stty
speed 1200 baud
erase = '^H'; kill = '^X'
-parenb -nl echo
```

Below, **stty** turns off (TAB)s so the appropriate number of (SPACE)s is sent to the terminal in place of a (TAB). Use this command if a terminal does not automatically expand (TAB)s.

```
$ stty -tabs
```

If you log in and everything that appears on the terminal is in uppercase letters, give the following command and then check the (CAPS LOCK) key. If it is set, turn it off.

```
$ STTY -LCASE
```

Turn on **lcase** if the terminal you are using cannot display lowercase characters.

tail

Display the last part (tail) of a file.

Format

tail [±[number]options] [file]

Summary

The **tail** utility displays the last part of a file. It takes its input from the file you specify on the command line or from its standard input.

Arguments

Without a **number** or **option**, **tail** displays the last ten lines of a file.

If a plus sign precedes the **option**, **tail** displays blocks, characters, or lines counting from the beginning of the file. If a hyphen precedes the **option**, **tail** counts from the end of the file. If a **number** precedes the **option**, that value is used in place of ten.

Options

Without any options, **tail** counts by lines. The options below must follow immediately after the **number** and not be preceded by a hyphen or a (SPACE). If **number** is omitted, **tail** uses a default value of ten.

b

blocks   This option causes **tail** to count by blocks.

c

characters   This option causes **tail** to count by characters.

l

lines   This option causes **tail** to count by lines (default).

f

follow   After copying the last line of the file, **tail** enters an endless loop. It waits and copies additional lines from the file if the file grows. This is useful for tracking the progress of a process that is running in the background and sending its output to a file. The **tail** utility continues to wait indefinitely, so you must use the interrupt key or **kill** command to terminate it.

r

reverse   Display lines in the reverse order.

Examples

The examples are based on the following **lines** file:

```
$ cat lines
line one
line two
line three
line four
line five
line six
line seven
line eight
line nine
line ten
line eleven
```

First, **tail** displays the last ten lines of the **lines** file (no options).

```
$ tail lines
line two
line three
line four
line five
line six
line seven
line eight
line nine
line ten
line eleven
```

The next example displays the last three lines (–3, no option) of the file.

```
$ tail -3 lines
line nine
line ten
line eleven
```

The example below displays the file, starting at line eight (+8, no option).

```
$ tail +8 lines
line eight
line nine
line ten
line eleven
```

The next example displays the last six characters in the file (–6c). Only five characters are evident (leven); the sixth is a (NEWLINE).

```
$ tail -6c lines
leven
```

The example below displays the last four lines in the file in reverse order (–4r).

```
$ tail -4r lines
line eleven
line ten
line nine
line eight
```

The final example demonstrates the –f option. Below, **tail** tracks the output of a **make** command, which is being sent to the file **accounts.out**.

```
$ make accounts > accounts.out &
$ tail -f accounts.out
        cc -c trans.c
        cc -c reports.c
  .
  .
(DELETE)
$
```

In the example above, using **tail** with –f has the same effect as running **make** in the foreground and letting its output go to the terminal; however, using **tail** has some advantages. First, the output of **make** is saved in a file. (The output would not be saved if you simply let it go to the terminal.) Also, if you decide to do something else while **make** is running and you do not have job control, you can kill **tail,** and the terminal will be free for you to use while **make** continues in the background. When you are running a large job, such as compiling a large program, you can use **tail** with the –f option to check on its progress periodically.

tar

Store or retrieve files from an archive file.

Format

tar key[options] [file-list]

Summary

The **tar** (tape archive) utility can create, add to, list, and retrieve files from an archive file. The archive file is often stored on tape.

Key

Use only one of the following keys to indicate what type of action you want **tar** to take. You can modify the action of the key by following it with one or more options. The key and options do not require a leading hyphen.

c

> **create**   **tar** creates a new tape, destroying any files that were previously written to the tape. This key implies the **r** key and, after creating a new tape, functions in the same way as **r**, writing the **file-list** to the tape.

r

> **write**   **tar** writes the **file-list** to the end of the tape. It leaves existing files intact.

t

> **table of contents**   With a **file-list**, **tar** displays the name of each of the files in the **file-list** each time it occurs on the tape. Without a **file-list**, **tar** displays the name of each of the files on the tape.

u

> **update**   The **tar** utility adds the files from the **file-list** if they are not already on the tape *or* if they have been modified since they were last written to the tape. Because of the checking it does, this option is slow.

x

> **extract**   **tar** reads the **file-list** from the tape. Without a **file-list**, it reads all the files from the tape. The **tar** utility attempts to keep the owner, modification time, and access privileges the same as the original file. If **tar** reads the same file more than once, the later versions of the file overwrite previous versions.

Options

You can specify one or more options following the key. The key and options do not require a leading hyphen.

0-8

> Use a number from 0 through 8 to indicate a drive other than the default, which is system-dependent (usually 8).

b

> **block** This option causes **tar** to use the next argument as a blocking factor for writing a tape. If you do not specify a blocking factor, **tar** assumes a blocking factor of 20. This option is effective only when you are writing to a raw device. The **tar** utility automatically determines the blocking factor when it reads a tape. Do not use this option if you will want to update the tape or if you are creating a disk file.

C

> This option causes **tar** to make the next argument the working directory. You can use the –C option several times on a command line, in front of different files in the **file-list**. This allows you to **tar** directories located in different parts of the filesystem hierarchy without using full pathnames. Refer to "Examples," below.

f

> **file** This option causes **tar** to write to or read from the next argument instead of the tape drive that the system is set up for **tar** to use. If you give a hyphen as an argument, **tar** uses the standard input or output.

h

> This option causes **tar** to follow symbolic links and to include the linked-to files as if they were normal files and directories.

l

> **links** This option causes **tar** to display messages if it cannot resolve all the links to files it is copying.

m

> **modification time** When you use this option, **tar** does not maintain the original modification times of files it is extracting. Instead, it sets the modification time to the time of extraction.

v

> **verbose** This option lists each file as **tar** reads or writes it. With the **t** key, this option causes **tar** to display additional information about each file.

w

> **wait**   This option asks you for confirmation before reading or writing each file. Respond with **y** if you want **tar** to take the action. Any other response causes **tar** not to take the action.

Arguments

If you use the **f** and/or **b** options, the first one or two arguments must correspond to the options you use. Following these arguments (if they are present) is the **file-list** that lists the filenames of the files you want to write out or read in.

You can use ambiguous file references when you write files but not when you read them.

The name of a directory file within the **file-list** references all files and subdirectories within that directory.

Notes

If you write a file using a simple filename, the file will appear in the working directory when you read it back. If you write a file using a relative pathname, it will appear with that relative pathname, starting from the working directory when you read it back. If you use an absolute pathname to write a file, **tar** reads it back in with the same pathname.

As you read and write files, **tar** attempts to preserve links between files. Unless you use the **l** option, **tar** does not inform you when it fails to maintain a link.

Examples

The following example makes a copy of the **/home/alex** directory, and all files and subdirectories within that directory, on the standard **tar** tape. The **v** option causes the command to list all the files it writes to the tape as it proceeds. This command erases anything that was already on the tape.

```
$ tar cv /home/alex
a /home/alex/letter 5 blocks
a /home/alex/memo 11 blocks
a /home/alex/notes 27 blocks
.
.
.
```

In the next example, the same directory is saved on the tape on device **/dev/rmt1** with a blocking factor of 10. Without the **v** option, **tar** does not display the list of files it is writing to tape. This command runs in the background and displays its only message after the shell issues a new prompt.

```
$ tar cbf 10 /dev/rmt1 /home/alex &
3452
$ blocking factor = 10
```

The next command displays the table of contents of the tape on device **/dev/rmt1**.

```
$ tar tvf /dev/rmt1
Tar: blocksize = 10
rw-rw-rw- 201/0    4720   Jul 25 6:59 1994 /home/alex/letter
rw-rw-rw- 201/0   10420   Jul 25 6:59 1994 /home/alex/memo
rw-rw-rw- 201/0   27471   Jul 25 6:59 1994 /home/alex/notes
 .
 .
```

In the next example, Alex creates a **tar** archive in a file, **/tmp/alex.tar**. This is a common way to bundle files together that you wish to transfer over a network or otherwise share with others.

```
$ tar cf /tmp/alex.tar literature
```

The next command checks the table of contents:

```
$ tar tvf /tmp/alex.tar
 .
 .
```

The way that **tar** reads arguments from the command line is different from most UNIX commands. The following two command lines are equivalent to those in the previous example:

```
$ tar fc /tmp/alex.tar literature
$ tar vft /tmp/alex.tar
```

The final example uses the –C option to change directories. The command below makes **/usr2** the working directory and copies all the files and subdirectories in the barbara directory to tape. Then it makes **/usr** the working directory and copies all the files and subdirectories in the **local** directory.

```
$ tar c -C /usr2 barbara -C /usr local
```

tee

Copy the standard input to the standard output and one or more files.

Format

tee [options] file-list

Summary

The **tee** utility copies its standard input to its standard output *and* to one or more files you specify on the command line.

Arguments

The **file-list** contains the pathnames of files that receive output from **tee**.

Options

Without any options, **tee** overwrites the output files if they exist and responds to interrupts.

–a

append   This option causes **tee** to append output to files (not overwrite them).

–i

ignore interrupts   With this option, **tee** does not respond to interrupts.

Example

In the following example, a pipe sends the output from **make** to **tee**, which copies it to its standard output and the file **accounts.out**. The copy that goes to its standard output appears on the screen. The **cat** utility displays the copy that was sent to the file.

```
$ make accounts | tee accounts.out
        cc -c trans.c
        cc -c reports.c
    .
    .
    .
$ cat accounts.out
        cc -c trans.c
        cc -c reports.c
    .
    .
    .
```

Refer to page 711 for a similar example that uses **tail –f** rather than **tee**.

telnet

Connect to a remote computer over a network.

Format

telnet **remote-computer**

Summary

The **telnet** utility uses a standard protocol, the Telnet Protocol, to connect to a remote system over a network. The **remote-computer** is the name or network address of the remote system. The **telnet** utility is commonly used to establish a login session on a remote system, provided you have an account on the remote system.

Arguments

If you specify a **remote-computer** on the command line, **telnet** will try to establish a connection to that system. If you do not specify the name of a remote computer, **telnet** will perform interactively, prompting you to enter one of the commands described below.

Description

You can put **telnet** into command mode after you are connected to a remote computer by typing an escape character. On UNIX systems, the escape character is usually (CONTROL)-]. When you connect to a remote system, it should report the escape character it recognizes. To leave command mode, type a (RETURN) on a line by itself.

In response to a telnet> prompt, you can use the following commands:

?

> **help**   Displays a list of commands recognized by the telnet utility on the local system.

close

> Closes the connection to the remote system. If you specified the name of a system on the command line when you started telnet, close has the same effect as quit—the **telnet** program will exit. If you used the open command instead of specifying a remote system on the command line, close will return telnet to command mode.

open **remote-computer**

> If you did not specify a remote system on the command line, or if the attempt to connect to the system failed, you can specify the name of a remote system interactively with the open command.

quit

>   Quits the **telnet** session.

z

>   If you were using the C Shell when you started **telnet**, you can sus-
>   pend your session with the remote system by using the z com-
>   mand. When you suspend a session, you will return to your login
>   shell on your local system. To resume your telnet session with the
>   remote system, type **fg** at a C Shell prompt.

Notes

Many computers, including non-UNIX systems, support the Telnet Protocol.
The **telnet** command is an implementation of this protocol for UNIX systems, allowing you to connect to many different types of systems. Although
you typically use **telnet** to log in, the remote computer may offer other services through **telnet**, such as access to special databases.

Examples

In the following example, the user connects to a remote system named
bravo. After running a few commands, the user escapes to command mode
and uses the z command to suspend the **telnet** session to be able to run a few
commands on the local system. The user gives the C Shell **fg** command to
resume using **telnet**. Finally, the C Shell **logout** command on the remote system ends the **telnet** session. A prompt from the local system appears.

```
kudos% telnet bravo
Trying 130.128.52.2 ...
Connected to bravo.
Escape character is '^]'.
SunOS UNIX (bravo)
login: watson
Password:
Last login: Wed Oct 6 22:07:20 from kudos
bravo%
   .
   .
bravo% (CONTROL)-]
telnet> z
kudos%
   .
   .
kudos% fg
bravo% logout
Connection closed by foreign host.
kudos%
```

test

Evaluate an expression.

Format

test **expression**
[**expression**]

Summary

The **test** command evaluates an expression and returns a condition code indicating that the expression is either true (= 0) or false (not = 0).

As the second format above shows, instead of using the word test when you use the **test** command, you can use square brackets around the expression ([]).

Arguments

The **expression** contains one or more criteria (see the following list) that **test** evaluates. A –a separating two criteria is a logical AND operator: Both criteria must be true for **test** to return a condition code of *true*. A –o is a logical OR operator. When –o separates two criteria, one or the other (or both) of the criteria must be true in order for **test** to return a condition code of *true*.

You can negate any criterion by preceding it with an exclamation point (!). You can group criteria with parentheses. If there are no parentheses, –a takes precedence over –o, and **test** evaluates operators of equal precedence from left to right.

Within the **expression**, you must quote special characters, such as parentheses, so that the shell does not interpret them but passes them on to **test**.

Because each element (such as a criterion, string, or variable) within the **expression** is a separate argument, you must separate each element from other elements with a (SPACE).

Following is a list of criteria you can use within the **expression**.

Criteria	Meaning
string	This criterion is true if **string** is not a null string.
–n **string**	This criterion is true if **string** has a length greater than zero.
–z **string**	This criterion is true if **string** has a length of zero.
string1 = **string2**	This criterion is true if **string1** is equal to **string2**.
string1 != **string2**	This criterion is true if **string1** is not equal to **string2**.
int1 relop int2	This criterion is true if integer **int1** has the specified algebraic relationship to integer **int2**. The **relop** is a relational operator from the list following this table.
–b **filename**	This criterion is true if the file named **filename** exists and is a block special file.

(Continued)

Criteria	Meaning
−c **filename**	This criterion is true if the file named **filename** exists and is a character special file.
−d **filename**	This criterion is true if the file named **filename** exists and is a directory.
−f **filename**	This criterion is true if the file named **filename** exists and is not a directory.
−g **filename**	This criterion is true if the file named **filename** exists and its set group ID bit is set.
−h **filename**	This criterion is true if the file named **filename** exists and is a symbolic link.
−k **filename**	This criterion is true if the file named **filename** exists and its sticky bit is set.
−p **filename**	This criterion is true if the file named **filename** exists and is a named pipe.
−r **filename**	This criterion is true if the file named **filename** exists and you have read access permission to it.
−s **filename**	This criterion is true if the file named **filename** exists and contains information (has a size greater than 0 bytes).
−t **file-descriptor**	This criterion is true if the open file with the file descriptor number **file-descriptor** is associated with a terminal. If you do not specify a **file-descriptor, test** assumes number 1 (standard output). The file-descriptor for standard input is 0, and for standard error it is 2.
−u **filename**	This criterion is true if the file named **filename** exists and its set user ID bit is set.
−w **filename**	This criterion is true if the file named **filename** exists and you have write access permission to it.
−x **filename**	This criterion is true if the file named **filename** exists and you have execute access permission to it.

Relop	Description
−gt	greater than
−ge	greater than or equal to
−eq	equal to
−ne	not equal to
−le	less than or equal to
−lt	less than

Note

The **test** command is built into the Bourne and Korn Shells.

Examples

The following examples show how to use the **test** utility in Bourne Shell scripts. Although **test** will work from a command line, it is more commonly used in shell scripts to test input or verify access to a file.

The first two examples show incomplete shell scripts. They are not complete because they do not test for upper- as well as lowercase input or inappropriate responses and do not acknowledge more than one response.

The first example prompts the user, reads a line of input into the user variable **user_input**, and uses **test** to see if the user variable **user_input** matches the quoted string yes. Refer to Chapter 10 for more information on variables, **read**, and If.

```
$ cat user_in
echo "Input yes or no: \c"
read user_input
if [ "$user_input" = yes ]
    then
          echo You input yes.
fi
```

The next example prompts the user for a filename and then uses **test** to see if the user has read access permission (–r) for the file *and* (–a) if the file contains information (–s).

```
$ cat validate
echo "Enter filename: \c"
read filename
if [ -r "$filename" -a -s "$filename" ]
    then
         echo File $filename exists and contains information.
         echo You have read access permission to the file.
fi
```

Without a number, the –t criterion assumes a value of 1 for the file descriptor and causes **test** to determine whether the process running **test** is sending output to a terminal. If it is, the **test** utility returns a value of *true* (0). Following is a listing of the shell script **term** that runs **test**.

```
$ cat term
test -t
echo "This program is (=0) or is not (=1)
sending its output to a terminal:" $?
```

First, **term** is run with the output going to the terminal; that is, the output is not redirected to a file. The **test** utility returns a 0. The shell stores this value in the shell variable that records the condition code of the last process, **$?**. The **echo** utility displays this value.

```
$ term
This program is (=0) or is not (=1)
sending its output to a terminal: 0
```

The next example runs **term** and redirects the output to a file. The contents of the file **temp** show that **test** returned a 1, indicating that its output was not going to a terminal.

```
$ term > temp
$ cat temp
This program is (=0) or is not (=1)
sending its output to a terminal: 1
```

touch

Update a file's modification time.

Format

touch [option] file-list

Summary

The **touch** utility updates the time a file was last accessed and the time it was last modified, setting it to the current time. This utility is frequently used with the **make** utility.

Arguments

The **file-list** contains the pathnames of the files **touch** is to update.

Options

When you do not specify the −c option, **touch** creates the file if it does not exist.

−c

no create   Do not create the file if it does not already exist.

Examples

The following examples demonstrate how **touch** functions. The first commands show **touch** updating an existing file. The **ls** utility with the –l option displays the modification time of the file. The last three command lines show **touch** creating a file.

```
$ ls -l program.c
-rw-r--r-- 1 jenny 136  Jul  25 16:48 program.c
$ touch program.c
$ ls -l program.c
-rw-r--r-- 1 jenny 136  Nov   7 16:33 program.c
$ ls -l read.c
read.c not found
$ touch read.c
$ ls -l read.c
-rw-r--r-- 1 jenny   0  Nov   7 16:35 read.c
```

tr

Replace specified characters.

Format

tr [option] [string1 [string2]]

Summary

The **tr** utility reads its standard input and translates each character in **string1** to the corresponding character in **string2**.

Arguments

The **tr** utility is typically used with two arguments, **string1** and **string2**. The position of each character in the two strings is important; **tr** replaces each character from **string1** with the corresponding character in **string2**.

With one argument, **string1**, and an option (see below), **tr** can be used to delete the characters specified in **string1**.

With no arguments, **tr** simply copies its standard input to its standard output.

Options

–d

> **delete**   This option causes **tr** to delete characters that match those specified in **string1**.

–s

> **squeeze**   This option causes **tr** to reduce sequences of multiple identical characters in **string2** to single occurrences.

Examples

You can specify a range of characters by hyphenating them and enclosing them in square brackets. The two command lines in the following example produce the same result.

```
$ echo abcdef | tr 'abcdef' 'xyzabc'
xyzabc
$ echo abcdef | tr '[a-c][d-f]' '[x-z][a-c]'
xyzabc
```

The next example demonstrates a popular method for disguising text, often called "rotate 13" (because it replaces the first letter of the alphabet with the 13th, the second with the 14th, and so forth).

```
$ echo The punchline of the joke is ... |
> tr '[A-M][N-Z][a-m][n-z]' '[N-Z][A-M][n-z][a-m]'
Gur chapuyvar bs gur wbxr vf ...
```

To make the text intelligible again, reverse the order of the arguments to **tr**.

```
$ echo Gur chapuyvar bs gur wbxr vf ... |
> tr '[N-Z][A-M][n-z][a-m]' '[A-M][N-Z][a-m][n-z]'
The punchline of the joke is ...
```

The **–d** option causes **tr** to delete selected characters.

```
$ echo If you can read this, you can spot the missing vowels! |
> tr -d 'aeiou'
If y cn rd ths, y cn spt th mssng vwls!
```

In the following example **tr** is used to replace characters and reduce pairs of identical characters to single characters.

```
$ echo tennessee | tr -s 'tnse' 'srne'
serene
```

tty

Display the terminal pathname.

Format

tty [option]

Summary

The **tty** utility displays the pathname of its standard input file if it is a terminal. The exit status of **tty** is 0 if the standard input file is a terminal, and 1 if it is not.

Arguments

There are no arguments.

Options

−s

> **silent**   This option causes **tty** not to print anything. The exit status of **tty** is still set, however.

Notes

If its standard input is not a terminal, **tty** displays the message not a tty.

Example

The following example illustrates the use of **tty**.

```
$ tty
/dev/tty11
$ echo $?
0
$ tty < memo
not a tty
$ echo $?
1
```

umask

umask

Establish file-creation permissions mask.

Format

umask [**mask**]

Summary

The **umask** command specifies a mask that the system uses to set up access permissions when you create a file.

Arguments

The **mask** is a three-digit octal number, with each digit corresponding to permissions for the owner of the file, members of the group the file is associated with, and everyone else. When you create a file, the system subtracts these numbers from the numbers corresponding to the access permissions the system would otherwise assign to the file. The result is three octal numbers that specify the access permissions for the file. (Refer to the **chmod** utility in Part II for a complete description and examples of these numbers.)

Without any arguments, **umask** displays the file-creation permissions mask.

Notes

The **umask** command generally appears in a **.profile** or **.login** file. The **umask** command is built into the Bourne, C, and Korn Shells.

Example

The following command sets the file-creation permissions mask to **066**. The command has the effect of removing read and write permission for members of the group the file is associated with and everyone else. It leaves the owner's permissions as the system specifies. If the system would otherwise create a file with a permission value of **777** (read, write, and execute access for owner, group, and everyone else), it will now create the file with **711** (all permissions for the owner and only execute permission for group and everyone else).

```
$ umask 066
```

uniq

Display lines of a file that are unique.

Format

uniq [options] [–fields] [+characters] [input-file] [output-file]

uniq

Summary

The **uniq** utility displays a file, removing all but one copy of successive re-peated lines. If the file has been sorted (refer to the **sort** utility), **uniq** ensures that no two lines that it displays are the same.

The **uniq** utility takes its input from a file you specify on the command line or from its standard input. Unless you specify the output file on the command line, **uniq** sends its output to its standard output.

Arguments

In the following description, a *field* is any sequence of characters not con-taining white space (any combination of (SPACE)s and (TAB)s). Fields are bounded by white space or the beginning or end of a line.

The **–fields** is a number preceded by a hyphen and causes **uniq** to ignore the first specified number of blank-separated fields of each line. When you use this argument, **uniq** bases its comparison on the remainder of the line.

The **+characters** is a number preceded by a plus sign and causes **uniq** to ignore the first specified number of characters of each line. If you also use **–fields**, **uniq** ignores the number of characters you specify after the end of the last field that it ignores. The **+characters** does *not* ignore blanks follow-ing the last ignored field. You must take these blanks into account when you specify the number of characters to ignore.

You can specify the **input-file** on the command line. If you do not spec-ify it, **uniq** uses its standard input.

You can specify the **output-file** on the command line. If you do not specify it, **uniq** uses its standard output.

Options

–c

> **count** This option causes **uniq** to precede each line with the num-ber of occurrences of the line in the input file.

–d

> **duplicate lines** This option causes **uniq** to display only lines that are repeated.

–u

> **unique lines** This option causes **uniq** to display only lines that are *not* repeated.

Examples

These examples assume the file named **test** in the working directory contains the following text.

```
$ cat test
boy took bat home
boy took bat home
girl took bat home
dog brought hat home
dog brought hat home
dog brought hat home
```

Without any options, **uniq** removes all but one copy of successive repeated lines.

```
$ uniq test
boy took bat home
girl took bat home
dog brought hat home
```

The –**c** option displays the number of consecutive occurrences of each line in the file.

```
$ uniq -c test
      2 boy took bat home
      1 girl took bat home
      3 dog brought hat home
```

The –**d** option displays only lines that are consecutively repeated in the file.

```
$ uniq -d test
boy took bat home
dog brought hat home
```

The –**u** option displays only lines that are *not* consecutively repeated in the file.

```
$ uniq -u test
girl took bat home
```

Below, the –**fields** argument (–1) skips the first field in each line, causing the lines that begin with boy and the one that begins with girl to appear to be consecutive repeated lines. The **uniq** utility displays only one occurrence of these lines.

```
$ uniq -1 test
boy took bat home
dog brought hat home
```

The final example uses both the –**fields** and +**characters** arguments (–2 and +2) to first skip two fields and then skip two characters. The two characters this command skips include the (SPACE) that separates the second and third fields and the first character of the third field. Ignoring these characters, all the lines appear to be consecutive repeated lines containing the string at home. The **uniq** utility displays only the first of these lines.

```
$ uniq -2 +2 test
boy took bat home
```

W

Displays information on system users.

Format

w [option] [login-name]

Summary

The **w** utility displays the names of users who are currently logged in, together with their terminal device numbers, the times they logged in, which commands they are running, and other information.

Options

–s

> **short** This option causes **w** to display less information—user name, terminal device, idle time, and the command names only.

Arguments

If a **login-name** is supplied as an argument to the **w** utility, the display is restricted to information about that user only.

Description

The first line that the **w** utility displays is the same as that provided by the **uptime** command. This report includes the current time of day, how long the computer has been running (in days, hours, and minutes), how many users are logged in, and how busy the system is (load average). From left to right, the load averages indicate the number of processes that have been waiting to run in the past minute, 5 minutes, and 15 minutes.

The format of the information that **w** displays for each user is shown below.

> **name line time activity cpu1 cpu2 command**

The **name** is the login name of the user. The **line** is the device name for the line on which the user is logged in. The **time** is the date and time the user logged in. The **activity** column indicates how long the person has been idle (how many minutes have elapsed since the last key was pressed on the keyboard). The next two columns, **cpu1** and **cpu2**, give measures of how much computer processor time the person has used during the current login session and on the tasks that are currently running. The **command** column displays what command that person is currently running.

Notes

If a user is running several processes on the same terminal, the **w** utility tries to determine which one is the current (foreground) process; sometimes it does not get the answer right.

Examples

The first example shows the full list produced by the **w** utility.

```
$ w
 9:19am  up 15 days, 12:24,  4 users,  load average: 0.15, 0.03, 0.01
User     tty         login@  idle   JCPU   PCPU  what
hls      ttyp0       8:34am     1     11      1  vi .profile
scott    tty02    Tue 3pm 23:48     16      1  -sh
jenny    tty03       9:07am                      w
alex     tty06       9:15am                      telnet bravo
```

The next example shows the use of the –s option to produce an abbreviated listing.

```
$ w -s
 9:20am  up 15 days, 12:25,  4 users,  load average: 0.15, 0.03, 0.01
User     tty   idle  what
hls      p0       2  vi
scott    02   23:49  -sh
jenny    03          w
alex     06          telnet
```

In the final example, only information about Alex is requested.

```
$ w alex
 9:21am  up 15 days, 12:26,  4 users,  load average: 0.15, 0.03, 0.01
User     tty         login@  idle   JCPU   PCPU  what
alex     tty06       9:15am                      telnet bravo
```

WC

Display the number of lines, words, and characters in a file.

Format

wc [options] file-list

Summary

The **wc** utility displays the number of lines, words, and characters contained in one or more files. If you specify more than one file on the command line, **wc** displays totals for each file and totals for the group of files.

The **wc** utility takes its input from files you specify on the command line or from its standard input.

Arguments

The **file-list** contains the pathnames of one or more files that **wc** analyzes.

Options

–c

characters   This option causes **wc** to display only the number of characters in the file.

–l

lines   This option causes **wc** to display only the number of lines (that is, (NEWLINE) characters) in the file.

–w

words   This option causes **wc** to display only the number of words in the file.

Notes

A word is a sequence of characters bounded by (SPACE)s, (TAB)s, (NEWLINE)s, or a combination of these.

Examples

The following command line displays an analysis of the file named **memo**. The numbers represent the number of lines, words, and characters in the file.

```
$ wc memo
      5       31      146 memo
```

The next command displays the number of lines and words in three files. The line at the bottom, with the word total in the right column, contains the sum of each column.

```
$ wc -lw memo1 memo2 memo3
     10       62 memo1
     12       74 memo2
     12       68 memo3
     34      204 total
```

who

Display names of users.

Format

who [am i]

Summary

The **who** utility displays the names of users currently logged in, together with their terminal device numbers, and the times they logged in.

Arguments

When given the two arguments **am i**, **who** displays the login name of the user who is logged in at the terminal the command is given on, the terminal device number, and the time the user logged in.

Notes

Two utilities, **w** and **finger** utility provide information similar to the information **who** provides. The **w** utility displays a summary of current activity on the system including information about what each user is doing. By default, the **finger** utility displays information about each user currently logged in, including the user's login name, full name, terminal name, how long the terminal has been idle, and the time the user logged in. The **finger** utility can also be used over a network to display information about users on a remote system. See **finger**, page 606 and **w**, page 729.

Examples

The following examples demonstrate the use of the **who** utility.

```
$ who
jenny       tty01    Jul 25 11:01
alex        tty11    Jul 25 18:11

$ who am i
alex        tty11    Jul 25 18:11
```

write

Send a message to another user.

Format

write **destination-user** [**tty-name**]

Summary

You and another user can use **write** to establish two-way communication. Both of you must execute the **write** utility, each specifying the other user's login name as the **destination-user**. The **write** utility then copies text, on a line-by-line basis, from each terminal to the other.

When you execute the **write** utility, a message appears on the **destination-user**'s terminal indicating that you are about to transmit a message.

When you want to stop communicating with the other user, press (CONTROL)-**D** once at the start of a line to return to the shell. The other user must do the same.

Arguments

The **destination-user** is the login name of the user you are sending a message to. The **tty-name** can be used as a second argument, after the user name, to resolve ambiguities if the **destination-user** is logged in on more than one terminal.

Notes

It may be helpful to set up a protocol for carrying on communication when you use **write**. Try ending each message with **o** for "over" and ending the transmission with **oo** for "over and out." This gives each user time to think and enter a complete message without the other user wondering whether the first user is finished.

While you are using **write**, any line beginning with an exclamation point causes **write** to pass the line, without the exclamation point, to the shell for execution. The other user does not see the command line or the shell output.

Each user controls permission to write to his or her own terminal. Refer to the **mesg** utility.

Another utility, **talk**, allows you to have a two-way conversation with another user if you both have display terminals. The **talk** utility divides the users' screens into two windows and displays the statements of the two users in different windows on both screens. Both users can type simultaneously. Users generally find it easier to hold a conversation with **talk** than with **write**. The **talk** utility (page 42) can also be used to communicate with a user on a remote system over a network.

Example

Refer to page 44 for a tutorial example of **write**.

APPENDIX A

Regular Expressions

A regular expression defines a set of one or more strings of characters. Several of the UNIX utilities, including **ed**, **vi**, **emacs**, **grep**, **awk**, and **sed**, use regular expressions to search for and replace strings. A simple string of characters is a regular expression that defines one string of characters: itself. A more complex regular expression uses letters, numbers, and special characters to define many different strings of characters. A regular expression is said to match any string it defines.

This appendix describes the regular expressions used by **ed**, **vi**, **emacs**, **grep**, **awk**, and **sed**. The regular expressions used in ambiguous file references with the shell are somewhat different. They are described in Chapter 5.

735

Characters

As used in this appendix, a *character* is any character *except* a (NEWLINE). Most characters represent themselves within a regular expression. A *special character* is one that does not represent itself. If you need to use a special character to represent itself, see "Quoting Special Characters," page 738.

Delimiters

A character, called a *delimiter*, usually marks the beginning and end of a regular expression. The delimiter is always a special character for the regular expression it delimits (that is, it does not represent itself but marks the beginning and end of the expression). You can use any character as a delimiter, as long as you use the same character at both ends of the regular expression. For simplicity, all the regular expressions in this appendix use a forward slash as a delimiter. In some unambiguous cases, the second delimiter is not required. For example, you can sometimes omit the second delimiter when it would be followed immediately by (RETURN). Delimiters are not used with any of the **grep** family of utilities (**grep**, **egrep**, and **fgrep**).

Simple Strings

The most basic regular expression is a simple string that contains no special characters except the delimiters. A simple string matches only itself.

In the following examples, the strings that are matched **look like this**.

Regular Expression	Matches	Examples
/ring/	**ring**	**ring**, sp**ring**, **ring**ing, st**ring**ing
/Thursday/	**Thursday**	**Thursday**, **Thursday**'s
/or not/	**or not**	**or not**, po**or not**hing

Special Characters

You can use special characters within a regular expression to cause it to match more than one string.

Period

A period (**.**) matches any character.

Regular Expression	Matches	Examples
/ .alk/	all strings that contain a (SPACE) followed by any character followed by **alk**	will**_talk**, may**_balk**
/.ing/	all strings with any character preceding **ing**	**sing**ing, **ping**, before**_ing**lenook

Square Brackets

Square brackets ([]) define a *character class* that matches any single character within the brackets. If the first character following the left square bracket is a caret (^), the square brackets define a character class that matches any single character not within the brackets. You can use a hyphen to indicate a range of characters. Within a character class definition, backslashes, asterisks, and dollar signs (all described in the following sections) lose their special meanings. A right square bracket (appearing as a member of the character class) can appear only as the first character following the left square bracket, and a caret is special only if it is the first character following the left bracket.

Regular Expression	Matches	Examples
/[bB]ill/	member of the character class **b** and **B** followed by **ill**	**bill**, **Bill**, **bill**ed
/t[aeiou].k/	**t** followed by a lowercase vowel, any character, and a **k**	**talk**ative, **stink**, **teak**, **tank**er
/number [6–9]/	**number** followed by a (SPACE) and a member of the character class **6** through **9**	**number 60**, **number 8**:, get **number 9**
/[^a–zA–Z]/	any character that is not a letter	**1**, **7**, **@**, **.**, **}**, Stop**!**

Asterisk

An asterisk can follow a regular expression that represents a single character. The asterisk represents *zero* or more occurrences of a match of the regular expression. An asterisk following a period matches any string of characters. (A period matches any character, and an asterisk matches zero or more occurrences of the preceding regular expression.) A character class definition followed by an asterisk matches any string of characters that are members of the character class.

A regular expression that includes a special character always matches the longest possible string, starting as far toward the beginning (left) of the line as possible.

Regular Expression	Matches	Examples
/ab*c/	**a** followed by zero or more **b**'s followed by a **c**	**ac**, **abc**, **abbc**, debbca**abbbc**
/ab.*c/	**ab** followed by zero or more other characters followed by **c**	**abc**, **abxc**, **ab45c**, x**ab 756.345 x** cat
/t.*ing/	**t** followed by zero or more characters followed by **ing**	**thing**, **ting**, I **thought of going**
/[a–zA–Z]*/	a string composed only of letters and (SPACE)s	1.**_any string without numbers or punctuation**!

(Continued)

Regular Expression	Matches	Examples
/(.*)/	as long a string as possible between (and)	Get **(this) and (that)**;
/([^)]*)/	the shortest string possible that starts with (and ends with)	**(this)**, Get **(this and that)**

Caret and Dollar Sign

A regular expression that begins with a caret (^) can match a string only at the beginning of a line. In a similar manner, a dollar sign at the end of a regular expression matches the end of a line.

Regular Expression	Matches	Examples
/^T/	a **T** at the beginning of a line	**T**his line..., **T**hat Time..., In Time
/^+[0–9]/	a plus sign followed by a number at the beginning of a line	**+5** +45.72, **+7**59 Keep this...
/:$/	a colon that ends a line	...below**:**

Quoting Special Characters

You can quote any special character (but not a digit or a parenthesis) by preceding it with a backslash. Quoting a special character makes it represent itself.

Regular Expression	Matches	Examples
/end\./	all strings that contain **end** followed by a period	The **end.**, s**end.**, pret**end.**mail
/ \\/	a single backslash	****
/ */	an asterisk	*****.c, an asterisk (*****)
/ \[5\]/	**[5]**	it was five **[5]**
/and \/or/	**and/or**	**and/or**

Rules

The following rules govern the application of regular expressions.

Longest Match Possible

As stated previously, a regular expression always matches the longest possible string, starting as far toward the beginning of the line as possible. For example, given the following string:

```
    This (rug) is not what it once was (a long time ago), is
it?
```

The expression /Th.*is/ matches:

This (rug) is not what it once was (a long time ago), is

and /(.*)/ matches:

(rug) is not what it once was (a long time ago)

however, /([^)]*)/ matches:

(rug)

Given the following string:

singing songs, singing more and more

The expression /s.*ing/ matches:

singing songs, singing

and /s.*ing song/ matches:

singing song

Empty Regular Expressions

An empty regular expression always represents the last regular expression that you used. For example, if you give **vi** the following Substitute command:

:s/mike/robert/

and then you want to make the same substitution again, you can use the following command:

:s//robert/

Alternatively, you can use the following commands to search for the string mike and then make the substitution:

/mike/
:s//robert/

The empty regular expression (//) represents the last regular expression you used (/mike/).

Bracketing Expressions

You can use quoted parentheses, \(and \), to *bracket* a regular expression. The string that the bracketed regular expression matches can subsequently be used, as explained in "Quoted Digits" below. A regular expression does not attempt to match quoted parentheses. Thus, a regular expression enclosed within quoted parentheses matches what the same regular expression without the parentheses would match. The expression /\(rexp\)/ matches what /rexp/ would match and /a\(bj\)c/ matches what /abjc/ would match.

You can nest quoted parentheses. The bracketed expressions are identified only by the opening \(, so there is no ambiguity in identifying them. The expression /\([a-z]\([A-Z]j\)x\)/ consists of two bracketed expressions, one within the other and matches 3 t dMNORx7] u.

The Replacement String

The **vi** and **sed** editors use regular expressions as Search Strings within Substitute commands. You can use two special characters, ampersands (&) and quoted digits (\n), to represent the matched strings within the corresponding Replacement String.

Ampersand

Within a Replacement String, an ampersand (&) takes on the value of the string that the Search String (regular expression) matched. For example, the following **vi** Substitute command surrounds a string of one or more numbers with **NN**. The ampersand in the Replacement String matches whatever string of numbers the regular expression (Search String) matched.

        :s/[0-9][0-9]*/NN&NN/

Two character class definitions are required because the regular expression [0–9]* matches *zero* or more occurrences of a digit, and *any* character string is zero or more occurrences of a digit.

Quoted Digit

Within the regular expression itself, a quoted digit (\n) takes on the value of the string that the bracketed regular expression beginning with the *n*th \(matched.

Within a Replacement String, a quoted digit represents the string that the bracketed regular expression (portion of the Search String) beginning with the *n*th \(matched.

For example, you can take a list of people in the form

        last-name, first-name initial

and put it in the following form:

        first-name initial last-name

with the following **vi** command:

        :1,$s/\([^,]*\), \(.*\)/\2 \1/

This command addresses all the lines in the file (**1,$**). The Substitute command (**s**) uses a Search String and a Replacement String delimited by forward slashes. The first bracketed regular expression within the Search String, \([^,]*\), matches what the same unbracketed regular expression, [^,]*, would match. This regular expression matches a string of zero or more characters not containing a comma (the **last-name**). Following the first bracketed regular expression are a comma and a (SPACE) that match themselves. The second bracketed expression \(.*\) matches any string of characters (the **first-name** and **initial**).

The Replacement String consists of what the second bracketed regular expression matched (\2) followed by a (SPACE) and what the first bracketed regular expression matched (\1).

Full Regular Expressions

The **egrep** (a variant of **grep**) and **awk** utilities provide all the special characters that are included in ordinary regular expressions, except for \(and \), as well as several others. Patterns using the extended set of special characters are called *full regular expressions*.

Two of the additional special characters are the plus sign (+) and question mark (?). They are similar to the *, which matches *zero* or more occurrences of the previous character. The plus sign matches *one* or more occurrences of the previous character, whereas the question mark matches *zero* or *one* occurrence. You can use all three of these special characters *, +, and ? with parentheses, causing the special character to apply to the string surrounded by the parentheses. Unlike the parentheses in bracketed regular expressions, these parentheses are not quoted.

Regular Expression	Matches	Examples
/ab+c/	<u>a</u> followed by one or more <u>b</u>'s followed by a <u>c</u>	y<u>abc</u>w, <u>abbc</u>57
/ab?c/	<u>a</u> followed by zero or one <u>b</u> followed by <u>c</u>	b<u>ac</u>k, <u>abc</u>def
/(ab)+c/	one or more occurrences of the string <u>ab</u> followed by <u>c</u>	z<u>abc</u>d, <u>ababc</u>!
/(ab)?c/	zero or one occurrences of the string <u>ab</u> followed by <u>c</u>	x<u>c</u>, <u>abc</u>c

In full regular expressions, the pipe (|) special character acts as an OR operator. A pipe between two regular expressions causes a match with strings that match either the first expression or the second or both. You can use the pipe with parentheses to separate from the rest of the regular expression the two expressions that are being ORed.

Regular Expression	Meaning	Examples
/ab|ac/	either <u>ab</u> or <u>ac</u>	<u>ab</u>, <u>ac</u>, <u>ab</u>ac
/^Exit|^Quit/	lines that begin with <u>Exit</u> or <u>Quit</u>	<u>Exit</u>, <u>Quit</u>, No Exit
/(D|N)\. Jones/	<u>D. Jones</u> or <u>N. Jones</u>	P.<u>D. Jones</u>, <u>N. Jones</u>

SUMMARY

A regular expression defines a set of one or more strings of characters. A regular expression is said to match any string it defines.

The following characters are special within a regular expression.

Special Character	Function
.	Matches any single character
[xyz]	Defines a character class that matches **x**, **y**, or **z**
[^xyz]	Defines a character class that matches any character except **x**, **y**, or **z**
[x–z]	Defines a character class that matches any character **x** through **z** inclusive
*	Matches zero or more occurrences of a match of the preceding character
^	Forces a match to the beginning of a line
$	A match to the end of a line
\	Used to quote special characters
\(xyz\)	Matches what **xyz** matches (a bracketed regular expression)
\<	Forces a match to the beginning of a word
\>	Forces a match to the end of a word

In addition to the above special characters (excluding quoted parentheses), the following characters are special within full regular expressions.

Special Character	Function
+	Matches one or more occurrences of the preceding character
?	Matches zero or one occurrence of the preceding character
(xyz)+	One or more occurrences of what <u>xyz</u> matches
(xyz)?	Zero or one occurrence of what <u>xyz</u> matches
(xyz)*	Zero or more occurrences of what <u>xyz</u> matches
xyz|abc	Either what <u>xyz</u> or what <u>abc</u> matches
(xy|ab)c	Either what <u>xyc</u> or what <u>abc</u> matches

The **vi** utility recognizes the following special characters as well as all the special characters recognized by ordinary regular expressions. Refer to page 194 for a description of regular expressions in **vi**.

The following characters are special within a Replacement String in **sed**, **vi**, and **ed**.

Character	Function
&	Represents what the regular expression (Search String) matched
\n	A quoted number, **n**, represents the *n*th bracketed regular expression in the Search String

APPENDIX B

DEC Ultrix

When the UNIX system was created at Bell Laboratories to run on a PDP-7 system from the Digital Equipment Corporation (DEC), the hardware was less powerful and less complicated than today's average personal computer. By the time the BSD system was available to run on DEC's VAX computers in the early 1980s, it was already becoming difficult for a small group of systems programmers to support the many models and special hardware devices that were available. Systems programmers who work for a manufacturer have some advantages. Not only do they have earlier access to the computer hardware, they also have access to the hardware designers and specifications that may not be released to the public.

743

Background

Most of DEC's customers ran DEC's proprietary operating system, VMS, on their VAX systems. A significant fraction of the systems DEC sold, however, were purchased to run UNIX software from Berkeley or AT&T. By the mid-1980's, DEC decided to market their own version of the UNIX system, Ultrix, based on BSD 4.2. Ultrix offered some advantages over the basic 4.2 BSD system available from Berkeley. One of the biggest advantages was DEC's support for a broader range of their computer systems and peripherals, but a disadvantage was a lack of support for add-on hardware from other vendors. Another major advantage was DEC's support for the Network File System (NFS) and Network Information Service (NIS), allowing Ultrix systems to interoperate readily with computers from Sun Microsystems and other vendors who supported those network services.

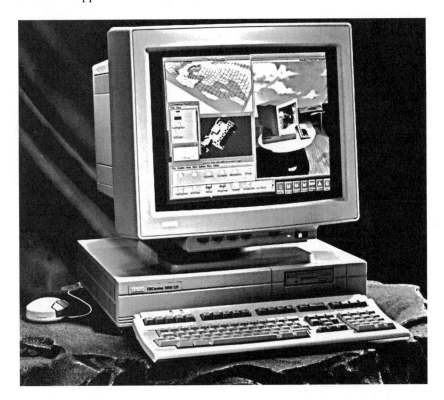

Figure B-1   DECstation 5000 Series 100 Workstation

In addition to making Ultrix systems compatible with other UNIX systems, DEC extended their version of UNIX to support other protocols (such as DECnet) and programming languages (Modula-2), and to make it easier for UNIX systems to interoperate with VMS systems. Over the years, DEC has added features from later versions of Berkeley UNIX (4.3), and moved toward compliance with standards such as POSIX, OSF/1, and ANSI C. Current releases of Ultrix are also System V compliant. Today, Ultrix runs on two of the three major hardware platforms available from DEC (VAX and Mips). DEC is moving away from Ultrix, however; their newest and most powerful hardware architecture, Alpha, runs a version of the Open Software Foundation's standard OSF/1 operating system.

Logging In

Most UNIX systems do not impose an arbitrary limit on how many users can log into the system at one time. With Ultrix, DEC chose to sell licenses that restrict access to the system. The least expensive license allows only two users on the system at one time; the most expensive license allows an unlimited number of users. The number of users does not correspond to the number of unique login names. With a two-user license, if one user logs into the system twice (from two different windows, for example), no one else will be able to access the system.

If you see the following message when you try to log in, you are being blocked by this limit.

```
Too many users logged on already.
Try again later.
```

Contact your system administrator for help with this problem.

User Utilities

If your search path includes the directories **/bin**, **/usr/bin**, and **/usr/ucb**, you will find the utilities that are described in this book, including **vi** and the Bourne, C, and Korn Shells. The tools should behave as they have been described in this text, but you may encounter occasional differences (such as missing or additional options). You may find other useful tools, such as a version of GNU **emacs**, in the directories **/usr/new** and **/usr/local/bin**. While DEC provides the software in the these directories, they do not offer support for it.

Ultrix includes two versions of the Bourne Shell, **sh** and **sh5**. The **sh** utility is an older version of the shell, whereas **sh5** includes enhancements that were introduced in later versions of System V (such as shell functions).

Graphical User Interface

The DECwindows package is DEC's enhanced Motif-based window manager, **dxwm**. By default, a DEC workstation is set up to run **dxwm**, which includes a menu bar at the top of the screen. If you choose the Applications item, you will see a menu that lists the most popular tools. Use the DECterm item to open another terminal emulator window (**dxwm** *may* open one for you automatically when it starts up). You will find windowing applications that have been customized by DEC in the **/usr/bin** directory; by convention, the first two characters of each of their names are dx. DEC's terminal emulator, for example, is named **dxterm** (the names on the Applications menu need not correspond to the filename for the actual program).

In addition to the customized applications provided by DEC in **/usr/bin**, the standard X11 applications are available in **/usr/bin/X11** (including the standard Motif window manager, **mwm**).

Programming Tools

On the VAX architecture the standard Ultrix C compiler, **cc**, supports the old version of the C language that is commonly referred to as "K & R C" (Kernighan and Ritchie C, named for the authors of the definitive book on the language). In the 1980s, a committee of the American National Standards Institute (ANSI) standardized an extended version of the language that is commonly referred to as ANSI C. Most UNIX C compilers support ANSI C today, often providing options to relax some of the stricter features of the language or to offer compatibility with old K & R C programs. On the MIPS architecture **cc** provides full ANSI C support. On the VAX architecture you must use the **vcc** compiler if you want full ANSI C support.

Compilers for other programming languages are also available from DEC, though they may not be available on every system (some are add-on packages). These include compilers for Lisp, Pascal, Fortran, and Modula-2.

Both the SCCS and RCS source code control systems are available on Ultrix systems, though RCS is not supported. If RCS has been installed on your system, you will find the tools in **/usr/new**.

System Administration

DEC provides many specialized tools to help system administrators install and configure software. The **setld** utility is used to install, inventory, and remove DEC software packages. Utilities exist to help configure complex packages such as NFS (**nfssetup**) and NIS (**ypsetup**). While these utilities are helpful, it is important to understand the underlying concepts and at least some of the details involved in configuring these subsystems, as the setup utilities are not designed to anticipate and cope with unusual or complicated environments.

One of the most visible differences for a system administrator on an Ultrix system is that system messages do not appear in plain text format in the usual place in /usr/adm (**messages** or **syslog** files). Instead, system messages are recorded in a special format in the directory **/usr/adm/syserr**, in a file named **syserr.**_hostname_, where _hostname_ is the hostname of your machine. To examine the contents of this file, you must use the Ultrix error report formatter, **uerf**.

For detailed information on configuring and administering your Ultrix system, refer to the manuals supplied with your system.

APPENDIX C

The POSIX Standards

The existence of different versions of the UNIX system has been a very fruitful source of creative and innovative software. However, it has also been a persistent source of frustration for users and programmers. Users who moved between different versions of the system (e.g., BSD and System V) would discover that commands that worked on one system did not work, or worked differently, on the other. Programmers found a similar phenomenon: programs that worked on one system would behave differently, or even fail to compile, on the other. In 1984 the users' group /usr/group (which is now called UniForum) started an effort to specify a "standard UNIX." This effort has expanded beyond the wildest dreams of its initiators as the POSIX series of standards.

Background

POSIX is the name for a collection of software standards, based on but not limited to the UNIX system. (POSIX is almost an acronym for Portable Operating System Interface.) The standards are developed by working groups of the Institute for Electrical and Electronics Engineering (IEEE); participation in these groups is open to everyone. For this and other reasons the POSIX standards are referred to as Open Systems Standards.

The explicit goal of the POSIX effort is to promote application portability. Thus the standards specify both program and user interfaces but not implementations. At this writing there are 7 adopted POSIX standards (see the table at the bottom of this page) and over 20 draft standards and profiles under development.

POSIX.1

POSIX.1 is the original POSIX standard. It was adopted in 1988 and revised in 1990. POSIX.1 is a C language programming interface standard. It specifies the syntax and semantics of 203 C language functions and the contents of various data structures. It also specifies the abstract structure of the filesystem. For example, a system that conforms to POSIX.1 must have a hierarchical filesystem with directories, FIFO files, and regular files. Each file must have attributes typical of UNIX system files, such as permission bits, owner and group IDs, and link counts. The programming interfaces refer to filenames using familiar UNIX-style pathnames such as **/home/alex/src/load.c.**

Adopted POSIX Standards	
Name	**Description**
POSIX.1	Base system interfaces for C programs. Adopted 1988, revised 1990.
POSIX.2	Shell and Utilities, including interactive utilities and a few C interfaces. Adopted 1992.
POSIX.3	Test methods for measuring conformance to POSIX. Adopted 1991.
POSIX.3.1	Test methods (assertions) for measuring conformance to POSIX.1. Adopted 1993.
POSIX.4	Real time extensions to POSIX.1. Adopted 1993.
POSIX.5	Ada language binding to POSIX.1. Describes the same functionality as POSIX.1, accessible from Ada programs. Adopted 1992.
POSIX.9	FORTRAN 77 language binding to POSIX.1. Describes the same functionality as POSIX.1, accessible from FORTRAN 77 programs. Adopted 1992.

Issues related to system administration are specifically excluded from POSIX.1, as are implementation details. After all, an application program does not need to know how to create a new device special file, and does not care how the **open()** function (which opens a file) works internally. By avoiding implementation issues, the standard allows systems that are not based on the UNIX system to conform to POSIX.1. There are several systems unrelated to the UNIX system that provide all the POSIX.1 interfaces and semantics.

The POSIX.1 committee was responsible for codifying existing practice, not engineering a new version of the UNIX system. During the development of the POSIX.1 standard, partisans of BSD and System V were forced to try to reconcile their differences. In some cases, this meant standardizing on behavior from one or the other version. In a few cases, the working group decided that both the BSD and System V implementations of some features were deficient, and created new interfaces, based on existing practice but with new syntax and semantics (e.g., terminal control). Where no compromise seemed to be reachable, the working group adopted optional behavior. For example, BSD has had job control since at least release 4.1, while System V.3 does not support job control. POSIX.1 makes job control an option.

One compromise took a unique form. POSIX.1 specifies formats for file archives. On UNIX System V, the preferred archive format is **cpio** (page 575). On BSD, the preferred format is **tar** (page 712). POSIX.1 requires that both formats be supported, in slightly modified forms. Because the specification of utilities is outside the scope of POSIX.1, neither the **cpio** nor the **tar** utility is mentioned; only the file formats for the archives are part of the standard. POSIX.1 requires that the implementation provide unnamed archive creation and archive reading utilities. See page 758 for a discussion of the **pax** utility specified by POSIX.2.

Although POSIX.1 is an adopted, published standard, it is (and will remain) subject to revision. The POSIX.1 working group is currently considering additions to the standard, including symbolic links (page 83), that were omitted from the original.

The POSIX.1 standard is available from the American National Standards Institute (ANSI) or from the IEEE. In addition, it has been adopted as an international standard by the International Standards Organization (ISO) and the International Electrotechnical Commission (IEC), which jointly coordinate international computing standards. The formal name for POSIX.1 is ISO/IEC IS 9945-1:1990. For a detailed description of the standard from a programmer's point of view, see *The POSIX.1 Standard: A Programmer's Guide*, Fred Zlotnick (Benjamin/Cummings 1991).

The POSIX.1 FIPS

POSIX.1 is a widely referenced standard. In particular, it is the subject of a Federal Information Processing Standard (FIPS) published by the United States Government. A FIPS specifies conformance requirements for computing systems procured by federal government agencies. FIPS 151-2 requires conformance to the 1990 version of the POSIX.1 standard and some of its optional features (e.g., job control and supplementary groups). The practical consequence is that just about every vendor who implements a POSIX.1 conforming system also implements the FIPS-required options. Thus FIPS 151-2 has become a de facto extended POSIX.1 standard.

The National Institute of Standards and Technology, which published the FIPS, has developed a conformance test suite. At this writing over one hundred systems have been certified as conforming to FIPS 151-2 or to its predecessor, FIPS 151-1. Most of these are UNIX systems, but versions of DEC's VMS and Unisys's CTOS operating system, which are not UNIX-based, have also been certified.

POSIX.2

POSIX.2, the Shell and Utilities standard, was formally approved as an IEEE standard in September 1992, and as an international standard in June 1993. For users, as opposed to application developers, POSIX.2 is the most important POSIX standard. Its principal purpose is to specify the semantics of a shell (based on the Korn Shell) and a collection of utilities that you can use to develop portable shell scripts. A secondary purpose is to promote user portability. This term refers to a standard specification for utilities such as **vi, man,** and **who** that are not very useful for scripts but are typically used interactively.

POSIX.2 is independent of POSIX.1, and a system can claim conformance to POSIX.2 without claiming conformance to POSIX.1. This is not true of most of the other POSIX standards, which take POSIX.1 as a base. In practice, you can expect virtually all UNIX systems to comply with both POSIX.1 and POSIX.2 within a few years. Many non-UNIX systems will also comply, making them "UNIX-like," at least on the outside.

Localization

One of the most important features of POSIX.2 is that it is fully localized. That is, it describes the behavior of the shell and utilities in the context of different character sets and locale-specific information (such as date and time formats). For example, the **grep** utility has a –i option that causes **grep** to ignore case in determining matches. POSIX.2 specifies what this means for alphabets in which the uppercase to lowercase mapping is either not defined or not one-to-one.

The general idea behind localization is that every process executes in a particular locale. The POSIX.2 standard defines a locale as "the definition of the subset of the environment of a user that depends on language and cultural conventions." The locale describes how the process should display or interpret information that depends on the language and culture, including character set and the method of writing times, dates, numbers, and currency amounts. Localization is not unique to POSIX.2; both the C Standard and POSIX.1 support it to a limited degree. However, POSIX.2 is much more specific in its description of how locale-specific information is provided to the system and how it affects the system's operation.

An important feature of POSIX.2 locales is that they are fragmented into categories. The standard specifies 6 locale categories and defines 6 environment variables corresponding to these categories.

Environment Variable	Locale Category
LC_CTYPE	Describes which characters are considered alphabetic, numeric, punctuation, blank, etc., and describes the mapping of uppercase to lowercase and vice versa.
LC_COLLATE	Describes the order of characters for sorting.
LC_TIME	Describes abbreviated and full names for months and days of the week, local equivalents of **AM** and **PM**, appropriate date representation, and appropriate 12- and 24-hour time representation.
LC_NUMERIC	Describes the character to use as a decimal point, the character to separate groups of digits (e.g., the comma in 65,536), and the number of digits in a group.
LC_MONETARY	Describes the currency symbol, where it is positioned, how negative values are written, the currency decimal point character, the number of fractional digits, and other details of how currency values are written.
LC_MESSAGES	Describes the formats of informative and diagnostic messages and interactive responses, and expressions to be interpreted as yes and no responses for those utilities that query the user.

Two more environment variables, **LC_ALL** and **LANG**, interact with these six to provide overrides and defaults. If **LC_ALL** is set, then its value is used in place of the value of any of the other six LC_* variables. If **LANG** is set, then its value is used in place of any LC_* variable that is not set.

Each of these environment variables can be set to a value that is the name of a locale, and that will cause features of the shell and some utilities to change behavior. For example, here is a fragment of a shell session on a system with POSIX.2 internationalization. (In this and the following examples assume that **LANG** and the LC_* variables have been exported. They must be exported, because they affect the standard utilities only when they are in the environment of those utilities.)

```
$ LC_TIME=POSIX
$ date
Thu Aug 25 21:21:03 1994
$ LC_TIME=Fr_FR # French
$ date
Jeu 25 Ao 21:21:12 PDT 1994
```

There are two standard locale names: POSIX and C. They describe the identical locale, which is a generic UNIX locale; setting all the locale environment variables to **POSIX** will result in traditional UNIX system behavior. Other locale names are implementation-defined. There is no standard format. Common conventions include the abbreviated language and country in the locale name. Thus **En_US** and **Fr_CA** might be locale names for locales describing English in the US and French in Canada.

An example that was actually run on a system that supports POSIX.2 style localization shows the results of mixing locales:

```
$ LC_TIME=Fr_FR
$ LANG=De_DE
$ cal 1 1993

        Janvier 1993
Dim Lun Mar Mer Jeu Ven Sam
                     1   2
 3   4   5   6   7   8   9
10  11  12  13  14  15  16
17  18  19  20  21  22  23
24  25  26  27  28  29  30
31

$ rm NoSuchFile
rm: NoSuchFile: Verzeichnis/Datei im Pfadnamen existiert nicht.
```

On some POSIX.2 systems it is possible for users to define their own locales in addition to those provided by the system; see the definition of the **localedef** utility on page 757.

The POSIX Shell

POSIX.2 specifies a shell based on the Korn Shell. The POSIX.2 shell is almost, but not quite, a subset of the System V.4 Korn Shell. Where the behavior differs, future releases of the Korn Shell will be modified to adopt the POSIX.2 changes. The Korn Shell is described in Chapter 12. Here is a brief description of some major differences between the Korn Shell and the POSIX.2 shell:

- The POSIX.2 shell does not support the **typeset** keyword.

- The POSIX.2 shell does not support the Select command.

- The POSIX.2 shell does not support the two-argument form of the **cd** command.

- The POSIX.2 shell does not automatically define and maintain the value of the **PWD** environment variable.

- The POSIX.2 shell has a different syntax for doing integer arithmetic. It does not use the **let** keyword. Arithmetic expressions are initiated by the symbols **$((** and terminated by **))**. Within the parentheses, you must refer to shell variables by using a **$** sign. For example, the following brief POSIX.2 shell dialogue,

```
$ x=3
$ y=4
$ z=$(($x + $y))
$ echo $z
7
```

will display the value 7. The equivalent Korn Shell sequence would be

```
$ x=3
$ y=4
$ let z="x + y"
$ echo $z
7
```

- In the Korn Shell you can also use double parentheses for arithmetic instead of **let**, but the syntax is different. Two ways to write the **let** statement in the Korn shell are

  $ z=$((x + y))

  and

  $ ((z=x + y))

- You can define shell functions in both the POSIX.2 Shell and the Korn Shell. The Korn Shell has two syntaxes for defining functions: the **function** keyword and the C-like notation described on page 387. Only the second syntax is supported in the POSIX.2 shell. For example, here is one way to define a shell function in either shell:

  ```
  parent()
  {
  _dir=$(dirname $1)
  echo $(basename $_dir)
  }
  ```

  The function above will print the name of the parent (last-but-one) component of a pathname argument.

  ```
  $ parent /home/alex/literature/moby_dick
  literature
  ```

- In the POSIX shell, functions execute in the caller's execution environment. This is largely but not entirely true for the Korn Shell; the principal exception is that traps set in Korn Shell functions apply to the execution of the function only. For example, consider the following shell dialogue:

  ```
  $ side_effect()
  > {
  > trap "rm /tmp/foo" 0 # on exit, remove it
  > }
  $ trap - 0              # on exit, no action
  $ side_effect
  ```

If the POSIX shell executes the **side_effect** function, when it returns from the function, the trap has been set for when the calling shell exits. If an earlier version of the Korn Shell executes it, the trap is set for the execution of the function and occurs when the function exits. This is not true in Korn Shell 93.

Utilities for Portable Shell Applications

POSIX.2 specifies 72 required utilities, referred to as Execution Environment Utilities. Most of them are familiar from UNIX System V.3 or BSD UNIX, or are derived from UNIX utilities. A few, such as **pathchk** and **printf** (see below), are inventions of the POSIX.2 committee. These were created to satisfy requirements that specifically relate to portability. Other utilities are adopted from the UNIX system but have changed semantics, either to resolve conflicts between System V.3 and BSD, to remove behavior that does not make sense in an internationalized context, or to fix inconsistencies (especially with the syntax of options).

The Execution Environment Utilities are shown below. Utilities that are not described in the main part of this text are marked with an asterisk (*). Utilities that have significant differences from their traditional UNIX semantics are marked with a dagger (†). Utilities that are new (i.e., inventions of the POSIX.2 working group) are marked with a double dagger (‡).

The Execution Environment Utilities			
awk	basename	bc*	cat
cd	chgrp	chmod	chown
cksum*‡	cmp*	comm	command*‡
cp	cut*	date	dd*
diff	dirname*	echo†	ed
env*	expr	false	find
fold*	getconf*‡	getopts	grep†
head	id*	join*	kill†
ln	locale*‡	localedef*‡	logger*‡
logname*	lp*	ls	mailx*
mkdir	mkfifo*‡	mv	nohup
od†	paste*	pathchk*‡	pax*‡
pr	printf*‡	pwd	read
rm	rmdir	sed	sh
sleep	sort	stty	tail
tee	test	touch	tr
true	tty	umask	uname*
uniq	wait	wc	xargs*

Brief descriptions of the utilities that are new with POSIX.2 follow.

cksum

The **cksum** utility computes a checksum for a file. It is useful when you are sending or receiving a file and want to ensure that it was not corrupted in transmission. The **cksum** utility replaces a utility named **sum** that was present in both BSD and System V Release 4. The POSIX.2 committee did not use **sum**, since BSD and System V had differing, incompatible implementations. The algorithm used by **cksum** is based on a cyclic redundancy check from the Ethernet standard ISO 8802-3.

The syntax is

cksum [**file...**]

You can name zero or more files on the command line. If you do not specify a filename, **cksum** computes a checksum for the standard input. For each input file, **cksum** writes to the standard output the file's checksum, byte count, and name. (Actually, it is not a byte count but an octet count. On those rare systems where a byte is not 8 bits, these will differ.)

command

The **command** utility executes any command line in a manner designed to guarantee that you are executing the version of the command that you would expect. If you type

command **command_name** [**arguments...**]

the shell executes **command_name** without looking for a shell function of that name. If you use the **–p** option, as in

command –p **command_name** [**arguments...**]

the shell searches for **command_name** using a special value for **PATH**, one that is guaranteed to find all the standard utilities. This protects you from accidentally invoking local utilities or functions with the same names as standard utilities.

If the system supports POSIX.2's User Portability Utilities Option (page 759), then **command** has two more option flags. With the -v option, **command** reports the absolute pathname of **command_name** without running it, using your **PATH** variable for the search. If **command_name** is a built-in shell utility, a reserved word, or a function, just its name is written. If **command_name** is an alias, the command line representing its alias definition is written. The **–V** option is similar but distinguishes between functions, reserved words, and built-in utilities.

getconf

The **getconf** utility lets you determine the values of various options and configuration-dependent parameters, such as whether or not the system supports the User Portability Utilities Option, or what maximum length filename the system supports. Some of these parameters may vary depending on where you are in the filesystem. For example, a UNIX system might support both traditional System V filesystems (in which filenames are limited to 14 characters) and BSD filesystems (in which filenames can be as long as 255 characters).

You invoke **getconf** in either of the following ways:

getconf **system_var**

getconf **path_var pathname**

The first syntax is used for system-wide variables. For example, you can determine the maximum number of simultaneous processes that any one user ID can own with the call

```
$ getconf CHILD_MAX
40
```

The second syntax is used to determine the values of variables that may vary from place to place in the file hierarchy. For example, you can determine the maximum permissible length of a filename in the **/tmp** directory with the command

```
$ getconf NAME_MAX /tmp
255
```

The set of symbols that you can query, which is too long to be listed here, can be found in the POSIX.2 standard (which refers directly to POSIX.1 for some of these symbols). Following is a list of some of the more useful symbols.

Symbol	Meaning
getconf PATH	Reports a value of the PATH variable that will find all standard utilities.
getconf LINE_MAX	Reports the maximum length of an input line that you can reliably pass to a standard utility that processes text files. It must be at least 2048.
getconf POSIX2_UPE	Displays the value 1 if the system supports the User Portability Utilities Option (page 759).
getconf POSIX2_LOCALEDEF	Displays the value 1 if the system supports the ability to define new locales using the **localedef** utility (page 757).
getconf PATH_MAX dir	Reports the length of the longest pathname that you can reliably use, relative to directory **dir**. This may vary from place to place in the filesystem.
getconf NAME_MAX dir	Reports the length of the longest filename that you can use in **dir**. This may vary from place to place in the filesystem.

locale

The **locale** utility is part of POSIX.2's effort to internationalize the UNIX environment. The **locale** utility exports information about the current locale. If invoked with no arguments or options, **locale** writes to standard output the values of the **LANG** and **LC_*** environment variables. This utility can also take options or arguments that allow you to write information about all available public locales or the names and values of selected keywords used in defining locales. The description of these keywords is beyond the scope of this book, but an example will illustrate their use. Suppose a user has typed a response to a question, and you want to determine, in a localized way, whether the response is affirmative or negative. The definition of the **LC_MESSAGES** locale category contains the keyword **yesexpr**. The value associated with this keyword is a regular expression describing the responses that should be treated as yes in the current locale. If the user's response is in a shell variable named **response**, then the following shell fragment will work:

```
yes=`locale yesexpr`
echo $response | grep "$yes" > /dev/null
if [ $? -eq 0 ]
then
echo "Answer was yes"
else
echo "Answer was no"
fi
```

localedef

The **localedef** utility allows users to define their own locales, if the implementation supports this facility. Such support is an option in POSIX.2. The information required to define a locale is voluminous, and its description is beyond the scope of this book. You can find a sample set of locale definition files, provided by the Danish Standards Association, in Annex G of the POSIX.2 standard.

logger

The **logger** utility provides a means for scripts to write messages to an unspecified system log file. The format and method of reading these messages are unspecified by POSIX.2, and will vary from one system to another. The syntax of **logger** is

logger **string** ...

The intended purpose of the **logger** utility is for noninteractive scripts that encounter errors to record these errors in a place where system administrators can later examine them.

mkfifo

POSIX.1 includes a **mkfifo()** function that allows programs to create FIFO special files (named pipes that persist in the filesystem even when not in use). This utility provides the same functionality at the shell level. The syntax is

mkfifo [–m **mode**] **file** ...

By default, the mode of the created FIFOs is 660 (rw-rw----), modified by the caller's **umask**. If the **–m** option is used, then the mode argument (in the same format as that used by **chmod**) is used instead.

pathchk

The **pathchk** utility allows portable shell scripts to determine if a given pathname is valid on a given system. The problem arises because the character set used in the pathname may not be supported on the system, or the pathname may be longer than the maximum **PATH_MAX** for this filesystem, or may have components (filenames) longer than the maximum **FILE_MAX** for this filesystem. The syntax of **pathchk** is

pathchk [–p] **pathname** ...

For each pathname argument, **pathchk** will check that the length is no greater than **PATH_MAX**, that the length of each component is no greater than **NAME_MAX**, that each existing directory in the path is searchable, and that every character in the pathname is valid in its containing directory. If any of these fail, **pathchk** writes a diagnostic message to the standard error. If you use the **–p** option, then **pathchk** performs a more stringent portability check: pathnames are checked against a maximum length of 255 bytes, filenames against a maximum length of 14 bytes, and characters against the portable filename character set (which consists of the lowercase and uppercase letters of the Roman alphabet, the digits 0-9, period, underscore, and hyphen). The limits 255 for **PATH_MAX** and 14 for **NAME_MAX** are the minimum that any POSIX-conforming system can support.

pax

The name **pax** is ostensibly an acronym for Portable Archive eXchange, but it is also a bilingual pun. The disputes between the advocates of the **tar** and **cpio** formats were referred to as the tar wars (in which 3-cpio did battle with tar-2-d-2), and **pax** is the peace treaty. The **pax** utility can read and write archives in several formats. These specifically include, but are not limited to, the POSIX.1 **tar** and **cpio** formats. Other formats are implementation defined. It is the stated intent of the POSIX.2 committee to define a new archive format in a future revision of the standard. That format will become the default for **pax**.

The syntax of the **pax** command is too complex to describe here (as you might expect from looking at all the options available to **tar** and **cpio**). If it exists in your system, consult the manual pages. The USENIX Association funded the development of a portable implementation of **pax** and placed it in the public domain, so this utility is now widely available.

printf

The **printf** utility was invented largely to deal with the incompatibility between the BSD and System V versions of **echo** (page 593). BSD **echo** treats a first argument of **–n** in a special fashion, while System V will echo it. System V **echo** treats certain strings starting with \ in a special fashion, while BSD will echo them. POSIX.2 states that any **echo** command line in which **–n** is the first argument or in which any argument starts with \ will have implementation defined behavior. To portably print any but the simplest strings, you should use **printf**.

The *f* in **printf** stands for **formatted**, and the **printf** utility allows you to print strings to the standard output under the control of a formatting argument. The syntax is

printf **format** [**string** ...]

Both the name printf and the syntax of the format string are borrowed from C.

The User Portability Utilities Option (UPE)

The UPE is a collection of 37 utilities and shell built-in commands for interactive use. This portion of the standard is an option. That is, a system can conform to POSIX.2 without providing these. Their purpose is to promote user portability by creating a uniform interactive command environment. All of the UPE utilities are listed below. Those that are not described in the main part of this text are marked with an asterisk (*).

UPE Utilities			
alias	at	batch*	bg
crontab	csplit*	ctags*	df
du	ex	expand*	fc
fg	file	jobs	man
mesg	more	newgrp	nice
nm*	patch*	ps	renice*
split*	strings*	tabs*	talk
time	tput*	unalias	unexpand*
uudecode*	uuencode*	vi	who
write			

Three of them, **bg**, **fg**, and **jobs** need only be supported if the system also supports job control. Two others, **ctags** and **nm**, need only be supported if the system also supports the Software Development Utilities option.

Many of the UPE utilities are affected by localization. For example, the **at** utility can accept names of days of the week as part of its time specification. The way one writes these names depends on the value of **LC_TIME**.

Software Development Utilities

As an option, POSIX.2 specifies the behavior of some utilities useful to software developers, such as **make**, **lex**, and **yacc**. In fact, there are three separate options in POSIX.2 that cover three distinct sets of development tools:

- The Software Development Utilities Option specifies the behavior of the **ar**, **make**, and **strip** utilities. These utilities are useful for software development in any programming language.

- The C-Language Development Utilities Option specifies the behavior of the **c89**, **lex**, and **yacc** utilities. The **c89** command invokes a C compiler that conforms to the 1989 C Standard (ANSI X3.159-1989, also ISO/IEC 9899-1990.) The **lex** and **yacc** utilities are useful high-level tools that parse input streams into tokens and take actions when a particular token is recognized. They have historically been available on UNIX systems.

- The FORTRAN Development and Runtime Utilities Option specifies the behavior of the **asa** and **fort77** utilities. The **asa** utility converts between FORTRAN's arcane printer control commands and ASCII output. The **fort77** command invokes a FORTRAN compiler that conforms to the FORTRAN 77 Standard (ANSI X3.9-1978).

POSIX.3

The POSIX standards developers recognized early in the process that testing systems for conformance to the standards was going to be essential. In the past, other standards efforts have suffered from lack of appropriately specified conformance tests or from conflicting conformance tests with different measures of conformance. The POSIX.3 standard specifies general principles for test suites that measure conformance to POSIX standards. For each standard, a set of assertions (individual items to be tested) is developed. For POSIX.1, a test methods standard with over 2,400 assertions has been adopted as POSIX.3.1. For POSIX.2, there is a draft test methods standard under development at this writing. It contains almost 10,000 assertions.

UNIX users who are involved in testing or procuring systems that must conform to standards need to be familiar with POSIX.3 and its associated test methods standards. For other UNIX users, these standards have little importance.

POSIX.4

The POSIX.4 standard is an addition to and modification of the POSIX.1 standard that describes C language interfaces for realtime applications. The standard defines realtime as "the ability of the operating system to provide a required level of service in a bounded response time." Realtime systems have historically been implemented as stand-alone systems controlling processes or machines, or as embedded systems (i.e., inside a microwave oven). However, there has always been a need for combined interactive and realtime systems, and the UNIX system has served as the base for many implementations of realtime facilities.

POSIX.4 was adopted in September 1993. The facilities specified in POSIX.4 are those that are commonly used by realtime applications such as semaphores, timers, interprocess communication, shared memory, and so on. Although there have been quite a few implementations of these and related facilities in various UNIX systems, there was no well-established and widely accepted set of UNIX realtime interfaces. Thus the routines specified in POSIX.4 are largely the invention of the POSIX.4 committee. They have already been implemented on a number of UNIX systems.

POSIX.4 is structured as a collection of optional extensions to POSIX.1. Thus a system can claim conformance to some parts of the standard and not others. However, it must claim conformance to POSIX.1. This has been a subject of some controversy, since many realtime applications, particularly for embedded systems, do not need the support of an operating system with all of the POSIX.1 machinery. One of the POSIX committees (POSIX.18) is currently considering how to divide POSIX.1 into consistent subsets that would be independently useful to applications.

A separate effort of the POSIX.4 committee is POSIX.4a, a specification of threads that is still in draft form. Support for threads allows a system to run programs in which several parts of the program can, in principle, execute in parallel. As more and more systems are developed that contain multiple processors, support for threads has grown in importance. Many implementations of the UNIX system, such as OSF/1, have had threads support for a long time. Others have recently added or are about to provide such support. The POSIX.4a effort is an attempt to avoid the creation of multiple, incompatible threads interfaces. At this writing, the POSIX.4a draft is being balloted. It will likely become a standard during 1994.

POSIX.5

POSIX.5 is an Ada Language version of POSIX.1. It specifies Ada routines that provide essentially the same functionality as the C routines of POSIX.1. The UNIX system itself is written in C, and C has always been the most widely used programming language on UNIX systems, but the Ada community has always been interested in the UNIX system and in providing a standard way for Ada programs to access UNIX system services. POSIX.5 provides that standard. In principle, POSIX.5 provides the exact functionality provided by POSIX.1. This does not mean that there is a precise one-to-one correlation between the interfaces in POSIX.1 and POSIX.5, because differences in the languages make that impossible.

The POSIX.5 working group is tracking changes to POSIX.1 and will keep the Ada version of the standard synchronized with the C version. The POSIX.20 working group, which works in concert with POSIX.5, is developing an Ada language version of POSIX.4 and POSIX.4a; this will provide Ada programmers with the ability to use standard interfaces for realtime applications on the UNIX system and UNIX-like systems. This is important to the

Ada community, since Ada has from its inception been used heavily in the development of realtime systems.

POSIX.9

POSIX.9 is a FORTRAN version of POSIX.1. It specifies routines in the FORTRAN 77 language that provide the same functionality as POSIX.1. FORTRAN was the "second language" on UNIX systems, in the sense that FORTRAN compilers have been available and widely used on UNIX systems almost as long as the UNIX system has been available. Nevertheless, there has not been a widely supported set of FORTRAN interfaces to UNIX system services. Thus there is no widespread existing practice to codify. The interfaces in POSIX.9 are essentially all inventions of the POSIX.9 working group. They correspond fairly closely to the C interfaces.

There is a new and more powerful version of the FORTRAN language, Fortran 90. (The name FORTRAN is properly written with all uppercase letters for versions of the language up through FORTRAN 77. Starting with Fortran 90, the name is spelled with a single uppercase letter.) There was some discussion about using Fortran 90 as the basis for POSIX.9. The consensus of the working group was that there was currently insufficient experience with Fortran 90. It would not be surprising to see POSIX.9 modified in a few years to use a more modern version of the Fortran language.

Draft POSIX Standards

The remaining POSIX standards committees are in various stages of preparing drafts of standards or of profiles. If you are interested in a particular standard or draft standard, you can contact the IEEE Computer Society in Washington, D.C., for more information.

Security

One area of current standards development is system security. Since early in its development, the UNIX system has had a simple and relatively effective security paradigm. File access permissions are assigned according to three levels of granularity (owner, group, and other—page 77), and certain actions require privileges. The privileges are monolithic; that is, either a process has all the privileges that the system supports (e.g., to add users, change the ownership of files, change its user ID) or it has none. One user ID is reserved for a privileged user, the superuser.

For most ordinary purposes, this paradigm works well, particularly in organizations where small groups cooperate on projects. However, it does not provide the level of security that some users need. The Department of Defense has defined several different levels of security in a document commonly referred to as the *Orange Book*. Some vendors have layered additional security features on top of UNIX systems to conform to the more secure levels of the *Orange Book*.

An important feature of all the POSIX standards is that they support an abstract privilege model in which privileges are discrete. Each time a POSIX standard describes an action that requires some privilege, the phrase *appropriate privileges* is used. Thus, POSIX.2 states that **chmod** can be used to change the mode of a file by the owner of the file or by a process with appropriate privileges. One model of these privileges is the superuser model, but there can be others. Thus POSIX allows many security paradigms.

The POSIX.6 committee is developing user interfaces, program interfaces, and structures to define higher levels of security. They include the following general areas:

Least Privilege

This is the idea that a process should only have the privileges that are absolutely necessary for its function. The monolithic nature of traditional UNIX system privileges is considered a security hazard. You may recall that in 1988, a "worm" program traveled across the Internet, crippling computers around the world. The worm exploited a feature of the **sendmail** program. Since **sendmail** has to write to all users' mail files, it must have some privileges. On a classical UNIX system, this means it has all privileges, and the worm used this fact to acquire all privileges itself.

Discretionary Access Controls (DACs)

These are additional access restrictions under the control of the creator of an object (such as a file). A typical DAC is an Access Control List, a list of user IDs permitted access to the file. This acts as an additional restriction to that imposed by the file's mode.

Mandatory Access Controls (MACs)

These are like two security levels. An object is created at some level, not under the control of its creator, and can only be accessed by processes at the same or a higher level. The level can be determined by the process' user or group ID or by the nature of the process itself.

Auditability Mechanism

This covers which types of objects or actions need to be audited, and the mechanisms for keeping track of the audit trail.

In all of these areas there is existing practice for UNIX systems; that is, you can find DACs, MACs, partitioned privilege, and audit mechanisms on secure UNIX systems today. The goal of POSIX.6 is to standardize the practices.

The POSIX.22 committee is addressing similar issues in a distributed environment. Clearly, network security adds its own layer of difficulties, including file access on remotely mounted systems.

System Administration

System administration was explicitly omitted from the scope of POSIX.1. In part this was because so many UNIX systems had developed incompatible tools, file hierarchies, and interfaces for system administration that there was little chance for quick agreement. Indeed, when the POSIX.7 committee first started work on system administration, it chose not to use any existing practice but rather to invent a new approach. That effort did not advance far. The POSIX.7 committee reorganized itself and selected three areas of system administration to be standardized separately, by three subcommittees. They are

- POSIX.7.1: Printing Administration
- POSIX.7.2: Software Installation and Management
- POSIX.7.3: User/Group Management

This by no means is intended to cover all system administration tasks. These three seem manageable now, while other issues (including device special files, filesystem management, and quotas) have been postponed for the time being.

The work on Printing Administration is the most advanced, with a draft standard currently in ballot. This draft standard specifies standard methods to send a file to a printer, query the print queue, and remove a file from the print queue, as well as other related tasks. The work on Software Installation will enter ballot during 1994. It includes standard ways to install applications, to recover from errors and roll back newly installed versions, and to patch and update programs. The User/Group management task is the newest subgroup, and the least advanced. It will address creation and administration of user accounts and groups in single systems as well as distributed environments. It will specifically exclude such subjects as mail, quotas, accounting, and software license usage, although these may be the subject of future work.

Networks

There are a number of POSIX groups working on different standards related to networks. The areas that need to be standardized occur at many different levels. Some are visible to users, some to application programs, and some only to the operating system.

The most visible network feature to a user is the availability of remote filesystems. There is well-established existing practice for this on UNIX systems, via packages such as NFS (page 164) and RFS. The purpose of remote filesystems is to enable file hierarchies on remote hosts to behave, to the extent possible, as if they are mounted on the local host. That is, the presence of the network should be transparent to the user and the user's programs. The POSIX.8 committee is charged with standardizing Transparent File Access.

There is also existing practice for allowing programs on two different hosts to communicate with each other, much as pipes or FIFOs allow programs on the same host to communicate. In fact, there are at least two competing approaches, Berkeley sockets and the XTI interface from X/Open. The POSIX.12 committee is trying to resolve the differences between these approaches. Sockets and XTI are referred to as Protocol Independent Interfaces, since they are above the level of the network protocol, the convention that describes precisely how hosts on the network communicate.

That protocol is also the subject of considerable standards effort. There is already an international standard for network protocols, the ISO OSI. However, most UNIX systems have historically used a different protocol, TCP/IP. Trying to resolve the differences between OSI, TCP/IP, and other network protocols will be difficult. The IEEE 1238 committee is working on part of this problem.

User Interfaces

Many modern applications have a graphical user interface (GUI—Chapter 6) that uses windows and a pointing device such as a mouse. There have been many competing GUIs on UNIX systems, including some based on the X Window System (such as Open Look and Motif) and some that stand alone (such as NeXTstep). The IEEE 1201.1 committee has been in the middle of what have been referred to as the GUI wars, trying to settle on a standard GUI toolkit for application programs. Recently, there appears to have been progress on making Motif the common window toolkit across all UNIX systems, and this will undoubtedly influence the work of the 1201.1 committee.

Profiles and POSIX Standards

An important concept in the POSIX lexicon is that of a profile. As the number of standards grows, the number of combinations of standards grows exponentially. However, the number of sensible, coherent combinations is much smaller. Many of the POSIX committees are developing AEPs, or Application Environment Profiles, rather than standards. An AEP is a "standard collection of standards" suitable for a particular application area. For example, the POSIX.10 committee is developing a supercomputing AEP. This profile references a number of standards that would be useful for applications that run on supercomputers. These include POSIX.1, POSIX.2, the ISO FORTRAN (Fortran 90) Standard, and the C Standard. A user who needs the resources of a supercomputer will typically also need the features provided by most or all of these standards.

Profiles are most useful as tools for procurements, particularly by large organizations such as government agencies. Typically such organizations find that requiring conformance to one or two standards does not adequately specify their needs. For example, although the POSIX.1 standard is quite useful and widely referenced, knowing that your system conforms to POSIX.1 does not, by itself, guarantee you much; most complex applications require facilities well outside the scope of POSIX.1. In fact, the NIST POSIX FIPS is really a profile. It requires conformance to POSIX.1, support for certain POSIX.1 options, and conformance to the C Standard.

If you are going to ask hardware vendors to propose systems to satisfy a complex set of requirements, using a profile makes your job much simpler. Thus it is not surprising that the U.S. government and the European Commission are actively involved in the development of POSIX profiles, and also develop profiles for their own purposes. As the number of POSIX standards grows, these standards are taking a more central place in government profiles.

SUMMARY

The IEEE POSIX committees have developed standards for programming and user interfaces based on historical UNIX practice, and new standards are under development. Most of the standards are compromises between versions of System V and versions of BSD, with a few innovations where compromise was not possible or was technically inadvisable. The standards have met with broad acceptance from government bodies and industry organizations.

POSIX.1 standardizes C language interfaces to the core UNIX system facilities; Ada and Fortran versions of these interfaces are specified by POSIX.5 and POSIX.9. POSIX.2 standardizes a shell and a collection of utilities useful for scripts and interactive use. It specifies how these tools should behave in international environments, where character sets and local conventions differ from those in the original UNIX environment. POSIX.4 specifies interfaces for realtime programs executing in UNIX-like environments.

Standards under development will cover parts of system administration, extended system security, networks, and user interfaces. Existing UNIX system practice in all of these areas will form the basis of the new standards. In turn, innovations from these standards will find their way into future UNIX systems.

Glossary

Absolute pathname A pathname that starts with the root directory (/). An absolute pathname locates a file without regard to the working directory.

Access In computer jargon, this word is frequently used as a verb to mean use, read from, or write to. To access a file means to read from or write to the file.

Access permission Permission to read from, write to, or execute a file. If you have "write access permission to a file," you can write to the file. Also, *access privilege*.

Alias A mechanism in the C and Korn Shells that enables you to define new commands.

Alphanumeric character One of the characters, either uppercase or lowercase, from A to Z and 0 to 9, inclusive.

Ambiguous file reference A reference to a file that does not necessarily specify any one file but can be used to specify a group of files. The shell expands an ambiguous file reference into a list of filenames. Special characters represent single characters (?), strings of zero or more characters (∗), and character classes ([]) within ambiguous file references. An ambiguous file reference is a type of *regular expression*.

Angle bracket There is a left angle bracket (<) and a right angle bracket (>). The shell uses < to redirect a command's standard input to come from a file, and > to redirect the standard output to a file. Also, the shell uses the characters << to signify the start of a here document, and >> to append output to a file.

Append To add something to the end of something else. To append text to a file means to add the text to the end of the file. The shell uses >> to append a command's output to a file.

Argument   A number, letter, filename, or another string that gives some information to a command and is passed to the command at the time it is called. A command line argument is anything on a command line following the command name that is passed to the command.

Arithmetic expression   A group of numbers, operators, and parentheses that can be evaluated. When you evaluate an arithmetic expression, you end up with a number. The Bourne Shell uses the **expr** command to evaluate arithmetic expressions; the C Shell uses @, and the Korn Shell uses **let**.

Array   An arrangement of elements (numbers or strings of characters) in one or more dimensions. The C and Korn Shells and **awk** can store and process arrays.

ASCII   This acronym stands for the *A*merican *N*ational *S*tandard *C*ode for *I*nformation *I*nterchange. It is a code that uses seven bits to represent both graphic (letters, numbers, and punctuation) and (CONTROL) characters. You can represent textual information, including program source code and English text, in ASCII code. Because it is a standard, it is frequently used when exchanging information between computers. See the file **/usr/pub/ascii** or give the command **man ascii** to see a list of ASCII codes.

There are extensions of the ASCII character set that make use of eight bits. The seven-bit set is common; the eight-bit extensions are still coming into popular use. The eighth bit is sometimes referred to as the meta bit.

Asynchronous event   An event that does not occur regularly or synchronously with another event. UNIX system signals are asynchronous; they can occur at any time, because they can be initiated by any number of nonregular events.

Background process   A process that is not run in the foreground. Also called a *detached process*, a background process is initiated by a command line that ends with an ampersand (**&**). You do not have to wait for a background process to run to completion before giving the shell additional commands. If you have job control, you can move background processes to the foreground, and vice versa.

Baud rate   Transmission speed. Usually used to measure terminal or modem speed. Common baud rates range from 110 to 19,200 baud. You can roughly convert baud rate to characters per second by dividing by ten (e.g., 300 baud equals approximately 30 characters per second).

Berkeley UNIX   One of the two major versions of the UNIX operating system. Berkeley UNIX was developed at the University of California at Berkeley by the Computer Systems Research Group. It is often referred to as *BSD* (Berkeley Software Distribution).

Bit   The smallest piece of information a computer can handle. A *bit* is a *b*inary dig*it*, either a 1 or 0 (on or off).

Bit-mapped display   A graphical display device in which each pixel on the screen is controlled by an underlying representation of zeros and ones.

Blank character   Either a (SPACE) or a (TAB) character, also called *white space*. Also, in some contexts, (NEWLINE)s are considered blank characters.

Block   A section of a disk or tape (usually 1024 bytes long, but shorter or longer on some systems) that is written at one time.

Block device   A disk or tape drive. A block device stores information in blocks of characters. A block device is represented by a block device (block special) file. See *Character device.*

Block number   Disk and tape blocks (see *Block*) are numbered, so that the UNIX system can keep track of the data on the device. These numbers are block numbers.

Boot   Load the UNIX system kernel into memory and start it running. Also *bootstrap.*

Bourne Shell   A UNIX command processor. It was developed by Steve Bourne at AT&T Bell Laboratories. See *Shell.*

Brace   There is a left brace ({) and a right brace (}). Braces have special meanings to the shell.

Bracket   Either a square ([) or angle bracket (<). See *Square bracket* and *Angle bracket.*

Branch   In a tree structure, a branch connects nodes, leaves, and the root. The UNIX filesystem hierarchy is often conceptualized as an upside-down tree. The branches connect files and directories. In a source code control system such as SCCS or RCS, a branch occurs when a revision is made to a file and is not included in other, subsequent revisions to the file.

Broadcast network   A type of network, such as Ethernet, in which any system can transmit information at any time, and all systems receive every message (but discard messages that were addressed to others).

BSD   See *Berkeley UNIX.*

Buffer   An area of memory that stores data until it can be used. When you write information to a file on a disk, the UNIX system stores the information in a disk buffer until there is enough to write to the disk or until the disk is ready to receive the information.

Built-in command   A command that is built into a shell. Each of the three major shells—the Bourne, C, and Korn Shells—has its own set of built-in commands. When the shell runs a built-in command, it does not fork a new process. Consequently, built-in commands run more quickly and can affect the environment of the current shell. Because built-in commands are used in the same way utilities are used, you will not typically be aware of whether a command is built in to the shell or a utility.

Byte   Eight bits of information. On most systems a byte can store one character.

C programming language   A modern systems language that has high-level features for efficient, modular programming as well as lower-level features that make it suitable as a systems programming language. It is machine-independent, so that carefully written C programs can be easily transported to run on different machines. Most of the UNIX operating system is written in C, and UNIX provides an ideal environment for programming in C.

C Shell   The C Shell is a UNIX command processor. It was originally developed by Bill Joy for Berkeley UNIX. It was named for the C programming language because its programming constructs are similar to those of C. See *Shell.*

Calling environment   A list of variables and their values that is made available to a called program. See "Executing a Command" in Chapter 10 and "Variable Substitution" in Chapter 11.

Case-sensitive   Able to distinguish between uppercase and lowercase characters. Unless you set the **ignorecase** parameter, **vi** performs case-sensitive searches. The **grep** utility performs case-sensitive searches unless you use the –i option.

Catenate   To join sequentially or end to end. The UNIX **cat** utility catenates files—it displays them one after the other. Also *concatenate*.

Character class   A group of characters in a regular expression that defines which characters can occupy a single character position. A character class definition is usually surrounded by square brackets. The character class defined by [abcr] represents a character position that can be occupied by **a**, **b**, **c**, or **r**.

Character device   A terminal, printer, or modem. A character device stores or displays characters one at a time. A character device is represented by a character device (character special) file. See *Block device*.

Child process   A process that was created by another process, the parent process. Every process is a child process except for the first process, which is started when the UNIX system begins execution. When you run a command from the shell, the shell spawns a child process to run the command. See *Process*.

Client   A computer (or program) that requests one or more services from a server.

Command   What you give the shell in response to a prompt. When you give the shell a command, it executes a utility, another program, a built-in command, or a shell script. Utilities are often referred to as commands. When you are using an interactive utility such as **vi** or **mail**, you use commands that are appropriate to that utility.

Command line   A line of instructions and arguments that executes a command. This term usually refers to a line that you enter in response to a shell prompt.

Command substitution   What the shell does when you surround a command with backquotes or grave accent marks. The shell replaces the command, including the backquotes, with the output of the command.

Concatenate   See *Catenate*.

Condition code   See *Exit status*.

Console terminal   The main system terminal, usually the one that receives system error messages. Also, *console*.

CONTROL **character**   A character that is not a graphic character such as a letter, number, or punctuation mark. Such characters are called CONTROL characters because they frequently act to control a peripheral device. RETURN and **FORMFEED** are CONTROL characters that control a terminal or printer.

The word CONTROL is shown in this book as a key cap because it is a key that appears on most terminal keyboards. It may appear as CTRL on your terminal. CONTROL characters are represented by ASCII codes less than 32 (decimal). Also nonprinting character.

Control flow commands   Commands that alter the order of execution of commands within a shell script or other program. Each one of the shells provides control structures, such as If and While, as well as other commands that alter the order of execution (e.g.,**exec**).

Control structure   A statement used to change the order of execution of commands in a shell script. Control structures are among the commands referred to as control flow commands. See *Control flow commands*.

Crash   The system stops unexpectedly.

.cshrc file   A file in your home directory that the C Shell executes each time you invoke a new C Shell. You can use this file to establish variables and aliases.

Current (process, line, character, directory, event, and so on)   The item that is immediately available, working, or being used. The current process is the process that is controlling the program you are running; the current line or character is the one the cursor is on; the current directory is the working directory.

Cursor   A small lighted rectangle or underscore that appears on the terminal screen and indicates where the next character is going to appear.

Daemon   A process that runs in the background, independent of a terminal, and performs a function. An example is the printer daemon, which controls the job queue for the printer.

Dataless   A computer, usually a workstation, that uses a local disk to boot a copy of the operating system and access system files but does not use a local disk to store user files.

Debug   To correct a program by removing its bugs (that is, errors).

Default   Something that is selected without being explicitly specified. For example, when used without an argument, **ls** displays a list of the files in the working directory by default.

Delta   A set of changes made to a file that has been encoded by the Source Code Control System (SCCS).

Detached process   See *Background process*.

Device   A disk drive, printer, terminal, plotter, or other input/output unit that can be attached to the computer.

Device driver   Part of the UNIX kernel that controls a device such as a terminal, disk drive, or printer.

Device file   Also called a *special file*. A file that represents a device.

Device filename   The pathname of a device file. All UNIX systems have two kinds of device files—block and character device files. Many versions of UNIX also have FIFOs (named pipes) and sockets. Device files are traditionally located in the /**dev** directory.

Device number   See *Major device number* and *Minor device number*.

Directory   Short for *directory file*. A file that contains a list of other files.

Disk partition   A portion of a disk. A disk partition can hold a filesystem or another structure, such as the swap area. Also, *disk slice*.

Diskless   A computer, usually a workstation, that has no disk and must contact another computer (a server) to boot a copy of the operating system and access the necessary system files.

Distributed computing   A style of computing in which tasks or services are performed by a network of cooperating systems, some of which may be specialized.

DNS   See *Domain Name Service.*

Domain   A name associated with an organization, or part of an organization, to help identify systems uniquely. Domain names are assigned hierarchically; the domain Berkeley.EDU refers to the University of California at Berkeley, for example (part of the higher-level education domain).

Domain Name Service   A distributed service that manages the correspondence of full hostnames (those that include a domain name) to IP addresses and other system characteristics.

Editor   A utility that is used to create and modify text files. The **vi** and **ed** editors are part of the UNIX system. Many UNIX systems also come with another popular editor, **emacs**. Also, *text editor.*

Element   One thing, usually a basic part of a group of things. An element of a numeric array is one of the numbers that are stored in the array.

Environment   See *Calling environment.*

EOF   An acronym for *End Of File.*

Ethernet   A type of local area network designed to transport data at rates up to 10 million bits per second over coaxial cable.

Exit status   The status returned by a process; either successful (usually 0) or unsuccessful (usually 1).

Expression   See *Logical expression* and *Arithmetic expression.*

FDDI   *Fiber Distributed Data Interface.* A type of local area network designed to transport data at the rate of 100 million bits per second over optical fiber.

File   A collection of related information, referred to by a filename. The UNIX system views peripheral devices as files, allowing a program to read from or write to a device, just as it would read from or write to a file.

Filesystem   A data structure that usually resides on part of a disk. All UNIX systems have a root filesystem, and most have at least a few other filesystems. Each filesystem is composed of some number of blocks, depending on the size of the disk partition that has been assigned to the filesystem. Each filesystem has a control block, the superblock, that contains information about the filesystem. The other blocks in a filesystem are *inodes*, which contain control information about individual files, and *data blocks*, which contain the information in the files.

Filename   The name of a file. A filename is used to refer to a file.

Filename completion   Automatic completion of filenames and user names after you specify unique prefixes.

Filename extension   The part of a filename following a period.

Filename generation   What occurs when the shell expands ambiguous file references. See *Ambiguous file reference.*

Filter   A command that can take its input from the standard input and send its output to the standard output. A filter transforms the input stream of data and sends it to the standard output. A pipe usually connects a filter's input to the standard output of one command, and a second pipe connects the filter's output to the standard input of another command. The **grep** and **sort** utilities are commonly used as filters.

Footer   The part of a format that goes at the bottom (or foot) of a page. See *Header*.

Foreground process   When a command is run in the foreground, the shell waits for the command to finish before giving you another prompt. You must wait for a foreground process to run to completion before you can give the shell another command. If you have job control, you can move background processes to the foreground, and vice versa. See *Background process* and *Job control*.

Fork   To create a process. When one process creates another process, it forks a process. Also, *spawn*.

Free list   The list of blocks in a filesystem that are available for use. Information about the free list is kept in the superblock of the filesystem.

Function   See *Shell function*.

Gateway   A device, often a computer, that is connected to more than one dissimilar type of network to pass data between them. Unlike a router, a gateway often must convert the information into a different format before passing it on.

Graphical User Interface   A graphical user interface provides a way to interact with a computer system by choosing items from menus or manipulating pictures drawn on a display screen, instead of by typing command lines. Also *GUI*.

Group   A collection of users. Groups are used as a basis for determining file access permissions. If you are not the owner of a file and you belong to the group the file is assigned to, you are subject to the group access permissions for the file. On most modern UNIX systems, a user may simultaneously belong to several groups. On older versions of the UNIX system, each user belongs to only one group at a time, although a user may temporarily change his or her group affiliation with the **newgrp** command.

Group ID   A number that is defined in the password database when a user is assigned a group number. The group database associates group IDs with group names.

GUI   See *Graphical User Interface*.

Hard link   A directory entry that contains the filename and inode number for a file. The inode number identifies the location of control information for the file on the disk, which in turn identifies the location of the file's contents on the disk. Every file has at least one hard link, which locates the file in a directory. When you remove the last hard link to a file, you can no longer access the file. See *Link* and *Symbolic link*.

Header   When you are formatting a document, the header goes at the top (or head) of a page. In electronic mail, the header identifies who sent the message, when it was sent, the subject of the message, and so forth.

Here document   A shell script that takes its input from the file that contains the script.

Hexadecimal number   A base 16 number. Hexadecimal (or *hex*) numbers are composed of the hexadecimal digits 0–9 and A–F. Refer to the following table.

Decimal	Octal	Hex	Decimal	Octal	Hex
1	1	1	17	21	11
2	2	2	18	22	12
3	3	3	19	23	13
4	4	4	20	24	14
5	5	5	21	25	15
6	6	6	31	37	1F
7	7	7	32	40	20
8	10	8	33	41	21
9	11	9	64	100	40
10	12	A	96	140	60
11	13	B	100	144	64
12	14	C	128	200	80
13	15	D	254	376	FE
14	16	E	255	377	FF
15	17	F	256	400	100
16	20	10	257	401	101

History   A mechanism provided by the C and Korn Shells that enables you to modify and reexecute recent commands.

Home directory   The directory that is the working directory when you first log in. The pathname of this directory is stored in the **HOME** shell variable.

Icon   An icon is a small picture drawn on a display screen as a placeholder for a larger window.

Indentation   See *Indention*.

Indention   When speaking of text, the blank space between the margin and the beginning of a line that is set in from the margin.

Inode   A data structure that contains information about a file. An inode for a file contains the file's length, the times the file was last accessed and modified, the time the inode was last modified, owner and group IDs, access privileges, number of links, and pointers to the data blocks that contain the file itself. Each directory entry associates a filename with an inode. Although a single file may have several filenames (one for each link), it has only one inode.

Internet   A wide area network that interconnects computers and local area networks around the globe, using the TCP/IP communications protocols.

Input   Information that is fed to a program from a terminal or other file. See *Standard input.*

Installation   A computer at a specific location. Some aspects of the UNIX system are installation-dependent. Also, *site*.

Interactive   A program that allows ongoing dialog with the user. When you give commands in response to shell prompts, you are using the shell interactively. Also, when you give commands to utilities such as **vi** and **Mail**, you are using the utilities interactively.

Interface   The meeting point of two subsystems. When two programs work together in some way, their interface includes every aspect of either program that the other deals with. The *user interface* of a program includes every aspect of the program the user comes into contact with—the syntax and semantics involved in invoking the program, the input and output of the program, and its error and informational messages. The shell and each one of the utilities and built-in commands has a user interface.

Invisible file   A file whose filename starts with a period. These files are called invisible because the **ls** utility does not normally list them. Use the –a option of **ls** to list all files, including invisible ones. Also, the shell will not expand a leading asterisk (∗) in an ambiguous file reference to match the filename of an invisible file.

I/O device   Short for *I*nput/Output device. See *Device*.

IP address   A four-part address associated with a particular network connection for a system using the *I*nternet *P*rotocol. A system that is attached to multiple networks that use IP will have a different IP address for each network interface.

Job control   A facility that enables you to move commands from the foreground to the background, and vice versa. The job control provided by the C and Korn Shells also enables you to stop commands temporarily.

Justify   To expand a line of type to the right margin in the process of formatting text. A line is justified by increasing the space between words and sometimes between letters on the line.

Kernel   The heart of the UNIX operating system. The kernel is the part of the operating system that allocates resources and controls processes. The design strategy has been to keep the kernel as small as possible and to put the rest of the UNIX functionality into separately compiled and executed programs.

Korn Shell   A command processor developed by David Korn at AT&T Bell Laboratories. It is compatible with the Bourne Shell, but includes many extensions. See *Shell*.

LAN   See *Local Area Network*.

Leaf   In a tree structure, the end of a branch that cannot support other branches. When the UNIX filesystem hierarchy is conceptualized as a tree, files that are not directories are leaves. See *Node*.

Link   A pointer to a file. There are two kinds of links—hard links and symbolic links. A hard link associates a filename with a place on the disk where the contents of the file are located. A symbolic link associates a filename with the pathname of a hard link to a file. See *Hard link* and *Symbolic link*.

Local Area Network   A network that connects computers within a localized area (such as a single site, building, or department).

Log in   To gain access to a UNIX system by responding correctly to the `login:` and `Password:` prompts.

Log out   To end your login session by exiting from your login shell; e.g., to stop using a terminal on a UNIX system so that another user can log in. Also, *log off*.

Logical expression   A collection of strings separated by logical operators (>, >=, =, !=, <=, and <) that can be evaluated as true or false.

.login file   A file the C Shell executes when you log in. You can use it to set environment variables and to run commands that you want executed at the beginning of each login session.

Login name   The name you enter in response to the `login:` prompt. Other users use your login name when they send you mail or write to you. Each login name has a corresponding user ID, which is the numeric identifier for the user. Both the login name and the user ID are established in the password database.

Login shell   The shell that you are using when you first log in. The login shell can fork other processes that can run other shells as well as running utilities and other programs.

.logout file   A file the C Shell executes when you log out, assuming the C Shell is your login shell. You can put commands in the **.logout** file that you want run each time you log out.

Machine collating sequence   The sequence in which the computer orders characters. The machine collating sequence affects the outcome of sorts and other procedures that put lists in alphabetical order. Many computers use ASCII codes, and so their machine collating sequences correspond to the ordering of the ASCII codes for characters.

Macro   A single instruction that a program replaces by several (usually more complex) instructions. The C compiler recognizes macros, which are defined using a **#define** instruction to the preprocessor.

Main memory   *R*andom *A*ccess *M*emory (RAM) that is an integral part of the computer. It is contrasted with disk storage. Although disk storage is sometimes referred to as memory, it is never referred to as main memory.

Major device number   A number assigned to a class of devices such as terminals, printers, or disk drives. Using the **ls** utility with the –l option to list the contents of the /**dev** directory displays the major and minor device numbers of many devices (as *major, minor*).

MAN   See *Metropolitan Area Network*.

Menu   A menu is a list of items from which you can choose to carry out common operations when working with a graphical user interface.

Metropolitan Area Network.   A network that connects computers and local area networks at multiple sites in a small regional area, such as a city.

Merge   To combine two ordered lists so that the resulting list is still in order. You can use the **sort** utility to merge files.

Metacharacter   A character that has a special meaning to the shell or another program in a particular context. Metacharacters are used in the ambiguous file references recognized by the shell and in the regular expressions recognized by several utilities. You must quote a metacharacter if you want to use it without invoking its special meaning. See *Regular character* and *Special character*.

(META) key   A key on the keyboard that is labeled (META) or (ALT). Use this key as you would the (SHIFT) key. While holding it down, press another key. The **emacs** editor makes extensive use of the (META) key.

Minor device number   A number assigned to a specific device within a class of devices. See *Major device number*.

Mount   To mount a filesystem is to make it accessible to system users. When a filesystem is not mounted, you cannot read from or write to files it contains.

Mouse   A mouse is a device that you use to point to a particular location on a display screen, typically so you can choose a menu item, draw a line, or highlight some text. You control a pointer on the screen by sliding a mouse around on a flat surface; the position of the pointer moves relative to the movement of the mouse. You select items by pressing one or more buttons on the mouse.

Multitasking   A computer system that allows a user to run more than one job at a time. The UNIX system is multitasking since it allows you to run jobs in the background while running a job in the foreground.

Multiuser   A computer system that can be used by more than one person at a time. The UNIX system is a multiuser operating system.

Network File System   A remote filesystem designed by Sun Microsystems, available on computers from most UNIX system vendors.

Network Information Service   A distributed service built on a shared database to manage system-independent information (such as login names and passwords).

NFS   See *Network File System*.

NIS   See *Network Information Service*.

Node   In a tree structure, the end of a branch that can support other branches. When the UNIX filesystem hierarchy is conceptualized as a tree, directories are nodes. See *Leaf*.

Nonprintable character   See (CONTROL) *character*. Also, *nonprinting character*.

Null string   A string that could contain characters but does not. A string of zero length.

Octal number   A base 8 number. Octal numbers are composed of the digits 0–7 inclusive. Refer to the table listed under *Hexadecimal number*.

Operating system   A control program for a computer that allocates computer resources, schedules tasks, and provides the user with a way to access the resources.

Option   A command line argument that modifies the effects of a command. Options are usually preceded by hyphens on the command line, and they usually have single character names (e.g., **–h**, **–n**). Some commands allow you to group options following a single hyphen (e.g., **–hn**).

Ordinary file   A file that is used to store a program, text, or other user data. See *Directory* and *Device file*.

Output   Information that a program sends to the terminal or to another file. See *Standard output*.

Parent process   A process that forks other processes. See *Process* and *Child process*.

Glossary

Partition   See *Disk partition.*

Pathname   A list of directories separated by slashes (/) and ending with the name of a directory or nondirectory file. A pathname is used to trace a path through the file structure to locate or identify a file.

Pathname element   One of the filenames that form a pathname.

Pathname, last element of a   The part of a pathname following the final /, or the whole filename if there is no /. A simple filename. Also, *basename.*

Peripheral device   See *Device.*

Physical device   A tangible device, such as a disk drive, that is physically separate from other similar devices.

PID   An acronym that stands for *Process ID*entification and is usually followed by the word *number*. The UNIX system assigns a unique PID number to each process when it is initiated.

Pipe   A connection between programs such that the standard output of one is connected to the standard input of the next. Also, *pipeline.*

Pixel   The smallest element of a picture, typically a single dot on a display screen.

Printable character   One of the graphic characters: a letter, number, or punctuation mark; contrasted with a nonprintable or (CONTROL) character. Also, *printing character.*

Point-to-point link   A connection limited to two endpoints, such as the connection between a pair of modems.

Process   The UNIX system execution of a program.

.profile file   A startup file that the login shell executes when you log in. Both the Bourne and Korn Shells execute the **.profile** file; the C Shell executes **.login** instead. You can use the **.profile** file to run commands, set variables, and define functions.

Program   A sequence of executable computer instructions contained in a file. UNIX system utilities, applications, and shell scripts are all programs. Whenever you run a command that is not built into a shell, you are executing a program.

Prompt   A cue from a program, usually displayed on the terminal, indicating that it is waiting for input. The shell displays a prompt, as do some of the interactive utilities, such as **Mail**. By default, the Bourne and Korn Shells use a dollar sign (**$**) as a prompt, and the C Shell uses a percent sign (**%**).

Quote   When you quote a character, you take away any special meaning that it has in the current context. You can quote a character by preceding it with a backslash. When you are interacting with the shell, you can also quote a character by surrounding it with single quotation marks. For example, the command **echo *** or **echo '*'** displays *. The command **echo *** displays a list of the files in the working directory. See *Ambiguous file reference, Metacharacter, Regular character, Regular expression,* and *Special character.*

Redirection   The process of directing the standard input for a program to come from a file rather than from the terminal. Also, directing the standard output or standard error to go to a file rather than to the terminal.

Regular character   A character that always represents itself in an ambiguous file reference or another type of regular expression. See *Special character.*

Regular expression   A string—composed of letters, numbers, and special symbols—that defines one or more strings. See Appendix A.

Relative pathname   A pathname that starts from the working directory. See *Absolute pathname*.

Remote filesystem   A filesystem on a remote computer that has been set up so that you can access (usually over a network) its files as though they were stored on your local computer's disks. An example of a remote filesystem is NFS.

Return code   See *Exit status*.

Root directory   The ancestor of all directories and the start of all absolute pathnames. The name of the root directory is /.

Root filesystem   The filesystem that is available when the system is brought up in single-user mode. The name of this filesystem is always /. You cannot unmount or mount the root filesystem.

Root login   Usually the login name of the superuser. See *Superuser*.

Router   A device, often a computer, that is connected to more than one similar type of network to pass data between them. See *Gateway*.

Run   To execute a program.

Scroll   To move lines on a terminal up or down one line at a time.

Server   A powerful, centralized computer (or program) designed to provide information to clients (smaller computers or programs) upon request.

Session   As used in this book, the sequence of events between when you start using a program, such as an editor, and when you finish, or between when you log in and the next time you log out.

Shell   A UNIX system command processor. There are three major shells: the Bourne Shell, the C Shell, and the Korn Shell. See *Bourne Shell*, *C Shell*, and *Korn Shell*.

Shell function   A series of commands that the shell stores for execution at a later time. Shell functions are like shell scripts, but they run more quickly because they are stored in the computer's main memory rather than in files. Also, a shell function is run in the environment of the shell that calls it (unlike a shell script, which is typically run in a subshell).

Shell script   A program composed of shell commands. Also, *shell program*.

Signal   A very brief message that the UNIX system can send to a process, apart from the process's standard input.

Simple filename   A single filename, containing no slashes (/). A simple filename is the simplest form of a pathname. Also, the last element of a pathname or the *basename*.

Single-user system   A computer system that only one person can use at a time, as contrasted with a *multiuser system*.

Sort   To put in a specified order, usually alphabetic or numeric.

(SPACE) character   A character that appears as the absence of a visible character. Even though you cannot see it, a (SPACE) is a printable character. It is represented by the ASCII code 32 (decimal). A (SPACE) character is considered a *blank* or *white space*.

Spawn   See *Fork*.

Special character   A character that has a special meaning when it occurs in an ambiguous file reference or another type of regular expression, unless it is quoted. The special characters most commonly used with the shell are ∗ and ?. Also, *metacharacter* and *wild card*.

Special file   See *Device file*.

Spool   To place items in a queue, each waiting its turn for some action. Often used when speaking about the **lpr** utility and the printer; that is, **lpr** spools files for the printer.

Square bracket   There is a left square bracket ([) and a right square bracket (]). They are special characters that define character classes in ambiguous file references and other regular expressions.

Standard error   A file to which a program can send output. Usually, only error messages are sent to this file. Unless you instruct the shell otherwise, it directs this output to the terminal (that is, to the device file that represents the terminal).

Standard input   A file from which a program can receive input. Unless you instruct the shell otherwise, it directs this input so that it comes from the terminal (that is, from the device file that represents the terminal).

Standard output   A file to which a program can send output. Unless you instruct the shell otherwise, it directs this output to the terminal (that is, to the device file that represents the terminal).

Startup file   A file that the login shell runs when you log in. The Bourne and Korn Shells run a file called **.profile**, and the C Shell runs a file called **.login**. The C Shell also runs a file called **.cshrc** whenever a new C Shell or a subshell is invoked. The Korn Shell runs an analogous file whose name is identified by the **ENV** variable.

Status line   The bottom (usually the 24th) line of the terminal. The **vi** editor uses the status line to display information about what is happening during an editing session.

Sticky bit   An access permission bit that causes an executable program to remain on the swap area of the disk. It takes less time to load a program that has its sticky bit set than one that does not. Only the superuser can set the sticky bit. If the sticky bit is set on a directory that is publicly writable, only the owner of a file in that directory can remove the file.

String   A sequence of characters.

Subdirectory   A directory that is located within another directory. Every directory except the root directory is a subdirectory.

Subshell   A shell that is forked as a duplicate of its parent shell. When you run an executable file that contains a shell script using its filename on the command line, a subshell is forked to run the script. Also, when you surround commands with parentheses, they are run in a subshell.

Superblock   A block that contains control information for a filesystem. The superblock contains housekeeping information, such as the number of inodes in the filesystem and free list information.

Superuser A privileged user who has access to anything any other system user has access to and more. The system administrator must be able to become a Superuser in order to establish new accounts, change passwords, and perform other administrative tasks. The login name of the superuser is typically *root*.

Swap What occurs when the operating system moves a process from main memory to a disk, or vice versa. Swapping a process to the disk allows another process to begin or continue execution.

Symbolic link A directory entry that points to the pathname of another file. In most cases, a symbolic link to a file can be used in the same ways a hard link can be used. Unlike a hard link, a symbolic link can span filesystems and can connect to a directory.

System administrator The person who is responsible for the upkeep of the system. The system administrator has the ability to log in as the superuser. See *Superuser*.

System console See *Console terminal*.

System V One of the two major versions of the UNIX system.

Termcap An abbreviation of *term*inal *cap*ability. The **termcap** file contains a list of various types of terminals and their characteristics. System V replaced the function of this file with the **terminfo** directory.

Terminfo An abbreviation of *term*inal *info*rmation. The **/usr/lib/terminfo** directory contains many subdirectories, each containing several files. Each of these files is named for, and contains a summary of the functional characteristics of, a particular terminal. Visually oriented programs, such as **vi**, make use of these files. Optionally available on SunOS, and other modern UNIX Systems, as an alternative to the **termcap** file.

Thicknet A type of coaxial cable (thick) used for an Ethernet network. Devices are attached to thicknet by tapping the cable at certain fixed points.

Thinnet A type of coaxial cable (thin) used for an Ethernet network. Thinnet cable is smaller in diameter and more flexible than thicknet cable. Each device is typically attached to two separate cable segments using a T-shaped connector; one segment leads to the device ahead of it on the network and one to the device that precedes it.

Token ring A type of local area network in which computers are attached to a ring of cable. A token packet circulates continuously around the ring; a computer can transmit information only when it owns the token.

Tty A terminal. Tty is an abbreviation for *tele*typewriter.

Usage message A message presented by a command when you call the command using incorrect command line arguments.

User ID A number that the password database associates with a login name. Also, *UID*.

User interface See *Interface*.

Utility A program included as a standard part of the UNIX system. You typically invoke a utility either by giving a command in response to a shell prompt or by calling it from within a shell script. Utilities are often referred to as commands. They are contrasted with built-in commands, which are built into the shell.

Variable   A name and an associated value. The shell allows you to create variables and use them in shell scripts. Also, the shell inherits several variables when it is invoked, and it maintains those and other variables while it is running. Some shell variables establish characteristics of the shell environment, whereas others have values that reflect different aspects of your ongoing interaction with the shell.

WAN   See *Wide Area Network.*

White space   A collective name for (SPACE)s and/or (TAB)s and occasionally (NEWLINE)s.

Wide Area Network   A network that interconnects LANs and MANs, spanning a large geographic area (typically in different states or countries).

Wild card   See *Metacharacter.*

Window   A region on a display screen that runs, or is controlled by, some particular program.

Window manager   A program that controls how windows appear on a display screen and how you manipulate them.

Word   A name for command line arguments, which are sequences of one or more nonblank characters separated by blanks. Also, a word is a Unit of Measure in **vi**. In **vi**, a word is similar to a word in the English language—a string of one or more characters that is bounded by a punctuation mark, a numeral, a (TAB), a (SPACE), or a (NEWLINE).

Work Buffer   A location where **ed** and **vi** store text while it is being edited. The information in the Work Buffer is not written to the file on the disk until you command the editor to write it.

Workstation   A small computer, typically designed to fit in an office and be used by one person. It is usually equipped with one display device and few peripherals (such as disks, printers, or modems).

Working directory   The directory that you are associated with at any given time. The relative pathnames you use are *relative to* the working directory. Also, *current directory.*

X terminal   A graphics terminal designed to run the X Window System.

X Window System   A design and set of tools for writing flexible, portable windowing applications, created jointly by researchers at the Massachusetts Institute of Technology and several leading computer manufacturers.

Index

L

M